Research on Schools, Neighborhoods, and Communities

Research on Schools, Neighborhoods, and Communities

Toward Civic Responsibility

William F. Tate IV
Editor

Published for the
American Educational Research Association

ROWMAN & LITTLEFIELD PUBLISHERS, INC.
Lanham • New York • Toronto • Plymouth, UK

Published for the American Educational Research Association

Published by Rowman & Littlefield Publishers, Inc.
A wholly owned subsidary of The Rowman & Littlefield Publishing Group, Inc.
4501 Forbes Boulevard, Suite 200, Lanham, Maryland, 20706
http://www.rowman.com

10 Thornbury Road, Plymouth PL6 7PP, United Kingdom

British Library Cataloguing in Publication Information Available

Library of Congress Cataloging-in-Publication Data
Research on schools, neighborhoods, and communities : toward civic responsibility / edited by William F. Tate IV.
    p. cm.
    Summary: "This volume focuses on research and theoretical developments related to the role of place or geography in matters of education, human development, and health. Multiple disciplinary perspectives are presented in order to provide different views of the strengths and problems in our communities. Research presented provides historical, moral, and scientifically based arguments organized to inform understandings of civic problems as well as to present possible solutions"— Provided by publisher.
  ISBN 978-1-4422-0467-6 (hardback) — ISBN 978-1-4422-0468-3 (paper) —
ISBN 978-1-4422-0469-0 (electronic)
  1. Community and school—United States. 2. Educational sociology—United States.
3. Educational equalization—United States. I. Tate, William F.
LC221.R47 2012
371.19—dc23   2011032848

∞™ The paper used in this publication meets the minimum requirements of American National Standard for Information Sciences—Permanence of Paper for Printed Library Materials, ANSI/NISO Z39.48-1992.

Printed in the United States of America

To the Cash, DeBerry, Jones, Legardy, Tate, and Terrell families, who have passed on their passion for schools and community.

And, as always, to Kimberly, for listening.

Contents

Acknowledgments

This book would not have been possible without the support of many people. First, I wish to extend my thanks to all of the authors of the volume. Second, I want to express my thanks to the reviewers for their insightful comments in the various production stages of the book. In particular, I wish to note my appreciation of the contributions and support of Celia Rousseau Anderson, Edna Cash, Linda Cottler, Jay Cummings, Carl Grant, Mark Hogrebe, Korina Jocson, Sheri Notaro, Catherine Striley, Allen R. Sullivan, William F. Tate III, and Daryl Tate. Also, the administrative and technical support of Marilyn Broughton, Natalia Kolk, Li Zou, and Brian Cohen was consistent throughout this project. Keith Griffin provided invaluable editorial assistance.

Many of the chapters in this book were presented during a 2009 conference held at Washington University in St. Louis—*America's Urban Infrastructure: Confronting Her Challenges, Embracing Her Opportunities*. I am grateful for the tremendous show of support by my colleagues from various programs, departments, centers, and schools at the university including: (1) Center for Regional Competitiveness in Science and Technology, (2) Center on Urban Research & Public Policy, (3) Program in African & African American Studies, (4) Office of Diversity Programs—School of Medicine, (5) Center for the Humanities, (6) Department of Education, (7) George Warren Brown School of Social Work, (8) School of Law, and (9) Office of Diversity Initiatives. I offer my thanks to the leadership of these units— Professors John Baugh, Garrett A. Duncan, Gerald Early, Will Ross, and Carol Camp Yeakey as well as Leah Merrifield and Deans Edward Lawlor and Kent Syverud. In addition, Professors Adrienne Davis, Anne Newman, Shanti Parikh, Itai Sened, Vetta L. Sanders Thompson, and Murray Weidenbaum helped in important ways to stimulate feedback for the conference presentations. In addition, Jeannie Oakes of the Ford Foundation provided insightful commentary and responses related to the conference paper presentations. The collective effort was intellectually rich and exciting.

I am thankful that Professor Ronald Walters made a determined effort to deliver his paper at the conference. Professor Walters's death after the conference was both a shock and loss. His contributions to our understanding of politics in the United States are significant.

In addition, I offer a special acknowledgment of gratitude to Chancellor Mark S. Wrighton, Provost Edward S. Macias, and Dean Gary S. Wihl for their support of and participation in the Washington University conference activities. The support I have received from Washington University's administration during my tenure as AERA president as well as through the preparation of this book allowed me to complete this project.

I wish to thank Felice J. Levine and Phoebe H. Stevenson for their support before, during, and after the 2008 AERA Annual Conference. In addition, Todd Reitzel displayed a significant level of patience as well as consistent encouragement in his role as AERA director of publications. I thank you, Todd, for the support. I also appreciate the affirming support of Cherry A. Banks, chair of the AERA Books Editorial Board, as well as the other members of the board. My experience as association president gave me a real appreciation for the entire AERA staff as well as the hundreds of colleagues who volunteer their time to serve on the council or the many other roles required to make the organization work well.

Last, but not least, I want to thank my family—Kimberly, Quentin, and Cameron—for their support of this project. My experiences with you made this work more relevant.

My research and development has been funded by the National Science Foundation under Award No. ESI-0227619. Any opinions, findings, and conclusions or recommendations expressed here are those of the author and do not necessarily reflect the views of the National Science Foundation.

Introduction

William F. Tate IV

Over 40 years ago, in response to a pressing concern for children living in disadvantaged conditions, Professor Edmond W. Gordon (1970) edited a special issue of *Review of Educational Research* (RER), a scholarly journal that is a part of the American Educational Research Association's (AERA) publication portfolio. Professor Gordon organized a collection of articles that explored a range of topics including: (1) immigrants and schools, (2) epidemiology and intelligence, (3) disadvantaged rural youth, (4) social class and socialization, (5) desegregation and minority group outcomes, (6) community participation in public education, and (7) school-to-college transitions. He lamented not being able to more directly examine a neglected area of education research—relationships between school performance and the health status of disadvantaged children. The content and research presented in this special *RER* issue have greatly informed my thinking about the field of education research in two ways. First, the topics highlighted in the special issue of the journal as well as the relationship between the health status of underserved children and education performance have persisted as public policy concerns (Hochschild & Scovronick, 2003; Irvin, Farmer, Leung, Thompson, & Hutchins, 2010; Mickelson, 2008; Payne, 2008; Tate & Striley, 2010). Second, these areas of concern as well as related processes and their impacts are situated in place, in neighborhoods and communities. However, the importance of geography is often not appropriately examined in education research. William Julius Wilson (1998) argued this very point as part of his call for more research that examines the association of environmental factors and academic achievement:

> The extent to which communities differ on some aspects of outlook and behavior depends in part on the extent of each community's social isolation from the broader society, the material assets or other resources that members of the community control, the privileges and benefits they derive from these resources, the cultural experiences community members have accumulated from political and economic arrangements, both current and historical, and the influence community members wield because of these arrangements. In the final analysis, the exposure to different cultural influences—as reflected in culturally shaped habits, styles, skills, values, and preferences—has to be taken into account and related to various types of social relations if one is to really appreciate and explain the divergent social outcomes of human groups. (p. 509)

During my tenure as the president of AERA, I sought to highlight the importance of environmental factors and schooling. The AERA Council approved my recommendation that the 2008 annual meeting theme be titled "Research on Schools, Neighborhoods, and Communities: Toward Civic Responsibility." My hope was that vigorous discussions about the geography of opportunity framed as a civic concern would occur across the Association. This edited book is an outgrowth of the 2008 annual meeting, and represents an effort to bring together scholars deeply interested in linking research and civic responsibility. The term *civic* is borrowed from Latin—of or for a citizen. The etymology of the word includes a Latin-to-English translation referring to the Roman civic crown. The civic crown was awarded to the individual who saved the life of a fellow citizen in battle. The notion of research focused on citizens or for citizens has a long history in the United States and abroad. For example, the efforts of political arithmeticians to use numbers as a means to better understand the quantity and character of British subjects inspired spirited debate. Political arithmetic was in part formed out of a desire to better understand how the state might address the concerns of citizens (Porter, 1986). Today, citizens are concerned about their opportunities to secure a quality education in their local communities (Bushaw & Lopez, 2010). However, the geography of opportunity has not been a central policy concern in the United States, as Briggs (2005) noted: "The risks posed by the uneven geography of opportunity, not to mention the challenges associated with changing it, are all but invisible on the public agenda as well as in the nation's intellectual life" (p. 5). This edited book was conceived as part of an effort to better understand what Yeakey (2000) referred to as "structure silences" related to research on education, schools, and communities. The volume seeks to explore understandings of the strengths and problems in our communities as an important civic function. As members of a research community, we have a civic responsibility to provide relevant and rigorous research that informs how we come to understand the social, cultural, and economic institution influences in our communities linked to educational processes and outcomes.

While the geography of opportunity has been somewhat underdeveloped as a policy and research topic, there has been an emerging treatment of place in the social science literature. The business and economic literature describes the role of industrial clusters and networks in communities (Gordon & McCann, 2000; Sorenson, 2003). The sociology literature examines social structures including the spatial dimensions of opportunity in communities (Foster-Bey, 2006; Pattillo, 2007). The political science literature is attentive to city and regional governance (Judd & Swanstrom, 2008; Stone, 1993). The public health literature examines the geography of medical resources, risk factors, and disease (Douglas, Esmundo, & Bloom, 2000; Jones-Webb & Wall, 2008). The psychology literature explores human development in a variety of contexts including the community setting (Spencer, Dupree, Cunningham, Harpalani, & Muñoz-Miller, 2003).

Education and education research are linked to the foregoing intellectual traditions. Historically, education research has both informed and encompassed social context frameworks associated with disciplinary-based scholarship and other professional literatures. Geographic factors are critical in discussions of social context. The noted urbanist Jane Jacobs underscores the importance of geography when she argues that community size is important and that policy and research generalizations across geographic types are unwise. She stated:

A successful city neighborhood is a place that keeps sufficiently abreast of its problems so that it is not destroyed by them. An unsuccessful neighborhood is a place that is overwhelmed by its defects and problems and is progressively more helpless before them. Our cities contain all degrees of success and failure. But on the whole we Americans are poor at handling city neighborhoods as can be seen by the long accumulations of failures in our great gray belts on the one hand, and by the Turfs of rebuilt city on the other hand. (Jacobs 1992, p. 112)

The social science literature suggests that civic problems are not self-defining. Research provides historical, moral, and scientifically based arguments with the potential to inform the actions of responsible citizens and many public and private institutions dedicated to the public good. The chapters in this volume represent an opportunity to present, rethink, and revise arguments associated with education, neighborhoods, and communities.

This book is organized, roughly, into five sections. The first section—comprising chapters 1 through 4—represents an effort to conceptualize place or geography and related mechanisms as central to the study of human development. Beginning in chapter 1 with Robert J. Sampson, several authors in this volume argue that communities can serve as a unit of social theory and policy intervention. Drawing on theoretical and empirical research associated with the Chicago School of urban sociology, in particular social disorganization theory, Sampson describes an alternative to an individualist perspective on social mechanisms and related policy strategies targeting individuals (vouchers and other choice options). Instead he puts forth an interpretation of environmental conditions that suggests changing the infrastructure of communities (or schools) themselves is the appropriate policy target. In addition, like the late Jane Jacobs, Sampson argues there is a need to better understand the state of neighborhoods and communities. He calls for a national strategy of community monitoring. To this end, he and Stephen W. Raudenbush (chapter 12) propose the development of a science of ecological assessment referred to as ecometrics to directly measure neighborhood processes. Consistent with the earlier statement by William Julius Wilson, this new science would examine neighborhood processes as collective phenomena rather than as replacements for individual traits. There is certainly a role for education researchers and other social scientists interested in human development broadly defined in this interdisciplinary area.

In chapter 2, "Toward a Theory of Place: Social Mobility, Proximity, and Proximal Capital," Odis D. Johnson continues the discussion of the importance of "place" in the context of the sociology of education literature. He offers an assessment of the development of a theory of "place" within the sociology of education while describing the distributive mechanisms that shape and economically stratify the social associations that make up ecological units (or places) and a type of endogenous capital called proximity capital. Johnson's analysis of the ecological units includes a discussion of how modes of social mobility convert proximity capital into proximal capital, resulting in differential educational opportunity and individual outcomes.

In chapter 3, "Urban Opportunity Structure and Racial/Ethnic Polarization," George C. Galster depicts "space" for low-income people of color as the emerging primary obstacle to socioeconomic progress and a central mechanism for maintaining racial/ethnic division. The foundational elements of space in this chapter are neighborhood and school segregation by race/ethnicity and class, and secondarily, the location of industry and employment. Galster suggests that these spatial considerations form a model of causation in which race-class prejudice, discrimination, segregation, and other disparities interact in a constraining fashion to limit the opportunity structures of low-income minorities living in cities across the United States. The chapter provides a conceptual framework for understanding the mutually reinforcing factors impacting many residents in urban America.

In chapter 4, "Racial Segregation in Multiethnic Schools: Adding Immigrants to the Analysis," Ingrid Gould Ellen and Katherine O'Regan with Amy Ellen Schwartz and Leanna Stiefel contribute to the literature focused on the racial segregation in American schools in their study of immigrant students in New York City's public schools. The authors use a student-level data set that includes all elementary and middle school students in the school district as part of a series of descriptive and exploratory analyses of both how segregated immigrants are and why. Their results indicate that foreign-born students are generally more racially isolated than their native-born counterparts, and this is not solely due to differences in income levels or language-skill differences. The findings suggest that this isolation decreases with time in the school system; however, the foreign-born/native-born differential is never eliminated. The study found substantial variation in racial isolation patterns when disaggregating immigrants by region of birth, suggesting a diversity of experiences that may indicate underlying causes. And finally, they discovered that clustering by region of birth is not the sole or even main source of this racial isolation, at least in most cases.

The next section of the book, chapters 5 through 8, is focused on the changing dynamics in metropolitan education, and suburban school districts in particular. In chapter 5, "Suburbanization and School Segregation," Sean F. Reardon, John T. Yun, and Anna K. Chmielewski examine the distribution of poor and minority students in suburban areas. Their analyses describe patterns and trends in suburban racial and socioeconomic segregation where segregation between and within suburban school districts is highlighted. Their demographic analysis sheds light on the relationship between socioeconomic segregation and racial segregation in suburban communities and schools.

In chapter 6, "Schools Matter: Segregation, Unequal Educational Opportunities, and the Achievement Gap in the Boston Region," John R. Logan and Deirdre Oakley describe their study of residential segregation focused on black and Hispanic children in the metropolitan Boston area. Their findings indicate that these children live in highly segregated neighborhoods where a number of risk factors are noticeable. Their regional analysis suggests the main source of segregation is minority exclusion from residential suburbs. School segregation is lower in Boston than in other portions of the region. This reflects the history of desegregation efforts in the city, despite erosion of these gains in the last decade.

In chapter 7, "Still Separate, Still Unequal, But Not Always So 'Suburban': The Changing Nature of Suburban School Districts in the New York Metropolitan Area," Amy Stuart Wells, Douglas Ready, Jacquelyn Duran, Courtney Grzesikowski, Kathryn Hill, Allison Roda, Miya Warner, and Terrenda White present the framework and early findings of a study being conducted on metro migrations and education. They are particularly interested in understanding the role public schools play in movers' decisions to pursue housing in various communities in the region. In addition, the study provides an account of the nature and extent of segregation and stratification across space and geopolitical boundaries. Ultimately, the research represents an effort to understand how educational opportunities are dispersed across a region.

In chapter 8, "Adding Geospatial Perspective to Research on Schools, Communities, and Neighborhoods," Mark C. Hogrebe argues that there is a role for geospatial methodology in education research as part of efforts to understand regional school quality. Education has spatial dimensions because schools are located in communities and neighborhoods across a metropolitan region. Recent advances in geographic information systems (GIS) make it possible to estimate effects with different study designs as well as illustrate the outcomes of analytical methods. The maps produced with GIS provide a method to share and democratize research findings with specialists in education as well as the public. The methodology provides a tool for researchers to inform civic decision-making. The chapter includes examples for scholars interested in adding this method to their scholarship.

The third section of the book—chapters 9 through 15—is oriented toward research on learning and teaching in social context. In chapter 9, "Conceptual and Methodological Challenges to a Cultural and Ecological Framework for Studying Human Learning and Development," Carol D. Lee contends that our most generative understandings of human learning develop as a result of examining multiple cultural communities. However, she makes a case that as studies move across diverse populations, new conceptual challenges will develop with regard to ecological validity. Examples of how scholars in several fields of study have handled this challenge are offered.

In chapter 10, "An Ecological and Activity Theoretic Approach to Studying Diasporic and Nondominant Communities," Kris D. Gutiérrez and Angela E. Arzubiaga examine the challenge of how to do empirical work that captures the complexity—the full range—of community activity toward deeper analyses of the community's ecology, the available affordances and constraints, and the influences on everyday practices. They argue that this task becomes more complicated when race and ethnicity are central to the empirical project. In addition, the chapter explores how the complexity of research grows as issues of racism and other forms of inequality are examined as well as when the investigation attempts to account for local, distal, and historical influences that mediate human activity.

In chapter 11, "Reconstructing Education in America," Henry M. Levin describes demographic and education trends that represent threats to the human capital infrastructure in the United States. He presents several education and human development interventions that have the potential to improve work force quality while ensuring equity across the population in terms of opportunity and productivity. Levin argues that these interventions should be implemented systematically in order to generate maximal effect and return on public investment.

In chapter 12, "Can School Improvement Reduce Racial Inequality?" Stephen W. Raudenbush questions why the progress in reducing racial inequality did not continue beyond 1990. He posits that social forces beyond the control of educators influenced important race-related outcomes. His chapter is largely a case for why in the face of these difficult social challenges it is feasible to conclude that school reform based on careful interpretations of research on the amount, quality, and distribution of school opportunities can support the reduction of racial inequality.

In chapter 13, "Seeing Our Way Into Learning Science in Informal Environments," Shirley Brice Heath provides a vision for a research program that is attentive to the potential and possibilities of learning in nonschool settings within the community. Offered here as a basis for this research agenda are current learning theories that account for (1) the interdependence of visual and gestural representation, (2) science identity, (3) organized attention to visual detail, and (4) distribution of identifiable functions of language chunks within deliberative discourse.

In chapter 14, "No Color Necessary: High School Students' Discourse on College Support Systems and College Readiness," Evellyn Elizondo, Walter R. Allen, and Miguel Ceja share findings from a project designed to identify factors related to the educational successes among African American and Latino students residing in Southern California. Their chapter describes the inconsistent and often contradictory role played by school agents such as counselors in the support systems offered Latino students in one high school setting. Their descriptive analysis suggests this is an important area for future research. Moreover, the findings in this chapter point to the need for the type of intervention described in chapter 15.

In chapter 15, "Taking Math and Science to Black Parents: Promises and Challenges of a Community-Based Intervention for Educational Change," Roslyn A. Mickelson, Linwood Cousins, Anne Velasco, and Brian Williams describe a community-based mathematics and science intervention organized to positively influence college preparatory course enrollments in the Charlotte-Mecklenburg schools. The Math/Science Equity Program (MSEP) was developed to encourage parental involvement in the mathematics and science course selection and placement processes. The underlying logic of this intervention is to foster civic engagement by equipping parents with knowledge about school operations and opportunity to learn factors in mathematics and science.

The fourth major section of this book, chapters 16–21, examines research on human development, health, and human services in a social context as part of an effort to better understand children, adolescents, and their families within community experiences. In chapter 16, "Maximizing Culturally and Contextually Sensitive Assessment Strategies in Developmental and Educational Research," Margaret Beale Spencer, Brian Tinsley, Davido Dupree, and Suzanne Fegley describe the theoretical and methodological traditions of the Center for Health, Achievement, Neighborhoods, Growth, and Ethnic Studies (CHANGES)—a culture- and context-sensitive programmatic research effort. The chapter includes a review of research on neighborhood contexts as well as the challenges of building relevant research infrastructure. Specific examples are provided to better illustrate the theoretical model guiding the center's investigations.

In chapter 17, "Immigrant Children: Hiding in Plain Sight in the Margins of the Urban Infrastructure," Michael A. Olivas details the implementation challenges facing immigrant children and their families in school settings in the post–*Plyler v. Doe* era. Despite the court ruling that undocumented children have the same right to a free public education as U.S. citizens and permanent residents, the chapter chronicles cases where implementation of the law has been impeded. The implications for failing to follow the court's ruling on human development and educational outcomes are significant.

In chapter 18, "Delivering High-Quality Public Services to Vulnerable Families and Children in America's Cities: The Lessons From Reforming Child Welfare," Olivia Golden features part of a larger project—specifically, case histories of social services agencies engaged in efforts to better address the needs of their respective communities. She brings both the experiences of a social services leader and scholar to bear on the complex issues of child welfare services, and highlights the importance of leaders and disciplined, evidence-based practices.

In chapter 19, "Health Disparities Among African Americans in Urban Populations," Sheri R. Notaro reviews several health-related factors influencing children and their families. She contends that health disparities can negatively impact development and opportunity to learn. In addition, the programmatic design and research on several health interventions created to better understand and alleviate disparities are explained.

In chapter 20, "A 'Tragic Dichotomy': A Case Study of Industrial Lead Contamination and Management in a Company Town," Jill McNew-Birren explains the political economy associated with Herculaneum, Missouri. She carefully documents the changing politics in state and federal lead regulation, including the influence of advances in the science associated with determining toxicity. The case is a complex story of civic engagement, economics, science, and human development.

In chapter 21, "Pandemic Preparedness: Using Geospatial Modeling to Inform Policy in Systems of Education and Health in Metropolitan America," I discuss a history of influenza in geographic context as well as related social outcomes. In addition, the chapter provides a set of visual models to explain access to health care for students and their families using the metro St. Louis region's demographics and resources. I call for greater reliance on geospatial tools to inform civic and interagency (e.g., health and education) planning.

The fifth major section of this book, composed of chapters 22 and 23, consists of two case studies of American urban cities that have experienced hardship and severe challenges. In chapter 22, "Urban America in Distress: A Case Study Analysis of Gary, Indiana: 1968–1987," Gail E. Wolfe presents a study of one Midwestern, industrial city in the latter half of the 20th century. The study examines Gary, Indiana, in the period between 1968 and 1987. Wolfe explores the political economy of the community, including metropolitan demographic shifts, housing, education, crime, and urban renewal. The detailed description of how numerous factors overlapped on the ground in Gary during this time interval provides a picture of the downward trends in the city's social, economic, and built infrastructure. The implications for education and human development are profound.

In chapter 23, "God's Will or Government Policy? Katrina's Unveiling of History and the Mass Dispersion of Black People," Jerome E. Morris chronicles a history of civic neglect in terms of the region's overwhelmingly poor and black residents. This case is an important reminder that civic actions as well as failures to act influence the life course of vulnerable populations with respect to education, housing, and employment opportunities. Morris provides an important pre-Katrina analysis of the city and region. This chapter is a powerful reminder that the interplay of research and policy should have a role in civic affairs.

In the first chapter of the epilogue section, chapter 24, "Research Infrastructure for Improving Urban Education," Larry V. Hedges and Nathan Jones provide alternative visions for building and organizing human capital with the expertise to conduct rigorous and relevant education research as part of the infrastructure supporting civic engagement related to urban education. In addition, they conducted an analysis that is an accounting of the doctoral productivity in various social science disciplines, including subfields of education. The study is a sobering account of the current boundaries of the education research enterprise in terms of human capital. If research on schools, neighborhoods, and communities is an important civic responsibility, then attention to the supply of social scientists is a primary consideration.

In the second chapter of the epilogue section, "The White House Office of Urban Affairs: Regionalism, Sustainability, and the Neglect of Social Infrastructure," the late Ronald Walters examines the aims and direction of a presidential initiative in an attempt to better understand its potential influence on challenging problems of race and poverty in metropolitan regions. Using the state of Maryland as an example, he argues throughout the chapter that neoliberal approaches have ignored important sociological factors linked to race, poverty reduction, and community development. A case study of Baltimore suggests that Smart Growth policies routinely neglected the neediest neighborhoods. The chapter concludes with a call for a sustainability movement where economic justice relates regional space to the health of the social infrastructure.

In the final chapter of the epilogue section, "Toward Civic Responsibility and Civic Engagement: Beyond the Business of Parallel Play," I conclude with reflections on the importance of research that is cross-disciplinary and attentive to geospatial considerations, as well as the need for scholarship focused on the most challenging social problems. I submit that to do so is the duty of researchers as part of fulfilling the commitment described in the AERA mission statement to "advance knowledge about education, to encourage scholarly inquiry related to education, and to promote the use of research to improve education and serve the public good."

REFERENCES

Briggs, X. (Ed.). (2005). *The geography of opportunity: Race and housing choice in metropolitan America*. Washington, DC: Brookings Institution Press.

Bushaw, W. J., & Lopez, S. J. (2010, September). A time for change, The 42nd annual Phi Delta Kappa/Gallup poll of the public's attitude toward the public schools. *Kappanmagazine.org*, 92(1), 8–26. Retrieved September 6, 2010, from http://www.pdkintl.org/kappan/docs/2010_Poll_Report.pdf

Douglas, L., Esmundo, E., & Bloom, Y. (2000). Smoke signs: Patterns of tobacco billboard advertising in a metropolitan region. *Tobacco Control, 9*, 16–23.

Foster-Bey, J. A. (2006). Did spatial mismatch affect male labor force participation during the 1990s expansion? In R. B. Mincy (Ed.), *Black males left behind* (pp. 121–147). Washington, DC: Urban Institute Press.

Gordon, E. W. (Ed.). (1970). Education for socially disadvantaged children [Special issue]. *Review of Research in Education, 40*(1), 1–179.

Gordon, I. R., & McCann, P. (2000). Industrial clusters: Complexes, agglomerations, and/or social networks? *Urban Studies, 37*(3), 513–532.

Hochschild, J., & Scovronick, N. (2003). *The American dream and the public schools*. New York, NY: Oxford University Press.

Irvin, M., Farmer, T., Leung, M., Thompson, J., & Hutchins, B. (2010). School, community, and church activities: Relationship to academic achievement of low-income African American early adolescents in the rural Deep South. *Journal of Research in Rural Education, 25*(4), 1–21. Retrieved September 6, 2010, from http://jrre.psu.edu/articles/25-4.pdf

Jacobs, J. (1992). *The death and life of great American cities* (2nd ed.). New York, NY: Vintage Books.

Jones-Webb, R., & Wall, M. (2008). Neighborhood racial/ethnic concentration, social disadvantage, and homicide risk: An ecological analysis of 10 U.S. cities. *Journal of Urban Health, 85*(5), 662–675.

Judd, D. R., & Swanstrom, T. (2008). *City politics: The political economy of urban America*. New York: Pearson.

Mickelson, R. (2008). Twenty-first century social science on school racial diversity and educational outcomes. *Ohio State University Law Jounal, 69*, 1173–1227.

Payne, C. M. (2008). *So much reform, so little change: The persistence of failure in urban schools*. Cambridge, MA: Harvard Education Press.

Pattillo, M. (2007). *Black on the block: The politics of race and class in the city*. Chicago, IL: University of Chicago Press.

Porter, T. M. (1986). *The rise of statistical thinking, 1820–1900*. Princeton, NJ: Princeton University Press.

Sorenson, O. (2003). Social networks and industrial geography. *Journal of Evolutionary Economics, 13*(5), 513–527.

Spencer, M. B., Dupree, D., Cunningham, M., Harpalani, V., & Muñoz-Miller, M. (2003). Vulnerability to violence: A contextually sensitive, developmental perspective on African American adolescents. *Journal of Social Issues, 59*(1), 33–59.

Stone, C. N. (1993). Urban regimes and the capacity to govern: A political economy approach. *Journal of Urban Affairs, 15*(1), 1–28.

Tate, W. F., & Striley, C. (2010). Epidemiology and education research: Dialoguing about disparities. *Teachers College Record*. Retrieved September 16, 2010, from http://www.tcrecord.org/content.asp?contentid=16036

Wilson, W. J. (1998). The role of the environment in black-white test score gap. In C. Jencks & M. Phillips (Eds.), *The black-white test gap* (pp. 501–510). Washington, DC: Brookings Institution Press.

Yeakey, C. C. (2000). Research, scholarship, and social responsibility: Social imperatives for a democratic society. In C. C. Yeakey (Ed.), *Edmund W. Gordon: Producing knowledge, pursuing understanding. Advances in education in diverse communities: Research, policy, and praxis* (Vol. 1, pp. 283–300). Stamford, CT: JAI.

I

CONCEPTUALIZING URBAN SPACE

1

Neighborhood Inequality, Violence, and the Social Infrastructure of the American City

Robert J. Sampson

Two venerable themes in American society—*community* and *inequality*—are linked now probably more than ever. The pursuit of "community" has been a perennial concern of both classical social theory and the general public for well over a century. Although urbanization and modernity have been said to weaken the realization of community bonds, with globalization dealing the final death blow (Giddens, 1990), the appeal of community has never gone away and if anything, is ascendant (Putnam, 2000). Indeed, the idea of a shared vision and community-level approaches to solving human problems is one that resonates widely. But pushing against the community ideal and pulling people apart is inequality. It is hard to achieve social unity and cohesive communities when sharp disparities in resources are associated with segregation by place. The economic implosion of 2008 has only worsened the trend toward increasing inequality in the United States, posing a further threat to promoting community efficacy.

The dominant policy approach to reducing inequality by place seems to be one largely of promoting individual choice. This dominance is highlighted most visibly and symbolically in the "voucher movement," whereby vouchers are increasingly advocated as a way to move individuals away from whatever bad school or bad community that inequality has wrought. "Escape" is the byword; choice is valorized. Consider, for example, how the federal government has spent millions of dollars on housing policy in the last 15 years. In the "Moving to Opportunity" housing program policymakers have promoted vouchers as a way to offer public housing residents a chance to escape concentrated poverty, improve their housing quality, and live in safety (Goering & Feins, 2003). Vouchers to attend charter schools have similarly taken hold of the public imagination and are now at the center of urban educational plans around the country, reinforced in part by the federal government's "Race to the Top" initiative. Despite mixed empirical evidence on effectiveness, vouchers have become the new policy paradigm.

A different approach to urban policy is to change the infrastructure of communities (or schools) themselves.[1] Rather than move people out, the idea is to fix what is already there. To be clear, I have no wish to argue against increasing individual opportunities. Rather than argue negatively, or against vouchers, this chapter instead tries to make a positive case by emphasizing a simple but overlooked point: communities too can serve as a unit of social science theory and policy intervention. There is good reason to consider the evidence on neighborhood-level variations in social outcomes and community-level interventions. Neighborhood inequality is highly durable and has a way of yielding unintended consequences for interventions that are targeted at individuals rather than social structures. I specifically argue that segregation and durable inequality by neighborhood transform well-intended individual-level interventions into continued processes of neighborhood stratification (see also Sampson, 2011). It follows that we need to take seriously the neighborhood contexts within which families live and make choices, treating those contexts as independent objects of theory and empirical study.

Equally important, I argue that we need to better appreciate the importance of the social fabric of cities. When urban infrastructure is discussed in macro-level or systemic terms, concerns often turn to its physical or material manifestation (e.g., roads, buildings, economic development). Physical infrastructure is crucial, of course, but so is social infrastructure. My guiding hypothesis is that neighborhoods and local communities are not just the backdrop or setting for current policies—they are active ingredients in constituting the social infrastructure of the American city. Overall, then, I make the case for community-level intervention instead of individual-level "escape hatches" and for a focus on the social infrastructure of American cities. Fortunately, a new set of urban policies, such as HOPE VI and "Promise Neighborhoods" are following this logic by intervening in the system-level and social dimensions of neighborhoods.

A few caveats are in order. Research on neighborhood effects and the concept of community cover a large volume of literature such that one essay cannot hope to do it justice as a whole. To gain focus I will zero in on neighborhoods as the social unit of analysis and violence as a key indicator given the importance of violence as a bellwether of urban livability, sustainability, and overall well-being. Before there can be a robust civic life and the next generation can learn, we must first have safe communities. A recent study demonstrates this stark reality—children exposed to violent events (homicide) less than a week prior to taking academic tests of vocabulary and reading perform much worse compared to those not exposed, by between one-half and two-thirds standard deviations (Sharkey, 2010). As I review below, violence has also been shown to undermine the social fabric of urban communities by inducing outmigration, fear, and moral cynicism, pointing to the relevance of a community-level approach to urban policy that addresses the causes and consequences of violence. In making my case I draw on research in Chicago, the site of a large-scale study that seeks to understand the social mechanisms behind neighborhood effects and crime—the "Project on Human Development in Chicago Neighborhoods" (Sampson, 2011). Although Chicago is not the country, it is a quintessentially American city and offers lessons that I believe are broadly relevant.

A final disclaimer up front—I will not argue for a specific policy as much as a family of policies linked to the idea of community intervention. The job of social scientists is not to dictate policy but to provide knowledge and guiding theoretical ideas. As the social psychologist Kurt Lewin wrote over 50 years ago, "There is nothing more practical than a good theory" (Lewin, 1951). I agree: Theory and ideas can shape the direction that policy takes.

PERSISTENT NEIGHBORHOOD INEQUALITY

Although there are many types of communities that one could define in terms of shared values or primary group ties, I define neighborhoods and local communities in spatial terms, letting properties of social organization vary. Sometimes neighborhoods make a community in the traditional sense of shared values, but often they do not—neighborhoods are variable in the nature and content of social ties, and they are nested within successively larger communities. This conception is consistent with the classic view that a neighborhood is a collection of both people and institutions occupying a spatially defined area influenced by ecological, cultural, market, and political forces (Park, 1915). Suttles (1972) refined this view by arguing that neighborhoods do not form their identities or composition simply as the result of free-market competition or internal dynamics. Many neighborhoods and local communities have their reputations and boundaries imposed on them by outsiders (e.g., police, real estate, city services).

Virtually all empirical studies of neighborhoods employ operational definitions that depend on geographic boundaries set by the government (e.g., the Census Bureau) or other administrative agencies (e.g., school districts, police districts). Although administratively defined units such as census tracts are reasonably consistent with the notion of nested ecological structures and permit the analysis of rich sources of linked data, researchers have become increasingly interested in strategies to define neighborhoods that respect the logic of street patterns and the social networks of neighbor interactions (Grannis, 1998). Still, there is no one correct definition of neighborhood that enjoys universal support—definitions vary according to the research question and theory just as they do for other social phenomena.

Research conducted in Chicago in the early part of the 20th century motivated a long line of American studies of neighborhoods, crime, and the social organization of the city. In *Juvenile Delinquency and Urban Areas* Shaw and McKay (1942/1969) argued that low economic status, ethnic heterogeneity, and residential instability led to the disruption of local community social organization, which in turn accounted for variations in crime and delinquency. They also demonstrated that high rates of delinquency in Chicago persisted in certain areas over many years, regardless of population turnover. More than any other, this finding led Shaw and McKay to question individualistic explanations of delinquency and focus on the processes by which criminal patterns of behavior, especially group-related, were transmitted across generations in areas of poverty, instability, and weak social controls (Bursik, 1988).

Neighborhood research in the post–Shaw and McKay era has tended to focus on the socially structured dimensions of disadvantage, especially the geographic isolation of the poor, and, in the United States, the racial isolation of African Americans in concentrated poverty areas (Massey & Denton, 1993; W. J. Wilson, 1987). The range of outcomes associated with concentrated disadvantage extends well beyond crime and violence to include infant mortality, low birth weight, teenage childbearing, dropping out of high school, and child maltreatment (Brooks-Gunn, Duncan, & Aber, 1997; Sampson, Morenoff, & Gannon-Rowley, 2002). Overall, the evidence thus suggests that multiple forms of disadvantage are geographically concentrated—especially violence (Reiss & Tonry, 1986)—and that disadvantage is surprisingly stable in its concentration over time (Sampson, 2011).

Research has also considered neighborhood social differentiation relating to life-cycle status, residential stability, home ownership, population density, and ethnic heterogeneity. The evidence on these factors is mixed, especially for density and ethnic heterogeneity (Morenoff, Sampson, & Raudenbush, 2001). Perhaps the most extensive area of ecological inquiry about disadvantage, dating back to the early Chicago School, concerns residential stability and home ownership. There is research showing that residential instability and low rates of home ownership are durable correlates of many problem behaviors (Brooks-Gunn et al., 1997), but that residential stability interacts with poverty. In contexts of deprivation and poverty, residential stability has been shown to correlate with negative rather than positive outcomes (Ross, Reynolds, & Geis, 2000), which makes theoretical sense if long-term exposure to concentrated disadvantage is a risk factor.

In brief, empirical research has established reasonably consistent patterns of crime and the well-being of communities. I would summarize them as follows (see also Sampson, 2011):

1. There is substantial inequality between neighborhoods in terms of economic status and correlated social resources. There is particularly strong evidence that links concentrated poverty, unemployment, and family disruption to the geographical isolation of racial minority groups—what is commonly called *concentrated disadvantage*.

2. Criminal violence is spatially clustered in the same neighborhoods that are characterized by severe concentrated disadvantage. So too are criminal justice sanctions in the form of arrest and imprisonment. The geographic intensity of crime and criminal justice intervention by the State is thus tightly coupled with concentrated disadvantage.

3. Multiple social problems besides crime tend to come bundled together geographically, including social and physical disorder, low birth weight, infant mortality, school dropout, and child maltreatment. Well-being is a general construct at the neighborhood level.

4. Although neighborhoods are constantly in flux with individuals moving in and out, there is simultaneously a general durability or stability in the relative social positions that neighborhoods hold: Disadvantage is both concentrated and cumulative in nature.

5. These broad empirical results have not varied much with the operational unit of analysis. Stratification of local communities with respect to violence, well-being, and social disadvantage is a robust phenomenon that emerges at multiple levels of geography.

SOCIAL MECHANISMS AND PROCESSES

While empirical evidence points to a number of durable neighborhood correlates of crime rates, it does not answer what is potentially the most important question: *Why* does community structure matter? What are the mechanisms and social processes that help explain why factors such as concentrated poverty lead to increases in crime and violence?

The most famous approach to mechanism-based theory can be traced back to those working in the tradition of *social disorganization theory* that emerged in the Chicago School of urban sociology. Social disorganization has been defined as the inability of a community structure to realize the common interests of its residents in maintaining effective social controls (Sampson & Groves, 1989). The social disorganization approach views local communities and neighborhoods as a complex system of friendship, kinship, and acquaintanceship networks, and formal and informal associational ties rooted in family life and ongoing socialization processes. From this view, both social organization and social *dis*organization are inextricably tied to systemic networks that facilitate or inhibit social control. When formulated in this way, social disorganization is analytically separable not only from the processes that may lead to it (e.g., poverty, residential mobility), but from the degree of criminal behavior that may be a result. This conceptualization also goes beyond the traditional account of community as a strictly geographical phenomenon by focusing on social networks and voluntary associations.

One of the most highly studied dimensions of community social organization is the density or "connectivity" of local friendship and acquaintanceship networks. Systemic theory holds that locality-based social networks constitute the core social fabric of human ecological communities (Bursik, 1988). When residents form local social ties, their capacity for social control is in theory increased because they are better able to recognize strangers and are more apt to engage in guardianship behavior against victimization. The greater the density and overlapping nature of interpersonal networks in a community, therefore, the greater the constraint on deviant behavior within the network, according to disorganization theory.

Social networks and closure are not sufficient to understand local communities, however. Networks are differentially invoked, and dense, tight-knit networks may impede social organization if they are isolated or weakly linked to collective expectations for rules of action. At the neighborhood level, the willingness of local residents to intervene on behalf of public safety depends, in large part, on conditions of mutual trust and shared expectations among residents. In particular, one is unlikely to intervene in a neighborhood context where the rules are unclear and people mistrust or fear one another. It is the linkage of mutual trust and the shared willingness to intervene for the common good that defines the neighborhood context of what Sampson, Raudenbush, and Earls (1997) term *collective efficacy*. Just as individuals vary in their capacity for efficacious action, so too do neighborhoods vary in their capacity to achieve common goals. Moreover, just as self-efficacy is situated rather than global (one has self-efficacy relative to a particular task or type of task), neighborhood efficacy exists relative to collective tasks such as maintaining public order. Collective efficacy with respect to crime is thus a task-specific construct that refers to shared expectations and mutual engagement by residents in local social control.

Moving from a focus on private ties to social efficacy signifies an emphasis on shared beliefs in neighbors' joint capability for action to achieve an intended effect, and hence an active sense of engagement on the part of residents. As Bandura (1997) argues, the meaning of efficacy is captured in expectations about the exercise of control, elevating the "agentic" aspect of social life over a perspective centered on the accumulation of "stocks" of social resources. Distinguishing between the resource potential represented by personal ties, on the one hand, and the shared expectations among neighbors for engagement in social control represented by collective efficacy, on the other, helps clarify the systemic model: Social networks foster the conditions under which collective efficacy may flourish, but they are not sufficient for the exercise of control. In this way collective efficacy may be seen as a logical extension of systemically based social disorganization theory. The difference is mainly one of emphasis: Locality-based networks may enhance neighborhood social organization, but the collective capacity for social action, even if rooted in weak personal ties, constitutes the more proximate social mechanism for understanding between-neighborhood variation in crime rates.

The theory of collective efficacy can ill afford to ignore institutions or the wider political environment in which local communities are embedded. Many neighborhoods exhibit intense private ties (e.g., among friends, kin) and yet still lack the institutional capacity to achieve social control or defend their interests (Granovetter, 1973). The institutional component is thus crucial and refers to the resource stock of neighborhood organizations and their linkages with other organizations both within *and* outside the community. Kornhauser (1978) argues that when the horizontal links among institutions within a community are weak, the capacity to defend local interests is weakened. Bursik and Grasmick (1993) highlight vertical links, or the capacity of local community organizations to obtain extra-local resources (police, fire services; block grants) that help sustain neighborhood social stability and local controls.

A large-scale study in Chicago ("Project on Human Development in Chicago Neighborhoods," or PHDCN) assessed many of these ideas with an original research design examining criminal behavior in community context. A major component of this study was a community survey of thousands of residents of 343 Chicago neighborhoods conducted in 1995 and again in 2002. Sampson et al. (1997) developed a two-part scale from this survey to examine rates of violence. One component was shared expectations about "informal social control," represented by a five-item Likert-type scale. Residents were asked about the likelihood ("Would you say it is very likely, likely, neither likely nor unlikely, unlikely, or very unlikely?") that their neighbors could be counted on to take action if: (i) children were skipping school and hanging out on a street corner, (ii) children were spray-painting graffiti on a local building, (iii) children were showing disrespect to an adult, (iv) a fight broke out in front of their house, and (v) the fire station closest to home was threatened with budget cuts. The second component was "social cohesion," measured by asking respondents how strongly they agreed (on a five-point scale) that "People around here are willing to help their neighbors"; "This is a close-knit neighborhood"; "People in this neighborhood can be trusted"; and (reverse coded): "People in this neighborhood generally don't get along with each other"; "People in this neighborhood do not share the same values." Social cohesion and informal social control were closely associated across neighborhoods, suggesting that they tapped aspects of the same latent construct. Sampson et al. (1997) combined the two scales into a summary measure termed "collective efficacy" and found that it varied widely across Chicago neighborhoods and was associated with significantly lower rates of violence. This association held up controlling for concentrated disadvantage, residential stability, immigrant concentration, and a comprehensive set of individual-level characteristics (e.g., age, sex, socioeconomic status [SES], race/ethnicity, home ownership) as well as indicators of personal ties and the density of local organizations. Whether measured by homicide events or violent victimization reported by residents, neighborhoods high in collective efficacy consistently had significantly lower rates of violence. Even after adjusting for prior violence, a two standard-deviation elevation in collective efficacy was associated with a reduction in the expected homicide rate by over 25 percent (Sampson et al.,1997).

Another key result was that the association of concentrated disadvantage and residential instability with higher violence declined after collective efficacy was controlled, suggesting a potential causal pathway at the community level. This pathway is presumed to operate over time, wherein collective efficacy is undermined by the concentration of disadvantage, racial segregation, family disruption, and residential instability, which in turn fosters more crime. Morenoff et al. (2001) also used PHDCN to show that the density of personal ties was associated with higher collective efficacy but did not translate directly into lower crime rates—the association of dense ties with lower crime was entirely indirect. These basic findings on collective efficacy and violence were replicated in the 2002 data and then extended to 2010 (Sampson, 2011).

We must bear in mind that social ties are neutral in the sense that they can be drawn upon for negative as well as positive goals. With this in mind Browning, Feinberg, and Dietz (2004) found that dense networks attenuate the effect of collective efficacy on crime, adding a twist to the idea that strong ties are not necessarily a good thing. In what is termed a *negotiated coexistence* model, collective efficacy is negatively associated with the prevalence of violent crime in urban neighborhoods but the density of exchange networks interacts with collective efficacy such that as network density increases, the regulatory effect of collective efficacy on violence declines. However, adding to the complexity, another study by Browning (2002) showed a direct association between collective efficacy and lower partner violence.

There is evidence that the civic infrastructure of local organizations and voluntary associations helps sustain the collective capacity for social action in a way that transcends traditional personal ties. Organizations are equipped to foster collective efficacy, often through strategic networking of their own or by creating tasks that demand collective responses (Small, 2009). Whether disorder removal, school improvements, or police responses, a continuous stream of challenges faces contemporary communities, challenges that no longer can be met by relying solely on individuals. Effective action can thus be conceived as depending in part on organizational settings and connections that are not necessarily reflective of the density of personal ties in a neighborhood. PHDCN-related research supports this position by showing that the density of local organizations as reported by residents along with their involvement in voluntary associations predicts higher levels of both collective efficacy and collective civic events, controlling for poverty, social composition, and prior crime rates (Sampson, 2011).

Taking Stock

There is evidence from beyond Chicago that supports these general observations on concentrated disadvantage, collective efficacy, and the general importance of community social processes. Rather than provide a review of the evidence from individual studies, I rely on an independent review of available empirical studies from 1960 to 1999 using the technique of meta-analysis (Pratt & Cullen, 2005). Collective efficacy emerged with an overall correlation of -.303 with crime rates across studies (95 percent confidence interval of -.26 to -.35). By meta-analysis standards this is a robust finding, and the authors rank collective efficacy number four in magnitude when weighted by sample size, slightly ahead of poverty's overall correlation of .25, family disruption, and race. Although the number of studies and hence the empirical base is limited, and while there is considerable variability in units of analysis across studies, the class of mechanisms associated with social disorganization theory and its offspring, collective efficacy theory, shows a robust association with lower crime rates (Kubrin & Weitzer, 2003; Sampson et al., 2002). Concentrated poverty and racial segregation also yield persistent associations with crime rates across a large number of studies, but it is important to note that assessing direct associations in meta-analysis is not the full picture. Concentrated disadvantage's influence may work through a number of mediating community processes such as collective efficacy.

Another community mechanism concerns culture. Harding (2010) shows a link between violence and heterogeneity in age-appropriate cultural scripts in Boston neighborhoods. A PHDCN study links moral cynicism about whether laws or collective moral rules are considered binding to higher violence. Respondents in Chicago were asked to report their level of agreement with statements such as "Laws were made to be broken"; "It's okay to do anything you want as long as you don't hurt anyone"; and "To make money, there are no right and wrong ways anymore, only easy ways and hard ways." In communities with high levels of cynicism and a perceived lack of legitimacy of legal rules, violent offending was significantly higher after controlling for demographic composition (Sampson, Morenoff, & Raudenbush, 2005). These findings and Harding's results suggest that where there is greater normative heterogeneity, violence is higher.

Summarized briefly, I would argue that the cumulative results of research support the claim that neighborhoods characterized by (a) mistrust, (b) perceived lack of shared expectations and cultural heterogeneity, (c) sparse acquaintanceship and exchange networks among residents, (d) attenuated social control of public spaces, (e) a weak organizational and institutional base, (f) low participation in local voluntary associations, and (g) moral/legal cynicism, are associated with an increased risk of interpersonal crime and public disorder within their borders. Moreover, the data suggest that key dimensions of social organization and collective action are influenced (although not determined) by neighborhood structural characteristics over long periods of time. Collective efficacy in particular appears to be undermined by concentrated poverty that is coupled with durable patterns of racial segregation, family disruption, and residential instability. Once again then, community and inequality are intimately connected in time and space.

EFFECTS OF CRIME ON SOCIAL AND ECONOMIC ORGANIZATION

It is important to recognize that crime and its consequences may themselves have important reciprocal effects on community. Skogan (1990) has provided an overview of some of the "feedback" processes that may increase levels of crime. These include the physical and psychological withdrawal from community life because of fear, a weakening of the informal social control processes that inhibit crime, decline in the organizational life and mobilization capacity of the neighborhood, deteriorating business conditions, and neighborhood out-migration.

For example, if people shun their neighbors and local facilities out of fear of crime, fewer opportunities exist for local networks and organizations to take hold. Street crime may be also accompanied by residential out-migration and business relocation from inner-city areas. As a result, crime can lead to demographic "collapse" and a weakening of the informal control structures and mobilization capacity of communities, which in turn fuels further crime.

Although the number of empirical studies is relatively small, there is evidence that crime can undermine the social and economic fabric of urban areas. One of the most important findings is that crime generates fear of strangers and a general alienation from participation in community life (Skogan, 1990). Besides weakening neighborhood social organization, high crime rates and concerns about safety may trigger population loss. For example, delinquency rates are not only one of the outcomes of urban change, they are also an important part of the process of urban change. Studying Chicago neighborhoods, Bursik (1986) observes that "although changes in racial composition cause increases in the delinquency rate, this effect is not nearly as great as the effect that increases in the delinquency rate have in minority groups being stranded in the community" (p. 73). In a study of 40 neighborhoods in eight cities, Skogan (1990) found that high rates of crime and disorder were associated with higher rates of fear, neighborhood dissatisfaction, and intentions to move out. Using the PHDCN, Morenoff et al. (2001) found a dynamic process where prior violence depressed collective efficacy (presumably because of fear or cynicism), even as collective efficacy helped stave off later crime. Similarly, Sampson and Raudenbush (1999) found a reciprocal negative relationship between collective efficacy and rates of violence in Chicago neighborhoods. While businesses may be less sensitive to crime than individual residents, they too are not immune from the social disorganization, fear, and social incivilities associated with street violence (Skogan, 1990).

The overall picture painted by prior research on the effects of crime on community is one of population abandonment of high-crime urban neighborhoods, business relocation to the suburbs, loss of economic revenue, a decrease in economic status and property values, and escalating levels of fear in central cities, at least in prior decades. Consider that many cities in the North and Midwest that lost population in the 1970s–1990s became increasingly poorer and racially isolated (Wilson, 1987). An important part of this racially selective decline in population and economic status apparently stems from violent crime. Interestingly, however, many of these same cities recovered and even thrived during the most recent era of the American crime decline (Blumstein & Wallman, 2000). New York City is perhaps the "poster city" for how low crime rates serve as a leading indicator of urban vitality. But it is not alone. Many cities are bucking dominant stereotypes and reporting record drops in violence, including Los Angeles and Chicago, the second and third largest cities in the country. In fact we are now at crime levels last seen in the 1950s. As Skogan (1990) has emphasized, crime is a salient event that has important symbolic consequences for perceptions of the inhabitability and civility of city life. Breaking the cycle of violence in communities and maintaining the declines in crime that have blessed many cities in recent years is thus crucial to a general strategy for urban policy, to which I now turn.

CHANGING PLACES, NOT PEOPLE

The logic of this essay points to efforts to change places rather than to change or move individuals. But efforts to intervene in communities face a large challenge. For starters, there is a consensus in evaluation research that community crime-prevention programs have achieved only limited success. Probably the most common crime-prevention approach is "neighborhood watch," where attempts are made to increase residents' participation in local efforts at social control (e.g., community meetings, neighborhood patrols). Other interventions have tried to increase social interaction among neighbors and instill concern for the public welfare of local residents. There have also been even more general efforts to change neighborhood opportunity structures, such as the classic Chicago Area Project patterned after Shaw and McKay's original delinquency theory. Yet evaluations of these programs are for the most part pessimistic about concrete reductions in crime (Bursik & Grasmick, 1993; Hope, 1995).

Although disappointing results from evaluation research could mean that neighborhood-level theories are wrong, another possibility is that programs were not implemented correctly. We know, for example, that community crime prevention is especially hard to implement in the areas that need them the most—poor, unstable neighborhoods with high crime rates—and that participation levels tend to fall off quickly once interventions are removed. Efforts to reduce crime are most likely to succeed if they are embedded in more comprehensive programs for neighborhood stabilization that local residents support. "One-shot" interventions that are externally imposed and simply try to reduce crime in the short run without confronting durable aspects of a neighborhood's vulnerability are, not surprisingly, highly susceptible to failure (Hope, 1995). Whether the poor track record of community interventions (similar to the poor track record of individual interventions) is due to a failure of theory or a programmatic failure of implementation is thus unknown. It is perhaps most likely that neighborhood-level interventions have pulled the wrong levers of change or targeted nonessential mechanisms.

I therefore examine some policy-related implications that attempt to move beyond past efforts. I focus primarily on community-level mechanisms reviewed above that are theoretically related, whether directly or indirectly, to the policy decisions of public officials. For the most part, these are policy domains that focus on crime prevention or the enhancement of community social organization from other than criminal justice agencies. Initiatives that rely on the police, prisons, and other agencies of social control have been reviewed at length many times, and hence I do not cover them here, except as they interface with neighborhood efforts. For example, I do not cover the traditional literature on neighborhood watch and community crime prevention. Rather, my discussion focuses on alternative neighborhood-level policies most directly related to crime and justice concerns, along with more comprehensive strategies that attack "root causes" of crime but that I argue are still amenable to community-level policy.

Neighborhood "Hot Spots" for Crime and Disorder

Research has long demonstrated that crimes are not randomly distributed in space. Rather, they are disproportionately concentrated in certain neighborhoods and "places" (e.g., taverns, parking lots). Ecologically oriented criminologists have dubbed these areas "hot spots" of crime (Sherman, Gartin, & Buerger, 1989). Drawing on community theory and advances in computer mapping technology, policing strategies can be more effective if they are implemented using information on neighborhood hot spots. For example, Sherman and colleagues (1989) advocated place-based interventions whereby hot-spot data are used to study the effects of differential patrol allocations, selective revocation of bar licenses, and removal of vacant "crack" houses. Recent experimental-based research shows that policing and situational crime-prevention strategies targeted to small ecological areas (about two blocks in size) reduces crime. Moreover, crime is not simply displaced elsewhere—instead, there is a spatial diffusion of safety (Braga & Bond, 2008; Weisburd et al., 2006).

But the logic of social disorganization theory and the extant evidence suggest that it is not just crime that is important to target. "Incivilities" and signs of disorder such as broken windows, trash, public drinking, and prostitution increase fear of crime and possibly crime itself (Skogan, 1990). One possibility is that potential offenders recognize such deterioration and assume that residents are so indifferent to what goes on in their neighborhood that they will not be motivated to confront strangers, intervene in a crime, or call the police (Wilson & Kelling, 1982). Another possibility is that physical and social elements of disorder comprise highly visible cues to which all neighborhood observers respond, potentially influencing migration patterns, investment by businesses, and overall neighborhood viability (Sampson & Raudenbush, 1999; Taylor, 2001). Thus if disorder operates in a cascading fashion by encouraging people to move (increasing residential instability) or discouraging efforts at building collective responses, it would indirectly have an effect on crime. To foster a climate of safety and order in public spaces, one could imagine collective strategies such as (a) cleaning up graffiti, trash, needles, and other elements of perceived disorder, (b) staggering bar closing times, (c) enactment of strict zoning/licensing, and (d) encouraging greater use of public spaces.

The optimal strategies for reducing disorder would appear to be those that involve both the police *and* community residents in the definition of the specific disorder problem to be solved and the planning of any interventions. The reason is that disorder is not a unitary concept, and people living in the same neighborhoods do not always agree on whether disorder is in fact a problem. Fortunately, there is evidence that community policing can be designed to encourage citizen participation in defining what are the problems to address, and ultimately to design solutions that reduce crime and increase community satisfaction (Skogan & Hartnett, 1997).

Informal Social Control and Collective Efficacy

A major dimension of social organization is the ability of a community to supervise and control teenage peer-groups. Communities characterized by a set of obligations, expectations, and social networks connecting the adults are better able to facilitate this task. For example, when the parents' friends or acquaintances are the parents of their children's friends, the adults have the potential to observe the child's actions in different circumstances, talk to each other about the child, compare notes, and establish norms (Coleman, 1988). This form of relation can provide reinforcement for inculcating positive youth outcomes, as found when parents in communities with overlapping social networks assume responsibility for the supervision of youth that are not their own. Closure of local networks provides youth with a social resource of a collective nature—a social good that is created when relations among persons facilitate action. One can extend this model to closure among networks involving parents and teachers, religious and recreational leaders, businesses that serve youth, and even agents of criminal justice.

Programs that might foster informal social controls and collective efficacy include:

- organized community supervision of leisure-time youth activities
- monitoring/reduction of street-corner congregation in high-crime areas
- staggered school closing times to reduce peer-control system
- parent surveillance/involvement in after-school and nighttime youth programs
- adult-youth mentoring systems; forums for parental acquaintanceship

The key here is to increase positive connections among youth and adults in the community. Curfews for adolescents in public areas have been proposed by some, but my focus is on informal social controls that arise from ongoing social interactions and community support. Consider as a possibility what Meares and Kahan (1998) describe as the emergence of a "working trust" between the police and residents of Chicago's poverty-stricken west side in the cocreation of zones of safety. Policies including juvenile curfews and policing of minor disorders were supported by residents largely because of the leadership role of the local police commander, who was a longtime resident. In fact, the police commander led a prayer vigil to protest the occurrence of drug dealing and crime in the community. Over 1,000 residents participated, and in groups of ten they marched and reclaimed street corners where drug dealers had previously dominated. Following the prayer vigil, over 7,000 residents retired to a local park for a celebration. Such a coalition is surely controversial, but from the perspective of collective efficacy theory coupled with the strength of the black church as a site for collective-action strategies, the Chicago alliance is a development that bears watching. Indeed, it appears that participation by residents in a newly constituted and legitimized community policing effort was in itself an action that increased community solidarity and collective efficacy.

Housing-Based Neighborhood Stabilization

A more general option for enhancing social organization is to focus on joint public/private intervention programs to help stabilize and revitalize deteriorating neighborhoods. My focus is primarily on investment in the housing structure of declining but still-reachable communities. As noted above, a long history of community-based research shows that population instability and housing decay are linked to crime and social problems among youth. This research becomes more salient in the era of housing foreclosures brought on by the 2008 economic collapse. The implication is that community-based policy interventions may help to reverse the tide of vacancies and deterioration in many neighborhoods across America, not just the concentrated poverty areas of our large cities. These policies might include:

- resident management of public housing
- tenant buy-outs of existing public units
- rehabilitation of existing low-income housing
- strict code enforcement

Low-income neighborhoods have historically suffered from severe population and housing loss of the sort that is disruptive of the social and institutional order. Bursik (1989) has shown that the planned construction of new public housing projects in Chicago's poor communities in the 1970s was associated with increased rates of population turnover, which in turn were related to increases in crime independent of racial composition. More generally,

Skogan (1990) has noted how urban renewal and forced migration contributed to the wholesale uprooting of many urban black communities, especially the extent to which freeway networks driven through the hearts of many cities in the 1950s destroyed viable, low-income communities. In Atlanta one in six residents were dislocated through urban renewal, the great majority of whom were poor blacks (Logan & Molotch, 1987). Nationwide, fully 20 percent of all central city housing units occupied by blacks were lost in the period 1960–1970 alone.

Recognizing these historical patterns, it would be wise to focus on the stabilization of existing areas—especially those at risk of a tipping point to widespread vacancy. When considered with the practices of redlining and disinvestments by banks and "block-busting" by real estate agents (Massey & Denton, 1993), local policies toward code enforcement—which on the surface are far removed from crime—have nonetheless contributed to crime through neighborhood deterioration, forced migration, and instability. By acting to reduce population flight, residential anonymity, and housing deterioration, my hypothesis is that neighborhood stabilization and ultimately a more cohesive environment for youth socialization will emerge.

Deconcentration of Poverty

As Wilson (1987) famously argued, the social transformation of the inner city in the late 20th century resulted in the disproportionate concentration and segregation of the most disadvantaged segments of the urban black population—especially poor, female-headed families with children. This social transformation was fueled by macro-structural economic changes related to the deindustrialization of central cities where disadvantaged minorities are concentrated (e.g., shift from goods-producing to service-producing industries; increasing polarization of the labor market into low-wage and high-wage sectors). But perhaps more important, the steady out-migration of middle- and upper-income black families from core inner-city areas may have removed a former source of institutional supports. Consistent with a social organizational approach, Wilson (1987) theorized that the basic institutions of a neighborhood (e.g., churches, schools, stores, recreational facilities) were more likely to remain viable if the core of their support came from economically stable families.

An understanding of concentration effects must also recognize not just voluntary migration decisions but also the negative consequences of policy decisions to concentrate minorities and the poor in public housing. Opposition from organized community groups to the building of public housing in their "backyard," de facto federal policy to tolerate segregation against blacks in urban housing markets, and decisions by local governments to neglect the rehabilitation of existing residential units, led to massive, segregated housing projects that became ghettos for the minorities and disadvantaged (Massey & Denton, 1993). The great American crime decline and the economic boom of the 1990s offered new opportunities to reverse these changes, and as noted above growing evidence shows real progress on the health of many U.S. cities. Building on the previous strategy, community-level approaches that merit further investigation are:

- dispersing concentrated public housing
- scattered-site, new, low-income housing
- mixed-income housing development and incentives for mixed-income neighborhoods

The evidence that dispersion policies, scattered-site and mixed-income housing can work is small but encouraging (Cisneros & Engdahl, 2009; Popkin & Cove, 2007). In a major example, the Chicago Housing Authority embarked on an ambitious plan to "scatter" tens of thousands of units of high-rise public housing in the city's ghetto as a means to break down the severe segregation that was firmly in place. The infamous Robert Taylor Homes that became a national symbol of urban despair no longer exists—in its place a black middle-class is now emerging (Sampson, 2011). Efforts to promote stable low-income neighborhoods are also now part of ambitious efforts in Chicago (e.g., the "New Communities Program" of the MacArthur Foundation).

Municipal Services

The provision of city municipal services for public health and fire safety—decisions presumably made with little if any thought to crime and violence—appear to be salient in the social (dis)integration of poor communities. As Wallace and Wallace (1990) argue based on an analysis of the "planned shrinkage" of New York City fire and health services in the 1970s:

> The consequences of withdrawing municipal services from poor neighborhoods, the resulting outbreaks of contagious urban decay and forced migration which shred essential social networks and cause social disintegration, have become a highly significant contributor to decline in public health among the poor. (p. 427)

The loss of social integration and networks from planned shrinkage of services may increase behavioral patterns of violence, which cause further social disintegration (Wallace & Wallace, 1990). This pattern of destabilizing feedback is central not only to an understanding of the role of municipal service policies in fostering the downward spiral of low-income, high-crime areas, but also, by implication, *the turnaround and stabilization of those areas*. Housing and community-based policies noted above should thus be coordinated with local policies regarding fire, sanitation, and other municipal services, especially in recessionary times.

Community Organizational Base

Stable interlocking organizations form a major linchpin of building social capital, collective efficacy, and effective social control (Small, 2009). When local organizations are unstable and isolated, and when the vertical links of community institutions to extra local sources of support are weak, the capacity of a community to defend its local interests is weakened. As Bursik and Grasmick (1993) argue along similar lines, public control refers to the regulatory capacities that develop from the networks among neighborhoods and between neighborhoods and public/private agencies. More specifically, this dimension "refers to the ability to secure public and private goods and services that are allocated by groups and agencies located outside of the neighborhood" (Bursik & Grasmick, 1993, p. 19). It follows that interventions promoting public control would work to increase citizen involvement in community organizations while at the same time promoting the integration of local institutions with extra-local or external resources. Collective action to change resource allocation strategies might also be targeted (e.g., mobilization of political allies to influence private community funding or city budget allocations). Although there is little if any evidence evaluating these kinds of mobilization strategies, even minor successes may produce cumulative changes that over time ultimately lead to a more stable and long-lasting social organization.

Community Justice and Prisoner Reentry

Imprisonment rates have soared in recent decades and may have contributed to the declining crime rate. But most prisoners return to a home community (Travis, 2005). The logic of this chapter calls for a community-level approach that seeks to reintegrate offenders and help counteract the hardships that already-disadvantaged neighborhoods face when unemployed ex-felons return home. Not only might concentrated incarceration have the unintended consequence of increasing crime rates through its negative impact on the labor market and social capital prospects of former prisoners (Clear, Rose, & Ryder, 2001; Western, 2006), but there is evidence that neighborhood context also helps explain the recidivism rates of ex-prisoners (Hipp, Petersilia, & Turner, 2010). It follows that a policy of integrating prisoner release programs with efforts to build community capacity and achieve community justice is an important step for policy (Clear & Karp, 1999; Clear et al., 2001). One can think of this as "collective efficacy meets prisoner reentry."

Ecometrics—Toward a National Strategy of Community Monitoring

Finally, community-based policy is not complete without a rigorous system of measurement and evaluation. Just like educational reform cannot proceed without a rigorous system for measuring growth in learning, so too community renewal cannot proceed without a rigorous metric for measuring community processes. One of the most important "first-order" findings from recent research is that community-based surveys can yield reliable and valid measures of neighborhood social and institutional processes. But unlike individual-level measurements in education that are backed up by decades of psychometric research into their statistical properties, the methodology needed to evaluate neighborhood mechanisms is not widespread. Stephen Raudenbush and I (Raudenbush and Sampson, 1999) thus proposed moving toward a science of ecological assessment, which we call "ecometrics," by developing systematic procedures for directly measuring neighborhood processes and by integrating and adapting tools from psychometrics to improve the quality of neighborhood-level measures. The important procedural point is that neighborhood processes can and should be treated as ecological or collective phenomena rather than as stand-ins for individual-level traits. A national or codified system of measurement, with standard protocols for evaluation, would enhance the science behind any community-based policy. Furthermore, local communities could use standardized measures for benchmarking or monitoring their progress or capacities in meeting stated goals.

CONCLUDING THOUGHTS

What seem to be "noncrime" policies—for example, where or if to build mixed-income housing, the enforcement of municipal codes, maintaining essential city services, the rehabilitation of existing residential units, the dispersal of concentrated poverty, building social connections among adults and youth, increasing collective efficacy to achieve common goals, and community monitoring through "ecometrics"—may have an important bearing on preventing crime and promoting general well-being. This conceptualization explicitly considers the role of political and urban planning, including their unintended social outcomes, in shaping local community structures. As argued above, residential instability and the concentration of poor, female-headed families with children were influenced by planned governmental policies at local, state, and federal levels even if not desired at the outset. Crime also generates a reciprocal feedback effect by undermining social and economic organization, which in turn can lead to further increases in crime. Even decisions to relocate businesses appear to be shaped in part by the corrosive impact of serious crime on the quality of life for workers and customers alike. Hence policies on urban development can ill afford to ignore the symbolic and economic consequences of crime for the habitability, civility, and economic vitality of city life.

The implication of this chapter's theoretical framework is that community-level policy options are a foundational way to think about improving collective efficacy, reducing concentrated poverty, and furthering the crime declines that are underway in American cities. The value of a community-level perspective is that it cautions against a simple "kinds of people" analysis by focusing on the social characteristics of collectivities and how they are interrelated. Based on the theory and research reviewed here, policymakers should pay special attention to integrating violence prevention and community prisoner reentry with more general noncrime policies that address mediating processes of social organization (e.g., intergenerational closure, control-of-street-corner peer groups, organizational participation and mobilization around local problems); the political economy of place (e.g., how concentrated poverty and vacancy rates are influenced by housing policy, municipal services, and code enforcement); community investments in early child development; and ecometric measurement. Perhaps then we can expect a more lasting effect of neighborhood-based interventions on the reduction of crime and disorder and the enhancement of urban social infrastructure. The widespread return migration to U.S. cities and the broad crime reductions of the early 21st century suggest that community-level approaches are not utopian and may even be responsible for some of these observed gains.

In effect, I am calling for a paradigm shift in urban policy and in the levels of policy manipulation. Interventions at the level of neighborhoods or other ecological units are possible, and some can even be accomplished in experimental fashion. Examples include the random assignment of neighborhoods to receive a network-based AIDS intervention, community policing, or an effort to mobilize collective efficacy. The theoretically implied unit of intervention is the community itself. If rates of sexually transmitted diseases or public violence were significantly reduced after a randomized intervention, or if dissimilar outcomes were affected (e.g., civic trust, social interactions), we may then speak of an emergent neighborhood-level effect. From a policy perspective, neighborhood-level interventions (not all of which need to be randomized) may be more cost effective than those targeted to individuals.

The good news is that community-level ideas and interventions are being combined in innovative programs around the country. One is the Harlem Children's Zone, a comprehensive school, child, and community-based program with encouraging early results on learning (Dobbie & Fryer, 2009). The Harlem Children's Zone did not start with the assumption that the poor neighborhood of Harlem was inherently a bad place and that people needed to simply move out. Rather, it attempted to improve the schools and community simultaneously, a bold move to invest in the children living there. Now people want to move to Harlem—yet just a few years back it would have been considered rational to flee by most observers! Other community interventions can be noted—community policing in Chicago, the deconcentration of public housing around the country, and the HOPE VI mixed-income program (Cisneros & Engdahl, 2009). The initiative of President Obama to create "Promise Neighborhoods" and "Choice Neighborhoods" in multiple cities is probably the most visible affirmation of the goal to create safe, educationally intensive communities with a commitment to the human and social capital development of the next generation.[2] The science is clear that human capital interventions are important for children—the earlier, the better (Heckman, 2006). As I have argued in greater depth elsewhere (Sampson, 2011), the structural logic of community-level intervention adds a powerful dimension to concern for child well-being in a way that goes well beyond the individual-level voucher logic that has until now dominated policy thinking.

NOTES

This chapter draws on the research in Sampson (2011) and is a revision of a paper presented at "America's Urban Infrastructure: Confronting Her Challenges, Embracing Her Opportunities," Washington University, St. Louis, MO, November 20, 2009.

1. I set aside schools even though the structural logic of my argument is relevant. See Raudenbush (2009 and this volume) for a discussion of educational policy at the school level.
2. As of early 2010, Congress has signed legislation to spend over $65 million to replicate the Harlem Children's Zone in 20 neighborhoods across the United States.

REFERENCES

Bandura, A. (1997). *Self efficacy: The exercise of control.* New York: W. H. Freeman.

Blumstein, A., & Wallman, J. (2000). *The crime drop in America.* New York, NY: Cambridge.

Braga, A., & Bond, B. J. (2008). Policing crime and disorder hot spots: A randomized controlled trial. *Criminology, 46,* 577–607.

Brooks-Gunn, J., Duncan, G., & Aber, L. (Eds.). (1997). *Neighborhood poverty: Policy implications in studying neighborhoods* (Vol. 2). New York, NY: Russell Sage Foundation.

Browning, C. R. (2002). The span of collective efficacy: Extending social disorganization theory to partner violence. *Journal of Marriage and the Family, 64*(4), 833–850.

Browning, C. R., Feinberg, S. L., & Dietz, R. (2004). The paradox of social organization: Networks, collective efficacy, and violent crime in urban neighborhoods. *Social Forces, 83*(2), 503–534.

Bursik, R.J., Jr. (1986). Delinquency rates as sources of ecological change. In J. M. Byrne & R. J. Sampson (Eds.), *The social ecology of crime.* New York, NY: Springer-Verlag.

Bursik, R. J., Jr. (1988). Social disorganization and theories of crime and delinquency: Problems and prospects. *Criminology, 35,* 677–703.

Bursik, R. J., Jr. (1989). Political decision-making and ecological models of delinquency: Conflict of consensus. In S. Messner, M. Krohn, & A. Liska (Eds.), *Theoretical integration in the study of deviance and crime.* Albany: State University of New York Press.

Bursik, R. J., & Grasmick, H. (1993). *Neighborhoods and crime: The dimensions of effective community control.* New York, NY: Lexington Books.

Cisneros, H. G., & Engdahl, L. (Eds.). (2009). *From despair to hope: Hope VI and the new promise of public housing in America's cities.* Washington, DC: Brookings Institution Press.

Clear, T., & Karp, D. (1999). *The community justice ideal: Preventing crime and achieving justice.* Boulder, CO: Westview.

Clear, T. R., Rose, D. R., & Ryder, J. A. (2001). Incarceration and community: The problem of removing and returning offenders. *Crime and Delinquency, 47,* 335–351.

Coleman, J. S. (1988). Social capital in the creation of human capital. *American Journal of Sociology, 94,* S95–120.

Dobbie, W., & Fryer, R. G., Jr. (2009). *Are high-quality schools enough to close the achievement gap? Evidence from a bold social experiment in Harlem.* Cambridge, MA: Harvard University.

Giddens, A. (1990). *Consequences of modernity.* Stanford, CA: Stanford University Press.

Goering, J., & Feins, J. (Eds.). (2003). *Choosing a better life? Evaluating the Moving to Opportunity social experiment.* Washington, DC: Urban Institute Press.

Grannis, R. (1998). The importance of trivial streets: Residential streets and residential segregation. *American Journal of Sociology, 103,* 1530–1564.

Granovetter, M. (1973). The strength of weak ties. *American Journal of Sociology, 78*(6), 360–380.

Harding, D. J. (2010). *Living the drama: Community, conflict, and culture among inner-city boys.* Chicago, IL: University of Chicago Press.

Heckman, J. J. (2006). Skill formation and the economics of investing in disadvantaged children. *Science, 312,* 1900–1902.

Hipp, J. R., Petersilia, J., & Turner, S. (2010). Parolee recidivism in California: The effect of neighborhood context and social service agency characteristics. *Criminology, 48*(4), 947–949.

Hope, T. (1995). Community crime prevention. In M. Tonry & D. Farrington (Eds.), *Building a safer society* (pp. 21–89). Chicago, IL: University of Chicago Press.

Kornhauser, R. R. (1978). *Social sources of delinquency: An appraisal of analytic models.* Chicago, IL: University of Chicago Press.

Kubrin, C. E., & Weitzer, R. (2003). New directions in social disorganization theory. *Journal of Research in Crime and Delinquency, 40*(4), 374–402.

Lewin, K. (1951). *Field theory in social science: Selected theoretical papers.* D. Cartwright (ed.). New York, NY: Harper & Row.

Logan, J., & Molotch, H. (1987). *Urban fortunes: The political economy of place.* Berkeley: University of California Press.

Massey, D. S., & Denton, N. (1993). *American apartheid: Segregation and the making of the underclass.* Cambridge, MA: Harvard University Press.

Meares, T., & Kahan, D. (1998). Law and (norms of) order in the inner city. *Law and Society Review, 32,* 805–838.

Morenoff, J. D., Sampson, R. J., & Raudenbush, S. (2001). Neighborhood inequality, collective efficacy, and the spatial dynamics of urban violence. *Criminology, 39,* 517–560.

Park, R. E. (1915). The city: Suggestions for the investigations of human behavior in the urban environment. *American Journal of Sociology, 20,* 577–612.

Popkin, S., & Cove, E. (2007). *Safety is the most important thing: How Hope VI helped families.* Washington, DC: Urban Institute, Metropolitan Housing and Communities Center.

Pratt, T., & Cullen, F. (2005). Assessing macro-level predictors and theories of crime: A meta-analysis. In M. Tonry (Ed.), *Crime and justice: A review of research* (Vol. 32, pp. 373–450). Chicago, IL: University of Chicago Press.

Putnam, R. (2000). *Bowling alone: The collapse and renewal of American community.* New York, NY: Simon and Schuster.

Raudenbush, S. (2009). *Reorganizing urban schools to reduce inequality.* Paper presented at America's Urban Infrastructure: Confronting Her Challenges, Embracing Her Opportunities, Conference at Washington University, St. Louis, MO.

Raudenbush, S. W., & Sampson, R. J. (1999). "Ecometrics": Toward a science of assessing ecological settings, with application to the systematic social observation of neighborhoods. *Sociological Methodology, 29,* 1–41.

Reiss, A. J. Jr., & Tonry, M. (1986). *Communities and crime* (Vol. 9). Chicago, IL: University of Chicago Press.

Ross, C. E., Reynolds, J. R., & Geis, K. J. (2000). The contingent meaning of neighborhood stability for residents' psychological well-being. *American Sociological Review, 65,* 581–597.

Sampson, R. J. (2011). *Great American city: Chicago and the enduring neighborhood effect.* Chicago, IL: University of Chicago Press.

Sampson, R. J., & Groves, W. B. (1989). Community structure and crime: Testing social-disorganization theory. *American Journal of Sociology, 94*(4), 774–802.

Sampson, R. J., Morenoff, J. D., & Gannon-Rowley, T. (2002). Assessing "neighborhood effects": Social processes and new directions in research. *Annual Review of Sociology, 28,* 443–478.

Sampson, R. J., Morenoff, J. D., & Raudenbush, S. W. (2005). Social anatomy of racial and ethnic disparities in violence. *American Journal of Public Health, 95,* 224–232.

Sampson, R. J., & Raudenbush, S. W. (1999). Systematic social observation of public spaces: A new look at disorder in urban neighborhoods. *American Journal of Sociology, 105,* 603–651.

Sampson, R. J., Raudenbush, S. W., & Earls, F. (1997). Neighborhoods and violent crime: A multilevel study of collective efficacy. *Science, 277,* 918–924.

Sharkey, P. (2010). The acute effect of local homicides on children's cognitive performance. *Proceedings of the National Academy of Sciences, 107,* 11733–11738.

Shaw, C. R., & McKay, H. D. (1942/1969). *Juvenile delinquency and urban areas.* Chicago, IL: University of Chicago Press.

Sherman, L., Gartin, P., & Buerger, M. (1989). Hot spots of predatory crime: Routine activities and the criminology of place. *Criminology, 27,* 27–56.

Skogan, W. (1990). *Disorder and decline: Crime and the spiral of decay in American cities.* Berkeley: University of California Press.

Skogan, W., & Hartnett, S. (1997). *Community policing, Chicago style.* New York, NY: Oxford University Press.

Small, M. (2009). *Unanticipated gains: Origins of network inequality in everyday life.* New York, NY: Oxford University Press.

Suttles, G. D. (1972). The defended community. In G. D. Suttles (Ed.), *The social construction of communities* (pp. 21–43). Chicago, IL: University of Chicago Press.

Taylor, R. B. (2001). *Breaking away from broken windows: Baltimore neighborhoods and the nationwide fight against crime, grime, fear, and decline.* Boulder, CO: Westview.

Travis, J. (2005). *But they all come back: Facing the challenges of prisoner reentry.* Washington, DC: Urban Institute Press.

Wallace, R., & Wallace, D. (1990). Origins of public health collapse in New York City: The dynamics of planned shrinkage, contagious urban decay and social disintegration. *Bulletin of the New York Academy of Medicine, 66,* 391–434.

Weisburd, D., Wyckoff, L., Ready, J., Eck, J., Hinkle, J., & Gajewski, F. (2006). Does crime just move around the corner? A controlled study of spatial displacement and diffusion of crime control benefits. *Criminology, 44,* 549–592.

Western, B. (2006). *Punishment and inequality in America.* New York, NY: Russell Sage Foundation.

Wilson, J. Q., & Kelling, G. (1982, March). Broken windows: The police and neighborhood safety. *Atlantic, 127,* 29–38.

Wilson, W. J. (1987). *The truly disadvantaged: The inner city, the underclass, and public policy.* Chicago, IL: The University of Chicago Press.

2

Toward a Theory of Place

Social Mobility, Proximity, and Proximal Capital

Odis D. Johnson Jr.

The growing interest in the relationship between one's context and opportunity has increased the need within the social sciences, and the sociology of education in particular, to explain social mobility according to "place," a term I use to identify ecological units in which populations are organized in accordance with economic and social forces and therefore distinguished by social, cultural, and economic characteristics. A number of conceptual advances have occurred in the last two decades that help explain how, why, and to what end place contributes to inequality in social outcomes and intergenerational transmissions of social status. Consequently we have theories of epidemic effects and threshold effects, spillover effects, endogenous group membership effects, and articulations of "social capital" within communities, just to name a few. While sociologists of education have advanced understandings of processes of differentiating youth through schooling according to race, gender, and class, theories of differentiation according to place remain conspicuously absent, especially in light of recent conceptual advances in neighborhood studies. Indeed, some sociologists of education have suggested an ecological perspective in education is not informative (Arum, 2000), though the extent to which one exists remains unclear. Urban sociologists, criminologists, and economists, on the other hand, have presented many elements fundamental to an ecological system of differentiation that await synthesis, coherence, recognition, and utility in explaining social mobility through a primary neighborhood institution, the educational institution. Thus, my task in this project is to (1) assess the development of a theory of "place" within the sociology of education; (2) describe the distributive mechanisms that fashion and economically stratify the social associations that constitute ecological units (or places) and a form of endogenous capital called "proximity capital"; and (3) within these units, describe the conditions that facilitate an individual's success and failure in converting proximity capital into social mobility.

"PLACE" AND PERSPECTIVES WITHIN THE SOCIOLOGY OF EDUCATION

Functional and Conflict Theories

The sociology of education has for more than half a century advanced thought on the crucial role of education in providing social mobility and enabling status attainment.

Functional and conflict theories, cultural studies, and the more emergent neo-institutional perspective have provided sociological theories that, while describing educational systems, also explain variability in educational performance. The earlier theories, functional theories, argued that the occupational structure's need for skilled labor provided a mandate for educational institutions to test, sort, and allocate individuals into occupations according to ability (Sorokin, 1959) and achievement (Parsons, 1959). Though the efficiency of schools in accomplishing this goal was doubted by some (Clark, 1960), what remains clear is that functional theories placed greater emphasis on the contribution of school outputs to the occupational structure and less on the contribution of social inputs, such as neighborhood resources, to school-based systems of student differentiation. The educational inputs that today form the basis of investigations of educational opportunity received little attention in functional theories. Instead the family seemed to be the only source of educational "materials" on which schools and their processes of differentiation relied. Functional theory held that families served as the first juncture within the distributive process where differentiation occurred, the variation often corresponding to differences in social class (Parsons, 1959; Sorokin, 1959).

As the importance of individual ascriptive traits increased within sociological studies, the functional conception of schooling processes came under criticism; where theory initially considered the relation between the products of schooling and the needs of the occupational structure, the social unrest of the 1960s demanded interrogation of associations between societal inputs represented by ascriptive characteristics and schooling outputs. Collins's (1977) explicit critique of "technical-function" theory highlighted its inability to explain persistent differences within educational performance according to class and ethnicity. From a Weberian perspective that stressed the importance of status groups over that of individuals, Collins (1977) argued "the power of 'ascribed' groups may be the *prime* [italics his] basis of selection in all organizations," making technical skills a secondary consideration dependent on the balance of power (p. 125). In Collins's view, social mobility in education was characterized by power struggles among status groups and was less reliant on the demonstration of technical skills, thus making less meritocratic the distributive processes within schools that claim to sort individuals according to ability.

Of course, there were other competing perspectives within conflict theory. Bowles and Gintis (1976) had advanced a more functional yet neo-Marxist understanding of schooling that relied heavily on the socializing influence of work, families, and schools on children. Capitalists socialized their employees in a fashion that ensured workers' dedication to a life of labor, and in so doing guaranteed profit generation and the maintenance of the stratified class structure in the interests of the elite. Workers in turn unconsciously socialized youth through child rearing practices and education to meet the demands of the occupational structure for appropriately socialized workers. Mobility through schooling, therefore, was reserved for the children of the elite, limited opportunity for the less fortunate, and social reproduction for everyone. The work of Bowles and Gintis (1976) received much attention and soon came to represent the vanguard of conflict theory. However, the potential creation of a niche for the consideration of place is more apparent in the neo-Weberian perspective in that its acknowledgment of status groups and their ability to represent social characteristics apart from class avoids a preoccupation with the individual and purely economic precursors of mobility. Weber enumerated multiple sources giving rise to status groups, including differences in life situations extending from geographic origin. Though alternative sources of status group formation were acknowledged by Collins (1977), the heavy investment of the field in the neo-Marxist class perspective left a neo-Weberian theory of place undeveloped. Such a perspective could have no doubt moved the field forward in understanding between-school variability in school functioning and educational performance and advanced its interrogation in educational theory as emblematic of place differentiation. Sociologists of education were not the only ones to overlook the applicability of Weber. As Blau and Duncan (1967) contend, sociologists in community and urban studies also overlooked the applicability of Weberian status-group theory in explanations of differentiation within communities (pp. 5–6). Still there are other factors within the field that presented both promise and problems for the emergence of a theory of place.

Complicating the formalization of a theory of place is the unparalleled development of urban and community sociology and the sociology of education. Functional and conflict theory emerged in the 1950s and 1960s respectively decades after the adoption and employment of the ecological perspective at the Chicago school of sociology. Inspired by the observations of their predecessors, Davis, Gardner, and Gardner (1941), Whyte (1943), Drake and Cayton (1945), and Warner et al. (1947), all with ties to the Chicago school of sociology, forged a tradition in examining the social structure of communities. It was at the conclusion of this era that Hollingshead (1948) completed *Elmtown's Youth*. Though Hollingshead was a sociologist from Yale, his study was guided by the Committee on Human Development at the University of Chicago and was one of many studies carried out by University of Chicago faculty in that community setting. Hollingshead's effort to understand how the social structure of the community gave rise to adolescent behavior led him to focus much attention on schooling, exploring its curriculum and the actions of personnel that enabled student mobility and their eventual status attainment. His work represented the earliest explicit coupling of the ethnographic community study and the sociological investigation of schooling. However, his micro-sociological perspective would not receive much attention from the educational sociologists of the 1950s and 1960s, who, at the time, were more interested in macro-sociological approaches to educational research and theory. Ecological research soon lost ground, even within the Chicago school, to the influence of economics, a growing interest in individual income, and the rise of empiricism—trends foregrounding the work of the Chicago school scholars Otis Dudley Duncan, Peter Blau, and James Coleman, who, along with Harvard professors, aided the ascent of the sociology of education.

Yet other lost opportunities to recognize the importance of place become a bit more difficult to explain. A limitation of early theory within the sociology of education was the creation of a somewhat simplified conceptualization of the opportunity structure that was often depicted as static with little variability in its structure across contexts. Opportunity, however, did not manifest in a similar fashion across all areas nor did it present the same opportunities to all populations. To be sure, the breadth of occupations available in the industrialized city of the mid-twentieth century was significantly different from those available in rural areas. As Park (1925) argued, the technical organization of the city demanded "exceptional skill," requiring "special preparation," and "called into existence the trade and professional schools, and finally bureaus for vocational guidance" (p. 13). If the demands of the occupational structure in fact induced schools to perform its sorting function, then rural schools were forced to comply with vastly different structural needs than city schools. Today, we still find that the quality of rural and urban schooling differs in significant ways and, added to that variability, that a relatively higher quality of schools is found in suburban areas.

This line of reasoning remained unapplied to concerns about variation in educational opportunity and outcomes across smaller environments. For instance, what Park (1925) identifies as the smallest ecological unit, the neighborhood, was a central organizing factor in the provision of education. Desires for local control of schooling in neighborhoods that, according to the earliest ecological studies (Drake & Cayton, 1945; DuBois, 1899), varied significantly in socioeconomic status, hint at a discernable if not systematic variation in the education the neighborhoods provided, its quality, and its relationship to the occupational structure through the schools' distributive function. For example, Drake and Cayton (1945) in their classic study of the black belt of Chicago in the 1930s would find thirteen of the city's fifteen schools needing multiple shifts to accommodate the large number of students located in the crowded and segregated African American community (p. 202). As the Chicago leadership preferred to build segregation into the sky through immense housing project developments in the 1950s and 1960s (Venkatesh, 2000) rather than allow the northern expansion of the African American community, obvious differences in the quality of education across communities persisted (Orfield, 1992) and paralleled educational inequities in other cities (Wells & Crain, 1997). It hardly seems possible that educational theorists were unaware of or uninterested in how the local provision of education corresponded to neighborhood quality through the maintenance of the "neighborhood school."

Nonetheless it would have been well within the interests of early educational theories to consider the role of neighborhoods in increasing the efficiency of institutional processes of differentiation. With the influence of place unacknowledged in early theories, schools are bequeathed the task of sorting children from families whose neighboring has no social explanation—as if families had been organized into residential groups randomly. Functional theory appropriately identified the family as a source of variation in society's distributive processes, yet it did not fully consider how and why families are organized and consequently how the sorting function of families is preceded by ecological processes that make unmistakable contributions to the end result. The exercise of residential preferences and enactment of place-based social policies such as redlining, the construction of public housing, and suburban development increased the more homogenous grouping of families according to social class (Goetz, 2003; Massey & Denton, 1993; Venkatesh, 2000; Wilson, 1987) and in doing so, also the efficiency of the processes of differentiation within schools.

Explanations of Social Mobility in Cultural Studies in Education

Due to the inability of early macro-sociological theory to explain persistent inequality, the next shift in educational theory occurring in the 1970s would begin to investigate what goes on in the "black box" that had come to symbolize educational institutions. Karabel and Halsey (1977) remarked that if functional and conflict theories considered *how* and *why* educational systems function as they do, cultural theories examine the content of those systems or *what* is taught. The field with its newfound interest in individual subjectivities, an orientation that seemingly moved the field further away from explaining variability according to place, did not altogether abandon macro-sociological explanations of mobility through schooling. Most importantly, however, the field progressed in defining the agents that fuel the advancement of individuals in education, departing from the functionalists' identification of ability, noting the importance of ascription, and finally exploring the conduit of capital.

The cultural capital concept is one of the most influential theories in cultural studies (Bourdieu, 1977b). In his account of social mobility through schooling, Bourdieu (1977a) argued that educational institutions are entrusted with the intergenerational transmission of cultural knowledge that reflects society's greatest cultural products or "high culture." Those born into economically advantaged families receive through rearing the instruments needed to appropriate the knowledge transmitted in schools, and those lacking capital and the cultivation of the requisite cultural tools unfortunately depend on schools to cultivate these dispositions, which according to Bourdieu (1977a) only transmit culture, not the instruments for its appropriation. Unlike early sociological theory, which tended to simplify or avoid detailed conceptualizations of the opportunity structure, Bourdieu argued that types of knowledge that differ in their reflection of dominant culture correspond to certain occupations within the stratified economic structure. Bourdieu (1977a), for example, pointed out that the least dominant form of cultural capital reflected knowledge commensurate with agriculture, craftsmanship, and small trades, categories that were "excluded from participation in high culture" (p. 488).

One can infer from Bourdieu's observations that areas with economies dominated by similar occupations reflect a similar culture and a need of workers with similar knowledge and skills for labor production. It follows that schools within these areas might also reflect a similar level of cultural capital in the skills they impart to their learners. This plausibility positions Bourdieu's thesis to figure prominently in explanations of differentiation between schools according to the needs of local markets. Though Bourdieu's thesis does not question how cultural capital plays out in neighborhoods where families with certain inculcating practices are concentrated, it nonetheless implies that it is according to place through social class that we find families of proximity with similarities in rearing practices, and providing schools with children who are predisposed in many instances to a similar level of learning. This perhaps is an important point of departure for the field in developing a theory of place, since others have used other concepts of Bourdieu's (1984) to recognize neighborhood differences in cultural capital (Blasius, 1993; Blasius & Friedrichs, 2008).[1] Bourdieu's thinking then has great potential and utility in revealing distinctions among areas according to the concentration of predispositions toward learning and academic performance levels among children.

In contrast, the most obvious incongruities between cultural capital theory and place stratification arise from the theory's marginal role for schools and between-school differences in the development of educational disparities. Bourdieu (1977a) maintains "the educational system reproduces all the more perfectly the structure of the distribution of cultural capital among classes in that the culture which it transmits is closer to dominant culture" (p. 493). Schools, their ecological type notwithstanding, simply transmit dominant cultural knowledge, and differentiation occurs according to the distribution of student predispositions that do or do not allow them to learn. Consequently, there is little room for one to argue that the structural qualities of schools and the quality of their immediate context covary, and that that variation contributes to achievement disparities across neighborhoods. A related complication is the claim that educational institutions make no refinements to their transmission of dominant culture according to the distribution of predispositions within the school as suggested in Bourdieu's (1977a) notion of "non-existent pedagogic action." Consequently, Bourdieu's theorized process of differentiation within schools becomes one of the more inefficient processes depicted within educational theory, since it contends that schools transmit only dominant culture although the populations they serve have already been sorted at the neighborhood level, in some instances quite decisively, according to their ability to appropriate such transmissions.

Associations in Educational Theory

The publication of Willis's (1977) *Learning to Labor*, one of the earliest ethnographic studies within the field, marked a new direction in the analysis of the intersection of culture and social class. Prior to its publication, educational theory envisioned mobility as exclusively arising from hierarchically arranged relationships between those with power and those without, and institutions and their subjects, rather than partly determined by the association of individuals and concentrations of social class among them. Though not explicitly stated, a presumption underlying educational theory up to this point is that one's social class is an individual possession—that is, a product of an individual's interaction with and valuation within institutions and the opportunity structure, rather than a creation, in part, of processes of collective capitalization arising from the concentration of capital within context-specific membership groups, networks, and units. For example, in describing the development of a counter–school culture among working-class boys, "the Lads," and how their peer relations were defined in contrast to those who conformed to the achievement ideology and schooling, Willis's analysis reveals how vital the associations among youth are in reinforcing dispositions that are inconsistent with mobility. In an effort similar to Willis's, MacLeod (1987) exposes similar collective processes leading to the development of limited aspirations within a group of adolescent boys, "the Hallway Hangers," from a low-income housing project, Clarendon Heights. Although Bourdieu's work did not make explicit ties between peer associations, the role of place, and the habitus, MacLeod (1987) did, arguing that student dispositions also reflect the experiences and attitudes of individuals in close proximity (p. 15). So MacLeod and Willis illustrate mobility as a mechanism reflecting interactions between institutions of power and individuals, as well as between individuals within institutions, the latter illustration being fundamental to an understanding of place, or processes dependent on the association of individuals inhabiting certain social class attributes.

The role that "lateral social organization" or associations perform in furthering social stratification grew in interest among sociologists and attracted the attention of cultural anthropologists. The cultural ecological model represents this theoretical development and emphasizes the importance of racial and ethnic group membership to differences in school outcomes. Ogbu (1987) hypothesized that youth acquire dispositions toward schooling via the cultural curriculum that accompanies minority group affiliation and that these dispositions often conflict with the behavior that is expected of them by individuals not of their community. While traditional ecological models emphasize the "relations of individuals affected by the selective, distributive and accommodative forces of the environment" (McKenzie, 1925, p. 64), Ogbu's rendition of ecology relies on populations' historical social "place" within processes of marginalization, not so much their physical place in the social environment. While informative, the emphasis placed on the historical marginalization of minorities in Ogbu's work presents a dilemma in that it implies that no matter where involuntary minorities may be physically located, they are subject to the same "ecological" forces and develop orientations to schooling that result in similar levels of academic performance.

Reconsidering the achievement of Ogbu's (2003) study participants in Shaker Heights, Ohio, with attention to place-based variability would complicate his assumption. Ogbu (2003) argued that African American youth in Shaker Heights developed dispositions toward achievement primarily through family life that did not support academic excellence relative to whites and that this was the primary contributor to the black-white test-score gap. Unfortunately, Ogbu (2003) had compared the performance of African Americans in Shaker Heights to their white counterparts, the latter coming from families earning twice the median income of the former and coming from more highly educated families. Census figures show that over 40 percent of white families in Shaker Heights had a household income over $100,000 in 1999 compared to 15 percent of African American households; yet, in Ogbu's analysis, the two groups were treated as social class equivalents. What complicated the cultural ecological model more in this case is that the average test performance of the African Americans he called "disengaged" exceeded the test performance of the average white student within the state of Ohio (CNN, 2004). The less sympathetic interpretation of this tension would question the application of the cultural ecological model if variability in African American performance across contexts is so great that what is identified as disengagement within one context could indicate excellence in another and in relation to white Americans in other contexts that, according to the cultural ecological model, are not subject to similar sociocultural determinants. One could, however, find common ground in these observations in noting that the presence of variability in the performance of racial and ethnic groups across places does not prove an absence of cultural ecological forces. After all, the performance of African Americans within advantaged areas could have been greater if it were not for the social dynamics that accompany their involuntary minority group status.

A more localized conceptualization of associations, social capital theory, was introduced by Loury (1977) and Bourdieu (1985) and defined in educational theory most notably by Coleman (1988). These theorists define social capital as the human capital, relationship norms, and possible mobility one acquires from interacting with another who possesses greater human or social capital. The "capital" in this case exists within the ties that enable the transfer of social resources. The bounty of social capital theory that was produced during this time identified several important features of it that enable social mobility, including the strength of the tie (which was wed with the work Granovetter [1978, 1983], produced a decade earlier); the intergenerational closure such ties produce (Coleman, 1987); and also the type of activity that ties enable (Portes & Landolt, 1996). Although Coleman (1988) did not specifically suggest that variability in social capital arises from differences in the context of the beneficiary, it is reasonable to expect that to some degree one's context populates the individuals with which ties are established, and through them, ties with others located beyond the context. Hence, even as networks extend beyond the immediate context of the beneficiary, it is possible that their composition is influenced heavily by that context. In another application, Granovetter (1983) suggests individuals in lower income areas have fewer weak ties and rely more heavily on their stronger ties with family, friends, and neighbors. Having weak ties in addition to the strong ones connects an individual to a larger and more heterogeneous network of resources and opportunities for advancement.

The Neo-Institutional Perspective and Educational Policy

The more recent shift in educational theory concerns the influence of educational institutions in educational production and extends from the work of organizational sociologists at Stanford University who pioneered the approach in the 1970s. Their efforts demonstrated that the social purpose of institutions was driven more by a concern for legitimacy (Meyer & Rowan, 1977) than the functionalists' concern for efficiency and that their organization was loosely structured, which allowed them to be responsive to external demands more than institutional ones (Weick, 1976). During the 1990s, educational researchers began to revisit earlier perspectives in organizational theory, noting that broader societal changes and policy decisions fundamentally altered the organization of schools (Rowan & Miskel, 1999). Among the new determinants of institutionalism was the introduction of greater accountability for school performance and student learning; a greater awareness of institutional cultures and their social construction; and the situation of institutions within a web of forces that have origin in other institutional structures, primarily of the political and market type (Meyer & Rowan, 2006). The resulting neo-institutional perspective implies a greater role for schools in educational production and, by extension, social stratification, though the perspective stops short of positing to what degree institutional change affects the big picture.

Functional theories and the macro-sociological works (as opposed to the ethnographic ones) of the cultural theorists gave little attention to the school as a determinant of educational production because it was viewed as a repository of information as opposed to a system that produced human capital. Neo-institutionalism may bring much-needed attention to the importance of schools within macro-sociological theory, though not all of the tenets are equally consistent with a theory of place. The most complementary current within neo-institutional thought is that schools enact institutional norms and cultures that compel the behavior of institutional actors. This tenet supports the development of between-school differences that could correspond to the context in which the school is embedded. Though the neo-institutionalists may prefer to think of institutional cultures as shielding schools from external forces, school populations are still largely determined by their location and play a role in shaping the culture of schools and the educational practices of staff. In the other extreme, the neo-institutional notion that schools are becoming more tightly coupled due to accountability policies and competition might suggest a more autonomous institutional role for them, but the lessening of institutional variability becomes a possibility as well. Here we find neo-institutionalism inadvertently aligning with other macro-sociological theories that find schools a less relevant factor in the equation, not because they do not affect educational production but because they all have similar effects, leaving only social background factors such as neighborhood quality to contribute inequitably to social mobility. This outcome, however, may be the ultimate goal of the neo-institutional perspective: to realize a more efficient and common social purpose of school sorting mechanisms, based less on legitimacy, perhaps more on the functionalists' ideal of individual ability, or Horace Mann's hope for a compensatory education.

Yet some proponents of the neo-institutional perspective contend its renaissance in educational theory leads to a diminished role for the importance of the neighborhood context. For example, Arum (2000) declares:

> Educational practices are more a reflection of a school's institutional community (e.g., state regulatory agencies, professional associations, training organizations, and market competition) than of a school's neighborhood demographic community. Neo-institutional educational research, therefore, offers an explicit challenge to traditional ecological educational research, which has conceptualized schools as being embedded primarily in localized community settings. Schools are organizations, and as such their communities are by definition largely institutional in character. (Arum, 2000, p. 396)

Arum's claim that educational practices reflect the nature of the institutional community more than the ecological one stops short of characterizing those actions of the institutional community that have often worked to reinforce geographic inequality in educational opportunity. For instance, it is far from unequivocal that educational policies have been as successful in increasing the heterogeneity of school populations as they were in increasing homogeneity prior to the civil rights movement. Despite Arum's (2000) appeal to desegregation efforts (p. 403), recent commentaries suggest schools desegregated little according to race (especially in the North) in the wake of *Brown v. Board*, less so according to social class, and today are becoming increasingly racially segregated (Orfield & Eaton, 1996). Remedies once mandated by the courts have lost their judicial appeal, as heightened individualism and increasing diversity among public school children have made the chances of achieving integration more remote. In many cases magnet programs have worked to gather students able to meet higher admission requirements from across the metropolis to attend programs that concentrate students of a higher social class within a few schools. School choice, the panacea of neoconservatives and the liberator of urban residents trapped within low-performing schools, has presented more promise than progress, especially as pursued in the No Child Left Behind legislation (Hammond, 2004). Research suggests higher-income groups are more likely than lower-income and minority groups to take advantage of school choice, using such policies to obtain educational environments of advantage (Lee, Croninger, & Smith, 1996). These organizations, enacting potentially transformative policy in support of the claims of the neo-institutionalists, have in the past brought attention to the influence of segregation and concentrated disadvantage in neighborhoods and schools. Yet it is unclear whether the results of their policy efforts should assuage our suspicion that these distributions remain entrenched and their influences problematic. In the absence of research that suggests social class has become less predictive in general, and more specifically as a result of organizational actions, and that variation in achievement and school quality according to context has diminished significantly, there will remain room for ecology to assume a prominent role in the sociology of education.

Those complications aside, the "challenge" Arum notes is more appropriately understood as an acknowledgment of the difficulty in modeling the complexity of nested social phenomena rather than an artificial binary that would have one tradition perish at the expense of the other. The true significance here is that institutional effects may mediate neighborhood influences as much as they might inspire them. A few neighborhood studies in education have already examined this possibility, exploring the bi-directional flow of violence between neighborhoods and schools (Mateu-Gelabert & Lune, 2003); the influence of educational policies and school reputations on the residential choices of parents and, by extension, the composition of neighborhoods (Bayoh, Irwin, & Haab, 2006) and school influences on the price of housing (Brunner & Sonstelie, 2003; Kane, Staiger, & Reigg, 2006; Nechyba, 2000). Placing conceptual limits on the importance of a school's demographic community, its larger social milieu, and built environment marginalizes the investigation of these important relationships and, in them, the importance of institutions.

TOWARD A THEORY OF PLACE: PROXIMITY AND PROXIMAL CAPITAL

The Formation and Distribution of Social Class Associations

Our movement toward a theory of place begins with an effort to identify the social laws, behavior, and accompanying social machinery that distribute individuals into positions within stratified structures, the one of most concern here being the grouping or "association" of individuals inhabiting social classes.[2] In Figure 2.1, I provide a general framework of relationships, conditions and social artifacts that work together somewhat systematically to sort individuals into ecological structures. As seen in Figure 2.1, we first start with the voluntary association that under ideal conditions would group individuals largely according to the satisfaction such associations bring (Duncan, 1928).[3] There are myriad "satisfactions" that represent organizing forces, but in the exploration of this heuristic I limit my concern to the capitals that are known to provide social advancement.

The most apparent of these capitals is of the economic kind that serves as a marker of individual socioeconomic status. Income and wealth continue to motivate the formation of associations of various types, from marriage to organizational affiliation. Next, cultural capital, as has already been discussed, often binds relationships between individuals who might share certain cultural tastes. Popularity, style, and command of certain cultural practices, for example, often provide youth with a means of enticing some to establish peer groups while dissuading others. Another capital, social capital, is itself a tie between individuals who together enable a transfer of opportunity or some resource necessary to the creation of human capital (Bourdieu, 1985; Coleman, 1988). Human capital being the last of these capitals is the investment in the cultivation of a person's skill, generally through education (Schultz,

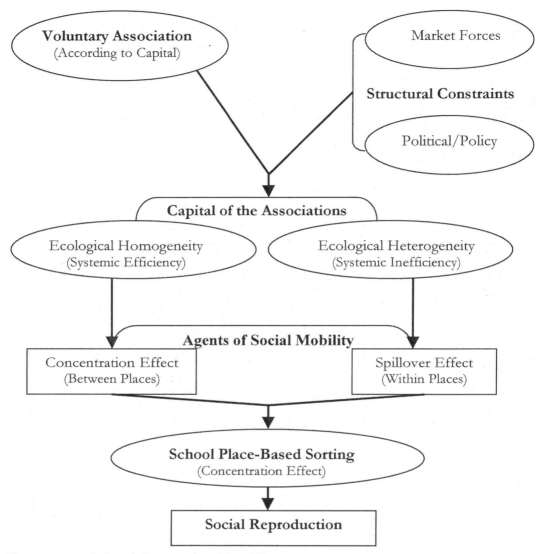

Figure 2.1. Depiction of Place-Based Social Mobility System

1960, 1961). In relation to the association, the demonstration of a person's human capital invites others to be mentored or taught or to join efforts to complete a task of mutual interest. Economic, cultural, social, and human capitals, then, are desirous and inspire one to build potentially beneficial associations. "Beneficial" here is ventured with the awareness that these associations are not always entered into with a perfect understanding of their social returns or consequences. Nondominant cultural capital, for example, may help young adolescents navigate the social preferences within their peer group, but it does little to help them academically (Carter, 2003). Likewise, social capital may provide the resources necessary for success as well as for potentially self-defeating behavior (Portes & Landolt, 1996). These capitals then supply the initial inclination among individuals that brings about the associations that form places.

There are other more systematic processes that determine the composition of these associations and amount to additional modes of associational distribution. Figure 2.1 accounts for the contravening influences of market forces and the making of public policy. Considering market forces first, inasmuch as individuals are motivated by the prospects of capital in entering association, capital also constrains their choice and ability to achieve access to the most exclusive, affluent, and rewarding associations. Market forces—consisting of a more explicit appraisal of the quality of associations—produce a purely economic standard for sorting and hence constitute another mechanism through which individuals are distributed into associations. It is through this distributive mechanism that economic capital rewards economic capital—those that have the most capital gain access to the associations of greatest value, while the less advantaged, being discouraged by the markets' high valuation of good neighborhoods and good schools, for example, are relegated to membership in associations of a lesser value.

Social policies at all levels of government differentiate associational opportunity through the implementation of discriminatory policies that, throughout history, have privileged the associational interest of white, Anglo-Saxon, male Protestants. In regard to race, for instance, FHA policy that discriminated in its extension of mortgage capital to individuals based on race and place; HUD policy that explicitly aided the concentration of low-income ethnic and immigrant populations (Goetz, 2003; Polikoff, 2006); and local agencies' zoning practices that denied minorities and low-income populations entry into neighborhoods whose residents desired exclusivity (Goetz, 2003; Massey & Denton, 1993; Wilson, 1987; Yinger, 2001), kept African Americans trapped within predominantly African American and low-income neighborhoods while supporting the creation of predominantly white suburbs. Affluence became increasingly concentrated at the urban fringe, leading to greater rates of economic segregation at the metropolitan level between and within racial groups (Massey, 1996; St. John, 2002).

Capital of the Associations: Endogenous Capital and Ecology

At this point in our theoretical model, individuals have been sorted into associations of social class, and as a whole compose a social class distribution of associations. There are a few qualities of this distribution of associations that are important to note. First, the distribution of capital among these associations is unequal primarily because people come to these associations with differing amounts of capital. In this case, the stratified social edifice supporting the organization of individuals has given rise to equally stratified structures of association. Consequently, as associations are formed and come to reflect the capital of their constituent members, the inequitable distribution of capital across them materializes.

Second, the capital of the association is endogenous in that its ability to support social mobility is contextually defined. Unlike traditional conceptualizations of social class that assume one's socioeconomic status is an exogenous individual-level attribute, endogenous capital recognizes that the economic returns to individual capital depend, in part, on the social class of the associations in which it is situated. We might find, then, that the benefits accruing to middle-class families residing in affluent communities are greater than those accruing to families of comparable income living among the less advantaged. Thus, this capital, having properties that are specific to places, can be considered a "capital of the associations" or for short, "proximity capital."

In just the past decade we have seen the formulation of theories of endogenous capital that are useful in illustrating the role capital plays in enabling status attainment for individuals and communities. Economists Lundberg and Startz (2000), for example, term the spatial situation of capital "community social capital" and define it as "the average stock of human capital" that one generation transmits to the next. One shortcoming of their approach, however, is that the processes of human capital acquisition among individuals of the same generation are not considered. Peer effects, for example, are intragenerational effects that emanate from decisions made contemporaneously among peers, and they make significant contributions to human capital outcomes (Manski, 1993). Lundberg and Startz's (2000) largely intergenerational definition of endogenous capital consequently is one that does not account for the influence of lateral relationships in social reproduction. Putnam (2000), in contrast, refers to community social capital as the prevailing "norms of reciprocity and trustworthiness" arising from relationships among individuals (p. 19). This articulation of endogenous capital, however, has come under fire because social capital in its earliest definition located the capital in human interactions, not within individuals or communities (DeFilippis, 2001; Durlauf, 1999).

Moreover, the aforementioned theories of endogenous capital mention little about the third quality of the association, that being their ecological nature. Associations are ecological in function in that they carry out the general aims of human sustenance and competition (Hawley, 1986). For example, qualitative research on adolescents found that their peer groups created structures of behavior and provided resources for their constituent members that ultimately lessened the adolescents' reliance on parents (Rainwater, 1970). Other investigations of male peer culture describe the competition for resources that seemingly instigate rivalries between adolescent groups (MacLeod, 1987; Willis, 1977). These associations are also ecological in nature, because once structures for sustenance and competition are created, they impose themselves on the associating members as an external fact (Park, 1925). W. E. B. DuBois (1899), writing over a century ago, said it first, surmising that the environment had an "immense effect"—perhaps of the greatest magnitude—on the thought, life, work, crime, wealth, and pauperism of the inhabitants of the ward he was observing (p. 44). In sum, once associations are established, structures arise in accordance with their capital, social processes ensue, and individual dispositions and behavior follow.

Social Mobility Under Assumptions of Ecological Homogeneity and Heterogeneity

At this point in the framework, I turn our attention to two concerns: one being the identification of agents of social mobility according to place, and the other being the circumstances in which the agents are likely to act. Starting with the latter of these first, the existence of social class heterogeneity within associations compels one to admit that the distributive mechanisms that group individuals according to social class are imprecise. The framework associates these imperfections with the existence of two conditions: ecologically homogeneous places represent a more efficient process of associational allocation, while heterogeneous ones suggest that market forces and political decisions have worked less efficiently (or perhaps less forcefully) in creating a more perfect distribution of associations according to social class. I will address both ecological circumstances, taking on first the possibility of social mobility within a more efficient system.

According to neighborhood and school effects research, the concentration of social class among associates brings about "effects" of various types on individuals that are greater than what can be explained by their individual characteristics. Consider, for example, the possibility that neighborhoods, through the attractiveness of affordable access, gather individuals who are predisposed to a certain achievement level and corresponding social status. Under these circumstances observations of variation in status attainment according to place become mere statements of aggregated exogenous behavior. The mode of mobility might not correspond to place in this situation because these individuals might experience the same (im)mobility if they were located within a much different socioeconomic environment. A discernable mode of mobility, therefore, is established not merely through the observation of place stratification and distributive systems, but through the observation of endogenous effects arising in places that vary in quality according to the social class of the associating individuals and inspiring complementary dispositions among its constituent members, who receive sanctions from schools fashioned by places specifically for that purpose. Wilson (1987) and Jencks and Mayer (1990) would refer to these effects as "concentration effects" and detail their influence within peer relations, role modeling, and institutional processes.

Concentration effects are the primary enabler of social mobility within homogeneous settings, the stratification of which across places leads to concentration effects of varying value, and consequently a more macro-level system of social mobility operating largely between places. To illustrate this point, consider that concentration effects emanate from high- and low-income communities. In affluent communities, for example, individual capital is used to gain access to places where it is rewarded through the externalities arising from its concentration among individuals. The power to form, maintain, and secede from social class associations, as well as exclude others and mitigate their associational preferences accrues to advantaged populations, reinforcing the spatial distribution of social class associations. This power is reflected in the political influence of communities of capital that protect their capitalizing interests; in the market that reflects and values exclusivity and place stratification; and in institutions that under the guise of meritocracy reward secession with the resources, knowledge, and socialization of greatest social value.

Those that are marginalized and disempowered in communities with little capital also contend with concentration effects that have been at times inappropriately reduced to a "contagion effect," a concept that suggests social immobility in low-income places arises from the presence of disadvantaged individuals. More recent alternative perspectives speculate that immobility in low-income places is more likely caused by the absence of proximity capital than by the presence of low-income populations or a corollary "bad proximity capital." As Massey (2001) and others have recognized, the most influential neighborhood characteristic in empirical research is the presence of individuals of a middle-class or affluent social standing. When the number of advantaged individuals falls to low levels in neighborhoods and schools, incidences of behavior inconsistent with social advancement increase dramatically (see Crane, 1991). My empirical synthesis of neighborhood effects finds the effects of neighborhood affluence to be more influential in determining education outcomes than any other neighborhood factor within neighborhood studies (Johnson 2008b). In comparison, the concentration of low-SES individuals is frequently insignificant in analyses of neighborhood effects in education and often in school effects research (Myers, Hyeonie, & Mandala, 2002). In short, it is more important to consider *who does not* live in places of concentrated poverty than *who does* in explanations of immobility.[4] Hence, positive externalities in places correspond to the existence of proximity capital whereas negative ones correspond to its absence.

As previously stated, the imperfections of stratification give rise to heterogeneous areas, requiring the articulation of a second system of mobility and corresponding externality. Key within this articulation is an accounting of social mobility within places—at a more micro level—as opposed to between them, since it is within this ecological condition that we find social class heterogeneity. Mobility within areas where the associations are more economically diverse rely on what Benabou (1993, 1996) and Durlauf (1994) term the "spillover"—an externality emanating from both social ties and structural considerations that positively affects the behavior and opportunity of individuals or groups with relatively less human capital in the proximity. Proximal capital extends from the concept of sociological and fiscal spillovers in that it explains the subsequent social upgrading of individuals of a lower socio-economic position with access to proximity capital. Proximal capital then is the conversion of proximity capital into social mobility.

The concept of proximal capital tempers the appearance that place-based distributive systems are overly deterministic with the suggestion that externalities can only be decisively controlled and guaranteed to avail those in power through the creation and maintenance of exclusive associations. Areas of economic heterogeneity represent the capitalists' apparent loss of exclusivity and, consequently, control over place-based agents of social advancement. Upon accessing proximity capital, less advantaged individuals may form relationships that enable mobility, though social interaction is not a prerequisite of mobility. Sociological spillovers may stem from the examples of behavior that local peers and adults unknowingly provide. In addition to the spillovers emanating from passive role modeling are those that extend from nonhuman environmental resources. African Americans, for example, who integrated hostile environments during the era of school desegregation may not have profited educationally as much from direct interaction with their white counterparts as they had from better facilities; updated and rigorous curricular materials; and, upon graduation, institutional prestige (Rosenbaum, 1995; Rosenbaum, Kulieke, & Rubinowitz, 1988; Wells, 1995; Wells & Crain, 1997).

There are, however, at least three factors that complicate the conversion of proximity capital into proximal capital (Johnson, 2008a). First, conversion requires individual capital to offset the economic costs of maintaining associations with better-off individuals. Gentrification is a process that epitomizes the struggle of individuals with less income to maintain their residency as they are eventually priced out of neighborhoods by rising property taxes and rents that accompany the influx of economically better-off individuals. Gentrification enables the spillover effect to give way to the concentration effect as fewer less advantaged individuals remain within proximity to benefit from its increasing capital. Second, as sociologists and community activists argue, the high social costs less advantaged individuals pay as they experience racial and class discrimination and isolation in economically heterogeneous areas may outweigh the sum of other environmental advantages (Fischer, 1991; Hamilton, 1968; Rosenbaum et al., 1988; Wells & Crain, 1997). Heterogeneous places may give rise to other norms such as cultural incongruities between school personnel and students as well as feelings of relative deprivation within individuals. These social effects represent a group of hypotheses called "conflict models" that acknowledge that the presence of middle-class and affluent individuals within proximity is not always beneficial for the less advantaged (Gephardt, 1997).[5]

Last but most importantly, our heuristic posits that a more systematic inhibitor to one's proximal capital can be found in the functioning of schools. Here we identify place as the axis of differentiation within schools in that it envelops other more popular candidates of differentiation, namely ability and achievement. Before they enter school, children are first distributed into relatively homogeneous or heterogeneous economic associations by larger distributive processes operating between neighborhoods and communities. Schools find children already situated, without the aid of indicators of ability or achievement, in the stratified ecological structure within environments that are concentrated in affluence and poverty or between them in economically heterogeneous environments.

Of the latter, scholars have noted that schools within heterogeneous areas are among the most stratified, primarily because affluent families demand student differentiation (Brantlinger, 2003; Jencks & Mayer, 1990). Consequently, and unlike cultural theory, a theory of place recognizes that heterogeneous schools, as socially efficient agents of stratification, function to dispel heterogeneous associations and spillover effects. Children from economically heterogeneous environments enter school and are physically allocated according to their individual social class into different classrooms, tracks, and programs—*places* within schools—that, through the degree to which classroom instruction, teacher qualities, and the types of knowledge correspond to the students' social class, *cause* them to perform at a certain academic level. Children accordingly experience the academic privileges of concentrated advantage in gifted programs and accelerated placement courses, or fewer or no relative benefits within remedial, special education, and vocational courses. The ecological forces that bring about the ordering and grouping of a setting's populations according to social class are ultimately expressed in the norms and social organization of schools.

Then what of achievement, the functionalists' arbiter of mobility? The function of achievement serves to exonerate schools of their rather blatant structural organization and fuel the yearly reproduction of a youth's social class associations. Achievement, then, rather than indicating merit and natural endowments, merely identifies the effectiveness and efficiency of ecological differentiation within schools; associates the effects of ecological differentiation with individual students; provides the individual access to the appropriate ecological strata in which students with a similar educational record and social class are concentrated; and, upon school completion, provides the individual with educational credentials that indicate her eligibility for membership in the appropriate institution and environment within the stratified opportunity structure. In this regard, schools represent another mode of associational distribution in that they are socially organized to correct the systemic inefficiencies of sorting at the macro level by finalizing the allocation of individuals into social class associations. After a more perfect sorting of individuals is achieved, the mode of social (im)mobility within heterogeneous schools relies primarily on concentration effects arising from the presence or absence of proximity capital within classrooms.

Here we find neo-institutionalists conflicted by artificial disciplinary terminology and the relatively small estimates of between-school variability in empirical studies as they announce the limits of ecological research. Undermining clarity in this case is the precarious decision of some researchers to treat ecology as merely an external school factor, as if the application of ecology lies dormant at the foot of the school door while on the other side "organization" takes over. Should we not acknowledge the shared defining features of the structures, processes, and resulting dispositions that vary according to places inside as well as outside of schools? That the majority of variation in student performance is often found within schools (with a few noteworthy exceptions) does not mark the limits of ecology: it suggests nothing other than that the system of student differentiation according to the distribution of proximity capital is more observable within neighborhood institutions than between them, because within there exists a relatively explicit distributive machinery that lends itself to our current methodological capabilities. Nonetheless, that the overwhelming majority of schools use classrooms to make distinctions in instructional quality, create hierarchically arranged educational programs, and allocate school resources in a manner consistent with the educational goals of these places suggests that within-school variability found amid economic diversity is also ecological variability.

Through these mechanisms, access to proximity capital for the less advantaged works to undermine the acquisition of human and social capital and later the economic capital necessary to gain access to other areas of capital. Heterogeneity in its most inequitable social function provides a context where the "have-nots" and "have-too-littles" have their greatest potential for social advancement through association with individuals possessing more human capital, yet the pay-offs are reserved for those who "have the most." These conditions serve to reify the structure of the distribution of social class associations.

NOTES

1. Bourdieu (1984) suggested in *Distinction* that the lifestyles of social classes differ in cultural taste, with low-income populations exhibiting a "taste of necessity." The suggestion implies that the prevalence of the taste of necessity might vary according to the concentration of low-income individuals across neighborhoods.

2. The conceptualization of association follows from the law of proximity, a Gestalt principle of organization that holds events or objects that are near to one another in space and time are perceived as forming a unit.

3. Duncan hypothesized that membership groups formed as persons united in groups that promised to satisfy "some wish" or desire, while other membership groups were avoided "offering no element of satisfaction" (p. 426).

4. This observation is consistent with the concerns expressed by Goetz (2003) and Benabou (1993) regarding the creaming effects of redistributive policy. Both authors point out that the consequences of individuals moving to more prosperous environments are greater for the communities left behind than for those being joined.

5. The work of O'Connor (1997) and Spencer (2001) find exceptions to the negative influence of these dynamics in the resiliency and cultivation of collective dispositions among African American youth.

REFERENCES

Arum, R. (2000). Schools and communities: Ecological and institutional dimensions. *Annual Review of Sociology, 26*, 395–418.

Bayoh, I., Irwin, E., & Haab, T. (2006). Determinants of residential location choice: How important are local public goods in attracting homeowners to central city locations? *Journal of Regional Science, 46*(1), 97–120.

Benabou, R. (1993). Workings of a city: Location, education and production. *The Quarterly Journal of Economics, 108*(3): 619–652.

Benabou, R. (1996). Equity and efficiency in human capital investment: The local connection. *Review of Economic Studies, 63*(2), 237–264.

Blasius, J. (1993). *Gentrification and lifestyles.* Opladen, Germany: Leske Budrich.

Blasius, J., & Friedrichs, J. (2008). Lifestyles in distressed neighborhoods: A test of Bourdieu's "taste of necessity" hypothesis. *Poetics, 36*, 24–44.

Blau, P., & Duncan, O. D. (1967). *The American occupational structure.* New York, NY: Wiley.

Bourdieu, P. (1977a). Cultural reproduction and social reproduction. In J. Karabel & A. Halsey (Eds.), *Power and ideology in education* (pp. 487–511). New York, NY: Oxford University Press.

Bourdieu, P. (1977b). *Outline of a theory of practice.* Cambridge, England: Cambridge University Press.

Bourdieu, P. (1984). *Distinction: A social critique of the judgment of taste.* Cambridge, MA: Harvard University Press.

Bourdieu, P. (1985). The forms of capital. In J. Richardson (Ed.), *Handbook of theory and research for the sociology of education* (pp. 241–258). New York, NY: Greenwood.

Bowles, S., & Gintis, H. (1976). *Schooling in capitalist America: Educational reform and the contradictions of economic life.* New York, NY: Basic Books.

Brantlinger, E. (2003). *Dividing classes: How the middle class negotiates and rationalizes school advantage.* New York, NY: RoutledgeFalmer.

Brunner, E., & Sonstelie, J. (2003). Homeowners, property values, and the political economy of the school voucher. *Journal of Urban Economics, 54*, 239–257.

Carter, P. (2003). "Black" cultural capital, status positioning, and schooling Conflicts for low-income African American youth. *Social Problems, 50*(1), 136–155.

Clark, B. (1960). The "cooling-out" function in higher education. *American Journal of Sociology, 65*(6), 569–576.

CNN. (2004). *CNN Presents:* The Gap: 50 years after the Brown ruling. Atlanta, GA: Cable News Network.

Coleman, J. (1987). The relations between school and social structure. In M. Hallinan (Ed.), *The social organization of schools* (pp. 177–204). New York, NY: Plenum Press.

Coleman, J. (1988). Social capital in the creation of human capital. *American Journal of Sociology, 94*(supplement), 95–120.

Collins, R. (1977). Functional and conflict theories of educational stratification. In J. Karabel & A.H. Halsey (Eds.), *Power and ideology in education* (pp. 118–136). New York, NY: Oxford University Press.

Crane, J. (1991). The epidemic theory of ghettos and neighborhood effects on dropping out and teenage childbearing. *American Journal of Sociology, 96*(5), 1226–1259.

Davis, A., Gardner, B. B., & Gardner, M. R. (1941). *Deep South: A social anthropological study of caste and class.* Chicago, IL: University of Chicago Press.

DeFilippis, J. (2001). The myth of social capital in community development. *Housing Policy Debate, 12*(4), 781–805.

Drake, S. C., & Cayton, H. (1945). *Black metropolis: A study of Negro life in a northern city*. Chicago, IL: University of Chicago Press.

DuBois, W. E. B. (1899). *The Philadelphia Negro: A social study*. Philadelphia: University of Pennsylvania Press.

Duncan, H. G. (1928). The concept of personal ecology. *Social Forces, 6*(3), 426–429.

Durlauf, S. (1994). Spillovers, stratification and inequality. *European Economic Review, 38*, 836–845.

Durlauf, S. (1999). The case "against" social capital. *Focus, 20*(3), 6–10.

Fischer, P. B. (1991). Is housing mobility an effective anti-poverty strategy? An examination of the Cincinnati experience. Department of Politics, Lake Forest, IL: Lake Forest College.

Gephardt, M. A. (1997). Neighborhoods and communities as contexts for development. In J. Brooks-Gunn, G. J. Duncan, & J. L., Aber (Eds.), *Neighborhood poverty: Context and consequences for children*. New York, NY: Russell Sage Publications.

Goetz, E. G. (2003). *Clearing the way: Deconcentrating the poor in urban America*. Washington, DC: Urban Institute Press.

Granovetter, M. (1978). Threshold models of collective behavior. *American Journal of Sociology, 83*, 1420–1443.

Granovetter, M. (1983). The strength of weak ties: A network theory revisited. *Sociological Theory, 1*, 201–233.

Hamilton, C. (1968). Race and education: A search for legitimacy. *Harvard Educational Review, 38*(4), 669–684.

Hammond, L. D. (2004). From "Separate but Equal" to "No Child Left Behind": The collision of new standards and old inequalities. In D. Meier & G. Wood (Eds.), *Many children left behind: How the No Child Left Behind Act is damaging our children and our schools*. Boston, MA: Beacon Press.

Hawley, A. H. (1986). *Human ecology: A theoretical essay*. Chicago, IL: University of Chicago Press.

Hollingshead, A. B. (1948). *Elmtown's youth*. New York, NY: John Wiley and Sons.

Jencks, C., & Mayer, S. (1990). The social consequences of growing up in a poor neighborhood. In L. E. Lynn Jr. & M. G. H. McGeary (Eds.), *Inner-city poverty in the United States* (pp. 111–186). Washington, DC: National Academy Press.

Johnson, O. (2008a). Ecology in educational theory: Thoughts on ecology, stratification and proximal capital. *Urban Review, 40*(3).

Johnson, O. (2008b). *The problem of concentrated advantage in a new understanding of educational inequality*. Paper presented at the Annual Meeting of the American Sociological Association, August 2, 2008, Boston, MA.

Kane, T., Staiger, D., & Reigg, S. (2006). *School quality, neighborhoods and housing prices: The impacts of school desegregation. American Law and Economics Review, 8*(2), 183–212.

Karabel, J., & Halsey, A. H. (1977). Educational research: A review and an interpretation. In J. Karabel & A. H. Halsey (Eds.), *Power and ideology in education* (pp. 118–136). New York, NY: Oxford University Press.

Lee, V., Croninger, R., & Smith, J. (1996). Equity and choice in Detroit. In B. Fuller and R. Elmore (Eds.), *Who chooses? Who loses? Culture, institutions, and the unequal effects of school choice*. New York, NY: Teachers College Press

Loury, G. (1977). A dynamic theory of racial income differences. In P. Wallace & A. LaMond (Eds.), *Women, minorities, and employment discrimination* (pp. 153–188). Lexington, MA: Heath.

Lundberg, S., & Startz, R. (2000). Inequality and race: Models and policy. In K. Arrow, S. Bowles, & S. Durlauf (Eds.), *Meritocracy and economic inequality* (pp. 269–295). Princeton, NJ: Princeton University Press.

MacLeod, J. (1987). *Ain't no makin it: Aspirations and attainment in a low-income neighborhood*. Boulder, CO: Westview Press.

Manski, C. F. (1993). Identification of endogenous social effects: The reflection problem. *Review of Economic Studies, 60*, 531–542.

Massey, D. S., & Denton, N. A. (1993). *American apartheid: Segregation and the making of the underclass*. Cambridge, MA: Harvard University Press.

Massey, D. (1996). The age of extremes: Concentrated affluence and poverty in the twenty-first century. *Demography, 33*, 395–412.

Massey, D. (2001). The prodigal paradigm returns: Ecology comes back to sociology. In A. Booth & A. Crouter (Eds.), *Does it take a village?: Community effects on children, adolescents, and families*. Mahwah, NJ: Lawrence Erlbaum Associates, Inc.

Mateu-Gelabert, P., & Lune, H. (2003). School Violence: The bidirectional conflict flow between neighborhood and school. *City & Community, 2*, 353–368.

McKenzie, R. (1925). The ecological approach to the study of the human community. In R. Park, E. Burgess, & R. McKenzie (Eds.), *The city: Suggestions for investigation of human behavior in the urban environment* (pp. 1–46). Chicago, IL: University of Chicago Press.

Meyer, H. D., & Rowan, B. (2006). *The new institutionalism in education*. Albany: State University of New York Press.

Meyer, J., & Rowan, B. (1977). Institutionalized organizations: Formal structure as myth and ceremony. *American Journal of Sociology, 83*, 340–363.

Myers, S. L., Hyeonie, K., & Mandala, C. (2002). The effect of school poverty on racial gaps in test scores: The case of the Minnesota Basic Standards Tests. Unpublished manuscript, University of Minnesota, Minneapolis/St. Paul.

Nechyba, T. J. (2000). Mobility, targeting, and private-school vouchers. *American Economic Review, 90*(1), 130–146.

O'Connor, C. (1997). Dispositions toward (collective) struggle and educational resilience in the inner city: A case analysis of six African-American high schools students. *American Educational Research Journal, 34*(4), 593–629.

Ogbu, J. U. (1987). Variability in minority school performance: A problem in search of an explanation. *Anthropology of Education Quarterly, 18*, 312–336.

Ogbu, J. U. (2003). *Black American students in an affluent suburb: A study of academic disengagement.* Mahwah, NJ: Lawrence Erlbaum Associates, Inc.

Orfield, G. (1992). Urban schooling and the perpetuation of job inequality in metropolitan Chicago. In G. E. Peterson & W. Vroman (Eds.), *Urban labor markets and job opportunity.* Washington, DC: Urban Institute Press.

Orfield, G., & Eaton, S. E. (1996). *Dismantling desegregation: The quiet reversal of Brown v. Board of Education.* New York, NY: The New Press.

Park, R. E. (1925). The city: Suggestions for investigation of human behavior in the urban environment. In R. Park, E. Burgess, & R. McKenzie (Eds.), *The city: Suggestions for investigation of human behavior in the urban environment* (pp. 1–46). Chicago, IL: University of Chicago Press.

Parsons, T. (1959). The school class as a social system: Some of its functions in American society. *Harvard Educational Review, 29*, 297–318.

Polikoff, A. (2006). *Waiting for Gautreaux: A story of segregation, housing and the black ghetto.* Chicago, IL: Northwestern University Press.

Portes, A., & Landolt, P. (1996). The downside of social capital. *American Prospects, 26*, 18–21.

Putnam, R. (2000). *Bowling alone: The collapse and revival of American community.* New York, NY: Simon and Schuster.

Rainwater, L. (1970). *Behind ghetto walls.* New York, NY: Columbia University Press.

Rosenbaum, J. E. (1995). Changing the geography of opportunity by expanding residential choice: Lessons from the Gautreaux program. *Housing Policy Debate, 6*(1), 231–269.

Rosenbaum, J. E., Kulieke, M. J., & Rubinowitz, L. S. (1988). White suburban schools' responses to low-income black children: Sources of successes and problems. *Urban Review, 20*(1), 28–41.

Rowan, B., & Miskel, C. (1999). Institutional theory and the study of educational organizations. In J. Murphy & K. S. Louis (Eds.), *Handbook of research on educational administration* (pp. 359–383). San Francisco: Jossey-Bass.

Schultz, T. (1960). Capital formation by education. *Journal of Political Economy, 6.*

Schultz, T. (1961). Investment in human capital. *American Economic Review, 51*, 1–17.

Sorokin, P. (1959). *Social and Cultural Mobility.* New York, NY: The Free Press.

Spencer, M. B. (2001). Resiliency and fragility factors associated with the contextual experiences of low-resource urban African American male youth and families. In A. Booth & A. Crouter (Eds.), *Does it take a village? Community effects on children, adolescents, and families.* Mahwah, NJ: Lawrence Erlbaum Associates, Inc.

St. John, C. (2002). The concentration of affluence in the United States, 1990. *Urban Affairs Review, 37*(4), 500–520.

Venkatesh, S. (2000). *American project: The rise and fall of a modern ghetto.* Cambridge, MA: Harvard University Press.

Warner, W. L., et. al (1947). *Democracy in Jonesville: A study in quality and inequality.* New York, NY: Harper.

Weick, C. (1976). Educational organizations as loosely coupled systems. *Administrative Science Quarterly, 21*, 1–19.

Wells, A. S. (1995). Re-examining social science research on school desegregation: Long- versus short-term effects. *Teachers College Record, 96*, 694–718.

Wells, A. S., & Crain, R. (1997). *Stepping over the color line: African-American students in white suburban schools.* New Haven, CT: Yale University Press.

Whyte, W. F. (1943). *Street corner society: The social structure of an Italian slum.* Chicago, IL: University of Chicago Press.

Willis, P. (1977). *Learning to labor: How working class kids get working class jobs.* New York, NY: Columbia University.

Wilson, W. J. (1987). *The truly disadvantaged: The inner-city, the underclass and public policy.* Chicago, IL: University of Chicago Press.

Yinger, J. (2001). Housing discrimination and residential segregation as causes of poverty. In S. Danziger & R. Haveman (Eds.), *Understanding poverty* (pp. 359–391). New York, NY: Russell Sage Foundation.

3

Urban Opportunity Structure and Racial/Ethnic Polarization

George C. Galster

In his seminal, if controversial, work published in 1978, *The Declining Significance of Race*, William Julius Wilson argued that individuals' minority status *per se* was becoming a relatively less important barrier to their socioeconomic advancement than their lower-income status (Wilson, 1978). In this chapter I offer a different conceptual perspective on the issue of race, class, and opportunity. I argue that, for people of color who also happen to have low incomes, *space* is increasingly becoming the primary barrier to their socioeconomic advancement and the central means for perpetuating racial/ethnic polarization. The key dimensions of space in this essay are segregation of neighborhoods and schools by race/ethnicity and by class and, secondarily, the location of economic activity. These spatial dimensions form the key links in a model of cumulative causation in which race-class prejudice, discrimination, segregation, and socioeconomic disparities interact in a mutually reinforcing fashion to constrain severely the opportunities of low-income minorities residing in the cores of American cities.

A visual portrayal of the subject of this chapter is presented in Figure 3.1. The opportunities of individuals can be thought of as being limited by two sets of personal characteristics—minority racial/ethnic status and socioeconomic status[1]—and two sets of spatial characteristics—segregation of neighborhoods and schools by race and class and the location of economic activity. The more limits to which one is subjected, the less her opportunities. Here I will explore the nature of the constraint occurring when one is at the intersection of all four sets of limitations (shown by the shaded area in Figure 3.1).

The chapter presents little new empirical evidence. Rather, its contribution is a new conceptual framework within which extant evidence can be organized and, hopefully, new insights gained. It is organized as follows. The first section presents a conceptual framework for understanding how individuals achieve a certain degree of socioeconomic status through the various choices they make within the spatially and racially contextualized constraints they perceive. The second section applies this framework to the issue of race, poverty, and urban polarization and brings to bear relevant evidence. The third section expands the notion of opportunity structure beyond the individual to the society-wide construct of cumulative causation, in which race-class segregation of neighborhoods and schools forms the key link in a process perpetuating urban polarization.

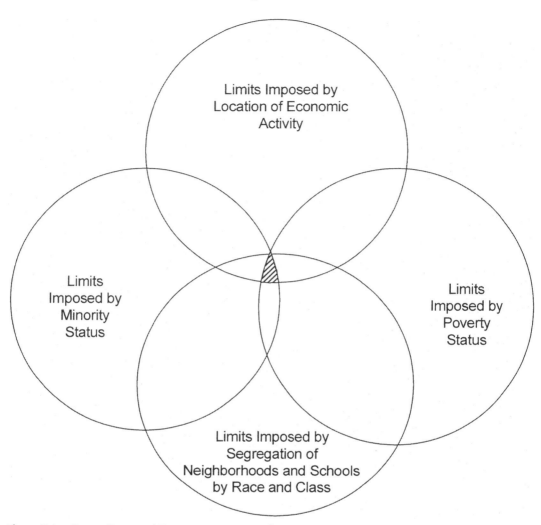

Figure 3.1. Space, Race, and Poverty: Key Intersections

LIFE CHOICES: A CONCEPTUAL FRAMEWORK
FOR UNDERSTANDING ACHIEVED STATUS

The central claim of this chapter is that persistent racial-ethnic polarization in our metropolitan areas can be illuminated by positing a conceptual model of individual decision-making about crucial issues affecting one's achieved socioeconomic status, a model of what I call "life choices." Central to this model is the notion that decisions are made rationally, but with imperfect information, in the context of the constraints and payoffs perceived by the decision-maker. Not only do these constraints and payoffs vary dramatically by the race and ethnicity of the decision-maker, but across various scales within a metropolitan area as well. Thus, observed behaviors that contribute to current and future socioeconomic achievements (for example, bearing children out of wedlock as a teen, acquiring more education, committing a crime, or participating in the labor force) are shaped not only by personal characteristics but also by the geographic context in which those decisions are made. Unfortunately, low-income racial/ethnic minorities often occupy residential niches wherein they encounter an inferior set of choices and associated payoffs. Just as space is warped in an Einsteinian universe, so urban space is warped in its structure of opportunities, to the disadvantage of poor minorities typically residing in core neighborhoods.

This section first sketches a model of life decisions in which geography creates constraints on individuals' feasible choices and on the payoffs they can reap from these choices. I term this aspect of geography the "urban opportunity structure." The model then is illustrated with a realistic hypothetical scenario.

Overview of the Conceptual Framework

To improve their socioeconomic status (and perhaps that of their children), individuals make many decisions relating to education, marriage, fertility, labor force participation, illegal activities, and sociopolitical participation (Galster & Killen, 1995). In making these life choices, individuals draw upon their values, aspirations, and preferences. Factors such as honesty, diligence, respect for authority and traditional institutions, risk-aversion and ability to plan and sacrifice for the future would also be important here. The nature of the person's parents and upbringing likely would be predictive of these traits.

Personal characteristics and contextual constraints determine the feasibility of choosing certain options and the prospective benefits associated with each. Some personal characteristics are indelible, such as age, gender, immigrant status, race, and ethnicity. Others are more malleable over a lifetime, in that they are the product of previous choices (even though, once acquired, these attributes may no longer be malleable), such as employment, criminal record, and educational credentials.

Contextual constraints refer to the *urban opportunity structure*: the geographically varying set of institutions, systems, and markets in a metropolitan area that affect personal and intergenerational socioeconomic advancement. The opportunity structure includes local politics; social networks; criminal justice and social service systems; education; and labor, housing, and financial markets.

This opportunity structure operates in dramatically varied ways across and within metropolitan areas, enhancing or eroding chances for socioeconomic advancement depending on one's place of residence. There are at least three spatial scales over which this variation occurs. Across neighborhoods, variations in peer groups, social organizations, and social networks occur. Across political jurisdictions, health, education, recreation, and safety programs vary. Across metropolitan areas, the locations of employment of various types and skill requirements vary.

Given their characteristics and a set of *perceived* personal and contextual constraints, individuals make a series of life choices during their lives. These choices may best be described as based on "bounded rationality": imperfect (perhaps even incorrect) information and varying degrees of dispassionate, analytical thought. Yet, it is clearly wrong to think of these choices as groundless or random. In conjunction with the associated payoffs from those choices permitted by the constraints, the particular combination and sequence of choices made will produce some level of achieved socioeconomic status, typically measured at young adulthood and thereafter.

Past choices may, in turn, reshape individuals' current aspirations, preferences, and achieved characteristics and, thereby, current choices. For example, the choice to raise children may intensify one's aversion to risky entrepreneurial ventures or participation in illegal activities. Similarly, if prior choices to seek long-term employment have consistently been frustrated, one's ability to plan and invest for the future and respect for civil authority may wane, and lack of job experience may constrain future job options.

Finally, the urban opportunity structure itself is malleable over time. Some of these alterations may be exogenous to the actions of households, such as technologically induced industrial restructuring. Other alterations, however, may be influenced by the aggregate behaviors of households within a metropolitan area. For example, the quality of the local public school system serving an individual's neighborhood constrains that individual's ability to gain skills. Yet, if many individuals decide to participate in a collective political process, the result may be a reallocation of fiscal resources to improve the local schools. The educational background of the parents of students living in the district also comprises an important element of constraint on school outcomes. Inasmuch as better-educated parents create more intellectually stimulating home environments, better monitor the completion of homework, and demonstrate more interest in what goes on in school, it is plausible that the quality of the classroom environment will be improved for many students. So if, in response to inferior public education, better-educated parents move out of the district or enroll their children in private schools, the constraint on all parents who remain in the public school system becomes tighter.

An Illustration of the Framework

To render the model less abstract, consider the following illustration of a hypothetical teenage female, graphically represented in Figure 3.2. The amount and composition of income this person will earn in her twenties will depend on her earlier life decisions about family structure, education, and labor force participation. Each of these sequential decisions[2] will be influenced by the urban opportunity structure as it is manifested in the young woman's neighborhood.

Decisions about fertility are the first set of life decisions that directly or indirectly affect socioeconomic status. The direct effect occurs because fertility determines the ability of the mother to work outside of the home and her potential for gaining nonwage sources of income (for example, government transfer payments). The indirect effect occurs because early fertility often reduces the mother's educational attainment (Upchurch & McCarthy, 1990).

As with other life decisions, those regarding fertility are shaped by personal and contextual constraints extant at the time of the decision in question. Imagine that this situation is portrayed diagrammatically as in Figure 3.2. The individual's values, self-esteem, and many other characteristics (often related to parental characteristics) undoubtedly play a role, as represented by causal paths A and B. But the spatial context that specifies opportunities also can be influential (paths C, D, and E). A teenage girl may choose childbearing (coupled with welfare support) as her best feasible course for personal fulfillment and socioeconomic stability if she believes there to be no legal, well-paying job opportunities for those who complete a high school such as hers (Galster & Killen, 1995). This choice will be further encouraged if neighborhood norms regarding out-of-wedlock childbearing are permissive (path C) or if the woman anticipates discrimination against her in the labor market because of her race or ethnicity (path E).

A second life decision that determines socioeconomic status relates to education. Success in finding high-paying, full-time employment depends upon the personality attributes applicants bring to the labor market, their educational credentials, and their attainment of reading, writing, communications, and critical thinking skills. Some research not only illustrates growing wage premiums for workers with college degrees and work experience, but also shows that earnings inequality has increased among workers with the same level of

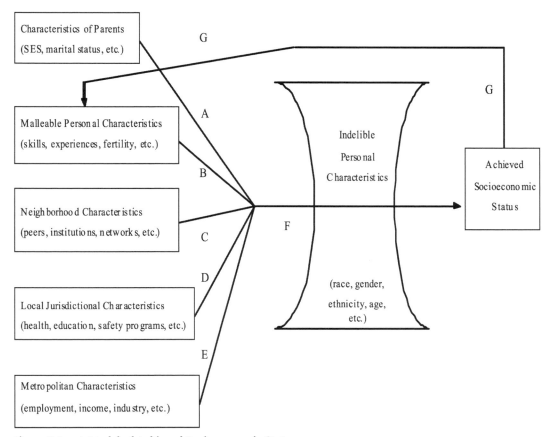

Figure 3.2. A Model of Achieved Socioeconomic Status

schooling and experience (Levy & Murnane, 1992). This suggests that employers are evaluating not just credentials but also the quality of the learning students obtain in school and the quality of the experience young workers obtain in their first jobs.

A teenage girl's choice of educational level depends on a host of spatial contextual constraints. The perceived payoff from any educational credential will be less if she believes that her only feasible educational institutions are of low quality (path D), if she has poor access to and information about employment, or if she believes she will face discrimination in the labor market once she graduates (path E). Peer effects seem especially potent influences upon educational attainment (path C) (Galster & Killen, 1995). Of course, educational choices also will be influenced by the malleable characteristics the teen has accumulated at the time in question, such as past fertility behavior (suggested by the feedback path G).

Lastly, decisions about work critically affect socioeconomic status. The particular labor force outcome will be influenced by the personal traits that the individual offers prospective employers. Those with the malleable traits of less experience and fewer credentials are less likely to be hired for the better-paying positions and more likely to face unemployment. Moreover, women or racial minorities may have their experience and credentials subjectively downgraded in a labor market that discriminates against these indelible traits. Historically, most people who decide to participate in the labor force find jobs quickly, but a fraction enter unemployment, which usually lasts a few months (U.S. Department of Commerce, 1992). Others suffer long spells of unemployment or drop out of the labor force entirely.

Labor market outcomes will also be influenced by residence (Galster & Killen, 1995). A teenage girl's neighborhood may be distant from job opportunities (path E) and be poorly served by public transit (path D). Her local social networks may be ineffective in transmitting information about potential jobs or may contain few role models of success achieved through diligent activities in the legal economy (path C). These networks may be especially weak in providing "bridging social capital" if they consist primarily of non-English speakers. Inferior local public services and schools may impair her health and intellectual development (path D). If she were to suffer from chronic unemployment or underemployment, she would receive an increasingly strong combination of incentives from the limits imposed by the metropolitan employment structure (path E), the failures of local human development and public safety systems (path D), and the potential temptations from peers (path C), which may induce her participation in criminal activities. When such choices result in a criminal record, the subsequent limitations of labor force choices and payoff potentialities become extreme (path G).

THE OPPORTUNITY STRUCTURE FRAMEWORK APPLIED TO URBAN POLARIZATION

Given this overview of the conceptual framework of opportunity structure, I return to the focus of this chapter: racial/ethnic status, poverty, and urban polarization. My thesis is that members of racial/ethnic minority groups who have low incomes—people unfortunate enough to be in the intersection of the four sets of constraints portrayed in Figure 3.1—face an urban opportunity structure that disproportionately offers more limited choices and smaller payoffs from the few choices that are feasible. Given this spatially biased opportunity structure that they confront, low-income urban minorities are more likely to make life choices that impede their chances for socioeconomic advancement and those of their children. They are seduced by a warped geography of opportunity into making decisions that, though rational from their perspective, are personally and socially inefficient and inequitable inasmuch as they perpetuate inequality. Even when they make the same choices as, say, higher-income whites residing in suburban areas, the payoffs they receive are limited by the conditions associated with their place of residence. The most important place-based constraints are associated with segregated housing and public schools. This subject will be the focus below.

As if these spatial penalties were not enough, racial-ethnic minorities, especially those with lower incomes, face the additional burdens of personal discrimination in a variety of markets. Some forms of housing and mortgage market discrimination tend to lock minorities into particular spatial niches; others in labor markets tend to erode the socioeconomic payoffs from certain choices and preclude other choices altogether.[3] The sorts of discrimination faced by low-income minorities have been well documented by numerous sources, and thus are not within the purview of this essay. This is not to minimize their significance, but merely to suggest that my focus is on the spatial dimensions of unequal opportunity in urban America today.

Race-Class Segregation of Neighborhoods

Where one lives is the most fundamental component of the opportunity structure because it significantly influences every other component. Unfortunately, the racial and class dimension of American metropolitan housing markets may be summarized with two words: segregation and centralization.

It is conventional to measure segregation with a "dissimilarity index," which shows how evenly various racial/ethnic groups are spread across neighborhoods within metropolitan areas. A score of zero on this index indicates that the proportion of any particular group is the same across all neighborhoods ("complete integration"); a score of 100 indicates that every neighborhood has residents of only one particular group ("complete segregation") (Massey & Denton, 1993). As Table 3.1 shows, our metropolitan neighborhoods remain highly segregated. Blacks are most segregated from whites (average score of 65), followed by Hispanics (52) and Asians (42). Although there have been modest reductions in dissimilarity among all groups during the 1990s, the situation in 2000 was little different than it was in 1960 (Jaynes & Williams, 1989).

Another useful measure of segregation is the "exposure index," which shows the percentage of residents of one racial-ethnic group who live in the "average" neighborhood of a designated group. Table 3.1 also shows these indices, which indicate that the average black person today lives in a neighborhood with virtually the same percentage of white neighbors (33 percent) as in 1990. Both the average Hispanic and Asian household live in a neighborhood with six

Table 3.1.   Residential Segregation (1990 and 2000) by Major Racial-Ethnic Groups

	1990	*2000*
BLACKS		
Dissimilarity with Whites	69.4	65.1
Dissimilarity with Hispanics	61.9	52.7
Dissimilarity with Asians	70.6	61.8
The average black lives in a neighborhood with . . .		
a % white of:	33.0	33.2
a % black of:	56.1	51.1
a % Hispanic of:	8.3	11.6
a % Asian of:	2.1	3.2
HISPANICS		
Dissimilarity with Whites	51.4	51.6
Dissimilarity with Blacks	56.2	49.1
Dissimilarity with Asians	51.8	49.7
The average Hispanic lives in a neighborhood with . . .		
a % white of:	41.5	36.4
a % black of:	10.1	10.6
a % Hispanic of:	42.8	45.8
a % Asian of:	5.1	5.8
ASIANS		
Dissimilarity with Whites	44.3	42.2
Dissimilarity with Blacks	60.3	54.2
Dissimilarity with Hispanics	48.8	47.6
The average Asian lives in a neighborhood with . . .		
a % white of:	59.9	53.9
a % black of:	8.3	9.0
a % Hispanic of:	16.2	17.6
a % Asian of:	15.2	18.0

Source: Iceland, Weinberg, & Steinmetz (2002)

percentage points *fewer* whites today than in 1990, due primarily to the rapid recent immigration and fertility of these groups.

Moreover, minorities not only tend to live apart from whites, but their residences tend to cluster in or near the older, core municipality of the metropolitan area, especially if minorities also have lower incomes. Even though more minorities than ever live in suburbs,[4] they remain relatively clustered near the core because whites of all incomes generally have increasingly moved out of the core and inner-ring suburbs and into metropolitan fringes (Galster, 1991a).

The segregation of neighborhoods on the basis of income has been rising dramatically since 1970. Abramson, Tobin, and VanderGoot (1995) found that the dissimilarity of poor versus nonpoor households rose from 1970 to 1990 in 72 of the 100 largest metropolitan areas, an average increase of 3.5 percentage points (11 percent) to a level of 36. At the same time there was a rapid expansion of the number and population living in neighborhoods having more than 40 percent poverty rates, especially among blacks and Hispanics (Jargowsky, 1997).

Census data do not permit for most census tracts the delineation of individuals by both racial status and poverty status, thus it is not possible to precisely compute segregation indices for the poor separately by race. Here I attempt a suggestive, second-best alternative, however. One can specify census tracts in 1990 as "majority black" (50 percent or more black residents), "majority Latino" (50 percent or more Hispanic residents) or "predominantly white" (90 percent or more non-Hispanic white residents), then, for each category, compute the isolation index of the poor for each neighborhood category. The results are shown in Table 3.2.

Table 3.2 shows that the average poor person living in a majority-black metropolitan neighborhood in 1990 experienced a neighborhood poverty rate of 38 percent. The corresponding figure for poor Hispanics living in a majority-Hispanic neighborhood was 34 percent. But the figure for poor whites in a majority-white neighborhood was only 12 percent. During 1980–1990 this figure has risen for all three groups, but especially for nonwhite poor. Thus, not only do our metropolitan areas' neighborhoods remain segregated by race and, increasingly, by class, but *poor minorities* are exceptionally (and increasingly) isolated residentially.

The causes of this phenomenon of racial and class segregation of neighborhoods are multiple and complex, and beyond the scope of this chapter. Suffice it to note here that interracial economic disparities, housing stocks increasingly separated into homogeneous value or rent groupings (often abetted by exclusionary zoning policies by suburban municipalities), most nonpoor whites' preferences for predominantly white, nonpoor neighborhood composition, and historical and continuing illegal racial discrimination by public and private parties all contribute (Emerson, Yancey, & Chai, 2001; Galster, 1992c; Massey & Denton 1993).

More importantly for this chapter, both segregation and centralization erect distinct obstacles to the socioeconomic advancement of minorities. Segregation can contribute to intergroup disparities in several ways (Galster, 1992b). First, separate informal networks and formal institutions serving the minority community, because they have a narrower scope and base of support, will have fewer financial, informational, and human resources to draw upon; therefore they will offer inferior options for the development of human capital and the discov-

Table 3.2. Average Percentage Poor in Typical Poor Person's Neighborhood by Predominant Racial-Ethnic Group in Neighborhood, 1970–1990

Neighborhood	1970	1980	1990
50%+ Black	34%	36%	38%
50%+ Hispanic	36%	33%	34%
50%+ White	11%	11%	12%

Note: Isolation index of poor persons
Source: Author's calculations based on U.S. census tract data in Urban Institute Under Class Database

ery of alternative employment possibilities.[5] Second, isolation can encourage and permit the development of distinct subcultural attitudes, behaviors, and speech patterns that may impede success in the mainstream world of work, either because they are counterproductive in some objective sense or because they are perceived to be so by prospective (often white) employers. Third, an identifiable, spatial labor market may be formed in the minority community and attract employers offering only irregular, low-paying, dead-end jobs.

The primary means by which the centralized pattern of minority residence affects minority well-being are twofold. First, minorities' employment opportunities will be restricted in light of progressive decentralization of jobs (especially those paying decent wages only with modest skill requirements) in metropolitan areas. The ability of minorities to both learn about and commute to jobs declines as proximity to them declines (Kain, 1992). Second, as we shall see below, location in the central city more likely confronts a financially distressed municipality and public school system. This means that inferior public services and high tax rates may be the unenviable situation facing centralized minorities.

The statistical evidence makes it clear that minority households are significantly affected by the constraints imposed by racial residential segregation and centralization. One study estimated, for example, that racial segregation increases the probability that a young black man does not work by as much as 33 percent, and the probability that a young black woman heads a single-parent family by as much as 43 percent (Massey, Gross, & Eggers, 1991). Other studies found that if we could cut racial residential segregation by 50 percent, the median income of black families would rise 24 percent (Galster & Keeney, 1988), the black homicide rate would fall by 30 percent (Peterson & Krivo, 1993), the black high school dropout rate would fall by over three-fourths, and poverty rates for black families would drop 17 percent (Galster, 1987; Galster, 1991b; Price & Mills, 1985). Thus, it is clear that the constraints imposed by racial segregation of neighborhoods play a major role in explaining persistent interracial socioeconomic disparities.

The effects of neighborhood economic class segregation have their own limitations on opportunities, independent of parental and other background characteristics. In neighborhoods characterized by concentrated poverty, chronic joblessness and welfare use, the limitations on opportunity are especially horrific (Wilson, 1987; Wilson, 1996). If few of one's neighbors work, there is little chance of learning through informal networks about job vacancies that may arise in employees' firms. If one's children play in a friend's home that is filled with lead paint dust, their mental capacity can be impaired. If students who do not come to school ready to learn dominate the local public school, the quality of education received by other students will be harmed. If neighborhood norms tolerate or even encourage teen childbearing out-of-wedlock, boys and girls will be more likely to become sexually active. If there is little social cohesion and collective efficacy, control of public spaces may default to criminal elements, whereupon some members of households may fear to leave their homes for work or recreation.

Commonsensical arguments such as these have garnered considerable support from statistical analyses (DeLuca & Dayton, 2009; Ellen & Turner, 1997; Gephart, 1997; Leventhal & Brooks-Gunn, 2000). Several studies have shown that, controlling for many (though certainly not all) parental and individual characteristics of importance, outcomes for people living in places of concentrated disadvantage are much less positive. A variety of social maladies—violence, crime, substance abuse, dropping out of school, not participating in the labor market, out-of-wedlock child bearing—are intensified in circumstances of concentrated poverty.[6]

There also is evidence that the likelihood that people will engage in such socially undesirable behaviors grows disproportionately as the percentage of disadvantaged neighbors exceeds a threshold point (Quercia & Galster 2000). The bulk of the evidence, albeit limited, implies a threshold around 20 percent poor in the neighborhood (Galster, 2002; Galster, Cutsinger, & Malega, 2008). This would be particularly important were it to garner an empirical consensus, for it suggests that deconcentrating poverty will not merely "move social problems around" while keeping their aggregate level unchanged. Rather, if neighborhoods exceeding the 20 percent threshold were eliminated by population redistributions, the overall incidence of social problems throughout metropolitan areas would be dramatically reduced (Galster, 2002; Galster & Zobel, 1998).

A complementary strand of research has investigated the issue of neighborhood effects by comparing the well-being of low-income households in high-poverty neighborhoods and the low-poverty neighborhoods to which they move as a result of a deconcentrating assisted housing initiative.

Perhaps the best-known evidence was produced by Rosenbaum and his collaborators during their multiple investigations of the Gautreaux program in Chicago. As a remedy to the 1969 lawsuit filed against the Chicago Housing Authority, the court ordered HUD to help thousands of black public housing residents move to neighborhoods located within the metropolitan area with low concentration of blacks (Goering, 1986). Ultimately, 7,100 families participated, with most moving to suburban areas with low concentrations of poverty and minorities. Interviews revealed that, compared to those moving out of public housing but remaining in the city, suburban participants: (1) felt significantly safer and their children were less vulnerable to gang recruitment, (2) were (eventually) socially integrated to some degree and not isolated, (3) had children who were more likely to be attending four-year colleges, taking college-track courses in high school, and working at a job with good pay and benefits (DeLuca & Dayton, 2009; Keels, Duncan, DeLuca, Mendenhall, & Rosenbaum, 2005; Rosenbaum, 1995; Rubinowitz & Rosenbaum, 2000).

Evidence emerging from the ongoing Moving To Opportunity demonstration echoes some of the Gautreaux findings of positive impacts, though the research methods and findings vary across the experimental sites in a way that generalizations are rendered precarious. Nevertheless, the results suggest that compared to the control group, the experimental MTO group moving to low-poverty neighborhoods experienced: (1) social interactions with neighbors that were not significantly different from their neighborhood of origin, (2) better physical health, lower reports of depressive or anxious behavior, (3) reductions in self-reported criminal victimization, (4) lower rates of welfare receipt, (5) increased standardized achievement scores of their young children, (6) lower rates of criminal offending and arrests for violent crimes for their young boys, and (7) fewer instances of behaving punitively toward their children or engaging in restrictive parenting practices (Briggs, Popkin, & Goering, 2010; DeLuca & Dayton, 2009; Goering & Feins, 2003; Katz, Kling, & Liebman, 2001; Leventhal & Brooks-Gunn, 2000; Ludwig, Duncan, & Pinkston, 2000; Ludwig, Duncan, & Hirschfield 2001; Ludwig, Ladd, & Duncan, 2001; Orr, Feins, Jacob, & Beecroft, 2003).

Studies of the impacts upon households participating in scattered-site public housing programs have generally reinforced the conclusions derived from research on tenant-based subsidy programs, though they have typically not been as comprehensive or methodologically rigorous (Varady & Preiser, 1998). Tenants living in scattered-site public housing generally: (1) experienced few problems with their move and felt welcome in their homes, (2) strongly preferred their new homes and neighborhoods to their former ones, (3) were generally satisfied with accessibility and public services with the exception of public transportation, (4) had minimal social interactions with their middle-class neighbors but were not socially isolated, and (5) expected their children to benefit in the long-term from the superior educational opportunities and neighborhood safety (Briggs, 1997; Hogan, 1996).

Race-Class Segregation of Schools

Education is a complicated channel for upward mobility. There are many schooling choices, and different subgroups of the urban population favor different paths. It appears that choices of public vs. private schools, various public school districts, and courses of study within a particular school all affect academic achievement and the likelihood of labor market success (Alexander & Pallas, 1985; Hanusheck, 1986; Hoffer, 1985). However, the possibility of exercising choice (by migration to the suburbs, enrollment in a private school, selection of a more academically oriented curriculum) often seems remote for urban, low-income minority groups (Darden, Duleep, & Galster, 1992; Hill & Rock, 1992; Jaynes & Williams, 1989). The result is a set of educational constraints profoundly differentiated by race and ethnicity.

Racial differences in enrollment patterns reveal one dimension of this differentiation. Dissimilarity indices of the degree of racial segregation among school districts for metropolitan areas with the largest numbers of minority pupils are presented in Table 3.3. They show that, when compared to white students in the 1999–2000 school year, black students are generally more unevenly distributed across districts than are Hispanic or Asian students (dissimilarity indices of 65, 58, and 50, respectively). All minority groups are highly segregated from whites across school districts, however, in rough correspondence to their degree of residential segregation (Orfield, 1983). Moreover, unlike the case of neighborhood racial segregation, all three minority groups' dissimilarity indices rose two or three points since 1989 in the areas where they constituted a sizable fraction of the enrollment (Lewis Mumford Center, 2002).

Similarly, the exposure of minority students to white students has been declining over the last decade (Orfield 1994). As shown in Table 3.3, in 1999 the percentage of students in one's own racial group in the typical school was 59, 55, and 21 percent for black, Hispanic, and Asian students, respectively (Lewis Mumford Center, 2002).

But where are minority students preponderantly concentrated? Nationally, two-thirds of African American students and nearly half of other minority students attend primary and secondary schools in central city districts; less than a quarter of white students do so (Hill & Rock, 1992). Given the centralized nature of poverty neighborhoods, these intersections generate center city schools with high proportions of *both* minority and low-income students.

Table 3.3. School Segregation in 1989 and 1999 by Predominant Racial-Ethnic Group

	1989	*1999*
BLACKS		
Dissimilarity with whites	61.7	64.5
Average black attends school with % black of:	56.6	59.2
HISPANICS		
Dissimilarity with whites	53.1	55.0
Average Hispanic attends school with % Hispanic of:	46.7	54.9
ASIANS		
Dissimilarity with whites	47.4	49.8
Average Asian attends school with % Asian of:	17.6	20.5

*For blacks and Hispanics, data show unweighted averages for 50 metro areas with largest numbers of black and Hispanic students, respectively; for Asians, data are averages for top 25 metro areas.
**For details, see Lewis Mumford Center, 2002, http://mumford1.dyndns.org, Tables 2–7.

During the 1999–2000 school year, the average black student in public school attended a school having 65 percent of its students from poor families; the corresponding figures for Hispanic and Asian students are 66 and 42 percent. By contrast, the average white student in public school attended a school having only 30 percent of its students from poor families (Lewis Mumford Center, 2002). In many large metropolitan areas, the gaps between school poverty rates experienced by minority and white public school students are even more dramatic. In Newark, Detroit, Philadelphia, Cleveland, Milwaukee, Boston, Baltimore, Cincinnati, Kansas City, Minneapolis, and St. Louis, the average school poverty rate to which black students are exposed exceeds that for white students by 40 percentage points or more. In Newark, Philadelphia, Orange County, Boston, Hartford, Los Angeles, Houston, and Bergen-Passaic, the average school poverty rate to which Hispanic students are exposed exceeds that for white students by 40 percentage points or more (Lewis Mumford Center, 2002, tables 8–10).

Thus, the educational constraints facing the vast majority of white students are quite different from those facing black and Hispanic students. The educational opportunities of most black and Hispanic students are intimately connected to inner-city districts in the largest metropolitan areas. Unfortunately, these districts tend to be racially, economically, and socially isolated and inferior providers of education on several counts.

The first area of inferiority involves funding. School districts with the fewest minority students spend $902 more state and local dollars per pupil annually than those with the most minority students. State aid typically does little but exacerbate this gap. Roughly 60 percent of states provide more than $100 per pupil more aid to districts with few poor or minority children than to districts with many (Schemo, 2002). Fiscal disparities between individual districts can be even more dramatic (Kozol, 1991). Inner-city students' teachers are, on average, less well prepared, come from inferior colleges, and are fewer in number in several critical subject areas. The same is true of guidance counselors (Orfield, 1992).

Second, racially-socially isolated school systems place more limits on the educational achievement and attainment of poor children from black and Hispanic families because these children have less contact with children from nonpoor families (Jencks & Mayer, 1990). Racial segregation makes it more difficult for nonpoor minority children to build on their parents' progress toward upward social mobility, because the critical mass that influences their education and social systems is more heavily influenced by children from poor families (Galster, 1991b; Wilson, 1987).

Finally, race-class segregation in schools can make it harder for minority children to acquire the "soft skills" valued in the labor market. These skills, especially styles of communication and interpersonal relationships, likely are derived from social patterns prevailing in white, middle-class culture. Children first may learn communication and interpersonal skills from family members and neighbors. Schools potentially give children a second chance to learn these skills, however, because students interact with schoolmates from other families and neighborhoods. The opportunity structure appears to provide poor white children with opportunities for economic integration in the school and neighborhood, but typically denies these opportunities to minority children. That is, many minority children have little exposure at home or in school to patterns that set the standard for workplace communication and interpersonal relationships. These children may therefore develop alterative patterns that may serve them well on the streets but hinder them in the workplace (Bleachman, 1991; Neckerman, 1991).

In combination, the aforementioned limitations on social, financial, and human resources produce the expected inferior school performance outcomes (Gottlieb, 2002; Moreau, 2002). For example, the "nonselective segregated high schools" serving about two-thirds of Chicago's students graduated only 8 percent of their students with reading ability at the national norm level. Nine out of ten Cleveland students (the vast majority of whom are minorities) failed the state proficiency exam in 1991 (Krumholz, 1992; Orfield, 1983). Unsurprisingly, disproportionate numbers of minority students find dropping out to be a rational decision in light of such school quality. Perhaps most damning of all, many employers appear to be writing off graduates of inner-city school systems as prospective employees. Minority students who pursue college find the combination of inferior training and limited exposure to whites a deterrent to persisting in college. Thus, not only have the African American and Hispanic vs. white gaps in college entrance rates been rising, but so have the gaps in college completion rates (Orfield, 1992).

URBAN POLARIZATION AS A PROCESS OF CUMULATIVE CAUSATION

Thus far I have argued that urban space is characterized by a warped opportunity structure that leads centralized minorities of low incomes to make choices that perpetuate their inferior socioeconomic status. The key structural element creating this warping is racial and class segregation of neighborhoods and schools. These interrelationships are portrayed diagrammatically in the three sections on the right of Figure 3.3 titled "segregation," "human consequences," and "socioeconomic disparities."

Here I introduce feedback loops into the picture.[7] In particular, race-class disparities work to reinforce the prejudices held by the dominant group—typically nonpoor whites of European ancestry—as shown by the arrow running from right to left at the bottom of Figure 3.3. Opinion polls have demonstrated how whites perceive blacks and Hispanics as less willing to work, more prone to gangs and drugs, less intelligent, less able to speak English well (Farley, 1998). To the extent that these stereotypical beliefs are supported by some empirical reality, it is precisely the reality as produced by the low-income, minority subcultural developments and constrained choices that emanate from their opportunity structure.

Prejudices, of course, motivate a variety of behaviors by whites, as shown by the arrows emanating from the "prejudices" box in Figure 3.3. Prejudice directly reinforces segregation in neighborhoods and schools through white "flight" and "avoidance": whites leave neighborhoods and schools when they exceed a threshold percentage of minorities or poor, and avoid such contexts when searching for alternatives (Ellen, 2000; Emerson et al., 2001; Galster, 1990). Prejudice indirectly reinforces segregation through motivating illegal behaviors in labor markets, housing markets, and schools, and through legal collective actions like exclusionary zoning and the establishment of private schools.

To paint the big picture more simply:

- Our society has created a warped metropolitan opportunity structure whose primary feature is race-class segregation of neighborhoods and schools.
- This structure induces many lower-income, minority households residing in core neighborhoods to make choices that are rational within their constrained set of options.
- But these choices perpetuate socioeconomic inequities among races and classes.
- These choices legitimate prejudices held by the dominant group against lower-income and minority households.
- These prejudices motivate and justify in the view of the dominant group legal and illegal acts and structures that reinforce segregation.

This dynamic may be labeled "cumulative causation."

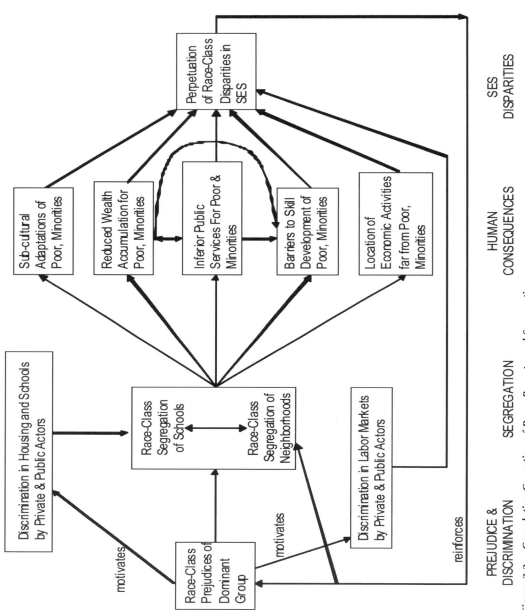

Figure 3.3. Cumulative Causation of Race, Poverty, and Segregation

POLICY IMPLICATIONS

If we take this analysis seriously, clear policy implications emerge. In this chapter I can only provide an outline of these implications; I have, however, provided more fleshed-out analyses elsewhere (Darden et al., 1992; DeMarco & Galster, 1993; Galster, 1990; Galster, 1992b; Galster, Tatian, Santiago, Pettit, & Smith, 2003).

Admittedly, combating a warped opportunity structure is controversial and complex. Some have suggested that the current race-class segregation of neighborhoods and schools can be continued if core communities' access to good jobs and schools is enhanced through, for example, new transportation schemes, empowerment zones, or school choice vouchers (Kingsley & Turner, 1993). I argue that such schemes, though worthy, are inferior to those that aim directly at expanding the residential and school choices of minorities and the poor, thereby desegregating communities and schools by class and by racial-ethnic composition (Galster, 1992b). The gist of the argument is that unless the iron grip of neighborhood and school segregation is released, all other ameliorative efforts will necessitate inefficient subsidies and distortions of the market, and will be blunted by elements of the opportunity structure that cannot easily be ruptured from the residential nexus, like local social networks. What is needed is a two-pronged initiative providing *both the means and the incentive to desegregate:* one aimed at individuals and the other at states, school districts, and municipalities.

Programs Encouraging Individual Desegregation

As for individuals, there are a variety of desegregation initiatives that federal, state, and local governments should adopt, some aimed at lower-income individuals and others at those in higher income groups. Consider first programs aimed at and providing the means and incentives for lower-income households to desegregate neighborhoods. At the federal level, there should be an intensified effort to expand geographically the housing choices for the less well-off through housing choice (formerly Section 8) voucher rent subsidies, coupled with affirmative efforts to market residential areas that might be unfamiliar to subsidy recipients, and to guarantee ongoing supportive counseling and social services to smooth recipients' transition into new environments (Briggs, Popkin, & Goering, 2010). Individuals receiving housing choice vouchers might also be encouraged to make desegregative moves by appending special bonus subsidies.

More broadly, there should be federal policies to encourage the movement of *all* households into neighborhoods where their racial-ethnic and/or income group is underrepresented. For example, those of any income or racial-ethnic group who make moves that promote race and/or class desegregation could be rewarded with a federal income tax credit based on their moving expense deduction.

States and localities have at their disposal several examples of successful neighborhood racial desegregation efforts, many of which could be tailored to encourage class desegregation as well (DeMarco & Galster, 1993). Governments could, for example, provide additional information to underrepresented home buyers about options in neighborhoods in which traditionally they would not have searched. Such affirmative marketing services have been successfully provided by the Leadership Council for Open Metropolitan Communities in the Chicago area and the East Suburban Council for Open Metropolitan Communities in the Cleveland area, for example. In addition, state and local governments could provide a variety of financial incentives to encourage desegregation. Oak Park, Illinois, provides rehabilitation subsidies to landlords who have racially-ethnically mixed apartment complexes. Cleveland Heights and Shaker Heights, Ohio, grant low-interest mortgages to house buyers moving into neighborhoods where their group is underrepresented. The State of Ohio allocates a share of its revenue bond funds to provide below-market-rate mortgages to first-time homebuyers making such desegregative moves (Chandler, 1992; Galster, 1992a).

As for encouraging class desegregation, there is several decades' worth of experience with state and local efforts to expand the geographic scope of assisted and affordable housing through mandates like "fair share" or "inclusionary zoning" laws, most notably in California, Maryland, Massachusetts, and New Jersey (Advisory Commission on Regulatory Barriers to Affordable Housing, 1991; Downs, 1973; Keating, 1994; Lake, 1981; Mallach, 1984; Schuetz, Meltzer, & Been, 2011). More recently, these efforts have been echoed in numerous federal court-ordered remedies in local housing authority segregation cases (Popkin et al., 2003). But more is required.

A variety of pilot programs should be initiated and funded by HUD or by state and local governments that provide substantial, behavior-modifying financial incentives for relevant parties to create opportunities for assisted housing where they are now sorely underrepresented. Local public housing authorities should have stronger incentives to recruit landlords for the Housing Choice Voucher program in lower-poverty neighborhoods and be rewarded for helping their assisted households make the corresponding sorts of poverty-deconcentrating moves (Briggs, 1997; Hartung & Henig, 1997; Turner, 1998). The reward structure should also facilitate the deconcentration of their existing public housing stock. Private developers of supportive housing for special needs populations should receive incentives if they produce in lower-poverty neighborhoods. Landlords of market-rate units should receive bonuses for participating in the Housing Choice Voucher program for the first time. Local governments should be financially encouraged to permit the development of rental housing that either provides site-based assistance (through public housing, HOME, or Low Income Housing Tax Credit programs) or is priced at Fair Market Rent levels that would permit its participation in the Housing Choice Voucher program (Pendall, 2000). Such financial incentives could emanate from either federal or state governments.

Programs Encouraging Institutional Desegregation

Federal programs should be designed to encourage lower levels of government to adopt coordinated desegregation programs that fit their local contexts. Encouragement could be supplied through the careful tailoring of intergovernmental transfers. Federal bonus funds to states might, for instance, be provided for establishing and/or supporting regional fair housing organizations (either public or private) that enforce antidiscrimination laws and promote neighborhood desegregation in their metropolitan areas. Similarly, direct federal financial aid to municipalities for any number of activities might be awarded for formal cooperation with such a regional organization.

Even more directly, federal and state governments should devise a system of grants that would be given to school districts and local governments progressing toward desegregation goals (Boger, 1996). Based on existing research (Galster, 2002), the goal should be to have no more than 20 percent of households in a neighborhood in poverty. A somewhat higher threshold might be contemplated regarding the maximum student body in a school building qualifying for free or reduced-price lunches (Gottlieb, 2002). Goals regarding racial mix would be tailored to the demographic particulars of each region. Incentives would take the form of annual grants to school districts and general-purpose local jurisdictions that voluntarily participated in the program. No entity would be penalized if it chose not to participate. The grants would be designed, however, to be sufficiently generous to convince many that it is in their fiscal self-interest to promote more diversity.

It is important to emphasize that diversity in this proposal is measured at the school building and neighborhood (census tract) levels. It would not be desirable for a school district or municipality to have a diverse aggregate profile, but to have particular types of students or households concentrated in a few schools or neighborhoods. It also should be recognized that the proposed grant incentives are designed to encourage the movement of different groups both within and among school districts and local jurisdictions, and to offer symmetric incentives to entities that have "too many" and "too few" low-income or minority people within them.

For local governments, the incentives could be administered through existing revenue-sharing programs. For each neighborhood (census tract) having less than the target percentages of certain households in the previous census, incentives would be provided for increasing the percentage; for each neighborhood having more than the target, incentives would be provided for decreasing that percentage until it no longer exceeded it.[8] Similarly, for school districts the incentives would be administered through existing school aid programs.

In closing, there is guidance provided by a proven array of programs instituted by a few progressive state and local governments that have reduced the segregation of neighborhoods by race and class. Recent retreats from the racial and class desegregation of schools suggests that more innovative strategies are called for in this arena. In both cases, there needs to be greater coherence, scope, and focus of desegregation policy; leadership at the federal level has been notably absent. Without serious efforts to disrupt segregation, the intersection of poverty and minority status will mockingly continue to transform "equal opportunity in America" from a hallowed premise into a hollow promise.

NOTES

The author wishes to thank Jackie Cutsinger for her research and manuscript production assistance.

1. There may be other important personal constraints, of course, such as gender, age, and disability status, but these are beyond the purview of this essay. For simplicity in this chapter I will use the term "race" to mean both racial and ethnic differences.

2. The decisions literally do not need to be sequential, and the sequence described here is typical but not necessary.

3. For reviews of the literature on personal discrimination, see Fix and Turner (1999) and Turner and Skidmore (1999).

4. In 2000, a majority of Asians, almost half of Hispanics, and over a third of blacks lived in suburbs (Institute on Race and Poverty, 2002).

5. This appears most strongly to be the case in large central cities of the Northeast and Midwest, and in African American areas. (See Fernandez & Harris, 1992; Peterson & Harrell, 1992; Taylor, Chatters, & Mays, 1988.)

6. In fairness it must be noted that the literature on concentrated poverty neighborhood effects is not without its weaknesses. Not all scholarly studies find that the characteristics of one's neighborhood have any identifiable impact on behavior. Some find identifiable but only small impacts, others find impacts on only certain low-income population groups, and all studies of neighborhood effects have important methodological weaknesses. (See Brooks-Gunn, Duncan, & Aber, 1997; DeLuca & Dayton, 2009; Ginther, Haveman, & Wolfe, 2000; Popkin, Buron, Levy, & Cunningham, 2000.)

7. Of course, segregation of neighborhoods and schools are mutually reinforcing. Households with children may choose neighborhoods on the basis of the race-class composition of schools. School enrollments in a system of neighborhood school assignments will reflect the race-class composition of the neighborhood. Another aspect of this interrelationship was revealed by South and Crowder (1997), who find that the racial segregation of neighborhoods impedes the ability of poor blacks to escape from neighborhoods of concentrated poverty.

8. With the planned advent of the Census Bureau's annual American Communities Survey later this decade, annually updated, five-year moving averages of population estimates at the census tract level will be available, instead of every ten years.

REFERENCES

Abramson, A. J., Tobin, M. S., & VanderGoot, M. R. (1995). The changing geography of metropolitan opportunity: The segregation of the poor in U.S. metropolitan cities, 1970–1990. *Housing Policy Debate, 6,* 45–72.

Advisory Commission on Regulatory Barriers to Affordable Housing. (1991). *Not in my backyard: Removing regulatory barriers to affordable housing.* Washington, DC: U.S. Department of Housing and Urban Development.

Alexander, K., & Pallas, A. (1985). School sector and cognitive performance. *Sociology of Education, 58,* 115–128.

Bleachman, E. (1991). Mentors for high-risk minority children. In *Mentoring program structures for young minority males.* Washington, DC: Urban Institute.

Boger, J. C. (1996). Toward ending residential segregation: A fair share proposal for the next reconstruction. In J. C. Boger & J. W. Wegner (Eds.), *Race, poverty, and American cities* (pp. 389–343). Chapel Hill: University of North Carolina Press.

Briggs, X. de Souza. (1997). Moving up versus moving out: Neighborhood effects in housing mobility programs. *Housing Policy Debate, 8,* 195–234.

Briggs, X. de Souza, Popkin, S., & Goering, J. (2010). *Moving to Opportunity: The story of an American experiment to fight ghetto poverty.* Oxford, England: Oxford University Press.

Brooks-Gunn, J., Duncan, G. J., & Aber, J. L. (1997). *Neighborhood poverty.* Vol. 1: *Context and consequences for children.* New York: Russell Sage Foundation.

Chandler, M. O. (1992). Obstacles to housing integration program efforts. In G. C. Galster & E. W. Hill (Eds.), *The metropolis in black and white* (pp. 286–305). New Brunswick, NJ: The Center for Urban Policy Research.

Darden, J., Duleep, H., & Galster, G. (1992). Civil rights in metropolitan America. *Journal of Urban Affairs, 14,* 469–496.

DeLuca, S., & Dayton, E. (2009). Switching social contexts: The effects of housing mobility and school choice programs on youth outcomes. *Annual Review of Sociology, 35,* 457–491.

DeMarco, D., & Galster, G. (1993). Prointegrative policy: Theory and practice. *Journal of Urban Affairs, 15,* 141–160.

Downs, A. (1973). *Opening up the suburbs: An urban strategy for America.* New Haven, CT: Yale University Press.

Ellen, I. G. (2000). *Sharing America's neighborhoods: The prospects for stable racial integration.* Cambridge, MA: Harvard University Press.

Ellen, I. G., & Turner, M. (1997). Does neighborhood matter? Assessing recent evidence. *Housing Policy Debate, 8,* 833–866.

Emerson, M. O., Yancey, G., & Chai, K. J. (2001). Does race matter in residential segregation? Exploring the preferences of white Americans. *American Sociological Review, 66,* 922–935.

Farley, R. (1998). *Testing for racial and ethnic discrimination in American economic life.* Paper presented at the Urban Institute Conference on Discrimination, Urban Institute, Washington, DC.

Fernandez, R., & Harris, D. (1992). Social isolation and the underclass. In A. V. Harrell & G. Peterson (Eds.), *Drugs, crime, and social isolation* (pp. 257–294). Washington, DC: Urban Institute Press.

Fix, M., & Turner, M. A. (1999). *A national report card on discrimination in America: The role of testing.* Washington, DC: The Urban Institute Press.

Galster, G. C. (1987). Residential segregation and interracial economic disparities: A simultaneous-equations approach. *Journal of Urban Economics, 21,* 22–44.

Galster, G. C. (1990). Federal fair housing policy: The great misapprehension. In D. DiPasquale & L. C. Keyes (Eds.), *Building foundations: Housing and federal policy* (pp. 132–155). Philadelphia: University of Pennsylvania Press.

Galster, G. C. (1991a). Black suburbanization. *Urban Affairs Quarterly, 26,* 621–628.

Galster, G. C. (1991b). Housing discrimination and poverty of urban African-Americans. *Journal of Housing Research, 2,* 87–122.

Galster, G. C. (1992a). The case for racial integration. In G. C. Galster & E. W. Hill (Eds.), *The metropolis in black and white* (pp. 279–292). New Brunswick, NJ: The Center for Urban Policy Research.

Galster, G. C. (1992b). A cumulative causation model for the underclass: Implications for urban economic development policy. In G. C. Galster & E. W. Hill (Eds.), *The metropolis in black and white* (pp. 190–215). New Brunswick, NJ: The Center for Urban Policy Research.

Galster, G. C. (1992c). Research on discrimination in housing and mortgage markets. *Housing Policy Debate, 3,* 639–684.

Galster, G. C. (2002). An economic efficiency analysis of deconcentrating poverty populations. *Journal of Housing Economics, 11,* 303–329.

Galster, G. C., Cutsinger, J., & Malega, R. (2008). The costs of concentrated poverty: Neighborhood property markets and the dynamics of decline. In N. Retsinas & E. Belsky (Eds.), *Revisiting rental housing: Policies, programs, and priorities* (pp. 93–113). Washington, DC: Brookings Institution Press.

Galster, G. C., & Keeney, W. M. (1988). Race, residence, discrimination, and economic opportunity: Modeling the nexus of urban racial phenomena. *Urban Affairs Review, 24,* 87–117.

Galster, G. C., & Killen, S. (1995). A geography of metropolitan opportunity: A reconnaissance and structural framework. *Housing Policy Debate, 6,* 7–43.

Galster, G. C., Tatian, P., Santiago, A., Pettit, K., & Smith, R. (2003). *Why NOT in my back yard? The neighborhood impacts of assisted housing.* New Brunswick, NJ: Rutgers University/Center for Urban Policy Research/Transaction Press.

Galster, G. C., & Zobel, A. (1998). Will dispersed housing programmes reduce social problems in the US? *Housing Studies, 13,* 605–622.

Gephart, M. A. (1997). Neighborhoods and communities as contexts for development. In J. Brooks-Gunn, G. J. Duncan, & J. L. Aber (Eds.), *Neighborhood poverty: Context and consequences for children* (pp. 1–43). New York: Russell Sage Foundation.

Ginther, D., Haveman, R., & Wolfe, B. (2000). Neighborhood attributes as determinants of children's outcomes: How robust are the relationships? *Journal of Human Resources, 35,* 603–642.

Goering, J. M. (1986). *Housing desegregation and federal policy.* Chapel Hill: University of North Carolina Press.

Goering, J., & Feins, J. (Eds.). (2003). *Choosing a better life? Evaluating the Moving to Opportunity social experiment.* Washington, DC: Urban Institute Press.

Gottlieb, A. (2002, May). Economically segregated schools hurt poor kids, study shows. *The Term Paper: News and Analysis on School Reform from the Piton Foundation,* 1–5.

Hanusheck, E. (1986). The economics of schooling. *Journal of Economic Literature, 24,* 114–177.

Hartung, J. M., & Henig, J. R. (1997). Housing vouchers and certificates as a vehicle for deconcentrating the poor: Evidence from the Washington, D.C., metropolitan area. *Urban Affairs Review, 32,* 403–419.

Hill, E. W., & Rock, H. M. (1992). Race and inner-city education. In G. C. Galster & E. W. Hill (Eds.), *The metropolis in black and white* (pp. 108–127). New Brunswick, NJ: The Center for Urban Policy Research.

Hoffer, T. (1985). Achievement growth and Catholic schools. *Sociology of Education, 58,* 74–87.

Hogan, J. (1996). *Scattered-site housing: Characteristics and consequences.* Washington, DC: U.S. Department of Housing and Urban Development, Office of Policy Development and Research.

Iceland, J., Weinberg, D. H., & Steinmetz, E. (2002). *Racial and ethnic residential segregation in the United States: 1980–2000.* U.S. Census Bureau (Census Special Report, CENSR-3). Washington, DC: U.S. Government Printing Office.

Institute on Race and Poverty. (2002). Racism and metropolitan dynamics. Minneapolis, MN: Institute on Race and Poverty.

Jargowsky, P. A. (1997). *Poverty and place: Ghettos, barrios, and the American city.* New York, NY: Russell Sage Foundation.

Jaynes, G., & Williams, R. (1989). *A common destiny.* Washington, DC: National Academy Press.

Jencks, C., & Mayer, S. (1990). The social consequences of growing up in a poor neighborhood. In L. E. Lynn & M. McGeary (Eds.), *Inner-city poverty in the United States* (pp. 111–186). Washington, DC: National Academy Press.

Kain, J. (1992). The spatial mismatch hypothesis. *Housing Policy Debate, 3,* 371–460.

Katz, L. W., Kling, J. R., & Liebman, J. R. (2001). Moving to opportunity in Boston: Early results of a randomized mobility experiment. *Quarterly Journal of Economics, 116,* 607–654.

Keating, W. D. (1994). *The suburban racial dilemma: Housing and neighborhoods.* Philadelphia, PA: Temple University Press.

Keels, M., Duncan, G., DeLuca, S., Mendenhall, R., & Rosenbaum, J. (2005). Fifteen years later: Can residential mobility programs provide a permanent escape from neighborhood crime and poverty? *Demography, 42,* 51–73.

Kingsley, T., & Turner, M. (1993). *Housing markets and residential mobility.* Washington, DC: Urban Institute Press.

Kozol, J. (1991). *Savage inequalities.* New York, NY: Crown Publishers.

Krumholz, N. (1992, June 3). Developing nightmare. *Cleveland Plain Dealer,* p. 3C.

Lake, R. W. (1981). *The new suburbanites: Race and housing.* New Brunswick, NJ: Rutgers University Center for Urban Policy Research.

Leventhal, T., & Brooks-Gunn, J. (2000). The neighborhoods they live in: The effect of neighborhood residence on child and adolescent outcomes. *Psychological Bulletin, 126,* 309–337.

Levy, F., & Murnane, R. (1992). U.S. earnings levels and earnings inequality: A review of recent trends and proposed explanations. *Journal of Economic Literature, 30,* 1333–1381.

Lewis Mumford Center. (2002). Spatial structures in the social sciences. Retrieved from http://mumford1.dyndns.org

Ludwig, J. O., Duncan, G. J., & Hirschfield, P. (2001). Urban poverty and juvenile crime: Evidence from a randomized housing-mobility experiment. *Quarterly Journal of Economics, 116,* 655–679.

Ludwig, J., Duncan, G., & Pinkston, J. (2000). *Neighborhood effects on economic self-sufficiency: Evidence from a randomized housing-mobility experiment.* Vol. 2001. Chicago, IL: Northwestern University, University of Chicago Joint Center for Poverty Research.

Ludwig, J., Ladd, H. F., & Duncan, G. J. (2001). Urban poverty and educational outcomes. In W. G. Gale & J. Rothenberg (Eds.), *Brookings-Wharton Papers on Urban Affairs: 2001* (pp. 147–201). Washington, DC: Brookings Institution Press.

Mallach, A. (1984). *Inclusionary housing programs: Policies and practices*. New Brunswick, NJ: Center for Urban Policy Research.

Massey, D., & Denton, N. (1993). *American apartheid*. Cambridge, MA: Harvard University Press.

Massey, D. S., Gross, A. B., & Eggers, M. L. (1991). Segregation, the concentration of poverty, and the life chances of individuals. *Social Science Quarterly, 20*, 397–420.

Moreau, C. (2002, October 19). Learning in mixed company. *Hartford Courant*.

Neckerman, K. (1991). *What getting ahead means to employers and disadvantaged workers*. Paper presented at the Urban Poverty and Family Life Conference, University of Chicago, Chicago IL.

Orfield, G. (1983). *Public school desegregation in the U.S., 1968–1980*. Washington, DC: Joint Center for Political Studies.

Orfield, G. (1992). Urban schooling and the perpetuation of job inequality in metropolitan Chicago. In G. Peterson & W. Vroman (Eds.), *Urban labor markets* (pp. 161–199). Washington, DC: Urban Institute Press.

Orfield, G. (1994). *The growth of segregation in American schools*. Alexandria, VA: National School Boards Association.

Orr, L., Feins, J., Jacob, R., & Beecroft, E. (2003). *Moving to Opportunity: Interim impacts evaluation, final report*. Washington, DC: U.S. Department of Housing and Urban Development.

Pendall, R. (2000). Why voucher and certificate users live in distressed neighborhoods. *Housing Policy Debate, 11*, 881–910.

Peterson, G., & Harrell, A. V. (1992). Introduction: Inner-city isolation and opportunity. In A. V. Harrell & G. Peterson (Eds.), *Drugs, crime, and social isolation* (pp. 1–26). Washington, DC: Urban Institute Press.

Peterson, R., & Krivo, L. (1993). Racial segregation and black urban homicide. *Social Forces, 71*, 1001–1026.

Popkin, S. J., Buron, L. F., Levy, D. K., & Cunningham, M. K. (2000). The Gautreaux legacy: What might mixed-income and dispersal strategies mean for the poorest public housing tenants? *Housing Policy Debate, 11*, 911–942.

Popkin, S., Galster, G., Temkin, K., Herbig, C., Levy, D., & Richer, E. (2003). Obstacles to desegregating public housing: Lessons learned from implementing eight consent decrees. *Journal of Policy Analysis and Management, 22*, 179–200.

Price, R. & Mills, E. (1985). Race and residence in earnings determination. *Journal of Urban Economics, 17*, 1–18.

Quercia, R. G., & Galster, G. C. (2000). Threshold effects and neighborhood change. *Journal of Planning Education and Research, 20*, 146–163.

Rosenbaum, J. E. (1995). Changing the geography of opportunity by expanding residential choice: Lessons from the Gautreaux program. *Housing Policy Debate, 6*, 231–269.

Rubinowitz, L. S., & Rosenbaum, J. E. (2000). *Crossing the class and color lines: From public housing to white suburbia*. Chicago, IL: University of Chicago Press.

Schemo, D. (2002, August 9). Neediest schools receive less money, report finds. *New York Times*, p. A-11.

Schuetz, J., Meltzer, R., & Been, V. (2011). Silver bullet or Trojan horse? The effects of inclusionary zoning on local housing markets. *Urban Studies, 48*, 273–296.

South, S. J., & Crowder, K. D. (1997). Escaping distressed neighborhoods: Individual, community, and metropolitan influences. *American Journal of Sociology, 102*, 1040–1084.

Taylor, R., Chatters, L. M., and Mays, V. (1988). Parents, children, siblings, in-laws, and non-kin as sources of emergency assistance to black Americans. *Family Relations, 37*, 298–304.

Turner, M. A. (1998). Moving out of poverty: Expanding mobility and choice through tenant-based housing assistance. *Housing Policy Debate, 9*, 373–394.

Turner, M. A., & Skidmore, F. (1999). *Mortgage lending discrimination: A review of existing evidence*. Washington, DC: The Urban Institute Press.

Upchurch, D., & McCarthy, J. (1990). The timing of first birth and high school completion. *American Sociological Review, 55*, 224–234.

U.S. Department of Commerce. (1992). *Statistical abstract of the United States*. Washington, DC: U.S. Bureau of the Census.

Varady, D. P., & Preiser, W. F. E. (1998). Scattered-site public housing and satisfaction: Implications for the new public housing program. *Journal of the American Planning Association, 64*, 189–207.

Wilson, W. J. (1978). *The declining significance of race*. Chicago, IL: University of Chicago Press.

Wilson, W. J. (1987). *The truly disadvantaged: The inner city, the underclass, and public policy*. Chicago, IL: University of Chicago Press.

Wilson, W. J. (1996). *When work disappears: The world of the new urban poor*. New York, NY: Alfred A. Knopf.

4

Racial Segregation in Multiethnic Schools

Adding Immigrants to the Analysis

Ingrid Gould Ellen and Katherine O'Regan,
With Amy Ellen Schwartz and Leanna Stiefel

The extensive and expanding literature examining racial and ethnic segregation in schools in the United States reveals that U.S. schools have extremely—and persistently—high levels of segregation (Orfield & Lee, 2004). This is true even as the composition of the student body has become increasingly diverse. While recent studies have moved beyond the traditional focus on blacks and whites to consider the segregation of Asian and Hispanic students as well, they typically ignore one of the largest compositional shifts currently affecting American schools: immigration. Yet immigrants may exhibit or invite different propensities for racial sorting and may therefore change patterns of racial interaction. If so, the increasing presence of immigrants in U.S. schools has the potential of altering these historically high levels of racial segregation.

This chapter attempts to shed light on this issue—whether and how racial segregation patterns of immigrant students differ from the native born, and what the implications are for racial segregation overall in U.S. schools. It does so by considering the segregation and distribution of immigrants in one very large and diverse urban public school system. Using a rich data set on elementary and middle school students in New York City public schools, where approximately 16 percent of the students are immigrants, this chapter presents a series of descriptive analyses that address two broad research questions. First, how does the racial isolation of immigrant students compare to that of the native born? Second, to the extent that patterns diverge, how can we explain the differences? While our cross-sectional analysis cannot definitively answer this second question, it does permit us to explore some possible contributing factors. Namely, do differences in population characteristics account for the different racial patterns? Do differences reflect temporary adjustments as immigrants first arrive in the United States? Do they simply reflect clustering by country of origin? In combination, these analyses shed light on whether the increased presence of immigrant students may lead to reductions in racial segregation, accomplishing what years of policies and court cases have not.

THEORY AND PAST LITERATURE

Many factors likely contribute to racial segregation in U.S. schools: explicit racial or ethnic preferences about the composition of the student body, which include both affirmative desires for ethnic clustering and inclinations to avoid particular groups; sorting by income; racial differences in preferences about school policies and characteristics; and underlying residential segregation (Benabou, 1996; Lankford & Wyckoff, 2000; Schneider, Teske, & Marshall, 2000; Weiher & Tedin, 2002).[1] Our interest here is in whether these factors differ for immigrant and native-born children—that is, do we see different patterns of racial sorting of immigrants, as compared to their native-born counterparts?

Previous research suggests that immigrants, especially recent immigrants, will exhibit a stronger inclination to cluster with others like them. When first coming to this country, immigrants are likely to be drawn toward the familiar and choose schools (as well as neighborhoods) where there are many others—friends, family, and so on—from their same country (Allen & Turner, 1996; Massey & Denton, 1987; Rosenbaum & Friedman, 2001). Given the link between nationality and race, such clustering is also likely to produce racial clustering. At the same time, while immigrants may gravitate toward schools with greater numbers of students from their same country of origin, they may in fact have less pronounced *racial* identities than the native-born or more established immigrants (Bashi Bobb, 2001; Waldinger, 2002). Thus, it is possible that they will be more comfortable sharing schools with students from other races and be less clustered along racial lines.

The racial attitudes of native-born families may also differentiate between native-born and immigrant racial groups. On the one hand, native-born families may be more resistant to sharing schools with other racial groups when those other racial groups are also foreign born, have greater difficulties with English, and are less familiar with American cultural norms. On the other hand, some researchers have suggested that foreign-born minority students are sometimes perceived as "higher-status minorities" (Waters, 1999). Thus, native-born families may in fact be more open to living with and having their children go to school with students from other racial groups when those students are immigrants.

Income might play a role too, since the incomes of immigrants are lower on average than those of the native born (Schmidley, 2001). We therefore expect immigrant children to attend schools with higher poverty rates, and given the association between poverty and race, we might also expect immigrant children to attend schools with fewer whites. For foreign-born minority students, their lower incomes would therefore translate into higher levels of racial segregation; for foreign-born whites, their lower incomes could lead them to be less racially segregated, or more exposed to minority students, than are native-born whites.

Finally, immigrants from different regions may also have distinct preferences about school programs and services. For example, immigrants may search for schools with specialized programs and services that cater to their particular language and culture (e.g., bilingual classes). Given the link between nationality and race, such differences in preference would also heighten racial clustering.

In sum, theory offers unclear predictions about whether immigrant students should be more or less racially segregated, and there is little empirical evidence to guide us either way.[2] Our search uncovered no studies exploring how immigration affects patterns of racial segregation in schools.[3] A number of papers have examined the residential segregation of immigrants, however, and most find evidence suggesting that immigrants, especially recent immigrants, are more racially segregated than their native-born counterparts.[4]

Specifically, several studies report a strong correlation between the percentage of Hispanics in a city that are foreign-born and levels of residential segregation among Hispanics (Farley & Frey, 1994; Massey, 1979; Massey & Bitterman, 1985). A few other studies find evidence that first-generation immigrants tend to be more residentially segregated than their later-generation counterparts (Aguirre, Schwirian, & La Greca, 1980; Allen & Turner, 1996; Massey, 1979; Taeuber & Taeuber, 1965). Finally, White and Omer (1996) compare the segregation levels of a variety of ethnic groups in New Jersey and report that groups that have been in the United States for longer tend to be less segregated.

BACKGROUND: DATA AND SEGREGATION IN
NEW YORK CITY SCHOOLS

New York City is an ideal city in which to investigate our questions. First, the New York City schools are extraordinarily racially diverse. Of the top ten urban school districts in the United States, New York, Dallas, and San Diego are the only three in which no single racial group comprises a majority (Orfield, 2001). In addition, unlike Dallas and San Diego, New York City's immigrant population is not only large but also highly diverse. In 2000, approximately 16 percent of the students in the city's elementary and middle schools are immigrants, from nearly 200 countries, territories, and semi-sovereign states. This large and diverse immigrant population offers an outstanding opportunity to examine school attendance patterns of immigrants in general as well as immigrants from distinct regions of the world. Further, this diversity permits us to examine multiple groups of foreign born of similar race but different regions of origin, helping distinguish ethnic segregation from racial segregation per se.

School Choice in New York City

Segregation patterns in schools will reflect a complicated set of choices (and lack of choices) both residentially and with respect to schools. In terms of choice of schools (for a given residential location), New York City resembles most school districts. It is divided into catchment-zones, which determine the school of default, especially for elementary school students. Children are guaranteed a spot in their zoned school, subject to space limitations. There is some level of choice, however—families can request waivers to attend other schools and there are several magnet programs. Still, while there is little direct evidence on these patterns, it seems likely that most children attend their zoned schools, given the bureaucratic difficulties of securing waivers as well as the greater travel time required to attend other schools (Cookson & Lucks, 1995).

Although data and evidence about school choice are very limited, the degree and nature of choice available at the elementary school level differs from that available at the middle school level, thereby suggesting important differences by type of schools for our analysis. For example, there are far fewer middle schools than elementary schools, and middle schools are more geographically dispersed. At the same time, it seems likely that middle school children have greater flexibility to act on choices than elementary school children, due in part to the ability of middle school children to use public transportation and the willingness of their parents to send them to schools farther from home. Because of such potential differences in choice mechanisms, we performed separate analyses for each set of schools (elementary and middle). Since the results were highly similar across the two types of schools, however, we have chosen to present results for the full sample of schools together.

Data

We use a rich, pupil-level data set that provides socioeconomic and academic information on all of the students attending a public elementary or middle school grade in New York City during the 1998–1999 school year. The data include the student's grade level, eligibility for free lunch (indicating family resources below 130 percent of the poverty line), race, and

Table 4.1. Summary Statistics for New York City Elementary and Middle School Students, 1998–1999 School Year

	All Students	Native Born	Foreign Born
% White	15.7	15.2	18.1
% Black	35.5	38.5	19.9
% Hispanic	37.7	38.1	35.5
% Asian	10.8	7.7	26.4
% eligible for free lunch (poor)	79.3	78.6	82.9
% limited English proficient (LEP)	16.1	7.6	31.2
N	608,568	510,386	98,182

*Note: Eligibility for free lunch percentages based on students with non-missing data. Approximately 95 percent of students overall and in each racial group have non-missing data. LEP students are students who scored at or below the 40th percentile on the Language Assessment Battery.

most relevant for our study, detailed information on student's place of birth, year of entry into the city school system, and whether or not a student is classified as having limited English skills.[5] Table 4.1 provides some summary statistics on these data.

As shown, our sample includes almost 609,000 students. Over 98,000, or roughly 16 percent, of these students are foreign born, and 16 percent are limited English proficient, or LEP.[6] As for racial composition, the students are largely nonwhite, with black and Hispanic students together comprising 73 percent of the population. (Note that in contrast to Census data, Hispanic is treated as a separate racial group by the school system, so students cannot be both black *and* Hispanic.) A large majority of students are eligible for free lunch. As for differences between native-born and foreign-born students, a much larger share of foreign-born students are Asian and a much smaller share are black. In addition, foreign-born students are somewhat more likely to be white; slightly less likely to be Hispanic; more likely to be eligible for free lunch; and, not surprisingly, far more likely to be classified as limited English proficient (LEP).

Measuring Segregation in New York Schools

A large literature exists on the various approaches to conceptualizing and measuring segregation.[7] The choice of measure should depend on the specific dimension of segregation one wishes to capture. One dimension of primary interest is *unevenness*, the extent to which students of different races or ethnicities are distributed quite differently across schools (attend different schools). The most common measure of unevenness is the dissimilarity index, a dichotomous measure of segregation between two groups. While this index has its weaknesses (see James & Taeuber, 1985; Reardon & Firebaugh, 2000), it has been used extensively in both the residential and school segregation literatures and has general intuitive appeal. The index can be interpreted as the share of one group that would have to be redistributed in order for both groups to have identical distributions. Thus, when there is perfect integration, the index is zero; with complete segregation, it equals one. In mathematical terms, the index between demographic group k (e.g., native born) and j (e.g., foreign born) is calculated as follows:

$$D = \frac{1}{2} \sum_{i}^{M} \left| \frac{N_{ki}}{N_k} - \frac{N_{ji}}{N_j} \right|$$

where

N_{ji}, N_{ki} = the number of students of group j, k in school i, M schools in total

N_j, N_k = the number of students of group j, k in aggregate

In much of this chapter, our focus is on a second (but related) dimension of segregation—the potential social contact between groups provided by their school environments. Here we measure the extent to which students of a particular race or ethnicity attend schools with students of different races or ethnicities, and are thereby exposed to others on a day-to-day basis. While unevenness in the distribution across schools is a large factor in shaping these environments, so too is relative size of the populations. If our interest in segregation is driven by concerns about interaction between groups, then exposure may be of greater interest.

We employ interaction indices to capture this exposure. Used extensively in both the literatures on schools and neighborhoods, interaction indices are both easy to interpret and compute. The index reports, for the average person in a group, the percent of population in a school that is of a different group (the exposure index) or of the "own" group (the isolation index).

Mathematically, the exposure index of group k to group j is as follows:

$$_k I_j = \sum_{i}^{M} \left| \frac{N_{ki}}{N_k} * \frac{N_{ji}}{N_i} \right|$$

where

N_{ji}, N_{ki} = the number of students of group j, k in school i, M schools in total

N_k = the number of students of group k in aggregate

N_i = the number of students in school i

The isolation index is the exposure of group k to itself:

$$_k I_k = \sum_{i}^{M} \left| \frac{N_{ki}}{N_k} * \frac{N_{ki}}{N_i} \right|$$

Segregation in New York City's Schools

We begin by first assessing overall levels of racial segregation in New York City's schools, using each of these measures in turn. Table 4.2 shows overall levels of racial segregation, or *unevenness*, in the city's schools, using the dissimilarity index. The first column shows the unevenness of the distribution of each racial group with respect to all others not in this

Table 4.2. Racial Segregation in New York City Elementary and Middle Schools, 1998–1999 (Dissimilarity Index)

	Segregation From All Others	Segregation From Whites	Segregation From Blacks	Segregation From Hispanics
White	0.682			
Black	0.585	0.798		
Hispanic	0.500	0.703	0.553	
Asian	0.587	0.493	0.766	0.608

group—for example, the segregation of black students from all nonblack students. The table shows that white students are the most segregated group; more than two-thirds of white students would have to switch to another school in order for each school in the city to have the same share of whites. Hispanic students appear to be the least segregated, with a dissimilarity index of 0.5.

The latter columns show segregation between specific racial groups. The first of these additional columns, for instance, shows the degree to which whites are separated from each of the other racial groups—blacks, Hispanics, and Asians. These measures show large and perhaps predictable variation. The most segregated pair is whites and blacks, followed by blacks and Asians.[8] The two least segregated pairs are Asians and whites, and blacks and Hispanics.

Table 4.3 presents exposure indices, or the racial composition of the school attended by the typical student in a given group. The first row, for example, indicates that the typical white student attends a school in which 48.4 percent of students are white, 13.3 percent are black, 22.4 percent are Hispanic, and 15.8 percent are Asian. While this may sound fairly integrated, it represents a considerable divergence from the racial breakdown of the student population as a whole (see bottom row). If schools were perfectly integrated, all students would attend schools that were just 15.6 percent white, 35.5 percent black, 37.8 percent Hispanic, and 10.7 percent Asian.

As a summary measure of lack of exposure to "others," the diagonal of the table (in bold) indicates exposure to one's own group, referred to as the isolation index. Blacks are the most isolated, followed by Hispanics. Recall that isolation reflects a combination of segregation and population size, so it is perhaps not surprising that the two largest groups should be the most racially isolated. Given that whites represent less than 16 percent of all students, the fact that the typical white student attends a school in which nearly half of the students are white suggests considerable segregation.

Table 4.3. Racial Exposure Levels in New York City Elementary and Middle Schools, 1998–1999

	Exposure to Whites	Exposure to Blacks	Exposure to Hispanics	Exposure to Asians
White	**0.484**	0.133	0.224	0.158
Black	0.059	**0.628**	0.265	0.044
Hispanic	0.093	0.250	**0.568**	0.086
Asian	0.230	0.144	0.303	**0.321**
Proportion of students	*0.156*	*0.355*	*0.378*	*0.107*

PATTERNS OF RACIAL ISOLATION

For foreign-born students to be more or less racially isolated than native-born students, it must be true that foreign-born and native-born students of any given race attend a different set of schools (or at least are distributed across those schools differently). In other words, foreign-born students must be segregated from native-born students, within a given racial group. Thus, our first question is to explore whether this is the case.

Table 4.4, which presents the within-race segregation of the native born from the foreign born, using the dissimilarity index, suggests that there is a good deal of segregation within racial groups. The most striking result is the extent to which foreign-born whites attend different schools than native-born whites. More than 50 percent of foreign-born white students would need to change schools to achieve the same distribution as native-born whites. Within other racial groups, the foreign born are also distributed differently across schools than are the native born, but the differences are not as stark.[9]

Table 4.4. Within Race Segregation Between Native Born and Foreign Born, Dissimilarity Index, 1998–1999

White	0.518
Black	0.342
Hispanic	0.270
Asian	0.265

Given that there are differences in the distributions of immigrants and native born, our next question is *how* their distributions differ, and in particular, whether foreign-born students attend schools in which they are more or less racially isolated. Table 4.5 provides racial exposure and isolation indices separately for the native- and foreign-born. It shows that foreign-born Hispanics and blacks are more racially isolated than their native-born counterparts. By contrast, there is little difference in isolation levels of foreign-born and native-born Asians, and foreign-born whites appear to attend schools with considerably fewer whites than their native-born counterparts.

Table 4.5. Racial Exposure Levels in New York City Elementary and Middle Schools, 1998–1999

	Actual Exposure Levels			
	Whites	*Blacks*	*Hispanics*	*Asians*
Native-born whites	**0.499**	0.132	0.217	0.151
Foreign-born whites	**0.418**	0.135	0.254	0.192
Native-born blacks	0.059	**0.622**	0.272	0.043
Foreign-born blacks	0.056	**0.676**	0.214	0.050
Native-born Hispanics	0.094	0.259	**0.561**	0.084
Foreign-born Hispanics	0.083	0.205	**0.610**	0.100
Native-born Asians	0.251	0.138	0.284	**0.324**
Foreign-born Asians	0.199	0.153	0.331	**0.316**

While foreign-born black and Hispanic students are more racially isolated than their native-born counterparts, their exposure to whites is quite similar. The typical black student—foreign born or not—attends a school in which less than 6 percent of students are white, while the typical Hispanic student—foreign born or not—attends a school in which 8 or 9 percent of students are white. Thus, if exposure to the majority white population is what's critical, then in New York City's schools, foreign-born blacks and Hispanics are not any more disadvantaged than their native-born peers (more aptly put, they are similarly disadvantaged). For blacks and Hispanics, the table shows that the real difference lies in their exposure to each other. The greater number of black peers experienced by foreign-born blacks as compared to native-born blacks is almost exactly offset by a smaller number of Hispanic peers. And similarly for foreign-born Hispanics.

Evolution of Patterns as Immigrants Spend More Time in U.S. Schools

It is possible that the heightened racial isolation among foreign-born blacks and Hispanics observed here may be only the temporary result of clustering among recent immigrants, and may disappear as new immigrants spend more time in this country. Table 4.6 explores this possibility, reporting exposure rates for recent and non-recent, or more established, immigrants by race.[10] Recent immigrants are foreign-born students who have entered the school system within the last three years.

There are several consistent findings across groups in this table. First, with the exception of whites, immigrants who are more established have somewhat more contact with those of other races (in aggregate) than do immigrants who have more recently arrived. Foreign-born minorities, in other words, appear to grow less racially isolated with time in the United States. Moreover, all groups of foreign-born students appear to gain some additional contact

Table 4.6. Exposure to Racial Groups by Nativity and Recent Immigrant Status, 1998–1999 (sample restricted to NYC students between third and eighth grade or higher)

| | Exposure to | | | |
	Whites	Blacks	Hispanics	Asians
Percent of population	*0.162*	*0.364*	*0.378*	*0.093*
White				
Non-recent foreign-born	**0.420**	0.143	0.248	0.188
Recent foreign-born	**0.395**	0.137	0.280	0.186
Black				
Non-recent foreign-born	0.063	**0.662**	0.221	0.051
Recent foreign-born	0.045	**0.681**	0.228	0.043
Hispanic				
Non-recent foreign-born	0.084	0.215	**0.612**	0.088
Recent foreign-born	0.081	0.187	**0.626**	0.104
Asian				
Non-recent foreign-born	0.208	0.165	0.333	**0.291**
Recent foreign-born	0.195	0.149	0.340	**0.315**

Note: Non-recent foreign-born are students who were not born in the United States but who have been in the U.S. school system for at least three years. Recent foreign-born are foreign-born students who have been in the school system for less than three years.

with whites as they spend more time in the country. However, it is worth noting that non-recent black and Hispanic immigrants are still more racially isolated than their native-born counterparts. To the extent that these patterns of segregation are decreasing over time, they do not come close to disappearing during the school life of one generation of immigrant students.

EXPLAINING PATTERNS OF RACIAL ISOLATION

In summary, our evidence suggests that foreign-born minorities tend to be more, not less, racially isolated, while foreign-born whites are less racially isolated. In the remainder of the chapter, we explore the root causes of these differences in racial patterns by nativity status to learn which of the potential sources outlined above seem to be most important. In particular, we consider three possibilities: differences in language skills; differences in income; and different tastes for ethnic clustering. While we cannot observe the latter (tastes for ethnic clustering), Table 4.7 provides some insight on the former. Specifically, it shows differences in the proportion of students eligible for free lunch and in the proportion classified as Limited English Proficient (LEP) between foreign-born and native-born students of different races.

Differences in Language Skills

As shown in Table 4.7, foreign-born students of all races are, not surprisingly, more likely to be classified as LEP than their native-born counterparts. It seems reasonable to assume that families with children with more limited English skills might choose schools with stronger LEP or bilingual programs that cater to their native language. They also might simply be more socially at ease in schools with other families who speak their native language. Finally, native-born families might be more resistant to share schools with families of other races if those families also have difficulties with English. For all these reasons, we might expect foreign-born families with more limited English skills to be more racially isolated. This would help to explain the heightened isolation levels of black and Hispanic foreign-born students, though not the lesser isolation of foreign-born whites.

To explore this possibility, we recalculated the exposure rates in Table 4.5 separately by English-language proficiency. The results (not shown) are essentially unchanged when we

Table 4.7. Selected Characteristics of Native-Born and Foreign-Born Elementary and Middle School Students, 1998–1999 (by Race)

	% Free Lunch Eligible	% Classified as LEP
White		
Native-born	38.4	1.3
Foreign-born	65.2	20.3
Black		
Native-born	86.6	1.1
Foreign-born	87.8	8.8
Hispanic		
Native-born	88.8	17.1
Foreign-born	92.9	49.0
Asian		
Native-born	63.3	6.0
Foreign-born	78.0	31.6

control for LEP status in this way—there is little difference in racial exposure rates of foreign-born students who qualify as LEP and those who do not.[11]

Differences in Income

We also learn from Table 4.7 that foreign-born students of all races are more likely to be poor, though differences are particularly pronounced for whites and Asians. As predicted above, the lower incomes of foreign-born families might lead foreign-born whites to be less racially isolated and foreign-born minorities to be more racially isolated—which is exactly the pattern that we see in our data. To test this possibility, we recalculate exposure rates by poverty level (not shown). After controlling for poverty, we find that while the differences in isolation between foreign-born and native-born minorities remain largely unchanged, the difference in isolation between native-born and foreign-born white students declines substantially. In other words, a large part of the reason that foreign-born white students are less racially isolated appears to be that they have lower incomes, and lower-income students of all races attend schools with fewer whites.

Preferences for Clustering by Region of Origin

The heightened levels of racial isolation that we observe on the part of black and Hispanic immigrants might be due to the preferences of immigrants to attend schools with other children from their same country or region of origin, who also typically belong to their same race. Such clustering cannot of course help us to explain the relatively *lower* isolation levels among white immigrant students. (Nativity differences for whites have largely been explained by income in any case.)

To examine the possibility that clustering by region helps to explain patterns of isolation, we grouped the nearly 200 countries and territories where New York City students were born into 12 regions based on geographic proximity and similarities in language and race/ethnicity (Conger, Stiefel, & Schwartz, 2003; Ellen et al., 2002). In this chapter, we focus on the nine regions that are racially homogenous. These nine regions account for 89 percent of all foreign-born students. (See the Appendix for region definitions and summary statistics.)

Table 4.8 reports racial exposure rates, further broken down by region of birth. The first column shows, for each immigrant group, the share of all students born in that region. Dominicans represent the largest group, representing about 3 percent of all students (and roughly 19 percent of the foreign-born), followed by students born in Latin American countries and students born in Caribbean countries. The second column shows levels of racial isolation for each of these groups. Some clear differences between regions emerge. Among black immigrants, for example, Caribbean students are far more racially isolated than are other black immigrants. The typical student born in a Caribbean country attends a school where 71 percent of the students are black. By contrast, the typical student born in sub-Saharan Africa attends a school where only 51 percent of students are black. In fact, black immigrants born in sub-Saharan Africa are actually *less* racially isolated than are native-born blacks. Within New York City public schools at least, the greater isolation of foreign-born black students is limited to those from the Caribbean.

We see stark contrasts among other racial groups as well. These results highlight the importance of getting below the aggregate racial/ethnic categories of immigrants. Our finding of greater racial isolation on the part of foreign-born blacks and Hispanics on average masks considerable variation within the groups. The racial segregation of immigrants depends on their region of origin, with some groups less racially segregated than are native-born stu-

Table 4.8. Exposure of New York City Elementary and Middle School Students by Region of Birth to Other Students, 1998–1999 (by Race)

	Share of Population	Same Race	Exposure to	
			Same Race Born in Home Region	Same Race Not Born in Home Region
Foreign-born white				
Former Soviets	0.016	0.464	0.174	0.291
Eastern Europeans	0.006	0.357	0.052	0.305
Native-born white		0.499		
Foreign-born black				
Caribbean	0.022	0.711	0.093	0.618
Sub-Saharan African	0.003	0.511	0.013	0.498
Native-born black		0.623		
Foreign-born Hispanic				
Dominicans	0.030	0.689	0.105	0.584
Latin Americans	0.024	0.532	0.071	0.461
Native-born Hispanic		0.560		
Foreign-born Asian				
Chinese	0.012	0.430	0.135	0.295
South Asian	0.015	0.267	0.065	0.202
East Asian	0.006	0.294	0.036	0.258
Native-born Asian		0.324		

dents of the same races, and others more. There are, of course, large differences in the characteristics of students born in different regions, which themselves may drive sorting across schools, such as poverty, LEP status, and year of entry to the school system. But further analysis suggests that the large differences in racial association by region of origin do not appear driven by differences in underlying but associated demographics.[12]

It is possible that differential tastes for clustering by birth region might help to explain the large variation in segregation levels. Perhaps Dominicans simply have a greater desire to attend schools with other students from their same country, and this explains their very high levels of racial isolation. That is, is the heightened isolation of Dominicans explained by the fact that Dominicans attend schools with other Dominicans, who are also Hispanic?

The remaining two columns of Table 4.8 explore this possibility. Specifically, the columns break down the isolation index into exposure to students of the same race born in the same region and to students of same race born elsewhere. As shown, every group exhibits some degree of regional clustering. In every case, students attend schools with much higher proportions of students born in their same region than they would if they were distributed evenly across schools (as seen in column 1, the share of the overall population for that group). This regional clustering is quite dramatic for some groups. For example, even though students from the former Soviet Union make up just over 1 percent of the student population, on average, they attend schools in which 17 percent of students are also from the former Soviet Union. Put another way, immigrants born in former Soviet countries are 17 times more likely to have Soviet peers in their schools as they would be if their distribution across schools was even. As for Chinese immigrants, despite being only 1.2 percent of the entire student body, they typically attend a school in which nearly 14 percent of students were also born in China.

To what extent does this regional clustering explain heightened isolation of students born in particular regions and in turn the heightened racial isolation of foreign-born black and Hispanic students? The last column of the table suggests that while clustering by region or country of origin contributes to heightened levels of racial isolation, it does not explain all of it.

As shown, there is considerable variation in exposure to students of the same race, even after subtracting out those born in the same region. Caribbean, Dominican, and Chinese students are considerably more isolated than foreign-born students of their same race born in other regions. For example, the typical Caribbean immigrant attends a school in which 62 percent of students are non-Caribbean black students. The typical black student born in Sub-Saharan Africa, meanwhile, attends a school in which less than half of students are black students born in the United States or other regions of the world. Even after taking out their fellow Caribbeans, that is, Caribbean blacks are still far more racially isolated than other black immigrants.

Similarly, the greater propensity of Dominican students to go to school with other Dominicans explains only a small portion of their greater racial isolation. To see this, note that Hispanic students born in Latin America typically go to schools in which 46 percent of students are Hispanic students not born in Latin America. Dominican students, meanwhile, typically attend schools in which the proportion of non-Dominican Hispanic students is 58 percent. In fact, the proportion of *non-Dominican* Hispanic students in the typical school attended by Dominican students exceeds the *total* share of Hispanic students in the typical school attended by native-born Hispanic students.

INTERPRETATIONS AND IMPLICATIONS

While this work is exploratory and descriptive, it offers insight into how the influx of immigrants is likely to affect future patterns of racial interaction in school systems around the country. While theoretical considerations do not lead to clear predictions, we find that foreign-born black and Hispanic students are more racially isolated than their native-born counterparts. This is particularly true for recent immigrants, although these differences persist past early years in the school system. While recent black and Hispanic immigrants are more racially segregated than those who are more established, time in U.S. schools mediates these differences only slightly.

These differences do not appear to be explained by LEP status or income, though they do appear to be linked partly to clustering of immigrants by country of origin. Interestingly, when looking at subgroups of immigrants, we find that only certain groups are more segregated than their native-born counterparts—in particular, immigrants born in China, the Dominican Republic, and other Caribbean countries. For whites, we find that the foreign born are less racially isolated than native-born whites, but this difference largely disappears once we control for poverty.

We caution against generalizing, however, since we find large differences in racial segregation across sub-groups. This means that the makeup of the foreign-born students entering a school system matters a great deal in determining resulting patterns of interaction. As Table 4.8 documents, the effects on the *racial* environments of students will depend not only on the race of immigrants, but on their specific country of origin. Some immigrant groups appear less racially isolated than even the native born of their similar race; others are far more isolated.

Finally, we also assess the extent to which clustering by region of birth might be the source of higher racial segregation. While we find high degrees of clustering for some groups (Dominicans, Chinese, and Russians), in general this regional clustering does not explain the racial segregation patterns. And again, we find diversity in the patterns.

In short, we find no single answer to the question of whether immigration as a whole is likely to mitigate or exacerbate patterns of racial segregation, suggesting caution for educators and researchers trying to draw conclusions about the impact of immigrants as a whole. White immigrants generally appear to be less segregated than their native-born counterparts, suggesting that the entry of white immigrants is likely to lessen overall segregation levels within a school district. The impact of minority immigrants is likely to be more varied, depending on the specific nationalities, but the evidence here suggests that the entry of certain groups of minority immigrants may lead to heightened levels of racial segregation within a school district.

APPENDIX A: REGIONS OF BIRTH

Table 4.A1.   Foreign-born Elementary and Middle School Students in New York City, 1998–1999

	Number of Students	*Percent of Foreign Born*	*Percent Poor*	*Percent LEP*
Dominican Republic	18,576	18.92	96.02	53.23
Latin America	15,808	16.10	89.13	45.24
Caribbean	15,067	15.35	87.76	7.11
Former USSR	10,117	10.30	62.96	15.81
South Asia	9,717	9.90	83.39	35.58
China Region	7,238	7.37	81.21	47.82
East Asia/Pacific	4,400	4.48	54.16	22.52
Eastern Europe	3,949	4.02	69.92	26.87
Sub Saharan Africa	2,401	2.45	84.39	23.91
Other regions	10,909	11.11	80.24	12.54

Note: Poor are students who are eligible for free lunch. LEP are students who scored at or below the 40th percentile on the Language Assessment Battery.

List of Countries in Nine Regions of Birth

Former Soviet Union: Armenia, Azerbaijan, Belarus, Georgia, Kazakhstan, Kyrgyzstan, Moldova, Russia, Tajikistan, Turkmenistan, Ukraine, USSR, Uzbekistan

East Europe: Albania, Bosnia and Herzegovina, Bulgaria, Croatia, Czech Republic, Estonia, Hungary, Latvia, Lithuania, Macedonia, Poland, Romania, Slovak Republic, Slovenia, Yugoslavia

China: China, Hong Kong, Taiwan

East Asia: Bhutan, Brunei Darussalam, Burma (Myanmar), Cambodia, Fiji, French Polynesia, Indonesia, Japan, Korea (North and South), Laos, Macao, Malaysia, Maldives, Marshall Islands, Micronesia, Mongolia, Nepal, Papua New Guinea, Philippines, Samoa, Singapore, Solomon Islands, Sri Lanka, Thailand, Vanuatu, Vietnam

South Asia: Bangladesh, India, Pakistan

Sub-Saharan Africa: Angola, Benin, Botswana, Burkina Faso (Upper Volta), Burundi, Cameroon, Cape Verde, Central African Republic, Chad, Comoros, Congo, Djibouti, Equatorial Guinea, Ethiopia, Gabon, Gambia, Ghana, Guinea-Bissau, Guinea, Ivory Coast, Kenya, Lesotho, Liberia, Madagascar, Malawi, Mali, Mauritania, Mauritius, Mozambique, Namibia, Niger, Nigeria, Rwanda, Sao Tome and Prin, Senegal, Seychelles, Sierra Leone, Somalia, Republic of South Africa, Sudan, Swaziland, Tanzania, Togo, Tonga, Uganda, Zaire, Zambia, Zimbabwe

Dominican Republic: Dominican Republic

Caribbean: Antigua and Barbuda, Bahamas, Barbados, British Virgin Islands, British West Indies, Cuba, Dominica, French Antilles, French West Indies, Grenada, Guadeloupe, Haiti, Jamaica, Nether Antilles, Saint Kitts and Nevis, Saint Lucia, Saint Vincent and Grenada, Trinidad and Tobago

Latin America: Argentina, Belize, Bolivia, Brazil, Chile, Colombia, Costa Rica, Ecuador, El Salvador, Guatemala, Honduras, Mexico, Nicaragua, Panama, Paraguay, Peru, Uruguay, Venezuela

NOTES

We thank Dylan Conger for excellent research assistance and the Spencer Foundation for their generous support of this work.

1. Most of the literature on school segregation has emphasized sorting across jurisdictions. Analyses consistently find that most public school segregation is attributable to segregation between districts, rather than within (Clotfelter, 1998; Lankford & Wyckoff, 2000; Reardon, Yun, & Eitle, 2000; Rivkin, 1994). But the same forces that drive segregation across districts probably also contribute to segregation within districts, especially in a system as large as New York City, which itself contains 32 distinct community school districts. (Tax differences of course do not come into play, and resource differences may be smaller.)

2. The presence of immigrants of one race may also lessen segregation between other racial groups. In particular, Farley and Frey (1994) argue that Hispanics and Asians serve as a buffer of sorts and may lessen traditional black/white hostility and segregation. This effect cannot be identified in our cross-sectional data, however.

3. Ellen, O'Regan, Schwartz, and Stiefel (2002) examine the segregation of immigrants in public schools, but the focus is on the extent to which immigrant students are clustered with other immigrants.

4. A few papers suggest that immigration may dampen black-white segregation levels through introducing new ethnic groups such as Hispanics and Asians. White and Glick (1999), for example, find that increases in immigrants as a share of the population decreases black/white residential segregation over time. Similarly, Farley and Frey (1994) find that larger proportions of nonblack minorities in a metropolitan area are significantly correlated with lower levels of black-white segregation.

5. Students who score less than 40 on the Language Assessment Battery are designated as limited English proficient (LEP). This set of tests is used to assess English proficiency and eligibility for specialized instructional services.

6. In addition, a large number of students are undoubtedly children of one or more foreign-born parents, but our data set does not identify this group.

7. For overviews of the issues and measures, see James and Taeuber (1985), Massey and Denton (1987), Taeuber and Taeuber (1965), White (1987), and Zoloth (1976).

8. As a comparison, Logan (2002) shows black-white school segregation for 56 central cities that enrolled more than 25,000 students and in which blacks comprised more than 10 percent of the population. Of these 56 cities, New York has the seventh-highest black-white segregation index.

9. Lobo and Salvo (2000) examine 1990 census tract data and find that native-born blacks are residentially segregated from foreign-born blacks. They estimate a dissimilarity index of 0.42, as compared to our school-level segregation that we find of 0.34. The greater degree of residential segregation is consistent with Logan (2002). He finds that in New York City, black-white neighborhood segregation is higher than school segregation.

10. Note that here we restrict our sample to third graders and beyond, so that all students could potentially have been in the school system three years, our measure of recent versus non-recent immigrant.

11. These and other results are available from authors upon request.

12. To test this, we have replicated these tables separately by poverty and by LEP status. The absolute levels of isolation change only slightly, and all key patterns remain the same.

REFERENCES

Aguirre, B. E., Schwirian, K., and La Greca, A. (1980). The residential patterning of Latin American and other ethnic populations in metropolitan Miami. *Latin American Research Review, 15*(2), 35–63.

Allen, J. P., & Turner, E. (1996). Spatial patterns of immigrant assimilation. *The Professional Geographer, 48*, 140–155.

Bashi Bobb, V. (2001). Neither ignorance nor bliss: Race, racism, and the West Indian immigrant experience. In Hector R. Cordero-Guzman, Robert C. Smith, & Ramon Grosfoguel (Eds.), *Migration, transnationalization, and race in a changing New York*. Philadelphia, PA: Temple University Press.

Benabou, R. (1996). Heterogeneity, stratification, and growth: Macroeconomic implications of community structure and school finance. *The American Economic Review, 86*(3), 584–609.

Clotfelter, C. T. (1998). *Public school segregation in metropolitan areas* (NBER Working Paper 6779). Cambridge, MA: National Bureau of Economic Research.

Conger, D., Stiefel, L., & Schwartz, A. E. (2003). *Who are our students? A statistical portrait of immigrant students in New York City's elementary and middle schools* (Working Paper, Taub Urban Research Center). New York: New York University.

Cookson, P. W., & Lucks, C. S. (1995). School choice in New York City: Preliminary observations. In Maureen T. Hallinan (Ed.), *Restructuring schools: Promising practices and policies*, New York, NY: Plenum Press.

Ellen, I. G., O'Regan, K., Schwartz, A. E., & Stiefel, L. (2002). Immigrant children and New York City schools: Segregation and its consequences. In William G. Gale & Janet Rothenberg Pack (Eds.), *Brookings-Wharton papers on urban affairs*. Washington, DC: Brookings Institution Press.

Farley, R., & Frey, W. (1994). Changes in the segregation of whites from blacks during the 1980s: Small steps toward a more integrated society. *American Sociological Review, 59*(1), 23–45.

James, D. R., & Taeuber, K. E. (1985). Measures of segregation. In Nancy Tuma (Ed.), *Sociological methodology* (pp. 1–32). San Francisco, CA: Jossey-Bass.

Lankford, H., & Wyckoff, J. (2000). *Why are schools racially segregated? Implications for school choice policies*. Paper prepared for Conference on School Choice and Racial Diversity, New York, NY.

Lobo, A. P., & Salvo, J. J. (2000). The role of nativity and ethnicity in the residential settlement patterns of blacks in New York City, 1970–1990. In Lydio F. Tomasi & Mary G. Powers (Eds.), *Immigration today: Pastoral and research challenges*. New York, NY: Center for Migration Studies.

Logan, J. R. (2002). The suburban advantage: New census data show unyielding city-suburb economic gap, and surprising shifts in some places. Albany, NY: Lewis Mumford Center for Comparative Urban and Regional Research, University at Albany.

Massey, D. S. (1979). Effects of socioeconomic factors on the residential segregation of blacks and Spanish Americans in U.S. urbanized areas. *American Sociological Review, 44*, 1015–1022.

Massey, D. S., & Bitterman, B. (1985). Explaining the paradox of Puerto Rican segregation, *Social Forces, 64*, 306–331.

Massey, D., & Denton, N. (1987). *American apartheid: Segregation and the making of the underclass*. Cambridge, MA: Harvard University Press.

Orfield, G. (2001, July). *Schools more separate: Consequences of a decade of resegregation*. Los Angeles, CA: The Civil Rights Project, UCLA. Retrieved from http://civilrightsproject.ucla.edu/research/k-12-education/integration-and-diversity/schools-more-separate-consequences-of-a-decade-of-resegregation/?searchterm=resegregation

Orfield, G., & Lee, C. (2004). *Brown at 50: King's dream or Plessy's nightmare?* Cambridge, MA: The Civil Rights Project, Harvard University.

Reardon, S. F., & Firebaugh, G. (2000). *Measures of multi-group segregation* (Working Paper). University Park: Population Research Institute, Pennsylvania State University.

Reardon, S. F., Yun, J. T., & Eitle, T. M. (2000). The changing structure of school segregation: Measurement and evidence of multiracial metropolitan-area school segregation, 1989–1995. *Demography, 37*(3), 351–364.

Rivkin, S. G. (1994). Residential segregation and school integration. *Sociology of Education, 67*(4), 279–292.

Rosenbaum, E., & Friedman, S. (2001). Mobility incidence and turnover as components of neighborhood racial and ethnic change in New York City, 1991–1996. *Journal of Housing Research, 12*(1), 27–53.

Schmidley, D. (2001). *Profile of the foreign-born population in the United States: 2000*. Current Population Reports. Washington, DC: U.S. Census Bureau, U.S. Department of Commerce.

Schneider, M., Teske, P., & Marshall, M. (2000). *Choosing schools: Consumer choice and the quality of American schools*. Princeton, NJ: Princeton University Press.

Taeuber, K. E., & Taeuber, A. F. (1965). *Negroes in cities: Residential segregation and neighborhood change*. Chicago, IL: Aldine.

Waldinger, R. (2002). *The remaking of America and immigrants: Old and new*. Paper prepared for the Henry Hart Rice Urban Policy Forum, Los Angeles, CA, April 11, 2003.

Waters, M. C. (1999). *Black identities: West Indian immigrant dreams and American realities*. New York, NY: Russell Sage Foundation Press.

Weiher, G. R., & Tedin, K. L. (2002). Does choice lead to racially distinctive schools? Charter schools and household preferences. *Journal of Policy Analysis and Management, 21*(1), 79–92.

White, M. J. (1987). *American neighborhoods and residential differentiation*. New York, NY: Russell Sage Foundation.

White, M. J., & Glick, J. E. (1999). The impact of immigration on residential segregation. In Frank D. Bean & Stephanie Bell-Rose (Eds.), *Immigration and opportunity: Race, ethnicity, and employment in the United States*. New York, NY: Russell Sage Foundation.

White, M. J., & Omer, A. (1996). Segregation by ethnicity and immigrant status in New Jersey. In Thomas J. Espenshade (Ed.), *Keys to successful immigration: Implications of the New Jersey experience*. Washington, DC: Urban Institute Press.

Zoloth, B. S. (1976). Alternative measures of school segregation. *Land Economics, 52*, 278–298.

II

THE GROWING COMPLEXITY OF METROPOLITAN AMERICA

5

Suburbanization and School Segregation

Sean F. Reardon, John T. Yun, and Anna K. Chmielewski

While issues of racial segregation in schools have been examined extensively in urban settings, we still know relatively little about the patterns, causes, and consequences of school segregation in suburban areas. In addition, we know little (in either urban or suburban settings) about the nature of the relationship between racial and socioeconomic segregation. These issues are becoming increasingly important as large numbers of low-income and minority families migrate from urban and rural areas to the suburbs, which have had very limited histories of, or structures for, equitably serving large populations of poor or minority students (Reardon & Yun, 2001).

In earlier work, Reardon and Yun (2001) found that suburban racial school segregation increased in response to increases in the proportion of minority group members enrolled in suburban schools. Suburban areas with growing minority populations experienced, on average, increasing segregation levels during the period 1987–1995. In this chapter, we extend this earlier work in several key ways. First, we use data from 1993 to 2005, adding 10 more years to the data used in our earlier work, exploring the relationship between suburban racial composition and school segregation.[1] Specifically, we address the question of the extent to which suburban segregation increases in response to growing poor and minority student populations. Second, we analyze the relationship between changes in racial segregation and socioeconomic segregation in suburban areas, investigating the extent to which suburban racial segregation can be attributed to patterns of socioeconomic segregation among and within suburban school districts.

SUBURBANIZATION AND
DEMOGRAPHIC CHANGE, 1980–2000

Between the 1980 and 2000 Censuses, the United States population grew by approximately 62 million people (Table 5.1). Virtually all of this growth was due to growth in the population of metropolitan areas. Moreover, most of the metropolitan growth was in turn attributable to growth of the suburban population, which grew from 99 million to 144 million, a growth rate of nearly 45 percent. Although central cities of metropolitan areas also experienced growth during this period, their growth was more modest—from 72 million

Table 5.1. Residential Racial Composition of the United States by Metropolitan Status, 1980–2000

	1980 Total (Millions)	1980 Percent of Total	1990 Total (Millions)	1990 Percent of Total	2000* Total (Millions)	2000* Percent of Total	1980–2000 Change (Millions)	1980–2000 Change (Percent)
U.S. Total								
White, not Hispanic	181.1	80.0	188.1	75.6	198.2	68.6	17.1	9.4
Black	25.7	11.3	29.2	11.7	35.4	12.3	9.7	37.7
Hispanic	14.6	6.4	22.4	9.0	37.7	13.0	23.1	157.9
Asian	3.5	1.5	7.0	2.8	11.6	4.0	8.1	230.9
Other	1.7	0.8	2.0	0.8	6.0	2.1	4.3	250.8
Total	*226.5*	*100.0*	*248.7*	*100.0*	*288.8*	*100.0*	*62.3*	*27.5*
Metropolitan Area								
White, not Hispanic	133.8	77.8	140.5	72.9	152.2	65.5	18.4	13.7
Black	21.1	12.3	24.4	12.7	30.5	13.1	9.4	44.7
Hispanic	12.9	7.5	20.2	10.5	34.3	14.8	21.4	166.1
Asian	3.2	1.9	6.5	3.4	11.0	4.7	7.8	244.5
Other	0.9	0.5	1.1	0.6	4.4	1.9	3.5	385.9
Total	*171.9*	*100.0*	*192.7*	*100.0*	*232.4*	*100.0*	*60.5*	*35.2*
Central Cities								
White, not Hispanic	47.3	65.2	46.0	59.1	45.2	51.1	-2.1	-4.5
Black	15.3	21.1	16.6	21.3	18.7	21.1	3.4	21.9
Hispanic	7.8	10.8	11.5	14.8	17.5	19.8	9.7	124.9
Asian	1.7	2.3	3.2	4.1	5.1	5.7	3.4	198.3
Other	0.4	0.6	0.5	0.6	2.0	2.2	1.6	389.8
Total	*72.5*	*100.0*	*77.8*	*100.0*	*88.4*	*100.0*	*15.9*	*21.9*
Suburbs								
White, not Hispanic	86.5	87.0	94.5	82.2	107.0	74.3	20.5	23.7
Black	5.8	5.8	7.8	6.8	11.9	8.2	6.1	104.7
Hispanic	5.1	5.1	8.7	7.6	16.8	11.7	11.7	229.0
Asian	1.5	1.5	3.3	2.9	6.0	4.1	4.5	296.9
Other	0.5	0.5	0.6	0.5	2.4	1.7	1.9	382.8
Total	*99.4*	*100.0*	*114.9*	*100.0*	*144.0*	*100.0*	*44.6*	*44.9*

Source: U.S. Bureau of the Census (1984, 1992, 2008).
*For the first time the 2000 Census allowed the choice of more than one racial classification, thus the "Other" category may be larger than in previous years. In addition, the racial categories (White, not Hispanic, Black, and Asian) also include those who answered in more than one category.

in 1980 to 88 million in 2000 (a gain of roughly 22 percent). During the same period, the nonmetropolitan area population grew at a rate of only 3 percent. By 2000, as many people lived in U.S. suburban areas as in central cities and rural areas combined.

Accompanying these large population shifts was a concomitant change in the racial composition of the nation and its metropolitan areas and suburbs. Whites made up 78 percent of the metropolitan population and 87 percent of the suburban population in 1980, but only 65 and 74 percent of the corresponding populations in 2000. The white metropolitan population grew by over 18 million, while the nonwhite metropolitan population grew by 42 million. During this same period, black, Hispanic, and Asian metropolitan populations increased by 45, 166, and 245 percent, respectively. This disproportionate growth of minority populations occurred primarily in the suburbs, where the white population increased by 24 percent while the black, Hispanic, and Asian populations increased by 104, 229, and 297 percent, respectively. As a result, the black, Hispanic and Asian suburban population proportions increased as well. By 2000, nearly 12 percent of the suburban population was Hispanic, 8 percent was black, and 4 percent was Asian. Given these important and very large shifts in population and composition, it continues to be critical to understand just how and in what ways these changes translate into patterns of school racial segregation.

These changes in metropolitan and suburban racial composition are well documented, although their consequences are less well understood. One potential consequence is an increase in racial segregation among suburban schools. In earlier work, we documented strong positive associations between increases in minority suburban racial composition and increases in racial school segregation during the period from 1987 to 1995 (Reardon & Yun, 2001). In that work, however, we did not examine the extent to which changes in the proportion of students in poverty may be related to changes in racial and socioeconomic suburban school segregation. Nor did we examine whether changes in suburban racial school segregation may be the result of increasing suburban socioeconomic segregation. Given that suburban black and Hispanic poverty rates are three to four times higher than suburban white poverty rates (Stoll, 2006), minority suburbanization may lead to an increase in the socioeconomic disparity between white and minority suburban populations. Because income inequality leads to income segregation (as a result of the suburban housing market and the placement of low-income suburban housing) (Reardon & Bischoff, 2011; Watson, 2009), racial income disparities may link changes in socioeconomic segregation to changes in racial segregation.

Our interest in examining the relationship between socioeconomic factors and racial segregation stems also from recent legal and policy interest in socioeconomic school integration policies. Policymakers and scholars have become increasingly interested in socioeconomic integration in recent years, for several reasons. First, many scholars have long warned of the negative effects of poverty concentration (Coleman et al., 1966; Entwisle, Alexander, & Olson, 1997; Kahlenberg, 1995). Second, the recent U.S. Supreme Court decision in the Seattle and Louisville voluntary desegregation cases (*Parents Involved in Community Schools v. Seattle School District No. 1*)[2] limits the way race can be used in school assignment. As a result, districts experiencing (or expecting to experience) rapid demographic change may increasingly look toward so-called "race-neutral" methods to achieve more diverse schooling environments (Kahlenberg, 1995; Reardon, Yun, & Kurlaender, 2006). Race-neutral methods are those that do not explicitly use race and that aim to desegregate schools on the basis of characteristics such as socioeconomic status or free/reduced-price lunch eligibility.

TRENDS IN SUBURBAN RACIAL AND SOCIOECONOMIC COMPOSITION

Figure 5.1 provides a graphical description of how racial/ethnic composition has changed in the suburbs of metropolitan areas from 1993 to 2005 (the time period covered by our analysis here). Each corner of the triangle represents 100 percent of a particular racial/ethnic group and 0 percent of the other groups (we exclude consideration of Asian and Native American students here because the figure can only accommodate three groups). The circles at the ends of each line represent the beginning and ending year of the data (the light circle is 1993, and the dark 2005), and the size of the circle the size of the suburban metropolitan enrollment. Thus, a metropolitan area with a large suburban enrollment that was 50/50 white/black in 1993 and 50/50 white/Hispanic in 2005 would be represented by a large light-colored circle at the midpoint of the bottom edge of the triangle and a large dark circle at the midpoint of the left edge, with a dark line connecting them, representing the shares of all three racial groups in the intervening years. While the figure is very crowded, there is a relatively clear trend away from the lower left, indicating decreasing white enrollment proportions. Most of the lines move toward the top of the triangle, indicating that Hispanic enrollment proportions grew rapidly while white enrollment proportions declined and black enrollment proportions remained relatively stable during that time.

Figure 5.2 plots the percentage of white in each metropolitan area in both 1993 and 2005 against the percentage of free-lunch eligible in the metropolitan area.[3] These points are connected with a line, and again the size of the circles represents suburban metropolitan enrollment, with larger circles representing larger enrollment. The figure shows a great

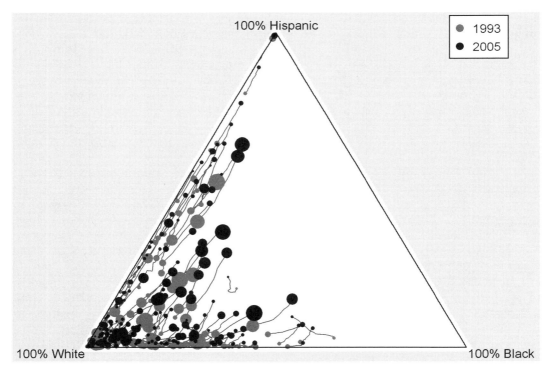

Figure 5.1.   Trends in White, Black, and Hispanic Suburban School Enrollment Proportions, 1993–2005 (*Source*: authors' calculations from Common Core of Data, 1993–2005)
* 217 metropolitan suburban areas in longitudinal sample

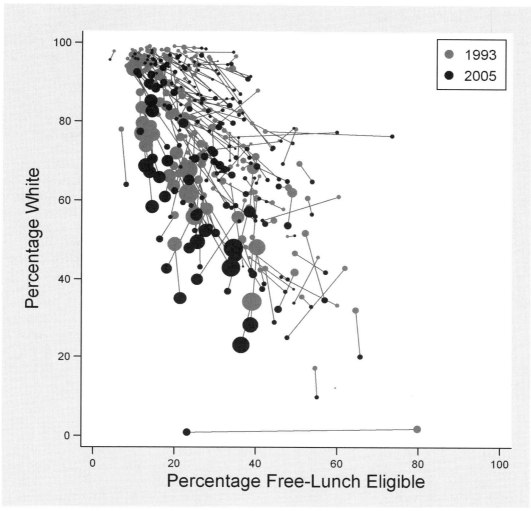

Figure 5.2. Trends in White and Free-Lunch-Eligible Suburban School Enrollment Proportions, 1993–2005
(*Source*: authors' calculations from Common Core of Data, 1993–2005)
* 217 metropolitan suburban areas in longitudinal sample

deal of variation in level of both the percentage of white and free-lunch eligibility, but the predominant direction of change is in the southeasterly direction, indicating increasing free-lunch-eligible proportions and decreasing white-student proportions.

THE LINK BETWEEN SUBURBAN RACIAL/SOCIOECONOMIC CHANGES AND SCHOOL SEGREGATION

In earlier work, Reardon and Yun (2001) examined the relationship between patterns of racial segregation and racial change in metropolitan areas. There were two key findings from these analyses. First, we found that increases in proportions of minority students in suburban areas were associated with increases in both within- and between-district suburban segregation. In addition, we found that these relationships differed in character among the three major racial/ethnic groups. Further, we suggested that although suburban districts had, on average, lower levels of school segregation than did urban areas, suburban segregation was increasing at a substantial rate, which might accelerate as migration of minority groups to the suburbs increased. As noted above, however, this work did not address issues of the relationship between racial and socioeconomic segregation.

Previous work on the relationship between socioeconomic segregation and racial segregation is relatively sparse. One argument made by proponents of socioeconomic desegregation is that since the shares of black, Hispanic, and Native American students who are poor is higher than the share of white and Asian students, socioeconomic desegregation will inevitably result in racial/ethnic desegregation (Chaplin, 2002; Kahlenberg, 2001). Reardon et al., (2006) showed that it is possible to achieve full socioeconomic desegregation while maintaining extremely high levels of racial segregation, depending on the correlation between race and poverty. If the correlation is high, racial/ethnic desegregation is an inevitable consequence of socioeconomic desegregation. The lower the correlation, however, the less tightly linked are socioeconomic and racial integration. Reardon, Yun, and Kurlaender showed that the correlation between race and poverty is not sufficiently high in most large school districts to guarantee that practical racial desegregation would result from socioeconomic integration.

The analysis in the Reardon, Yun, and Kurlaender paper was based largely on a theoretical analysis of what link between racial and socioeconomic segregation was possible, given existing socioeconomic differences among racial groups. Moreover, that analysis focused primarily on within-district patterns in large school districts. Suburban segregation patterns, however, are largely the result of between-district patterns (Reardon, Yun, & Eitle, 2000). As a result, our earlier analyses do not provide clear evidence of the extent to which socioeconomic and racial segregation are linked in suburban areas.

Segregation Between and Within Districts

The structure of suburban school systems varies widely across metropolitan areas in the United States. In some areas, particularly in metropolitan areas in the Northeast and Midwest, suburban schools are administered by dozens—in some cases more than 100—school districts (Bischoff, 2008). In other metropolitan areas, a few relatively large school districts serve all suburban students. This difference has important policy implications. Within-district segregation can be addressed by school assignment policies (although given the recent Supreme Court decisions those options are becoming more limited), while between-district segregation is largely due to residential patterns within metropolitan areas. Since the Supreme Court's *Milliken v. Bradley*[4] decision effectively outlawed mandatory between-district desegregation plans, historically, policies have been much more effective at dealing with within-district segregation than between-district segregation. Given the differences in the causes of between- and within-district suburban segregation, we examine both components of segregation in our models, as measuring total suburban segregation alone may mask important differences between them. For example, it is possible that any increases in between-district suburban segregation may be offset by reductions in within-district suburban segregation, resulting in zero change in total segregation. By simply measuring total segregation we would miss the important changes, and the key policy implications for each—residential patterns for between-district segregation and school assignment for within-district segregation.

DATA AND METHODS

Data and Sample Criteria

We use data from the Common Core of Data (CCD) for the school years 1993–1994 through 2005–2006 (see Sable, Gaviola, & Garofano, 2007). The CCD includes race/ethnic and free-lunch-eligible enrollment counts[5] for each public school in the United States in each year since 1987–1988. We use these data to compute segregation levels and enrollment composition for each suburban area. For the years 1993–1994 through 1997–1998, we use data from the CCD Longitudinal Data File; for later years, we use CCD data from each individual year. Because the CCD Longitudinal Data File has imputed racial and free-lunch-enrollment data for many schools, particularly in the early years of the data, we excluded the years 1987–1988 through 1992–1993 because they had a great deal of imputed data.

We use 2003 OMB definitions of metropolitan areas. Specifically, we use 337 metropolitan areas (technically called Core-Based Statistical Areas [CBSAs])[6] in the 2000 Census that include at least two school districts serving primarily suburban students. We exclude metropolitan areas that have fewer than two suburban school districts, since it would be impossible to calculate between-district segregation in such areas. We use the 2003 boundary definitions for each year, ensuring that the same physical area and the same school districts are included in a given metropolitan area over time. For each metropolitan area, we include school districts that are defined as "typical" local school districts or districts consisting of charter schools (i.e., those that have an agency type code [TYPE] of 1, 2, or 7 in the CCD), and that are defined as serving primarily suburban students (i.e., those that have a metro status code [MSC] of 2 in the CCD).

Each observation in our data is a suburban area × year, for a total of 4,381 observations (337 suburban areas × 13 years). However, the CCD is missing racial and free-lunch-enrollment data for some schools and, as noted above, has imputed data for many schools drawn from the CCD Longitudinal Data File. We use data only from suburban areas and years where we have non-missing, non-imputed race and free-lunch data for at least 90 percent of students. Moreover, we exclude from our analysis metropolitan areas that do not meet the 90 percent threshold of valid data in at least 10 of the 13 years. Of the 337 suburban areas, we exclude 120 that have insufficient data in 4 or more of the years from 1993–2005. This leaves 217 suburban areas and a total of 2,670 suburban-area years in our sample. In our regression analyses, we also exclude suburban areas that do not have at least 3 percent of the relevant minority group in at least one year observed. As a result, our analyses include different numbers of metropolitan areas for black-white segregation (144 metropolitan areas), Hispanic-white segregation (140 metropolitan areas), Asian-white segregation (53 metropolitan areas), and poor-nonpoor segregation (217 metropolitan areas).

We measure segregation using the information theory index (H) (Theil, 1972; Theil & Finezza, 1971).[7] The information theory index is a measure of the extent to which two (or more) groups are evenly distributed among schools in a region; it measures how much less diverse schools are, on average, than is the regional student population as a whole. H ranges from a minimum of 0, obtained only if all schools in the region have identical racial compositions, to a maximum of 1, obtained only if each school in the region is mono-racial (if no student attends school with any student of another race/ethnicity).

Although H is highly correlated with the dissimilarity index and the variance ratio index, two other measures of segregation commonly used in the literature, we use it because it is additively decomposable into between-district and within-district components (Reardon & Firebaugh, 2002), a feature that enables us to determine the extent to which any effects of changing racial composition on segregation are due to changes in segregation between or within suburban school districts. The within-district component of H indicates the extent by which H would be reduced if all schools in each district had the same racial composition as their district as a whole—the portion of segregation that is due to unevenness in racial composition among schools within the same district. The between-district component, in contrast, indicates the portion of segregation that would remain if all within-district segregation were eliminated; it is the portion of segregation due to uneven racial composition across districts.

Models

In order to describe the association between suburban racial and socioeconomic composition and segregation, we fit two series of models. Our basic model has this form:

$$S_{it}^{wm} = \alpha + \delta P_{it}^m + \mathbf{X}_{it}\mathbf{B} + \Gamma_i + \Lambda_{rt} + \epsilon_{it} \qquad [5.1]$$

Where i indexes suburban areas, t indexes years, S_{it}^{wm} is a measure of the segregation of white students from students of race group m in area i and year t, P_{it}^m indicates the proportion of students in suburban area i and year t of race group m, X_{it} is a vector of covariates (total enrollment, racial/ethnic proportions, and free-lunch-eligible proportion) for area i and year t, Γ_i is a vector of suburban area fixed effects, Λ_{rt} is a vector of region-by-year fixed effects, and ε_{it} is an error term. The parameter of interest is δ, which indicates the average change in segregation associated with a unit change in the proportion of group m in the suburban area, net of stable suburban area characteristics, region-specific temporal trends, and the vector of time-varying covariates X. A positive value of δ indicates that, on average, within a given suburban area, segregation increases when the proportion of group m grows faster than the regional average.

We fit versions of model 5.1 using each of black-white, Hispanic-white, and Asian-white segregation as outcome variables. In the case of the black-white models, we are particularly interested in the coefficient δ on the variable indicating the proportion of students in the suburban area who are black, while in the case of the Hispanic-white models, we are interested in the coefficient δ on the variable indicating the proportion of students in the suburban area who are Hispanic, and so on. In addition, we fit a set of models where the outcome variables are measures of segregation between poor (free-lunch-eligible) and non-poor students rather than measures of racial segregation. In these models, the parameter of interest is the coefficient on the variable indicating the proportion of free-lunch-eligible students in a suburban area.

For each segregation measure (white-black, white-Hispanic, white-Asian, poor-nonpoor), we fit three models. The first uses total between-school segregation as the outcome measure. The second uses between-district school segregation as the outcome measure. And the third uses the component of segregation due to within-district segregation as the outcome measure. Because the latter two components sum to the first measure (total school segregation), the coefficients in the latter two models will also sum to the corresponding coefficient in the first model, allowing us to compare the magnitude of the coefficients across the models in order to determine the extent to which the overall associations between composition and segregation are due to between- or within-district associations (see Reardon and Yun, 2001, for proof and discussion of such a regression decomposition).

Our first series of models consists of 12 models, then—three models (total, between-district, and within-district) for each of the four segregation measures (white-black, white-Hispanic, white-Asian, poor-nonpoor). One concern with these models may be that any associations between racial composition and racial segregation may be driven, at least in part, by the fact that racial composition is somewhat correlated with economic composition (suburban areas with more minority students also tend to have more poor students, see Figure 5.2). In order to assess this, we fit a second series of models of the form:

$$S_{it}^{wm} = \alpha + \delta P_{it}^m + \mathbf{X}_{it}\mathbf{B} + \gamma_b S_{it}^{pb} + \gamma_w S_{it}^{pw} + \Gamma_i + \Lambda_{rt} + \epsilon_{it} \qquad [5.2]$$

S_{it}^{pb} and S_{it}^{pw} are the between- and within-district segregation, respectively, between poor and nonpoor students in suburban area i in year t. Model 5.2 is identical to 5.1 but controls for socioeconomic segregation among schools in each suburban area. The coefficients γ_b and γ_w indicate the associations between the between- and within-district segregation of the poor, respectively, in the suburban area, net of stable suburban area characteristics, region-specific temporal trends, and the vector of time-varying covariates $\mathbf{X}$ (including racial composition). Positive values of γ_b and γ_w indicate that, on average, within a given suburban area, racial segregation between whites and minority group m increases when socioeconomic segregation grows faster than the regional average. As before, the parameter indicates the average change in segregation associated with a unit change in the proportion of group m in the suburban area, net of stable suburban area characteristics, region-specific temporal trends, the vector of time-varying covariates $\mathbf{X}$, and levels of socioeconomic segregation. Again, these models are fit for total, between- and within-district segregation resulting in nine additional models. A comparison of the estimated δ from model 5.2 with that from model 5.1 describes the extent to which changing patterns of socioeconomic segregation account for the association between racial composition and racial segregation.

The parameter γ_w in the within-district segregation models is of interest as well. It describes the extent to which changes in within-district socioeconomic segregation are associated with within-district changes in racial segregation. Although the parameter γ_w cannot be interpreted causally without some strong assumption about the exogeneity of changes in the segregation of the poor, it may nonetheless be informative regarding the potential for socioeconomic integration policies within suburban districts to affect racial segregation. If $\gamma_w = 1$, then unit decreases in socioeconomic segregation correspond to equally large decreases in racial segregation. Associations of this order of magnitude would suggest that strategies that reduced within-district socioeconomic segregation might yield very large reductions in racial segregation as well, thereby achieving some racial integration via race-neutral means. The smaller the coefficient γ_w, however, the less likely such effects might be. If $\gamma_w = 0$, for example, changes in socioeconomic segregation are unrelated to changes in racial segregation, implying little reason to expect that student assignment plans aimed at reducing the segregation of poor from nonpoor students will reduce racial segregation in the process.

Finally, while the association of changes in between-district socioeconomic segregation with changes in between-district racial segregation (the parameter γ_b above) is of substantive interest (it helps us understand the extent to which between district racial segregation is driven by between-district poverty segregation), it is of perhaps less educational policy interest because of the Supreme Court's limitation on mandatory between-district desegregation plans. Nonetheless, the coefficient on between-district poverty segregation may be informative about the extent to which housing policies that encourage socioeconomic integration in the suburbs (such as policies requiring a number of affordable housing units in each suburban municipality) might lead to reductions in between-district racial segregation.

RESULTS

Before we examine the analytic questions in this chapter (whether changes in suburban racial enrollment shares are related to changes in racial segregation, and to what extent socioeconomic segregation mitigates or contributes to that relationship) it is very useful to examine general trends in school segregation over time.

Figure 5.3 shows the trends in suburban school segregation between white students and black, Asian, and Hispanic students, as well as the trends in poor and nonpoor segregation from 1993 to 2005. In general, levels of segregation as measured by the information theory index (H) above 0.40 are considered high or extreme, values between 0.25 and 0.40 moderate and changes in segregation levels of approximately 0.05 represent important changes in segregation levels (Reardon & Yun, 2003). Over this 13-year time-span, white-black suburban segregation levels were relatively stable, averaging 0.22 to 0.24 across suburban areas with black student proportions of at least 3 percent. On average, white-Asian and white-Hispanic segregation levels were lower, ranging from approximately 0.15 to 0.17. In addition, segregation levels between white students and both Asian and Hispanic students have gradually increased from 1993 to 2005, though the magnitude of the increases (approximately 0.02–0.03) is modest. Finally, the segregation between poor (free-lunch-eligible) and nonpoor students has been generally low and relatively stable from 1993–2005.

Table 5.2 describes trends in segregation levels by region of the country, and indicates the proportion of suburban school segregation that is between, rather than within, districts. Several key findings are evident. First, racial suburban segregation levels vary considerably

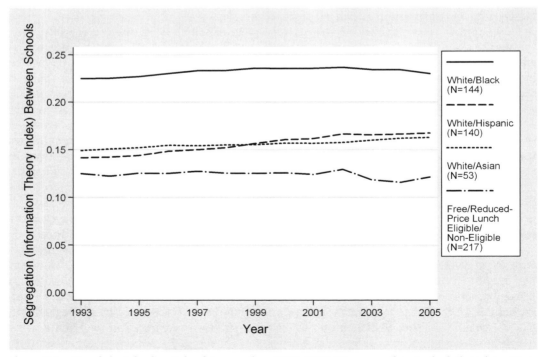

Figure 5.3.   Trends in Suburban School Segregation, 1993–2005 (*Source*: authors' calculations from Common Core of Data, 1993–2005)

across regions. For example, white-black suburban segregation in the South, Border, and West in 2005 was approximately 0.20 but in the Midwest was about 0.34. White-Hispanic segregation in the South and Midwest in that same year was approximately 0.15 while in the Northeast it was 0.24. Second, there is a great deal of regional and group variation in the proportion of segregation that is due to between-district segregation patterns. In both 1993 and 2005, between-district segregation comprises a very large portion of suburban segregation in the Northeast (over 80 percent for some groups) and much less in the South and Border states (as low as 50 percent and 35 percent respectively). These differences are likely due to the relatively high degree of school district fragmentation in the Northeast relative to the South and Border states, where many school districts encompass entire counties (Bischoff, 2008). As noted above, high fragmentation allows for more residential sorting among school districts (and more race/ethnic homogeneity within districts).

Table 5.2. Trends in Suburban School Segregation and Proportion of Segregation Between Districts by Region, 1993–2005

	White/Black				White/Hispanic			
	N (metros)	1993	2005	Change	N (metros)	1993	2005	Change
Average Between-School Segregation (Information Theory Index)								
Total	144	0.225	0.230	0.005	140	0.142	0.167	0.025
South	76	0.193	0.202	0.010	56	0.118	0.141	0.023
Border	12	0.208	0.206	-0.003	9	0.104	0.113	0.009
Northeast	17	0.237	0.243	0.006	13	0.229	0.235	0.006
Midwest	23	0.348	0.335	-0.013	22	0.127	0.153	0.026
West	16	0.198	0.214	0.016	40	0.163	0.201	0.038
Average Proportion of Segregation that is Between Districts								
Total	144	0.623	0.619	-0.005	140	0.581	0.607	0.026
South	76	0.520	0.512	-0.008	56	0.483	0.494	0.011
Border	12	0.539	0.545	0.007	9	0.328	0.445	0.117
Northeast	17	0.846	0.858	0.013	13	0.843	0.857	0.014
Midwest	23	0.812	0.826	0.014	22	0.698	0.768	0.071
West	16	0.671	0.627	-0.044	40	0.625	0.631	0.006

	White/Asian				FLE/non-FLE			
	N (metros)	1993	2005	Change	N (metros)	1993	2005	Change
Average Between-School Segregation (Information Theory Index)								
Total	53	0.149	0.163	0.014	217	0.121	0.119	-0.002
South	11	0.158	0.166	0.009	86	0.113	0.107	-0.006
Border	3	0.123	0.141	0.018	14	0.088	0.076	-0.012
Northeast	9	0.109	0.137	0.028	26	0.129	0.129	0.000
Midwest	4	0.148	0.190	0.042	49	0.111	0.107	-0.004
West	26	0.162	0.168	0.006	42	0.157	0.168	0.010
Average Proportion of Segregation that is Between Districts								
Total	53	0.638	0.653	0.015	217	0.473	0.525	0.052
South	11	0.500	0.546	0.046	86	0.390	0.427	0.037
Border	3	0.398	0.408	0.011	14	0.360	0.419	0.059
Northeast	9	0.790	0.804	0.015	26	0.704	0.776	0.071
Midwest	4	0.711	0.751	0.039	49	0.502	0.559	0.057
West	26	0.661	0.660	-0.001	42	0.502	0.567	0.065

Source: Author's calculations from Common Core of Data, 1993–2005

Table 5.2 suggests that, on average, segregation patterns have not changed dramatically in any region of the country during the 1993–2005 period, with a few exceptions. None of the regions saw changes in segregation of greater than 0.04 for any group. The share of segregation between districts changed relatively little except for sizeable increases in the between-district share of segregation between white and Hispanic students in the Border and Midwest states (which increased by 11.7 and 7.1 percentage points respectively) and between poor and nonpoor students in most regions. Nonetheless, these numbers tell us nothing about the relationship between changes in segregation and changes in the racial/ethnic and socioeconomic composition of the student population. For that, we turn to our regression results.

Table 5.3 reports the estimated coefficients from the regression models described above in Equation 5.1. These models address the question of whether changes in the racial/ethnic and socioeconomic composition of suburban students predict changes in suburban segregation levels, net of stable suburban area characteristics, region-specific temporal trends, and changes in the overall enrollment. The table is broken down into four sections by group-specific segregation outcome (white-black, white-Hispanic, white-Asian, poor-nonpoor) and within each of these sections by total segregation, between-district, and within-district segregation.

The key finding from Table 5.3 is that changes in the suburban enrollment share of all three racial groups predict statistically significant and numerically substantial changes in the total segregation of that particular group relative to white students. (See the bolded estimates in the first column of the black, Hispanic, and Asian sections of Table 5.3.) This suggests that the growth of any minority group population in a suburban region leads to increased segregation of that group from white students. For example, our results indicate that, on average, an increase of one percentage point in the proportion of students in a suburban area who are black leads to an increase of roughly 0.0038 in the overall level of black-white segregation (note that the proportion variables are scaled from 0 to 1, so a one-percentage-point change corresponds to a change of only 1/100th the magnitude of the coefficient shown in Table 5.3). This may seem small, but note that among the 144 metropolitan areas in the black-white segregation sample (those where at least 3 percent of suburban students are black), the average proportion of blacks increased by 1 percentage point (from 15.2 percent to 16.2 percent), and the average segregation level increased by 0.005 (from 0.225 to 0.230; see Table 5.2). This implies that changes in suburban black proportions account for three-quarters (0.0038 of 0.0050) of the average change in black-white segregation levels.

Similarly, a change of one percentage point in the proportion of suburban students who are Hispanic leads to an estimated increase in overall white-Hispanic segregation levels of 0.0052. The average proportion of Hispanics in the 140 suburban areas in our Hispanic sample increased from 12.6 percent to 19.2 percent, an increase of 6.6 percentage points. The regression results in Table 5.3 imply that this would lead to an increase in white-Hispanic segregation of 0.034 (0.066 × 0.515) points. Table 5.2 indicates the actual average increase in white-Hispanic segregation levels in our sample was 0.025 points, suggesting that the increases in Hispanic-white segregation levels more than accounted for the average increase in white-Hispanic suburban segregation.

For Asians, the estimated effect of changes in Asian composition on Asian-white segregation is similar in magnitude to the effect of changes in black student composition in the black-white segregation models, but it accounts for less of the overall change in Asian-white segregation levels. On average, in the 53 suburban areas in our Asian sample, the proportion of students who were Asian increased by 1.5 percentage points. The results in Table 5.3 imply that this would produce an increase of roughly 0.0055 (0.015 × 0.371) points in the average segregation levels between Asian and white students. In fact, Asian-white segregation increased by an average of 0.014 points from 1993 to 2005 in our sample, suggesting

Table 5.3. Estimated Associations Between Racial and Socioeconomic Composition and Segregation, Suburban Areas, 1993-2005 (Model 1)

	White/Black			White/Hispanic		
	Total Seg.	Between-District Seg.	Within-District Seg.	Total Seg.	Between-District Seg.	Within-District Seg.
Proportion Black	**0.384***	**0.200***	**0.183***	0.107	0.021	0.087
	(0.052)	**(0.042)**	**(0.037)**	(0.064)	(0.044)	(0.046)
Proportion Hispanic	0.473***	0.394***	0.079*	**0.515***	**0.291***	**0.224***
	(0.055)	(0.045)	(0.039)	**(0.046)**	**(0.031)**	**(0.033)**
Proportion Asian	0.235	0.275*	-0.041	0.731***	0.295**	0.436***
	(0.138)	(0.113)	(0.098)	(0.137)	(0.094)	(0.098)
Proportion Native American	-0.529*	-0.462*	-0.068	-0.005	0.025	-0.031
	(0.219)	(0.179)	(0.155)	(0.133)	(0.091)	(0.095)
Proportion FLE	-0.130***	-0.096***	-0.035	-0.002	-0.004	0.002
	(0.027)	(0.022)	(0.019)	(0.023)	(0.016)	(0.016)
Log_{10} (Total Enrollment)	-0.123***	-0.115***	-0.007	0.022	-0.002	0.024
	(0.027)	(0.022)	(0.019)	(0.025)	(0.017)	(0.018)
N (metros)	144	144	144	140	140	140
N (metro years)	1764	1764	1764	1735	1735	1735

(continued)

Table 5.3. *(continued)*

	White/Asian			FLE/non-FLE		
	Total Seg.	Between-District Seg.	Within-District Seg.	Total Seg.	Between-District Seg.	Within-District Seg.
Proportion Black	0.146	0.314***	-0.168***	0.053	0.085*	-0.032
	(0.080)	(0.076)	(0.037)	(0.049)	(0.035)	(0.033)
Proportion Hispanic	0.057	0.051	0.006	-0.021	-0.005	-0.016
	(0.057)	(0.054)	(0.026)	(0.037)	(0.027)	(0.025)
Proportion Asian	**0.371***	**0.252***	**0.118***	0.036	-0.070	0.106
	(0.107)	**(0.102)**	**(0.050)**	(0.120)	(0.087)	(0.082)
Proportion Native American	-0.036	-0.036	-0.001	0.030	0.064	-0.034
	(0.124)	(0.118)	(0.057)	(0.115)	(0.083)	(0.079)
Proportion FLE	0.004	0.012	-0.008	**-0.005**	**0.043***	**-0.048***
	(0.030)	(0.028)	(0.014)	**(0.018)**	**(0.013)**	**(0.013)**
Log$_{10}$ (Total Enrollment)	0.013	-0.033	0.045*	0.090***	0.052***	0.038
	(0.038)	(0.036)	(0.014)	(0.020)	(0.014)	(0.014)
N (metros)	53	53	53	217	217	217
N (metro years)	656	656	656	2670	2670	2670

Note: * p < .05; ** p < .01; *** p < .001 (two-tailed test). Standard errors in parentheses. All models include metropolitan area and region-x-year fixed effects. FLE: Free-Lunch Eligible. See text for definition of sample criteria.

that increases in Asian proportions in the suburbs account for only about 40 percent of the overall average change in Asian-white segregation.

Next, note that changes in the proportion of students who were eligible for free lunch had no statistically significant relation to changes in the overall segregation of the poor from the nonpoor.

The second key finding in Table 5.3 is that changes in suburban minority student composition were positively associated with both the between- and within-district components of segregation. (See the bolded estimates in the second and third columns of the black, Hispanic, and Asian sections of Table 5.3.) Roughly half of the overall effect of changes in black and Hispanic proportions on segregation was due to their effects on between-district segregation and roughly half was due to their effects on within-district segregation. For Asians, however, roughly two-thirds of the effect of increasing proportions was due to its effect on between-district segregation.

The pattern of effects of increasing poverty on the segregation of the poor from the nonpoor, however, is somewhat different. In this case, increases in the proportion of students in a suburban area who are free-lunch eligible are positively associated with changes in between-district segregation, but negatively associated with within-district segregation. These two effects are both quite small in comparison to the effects of changes in racial composition on racial segregation. Moreover, they cancel one another out, leading to no overall effect of changes in poverty composition on poor-nonpoor segregation.

Above we have described the associations between changing suburban student racial/ethnic composition and changing segregation levels as causal, but it may be that some other factor that is correlated with both changing student racial/ethnic composition and changing segregation drives these patterns of association. One possibility is that it is not changes in racial/ethnic composition *per se* that lead to changes in segregation levels, but rather it is that changes in racial composition are associated with changes in the segregation of the poor from the nonpoor (because black and Hispanic suburban students are, on average, more likely to be poor than their white suburban counterparts), and it is the segregation of the poor which leads to the association between racial composition and racial segregation. Our next set of regression models tests this possibility.

Table 5.4 reports the results of regression models of the form shown in Equation 5.2 above. Here we include between- and within-district poor-nonpoor segregation as an additional covariate. The first finding here is that the coefficients on the racial composition variables are virtually unchanged when we add socioeconomic segregation terms to the model. In other words, the association between racial composition and racial segregation cannot be attributed to segregation between the poor and the nonpoor. This suggests that there is an independent effect of racial/ethnic compositional changes on racial/ethnic segregation holding the changes in socioeconomic segregation constant.

Table 5.4 also provides some evidence regarding the question of whether changes in socioeconomic segregation may induce changes in racial segregation as a by-product. As we noted above, this question has increasing salience as districts move away from policies that desegregate on the basis of race and toward socioeconomic desegregation plans. We find that in the case of black-white and Hispanic-white segregation, changes in both between- and within-district socioeconomic segregation are positively related to changes in racial/ethnic segregation. Moreover, the effect of between-district socioeconomic segregation is related to between-district (but not to within-district) racial segregation, while the opposite is true for the effect of within-district socioeconomic segregation, as we would expect. The associations between socioeconomic and racial segregation within districts (where desegregation policies are more relevant) are, however, relatively modest in size. For white-black and white-Hispanic segregation the estimated coefficients are 0.174 and 0.151 respectively,

Table 5.4. Estimated Associations Between Racial and Socioeconomic Composition and Segregation, Controlling for FLE Segregation, Suburban Areas, 1993–2005 (Model 2)

	White/Black			White/Hispanic			White/Asian		
	Total Seg.	Between-District Seg.	Within-District Seg.	Total Seg.	Between-District Seg.	Within-District Seg.	Total Seg.	Between-District Seg.	Within-District Seg.
Between-District FLE Seg.	0.242*** (0.034)	0.239*** (0.028)	0.003 (0.024)	0.091* (0.036)	0.112*** (0.025)	-0.021 (0.026)	-0.012 (0.031)	-0.012 (0.030)	-0.001 (0.015)
Within-District FLE Seg.	0.162*** (0.037)	-0.012 (0.030)	0.174*** (0.026)	0.202*** (0.045)	0.052 (0.031)	0.151*** (0.032)	-0.167*** (0.042)	-0.127** (0.040)	-0.040 (0.020)
Proportion Black	**0.386*** (0.051)**	**0.186*** (0.042)**	**0.200*** (0.036)**	0.113 (0.063)	0.023 (0.043)	0.090* (0.045)	0.126 (0.081)	0.299*** (0.077)	-0.174*** (0.038)
Proportion Hispanic	0.485*** (0.054)	0.407*** (0.044)	0.078* (0.039)	**0.524*** (0.046)**	**0.297*** (0.031)**	**0.266*** (0.033)**	0.035 (0.056)	0.034 (0.054)	0.000 (0.027)
Proportion Asian	0.246 (0.135)	0.310** (0.111)	-0.065 (0.097)	0.723*** (0.136)	0.295*** (0.093)	0.429*** (0.098)	**0.361*** (0.106)**	**0.245* (0.101)**	**0.116* (0.050)**
Proportion Nat. Am.	-0.569*** (0.214)	-0.534** (0.176)	-0.035 (0.154)	0.000 (0.132)	0.018 (0.091)	-0.018 (0.095)	-0.043 (0.122)	-0.040 (0.117)	-0.002 (0.057)
Proportion FLE	-0.163*** (0.027)	-0.116*** (0.022)	-0.047* (0.019)	0.016 (0.023)	0.002 (0.016)	0.014 (0.016)	0.026 (0.030)	0.029 (0.028)	-0.002 (0.014)
Log$_{10}$ (Total Enrollment)	-0.144*** (0.026)	-0.132*** (0.021)	-0.012 (0.019)	0.007 (0.025)	-0.01 (0.017)	0.017 (0.018)	0.029 (0.038)	-0.020 (0.036)	0.049** (0.018)
N (metros)	144	144	144	140	140	140	53	53	53
N (metro years)	1764	1764	1764	1735	1735	1735	656	656	656

Note: * p < .05, ** p < .01, *** p < .001 (two-tailed test). Standard errors in parentheses. All models include metropolitan area and region-x-year fixed effects. FLE: Free-Lunch Eligible. See text for definition of sample criteria.

suggesting that decreases in socioeconomic segregation might yield decreases in racial/ethnic segregation of about 15 to 17 percent of the change in socioeconomic segregation.

For white-Asian segregation, however, changes in between-district socioeconomic segregation have no relationship to white-Asian segregation, while changes in within-district socioeconomic segregation have a negative relationship with white-Asian segregation, a pattern driven primarily by changes in between-district white-Asian segregation. Given that it is not clear how within-district socioeconomic segregation might affect between-district racial segregation, we suspect this is not reflective of a causal relationship. This suggests (as do many of our findings) that there is much more research that must be done to parse out the most likely causal mechanisms that result in these important demographic shifts and that the mechanisms are unlikely to be the same for each of the racial groups in our study.

CONCLUSION

Rapid suburbanization and, in particular, the rapid suburbanization of minority populations in the last few decades, is one of the most significant demographic shifts in the United States, yet we understand relatively little about its consequences for schooling, segregation, and equal opportunity. Our goal in this chapter was to examine the relationships among racial/ethnic and socioeconomic diversity and racial/ethnic and socioeconomic school segregation in the suburbs.

Our primary finding was that minority suburbanization leads to increased segregation of black, Hispanic, and Asian students from white students. This finding, based on more recent, and better, data than our earlier work confirms the finding of that earlier work, but extends it in several important ways. Notably, we find that increases in poverty rates (measured here by free-lunch-eligibility rates) do not lead, on average, to increases in socioeconomic school segregation, though they do appear to lead to some increase in the proportion of socioeconomic segregation that is due to between-, rather than within-district sorting. It is not clear what mechanisms drive this, but prior research has found some evidence that school district fragmentation leads to increased between-district residential sorting (Bischoff, 2008); real or perceived differences in school quality may exacerbate disparities in housing prices between districts, which may in turn lead to increased between-district socioeconomic segregation. The fact that racial segregation grows in response to changes in racial composition, while socioeconomic segregation does not grow in response to similar changes in socioeconomic composition, however, suggests that racial segregation is driven by factors other than socioeconomic differences.

A second important finding here is that racial segregation does not appear to change much in response to socioeconomic segregation patterns. That is, socioeconomic segregation does not appear to serve as a strong proxy for racial segregation. This finding, if supported in other empirical research, casts doubt on the hope that race-neutral strategies (whether housing policies or student assignment policies) can be effective in producing substantial racial desegregation as an inevitable result.

NOTES

An earlier version of this chapter was presented at the Annual Meeting of the American Educational Research Association, New York City, March 24–28, 2008. The paper was prepared with support from the William T. Grant Foundation (grant to Reardon). All errors remain our own.

1. We exclude the years 1987–1992 from the analysis in this chapter because of missing data; see the "Data" section below.

2. 551 U.S. 701 (2007).

3. We use free-lunch eligibility here because reduced-price lunch eligibility data are not available prior to 1998.

4. 418 U.S. 717 (1974).

5. Because the CCD does not include reduced-price lunch eligible counts prior to 1998–1999, we use free-lunch-eligible counts (rather than the sum of the counts of free- and reduced-price-lunch eligible) throughout for consistency.

6. See definitions at http://www.census.gov/population/www/metroareas/aboutmetro.html.

7. The information theory index is defined as $H = \sum_j \frac{T_j(E - E_j)}{TE}$, where j indexes schools; T and T_j denote the total enrollment in the region and in school j, respectively; and where E and E_j denote the entropy (a measure of racial diversity) in the region and in school j, respectively. The entropy is defined as $E = \sum_m [p_m \cdot \log_m(p_m) + (1 - p_m) \cdot \log_m(1 - p_m)]$, where m indexes racial groups and p_m denotes the proportion of group m in the population.

REFERENCES

Bischoff, K. (2008). School district fragmentation and racial residential segregation: How do boundaries matter? *Urban Affairs Review, 44*(1).

Chaplin, D. (2002). Estimating the impact of economic integration of schools on racial integration. In Century Foundation Task Force on the Common School (Ed.), *Divided we fail: Coming together through public school choice.* New York, NY: The Century Foundation Press.

Coleman, J. S., Campbell, E. Q., Hobson, C. J., McPartland, J., Mood, A. M., Weinfeld, F. D., et al. (1966). *Equality of educational opportunity.* Washington, DC: U.S. Department of Health, Education, and Welfare, Office of Education.

Entwisle, D. R., Alexander, K. L., & Olson, L. S. (1997). *Children, schools, and inequality.* Boulder, CO: Westview Press.

Kahlenberg, R. D. (1995). *The remedy: Class, race, and affirmative action.* New York, NY: BasicBooks.

Kahlenberg, R. D. (2001). *All together now: Creating middle-class schools through public school choice.* Washington, DC: Brookings Institution Press.

Reardon, S. F., & Bischoff, K. (2011). Income inequality and income segregation. *American Journal of Sociology, 116*(4), 1092–1153.

Reardon, S. F., & Firebaugh, G. (2002). Measures of multi-group segregation. *Sociological Methodology, 32,* 33–67.

Reardon, S. F., & Yun, J. T. (2001). Suburban racial change and suburban school segregation, 1987–1995. *Sociology of Education, 74*(2), 79–101.

Reardon, S. F., & Yun, J. T. (2003). Integrating neighborhoods, segregating schools: The retreat from school desegregation in the South, 1990–2000. *North Carolina Law Review, 81*(4), 1563–1596.

Reardon, S. F., Yun, J. T., & Eitle, T. M. (2000). The changing structure of school segregation: Measurement and evidence of multi-racial metropolitan area school segregation, 1989–1995. *Demography, 37*(3), 351–364.

Reardon, S. F., Yun, J. T., & Kurlaender, M. (2006). Implications of income-based school assignment policies for racial school segregation. *Educational Evaluation and Policy Analysis, 28*(1), 49–75.

Sable, J., Gaviola, N., & Garofano, A. (2007). *Documentation to the NCES Common Core of Data Local Education Agency Universe Survey: School year 2005–06.* National Center for Education Statistics.

Stoll, M. A. (2006). *Race, place and poverty revisited* (Working Paper No. 06-14). Ann Arbor, MI: National Poverty Center, University of Michigan.

Theil, H. (1972). *Statistical decomposition analysis* (Vol. 14). Amsterdam, The Netherlands: North-Holland Publishing Company.

Theil, H., & Finezza, A. J. (1971). A note on the measurement of racial integration of schools by means of informational concepts. *Journal of Mathematical Sociology, 1,* 187–194.

U.S. Bureau of the Census. (1984). *Statistical Abstract of the United States, 1984.* Washington, DC: U.S. Government Printing Office.

U.S. Bureau of the Census. (1992). *1990 census of the population: General population characteristics, United States.* Washington, DC: U.S. Government Printing Office.

U.S. Bureau of the Census. (2008). *Table from American Fact Finder Data Tool.* Retrieved on March 15, 2008, http://factfinder.census.gov/servlet/DTTable?_bm=y&-show_geoid=N&-tree_id=4001&-gc_url=010:00|64|72|84|&-_showChild=Y&-context=dt&-state=dt&-all_geo_types=N&-mt_name=DEC_2000_SF1_U_P010&-redoLog=false&-transpose=N&-_lang=en&-geo_id=01000US&-CONTEXT=dt&-format=&-search_results=01000US&-CHECK_SEARCH_RESULTS=N&-ds_name=DEC_2000_SF1_U

Watson, T. (2009). Inequality and the measurement of residential segregation by income. *Review of Income and Wealth, 55*(3), 820–844.

6

Schools Matter

Segregation, Unequal Educational Opportunities, and the Achievement Gap in the Boston Region

John R. Logan and Deirdre Oakley

It is common knowledge that school quality has a profound impact on the academic achievement of children and adolescents. In an effort to ensure that all public school students receive a decent education the No Child Left Behind Act (NCLB) signed into law in 2002 requires that all students meet "high academic standards" by 2014, including subgroups of students with traditionally low levels of achievement through annual testing in reading and math (Borman et al., 2004). Although the NCLB acknowledged that students' performance was constrained by the quality of their schools, and introduced mechanisms to identify "failing schools," it did not provide new federal support to address the high degree of stratification of American public school systems by race and class (Mickelson, 2003).

This study addresses the question of what kinds of public elementary schools students in the Boston metropolitan region are enrolled in. It evaluates school characteristics for non-Hispanic white, black, Hispanic, and Asian students, and distinguishes between patterns in the central city and the suburbs. Our purpose is to understand the extent to which these students attend unequal schools. Other important questions—why schools are unequal or how the inequalities may contribute to racial disparities in educational outcomes for individual students—also should be addressed, but they require different information than we have available here.

We characterize schools by their degree of poverty concentration, racial composition, and student performance on statewide standardized tests. We focus on these characteristics because there are strong reasons to suspect that each of them may have independent effects on student outcomes.

WHY SCHOOLS MATTER

There is no doubt about the extent of racial/ethnic disparities in educational outcomes (Hallinan, 2001; Henderson, 2002; Jencks & Phillips, 1998; Maruyama, 2003; Rumberger & Palardy, 2005). One review of recent results from the National Assessment of Educational Progress (NAEP) showed that nationwide only 54 percent of black students performed at or above the basic level on the 2003 eighth-grade reading exam compared to 87 percent of white students (Stiefel, Schwartz, & Chellman, 2008, p. 527). Dropout rates are much higher among black and Hispanic students than among white and Asian students (Mickelson, 2003). The source of these racial/ethnic differences has not been clearly established. Researchers have long suspected that socioeconomic factors and family background play an important role. However, Roscigno and Ainsworth-Darnell (1999), analyzing survey data from the National Educational Longitudinal Survey (NELS), found that although black-white differences in socioeconomic standing have strong effects on racial variations in cultural capital and household educational background, these resources have little mediating effect on the black-white achievement gap.

A different approach is to ask how schools themselves matter. In the landmark case of *Brown v. Board of Education of Topeka* (1954), the U.S. Supreme Court officially declared that the "separate but equal" doctrine established 58 years earlier in *Plessy v. Ferguson* (1896) had no place in the field of public education (Whitman, 1998). Racially segregated schools, according to the Court, were inherently unequal. There was little empirical basis at the time for this claim. But since racial segregation persists at fairly high levels despite the widespread desegregation of schools following the *Brown* decision (Logan, Oakley, & Stowell, 2008), many scholars have sought to evaluate its effect (Armor, 1995; Bifulco & Ladd, 2006; Cutler & Glaeser, 1997; Mercer & Scout, 1974; Orfield & Eaton, 1996; Rumberger & Palardy, 2005; Schofield, 1995; Wells & Crain, 1994).

Several studies suggest a direct and independent effect of racial composition on student performance. Bankston and Caldas (1996, 1997) and Rumberger and Williams (1992) showed that minority concentration is associated with lower achievement on standardized tests. Academic outcomes are generally better for blacks in racially integrated schools (Armor, 2002; Dawkins & Braddock, 1994). Further, blacks' higher achievement when they attend majority white schools also does not harm white outcomes (McPartland, 1969; Spady, 1973; St. John & Hoyt, 1975). Stiefel and colleagues find that the achievement gap between white and nonwhite children is greatest among racially segregated schools (Stiefel et al., 2008). Card and Rothstein (2005) concluded that segregation continues to be a major obstacle to equal educational opportunities for minority children and a source of gaps in academic achievement. More broadly, it has been argued that black and Hispanic students in segregated schools may be disadvantaged by their lack of connection to the mainstream culture and the social ties that accompany it. In the long run, according to Ellen, O'Regan, Schwartz, and Stiefel (2002), they may find themselves with fewer connections to jobs and less facility interacting with the dominant group that includes a majority of potential employers and supervisors.

Of course the racial composition of schools is strongly correlated with other school characteristics, such as class composition. The classic study of school effects, the Coleman Report (Coleman et al., 1966) provided evidence that the racial isolation of black children in majority minority schools is associated with lower academic achievement. But Coleman demonstrated that these racial differences were primarily attributable to socioeconomic differences between races. He argued that predominantly white schools tended to enroll students from higher socioeconomic backgrounds and it was for this reason that these schools' academic performance was better than that of predominantly minority schools. He found, in short, that apparent contextual effects were really compositional (see also Hauser, Sewell, & Alwin, 1976). If there was a contextual effect, in Coleman's view, it was the effect of class composition. A recent study of this question (Chaplin, 2002) found that the concentration of poverty within a school is negatively associated with student performance and later outcomes, even after controlling for a student's own family background (see also a number of prior studies, including Chubb & Moe, 1990; Gamoran, 1996; Jencks & Mayer, 1990; and Lee & Smith, 1997).

But studies have continually demonstrated that minority children are more likely to be in high-poverty schools (Orfield & Lee, 2005). In fact Saporito and Sohoni (2007) found that unlike the typical white child, who attends a public school in which most of the children are above the poverty line, the typical black or Hispanic child attends a public school in which most of the children are below the poverty line. This study also found that the gap in poverty rates between schools and their corresponding neighborhoods is greater in schools with higher percentages of nonwhite students than it is in areas with higher percentages of white students (Saporito & Sohoni, 2007).

Another relevant factor is metropolitan location, which is related to both racial and class composition and strongly associated with educational outcomes. For example, Swanson (2008) found that high school graduation rates are 15 percentage points lower in the nation's urban schools compared with those located in the suburbs. And in 12 cities, 9 of which are in the Northeast and Midwest, the city-suburban graduation gap exceeds 25 percentage points. It is well known that black and Hispanic students are more likely to attend city schools. In fact, the 24 largest central cities (with 4.5 million students) have an enrollment that is more than 70 percent black and Hispanic. In 20 of these districts the student population is 90 percent black (Orfield & Lee, 2005). Orfield and Lee pointed out that more than 60 percent of black and Hispanic students attend high-poverty schools (defined as more than 50 percent poor). In contrast, white public school students are highly concentrated in more affluent suburban districts, and only 18 percent of white students and 30 percent of Asian students attend high-poverty schools. In addition to the contextual effects of concentrated poverty, it is argued that poor central-city schools are more likely to have inadequate resources and funding as well as a less qualified teaching staff compared to suburban school systems (Eaddy et al., 2003; Hochschild & Scovronick, 2003).

Another series of studies have examined the connection between school segregation and racial disparities in achievement by analyzing trends in outcomes in districts that are desegregated. In the decades that followed the *Brown* decision more than 700 separate court cases involving several thousand school districts enforced the requirement to desegregate (Logan & Oakley, 2004). There are mixed results (see the review by Crain & Mahard, 1978). One study found positive effects of desegregation for blacks, especially for desegregation plans with a metropolitan scope (Longshore & Prager, 1985). But Longshore and Prager caution that this finding could be due to the fact that metro-wide plans reach more middle-class whites and desegregation is therefore socioeconomic as well as racial, or because metro plans assign more black students to high-quality suburban schools. Distinguishing effects of race, class, and metropolitan location is difficult.

Grissmer, Flanagan, and Williamson (1998) believe that long-term time trends in the course of school desegregation offer indirect evidence of positive effects. NAEP test scores have improved especially for blacks, with significant but smaller gains for Hispanics and lower-scoring white students, and small or no gains by other white students. These scholars noted that black gains were limited to cohorts entering school around 1970–1980, when desegregation was first implemented, and that there has been little improvement for subsequent cohorts. They argued that this pattern could be due to time-bound changes engendered by the Civil Rights movement and War on Poverty initiatives through the 1970s, including direct effects related to school desegregation, especially in the South.

Another approach to evaluating the historical evidence was a meta-analysis of more than 300 samples of black students experiencing desegregation, derived from 93 research studies (Crain & Mahard, 1983). Crain and Mahard found that black students who received only a "partial treatment" (i.e., they experienced desegregation after they had completed one or more years of segregated schooling) had weaker treatment effects. Studies that used random-assignment experimental designs found significant positive treatment effects. But studies that compared black achievement gains in relation to white students or to achievement test norms found much weaker (usually negative) effects of being in desegregated schools. Similarly Rivkin (2000) found little support for the belief that mandatory desegregation programs are likely to increase the life chances and earning power of blacks. Levine and Eubanks (1990) pointed out that even in some desegregated suburban schools middle-class blacks do not do as well as their white classmates with similar class backgrounds (though they do outperform less affluent black students in weaker schools).

These studies lead to the conclusion that some combination of school racial composition, class composition, and metropolitan location—perhaps linked with variations in resources and teacher quality—are part of the source of racial/ethnic disparities in school achievement. This conclusion is the starting point for our research in the Boston region: if schools matter, what are the differences in the schools attended by white, black, Hispanic, and Asian students, and what are their sources in residential and school segregation?

DATA AND MEASURES

This study uses data about neighborhoods from the census (United States Census Bureau, 1990, 2000); corresponding data on public elementary schools gathered by the National Center for Education Statistics (NCES, n.d.); and school rankings on standardized tests for 2004.

We use reading and math rankings for the elementary level. We also include middle and high school math rankings for comparison purposes to determine whether disparities at the elementary level persist (reading rankings are not available at these school levels). This data is organized as percentiles of school performance, standardized within each state—in our case Massachusetts. The test score data comes from the Massachusetts school report cards and were assembled by the School Matters Project of the National Education Data Partnership (2004). This is a collaborative effort of the Council of Chief State School Officers, Standard & Poor's School Evaluation Services, the CELT Corporation, the Broad Foundation, the Bill & Melinda Gates Foundation, and the U.S. Department of Education to provide school-level performance data for every public school in the country (http://www.schoolmatters.org). Because test score data was not systematically collected for the 1990 period, we can only include the latter time period. Thus we cannot look at the relationship between test scores and trends in segregation over the ten-year period, but these data provide a useful and current indicator of the status of the achievement gap broken down by race and ethnicity.

The NCES racial and ethnic composition data is classified as non-Hispanic white, non-Hispanic black, Hispanic, Asian, and other races. We have organized census data into these same categories, although shifts in census reporting between 1990 and 2000 complicate matters. In 2000 for the first time the census tabulated multiple races for individuals. In this study we treat as "Hispanic" all persons who identified themselves as Hispanic or Latino origin, regardless of their reported race. "Non-Hispanic blacks" are those who identified as black, alone or in combination with any other race. "Non-Hispanic whites" are those who identified as white alone. "Asians" include Asians and Pacific Islanders, alone or in combination with another race; these also include a small number of Hispanic Asians, who are therefore double-counted in this study. "Other race" is calculated as the difference between the sum of these four groups and the total population. This coding creates as much consistency as possible between 1990 and 2000 population counts, and between the census and school data sources. The test score data utilizes the Census 2000 categorization of race and ethnicity.

The region studied includes a seven-county area around Boston (formally, the Boston NECMA), with a total population of over 5 million. The city of Boston is by far the single largest community in this area, but with a population under 600,000 it accounts for only about a tenth of the region's residents. The region also includes a number of densely settled cities and towns, many with roots in the 19th century and some that are officially designated as "central cities" by the federal government. Closest to Boston itself are Cambridge, Chelsea, Everett, Lynn, Malden, Somerville, and Waltham. Further west are Worcester, Leominster, and Fitchburg. Gloucester, Lawrence, and Lowell are to the north, and Attleboro, Brockton, Fall River, and New Bedford to the south. Altogether these 17 "other cities" have well over a million residents, considerably outnumbering the City of Boston. The rest of the region, with over 3 million people, is treated here collectively as residential suburbs, or more simply, the suburbs. As we will see, distinguishing between the city of Boston, other cities, and suburbs is central to understanding how segregation and place inequality are organized in this metropolis.

To measure segregation we utilize two indices. The first is the Index of Dissimilarity (D). This is the most commonly used measure of segregation and is an indicator of the "unevenness of the distribution" of children of different races across neighborhoods. If all neighborhoods had the same racial composition, D would have a value of 0. In a situation of complete apartheid (for example, where neighborhoods were either all white or all black) D would have a value of 100. Based on many studies of different racial and ethnic groups, researchers generally consider values below 30 to represent a low level of segregation (typical, for example, of separation between different white ethnic groups in most cities). Values between 30 and 55 are interpreted as moderate segregation. Higher values are considered extreme levels of segregation. This index is not affected by the relative size of the white or black or other populations. Whatever the diversity of the population, it measures whether they are similarly distributed across neighborhoods.

The second measure we use determines the racial composition of the neighborhood where the average person lives. This is called the Index of Isolation, because at the extreme value (100) it means all children in the neighborhood have the same race. This measure depends in part on how diverse is the population in the region as a whole—for example, if the percentage of black residents is very low, it would be unlikely for blacks to live in majority-black neighborhoods, even if segregation (thinking now of segregation as unevenness of distribution) were quite high.

FINDINGS

Before examining the trends in segregation and academic achievement we briefly review the racial and ethnic composition of the Boston region, which historically has had only modest minority populations. Table 6.1 shows that as recently as 1990 nearly 90 percent of the population was non-Hispanic white. Blacks and Hispanics each accounted for close to 5 percent of the total, and Asians were 2.7 percent. During the 1990s, as the region grew slowly, the white population actually declined by about 60,000, while minorities grew at a rapid rate. Hence whites now are only 81.2 percent of the total. Hispanics are the largest minority with 6.6 percent, followed by blacks (5.9 percent) and Asians (4.7 percent). The decline in the white population stems partly from the fact that this is an older group, and Table 6.1 shows that the under-18 population is substantially less white than the total. By

Table 6.1. Racial and Ethnic Composition of the Boston Region

	Population All Ages				Population Under 18			
	1990		*2000*		*1990*		*2000*	
White	4,349,389	87.4%	4,272,023	81.2%	910,024	82.0%	934,676	75.0%
Black	233,732	4.7%	311,354	5.9%	70,185	6.3%	100,401	8.1%
Hispanic	232,964	4.7%	346,866	6.6%	83,418	7.5%	123,505	9.9%
Asian	132,407	2.7%	245,412	4.7%	38,284	3.4%	65,161	5.2%
Other races	26,788	0.5%	84,150	1.6%	8,412	0.8%	22,491	1.8%
Total	*4,975,280*	*100%*	*5,259,805*	*100%*	*1,110,323*	*100%*	*1,246,234*	*100%*

Source: United States Census Bureau

2000 whites were only 75 percent of the children in the region, while Hispanics were almost 10 percent, blacks 8.1 percent and Asians 5.2 percent. So there is now considerable racial and ethnic diversity among children in the region.

NEIGHBORHOOD SEGREGATION

Growing diversity in the region as a whole is not very well reflected at the level of neighborhoods. Instead, there is a strong tendency for children to live separately from those of other backgrounds. We measure this tendency in Table 6.2 with both the Index of Dissimilarity and the Index of Isolation at the level of census tracts (geographic areas that typically have 3,000–4,000 residents).

The upper panel of Table 6.2 lists the Index of Dissimilarity for the Boston region. Nationally black-white segregation averages around 65; Hispanic-white segregation averages just over 50; and Asian-white segregation averages about 40, which is considered moderate. In Boston, although black-white segregation is falling slowly, it remains very close to the national average. Segregation of Hispanics and Asians is above the average and rising. Most important for our purpose, levels of segregation are higher than this for minority children—values of dissimilarity vis-à-vis white children are between 65 and 70 for both black and Hispanic children. This means that the experience of separated neighborhoods is felt most keenly by children.

The lower panels of Table 6.2 list values of the Isolation Index, showing that Boston's average white child lives in a neighborhood where 85 percent of children are white (though in the region only 75 percent of children are white). The average black and Hispanic children are in neighborhoods where more than a third of other children are black or Hispanic, respectively—three or four times their representation in the region. And Asian children, while only 5.2 percent of the region's total, live in neighborhoods where 14.5 percent of children are Asian. Again, minority children are somewhat more isolated than the minority population of all ages. However, reflecting changes in overall population composition, isolation is declining slowly over time for whites and blacks.

A major reason why children of different races live so separately is the extreme concentration of white children in the region's suburbs, while minority children are very much underrepresented in the suburbs. Figure 6.1 illustrates these patterns. Boston is not the only case

Table 6.2.   Residential Patterns of Groups in the Boston Region

	All Ages		Under 18	
Segregation from Whites	*1990*	*2000*	*1990*	*2000*
Index of Dissimilarity				
Black	66.5	62.9	70.9	67.9
Hispanic	57.6	60.3	64.8	66.8
Asian	45.6	46.0	48.3	48.1
Isolation: The average group member lives in a neighborhood with this percentage of the same group:				
Whites	91.4	86.9	89.4	85.0
Blacks	39.5	33.1	43.4	36.7
Hispanics	20.4	25.8	30.5	34.4
Asians	9.7	12.2	12.8	14.5

Source: United States Census Bureau

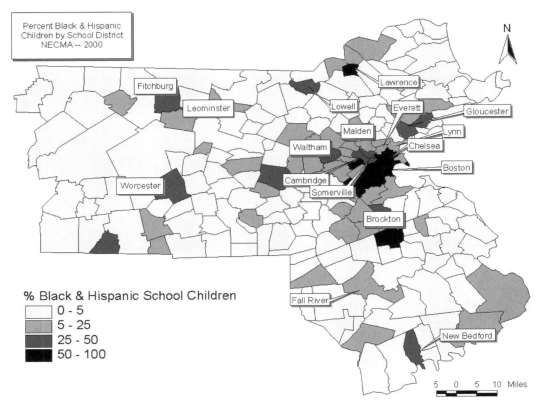

Figure 6.1. Neighborhood Segregation of Children (U.S. Census Bureau)

like this in the country; other areas where minorities still have not gained much access to suburban communities include Detroit, Milwaukee, and several upstate New York cities. But 40 percent or more of minorities nationally now live in the suburbs, and Boston is clearly out of step with the nation in this respect.

The Boston pattern is depicted visually in the map showing where black and Hispanic children lived in 2000. There is a large area including Boston and the cities and towns immediately adjacent to Boston where these groups account for a majority of the child population. In addition the "satellite" minority communities to the north, west, and south are shown very distinctly. Generally these are 19th-century suburbs or mill towns that now have an older, denser, and less desirable housing stock than the suburban towns around them.

Table 6.3 tracks the location of the under-18 population across the different sectors of the Boston metropolis in 1990 and 2000. Already in 1990 about three times as many white children lived in the suburbs than in the city of Boston and other cities combined. In the 1990–2000 decade, their number in cities dropped by about a third, while continuing to grow in suburbs. Indeed, very few white children remained in Boston itself by 2000, under 30,000 and about a quarter of the Boston population. Though we think of Boston as the major population center in the region, it is not so significant for white children—only about 3 percent of white children in the region live in the city.

A majority of Asian children, too, live in suburbs. But black children are most likely found in Boston proper, where they are fully 40.3 percent of the total, vs. the suburbs where they are only 2.6 percent of the child population. A majority of Hispanic children live in the

Table 6.3. Racial and Ethnic Composition of the Under-18 Population

		White	Black	Hispanic	Asian	Other	Total
City of Boston	1990	40,271	40,957	19,836	6,595	2,174	109,833
		36.7%	37.3%	18.1%	6.0%	2.0%	100.0%
	2000	29,644	46,961	27,831	8,354	3,769	116,559
		25.4%	40.3%	23.9%	7.2%	3.2%	100.0%
Other Cities	1990	193,025	17,919	44,503	14,132	3,520	273,099
		70.7%	6.6%	16.3%	5.2%	1.3%	100.0%
	2000	158,025	31,962	65,891	23,285	9,865	289,028
		54.7%	11.1%	22.8%	8.1%	3.4%	100.0%
Suburbs	1990	678,122	11,315	19,095	17,560	2,729	728,821
		93.0%	1.6%	2.6%	2.4%	0.4%	100.0%
	2000	747,007	21,478	29,783	33,522	8,857	840,647
		88.9%	2.6%	3.5%	4.0%	1.1%	100.0%

Source: United States Census Bureau

smaller cities, places like Lynn, continuing a pattern already found in 1990. Hispanics are just under a quarter of the child population in the city of Boston and other cities, compared to 3.5 percent in the suburbs.

In addition to these broad differences across geographic sectors, Table 6.4 shows that there is considerable segregation within them—especially in Boston, where black-white segregation of the under-18 population was at the extreme of 79.1 in 1990, and remains above 70 in 2000. For all minority groups, segregation is lower in the other cities and in the suburbs, generally in the 40–50 range. This reflects the national phenomenon that minorities tend to be less segregated in areas where they are fewer in number. Nevertheless, despite lower segregation as measured by the Index of Dissimilarity, white children are much more isolated in the suburbs than in Boston. Because there are so few suburban minority children, even if they were thoroughly dispersed among suburbs (that is, if segregation within suburbia were very low), there would hardly be a minority presence anywhere in the suburban zone. In the cities, despite higher segregation, neighborhoods still turn out to be more diverse.

One of the costs of segregation, paid by children of all races, is that young people are insulated from interracial contact. Neither whites nor blacks nor Hispanics nor Asians come into daily contact with a mix of people that fully reflects the growing diversity of the region. But white children reap advantages from segregation because they live in the most privileged areas, while black and Hispanic children live in worse neighborhoods. The situation of Asian children, as we will see, depends on whether their families live in the central city or in the suburbs.

Neighborhood inequality is demonstrated in Table 6.5 for selected indicators of neighborhood character: median income (using *constant 2000 dollars*), poverty, education level,

Table 6.4. Segregation of Children by Sector in the Boston Region

Segregation from Whites
Index of Dissimilarity

		Blacks	Hispanics	Asians
City of Boston	1990	79.1	63.1	53.6
	2000	72.7	56.4	50.8
Other Cities	1990	47.5	54.2	48.1
	2000	42.4	52.1	43.8
Suburbs	1990	42.8	42.1	39.8
	2000	43.1	45.2	41.3

Isolation: The average child lives in a neighborhood with this percentage of the same group:

		Whites	Blacks	Hispanics	Asians
City of Boston	1990	70.2	65.8	30.7	26.0
	2000	55.9	60.7	34.3	22.2
Other Cities	1990	78.4	16.1	38.6	14.7
	2000	65.7	19.8	43.1	18.4
Suburbs	1990	93.6	5.5	11.4	6.3
	2000	90.2	9.5	15.2	9.8

Source: United States Census Bureau

Table 6.5. Neighborhood Characteristics for Children in the Boston Region

The average child lives in a neighborhood with these characteristics:		City of Boston		Other Cities		Suburbs		Region total	
		1990	2000	1990	2000	1990	2000	1990	2000
Median income	White	$42,014	$46,969	$40,124	$41,789	$61,560	$68,205	$56,162	$63,065
	Black	$33,894	$33,665	$35,026	$36,765	$56,338	$58,943	$37,800	$40,060
	Hispanic	$33,219	$33,411	$29,277	$31,225	$50,816	$52,964	$35,140	$36,960
	Asian	$33,515	$36,240	$34,423	$38,499	$64,760	$71,109	$48,180	$54,985
% Poor	White	13.6	13.8	12.8	13.3	4.5	4.5	6.6	6.3
	Black	24.4	22.6	18.1	17.8	6.2	6.7	19.9	17.6
	Hispanic	24.6	24.0	26.3	23.3	9.2	10.2	22.0	20.3
	Asian	21.6	22.6	20.7	17.2	5.3	5.3	13.8	11.8
% College educated	White	26.7	35.3	17.2	21.3	30.4	38.5	27.4	35.5
	Black	15.7	18.4	18.3	19.9	29.4	34.1	18.6	22.2
	Hispanic	19.7	21.7	11.7	13.6	25.4	29.6	16.7	19.3
	Asian	27.6	29.7	16.2	19.9	36.9	46.1	27.7	34.6
% Other language	White	21.2	29.2	25.0	29.1	9.3	10.9	13.2	14.6
	Black	27.0	35.4	28.6	36.4	12.5	17.7	25.1	31.9
	Hispanic	36.9	42.5	42.6	49.4	17.1	22.2	35.4	41.3
	Asian	38.1	41.6	33.8	40.1	12.6	17.2	24.8	28.5

Source: United States Census Bureau

and incidence of speaking a language other than English at home. The first three of these certainly reflect the conventional measures of neighborhood quality; language use has some links to socioeconomic success, but it is used here mainly to indicate the degree of formation of immigrant residential enclaves that may offer both advantages and disadvantages to residents.

One way to interpret this table is to ask how different sectors of the metropolis compare to each other. Let us begin by focusing on the characteristics of neighborhoods where white children lived in 2000. The suburbs, which are where most lived, stand out from Boston and other cities. Compared to white children in Boston and other cities, those in the suburbs lived by far in the most affluent neighborhoods (median income of $68,205), with the lowest poverty rate (4.5 percent), highest share of college-educated residents (38.5 percent), and with the least exposure to non-English-speaking people (10.9 percent). White children's neighborhoods in Boston and other cities were rather alike in terms of poverty and language use. But children in the city of Boston lived in neighborhoods with higher average incomes and a much higher share of college-educated residents. Because in both of these respects the values for Boston in 2000 represent considerable gains from just ten years before, we interpret the pattern as evidence of a degree of gentrification of whites' neighborhoods. Perhaps as some of the older white working-class zones of the city have lost many white residents, other newly popular neighborhoods have attracted more affluent white families back into the city. For white children in such families, living in Boston may offer some real advantages over living in the smaller cities of the region, though not nearly equal to suburban contexts.

The suburban advantage is also very clear for minorities. For black children, for example, living in the suburbs compared to the city of Boston provides a $25,000 improvement in the average income of their neighborhood, a 16-point reduction in poverty rate and a 16-point improvement in percent with a college education. The relative status of neighborhoods in Boston and other cities varies across groups and indicators. But black children in Boston live in lower-income neighborhoods with higher poverty and fewer college-educated neighbors than do the smaller number of black children in the other cities. Hispanic children in the other cities live in neighborhoods with higher concentrations of non-English speakers, lower college rates, and lower incomes than do the smaller number of Hispanic children in Boston. So the variations seem to place black and Hispanic children in precisely the setting where they are most disadvantaged.

The very high degree of suburbanization of white children, in contrast to minority children, puts them in more desirable residential settings. At the same time, regardless of which sector of the metropolis they live in, white children's neighborhoods are very different from those of blacks and Hispanics. Suburban Asian children actually live in better neighborhoods than suburban white children, but the situation is reversed elsewhere.

The contrasts are generally most severe for white versus Hispanic children's neighborhoods. In terms of median income, Hispanic children's neighborhoods are about $15,000 below whites' neighborhoods in the suburbs, $10,000 below in smaller cities, and $13,000 below in Boston. Their poverty rates are 6 points higher in the suburbs, 10 points higher in smaller cities, and 8 points higher in Boston. They average 9 percent fewer college-educated neighbors in the suburbs, 10 percent fewer in smaller cities, and 14 percent fewer in Boston. All of these contrasts are probably associated with the presence of Hispanic enclaves in each of these segments, since Hispanic children's neighborhoods also have 12 percent more residents speaking another language in the suburbs, 20 percent more in smaller cities, and 13 percent more in Boston.

The result is that residential segregation within each portion of the metropolis also contributes to place advantages for white children and disadvantages especially for black and

Hispanic children. These disparities have in some respects deepened in the last decade, especially in Boston and in the suburbs. For example, white children's neighborhood median income increased by about $5,000 in Boston and $7,000 in the suburbs; the figures for black and Hispanic children did not change appreciably in Boston, and increased by only about $2,000 in the suburbs. Rather than catching up, we see signs that these children fell further behind in the 1990s.

SEGREGATION IN PUBLIC ELEMENTARY SCHOOLS

School segregation often replicates neighborhood patterns. However, the assignment of children to schools within school districts varies according to administrative policies, and in a region like Boston with a heritage of court-ordered school desegregation we might expect to see some continuing impacts of efforts to equalize educational opportunities. But this analysis is complicated by white students' continuing avoidance of public schools in the city of Boston. Aside from white flight out of the city, we see in Table 6.6 that white students are only 13.6 percent of total public elementary enrollment in Boston, whereas white children are 25.4 percent of the under-18 population. In 1990 whites were 36.7 percent of under-18 children, but only 23.5 percent of elementary enrollment. Presumably these differences reflect disproportionate private school attendance by a substantial share of white children whose families have remained in the city. About half of Boston's white children attend private schools rather than public schools.

Table 6.7 displays levels of school segregation and isolation indices that can be compared to the neighborhood indices discussed above in Tables 6.2 and 6.3. There are some similarities as well as startling contrasts. For the region as a whole, segregation of black and Hispanic schoolchildren is similar to the segregation of children across neighborhoods. Asian school segregation (54.9) is somewhat higher than Asian children's residential segregation (48.1). All of these segregation scores for the Boston region are higher than the national metropolitan averages: about 3 points higher for blacks, 7 points higher for Asians, and 12 points higher for Hispanics (for national figures, see Logan, 2002). Hence Hispanic school segregation is the dimension on which the Boston region most stands out.

School segregation within the city of Boston is much lower than this. Especially for black children, the value in 1989–1990 was remarkably low, clearly reflecting the desegregation policies that were in effect at that time. In the last decade, typical of many big-city school systems in the 1990s, segregation in Boston schools jumped noticeably (the Index of Dissimilarity increased from 32.8 to 45.1). But it is still low in comparison to most comparable cities. Black-white segregation among schools in the smaller cities and in the suburbs is also in the moderate range (though in these cases it is somewhat higher than residential segregation). Lynn, Massachusetts, is one of the smaller city school districts (with 23 elementary schools) with the most racially diverse student populations—about 15 percent black and 14 percent Asian, 27 percent Hispanic, and 44 percent white. Segregation scores are all below 40 in Lynn. In Worcester, schools, which are 53 percent white and 10 percent black, have a black-white segregation score of only 15.5. In Cambridge, black-white segregation is only 14.6.

Clearly, then, a major component of school segregation in this region is across school districts rather than within them, and a very important contributor to this is the low representation of whites in the city of Boston public schools and of minorities in the suburban schools. This pattern is depicted in Figure 6.2, which maps school districts in the Boston region in the 1999–2000 academic year. School districts are typically much larger than census tracts,

Table 6.6. Composition of Public Elementary Schools in the Boston Region

		White	Black	Hispanic	Asian	Other	Total
Region total	1989–1990	8,212	16,514	7,311	2,753	129	34,919
		23.5%	47.3%	20.9%	7.9%	0.4%	100%
	1999–2000	5,041	18,335	10,677	2,924	169	37,146
		13.6%	49.4%	28.7%	7.9%	0.5%	100%
City of Boston	1989–1990	60,099	7,574	15,132	5,712	104	88,621
		67.8%	8.5%	17.1%	6.4%	0.1%	100%
	1999–2000	54,754	13,715	27,021	8,806	385	104,682
		52.3%	13.1%	25.8%	8.4%	0.4%	100%
Other Cities	1989–1990	197,121	5,395	5,021	5,531	86	213,154
		92.5%	2.5%	2.4%	2.6%	0.0%	100%
	1999–2000	273,143	10,250	13,519	11,057	453	308,423
		88.6%	3.3%	4.4%	3.6%	0.1%	100%
Suburbs	1989–1990	303,221	30,065	27,755	14,410	337	375,788
		80.7%	8.0%	7.4%	3.8%	0.1%	100.0%
	1999–2000	325,578	40,654	47,182	21,532	977	435,923
		74.7%	9.3%	10.8%	4.9%	0.2%	100.0%

Source: National Center for Education Statistics

Table 6.7.   Segregation in Public Elementary Schools in the Boston Region

Segregation from Whites
Index of Dissimilarity

		Blacks	Hispanics	Asians
Region total	*1989–1990*	67.5	70.3	55.0
	1999–2000	67.5	69.6	54.9
City of Boston	*1989–1990*	32.8	48.8	55.6
	1999–2000	45.1	46.4	46.8
Other Cities	*1989–1990*	44.7	51.9	53.0
	1999–2000	42.4	47.8	44.9
Suburbs	*1989–1990*	46.0	56.5	44.8
	1999–2000	48.3	60.6	48.0

Isolation: The average child attends a school with this percentage of the same group:

		Whites	Blacks	Hispanics	Asians
Region total	*1989–1990*	88.4	35.8	33.2	17.4
	1999–2000	85.5	38.0	39.2	16.8
City of Boston	*1989–1990*	33.8	54.5	33.9	28.5
	1999–2000	23.6	60.1	44.3	27.5
Other Cities	*1989–1990*	74.8	18.2	39.7	20.9
	1999–2000	62.1	25.7	46.3	20.5
Suburbs	*1989–1990*	93.2	6.5	13.5	9.5
	1999–2000	90.7	11.2	25.2	10.8

Source: National Center for Education Statistics

with the result that this map smoothes over the variations within districts that appeared in the residential map in Figure 6.1. But the same overall pattern is apparent—strong concentrations of black and Hispanic children in the Boston School District, in some districts adjacent to Boston, and in the region's outlying cities, juxtaposed to very low representation in suburban districts.

The observation that school segregation is derived in large part from interdistrict differences also applies very clearly to school inequality. As previous research has demonstrated, a strong indicator of the educational challenges in them is the concentration of poverty among students. Table 6.8 reports the percent of students eligible for free or reduced-price lunches in the schools where students of different racial/ethnic groups attend. Within Boston schools, these figures are almost uniform across groups, around 80 percent. In the smaller cities' schools, there is more variation—below 50 percent for white students' schools, somewhat higher than that for black and Asian students' schools, and above two-thirds for Hispanic children. There are also some variations across suburban schools. But the

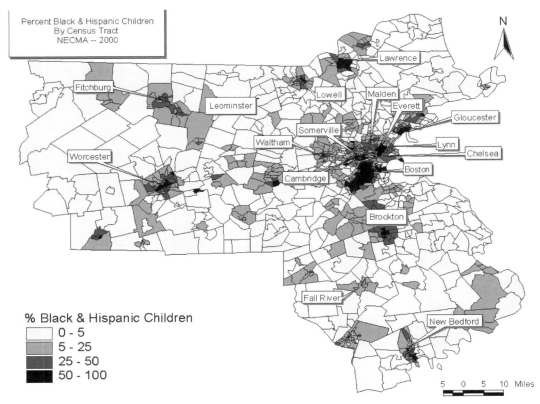

Figure 6.2.   Segregation of Elementary School Children across School Districts (National Center for Education Statistics)

biggest gaps are across segments of the metropolis: 78.3 percent in Boston, 52.7 percent in other cities, and only 13.9 percent in suburbs. This is the principal reason why in the region overall less than 20 percent of the average white child's classmates are poor, while around 60 percent of the average black or Hispanics' classmates are poor.

ACADEMIC ACHIEVEMENT

Our findings clearly show that minority children in the Boston region, especially black and Hispanic children, are highly segregated from other children, excluded from the more ad-

Table 6.8.   Percent Eligible for Free/Reduced Price Lunches in the Elementary School of the Average Child, 1999–2000

	White	Black	Hispanic	Asian	Total
Region total	18.5	58.9	62.5	40.5	26.8
City of Boston	78.7	80.5	82.7	81.0	78.3
Other cities	49.3	55.2	67.4	55.7	52.7
Suburbs	12.1	24.8	41.1	19.1	13.9

Source: National Center for Education Statistics

Table 6.9. Test Scores in the School Attended by the Average Student of Each Race/Ethnicity, 2004 (Percentiles)

| | Elementary Schools | | Middle Schools | High Schools |
	Reading	Mathematics	Mathematics	Mathematics
Boston Metropolis				
White	65.1	65.8	64.2	65.6
Black	29.1	30.9	33.9	37.0
Hispanic	28.5	33.7	32.2	34.4
Asian	54.4	58.5	59.6	61.2
Boston City				
White	25.7	34.1	55.2	57.4
Black	14.2	17.5	18.7	26.2
Hispanic	11.4	21.5	18.7	23.5
Asian	20.1	35.8	56.2	68.1
Boston Suburbs				
White	66.0	66.5	64.5	65.9
Black	48.0	48.2	49.9	50.4
Hispanic	40.1	42.0	41.0	41.3
Asian	62.3	63.5	60.5	59.0

Source: School Matters Project

vantaged suburban portion of the metropolis, and concentrated in schools where poverty is the norm. These trends strongly suggest disparities in access to equal education opportunities. But how do these trends line up with academic achievement in the schools that these children attend? Table 6.9 shows the 2004 elementary school rankings in reading and math as well as the middle and high school rankings in math in the schools that the average white, black, Hispanic, and Asian students attended. As described above, these rankings are computed as statewide percentiles for the schools.

Gaps in achievement are striking, with rankings in both reading and math for schools attended by white elementary students over twice as high as those for black and Hispanic students' schools. Percentile rankings for black and Hispanic students' schools are under 30 for reading and under 35 for math. In contrast, white students on average attended schools with scores around the 65th percentile for the state. Schools attended by the average Asian student were about 10 points lower than for whites. Disparities in school rankings on math scores persist through middle and high school, with a slight improvement for schools attended by black students.

The table shows the same rankings for schools within Boston proper. Elementary school rankings are much below those for the metropolitan region for the schools of every group. At the extreme, reading scores for the Boston city schools attended by the average Hispanic student were at the 11th percentile. Even white students' schools averaged only at the 25th percentile. Note, however, that at the middle school and high school levels the average white or Asian child attended a school with much higher performance, not far below the levels of suburban schools.

Table 6.9 also shows the same rankings for schools in the Boston suburbs. To the extent that differences in socioeconomic status are primarily responsible for school disparities, we should see a much narrower gap across racial and ethnic groups within suburbia. Rankings for schools at all levels are significantly higher than those for the city. Whites and Asians still perform much better than blacks and Hispanics in both reading and math. At the same time, disparities between schools attended by Asians and whites are not apparent in the suburbs.

At the middle school and high school levels, the disparities for schools attended by Hispanics and blacks are attenuated compared to those seen in the metropolis as a whole or in the central city, but they remain large.

CONCLUSION AND POLICY IMPLICATIONS

Taken together, our findings indicate that spatial segregation and inequality reduces the life chances for minority children, even for those whose families have found homes in suburban areas. Findings imply a close link between segregation and unequal access to economic and education resources. In addition, the disparities in academic achievement in the schools attended by children of different racial/ethnic backgrounds strongly suggest unequal educational opportunity.

Thus, it is important to ask what the underlying causes of segregation are and how public policy could equalize opportunities for all children. Most Americans presume that we have entered an era when the civil rights struggles of the mid-20th century protect minorities from unequal treatment in jobs, housing, and schools. Differences in where people live and in the neighborhood and school resources available to them are widely thought to stem from simple economic forces—especially the fact that black and Hispanic families have lower incomes than whites and Asians, which inevitably puts them at a disadvantage in the housing market.

In other research we have demonstrated that this "class interpretation" does not explain much of the locational inequality shown here (Logan 2002). Nationally, the average black family earning over $60,000 lives in a neighborhood with a higher poverty rate than the average white family earning under $30,000. In the greater Boston metropolis, there certainly are income differences across racial groups—blacks and Hispanics on average have household incomes only 55 percent to 60 percent as high as do whites. But even if we restrict our attention to the most successful households, we find huge differences in the character of neighborhoods.

The average white household in the Boston metropolis with an income over $60,000 lives in a neighborhood where the average household income is over $67,000 and 45 percent of residents have a college degree (American Communities Project, n.d.). With the same income, the average black household lives in a neighborhood with an average income of only $45,000 and only 29 percent of neighbors have a college education. The average Hispanic household in this income bracket lives in a neighborhood with an average income of $49,000 and 33 percent of neighbors have a college degree.

Even having a good job and a high income does not bring these minority households into equivalent neighborhoods. Probably differences in wealth and access to mortgage loans also play a role, though studies that also control for whether people are homeowners or renters reveal similar net racial disparities in the kinds of neighborhoods where people live (Logan, Alba, McNulty, & Fisher, 1996). There are two main reasons. One is typical of American metropolitan areas—the racial segregation experienced by black and Hispanic residents regardless of which part of the metropolis they live in. The other is unique to Boston and a few other spots in the country, like Detroit, Milwaukee, and much of upstate New York: in these places minorities have not yet gained significant access to suburbs, where the great majority of whites in the region now live.

This means that the one arena in which tremendous efforts have been made over the past several decades—the desegregation of public school systems within school districts—has scarcely affected racial inequality. Simply put, the achievements of Boston or Lynn or Cambridge, or any community that has managed to limit inequalities within its boundaries, are countermanded when the most affluent school systems where most white children go to school are largely off-limits to minority children. The only way that desegregation plans could substantially reduce the separate and unequal character of public education is if they were applied region-wide.

It also means that the longer-term solution of equalizing educational opportunity by integrating neighborhoods has made little headway, and it cannot progress more substantially until the barriers to minority suburbanization are discovered and attacked. We stress that it is not so much a question of affordability as it is race and ethnicity, based on mechanisms ranging from outright discrimination to historic color lines that people hesitate to cross. Until this does change, it is minority children who pay the highest price of the status quo as evidenced by the persistence of the academic achievement gap.

The substantive importance of regional patterns was recognized early in the history of desegregation. Plaintiffs in the case of *Milliken v. Bradley* (1974) argued that the Detroit School District could not be successfully desegregated unless all public schools in the entire metropolitan area were subject to a common desegregation order. But the Court ruled against this argument, setting a precedent that prevented most desegregation plans from extending beyond district boundaries. Although some subsequent court cases sought interdistrict remedies, especially linking central city school districts with surrounding suburbs, constitutional law has mostly been interpreted to bar such action (Hankins, 1989). There have been several voluntary interdistrict desegregation remedies, most notably in the St. Louis, Missouri, metropolitan region; however, most voluntary remedies—like court remedies—are implemented at the district level (Clotfelter, 2004; Flicker, 1990). In contrast, many Southern states have large countywide school systems that cross city-suburb boundaries, greatly increasing the reach of within-district desegregation efforts. Although there is no likelihood of countywide or metropolitan reorganization of schools in other states in the near future, there is no constitutional impediment to legislative action to mandate consolidation of the current system of local districts. Perhaps some years from now, if headway is not made to reduce educational disparities through other means, this policy option will resurface.

REFERENCES

American Communities Project. (n.d.). Spatial structures in the social sciences. Brown University. Retrieved from http://www.s4.brown.edu/S4/Projects_ACP.htm

Armor, D. J. (2002). Desegregation and academic achievement. In C. H. Rossell, D. Armor, & H. Walberg (Eds.), *School desegregation in the 21st century* (pp. 147–188). Westport, CT: Praeger.

Armor, D. J. (1995). *Forced justice: School desegregation and the law.* New York, NY: Oxford University Press.

Bankston, C., & Caldas, S. (1996). Majority African American schools and social injustice: The influence of de facto segregation on academic achievement. *Social Forces, 75*(2), 535–555.

Bankston, C., & Caldas, S. (1997). The American school dilemma: Race and scholastic performance. *Sociological Quarterly, 38*(3), 423–429.

Bifulco, R., & Ladd, H. (2006). School choice, racial segregation, and test-score gaps: Evidence from North Carolina's charter school program. *Journal of Policy Analysis and Management, 26*(1), 31–56.

Borman, K., Eitle, T., Michael, D., Eitle, D., Lee, R., Johnson, L., et al. (2004). Accountability in a post-desegregation era: The continuing significance of racial segregation in Florida's schools. *American Educational Research Journal, 41*(3), 605–631.

Brown v. Board of Education of Topeka, 347 U.S. 483 (1954).

Card, D., & Rothstein, J. (2005). *Racial segregation and the black-white test score gap* (CEPS Working Paper No. 109). Princeton, NJ: Center for Economic Policy Studies.

Chaplin, D. (2002). Estimating the impact of economic integration. In Century Foundation (Ed.), *Divided we fail: Coming together through public school choice* (pp. 87–113). New York, NY: Century Foundation Press.

Chubb, J. E., & Moe, T. M. (1990). *Politics, markets and America's schools*. Washington, DC: The Brookings Institution Press.

Clotfelter, C. T. (2004). *After Brown: The rise and retreat of school desegregation*. Princeton, NJ: Princeton University Press.

Coleman, J. S., Campbell, E., Hobson, C., McPartland, J., Mood, A., Weinfield, F. D., et al. (1966). *Equality of educational opportunity*. Washington, DC: U.S. Government Printing Office.

Crain, R. L., & Mahard, R (1978). Desegregation and black achievement: A review of the research. *Law and Contemporary Problems, 42*, 17–56.

Crain, R. L, & Mahard, R. (1983). The effect of research methodology on desegregation-achievement studies: A meta-analysis. *American Journal of Sociology, 88*(5), 839–854.

Cutler, D., & Glaeser, E. (1997). Are ghettos good or bad? *Journal of Economics, 112*(3), 827–847.

Dawkins, M., & Braddock, J. (1994). The continuing significance of desegregation: School racial composition and African American inclusion in American society. *Journal of Negro Education, 63*(3), 394–405.

Eaddy, R., Sawyer, C., Shimizu, K., McIlwain, R., Wood, S., Segal, D., et al. (2003). *Residential segregation, poverty, and racism: Obstacles to America's Great Society*. Washington, DC: Lawyers' Committee for Civil Rights Under Law.

Ellen, I. G., O'Regan, K., Schwartz, A. E., & Stiefel, L. (2002). *Racial segregation in multiethnic schools: Adding immigrants to the analysis*. New York: New York University, Wagner School of Public Service.

Flicker, B. (1990) *Justice and school systems*. Philadelphia, PA: Temple University Press.

Gamoran, A. (1996). Effects of schooling on children and families. In A. Booth and J. F. Dunn (Eds.), *Family-school links: How do they affect educational outcomes?* (pp. 107–114). Hillsdale, NJ: Erlbaum.

Grissmer, D. W., Flanagan, A., & Williamson, S. (1998). Why did the black-white test score gap narrow in the 1970s and 1980s? In C. Jencks and M. Phillips (Eds.), *The black-white test score gap* (pp. 182–228). Washington, DC: Brookings Institution Press.

Hallinan, M. T. (2001). Sociological perspectives on black-white inequalities in American schooling. *Sociology of Education, 74*, 50–70.

Hankins, G. G. (1989). Like a bridge over troubled waters: New directions and innovative voluntary approaches to inter-district school desegregation. *The Journal of Negro Education, 58*(3), 345–356.

Hauser, R., Sewell, W., & Alwin, D. (1976). High school effects on achievement. In W. Sewell, R. Hauser, & D. Featherman (Eds.), *Schooling and achievement in American society* (pp. 309–342). London, England: Academic Press.

Henderson, W. D. (2002). Demography and desegregation in the Cleveland public schools: Toward a comprehensive theory of educational failure and success. *Review of Law and Social Change, 26*(4), 460–568.

Hochschild, J., & Scovronick, N. (2003). *The American dream and the public schools*. New York, NY: Oxford University Press.

Jencks, C., & Mayer, E. (1990). The social consequences of growing up in a poor neighborhood. In L. E. Lynn & M. McGeary (Eds.), *Inner-city poverty in the United States* (pp. 111–186). Washington, DC: National Academy Press.

Jencks, C., & Phillips, M. (Eds.). (1998*). The black-white test score gap*. Washington, DC: Brookings Institution Press.

Lee, V., & Smith, J. (1997). High school size: Which works best and for whom? *Educational Evaluation and Policy Analysis, 19*(3), 205–227.

Levine, D., & Eubanks, E. (1990). Achievement disparities between minority and nonminority students in suburban schools. *Journal of Negro Education, 59*, 186–194.

Logan, J., Alba, R. D., McNulty, T., & Fisher, B. (1996). Making a place in the metropolis: Locational attainment in cities and suburbs. *Demography, 33*, 443–453.

Logan, J., Oakley, D., & Stowell, J. (2008). School segregation in metropolitan regions, 1970–2000: The impacts of policy choices on public education. *American Journal of Sociology, 113*(6), 1611–1644.

Logan, J., & Oakley, D. (2004). *The continuing legacy of the Brown decision: Court action and school segregation, 1960–2000*. Report of the Lewis Mumford Center, January 28. Retrieved from http://mumford.cas.albany.edu/schoolsegregation/reports/brown01.htm

Logan, J. (2002). *Choosing segregation: Racial imbalance in American public schools, 1990–2000*. Report of the Lewis Mumford Center, March 29. Retrieved from http://mumford1.dyndns.org/cen2000/SchoolPop/SPReport/page1.html

Longshore, D., & Prager, J. (1985). The impact of school desegregation: A situational analysis. *American Review of Sociology, 11*, 75–91.

Maruyama, G. (2003). Disparities in educational opportunities and outcomes: What do we know and what can we do? *Journal of Social Issues, 59*(3), 653–676.

McPartland, J. (1969). The relative influence of school desegregation and of classroom desegregation on the academic achievement of ninth grade Negro students. *Journal of Social Issues, 25*, 93–103.

Mercer, J., & Scout, T. (1974). *The relationship between school desegregation and changes in the racial composition of California school districts 1963–73*. Unpublished paper, University of California, Riverside.

Mickelson, R. (2003). When are racial disparities in education the result of racial discrimination? A social science perspective. *Teachers College Record, 105*(6), 1052–1086.

Milliken v. Bradley, 418 U.S. 717. (1974).

National Center for Education Statistics. (n.d.). Common Core of Data, 1990 & 2000. Retrieved from http://nces.ed.gov/ccd/

Orfield, G., & Eaton, S. (1996). *Dismantling desegregation: The quiet reversal of Brown v. Board of Education.* New York, NY: New Press.

Orfield, G., & Lee C. (2005). *Why segregation matters: Poverty and educational inequality.* Cambridge, MA: The Civil Rights Project at Harvard University.

Plessy v. Ferguson, 163 U.S. 537 (1896).

Rivkin, S. G. (2000). School desegregation, academic attainment, and earnings. *Journal of Human Resources, 35*(2), 333–346.

Roscigno, V. J., & Ainsworth-Darnell, J. (1999). Race, cultural capital, and education resources: Persistent inequalities and achievement returns. *Sociology of Education, 72*(3), 158–178.

Rumberger, R., & Palardy, G. (2005). Does segregation still matter? The impact of student composition on academic achievement in high school. *Teachers College Record, 107*(9), 1999–2045.

Rumberger, R., & Williams, J. (1992). The impact of racial and ethnic segregation on the achievement gap in California high schools. *Educational Evaluation and Policy Analysis, 14*(4), 377–396.

Saporito, S., & Sohoni, D. (2007). Mapping educational inequality: Concentrations of poverty among poor and minority students in public schools. *Social Forces, 85*(3), 1227–1253.

Schofield, J. (1995). Review of research on school desegregation's impact on elementary and secondary school students. In J. A. Banks & C. A. McGee-Banks (Eds.), *Handbook of research on multicultural education* (pp. 597–617). New York, NY: Macmillan.

School Matters Project of the National Education Data Partnership. (2004). School Data Direct. Retrieved from http:www.schooldatadirect.org

Spady, W. (1973). The impact of school resources on students. In F. Kerlinge (Ed.), *Review of research in education* (pp. 135–177). Itasca, IL: F.E. Peacock.

Stiefel, L., Schwartz, A., & Chellman, C. (2008). So many children left behind: Segregation and the impact of subgroup reporting in No Child Left Behind on the racial test score gap. *Educational Policy, 21*, 527–541.

St. John, N., & Hoyt, N. (1975). *School desegregation: Outcomes for children.* New York, NY: Wiley.

Swanson, C. (2008). *Cities in crisis: A special analytic report on high school graduation.* Washington, DC: Editorial Projects in Education Research Center.

United States Census Bureau. (2000). Summary files 1 & 3. Retrieved from http://www.census.gov/census_2000/datasets

United States Census Bureau. (1990). Summary tape files 1 & 3. Retrieved from http://www.census.gov/main/www/cen1990.html

Wells, A., & Crain, R. (1994). Perpetuation theory and the long-term effects of school desegregation. *Review of Educational Research, 64*, 531–555.

Whitman, M. (1998). *The irony of desegregation law: 1955–1995.* Princeton, NJ: Markus Wiener Publishers.

7

Still Separate, Still Unequal, But Not Always So "Suburban"

The Changing Nature of Suburban School Districts in the New York Metropolitan Area

Amy Stuart Wells, Douglas Ready, Jacquelyn Duran, Courtney Grzesikowski, Kathryn Hill, Allison Roda, Miya Warner, and Terrenda White

Woven throughout the history of the United States is a narrative of human movement. The story of this country, we argue, is a tale of the constant flow of people across geographic spaces—both voluntary and forced immigrations, migrations, and the settlements of villages, city neighborhoods, and suburban communities. Beginning with Native Americans' ancestors who traversed the Bering Straight, "movement" has been a central, identifying theme of this nation.

The flow of several waves of European immigrants onto colonial shores and across the plains and the haulage of millions of Africans via the slave trade redefined the United States demographically and geopolitically, as did the mass migration of freed African Americans from the South to the North and from the farms to the cities in the 20th century. The post–World War II construction of suburbia enabled the European immigrants and their decedents to migrate from the cities to the suburbs en masse, changing not only the character of suburbia but also the cities and ethnic enclaves they left behind. As if choreographed by the federal government, local zoning laws and real estate markets, this flow of whites to the suburbs was synchronized with the arrival of African American migrants into specific and highly contained city neighborhoods.

But even the resulting racially segregated pattern of "vanilla suburbs" and "chocolate cities" that seemed fairly stable by the late 1970s across most metro areas was subject to change. Beginning in the late 1960s, new waves of immigrants, primarily from Latin America and Asia, entered the urban neighborhoods abandoned by their European immigrant predecessors. By the 1980s, growing numbers of African Americans had begun migrating to the suburbs. And, in the last decade, more Latino and Asian immigrants have chosen suburban communities as their port of entry to the United States. At the same time, whites—particularly affluent and well-educated professionals—are migrating back into cosmopolitan and gentrified city neighborhoods, opting out of increasingly diverse suburbs.

Within these patterns of movement and change, human agency—manifested in the desire or need to leave one place and seek another—has been shaped, contorted, and compromised by social structures and powerful norms that create, maintain, and legitimize deep-seated inequalities in our society. This intersection between migration patterns and their spatial outcomes—for example, the dispersal of people across separate and often unequal places according to variables such as race/ethnicity, class, and social status—is central to our work. The complicated intermingling of "coercion" and "choice"—and the distinction between them in terms of who has real, meaningful choices and who does not—shape these migration patterns and the consequences of those moves (or lack thereof) for them and for the rest of society. Furthermore, the divergent habits of people moving into and out of suburbia—their schemes of perception about where they "fit" within a status hierarchy created by racially and socioeconomically stratified society—foster a clear understanding of the "multiple markets" for homes that are in some cases dictated more strongly by school district boundaries than by the characteristics of available housing units.

Our "Metro Migration" research project focuses on the most recent iterations of this long history of human movement, namely increasingly racially, ethnically, and socioeconomically diverse suburbs and gentrifying urban neighborhoods within four distinct metropolitan areas. These current migration patterns intersect with physical and symbolic boundary lines that divide space and opportunities. Although some of these boundaries and their symbolic meanings change over time—often because of the movement of people within and between them—they remain powerful dividing lines that circumscribe mobility and chance. Exactly how such boundaries have become so powerful in hording and denying opportunities in a society dedicated to an ethos of freedom, liberty, and individual choice is what we have set out to learn. When boundaries divide people not just in terms of which public utilities they use or the value of the property they own, but also the quality and reputation of the public schools their children attend, they have long-term implications for the health and well-being of the society as a whole. Thus, they must be more thoroughly interrogated and understood.

In this chapter, we present the framework and overview of our five-year study designed to examine these issues, followed by a discussion of the emerging themes and findings thus far, in this early stage of data collection and analysis on Long Island, New York.

21ST-CENTURY METRO MIGRATIONS AND THE PUBLIC SCHOOLS

Within the context of our national history of human movement, recent migration patterns are more demographically and spatially complex, with growing income inequality and large numbers of immigrants—both affluent and poor—adding several layers of diversity to the mix. Thus, our increasingly diverse and divided population is both shaped by and shapes local contexts, particularly the physical and legal boundary lines that define associations, resources, and life chances in both urban and suburban settings.

The interaction between the movement of people with different degrees of power and status across metropolitan spaces and the boundary lines that divide them and their access to opportunities is the central focus of this study. Place matters, we know, because where people live relates to so many of their life chances (Drier, Mollenkopf, & Swanstrom, 2004). Public schools, with their physical grounding within communities and boundary lines, are an increasingly important place-based resource that transmits differential opportunities across geographies and generations. We argue, therefore, that understanding the role that public schools, as geographically grounded institutions with strict boundaries, play within recent metro migration patterns is central to explaining ongoing racial/ethnic and social-class segregation.

Thus, we are conducting a study of both suburban and urban public school boundaries in four metropolitan areas. As families migrate to new communities across urban and suburban lines, our research project is designed to examine the relationship between migration patterns, school district boundaries, and patterns of segregation by race/ethnicity and social class. In other words, we want to understand the role of school district boundaries—their prevalence or scarcity—in the process of sorting people in terms of status and privilege. In what ways, then, are status and privilege maintained and reproduced as a result of this sorting and its consequences?

Postwar Metro Migrations

Since the end of World War II, U.S. metropolitan areas have changed dramatically as millions of residents have traversed urban and suburban boundaries. These post-war periods of movement resulted in considerable shifts in the demographic compositions of both cities and suburbs. The first phase was characterized by the rise of suburbia with much assistance from supportive federal policies. This post–World War II phase is characterized by the rapid development of suburban neighborhoods comprised of multiple single-family homes and occupied by mostly white residents fleeing urban centers. Whites' abandonment of cities was both a cause and effect of a common understanding that had developed by the 1960s—cities were undesirable and suburbs were places where those with resources and options fled. These images had strong racial overtones, as the skin color of those who lived across these separate and often unequal spaces became a central distinction.

Indeed, by 1980 many cities had become predominantly African American and/or Latino, with 67 percent of blacks and 50 percent of Latinos, but only 24 percent of whites, living in central cities (Harrigan & Vogel, 1993; U.S. Census Bureau, 1980).[1] At that time, only 23 percent of blacks lived in the suburbs. Furthermore, the black suburbanization rates were even lower—12–15 percent—in the Northeast (Harrigan & Vogel, 1993).[2]

After 1980, however, metro migrations included increasing minority suburbanization. During this time, growing numbers of middle-class black, Latino, and Asian families left urban communities for the suburbs, seeking the lifestyle advantages whites had sought decades earlier—larger homes with yards, lower crime rates, less noise and dirt, and, the perception of better public schools. By 2000, nearly 40 percent of blacks were living in the suburbs. Suburbanization has also increased among immigrant families—mostly Latino and Asian—and by 2000, 48 percent of immigrants were residing in suburban areas (Frey, 2001).

At the same time that blacks and Latinos were migrating to suburbs, a trickle of upper-middle-class and more affluent whites began moving back into select urban communities (Lees, Slayter, & Wyly, 2008). Much like the postwar era when whites left cities as more blacks poured in from the farms, we conceptualize the current era as a new "trading spaces" phase. Lured by the convenience, excitement, and culture of city living, increasing numbers of highly skilled whites in so-called "global cities" such as New York and San Francisco have opted out of long daily commutes by living in nearby urban, and often gentrified, neighborhoods (Sassen, 2006). City life, once considered by most whites as dangerous, dirty, and crowded, is now increasingly associated with excitement, fun, and convenience (see Leinberger, 2008). This 21st-century urban aristocracy—or "gentry"—is driving up home prices in select city neighborhoods, sometimes pushing lower-income residents—mostly black and Latino—into outlying urban and inner-ring suburban communities (Freeman, 2006). And so the cycle of segregation and resegregation continues, even as the occupied spaces change.

While whites began moving back into so-called gentrified areas of cities as early as the late 1970s, the pace of gentrification accelerated in the early 2000s (Lees et al., 2008). The New York City metropolitan area represents a good example: the percentage of whites in Manhattan increased 28 percent between 2000 and 2006, while it declined in nearby suburban Nassau County. During the same six-year period, the Hispanic population declined by 2 percent in Manhattan, but increased 20 percent in Nassau.

Overall, these fluctuating metropolitan characteristics suggest that traditional paradigms of "cities" versus "suburbs" are rapidly evolving in ways we cannot yet completely comprehend. The advent of the trading places phenomenon, in particular, complicates our 50-year-old notions of clearly delineated urban-suburban boundaries—in terms of not only demographics but also economic transformations. Thus, common categorizations of cities versus suburbs—one poor, with high-rise housing projects and dire need, and the other middle-class (or better) with single-family homes and peaceful neighborhoods—may have outlived its usefulness. Indeed, it is increasingly clear that contemporary urban and suburban communities *each* contain pockets of poverty and affluence, often functioning as racially and ethnically distinct spaces. In fact, by 2005, one million more poor people lived in suburban compared to urban areas (Berube & Kneebone, 2006).

Journalists and researchers now report on the growing number of distressed suburbs that are coming to resemble poor inner-city communities. For instance, Lucy and Phillips (2003) write that from 1990 to 2000, while some newly developing suburbs experienced rapid growth in people and jobs, "many older suburbs experienced central-city-like challenges, including an aging infrastructure, inadequate housing stock, deteriorating schools and commercial corridors—and population decline" (p. 117). Leinberger's 2008 article highlighted the impact of the subprime mortgage crisis on suburban communities experiencing high rates of foreclosures. But the author is quick to note that declining suburban neighborhoods did not begin with the mortgage crisis, and will not end with it as more people with high incomes move into the cities.

Thus, while much has changed in both urban and suburban communities since World War II, much has also stayed the same. In fact, the most consistent finding to emerge from research across these three phases of metropolitan change is that segregation along racial/ethnic lines has remained fairly constant in both urban and suburban contexts. In fact, there is strong evidence that African Americans, in particular, remain highly segregated in both urban *and* suburban contexts. Numerous authors have noted that black suburbanization is rarely accompanied by racial integration, and that even middle-class African Americans remain highly segregated (Adelman, 2005).

It is true that in the midst of migrations within local sites, segregation usually lessens to some degree when blacks or Latinos first move into predominantly white suburbs or whites begin to inhabit mostly black or Latino gentrifying urban neighborhoods. But over time, these neighborhoods, more often than not, become resegregated as whites depart economically declining suburbs and minorities become priced out of gentrified urban spaces (Farley & Squires, 2005; Freeman, 2006; Sethi & Somanathan, 2004).

Meanwhile, the rapid increase in income inequality in the United States appears to be accompanied by a related increase in residential segregation by class. According to Reardon and Bischoff (2009), both income inequality and income segregation grew substantially in the decades from 1970 to 2000, the result of spatial concentration of the most affluent residents.

The Role of Public Schools

Thus, migration patterns have changed and even reversed while patterns of segregation continue and worsen in some instances. A critical question remains unanswered by the existing research on these population shifts: *What role do public schools play in movers' decisions about ongoing segregation and stratification across space and boundaries?*

While a growing number of social scientists are attempting to explain these urban-suburban changes in terms of demographics, segregation patterns, housing, and labor markets, there has been little systematic study of the impact of public schools—their reputations, resources, and enrollments in particular—on the movement of families across urban and suburban school district boundary lines. Nor do we really understand how racial/ethnic, socioeconomic, and political shifts across urban-suburban lines are impacting educators and their ability and/or willingness to serve rapidly changing student populations. If, as Leinberger (2008) suggests, the impact of these recent migration patterns on cities and suburbs is likely to be profound, no less can be said of their potential impact on public schools.

Furthermore, we do know that, as with residential segregation, segregation in public schools appears to persist across urban and suburban contexts. For instance, Reardon and Yun's (2001, 2008) work demonstrates that suburban public schools tend to become more racially diverse initially as African Americans or Latinos move into formerly white suburban enclaves. But over time, whites flee these public schools, as they did in urban school districts in the 1950s, 1960s, and 1970s, leaving pockets of separate and unequal black and brown schools and whole school districts in suburbia. We also know that racial segregation in public schools overall is on the rise (Orfield & Lee, 2007), suggesting that the movement of people over city-suburban boundaries is not leading to more integrated educational experiences for most students.

We also know that suburban school districts tend to be smaller because suburban counties—especially in the North and Midwest—are far more fragmented or divided into tiny jurisdictions (Bischoff, 2008). This means that school segregation in suburbia is, on average, more insidious than it was in the large urban school districts in the 1950s and 1960s because any effort to "desegregate" students would require crossing legal, impenetrable, and highly symbolic school district boundaries (see Bischoff, 2008).

Research also strongly suggests that race/ethnicity continues to play a central role in how parents choose schools for their children—whether they are purchasing or renting a new home in a new school district or choosing among schools of choice where they already live—and that school choice or housing policies that do not take race/ethnicity into account within and across schools may exacerbate segregation and stratification (see Mickelson, Bottia, & Southworth, 2008; Ready & Lee, 2008; Wells & Roda, 2008, for reviews).

Furthermore, we know from recent research on adult graduates of desegregated schools that many parents believe the educational stakes are much higher today than they were in public schools 30 to 40 years ago, which, in turn, influences the school choices they make for their own children (see Wells, Holme, Revilla, & Atanda, 2009). In fact, Wells et al. (2009) learned that the school accountability measures put in place since these adults graduated from high school in 1980, along with the increasing inequality in the U.S. society since that time, had made these alumni of desegregated schools far more anxious about what to do with their own children. In other words, the broader societal changes and educational policy development since they were in school in the 1960s and 1970s led many of the graduates to focus on narrow measures of school quality, namely average standardized test scores by school or district, and to weigh these achievement indicators against school diversity (also see Wells & Holme, 2006).

In addition, there is a growing body of work documenting the rising anxiety levels of middle- and upper-middle-class white parents in particular when it comes to their children's education. Middle- and upper-middle-class white families are increasingly stressed about how competitive their children are in the race to the top of the increasingly stratified social hierarchy (see Demerath, 2009; Lareau, 2003; Wells and Roda, 2008). Such anxiety, we argue, must contribute to the parents' need to have their children enrolled in schools—public or private—with the most competitive advantage. This larger context of schooling in the early 21st century surely shapes the residential choices of these more affluent, high-status parents as they move or stay put within or between metropolitan areas. To better explain this relationship between parental anxiety and family migration patterns by race and income across school district boundary lines, we look to the literature on the symbolic and tangible meanings of space, place, and boundaries.

Space and Bounded Migration Patterns

We know that the outcome of metro migrations is an ongoing *cycle of segregation and inequality* by race/ethnicity, class, and status. We also know that there is a strong relationship between this segregation and the degree of fragmentation in a given context (Bishoff, 2008). The next logical empirical step, therefore, is to better understand the relationship between the local municipal boundaries that define fragmentation and a deeper understanding of how people of different racial/ethnic and social class backgrounds end up where they do in relation to these boundaries, as well as the consequences of those patterns. Such an analysis is particularly important in the field of education where the consequences of the boundaries are both tangible and intangible.

The perceived "quality" of public schools—at least as measured by test score data and, too often, the race and class of the students who attend—can strongly influence "place," especially who chooses to live there, the value of the property, and the degree of public and private investment in the community. As Tickamyer (2000) notes, "Relations of power, structures of inequality, and practices of domination and subordination are embedded in spatial design and relations" (p. 806).

In this way, the meaning that people ascribe to a school and its local community affects both in a complicated and iterative way. Understandings of the places where schools are located and how those places are changing certainly guide parents' behavior about where to live and thus where to send their children to school (Gotham, 2003), but we know little about how this process works or the role that schools themselves can or cannot play.

The cycle begins with the separate and unequal tangible, material conditions across existing boundary lines. These tangible factors, which include everything from facilities to supplies and equipment to teacher credentials—become the "proof" or the "evidence" that legitimizes several critical intangible factors—for example, the reputations, status, and prestige of the districts. In this way, the physical, legal, or social boundaries become the "symbolic boundaries"—symbols of "good" communities, schools, and residents (people who work hard, pay high taxes, and have the right values and priorities). At the same time that both the physical and symbolic boundaries create deep racial divides, they are talked about in a race-neutral, "color-blind" manner that explains away the stark racial/ethnic segregation across them (Lamont, 2007; Lewis, 2003).

We argue, however, that not only were the physical legal boundaries of municipalities and school districts in highly fragmented suburban counties constructed in a racialized manner, but they are maintained in a racialized manner through policies, meanings, and discourses that are on the surface color-blind or post-racial (powell, 2007). But the symbolic boundaries, embedded within and supported by the physical boundaries, are actually manifestations of the intricate relationship between race, class, and social status in the United States. And, in an era of increasing inequality, maintaining high social status is of utmost importance to anxious white, middle- and upper-middle-class parents. Boundaries—both physical and symbolic—shape and protect their association with each other and their disassociation with people of color and the poor. These associations are critical to status maintenance—in terms of their symbolic values of "who they are" and the tangible resources/factors they accumulate and maintain in separate spaces. The significance of these associations/disassociations shape the processes of boundary maintenance despite expressions of dismay and longing related to the lack of "diversity" in their all-white communities and schools, sometimes referred to as their "bubbles" (Gutmann, 1998; Wilkinson & Pickett, 2010; Wells & Roda, 2008).

By studying the meso level of school segregation, namely municipal and school district boundary lines, we seek to understand the multiple ways in which the structures—that is, the physical legal boundaries between districts and students' educational opportunities—are cyclically created, re-created, and legitimized. In a mixed-methods study such as ours, we can more carefully examine the places where the quantitative and qualitative data meet—at the meso level. Thus, we rely on the quantitative data—census data, school demographic and outcome data, and so on—to illustrate *what* the between-district segregation looks like. We also rely upon qualitative data, which explore *how* the boundaries circumscribe resources and access as well as the reputation, status, prestige, and symbols of the different school districts. If we are to truly understand the relationship between separateness and inequality, we need to more fully understand and interrogate the dividing lines—how they are created, codified, maintained, legitimized, and re-created.

THE RELATIONSHIP BETWEEN THE SOCIAL AND SYMBOLIC, THE TANGIBLE AND INTANGIBLE

The data we are collecting for our study of metro migrations at the county and school-district level illustrate both the "symbolic" and "social or physical" meanings of school boundaries. As Lamont and Molnár (2002) note, *symbolic* boundaries are conceptual distinctions made by social actors: "They are an essential medium through which people acquire status and monopolize resources" (p. 2). *Social* boundaries—or what we often refer to as physical or legal boundaries, on the other hand, are objectified forms of social differences manifested in unequal access to and distribution of material and nonmaterial resources. They also mold stable "patterns of association" (p. 2).

One underlying but often unexamined theme that runs throughout the literature on segregation and inequality is the role of symbolic resources (e.g., conceptual distinctions, interpretive strategies, cultural traditions) in creating, maintaining, or even contesting institutionalized social differences (e.g., class, gender, race, territorial inequality). In order to capture this process, we think it is useful to introduce a distinction between symbolic and social boundaries. *Symbolic boundaries* are conceptual distinctions, social constructions used to categorize objects, people, practices, and even time and space. They are tools individuals and groups struggle over and come to agree upon in definitions of reality. Documenting how people make sense of them allows us to capture the dynamic dimensions of social relations, as groups compete in the production, diffusion, and institutionalization of alternative systems and principles of classifications. Symbolic boundaries also separate people into groups and generate feelings of similarity and group membership (Epstein, 1992, p. 232). They are an essential medium through which people acquire status and monopolize resources.

Social boundaries—or physical/legal boundaries—are objectified forms of social differences manifested in unequal access to and unequal distribution of resources (material and nonmaterial) and social opportunities. They are also revealed in stable behavioral patterns of association, as manifested in connubiality and commensality. Only when symbolic boundaries are widely agreed upon can they take on a constraining character and pattern social interaction in important ways. Moreover, only then can they become social boundaries: that is, translate, for instance, into identifiable patterns of social exclusion or class and racial segregation (Lamont and Molnár, 2002; Massey & Denton, 1993; Stinchcombe, 1995; Logan, Alba, McNulty, & Fisher, 1996).

In this way, social boundaries are synonymous with "borders," which "provide most individuals with a concrete, local, and powerful experience of the state" (Lamont & Molnár, 2002, p. 183). Whether state-imposed segregation or state-supported school district boundary lines that divide students by race, class, and opportunities, *social boundaries have legal, physical realities that shape not only opportunities but the very meaning of schooling and education.*

Thus, symbolic and social boundaries should be viewed as equally real: the former exist at the intersubjective level, whereas the latter manifest themselves as groupings of individuals. At the causal level, symbolic boundaries can be thought of as a necessary but insufficient condition for the existence of social boundaries (Lamont & Fournier, 1992).

We argue that social boundaries serve to perpetuate unequal material conditions across district lines and thus help to legitimize the symbolic boundaries woven into the identities of "place" within the field of education. These symbolic boundaries formulate many *intangible* factors, including the reputation and status of an institution, which in turn shape and constrain the distribution of *tangible* factors such as material resources, teacher quality, and curricular offerings. In an iterative manner, therefore, these symbolic boundaries also legitimize and become social boundaries, as those with power and status in the society have the means to disassociate with people who lack status and honor (Lamont & Fournier, 1992).

In the U.S. Supreme Court's ruling in the landmark *Brown v. Board of Education* case and several pre-Brown cases addressing racial segregation in higher education, the justices noted that the harms of school segregation by race were not merely related to the "tangible" factors such as facilities, resources, supplies, and so on. The Court noted that "intangible" factors—for example, the reputation and status of an institution in society—matter a great deal as well. The *tangible* or material factors that are constrained by a school district's social boundaries have been highlighted in school finance literature in particular. They separate those districts that have a strong tax base with affluent residents and/or commercial property from the districts that are property poor and have low-income residents. The consequences of these boundaries are measured primarily in terms of each school district's ability to generate local funding and the disparities across districts in their ability to do so. For instance, they include discussions of local property values; property taxes; per-pupil funding; and specific resources such as books, buildings, technology, teachers' salaries, or athletic equipment.

But school district boundaries also constrain and shape *associations* between people. Thus, they constrain student access to certain schools, resources, opportunities, and peers, but they also constrain student access to school reputations and status—or intangible factors. According to Lamont and Molnár (2002), "it is often posited that identification generally proceeds through exclusion and that boundaries are salient and mostly have to do with demarcation" (p. 186).

These issues of association relate to differently valued cultural capital, such as lifestyle, language, education, race or religion—cultural indicators we use to identify those within our status group and thus those with whom we wish to associate (Lamont, 2007). As a result, such characteristics become the mechanisms that produce boundaries—both legal and symbolic—between status groups of race, class, gender, and so forth. These associations and their relationships to intangible factors in the field of education are part of the process by which schools serving students of color from poor families become labeled "bad" schools despite the teaching and learning taking place within them.

In the case of school district boundaries, these distinctions are clearest on the tail ends of the distribution of privileged versus nonprivileged districts, with the highly affluent, predominantly white districts on one end and the impoverished, mostly black and Latino school districts on the other. The contrast between such districts and their stability over time make them important sites to study in our effort to understand the significance of boundaries and how they are maintained.

Meanwhile the districts in the middle—those that are more diverse, whether they are stable or not—are the sites where symbolic and social boundaries are contested and often recreated on a smaller scale across schools and classrooms. These racially and ethnically diverse school districts are the places where the racial boundaries are both more vulnerable and where they are actively being sustained or remade, reinforced or legitimized.

Our research examines those districts in the middle-to-higher-end of the distribution in terms of test scores and other educational outcomes as well as the social class of their residents. Several of these districts are in a state of flux, as older white residents move out and younger families of varied racial/ethnic and country-of-origin backgrounds move in to take their places. What is most interesting about these districts is that "on paper" (or actually "online"), their outcome data are not that disparate, but their reputations and social status are strikingly different—a factor that appears thus far to have far more to do with the race/ethnicity and socioeconomic status of the families who live there. By designing a study that "controls" on the easy-to-access outcome data of schools, we are able to look more closely at the role that race and class play in the school and district choice process amid rapid migrations across school district boundaries.

METRO MIGRATIONS RESEARCH DESIGN AND OVERVIEW

Using the framework described above, we have designed a multisite, mixed-methods study of school district boundaries within four metropolitan areas that are experiencing some degree of migration and change across urban-suburban contexts. In sampling these metro areas, we sought cities and suburbs that differ fundamentally in terms of their (1) degree of fragmentation, (2) racial/ethnic composition and complexity, (3) geographic/regional and political orientation, and (4) economic positioning in a global economy. Thus, the four metro areas we are planning to study are New York, San Francisco, Detroit, and Louisville.

Our unit of analysis and thus focal point for this large-scale research project is *the relationship between metro migration patterns, racial/ethnic and socioeconomic segregation, school district boundaries, and movers' understandings of what those boundaries mean.*

Research Questions to Frame Our Work

We are further guided in our work by a set of research questions that speak to both the quantitative and qualitative nature of our research:

1. Within each of the four metropolitan areas in our study, what are the historic and current urban/suburban migration patterns and their relationship to physical/legal boundary lines—municipal or school district boundaries—and the degree of fragmentation? What factors shape the relationship between migration patterns, segregation—both racial/ethnic and socioeconomic—and boundary lines? Has that relationship changed over time? How does residential change or stability relate to race, class, school district boundary lines, and housing prices?

2. What role do public schools—the construction of their boundary lines, their tangible resources, public perception of their quality (or intangible factors), their racial and so-cial-class makeup, and so on—play in the demographic shifts occurring across urban-suburban contexts in many metropolitan areas today? Why are some school districts experiencing more demographic changes than others?

   A. How do public school educators and district officials respond (or not) to demo-graphic changes within their district?

   B. How do parents of preschool and school-age children make choices about where they live in relationship to public school district boundaries?

In order to answer these unasked questions, we are looking across urban and suburban counties within four U.S. metro areas, examining the political, social, and demographic context of public schools and the role their boundaries play in these changes. This larger context of change, explored through the first question, therefore, leads us to the second re-search question and its two critical sub-questions noted above about the role and decisions of educators and families within the metro migration process.

Four Distinct Metro Areas

1. New York City and Nassau County
2. San Francisco and San Mateo County
3. Detroit and Wayne County
4. Louisville and Jefferson County

The four metro areas—New York, San Francisco, Detroit, and Louisville—we have chosen to study differ in terms of key characteristics that relate to our research questions and unit of analysis. Most importantly for this study, these metro areas differ in terms of their degree of suburban _fragmentation_—with New York and its adjacent Nassau County on the highly fragmented end of the spectrum and Louisville, with its single, urban-suburban school dis-trict on the other. Nassau County is home to 56 school districts; San Mateo County, just south of San Francisco, has a total of 25. Meanwhile, Wayne County outside of Detroit houses 34 school districts, and Louisville has one large urban-suburban school system. As is illustrated in Table 7.1, each of these four metro areas differs in important ways on these measures of fragmentation, particularly when it comes to public school districts.

These four metro areas also differ demographically—for example, in their racial/ethnic composition, their income distribution, and their immigrant populations. New York and

Table 7.1. Fragmentation Sampling Characteristics of Four Metro Areas

Suburban County	# of School Districts	Land Area	Average Land Area of District	Public School Enrollment 2000	Average Enrollment per District (2000)
Nassau County	56	287 sq mi	5.1 sq mi	218,725	3,905
San Mateo County	23	449 sq mi	19.5 sq mi	99,220	4,314
Wayne County*	33	475 sq mi	14.4 sq mi	190,700	5,779
Jefferson County/ Louisville	1	385 sq mi	385 sq mi	100,005	100,005

*Does not include Detroit

San Francisco are much more racially/ethnically complex than Detroit and Louisville, but they also differ from each in terms of the number of African Americans and the ethnic mix and percentage of their Asian and Latino residents. For instance, within these two global cities, nearly 32 percent of San Franciscans are Asian, but only about 10 percent of New Yorkers are. Meanwhile, nearly 30 percent of New Yorkers are African American, compared to less than 7 percent of San Franciscans. New York also has a higher percentage of Latinos—about 30 percent compared to about 14 percent of San Franciscans—most of whom are Puerto Rican or Dominican and not Mexican.

The suburban counties we chose to study within each of these metro areas also differ in terms of their overall demographics, but each shares a border with their nearby city. And, with the exception of Jefferson County, which is part of the city-suburban school district, they all house an array of public school districts that vary in terms of their racial/ethnic makeup and student outcome data.

Furthermore, these four metro areas are also distinct geographically, regionally, and politically. Even though Detroit and Louisville are both in the middle of the country, they have distinct north-south histories and legacies, particularly when it comes to school desegregation. These distinctions in school desegregation histories are underscored by the divergent local responses to the U.S. Supreme Court rulings related to these two metro areas. For instance, the Detroit metro area is the site of the 1974 *Milliken v. Bradley* Supreme Court ruling that made interdistrict school desegregation all but impossible, whereas Louisville, with its less fragmented, countywide educational system, was the site of one of the within-district voluntary school desegregation cases involved in the U.S. Supreme Court's *Parents Involved in Community Schools (PICS)* decision of 2007. In this more recent PICS decision, the Supreme Court issued a complicated ruling that was more opposed to than supportive of school desegregation policies. Thus, both of these metro areas are sites of critical and problematic Supreme Court rulings regarding race and education, but their leaders' responses to these rulings differed radically. In Detroit, the Milliken decision marked the end of efforts to desegregate public schools in the city or the suburbs. In Louisville, on the other hand, local leaders accepted the legal setback embodied in the Court's *PICS* ruling and worked together to devise a legally acceptable plan that would avert the creation or perpetuation of racially isolated public schools.

Related to these geographic distinctions, therefore, are important economic/labor market distinctions that would affect the migration and immigration trends. For instance, at the center of two of these metro areas are "global cities"—New York and San Francisco—that are experiencing a rapid degree of gentrification and attracting white residents back into urban neighborhoods as growing numbers of blacks and Latinos move to the suburbs (Sassen, 2006).

Detroit, meanwhile, is a declining industrial Midwestern city surrounded by a mix of small, poor, and affluent suburban communities and school districts. The fourth metro area, Louisville, Kentucky, is centered on neither a global city nor a dying industrial city, although it has historically been a manufacturing hub. More recently, Louisville has attracted and retained major service economy corporations, allowing its economy to remain relatively strong compared to other Midwestern cities such as Detroit.

Each city, suburban county, district, and school within these metro areas will constitute an embedded case, with the districts embedded in the counties and the schools within the counties *and* districts. Such a design allows for us to examine themes of segregation, change, and inequality within and across contexts. Our data collection entails two levels of analysis—the metro and county level of data collection and analysis and the local district level data—that allow us to examine suburban and urban schools from the macro and micro perspectives, embedded in different spaces within the same metro areas. Thus, much of our quantitative analysis is conducted at the county level examining demographic and outcome data across the school districts. We have also conducted county level interviews, but the bulk of our qualitative data collection will focus on how people make sense of school districts and their boundaries.

Thus far, aside from historical case reports we have written on each of the four metro areas, most of our data collection has focused on Nassau County, New York, where we have conducted more than 125 interviews. In 2008, we began to study five school districts in Nassau County for a report that a local foundation was publishing on public schools on Long Island. We considered that preliminary investigation to be a pilot study for the larger project. Since we published a policy report from the pilot study in fall 2009, we have refocused our efforts with a better sense of how to examine the issues we are trying to understand. By early in 2010 we had moved forward with our data collection of six Nassau County school districts (only one of which was part of our original pilot study). The remainder of this chapter discusses the themes to emerge from both the pilot study and our more recent data collection.

EMERGING THEMES/FINDINGS FROM NASSAU COUNTY, NEW YORK

We know from existing research and our own analysis of data that Nassau County, New York (see Map 7.1 for a visual image), is one of the most fragmented and racially and socioeconomically segregated counties in the United States (Bischoff, 2008; Ready, Wells, Warner, & Grzesikowski, 2010). The question is, of course, what is the relationship between the educational and residential segregation that defines Nassau County and its political fragmentation into several local governments and school districts? A macro-analysis of fragmentation and segregation suggests that the relationship between the two is very strong (see Bischoff, 2008). Our early findings in Nassau suggest that fragmentation of Nassau County into many municipal and educational jurisdictions has been critical to the process of building and maintaining racial and, increasingly, socioeconomic segregation there.

The historical process by which this fragmentation occurred is still unfolding in our research and analysis. Still, the pieces of the story that we have suggest that, more often than not, the push to build multiple boundaries—boundaries between multiple towns, villages, hamlets, and school districts in this relatively small county (220 square miles)—was driven by the efforts of those with economic and political power to exclude themselves and disassociate from those who had less. Furthermore, the rationale for maintaining these dividing lines or boundaries is often grounded in the distinctions between people and property values across these spatial entities, especially school districts.

The seeds of fragmentation on Long Island were planted long before the first phase of postwar suburbanization began. By the late 1800s some of the wealthiest men in the United States, including J. P. Morgan, William Randolph Hearst, Russell Sage, and Vincent Astor, had erected large estates on Long Island's North Shore—also known as the "Gold Coast." According to one account, although these tycoons also built summer homes in places like Newport, Rhode Island, and Bar Harbor, Maine, their Long Island estates were ideal for the spring and fall seasons and many winter weekends because the rolling and wooded landscape of the island's North Shore was seen as ideal for "golf courses, polo grounds, boating, and bridal paths" (Baxandall & Ewen, 2001, p. 5). These palatial estates required a large labor force, including butlers, chauffeurs, gardeners, horse trainers, dog trainers,

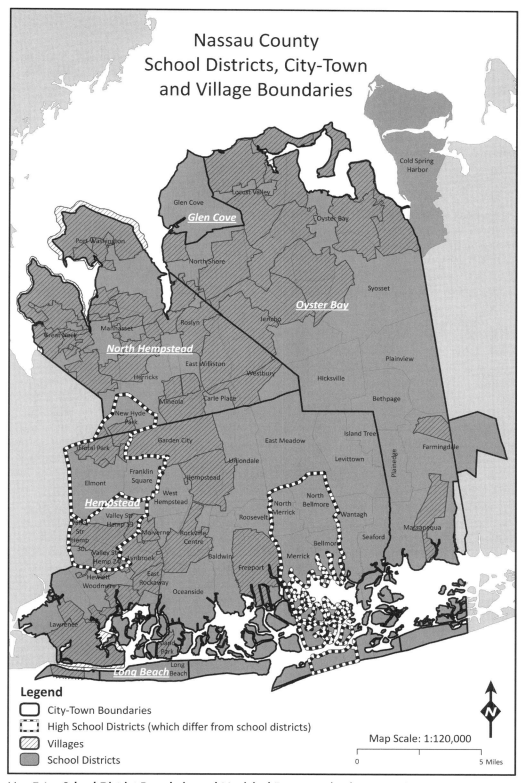

Nassau County
School Districts, City-Town and Village Boundaries

Cold Spring Harbor

Glen Cove

Glen Cove

Locust Valley

Oyster Bay

North Shore

Syosset

Oyster Bay

Port Washington

Manhasset

Roslyn

Jericho

Great Neck

North Hempstead

East Williston

Westbury

Hicksville

Plainview

Herricks

Mineola

Carle Place

Bethpage

New Hyde Park

Garden City

East Meadow

Island Tree

Farmingdale

Floral Park

Franklin Square

Unified

Levittown

Planedge

Elmont

Hempstead

West Hempstead

Hempstead

North Merrick

North Bellmore

Massapequa

Valley Str Hemp 13

Roosevelt

Wantagh

Valley Str Hemp 30

Malverne

Rockville Centre

Seaford

Hemp Str Hemp

Lynbrook

Baldwin

Bellmore

Merrick

Freeport

East Rockaway

Hewlett Woodmere

Oceanside

Lawrence

Island Park

Long Beach

Long Beach

Legend

▢ City-Town Boundaries

▢ High School Districts (which differ from school districts)

▨ Villages

▨ School Districts

N

Map Scale: 1:120,000

0 — — 5 Miles

Map 7.1. School District Boundaries and Municipal Fragmentation in Nassau County

cooks, house servants, wood haulers, planters, and fireplace tenders. Preferences for workers of certain ethnicities for particular jobs on the part of the estate owners led to an ethnically (but not racially) diverse labor force. For instance, according to Baxandall and Ewen (2001), the estate owners "preferred their superintendents and butlers to be English; their gardeners, Scottish; their servants, Irish; and their common laborers, Polish or Italian" (p. 6). Thus, the rise of the Gold Coast and the robber baron estates brought with it an influx of new low-income Long Island residents, mostly recent immigrants from Europe. The "estate" economy, therefore, yielded a more divided labor market and population, devoid of any meaningful middle class.

The fragmentation of Nassau County into separate, clearly demarcated and politicized spaces was also encouraged in 1898 when the historic charter of New York City amalgamated the city's five boroughs. Nassau County, which up until that time had been part of Brooklyn, was deliberately carved out as a separate entity from New York City. A major reason for this was that the affluent Gold Coast estate owners on Long Island wanted to separate their land from the City. Once Nassau County was independent of New York City, the Gold Coast property holders, hostile toward both taxation and the increase of the population in their dominions, used whatever political or economic leverage they had to change state and local policies to work more in their favor.

For instance, they recognized early on that the mechanism of incorporating small areas of land into villages that controlled their own zoning and housing policies could be quite useful. At the time, however, early in the 20th century, the New York State law called for a village to have at least 250 residents to become incorporated. The Gold Coasters wanted to reduce this number so that they could incorporate the land around their estates into villages, and thus control who lived in, what was built in, and even who walked through their communities. The Republican politicians who represented the interests of the estate owners successfully passed a new law in Albany that changed the minimum residency to 50. Many large estates met this threshold requirement when large extended families and employees were included in the calculation. Once the new policy was in place, many robber barons incorporated their estates and then "went to great lengths to keep it so, building huge walls around their estates and posting armed guards at the borders to prevent errant day trippers from meandering onto the grounds" (Baxandall & Ewen, 2001, p. 9).

As the 20th-century suburbanization process evolved, this amended state policy on incorporation became increasingly important to the maintenance of separate and unequal spaces, communities, and schools. Up until the mid-1960s, when the law was amended yet again to restrict the zoning powers of incorporated villages, any areas of Nassau County that successfully incorporated were able to develop strict zoning regulations that severely limited the types of homes constructed and the types of homebuyers who had access to these communities. For instance, these local zoning regulations would require new homes to have a minimum square footage and/or lot size, which partly dictates home prices, and therefore which families are able to reside in which neighborhoods. Yet another regulation not unique to Nassau County is the prohibition of multifamily housing units, and the refusal to allow low-income housing units funded by local, state, or federal governments (Kirp, Dwyer, & Rosenthal, 1995).

According to one Long Island historian we interviewed, the process of village incorporation was rampant from the 1920s until the 1960s when the law was changed. This was also a time of severe population shifts in Nassau County, as we have noted. The historian noted that once a village was incorporated it gained the right to maintain whatever zoning codes and laws the residents desired as well as the ability to develop its own police force and other municipal services. The "unincorporated" areas of Long Island, on the other hand, were under the jurisdiction of one of the four "towns" that cover every square mile of Nassau County. These unincorporated areas, known as "hamlets," are in fact more numerous than the incorporated villages. For instance, the Town of Hempstead includes 56 hamlets and 22 villages. There is, according to this historian and our analysis, a direct but imperfect correlation between affluence and incorporation on Long Island. He noted: "The incorporated villages in this town, and also the incorporated villages in the town of North Hempstead seem to have more wealth. I can only assume that the wealth came first and therefore that whole—again, this is my thought—that whole protectionism kinda thing. Like here we are, let's protect, let's build a fence around ourselves so to speak, and that fence is incorporation."

Furthermore, in terms of the "benefits" of incorporation, in addition to the control over zoning, the villages have more control over their local elections—of mayors and other local policymakers—and thus many more local decisions. Residents in the unincorporated areas, on the other hand, have to go to the town policymakers to effect change. This is a larger political body with other interests to answer to when decisions are made. The historian noted that in the unincorporated areas of the county, the town can decide to do whatever it wants to do. Still, the historian noted, zoning rights seemed to be one of the major motivating factors behind local citizens' efforts to incorporate their communities. This is evident in the fact that once the state law was changed in the 1960s to disempower any newly formed villages from having the control over their zoning (villages incorporated prior to the change in the law still maintain these zoning powers), no new villages were incorporated in Nassau County. Clearly the demand for incorporation died off once the state said that after a certain date *incorporated villages would have all the other rights of other incorporated villages with the exception of zoning matters."*

Today, Nassau County is a patchwork of local governments, including school districts, each with their own sets of rules and regulations, some of which are designed to influence who lives and goes to school within each piece of the multicolored but highly segregated quilt. According to a key administrator in the former Nassau County Executive's Office:

> In Nassau we have anywhere, depending on how you count, from two hundred to seven hundred [local governments]. . . . We've got one county, three towns, two cities, sixty-four villages. . . . Then you have fifty-six school districts, forty-five, give or take, water purveyors, seventy-seven give or take fire districts. Some of them are village fire districts. . . . These are all different levels of government.

While the specifics of the zoning laws of New York State and the politics, history, and demographics of Nassau County make some aspects of this story unique, the intricate relationship between fragmentation and racial/ethnic and socioeconomic segregation on Long Island is clearly not unique to Nassau County. Due in part to these village-specific zoning laws and in part to the practices of developers and real estate agents, the pattern of segregation began early and has been maintained and even reinvented as the decades have unfolded. For instance, the home-building industry was tightly tied to and coordinated with the local municipal zoning ordinances and the spatialized construction of the housing market. Thus, as in most parts of the United States, builders in Nassau County continue to design neighborhoods with finely grained differences in home price. For example, a housing development may offer homes for $300,000, while an adjacent set of homes costs $350,000. This obviously allows for economic segregation by quite minute strata of income, or what developers prefer to label "market segments." This is in contrast to many urban neighborhoods, which often provide housing for residents across a wide range of incomes, even on a single city block (see Duany, Plater-Zyberk, & Speck, 2000).

Yet we find today that even in places where the quality and size of housing differs very little across school district boundaries, the prices do. At a recent real estate open house on

Long Island, we saw one spacious and well-built home of four bedrooms and 4.5 baths that was one block from the boundary of a predominantly white and well-reputed school district. This house was physically located within the boundaries of a less prestigious school district with above-average test scores, but a rapidly declining white population. The real estate agent showing the house noted that if this same house, with an asking price of approximately $650,000, were located one block to the east in the more desired school district, the owners would be asking double that price for the house. The question for our project to answer is what role the school districts—their boundaries, their demographics, their reputations, and so on—play in the efficient sorting process that occurs on Long Island. The following five emerging themes from our research help illustrate our early understanding of how this process occurs.

Changing Demographics of Nassau County and the Simultaneous Segregation

The waves of residential and economic growth described above were accompanied by equally stark racial/ethnic and socio-demographic changes to Nassau's population. Mirroring the massive population growth of the first phase of metro migrations and the rise of suburbanization, school enrollments peaked at roughly 340,000 total in all 56 districts in 1968, but fell to roughly 170,000 only twenty years later—a dramatic decline of 50 percent. Enrollments rebounded somewhat from the late 1980s through 2000, where they have remained at about 210,000 students. An important demographic change that continues to influence these declines in school enrollments is the aging of Nassau County's population. The county's median age has been steadily increasing since 1970, when it was just under 31 years of age, to almost 42 today. This shift reflects the "empty nester" phenomenon, as well as a general increase in life expectancy.

These dramatic socio-demographic changes were accompanied by equally striking transformations of Nassau's racial/ethnic landscape. As indicated in Figure 7.1, the county was virtually all white throughout the first half of the 20th century. Residential growth during the 1950s was due overwhelmingly—indeed, almost exclusively—to expansions in the number of white residents. From 1950 to 1960 the proportion of white residents declined by less than 1 percent, while the overall population doubled. As late as 1970, roughly 19 out of every 20 residents in Nassau County were white. Soon thereafter, however, Nassau experienced sizeable increases in its nonwhite population. Recent estimates suggest that today almost one-third of the county's population is nonwhite. This represents an extraordinary departure from 50 years earlier, when barely 3 percent of Nassau's residents were nonwhite.

Figure 7.1 also highlights the historical parallels between decreases in the proportion of white residents and the proportion of white public school students. In 1970, the racial/ethnic composition of public school students essentially mirrored that of the general population. By 1990, however, white enrollment in Nassau County's public schools was 10 percent below the overall white enrollment. This reflects several economic and demographic forces. First, the rise in empty-nest households mentioned above was necessarily more common among white families, who were the overwhelming majority of families with children in schools during the peak enrollment years of the late 1960s. Second, as is true nationally, white families in Nassau County are somewhat more likely to enroll their children in private schools. Over the past two decades, however, the racial/ethnic makeup of Nassau's public schools is slowly coming to again reflect the overall population. Older white residents who pass away or retire to other states are replaced by new residents who are more likely to be nonwhite and to enroll their children in Nassau's public schools.

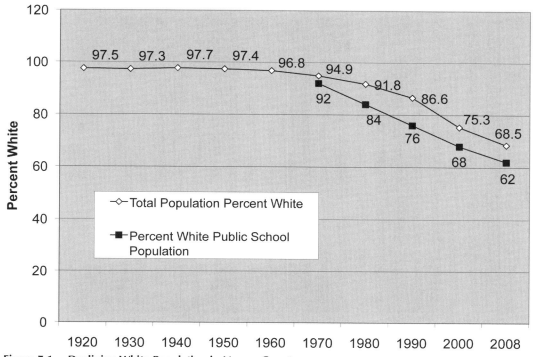

Figure 7.1. Declining White Population in Nassau County

Figure 7.2 provides a more nuanced picture of racial/ethnic changes across Nassau County's 56 public school districts. We find again the consistent theme of gradual declines in white student enrollments. Importantly, proportional declines in white students have been driven by increases in the proportion of Hispanic students rather than increases in black student enrollments. Between 1988 and 2007, the proportion of Hispanic students tripled, while the proportion of black students remained relatively stable. Note also the considerable increases among Asian students, whose proportional representation more than doubled over the past two decades. These patterns reflect national trends. Between 1993 and 2005, the proportion of white students declined by 8.5 percent, while the Hispanic student population increased from 12.1 to 18.9 percent (An & Gamoran, 2009). Decreases in the proportions of both white and black suburban residents, accompanied by increasing Hispanic populations, have also characterized suburban changes across many U.S. metropolitan areas. Analyses of the 100 largest U.S. metropolitan areas indicate that from 1990 to 2000, both black and white suburban populations declined, while Hispanic populations increased (Katz & Lang, 2003).

RACIAL/ETHNIC SCHOOL SEGREGATION IN NASSAU COUNTY

In this section we dig deeper to determine the extent to which Nassau County's public school districts experienced these demographic transformations equally. The analyses presented here employ data from the Common Core of Data (CCD), which is collected through the U.S. Department of Education's National Center for Education Statistics (NCES). The CCD, an annual census of U.S. public schools, provides basic school-level socio-demographic

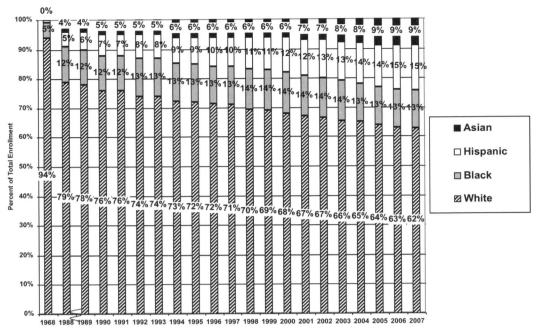

Figure 7.2.   Declining White Population in Nassau County Public Schools

information. We used Theil's *H*, an entropy index of segregation, which indicates the extent to which racial/ethnic groups are equally distributed across schools (Theil, 1972; also Reardon & Yun, 2001; Reardon, Yun, & Eitle, 2000). *H* possesses two quite useful properties. First, the indicator is not dependent on the overall racial/ethnic composition of a given population. Because student enrollments in Nassau County have become increasingly nonwhite over the past four decades, simple indicators of the proportion of schools that are majority nonwhite do not provide useful information. For example, a finding that more schools are currently nonwhite compared to a decade ago tells us nothing about increases in segregation, as all schools may have experienced similar increases in their nonwhite populations (An & Gamoran, 2009). Rather, such contexts require a measure of segregation that is less sensitive to overall racial/ethnic changes within a given population, and that instead considers how the proportional representation of students both within and across districts changes over time.

Figure 7.3 displays the historical patterns of white/nonwhite segregation in Nassau County. We see a gradual increase in segregation from the late 1980s through the 1990s, but segregation has remained somewhat stable—at very high levels—since 1999. In looking across years, consider that a 0.05 change in *H* is considered to be substantively meaningful (see Reardon & Yun, 2001). Such a change is roughly the equivalent to transferring 10 percent of the minority population from schools in which they were overrepresented to schools where they were underrepresented. A much more dramatic increase in segregation occurred between 1968 and 1988, a period (not coincidentally) during which Nassau County witnessed its greatest nonwhite population growth. Specifically, from 1970 to 1990, the nonwhite population increased from 8 percent to 24 percent. Note also that segregation between elementary schools is greater than that between schools in general. This flows largely from the fact that elementary school attendance boundaries are more closely tied to

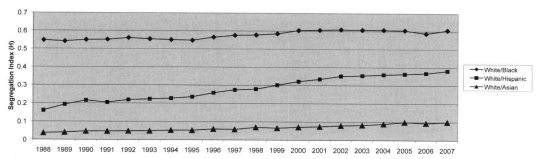

Figure 7.3.   White–Non-White Segregation Indices Over Time in Nassau County's 56 School Districts

home residence than is the case with middle and high schools, which tend to draw from larger geographic areas, due to their generally larger sizes.[3]

In Figure 7.4 we decompose the white/nonwhite segregation in Nassau County into the portion that lies between schools within school districts, and the portion that exists between school districts. The obvious revelation here is the extent to which segregation in Nassau County is a between-district phenomenon. The top line represents total segregation. The bottom line represents the proportion of segregation that lies between schools in the same school district. Since 1988, less than 10 percent of white/nonwhite segregation has been located between schools in the same school district, while more than 90 percent has been located between school districts. Given the Milliken decision, this has obvious implications for efforts to create more racially and ethnically integrated schools. In a highly fragmented county with 56 school districts that are roughly, but far from perfectly, tied to local municipal jurisdictions such as villages and hamlets, the high level of racial segregation between school district boundary lines should not be surprising. The fact that this fragmentation intersects with an increasingly racially/ethnically diverse school-age population, however, makes the segregation all the more probable and all the more problematic.

Changing Significance of Public School Boundaries

As public school districts interact with this complex landscape of highly fragmented local governance systems, we have been trying to better understand what role the school districts and their boundaries play in the mosaic of segregation and separation. As a former president of the Nassau County Superintendents Association noted, school governance on Long Island

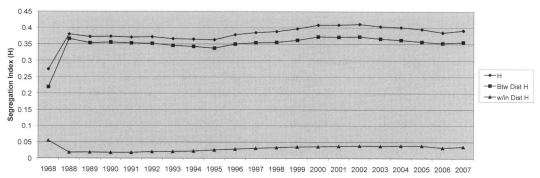

Figure 7.4.   White–Non-White Segregation—Within Versus Between Districts—in Nassau County's 56 School Districts

is very complex because district leaders are constantly negotiating multiple layers of politics. These layers include the state government, especially state legislators, who make the laws that affect education but who have no say over anything that goes on at the county level, where the municipal mosaic of local power—at the town, city, and village or hamlet level— are mind boggling. For instance, this superintendent noted that one school district in Nassau includes nine incorporated villages, and then there are districts that have no villages—or even a part of a village—within their boundaries. Whether or not they overlap with any of the villages, most of the school districts are nested within one of the four towns, which are responsible for trash pick up, snow shoveling, etc. And then there are some school districts (see Map 7.1) that actually straddle more than one town.

What we learned from our county- and district-level interviews was that in a suburban county in which most residents are fiercely committed to the idea of local control— particularly for those who live in villages and thus *have* a great deal of local control—residents are extremely wedded to their local government, especially their school districts. According to the education advisor to the former Nassau County Executive, "the villages are really at the heart of what Nassau County is all about . . . you know local control and all of that. . . . You have some very, very passionate local leaders. You know mayors love their villages. People love them. Of everything people want to protect in Nassau County, villages are probably second only to schools."

In fact, in part because of the multilayered configuration of local, municipal government structures in Nassau County, school districts, which collectively cover every square mile of the county and transcend all of the other uneven layers of local control, have become the focal points of local control and identity across the boundaries. While school districts have always been important to people migrating to Long Island, our data collection suggests that in this era of rampant income inequality, test score data overload, and high anxiety due to these factors on the part of many upper-middle-class parents, they matter more today than ever before (see Wells et al., 2009)

This is certainly true when it comes to buying and selling homes on Long Island. According to a local real estate agent who serves a wide range of clientele, from upper-middle-class to recent lower-income immigrant families, if someone asks him how "*the*" housing market on Long Island is doing, he replies that every zip code is different and that much of that difference is related to school districts:

> I could give you a report within a minute that I'll tell you what the zip code is doing. . . . I hate when someone gives me . . . well this is what's happening in Nassau County. Nassau County? There's hundreds and hundreds of towns. No. There's lousy school districts going bankrupt. There's excellent school districts. There are so many things that create value, and school districts are one of the things that do create value. It may be reputation or may be factual but they do create value and people are drawn to it.

This real estate agent and others familiar with the housing market on Long Island stated in interviews that most young couples and parents of school-age children looking to purchase or rent homes are more interested in school district boundaries than anything else. The real- tor noted that many consumers don't necessarily know the difference between a village and an unincorporated area of the county—or a hamlet—but they will often know about the school district. The link between housing values across boundaries in this small fragmented county and perceived school quality appears to be getting tighter.

As a superintendent of a school district with high test scores noted, the housing prices do change based on the school district outcome—the "school district is a big thing." This super- intendent and others like him in districts with high test scores conduct annual get-togethers with the realtors in their area. He is also a member of the local chamber of commerce, which includes many realtors. "So there is a connection, and they're [the realtors] very aware of the status of our budget, our scores, and all of those things that people come and ask them about. I'll do a presentation for them and . . . I'll give them a handout which describes some of the things that people ask them."

As the Long Island historian noted, during the age of mass suburbanization—the first phase of white flight to the suburbs in the 1950s and 1960s—the quality of the public schools in a given area were not so important, nor was that "quality" so easily measured prior to the accountability movement. But today, he noted, is a different time. Parents have greater access to test score data and other information than in the past, and, he said, education is seen as being more critical to children's chances of success as adults: "I think [the] school district is probably one of the most important [factors] because no matter what, we do care about the education system. I'd say that people are probably most conscious of that."

We know, for instance, from our early data collection with real estate agents on Long Island that there are school district boundaries that can double the asking price of structurally similar houses. As one real estate agent told us, a large four-bedroom home we visited with a large yard and a huge back porch would be double its asking price of $650,000 if it were located one block to the east, in a highly reputable and 98 percent white school district, as opposed to the more racially, ethnically, and socioeconomically diverse district in which it is located.

Similarly, a parent in a nearby district with declining test scores and white flight noted, "Our district's being judged, and then our housing prices, the prices of our homes and the values of our homes go down, because who wants to go to a district where the kids aren't getting good grades?"

Another important finding related to the increasing significance of school district boundaries on Long Island is the growth of the school district "border patrol" industry there. Previously all-white school districts receiving a growing number of students from New York City and Central America have now hired residency officers (a.k.a. border patrollers) to monitor legal versus illegal enrollments. These are growing operations in at least 6 of the 56 school districts' budgets. One of these 6 districts, after sending border patrollers into homes on "home visits," which can entail searches of students' bedrooms and closets to make sure they live there, also contracts out to private investigators for more in-depth surveillance, which can include videotaping a house for a 24-hour period. As one of these officials explained, border patrol is a booming industry on Long Island, as school districts must ensure there are no illegitimate students in their schools. He and others in this now 70 percent "minority" school district noted that the idea, funding, and ongoing support for this effort come from the all-white school board. Race, class, and school boundaries are, we argue, of increasing significance on Long Island.

The Interplay of Public and Private Resources in Separate and Unequal School Districts

This theme emerges from our initial examination of five Long Island school districts that varied tremendously in terms of the wealth of their constituents. Looking across these five districts, we realized that they differed not only in terms of their public funding and resources, but also the private resources within the community that flowed—directly and indirectly—into the schools. In other words, we learned the multiple ways in which public resources and private wealth are often discretely comingled to give students who attend schools of concentrated privilege even greater resource advantage. In other words, a public education system in which those with more resources are able to generate higher levels of public funding creates inequality in and of itself. But when that system is supplemented and reinforced by private resources—both tangible and intangible—from parents, community members, and other donors who are connected to the district through social networks, the mounting inequities are even more appalling.

We saw these private resources pour into the most affluent school district both through major donations and through the support systems that parents were able to give their children to enhance their achievement and school success. These affluent parents made sure their children had what they needed to succeed—everything from $200-an-hour private tutors to $300-an-hour therapies of all kinds—for example, psychological, physical, or occupational. A high school social worker in this affluent district, who used to work in a poor community, explained that while many problems adolescents face, including drug or alcohol use or divorcing parents, transcend the poor-affluent boundaries, it is the students in the affluent district whose parents can buy them a safety net that keeps them from failing:

> What I think is different . . . here, the families have the money to help them get through it. . . . The issues are the same. . . . They've got the students who are socially awkward, they've got students who need special ed. services, they've got parents who are divorcing. . . . But here, if your parents are divorcing, you may have the financial means to go to a therapist outside of school, you know. If you're autistic, your family has gone to the best specialists and they have you with the best medications, and you're going to special camps over the summer to really develop your social skills, and I think that's what separates the districts. It's really the resources.

While most people know about this comingling of public and private resources at an intuitive level, if not from systematic research, it is important to document the extent to which such layered inequality defines the separate and unequal educational opportunities across school boundaries. *Indeed, what we learned is that this understanding becomes a mechanism through which the system is legitimized and maintained by those with the power to change it.*

Perceptions of Good Schools and Their Tangible and Intangible Consequences

Related to the theme about the dramatically different educational opportunities available to students across these separate school districts, this theme examines the ways in which those who live and work in these distinct spaces understand the reputations of their school districts on Long Island. Documenting how people articulate their school districts' reputations may not seem empirically or scientifically important—nothing more than people's perceptions, which may or may not be "valid" in some more concrete sense. But we argue that "intangible" factors such as districts' or schools' reputations—for example, the way in which people make sense of particular public schools versus others, whether they know much about them or not—matter a great deal in terms of people's willingness to move into or out of a particular school district as well as their resistance to changing existing boundaries. *In some ways, therefore, perceptions are more powerful than "reality."*

Related to this theme and the larger body of research on race and education, we found in our study of Long Island that the reputations of schools and school districts are highly correlated with the status of the students who attend them and thus the families associated with them. It is the case that these reputations are also correlated with some objective measures of "school quality" as measured in terms of mostly tangible factors, since mostly poor, black, and Latino schools continually lack resources, well-prepared teachers, high-status curriculum, and so forth. But such bad reputations are, we suggest, more strongly correlated with the race/ethnicity and poverty rates of the students served than with an objective measure of school or district quality per se. In this way, school and district reputations can become self-fulfilling prophecies—with poorer districts unable to attract more affluent residents or more prepared educators. As a result, these ways of "knowing" school districts through their reputations helps to legitimize the separation and inequality across districts that so many people on Long Island say is morally wrong. It is in fact a vicious cycle of bad reputations begetting bad schools and vice versa. One thing that these data on public school districts' reputations clearly underscore is the harms of racial/ethnic segregation across the disparate villages and hamlets of Long Island.

CONCLUSION

We have begun on a five-year journey to figure out how and why school district boundaries matter amid massive metro migration patterns and ongoing racial/ethnic and increasing socioeconomic segregation. We know intuitively, if not empirically, that they surely do. What has been missing in the social science and education research literature for too long is a careful, systematic examination of *why* they matter so much. Our study is designed to answer that very question through a vast array of mixed methods applied to four different contexts.

This chapter represents our first leg of that journey—our evolving framework and methods—as well as early quantitative and qualitative findings from Nassau County—the most fragmented county in the United States. We hope our description of our study and these early findings both pique interest in such work in other contexts and inspire education researchers in particular to ask hard questions and collect data on issues that are not the most salient to policymakers in Washington, D.C., and the state houses right now, but which are critically important to the future of our increasingly racially and ethnically diverse society.

NOTES

1. We use the term "white" to describe "whites not of Hispanic origin" unless otherwise noted. We also use the terms "black" and "African American" interchangeably, as we do with "Latino" and "Hispanic," knowing that people who identify with these racial/ethnic groups are not uniform in their preference for one term or the other.

2. It is important to bear in mind, however, that many "black suburbs" are simply smaller, high-poverty cities located near large cities (e.g., Camden, New Jersey, and East St. Louis, Illinois; Massey & Denton, 1993). Areas that experienced substantial growth in black populations during this second phase of metropolitan change also tended to be older, "inner-ring" suburbs that were poor, experiencing social and economic decline, and rarely called to mind the "suburban ideal."

3. We are currently conducting analyses that incorporate Nassau County's private schools and that specifically explore white/black, white/Hispanic, and white/Asian segregation. In most instances, these analyses suggest more severe segregation—for example, higher values of H—as Asian students in Nassau County are far more likely than black or Hispanic students to attend school with whites.

REFERENCES

Adelman, R. (2005). The role of race, class and residential preferences in the neighborhood racial composition of middle-class blacks and whites. *Social Science Quarterly, 86*(1), 209–228.

An, B. P., & Gamoran, A. (2009). Trends in school racial composition in the era of unitary status. In C. Smrekar & E. B. Goldring (Eds.), *From the courtroom to the classroom: The shifting landscape of school desegregation*. Cambridge, MA: Harvard Education Press.

Baxandall, R., & Ewen, E. (2001). *Picture windows: How the suburbs happened*. New York, NY: Basic Books.

Berube, A., & Kneebone, E. (2006). *Two steps back: City and suburban poverty trends, 1999–2005.* Living Cities Census Series. Washington, DC: Brookings Institution Press.

Bischoff, K. (2008). School district fragmentation and racial residential segregation: How do boundaries matter? *Urban Affairs Review, 44*(2), 182–217.

Demerath, P. (2009). *Producing success: The culture of personal advancement in an American high school.* Chicago, IL: University of Chicago Press.

Drier, P., Mollenkopf, J., & Swanstrom, T. (2004). *Place matters: Metropolitics for the twenty-first century.* Lawrence: University Press of Kansas.

Duany, A., Plater-Zyberk, E., & Speck, J. (2000). *Suburban nation: The rise of sprawl and the decline of the American dream.* New York, NY: North Point Press.

Epstein, C. F. (1992). Tinkerbells and pinups: The construction and reconstruction of gender boundaries at work. In M. Lamont & M. Fournier (Eds.), *Cultivating differences: Symbolic boundaries and the making of inequality* (pp. 232–256). Chicago, IL: University of Chicago Press.

Farley, J. E., & Squires, G. D. (2005). Fences and neighbors: Segregation in 21st-century America. *Contexts, 4*(1), 33–39.

Freeman, L. (2006). *There goes the 'hood: Views of gentrification from the ground up.* Philadelphia, PA: Temple University Press.

Frey, W. (2001). *Melting pot suburbs: A census 2000 study of suburban diversity.* Washington, DC: The Brookings Institution, Center on Urban & Metropolitan Policy.

Gotham, K. F. (2003). Toward an understanding of the spatiality of urban poverty: The urban poor as spatial actors. *International Journal of Urban and Regional Research, 27*(3), 723–737.

Gutmann, A. (1998). Freedom of association: An introductory essay. In A. Gutmann (Ed.), *Freedom of association* (pp. 3–35). Princeton, NJ: Princeton University Press.

Harrigan, J. J., & Vogel, R. K. (1993). *Political change in the metropolis.* New York, NY: Longman.

Katz, B., & Lang, R. E. (2003). *Redefining urban and suburban America: Evidence from the Census 2000, vol. 1.* Washington, DC: Brookings Institution Press.

Kirp, D. L., Dwyer, J. P., & Rosenthal, L. A. (1995). *Our town: Race, housing, and the soul of suburbia.* Piscataway, NJ: Rutgers University Press.

Lamont, M. (2007). Euphemized racism: Moral qua racial boundaries. In J. F. Healey and E. O'Brien (Eds.), *Race, ethnicity and gender* (pp. 385–405). Thousand Oaks, CA: Pine Forge Press.

Lamont, M., & Fournier, M. (Eds.). (1992). *Cultivating differences: Symbolic boundaries and the making of inequality.* Chicago, IL: University of Chicago Press.

Lamont, M., & Molnár, V. (2002). The study of boundaries across the social sciences. *Annual Review of Sociology, 28*, 167–195.

Lareau, A. (2003). *Unequal childhoods: Class, race and family life.* Berkeley: University of California Press.

Lees, L., Slayter, T., & Wyly, E. (2008). *Gentrification.* New York, NY: Routledge.

Leinberger, C. B. (March, 2008). The next slum? *Atlantic Monthly.* Retrieved March 5, 2008, from http://www.the atlantic.com/doc/200803/subprime.

Lewis, A. (2003). *Race in the schoolyard: Negotiating the color line in classrooms and communities.* Piscataway, NJ: Rutgers University Press.

Logan, J. R., Alba, R. D., McNulty, T., & Fisher, B. (1996). Making a place in the metropolis: Locational attainment in cities and suburbs. *Journal of Demography, 33*(4), 443–453.

Lucy, W. H., & Phillips, D. L. (2003). Suburbs: Patterns of growth and decline. In Bruce Katz & Robert E. Lang (Eds.), *Redefining urban and suburban America.* Washington, DC: Brookings Institution Press.

Massey, D., & Denton, N. (1993). *American apartheid: Segregation and the making of the underclass.* Cambridge, MA: Harvard University Press.

Mickelson, R. A., Bottia, M., & Southworth, S. (March, 2008). School choice and segregation by race, class, and achievement. Tempe: Arizona State University Education Policy Research Unit.

Orfield, G., & Lee, C. (2007). *Historic reversals, accelerating resegregation, and the need for new integration strategies.* Los Angeles, CA: Civil Rights Project/Proyecto Derechos Civiles, UCLA.

powell, j. (2007). *Race, poverty and urban sprawl: Access to opportunities through regional strategies.* Presentation at the Forum for Social Economics, Minneapolis, MN.

Ready, D. D., & Lee, V. E. (2008). Choice, equity, and the schools-within-schools reform. *Teachers College Record, 110*(9), 1930–1958.

Ready, D., Wells, A. S., Warner, M., & Grzesikowski, C. (2010). *Metro migrations, suburban fragmentation and racial/ethnic segregation: Nassau County as both typical and extreme.* Paper presented at American Educational Research Association Conference Annual Meeting, Denver, CO.

Reardon, S. F., & Bischoff, K. (2009). *Income inequality and income segregation.* Palo Alto, CA: Stanford University.

Reardon, S. F., & Yun, J. T. (2001). Suburban racial change and suburban school segregation, 1987–95. *Sociology of Education, 74*, 79–101.

Reardon, S. F., & Yun, J. T. (2008). *Changing patterns of race, class, and school segregation in the suburbs, 1990–2006.* Paper presented at the American Educational Research Association Annual Meeting, New York, NY.

Reardon, S. F., Yun, J. T., & Eitle, T. M. (2000). The changing structure of school segregation: Measurement and evidence of multi-racial metropolitan school segregation, 1989–1995. *Demography, 37*(3), 351–364.

Sassen, S. (2006). *Cities in a world economy.* Thousand Oaks, CA: Pine Forge Press.

Sethi, R., & Somanathan, R. (2004). Inequality and segregation. *Journal of Political Economy, 112*(6), 1296–1322.

Stinchcombe, A. L. (1995). *Sugar Island slavery in the Age of Enlightenment: The political economy of Caribbean world.* Princeton, NJ: Princeton University Press.

Theil, H. (1972). *Statistical decomposition analysis.* Amsterdam: North-Holland Publishing Company.

Tickamyer, A. R. (2000). Space matters! Spatial inequality in future sociology. *Contemporary Sociology, 29*(60), 805–813.

United States Census Bureau. (1980). *1980 Decennial Census of Population and Housing.* Washington, DC: United States Census Bureau.

Wells, A. S., & Holme, J. J. (2006). No accountability for diversity: Standardized tests and the demise of racially mixed schools. In Jack Boger and Gary Orfield (Eds.), *The resegregation of the American South.* Chapel Hill: University of North Carolina Press.

Wells, A. S., Holme, J. J., Revilla, A. T., & Atanda, A. K. (2009). *Both sides now: The story of school desegregation's graduates.* Berkeley: University of California Press.

Wells, A. S., & Roda, A. (2008). *Colorblindness and school choice: The central paradox of the Supreme Court's ruling in the Louisville and Seattle school integration cases.* Paper presented at the American Educational Research Association Annual Meeting, New York, NY.

Wilkinson, R., & Pickett, K. (2010). *The spirit level: Why greater equality makes societies stronger.* New York, NY: Bloomsbury Press.

8

Adding Geospatial Perspective to Research on Schools, Communities, and Neighborhoods

Mark C. Hogrebe

WHY DOES EDUCATION RESEARCH NEED GEOSPATIAL PERSPECTIVE?

In education research, we use many types of data to measure and quantify processes and outcomes related to the education enterprise and its schools, teachers, and students. These data can be measured at the individual student level, or aggregated by teacher, classroom, school, district, or state. The data are typically "nonspatial," or "aspatial," and consist of variables related to factors such as student achievement, pedagogy, curricula, teacher training, and professional development. Data are analyzed by many descriptive and inferential methods designed to examine variable relationships and differences. Each type of data must be properly paired with the correct method of analysis in the context of the research question and design. However, there is an additional perspective that is frequently overlooked in education research—namely that variables typically occur in a physical, geographic location. Even though variables are most often analyzed as "nonspatial," they almost always can be associated with a place and thus have an intrinsic spatial component.

The purpose of this chapter is threefold. First, it discusses the significant value of adding geospatial perspective in education research to better understand the context in which education occurs. Second, it uses examples to demonstrate how incorporating a geospatial approach can enhance research on policies and segregation over sole reliance on global statistics. Lastly, geographic information systems (GIS) concepts used to generate spatial maps are introduced, followed by a discussion of several categories of GIS applications.

Geospatial perspective introduces regional, community, or neighborhood context as a factor that potentially moderates the relationships between the nonspatial education variables that are typically studied. If community or neighborhood context interacts with education variables at the individual or school level, then the relationships will differ across schools and vary by location. There has been increased emphasis in social science disciplines on the role that community and neighborhood context effects have on influencing behavior in specific locations (Coulton, 2005; Morenoff, Sampson, & Raudenbush, 2001; Sampson, 2003; Sampson, Morenoff, & Gannon-Rowley, 2002). Berry (2004) summarizes the importance of considering spatial context by saying that "it now is accepted as axiomatic, not simply by geographers but also by the broader social science community, that *space matters*, that geographic units cannot be treated as independent units of observation, that spatial autocorrelation is important . . . and that it cannot be ignored if statistical models are to be efficient and properly specified" (p. 444). However, just 5 years prior, Anselin (1999) stated that the notion that "space does matters . . . is by far not a widely accepted notion in the mainstream of the social sciences" (p. 74). The phrase "space matters" is founded on the idea that what occurs at a school or district will vary according to differences in community and neighborhood contexts.

The variation that exists between neighborhoods surrounding three schools just 15 miles apart is transparent in the dramatic physical differences seen in Figures 8.1(a), 8.1(b), and 8.1(c) for schools in one metropolitan area. The high school in Figure 8.1(a) is located near the intersection of two major interstate highways. There is a large rock quarry located to the north and west of the school and the only adjacent residential area is directly south. In contrast, the high school in 8.1(b) is surrounded by agricultural fields with limited road access and no nearby large residential areas. The high school in 8.1(c) is located in the inner city surrounded by city blocks populated with many older dwellings very close together. What role does the geographic location and physical context play in shaping the students and teachers that learn and teach in these schools?

While it may seem obvious that schools are largely influenced by the context in which they reside, the incorporation of neighborhood context into research has been difficult and in past decades largely ignored (Coulton, 2005; Sampson, 2003; Sampson et al., 2002). Raudenbush and Sampson (1999) discuss the quantitative assessment of ecological settings and have used the term "ecometrics" to describe the science of assessing neighborhood context. Neighborhood context is difficult to assess because there are so many factors contributing to the composition of the physical, social, and economic local environment. The diagram in Figure 8.2 attempts to show the myriad of factors that may potentially contribute to the composition of the neighborhood context. The diagram is *not* intended to be a comprehensive model of all factors, but it demonstrates the complexity of specifying them. Identifying, measuring, and assessing the effects of these factors can be a sizeable task.

It is because of this complexity that incorporating location into an analysis can be very valuable. The geospatial context of location may serve as a proxy variable to represent the effects of many factors and their complicated interactions. If schools differ by location, it may be that the local or neighborhood contexts in which the schools exist have an important influence on the student, teacher, and school variables and outcomes. The local context may moderate the school context and affect how the student and teacher variables are related. For example, neighborhoods that have higher household incomes, lower crime, higher real estate values, fewer mobile residents, and greater collective efficacy of residents' social control and cohesion, may be able to attract and retain more teachers who are highly qualified to teach in specific content areas. In turn, students taking courses from highly qualified teachers who are proficient in content areas will perform better in those courses and on content assessments.

If it is not possible to initially identify and assess variables based on a comprehensive model of neighborhood context effects, then the first step is to include location in the analysis to determine if there are spatial effects. Measures exist to determine if there is clustering by location across all of the data. These "global" measures calculate a single statistic summarizing the degree of clustering for the study area—for example, Moran's I. Also, there are measures of "local" clustering that disaggregate the global version of Moran's I into component parts in order to show where locations have similar and dissimilar values (Mitchell, 2005).

When there are differences by location, then neighborhood context is likely influencing individual schools and moderating variable relationships. At this point, one can use spatial

8.1(a)

School Campus

8.1(b)

School Campus

Figure 8.1. Variation in neighborhood contexts of school campuses located approximately 15 miles apart in a metropolitan area. School 8.1(a) located near two major interstate highways and rock quarry; school 8.1(b) surrounded by agricultural fields; and school 8.1(c) is an inner city school.

School Campus

8.1(c)

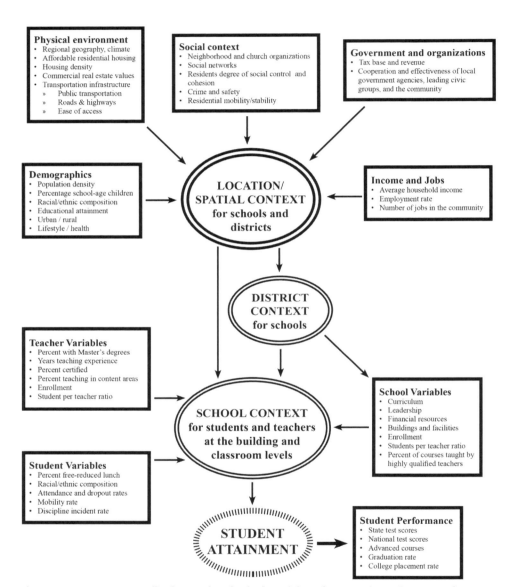

Figure 8.2. Factors contributing to the physical, social, and economic environment that comprise the community and neighborhood context are shown. The model does not claim to include every variable, but is intended to show the complexity of interactions that location represents.

statistical methods designed to incorporate the multilevel structure of the data for schools nested within different neighborhood contexts. Spatial statistics such as geographically weighted regression (Fotheringham, Brunsdon, & Charlton, 2002) and spatial regression models (Anselin, 2005; Ward & Gleditsch, 2008) take into account that relationships vary by location. The fact that nearby locations can be correlated is referred to as spatial autocorrelation and needs to be considered in models that attempt to account for variation among schools.

"ADDING VALUE" THROUGH GEOSPATIAL PERSPECTIVE

The premise that locations close together are more similar than those farther apart means that over a larger area or region, there will be variation by location. If local contexts vary, then the relationships between variables may also differ by location. These concepts of correlated locations and potentially different variable relationships that depend upon location are similar to those found in multilevel modeling. Students within the same classroom are more similar than students in different classrooms. Classrooms in the same school are more alike than those between schools. In addition to similarity of students or classrooms from the same school potentially producing correlated error terms, variable relationships may also differ depending on the school. For example, the relationship between time spent on homework and achievement might vary for schools of different socioeconomic levels (Kreft & De Leeuw, 2002). Location would be important in this example because schools closer together in the same district would tend to have similar socioeconomic levels, while schools farther apart would likely have different socioeconomic levels and potentially a different homework-achievement relationship.

The concept that location is important because local contexts vary is referred to as "non-stationarity" (Fotheringham et al., 2002). Non-stationarity means that variable values and their relationships depend on *where* measurements are taken. It is critical not to ignore this local variation by using only global statistics to arrive at one number to describe the data. While a global statistic such as the average of a distribution conveys important information, it is not sufficient. A description of the variance such as the standard deviation "adds-value" to our understanding of the data, in addition to the mean. For example, the average temperature for the United States in June is a global statistic that tells us something about the U.S. temperature, but for most purposes is useless at a local or even regional level. Knowing the standard deviation adds to our understanding about the extent of temperature variation across the country. However, most of us want to know the temperature for our region, county, city, and neighborhood. Reporting temperature variation by location clearly adds value to the weather report.

Using approaches that rely solely on global statistics can lead to an error of "ecological fallacy" (Robinson, 1950) in which results from a large group are used to make inferences about subgroups. This type of cross-level inference can be misleading in that subgroup characteristics may be very different from the large group average (Pedhazur, 1997, ch. 16). Another potential pitfall of relying exclusively on global statistics is Simpson's Paradox (De Veaux, Velleman, & Bock, 2005) in which the relationship between variables may differ within subgroups compared to when the data are aggregated. These potential problems can be mitigated if the data are disaggregated by location and local variation is included in the geospatial analysis.

Education researchers can use more than global statistics to gain a greater understanding of the role location plays in explaining variance. Incorporating location adds value to a research analysis strategy by extending the information provided by global statistics. For example, while it is good to have an overall average assessment for the country's high school seniors' mathematics achievement, we are all interested in the scores for the students in our city, district, and local school. We want to know not only the achievement at the local level, but also the characteristics of the students, school, teachers, and community—the factors that combine to create the local context.

Incorporating location into the analysis brings spatial dimension to the data and allows us to see variation in geographic space rather than in an abstract frequency distribution curve. The geospatial perspective adds value to global statistical methods by helping us visualize variation by geographic location. When we can see variation from geospatial reference points, variable relationships become apparent that may be overlooked with data in tabular form. This inductive approach to research is greatly facilitated through the geospatial display of variable relationships in maps (Goodchild & Janelle, 2004) and stimulates creative generation and exploration of hypotheses. Many times just seeing the spatial relationships on a map will spark an idea or produce an insight that otherwise would remain buried in a database. So in addition to providing a powerful dimension to descriptive research, the geospatial display of data can actually help shape and answer research questions. Preliminary descriptive spatial displays can lead to the use of spatial analysis as the primary research methodology. Geospatial analysis is a research tool that can complement the many quantitative and qualitative methods that are presently used in education research. In terms of different analytic perspectives, quantitative methods focus on the aggregate view and qualitative methods focus on the individual or small group view. In a sense, geospatial methods give a real, physical world dimension to the "X" and "Y" variables.

THREE EXAMPLES DEMONSTRATING THE
VALUE OF GEOSPATIAL PERSPECTIVE

The following examples show the value of using geospatial perspective in a research project and the powerful effect that visualizing data spatially on a map can have on improving communication and increasing understanding of the data. Data that are typically treated as nonspatial almost always are associated with a place in which they occur. Associating location with variables such as student achievement, race/ethnic percentages, and unemployment and then adding the spatial dimension through mapping will result in better understanding and communication of variable relationships. The examples demonstrate how the analysis and discussion of policies and politics can be significantly enhanced when the issues and corresponding variables are framed in the context of geographic space.

The first example of how the use of geospatial perspective through mapping can add significant value to a research project is found in the book *American Metropolitics: The New Suburban Reality*, by Myron Orfield (2002). Orfield describes the overall problem:

> An evolving pattern of intense, unequal competition and inefficient, environmentally damaging local land use threatens every community and region, undermining the nation's promise of equal opportunity for all. Geographic stratification has already had devastating consequences for the minority poor. Now it has begun to diminish the quality of life of working- and middle-class Americans and to circumscribe their opportunities. Sprawling development is gobbling up land with no corresponding growth in supporting infrastructure—schools, roads, transportation, sewage. This unplanned growth endangers public health, the environment, and the quality of life for people in every region. (p. 1)

Orfield's book is divided into three sections: metropatterns, metropolicy, and metropolitics. The metropatterns section uses 38 maps for six major U.S. regions (Atlanta, Chicago, Denver, Minneapolis–St. Paul, New York, and San Francisco) to show the unequal distribution of poverty, race, and tax capacity across these regions. Maps include variables such as the percentage of elementary students eligible for free lunch (by school) and the percentage of non-Asian minority students. It is one thing to describe these disparities, but it is much more powerful to see them in geographic space. Orfield uses the maps to highlight the patterns of diversity and segregation across the cities and suburbs and to anchor his analyses and discussion about trends. The metropatterns section also has an excellent example of using the traditional quantitative analysis technique of cluster analysis to identify six types of suburban communities: at-risk, segregated; at-risk, older; at-risk, low-density; bedroom-developing; affluent job center; and very affluent job center. The subsequent maps that provide the geospatial perspective for the cluster analysis results are very illuminating about the patterns of suburban community development across these six metropolitan regions.

The "metropolicy" section of the book uses the findings based on geographic patterns of suburban diversity as the foundation for a discussion of policies related to taxes, land use, and governance that create and maintain undesirable regional inequalities. The last section on "metropolitics" uses maps of electoral districts to demonstrate the importance of "swing" voters who vote for candidates from either political party. One of Orfield's conclusions is that metro politicians must "understand the diversity of U.S. suburbs and build a broad bipartisan movement for greater regional cooperation." The use of maps in Orfield's work demonstrates how incorporating geospatial perspective can greatly enhance the theoretical discussion, analysis, and presentation of social science issues dealing with diversity and inequality.

While Orfield's work examined six large metropolitan areas in studying the diversity of suburbs and related policies, the second example by Gordon (2008) focuses on one metro region. In his book, *Mapping Decline: St. Louis and the Fate of the American City*, Gordon crafts a compelling picture as he recreates the policies and practices that shaped the St. Louis region over the past 100 years. An outstanding example of integrating geospatial perspective with policy analysis, Gordon uses 68 maps from different decades to demonstrate the deleterious effects of fragmented local governance and taxation. The fragmented governance structure of many small municipalities produced local real estate restrictions and zoning ordinances that were designed to create demographic patterns of racial segregation and large inequalities. Gordon's analyses become significantly more impactful and transparent as the effects of the policies are displayed on maps in geographic space. Gordon's discussion reveals how policies and practices affect schools, neighborhoods, and cities. Their effects are evident in both the realities of physical locations and the geospatial perspective communicated in the maps.

The final example further demonstrates the value of using geospatial perspective in education research. In his article, "Geography of Opportunity: Poverty, Place, and Educational Outcomes," William Tate (2008) demonstrates how clusters of biotechnology companies have developed across the St. Louis metropolitan area including the largest cluster in the inner city urban core. A series of maps give spatial perspective to the census block group variables of percent unemployed, percent with bachelor's degrees, household income, as well as school variables relating to student performance on the state science proficiency assessment and the percentage of students receiving free or reduced-price lunches. These maps clearly show the uneven distribution of the geography of opportunity across the region. Clusters of biotech companies in the western suburbs are surrounded by areas of high employment, high household income, and greater percentages of bachelor's degrees together with fewer students receiving free or reduced-price lunches. In contrast, the largest biotech cluster located in the inner city urban core is surrounded by an area of low employment, low household income, and low percentage of bachelor's degrees, coupled with many students receiving free or reduced-price lunches and very low student proficiency in science. The maps highlight the uneven geography of opportunity as depicted by the large, inner-city biotech cluster located in an area surrounded by poverty and low educational outcomes in contrast to other suburban biotech clusters encompassed by more prosperous communities.

RESEARCH ON SEGREGATION NEEDS GEOSPATIAL PERSPECTIVE

Research designed to study racial or socioeconomic composition has an inherent geographic component because factors such as these vary across neighborhoods, schools, districts, cities, and regions. Segregation and diversity are intertwined with places that have geographic reference points. These locations can be used to generate maps that show the spatial distribution or clustering of racial and socioeconomic groups. While global measures of segregation like the dissimilarity index provide valuable information, they do not present the complete picture (see earlier discussion on global statistics). In the study of segregation across schools, we need to see which schools are segregated and where they are located in relation to other schools. Segregation does not occur in a vacuum, but is the result of many variables interacting in the local context. We need to visualize segregation and composition variables simultaneously with other local context variables to see how they vary within and between geographic entities (i.e., schools, districts, cities).

Three chapters in this volume study some type of segregation (e.g., racial, socioeconomic, immigrant). All use a global measure to develop a compelling analysis of segregation and its implications, but only one attempts to use spatial maps to portray segregation's geographic aspect. Incorporating the geospatial perspective into the discussions about the variation of segregation between and within schools or districts could add significant value and understanding to the presentations. Being able to see the variation across locations in combination with other contextual variables would certainly increase the probability of comprehending relationships and give greater meaning to the global statistics. The value of adding the geospatial perspective is clearly demonstrated in the three examples described in the previous section. The reader is strongly encouraged to experience the power of the geospatial presentations in these works.

As an example of how a spatial presentation could enhance the chapter by Reardon, Yun, and Chmielewski in this volume, let us focus on one of their important findings: "That is, socioeconomic segregation does not appear to serve as a strong proxy for racial segregation." While their results and conclusions are based on global statistical models, including geospatial maps that demonstrate segregation in key metropolitan areas would help the reader visualize the findings. As an example, the fact that economic and racial segregation does not align within coterminous boundaries is demonstrated in Figure 8.3 for the St. Louis metropolitan region. In Figure 8.3(a), the segregation of black residents can be seen in the concentration of adjacent census block groups in the northeastern section of the metro area with almost no diversity across the rest of the region. Figure 8.3(b) shows the distribution of the population with income below 185 percent of the poverty level (U.S. Census, 2000). This measure of low socioeconomic status reveals greater diversity across the area. The comparison of Figures 8.3(a) and 8.3(b) demonstrates that the highly racially segregated census block groups in the northeastern section do not align neatly with the low socioeconomic block groups. This spatial picture seems to support Reardon and colleagues' finding above that socioeconomic segregation does not serve as a strong proxy for racial segregation. The maps also show the geographic size differences between the large and small districts as well as the variation in racial and socioeconomic diversity within and between districts. Segregation is local in that it varies by

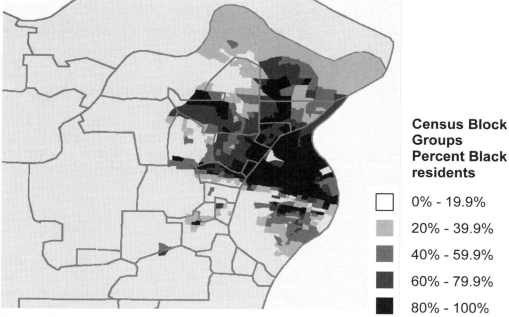

**Census Block
Groups
Percent Black
residents**

☐ 0% - 19.9%

▨ 20% - 39.9%

▨ 40% - 59.9%

▨ 60% - 79.9%

■ 80% - 100%

Figure 8.3(a)

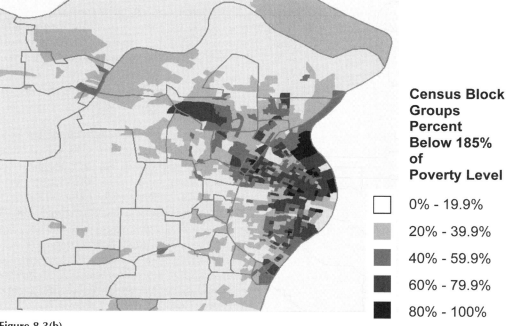

**Census Block
Groups
Percent
Below 185%
of
Poverty Level**

☐ 0% - 19.9%

▨ 20% - 39.9%

▨ 40% - 59.9%

▨ 60% - 79.9%

■ 80% - 100%

Figure 8.3(b)

Figure 8.3.   In Figure 8.3(a), the segregation of black residents can be seen in the concentration of adjacent census block groups in the northeastern section of the St. Louis, Missouri, metro area with almost no diversity across the rest of the region. Figure 8.3(b) shows the distribution of the population with income below 185 percent of the poverty level (2000 U.S. Census). This measure of low socio-economic status reveals greater diversity across the area. The comparison of Figures 8.3(a) and 8.3(b) demonstrates that the highly racially segregated census block groups in the northeastern section do not align neatly with the low socioeconomic block groups.

school, district, city, and region. Research on segregation should incorporate the study of local patterns by using a geographic lens.

USING GIS TO GENERATE GEOSPATIAL PERSPECTIVE

Geographic information systems (GIS) refers to the technology and processes for collecting, analyzing, interpreting, communicating, and using geospatial data (Maantay & Ziegler, 2006). GIS is based on the philosophy that location is important because many factors and their relationships vary by place and distance. Essentially, GIS is a powerful tool that can be used to generate geospatial perspective through mapping. There are three basic components to GIS: geography, information, and systems.

Geography

Geography refers to feature classes or themes. Traditionally, geography is represented by feature classes such as topography (physical features like mountains and valleys), hydrology (rivers and lakes), and ecology (vegetation and wildlife). Feature classes are also manmade entities like cities, neighborhoods, buildings, streets, and highways. Geography can represent the location of feature classes that refer to human characteristics and activities. For example, demographic variables like age, gender, and ethnicity represent characteristics of people who live and work in places—locations that have geographic reference points. Other variables such as income, consumer behavior, and voting patterns all occur in geographic space. And of course education occurs in schools, which are located in neighborhoods and districts. Therefore, all school, teacher, and student variables are associated with a building location that can be mapped in geographic space. Basically, almost any behavior or activity can be tied to a location.

Information

The second component of GIS is information about places, people, and things. Locations or places can be referenced as values and stored in a database. The GIS uses this database to produce the spatial map. The database is composed of several "attribute" tables, one for each feature class or theme. One feature class represented in an attribute table might be all the school locations in a metropolitan area. Another feature class could be the census block groups within the school districts. Streets and highways might be a third feature class. The attribute tables are spreadsheet-type files in which each row represents one "feature" from the feature class with a specific location such as a school building, census block group, or school district. Each column is an attribute or variable that contains one type of specific data such as geographic coordinates, shape and area information for polygons, federal and state identifying numbers, and other nonspatial characteristics paired with the specific location of the feature (see Figure 8.4). Each row in Figure 8.4 represents one school district and the columns contain the data for the attributes that describe the districts. Notice that the columns represent identifying data (ID and name columns), shape and location data, as well as nonspatial data associated with the districts—that is, enrollment and FRL percentage.

Multiple feature classes are used as layers in a GIS project. From the example above, the three layers might be schools, census block groups, and roadways. Each of these layers produces vector images that are defined mathematically. The schools are points, census block groups are polygons, and roadways are lines. A fourth layer could be added that is an actual

FID	GEOID	Shape	CENTROID_X	CENTROID_Y	SHAPE_LENG	COUNTY_ID	DIST_ID	DIST_NAME	ENROLLMENT	FRL_PCT
0	2918331650	Polygon	-90.863318	38.794922	0.812763	29183	31650	WENTZVILLE R-IV SCHOOL	8720	17
1	2918308370	Polygon	-90.714383	38.843829	1.202810	29183	08370	FT. ZUMWALT R-II	18496	11
2	2918323160	Polygon	-90.375036	38.879106	1.251370	29183	23160	ST. CHARLES COUNTY R-V	1227	32
3	2918913830	Polygon	-90.300227	38.810139	1.018856	29189	13830	HAZELWOOD	19315	39
4	2951029280	Polygon	-90.244951	38.635563	0.652301	29510	29280	ST LOUIS CITY	39438	87
5	2918912010	Polygon	-90.319204	38.763799	0.467696	29189	12010	FERGUSON-FLORISSANT	12220	57
6	2918926670	Polygon	-90.236934	38.749497	0.247189	29189	26670	RIVERVIEW GARDENS	7981	77
7	2918916290	Polygon	-90.262829	38.722584	0.134230	29189	16290	JENNINGS	3227	82
8	2918931590	Polygon	-90.292419	38.674909	0.072230	29189	31590	WELLSTON	561	83
9	2918930660	Polygon	-90.332394	38.666184	0.183055	29189	30660	UNIVERSITY CITY	3784	59
10	2918922650	Polygon	-90.307106	38.699473	0.235764	29189	22650	NORMANDY	5290	83
11	2918926640	Polygon	-90.367539	38.709889	0.256638	29189	26640	RITENOUR	6101	56
12	2918923700	Polygon	-90.435475	38.732882	0.407840	29189	23700	PATTONVILLE	5690	32
13	2918909720	Polygon	-90.328622	38.642399	0.159203	29189	09720	CLAYTON	2558	17
14	2918905880	Polygon	-90.347775	38.619229	0.103148	29189	05880	BRENTWOOD	812	26
15	2918920010	Polygon	-90.323901	38.619194	0.123167	29189	20010	MAPLEWOOD-RICHMOND HEI	1001	52
16	2918917820	Polygon	-90.392389	38.647063	0.314130	29189	17820	LADUE	3293	9
17	2918931530	Polygon	-90.356705	38.591351	0.263120	29189	31530	WEBSTER GROVES	4105	20
18	2918913620	Polygon	-90.275770	38.533009	0.115659	29189	13620	HANCOCK PLACE	1878	72
19	2918904500	Polygon	-90.299342	38.549455	0.128618	29189	04500	BAYLESS	1596	49
20	2918902910	Polygon	-90.327284	38.560915	0.215596	29189	02910	AFFTON	2481	27
21	2918918690	Polygon	-90.394799	38.530355	0.379321	29189	18690	LINDBERGH R-VIII	5488	18
22	2918916770	Polygon	-90.420308	38.587259	0.281016	29189	16770	KIRKWOOD	5027	19
23	2918930690	Polygon	-90.484996	38.557449	0.147038	29189	30690	VALLEY PARK	1018	50
24	2918926850	Polygon	-90.623718	38.570740	1.136213	29189	26850	ROCKWOOD	21871	12
25	2918328920	Polygon	-90.524515	38.794763	0.392223	29183	28920	ST. CHARLES R-VI	5881	28
26	2918329580	Polygon	-90.499172	38.644943	0.718277	29189	23580	PARKWAY	18994	16
27	2918328950	Polygon	-90.750250	38.701384	1.420172	29183	28950	FRANCIS HOWELL	18336	9
28	2918920670	Polygon	-90.332284	38.474584	0.587682	29189	20670	MEHLVILLE	11582	21
29	2909912300	Polygon	-90.442827	38.403608	0.813066	29099	12300	FOX C-6	11239	25

Record: ‖◂ ◂ [1] ▸ ▸‖   Show: All Selected   Records (0 out of 30 Selected.)   Options ▾

Figure 8.4. Attribute table for school districts. Each row represents one district and the columns contain the data for the attributes (variables) that describe the districts. The columns represent identifying data (ID and name columns), shape and location data, and also non-spatial data associated with the districts—that is, enrollment and FRL percentage.

image of the location. This layer would consist of a raster image composed of pixels (like from a digital camera) similar to the imagery seen in Google Earth. GIS can make all four layers visible simultaneously or turn them on one at time. GIS uses the information in the attribute tables for the feature classes to generate the spatial maps.

Systems

The third component of GIS is systems and refers to the integration of computer software, hardware, data, GIS users, and people managing the whole process. In some occupations, GIS is used to manage the data and workflow for multiple facets of an entire organization. In order to make GIS work as an important organization-wide tool, all of the components must be coordinated as a system. Viewing and analyzing data spatially is essential for companies involved in things like traffic, transportation, and distribution; urban and regional planning; utilities and construction; and public safety/law enforcement to mention just a few. Some school districts use GIS as a comprehensive tool to integrate functions such as enrollment projections, reconfiguring attendance zones, planning transportation and bus routes, and building/facilities management. Individual student home addresses can be "geocoded" so that each address appears as a point on the map, making it easy to see where students live in relation to each other and the school they attend. For an example of how GIS can be implemented in school districts, see http://www.schoolsiteonline.com.

GIS "systems" is the product of GIS "science." In GIS systems, the emphasis is on the technology, function, and application of mapping and spatial analysis in real-world settings. GIS science is concerned with the theory and decision-making that underlies GIS systems. For example, GIS science develops data transformations used in map projections or new spatial analysis methods. It integrates knowledge from fields such as geography, computer science, statistics, data modeling, cognition, and information systems (Schuurman, 2004).

GIS GOES BEYOND GLOBAL STATISTICS

The following examples demonstrate how using GIS to create geospatial perspective generates a great deal of additional information over and above global statistics. The examples are based on public accessible data downloaded from the Missouri Department of Elementary and Secondary Education (DESE) website (http://dese.mo.gov) in 2007 and focus on the spatial presentation of the data. The theme for the examples is the comparison of St. Louis City schools versus other schools in the metropolitan region on key student and teacher variables at the school level. Figure 8.5 shows a bar graph for a global statistic that compares the average percentage of students receiving free or reduced-price lunches (FRL) versus the average percentage for all other metro schools at the elementary, middle, and high school

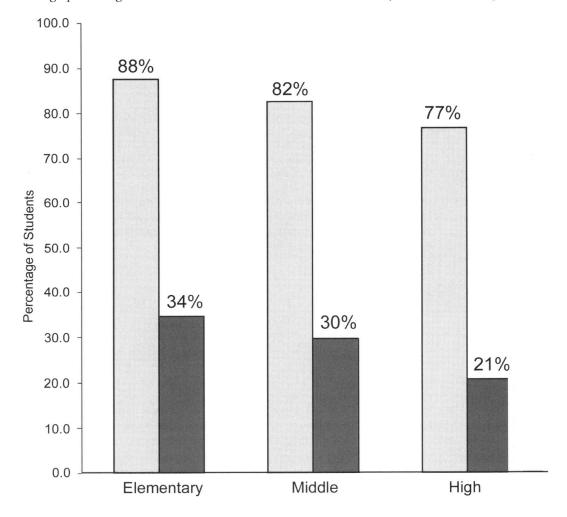

Figure 8.5.   The average percentage of students receiving free or reduced-price lunches in St. Louis City schools versus the average percentage for all other metro schools at the elementary, middle, and high school levels.

levels. The bars represent mean percentages across schools and clearly show that the average percentage of FRL students in St. Louis City schools is much higher than for other schools in the area (e.g., elementary, 88 percent versus 35 percent).

Now examine the geospatial presentation in Figure 8.6 from the same data set, which incorporates more information about FRL percentages between and within schools. First, the variation in FRL percentage among districts is shown on the background map. The second information source is the location and relative size of the schools in terms of enrollment. If bigger circles equal larger enrollment, then St. Louis City elementary schools generally have smaller enrollments. Third, the FRL percentage within schools is depicted by the darker slice of the circle. Most all of St. Louis City schools have a high percentage of FRL students, while the reverse is true for most other schools. However, there are a number of schools at the elementary level just to the north and west of St. Louis City that also have a high percentage of FRL students. Finally, the map shows the variation in FRL percentage between schools across the area and reveals the obvious clustering of high-FRL schools in St. Louis City and nearby non–St. Louis City schools to the north and west.

The second example for average teacher salaries is from the same data set for St. Louis City schools versus other metro schools. The bar graph in Figure 8.7 shows the lower aver-

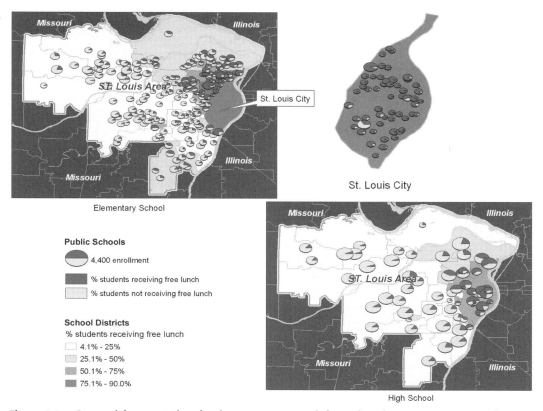

Figure 8.6. Geospatial presentation that incorporates more information about FRL percentages between and within schools. First, the variation in FRL percentage among districts is shown on the background map. School location is shown as well as relative size of schools in terms of enrollment. The FRL percentage within schools is depicted by the darker slice of the circle. Finally, the map shows the variation in FRL percentage between schools across the area and reveals the obvious clustering of high-FRL schools in St. Louis City and nearby non–St. Louis City schools to the north and west.

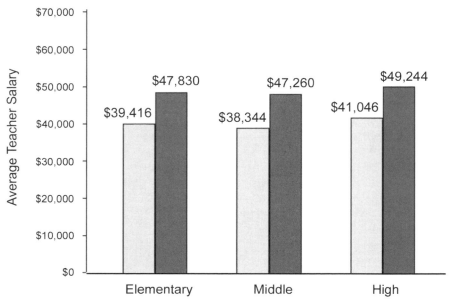

Figure 8.7. The average teacher salary for St. Louis City schools versus the average teacher salary for all other metro schools at the elementary, middle, and high school levels.

age teacher salaries in St. Louis City schools. The background geospatial map in Figure 8.8 portrays variation in average salaries across districts. The circles are schools, and their relative size represents the average teacher salary at that school. There is little variation between the lower average salaries for St. Louis City schools; however, an abrupt increase in salaries occurs in schools immediately surrounding St. Louis City schools, even in the adjacent schools with a high percentage of FRL students (Figure 8.6). The average teacher salaries in schools outside of St. Louis City are by no means evenly distributed. At the elementary level, there are three groups of districts with different average salaries in their schools. Several districts in the far western part of the metro region have lower salaries across schools that are similar to those in St. Louis City.

Correlations between variables can also be given spatial perspective. Hogrebe, Kyei-Blankson, and Zou (2008) demonstrated several examples of how to map variable relationships that are summarized as correlation coefficients. They show in geographic space the relationships between the percentages of students scoring proficient or advanced on Missouri's high-stakes science test and variables such as FRL percentage, instructional expenditures per student, percentage of teachers with master's degrees, average years of teaching experience, and teachers' average salary. Mapping these variables in geographic space reveals how they change across districts and where the associations are strong and weak.

TYPES OF GIS APPLICATIONS

GIS Desktop Software

The broad category of desktop applications refers to GIS software that is loaded onto a local computer. This local software, such as ArcView by ESRI (http://www.esri.com) allows the user to define the overall purpose of the spatial database and to select the variables to

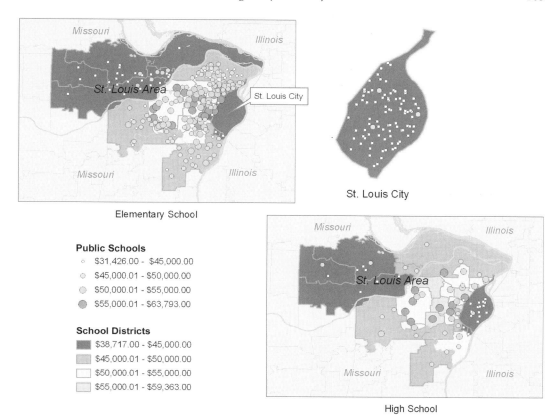

Figure 8.8. The background geospatial map shows variation in average salaries across districts. The circles are schools and their relative size represents the average teacher salary at that school. There is little variation between the lower average salaries for St. Louis City schools; however, an abrupt increase in salaries occurs in schools immediately surrounding St. Louis City schools. The average teacher salaries in schools outside of St. Louis City are not evenly distributed. Several districts in the far western part of the metro region have lower salaries across schools that are similar to those in St. Louis City.

be included. The desktop software puts the user in control of all aspects of a GIS project such as gathering, in-putting, analyzing, interpreting, and communicating geospatial data. It allows the user to develop and explore specific research questions of interest and to perform a variety of spatial and statistical analyses appropriate to the questions. In order to use most GIS desktop software, there is a learning curve in which the user needs some training to understand GIS concepts, navigate the software, know where to get data and how to import it, perform analyses, and generate maps. The primary advantage in learning to use a GIS software application is the tremendous flexibility it provides the user to define research questions, types of data, methods of analyses, map content, and presentation.

GIS Internet Applications

GIS Internet applications are websites that allow users to create real-time interactive maps. These Internet applications are developed by programmers with special software designed to run GIS on a server. The applications generally focus on a particular theme such as census data, schools, crime in a specific city, or local points of interest. The user selects from an existing list the variable or combination of variables to display on the map based on their own questions of interest related to the theme of the website. The advantage of the GIS Internet application is that no GIS or technical experience is required to use the interface and generate maps. The primary purpose is to communicate data in a spatial format. Internet GIS applications are best suited for descriptive research and information gathering. Probably the most familiar GIS Internet application is Google Earth (http://earth.google.com). Other popular GIS Internet sites include state and district education data at http://nces.ed.gov/surveys/sdds/ed/index.asp and census data at http://www.socialexplorer.com.

An example of a comprehensive GIS Internet application that focuses on St. Louis, Missouri, metropolitan schools and districts is located at http://maps.wustl.edu/cistl. The purpose of this interactive GIS website is to give teachers, administrators, parents, and other educational stakeholders immediate access to hundreds of variables about students, teachers, and schools located in 57 metropolitan school districts. The data are available to the general public on the Missouri Department of Elementary and Secondary Education website (http://dese.mo.gov), but not in a format that is easily accessible for regional study. Using these data, the site displays multiple variables in spatial format on maps that allow users to visually compare schools within and outside a district. The strength of this approach is that users with no GIS training can generate sophisticated maps that instantly project variable relationships and their spatial distribution across schools, districts, and the community.

The interface asks the user to select variables for districts and schools from a drop-down list. The user selects the year, the grouping method (i.e., equal interval, quantile, user-defined), and the number of groups (i.e., 3, 4, or 5). Pressing the "display" button generates a complete spatial map showing variation across schools and districts (see Figure 8.9). After the map is displayed, the user has access to navigation tools such as zooming and panning

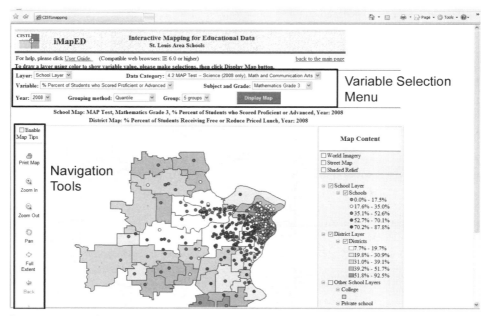

Figure 8.9. Interface for a comprehensive GIS Internet application that focuses on St. Louis, Missouri, metropolitan schools and districts that is located at http://maps.wustl.edu/cistl. The "iMapED" (Interactive Mapping for Educational Data) website gives immediate access to hundreds of variables about students, teachers, and schools located in 57 metropolitan school districts.

and the school and district layers can be turned on or off. There is a street layer and a satellite image layer that can be turned on to give more spatial context to the schools and districts.

More detailed analyses can be performed with this interface, such as in Figure 8.10, which shows the results of combining census block group data for the percentage of population 25 years of age or older who have a bachelor's degree, with data for individual schools about the percentage of students receiving free or reduced-price lunches (FRL). It is clear from the map that schools with a lower percentage of FRL students tend to be located in neighborhoods with higher percentages of bachelor's degrees.

The main point is that this type of Internet GIS application requires no training, but at the same time brings together large amounts of data from different sources and integrates them into a sophisticated and user-friendly research tool. It empowers those with minimal GIS experience to ask their own educational questions about students, teachers, and schools, and then to visualize the relationships in the geospatial context of neighborhoods and communities. This simplified approach allows educators, policymakers, and community leaders to have instant access to important educational data presented spatially that can enhance understanding of factors related to schools, neighborhoods, and student performance.

GIS Applications in K–12 Curricula

A third category of GIS applications for educators pertains to GIS in K–12 classrooms and can include the use of both desktop and Internet GIS applications. GIS is used by teachers to explain and demonstrate concepts and processes in content areas such as ecology, biology, geography, social sciences, and agricultural education. There are many content area lessons online that were developed for classroom use with GIS. Students learn to use GIS as a research methodology that requires them to become active learners in managing a project. GIS

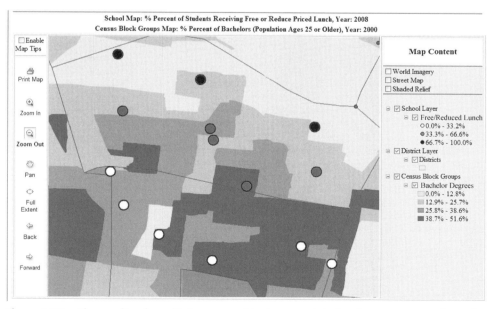

Figure 8.10. **The results of combining census block group data for the percentage of population 25 years of age or older who have a bachelor's degree, with FRL data for individual schools. Schools with lower percentage of FRL students tend to be located in neighborhoods with higher percentages of bachelor's degrees.**

is a great way to implement inquiry-based learning because it makes students define problems in specific content areas, develop research strategies, decide on which data to collect and how, analyze data, and communicate the results through the use of GIS applications. GIS demands an active, integrated approach to problem solving that relies on qualitative, quantitative, and spatial analysis of data.

CONCLUSION

The goal of this chapter was to demonstrate the significant value of adding a geospatial perspective in education research to better understand the different contexts that influence schools, teaching, and learning. Schools have physical locations in communities and neighborhoods that help shape the educational context. The GIS approach to studying and presenting data incorporates location and uses maps to visualize relationships for spatial and nonspatial variables. When GIS provides a geospatial dimension to the data, insights and hypotheses frequently emerge that lead to additional research questions. Spatial analysis complements other quantitative and qualitative research methods and can generate significant impact in presenting and communicating research findings. A geospatial perspective adds value to analysis methods that rely on global statistics and can enhance policy and segregation research by showing local variation and effects.

GIS interactive Internet applications are an easy and quick way to produce basic descriptive maps for census and school location variables, and some websites have additional variables related to a specific theme. In contrast, GIS desktop software applications require more training and practice, but give the user control over all aspects of data collection and map generation, as well as provide many spatial analysis tools for answering research questions. Spatial perspective and analysis using GIS research tools are widely used in many disciplines and industries. The time has come for education researchers to incorporate the geospatial perspective, which facilitates the understanding of the influence that neighborhoods and communities have in shaping the educational context.

REFERENCES

Anselin, L. (1999). The future of spatial analysis in the social sciences. *Geographic Information Sciences, 5*(2), 67–76.

Anselin, L. (2005). Spatial statistical modeling in a GIS environment. In D. J. Maguire, M. Batty, & M. F. Goodchild (Eds.), *GIS, spatial analysis, and modeling* (pp. 93–111). Redlands, CA: ESRI Press.

Berry, B. J. (2004). Spatial analysis in retrospect and prospect. In M. F. Goodchild & D. G. Janelle (Eds.), *Spatially integrated social science* (pp. 443–445). New York, NY: Oxford University Press.

Coulton, C. (2005). The place of community in social work practice research: Conceptual and methodological developments. *Social Work Research, 29*(2), 73–86.

De Veaux, R. D., Velleman, P. F., & Bock, D. E. (2005). *Stats: Data and models.* Boston, MA: Pearson Addison Wesley.

Fotheringham, A. S., Brunsdon, C., & Charlton, M. (2002). *Geographically weighted regression: The analysis of spatially varying relationships.* West Sussex, England: John Wiley & Sons.

Goodchild, M. F., & Janelle, D. G. (2004). Thinking spatially in the social sciences. In M. F. Goodchild & D. G. Janelle (Eds.), *Spatially integrated social science* (pp. 3–17). New York, NY: Oxford University Press.

Gordon, C. (2008). *Mapping decline: St. Louis and the fate of the American city.* Philadelphia: University of Pennsylvania Press.

Hogrebe, M. C., Kyei-Blankson, L., & Zou, L. (2008). Examining regional science attainment and school-teacher resources using GIS. *Education and Urban Society, 40*(5), 570–589.

Kreft, I., & De Leeuw, I. (2002). *Introducing multilevel modeling.* Thousand Oaks, CA: Sage Publications, Inc.

Maantay, J., & Ziegler, J. (2006). *GIS for the urban environment.* Redlands, CA: ESRI Press.

Mitchell, A. (2005). *The ESRI guide to GIS analysis, volume 2: Spatial measurements & statistics*. Redlands, CA: ESRI Press.

Morenoff, J. D., Sampson, R. J., & Raudenbush, S. W. (2001). Neighborhood inequality, collective efficacy, and the spatial dynamics of urban violence. *Criminology, 39*(3), 517–560.

Orfield, M. (2002). *American metropolitics: The new suburban reality*. Washington, DC: Brookings Institution Press.

Pedhazur, E. J. (1997). *Multiple regression in behavioral research: Explanation and prediction* (3rd ed.). Fort Worth, TX: Hartcourt Brace College Publishers.

Raudenbush, S. W., & Sampson, R. J. (1999). Ecometrics: Toward a science of assessing ecological settings, with application to the systemic social observation of neighborhoods. *Sociological Methodology, 29*, 1–41.

Robinson, W. S. (1950). Ecological correlations and the behavior of individuals. *American Sociological Review, 15*, 351–357.

Sampson, R. J. (2003). The neighborhood context of well-being. *Perspectives in Biology and Medicine, 46*(3), 53–64.

Sampson, R. J., Morenoff, J. D., & Gannon-Rowley, T. (2002). Assessing neighborhood effects: Social processes and new direction in research. *Annual Review of Sociology, 28*, 443–478.

Schuurman, N. (2004). *GIS: A short introduction*. Malden, MA: Blackwell Publishing.

Tate, W. (2008). Geography of opportunity: Poverty, place, and educational outcomes. *Educational Researcher, 37*(7), 397–411.

U.S. Census Bureau. (2000). *Census 2000 summary file 3 for St. Louis City and St. Louis County, MO block groups: Variable P88 ratio of income in 1999 to poverty level* (data file). American Fact Finder data download center. Available from http://factfinder.census.gov/servlet/DownloadCenterServlet?_ts=340543733936

Ward, M. D., & Gleditsch, S. K. (2008). *Spatial regression models*. Thousand Oaks, CA: Sage Publications.

III

TEACHING AND LEARNING RESEARCH IN SOCIAL CONTEXT

9

Conceptual and Methodological Challenges to a Cultural and Ecological Framework for Studying Human Learning and Development

Carol D. Lee

Human learning and development are complex. While this proposition on the surface would appear to be pretty much common sense, how researchers examine this phenomenon often does not address the complexity and diversity of what and how humans learn across time. As researchers, we are often driven by the singular focus of our disciplinary training, in terms of the questions we ask, the concepts and theories upon which we draw, and the research designs and analytic methods we employ. It would be naive to assert that we have learned little from such disciplinary foci. Indeed we have. At the same time, there remain many unanswered questions and what I deem to be many misconceptions that impact how we evaluate groups of people, including how we understand the geopolitical spaces they occupy. Such evaluations play out in consequential ways in recommendations and traditions of practice, whether it's how we think about learning in school, how we think about socialization in families and peer groups, or the resources and constraints of neighborhoods. Such evaluations often position particular kinds of knowledge, particular ways of communicating, particular ways of learning, and particular institutional resources as privileged and inevitable for meaningful learning to occur. As a consequence, in school settings especially, there are often disconnects between the indicators of knowledge competence and socio-emotional self-regulation that youth from nondominant communities and youth who are poor display when they are in school versus when they are in nonschool contexts (Nasir & Saxe, 2003).

I begin this discussion about such disconnects in displays of competence for two reasons. First, failure to thrive in school has detrimental life course outcomes, especially for youth from nondominant groups (e.g., persistent poverty, disparities in health status, greater likelihood of imprisonment—especially for males) (Boykin, 1986; McKinsey & Company Social Sector Office, 2009). The persistent achievement gap in the United States based on race, ethnicity, and class remains a dilemma of both educational practice and research (Ramani, Gilbertson, & Fox, 2007). Explanations for this achievement gap more often than not focus on the negative impacts of poverty (Coleman et al., 1966; V. Lee & Burkham, 2002; Massey & Denton, 1993; Wilson, 1987), on negative attributions with regard to family socialization (Furstenberg & Hughes, 1995; Jencks, 1972; Lareau & Horvat, 1999; Phillips, Brooks-Gunn, Duncan, Klebanov, & Crane, 1998), or inadequate knowledge or linguistic preparation for school (Bereiter & Engelmann, 1966; Bernstein, 1961; Deutsch & Brown, 1964), and on negative attributions to the internal states of students (e.g., not valuing school, low self-esteem, lack of emotional self-regulation) (Fordham, 1996; Ogbu, 1981). Each of these explanations typically focuses on singular institutions (e.g., the quality of schools, family functioning, or neighborhood climate). These explanations are complex in that each holds some aspect of truth, and yet many are also clouded by a broad narrative of cultural-deficit thinking that has characterized social, intellectual, and political history in the United States, indeed the Western world (Mills, 1997). Each explanation is rooted in some disciplinary tradition (i.e., sociology, cognitive psychology, child and adolescent development, education, etc.) that typically examines individuals within a singular setting, considers groups based on ethnicity and race as homogeneous, and conceptualizes learning as based on singular normative pathways. I am arguing that each of these assumptions, and especially if one considers them simultaneously, entails very narrow and constraining views that shift our attention away from the dynamic and diverse nature of human development. For that reason, I argue that both our ability to influence practice (that is, optimal conditions for learning in school and in families as two fundamental and influential settings) *and* our ability to construct robust and generative theories about human learning and development over time and space are equally constrained (C. D. Lee, 2008; C. D. Lee, in press). For example, while Piaget's experiments with his own children and children with similar life experiences unearthed powerful insights about mechanisms that triggered conceptual reorganization of understanding of such phenomena as conservation of matter, attempts to extrapolate his theories writ large across diverse populations proved problematic (Rogoff & Chavajay, 1995). It was not the case that his ideas about assimilation and accommodation or developmental pathways toward the ability to engage in formal logic were wrong, but rather that the pathways through which such processes occur and the valued outcomes of mature reasoning differed substantively across different cultural communities. And it is precisely a dynamic view of cultural practices that led Piagetian-trained scholars in the 1970s to think critically about how to examine competence in reasoning in ways that situated elicitation tasks and methods of analysis to be as responsive as possible to the contexts in which such reasoning occurred and to understand that when such reasoning (as in the case of logical syllogisms) did not occur in everyday or institutional practices, it was not due to a fundamental inability, but rather to the history of peoples' participation in particular practices, practices that served contextually responsive functions. This conceptual and methodological transition by scholars such as Michael Cole (1996), Barbara Rogoff (2003), Geoffrey Saxe (1991), Patricia Greenfield (2004), Jean Lave (1988), and others led to the emergence of fields such as everyday cognition and situated cognition. At the same time, in part because of our disciplinary silos, this shift to more cultural and ecological orientations of research on human learning and development has had little impact on practice, whether the practice of schooling or efforts to influence or understand the practices of families.

So I seek here to revisit questions of culture and ecology as the highly intertwined medium through which learning and development occur, and in doing so to explore the challenges that thinking in dynamic ways about culture and ecology pose with regard to relevant constructs, theoretical frameworks, research designs, and methods of analysis.

WHAT DO WE MEAN BY A CULTURAL AND ECOLOGICAL FRAMEWORK FOR HUMAN LEARNING AND DIVERSITY?

The fundamental idea is that people learn and mature as a consequence of the interplays among individual characteristics (genetic, physiological, psychological); characteristics of the groups to which the individual belongs (either by self-identification or ascription by others); and the characteristics of settings (e.g., social, physical, cognitive) (Cole, 2007; Quartz & Sejnowski, 2002; Rogoff, 2003; Saxe, 1999). This interplay is dynamic in that people influence settings and settings influence people. This interplay entails peoples' participation within and across multiple settings, within and across multiple dimensions of time (e.g., phylogenetic [the history of humans as a species], cultural historical [particular historical time periods], ontogenetic [over an individual's life course], and microgenetic [interactions in the moment]) (Bronfenbrenner & Morris, 1998). The fact that human learning and maturation occur within and across various routine settings indicates that it is the ecology of peoples' lives that matters, rather than a singular impact of participation in any one setting. The fact that participation in these various settings always entails shared (or for that matter contests over presumptions about what is or is not shared) knowledge, beliefs, dispositions, artifacts, and ways of using language means that participation in these settings is cultural. The tools of cultural participation are most often passed on across generations.

The idea that what is shared can also be contested is one of the more difficult big ideas to understand about how participation in cultural practices takes place. It is the contestation and transformation of knowledge, beliefs, artifacts, ways of using language, and indeed goals for participation that form the basis for the generation of new cultural knowledge, knowledge that has shifted over time as a consequence of efforts of both individuals and groups to respond to shifts in life conditions.

Humans are genetically oriented to make meaning of experience, to impose salience on experience as a guide for future actions, with the purpose of fulfilling fundamental goals of development (e.g., a sense of physical well-being, of belonging, of efficacy, of impact on the environment, of self-worth) (Maslow, 1954; Quartz & Sejnowski, 2002; Spencer, 2006; Weiner, 1985). We have survived as a species because of our ability to adapt to new circumstances. In early human history, the circumstances required for physical survival not only changed over time, but differed substantially in various parts of the world. As a consequence, human communities have and continue to differ substantively in terms of valued forms of social organization (e.g., family life, institutional configurations, forms of economic production) (Super & Harkness, 1986). While it may be easier for us to think about differences among human communities living in different regions of the world during different historical periods, we struggle to conceptualize what diversity in human communities means in the contemporary United States. This includes thinking about when, where, and why such differences matter.

Human communities or cultural groups may be defined by ethnicity (including pan-ethnicity), nationality, gender, age cohort (such as current elders who grew up during the Great Depression), class, religion, sexual orientation, political persuasions, as well as specialized professional or personal interests and skills. I have consciously not included race in this typology because I argue that race is a political construct, historically and currently used to create perceptions about dichotomies based on phenotype; and to propagate differential statuses with regard to power, wealth, and access. Race requires political, sociological, and economic analyses (Ladson-Billings & Tate, 1995; Mills, 1997). Its impact on fundamental issues of learning and development are a consequence of its political and economic influences on opportunity and on development (i.e., the kinds of challenges with which people must learn to wrestle because of the stereotypes and constraints that racism perpetuates) (Graham & Hudley, 2005; Spencer, 1987; Steele, 2004). Thus I prefer to address it from a different lens. For example, instead of a cultural focus on race, I propose that people of African descent living in the diaspora can be understood in terms of cultural practices in more appropriate ways as a pan-ethnic community (based on routine and shared cultural practices) (Akbar, 1979; Asante & Asante, 1990; Hatchett & Jackson, 1999; Hilliard, 1998;

Holloway, 1990; Smitherman, 2000) and as individual ethnic communities (e.g., blacks descended from the African holocaust of enslavement, and more recent black immigrants from the Caribbean, South and Central America, and Africa) (Cross, 1991; Dodoo, 1997; Rong & Brown, 2001; Sellers et al., 1998). There is no doubt that constructions around race directly impact these African-descent communities, but as a consequence of attributions from outside the community as opposed to self-attributions based on intergenerational beliefs and practices.

Indeed this discussion of the ecology of peoples' lives and the role of culture on their participation in the practices associated with the various settings of their lives sounds overwhelmingly complicated (Rogoff, 2002). And it is precisely that complexity that has challenged and continues to challenge how researchers interested in human learning and development (including its implications for practice) are able or even willing to try and tackle its implications.

I agree with Rogoff's metaphor about tackling such complexity. She argues against representations of ecological contexts (i.e., the Bronfenbrenner concentric circles) as nested boxes or circles. Such representations do not capture the dynamic relations among levels of context (e.g., societal, neighborhood, family) or relations across contexts (e.g., family, school, community organizations, peers, social networks, etc.); nor do they capture the all-important role of time (as I have already discussed). Rather she offers a representation of a whole activity—in her example a child with other children in a classroom—inscribed onto a film image to suggest movement over time. She then uses the metaphor of a lens through which the researcher can foreground and background particular aspects of the context (i.e., the individual, the group, interactional processes at play, artifacts being used) (Rogoff, 1995). This representation is useful, but still does not capture the presence of other settings on which the lens can be directed (e.g., the child at school and at home; the neighborhood and the school, etc.).

However, I do think the metaphor of a lens can serve as a useful heuristic, especially if we can figure out some way to represent a person in various settings across time. Whether through the arduous description I have offered so far, or some other representation, we are able to conceptualize the wholeness of an ecology and its cultural foundations, such a conceptualization can help to influence the range of questions we may pose to investigate. In addition, the fundamental assumptions that undergird such a framework or orientation, I think, also lead us to raise at least a minimal set of possible threats to validity and reliability in our research designs and analytic methods. For example, influenced in large part by sociocultural traditions inspired by Vygotsky and being disseminated through translations from the Russian (of Vygotsky, Luria, and others) through efforts of Michael Cole, James Wertsch, and others, a generation of researchers in what would become an emerging field of cultural psychology engaged in exactly the kind of reasoning I am proposing (Vygotsky, 1978, 1981; Wertsch, 1985). For example, when Scribner and Cole found that the instruments they were using, based on European samples, to examine the ability to engage in syllogistic reasoning among the Vai of Liberia suggested that the Vai were incapable of such reasoning, they chose a very revolutionary path (Scribner & Cole, 1981). They asked a basically different set of questions founded on a fundamental belief that competence is context dependent, rather than abstractly monolithic and universal. I believe it was their orientation to understanding culture and people's participation in routine practices across the settings of their lives that mattered and inspired a qualitatively different kind of thinking that led them to question the validity of their earlier design. It was an orientation based on the fundamental assumption that human communities engage in and value different pathways through which basic psychological needs are met.

We can contrast this cultural and ecological orientation to more traditional and indeed pervasive studies of human learning and development, including family functioning. I choose to illustrate this point through a brief discussion of research that currently informs educational practice, particularly with regard to subject matter learning in school.

Learning to read is perhaps the most basic skill to be learned in school because success in almost every subject requires the ability to comprehend written texts. While there are children (typically middle and upper-middle class) who learn to read at home through sustained interactions with parents, most children learn to read in school. There is an influential school of thought that argued middle-class children bring a significantly more advanced vocabulary to school than poor children (Hall & Moats, 1999; Hart & Risley, 1995). This difference in vocabulary development is theorized as a function of middle-class parents engaging their children in talk that mirrors the kinds of dialogues that characterize instruction in school. Specifically, it is contended that middle-class parents ask known-answer questions, use didactic questions to direct children's problem-solving behavior, focus on metacognitive talk in which children explain their reasoning, and scaffold linear oral narratives with an emphasis on a literal representation of events. Further, middle-class parents have many books in the home and read to their children to introduce them to texts. The researchers then extrapolate from these propositions to argue that poor children (and by extension children from particular ethnic minority communities because poverty and racial/ethnic status are so tightly intertwined in the United States) come to school ill prepared to learn to read.

I believe there are several fundamental flaws to this argument from a cultural and ecological perspective. First, it posits class status as monolithic. To presume that family economic status is deterministic of academic outcomes can blind our attention to variation among middle-class samples (Patillo, 1999). It also blinds us from even asking the question whether there are other repertoires that children living in poverty (even considering how differentiated such a group may be) construct out of their experiences in families, community organizations, churches, neighborhood life, or popular culture (such as media exposure) that may represent knowledge, ways of using language, dispositions or habits of mind that may be useful for learning to read (both to decode and to comprehend within and across an array of kinds of texts) (C. D. Lee, 2005a, 2005b, 2005c; Nasir, Rosebery, Warren, & Lee, 2006). Efforts to conceptualize what such relevant repertoires may be invite a reexamination of what is entailed in learning to read with understanding (C. D. Lee, 1997). These efforts have proven useful in expanding our understanding of reading processes and as a consequence to finding ways to incorporate such everyday repertoires as resources for learning (Au, 1980; Gutiérrez, Baquedano-Lopez, & Tejeda, 1999).

There are several programs of research in the area of reading that illustrate this point. Sarah Michaels and Courtney Cazden studied a practice in primary classrooms called sharing time (Cazden, Michaels, & Tabors, 1985; Michaels, 1981). The idea is that children bring objects from home and tell stories before their peers about these objects. Teachers use these personal narratives as an opportunity to provide children with feedback that scaffolds being explicit in describing events and characters and in sequencing events of the narrative. In their sample, white middle-class children told linear stories and teachers responded with guidance for improving. The African American children who were speakers of African American English told stories that on the surface appeared to meander and teachers found it difficult to provide the children with guidance because they thought the stories did not make sense. Michaels distinguished between the two types of narratives as topic centered versus topic associative. In a later analysis of the Michaels and Cazden data, James Paul Gee (1989) reexamined the stories of the African American children using literary theory and narrative analysis. Gee concluded that these stories were structurally more complex, examined issues of point of view in multilayered ways, and were actually more like literary narratives than the topic-centered stories that the school had valued. Similar work of the structure of oral narratives among children who are speakers of African American English Vernacular (AAEV) has been conducted by Tempii Champion (Champion, 1998, 2003; Champion, Seymour, & Camarata, 1995). While it is not clear that there has been any substantive uptake of these insights, efforts to understand the repertoires (knowledge, linguistic, dispositional) that children from diverse backgrounds bring to the learning of disciplines in schools in the case of Michaels, Cazden, Champion, and Gee are insightful.

In a similar vein, Kathy Au (1980; Tharp & Gallimore, 1988) working with native Hawaiian children in the Kamameha Project drew on an indigenous speech genre called talk story. Teachers in the project designed instructional conversations along the lines of talk story and students were found to be more deeply engaged in communicating about their reading and to make substantive improvements in their comprehension.

In the Cultural Modeling project (C. D. Lee, 1993, 1995a, 1995b, 2007), the tacit knowledge AAEV speakers use to produce and comprehend figurative language was scaffolded to support literary reasoning of canonical texts. Besides the opportunities that the Cultural Modeling design afforded students, these efforts also led to a reexamination of the kinds of problems that canonical texts posed to novice readers. The efforts to understand these everyday strategies then led to the development of heuristics for tackling generative interpretive problems in literature. This focus on heuristics is not common in the pedagogy of English teachers in contrast to a dominant focus on heuristics in domains like mathematics.

The point of these examples is to illustrate the kinds of new knowledge that can be generated when attention is directed to the cultural foundations of experiences distributed across people's participation in multiple settings. A central feature of these examples is that they demonstrate how prior knowledge embedded in everyday experience is connected to disciplinary knowledge.

Such a research focus also invites studies about how knowledge is distributed across settings and how the organization of particular settings may facilitate or constrain the uptake or transformation of what learners bring to new tasks. When settings are sufficiently dynamic, they invite adaptation of old knowledge to new forms of representation or to serve new functions. Saxe (1991) refers to this as a form-function shift of knowledge representations across time. The narrow views of learning that I have critiqued seem to view schooling as static, to see the work of learning academic knowledge like putting together a puzzle in which all the pieces have been predefined. On the other hand, we have abundant evidence of settings other than schools reflecting the kind of adaptive and dynamic learning conditions to which I am referring. These include community organizations, churches, and routine sites where people learn to play games and sports (A. Ball, 1995; Heath, 2004; Heath & McLaughlin, 1994; McLaughlin, Irby, & Langman, 1994; Nasir, 2000, 2002, 2005; Nasir, Hand, & Taylor, 2008). Many view the knowledge constructed in such everyday settings as less rigorous and demanding than learning in school; or that such knowledge is concrete and practical versus the knowledge of schooling seen as decontextualized and abstract. That body of research documenting everyday cognition, however, belies such claims. While Vygotsky made a similar distinction between what he called spontaneous (i.e., informal and intuited from everyday practice) and scientific concepts (formal and typically learned in school), he also argued that spontaneous concepts formed the foundation on which scientific concepts are built (Wertsch, 1985). Despite these controversies, a fundamental question remains. What features of a given setting facilitate the transformation of existing knowledge to new forms? I will argue that how we conceptualize our research will inform the response to this question.

CONCEPTUAL CHALLENGES TO THE CONDUCT OF RESEARCH FROM A CULTURAL AND ECOLOGICAL FRAMEWORK

There are many conceptual challenges to be considered when conducting research. Among the most difficult is how we conceptualize the idea of culture and cultural membership. I have discussed this idea somewhat in the earlier section of this chapter.

We have been socialized to think of culture as static and of cultural membership as homogenous (Gutiérrez & Rogoff, 2003). It has proven difficult to take into account the fact that culture has the heavy hand of history and tradition behind it. This means that institutional configurations (whether family life, schools, church, bookstores, basketball teams, etc.) have patterned ways of being that continue across generations. St. Patrick's Day continues to be celebrated in the United States among people who have never set foot in Ireland and have little idea about its history and meaning. Many African American families and families whose ancestors grew up in the South will eat black-eyed peas and greens for dinner for New Year's Day. Wherever in the world you find communities of African descent, you will also find a devotion to polyrhythmic music. I can see in me so many ways not only of my mother, but of my maternal grandmother whom I never knew.

At the same time, cultures are always in a state of change (Rogoff, 2003). Sometimes these changes are minor due to the adaptations that individuals always make to perceived norms. Sometimes because of bigger historical, political, economic, or physical changes in the environment, we see big changes. Certainly the introduction of new artifacts, new technologies, often will spark substantive changes in cultural practices. For example, the evolution and ubiquity of digital technologies is introducing huge changes in literacy practices and forms of social organization attached to these emerging literacy practices; such changes are easily tantamount to, if not greater than, the impact of the introduction of the printing press (Alvermann & Hagood, 2000; Alvermann, Hinchman, Moore, Phelps, & Waff, 2006; Resnick & Resnick, 1977). Whether the research questions about which we are interested should focus on that which is stable or on that which is in the midst of change is one of the issues with which researchers need to wrestle when adopting a cultural and ecological framework.

Another conceptual challenge has to do with how we think about cultural membership. In fields like psychology and sociology, there is a dominant focus on categorizing people according to some presumed cultural membership. Studies abound that presume to control for the influences of race, ethnicity, or some aspect of the construct of socioeconomic status on an outcome of interest. Orellana and Bowman (2003) make a compelling critique of such approaches. They argue that often researchers do not have sufficient knowledge of the array of kinds of practices in which people are engaged to be able to disentangle whether the set of variables being measured are sufficient to account for the correlations with the outcomes of interest. We often do not know how the variation in correlations with race or family configuration may actually subsume some other set of explanatory practices. For example, while studies may account for single- versus two-parent households, they often do not investigate the range of social capital of extended family networks involved in single-parent households (e.g., grandparents, aunts, and uncles who may play an active role in child socialization or the economic well-being of the target family). On a personal note, as a young child I was in a single-parent household, but my extended family of grandparents, aunts, uncles, and cousins showered me with physical, social, emotional, and cognitive resources that my mother alone could never have done. Studies that examine how many words children have learned upon entering school often do not gather data on other language practices that may yield relevant information about the kinds of metalinguistic knowledge related to reading that children bring as resources when they enter school; for example, Michaels's (1981),

Cazden's (Cazden et al., 1985), and Gee's (1989) research on the structure of oral narratives among speakers of African American English or Orellana's (2009; Orellana, Reynolds, Dorner, & Meza, 2003) and Valdes's (1996, 2001, 2002) research on kinds of knowledge that bilingual children who translate for their families develop.

Orellana and Bowman (2003) propose that we would do better to gather as extensive a body of knowledge about the range of practices in which people routinely engage first and then see how these practices map out with regard to particular configurations of cultural membership. We might find from such an approach that practices which seem on the surface to be different might actually cohere under broader explanatory constructs that might in fact produce insights that are more generalizable across populations. The bottom line is to avoid what Gutiérrez and Rogoff (2003) call the box problem, wherein we focus only on the patterned ways of particular groups and ignore the variation within groups, or where we think of people as only belonging to a single group, often based on race, ethnicity, or class.

A second conceptual challenge has to do with constructing representations or frameworks that can serve as heuristics or guideposts for thinking about the universes of complexity that I have been describing. Such representations or conceptual frameworks, I argue, need to meet the following minimal criteria. They should draw our attention to as many of the following as seems feasible and applicable to the phenomena of interest:

- The consequences of peoples' participation in more than one setting
- The role of identity, beliefs and perceptions
- Processes within and across settings that help to shape forms of participation, including shared and contested norms and also including what facilitates the uptake, transformation, or constraint on prior knowledge or dispositions that new participants to the setting bring
- Configurations of settings, including spatial and physical dimensions and artifacts used
- The role that some dimension of time may play (e.g., where developmentally in the life course are key players; influences that result from when in cultural historical time the activity takes place; how changes in forms of participation unfold over shorter or longer stretches of time)

Conceptual frameworks that draw our attention to such issues offer opportunities to examine how new ideas and understandings emerge for individuals, for groups, for settings. They can also help us understand how the cognitive, social, and emotional dimensions of learning are intertwined, and how such dimensions are embodied in practice, with what consequences for forms of participation.

I will point to several examples of such conceptual frameworks that I have found very informative for my own research. These include Saxe's four-parameter model (Saxe, 1991), Margaret Spencer's PVEST (Spencer, 2006), and Eccles's subjective task value model (Eccles, Wigfield, & Schiefele, 1998). I offer a very abbreviated description of each and point out how some of the criteria I outlined below are captured in these models. I think of them not only as hypotheses to be tested, but also as heuristics or guideposts about the kinds of variables that need attention. Each in its own way takes on the conceptual challenges of a cultural-ecological orientation to human learning and development.

Saxe (1991) identified three components that need to be examined in order to understand the cultural and ecological foundations of what and how children learn. The first component refers to the kind and structure of goals that emerge in goal-directed behavior. The second component refers to the knowledge, or what he calls cognitive forms, and the functions they serve as people engage in activity. With this second component, Saxe is interested in what he calls shifts in the form and function that particular kinds of knowledge serve as children move within and across settings, or as children develop over time. The third component involves understanding the range of cognitive forms that children learn as they participate in different cultural practices. This third component addresses the problem of transfer, or how what one learns in one setting may be taken up and used in another setting. These areas addressed by Saxe sit centrally in a cultural and ecological orientation to human learning and development. Both the three-component model described here and the four-parameter model discussed in the next paragraph can serve as useful heuristics for the kinds of questions we can ask and have implications for relevant kinds of data and analytic methods.

In order to analyze how goals emerge inside of goal-directed behavior, Saxe offers four parameters that influence the focus, emergence, and even transformation of goals. Saxe's four-parameter model aims to provide a structure through which we can understand how new goals emerge in the midst of practices, as shown in Figure 9.1.

The model represented in Figure 9.1 identifies four variables that influence what Saxe calls emergent goals—that is, goals that emerge as people are engaged in an activity. The first variable is the prior understandings the learner brings to the activity. The second variable is how the activity setting is organized. The third is the nature of social interactions within the activity, and the fourth are the artifacts being used or conventions that embody ways of doing things together. I find the idea of emergent goals particularly compelling because so much research on learning in situ does not focus on the idea of emergence as a negotiation that always occurs, situating all parties as agentive. Saxe used the model as a heuristic for understanding how poor children selling candy on the streets of a city in Brazil developed and learned to carry out new goals for selling (e.g., figuring out that how the candy was packaged mattered for profit or how the foreign exchange rate mattered for the price when selling to foreigners).

Eccles (Eccles, 2005; Eccles & Midgley, 1989; Eccles et al., 1993; Eccles et al., 1998) offers a model for the multiple sources of influence that help to shape children's motivation

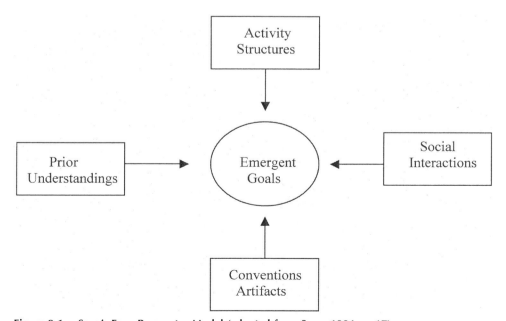

Figure 9.1.   Saxe's Four Parameter Model (adapted from Saxe, 1991, p. 17)

to achieve academic goals. It posits that beliefs and perceptions of children and those who socialize them matter. It goes beyond focusing on the child, the classroom or the family as the singular influence on children's motivation. Instead the model embodies the idea that it is the dynamic relationships among the child, those who socialize them (i.e., parents, teachers, other adult caregivers) that are sources of motivation. The model posits that academic motivation is influenced by cultural factors (e.g., the cultural beliefs, values, and stereotypes that are a part of the child's environment). Such cultural beliefs, values, and stereotypes can include ideas like girls are not good at mathematics, that learning is based on innate ability and therefore effort doesn't really matter. The Eccles model focuses on the child's participation in more than one setting in looking at the broader cultural milieu and the child's participation in prior achievement-related activities (which can be offered in any number of settings). It certainly focuses on issues of identity, beliefs, and perceptions. Because the child's prior experiences are embedded in the model, dimensions of time are incorporated. As a developmental psychologist, Eccles is keenly aware that how this model plays out will differ for children of different age cohorts. And finally, this is largely a process model, drawing our attention to the cultural and ecological factors that will play out in the face-to-face interactions in classrooms or other sites where there is explicit attention to learning. Figure 9.2 represents the elements of that model.

Finally, the PVEST model of Margaret Spencer has been extremely influential in my own thinking (Spencer, 1985, 1987, 1995, 1999, 2001, 2006, 2008). Margaret and I have collaborated on several publications and research efforts because I have been intrigued by what I see as complementary about my own Cultural Modeling Framework and PVEST (C. D. Lee, Spencer, & Harpalani, 2003). I will not address PVEST in great detail because Professor Spencer has a chapter in this volume. PVEST focuses on the role of identity processes in how people learn to cope over time. It emphasizes the fundamental role of perception, particularly perceptions of threat, and employs a risk-resiliency model to account for how the experience of challenge can be moderated by the balance and nature of risks and protective factors in one's environment. She argues that the coping strategies we develop over time become part of an emergent identity, a kind of tacit guidepost that we use to monitor what we perceive as threatening and what kinds of responses we think are appropriate. She situates this model in terms of the broader ecology of people's lives and how living under conditions of poverty, racism, and sexism complicate the normative challenges of life course development. PVEST focuses on more than one setting in accounting for how people's past experiences and perceptions influence what they make of new settings, experiences, and tasks. It most fundamentally focuses on identity processes as the underlying mechanism that influences if and how we cope. PVEST is a process model, here a model of psychological processes that occur not just in the "minds" of individuals, but that are also situated in relationships. PVEST addresses issues of time because it is posited as a recursive model across the life course. I will discuss later what I have found to be useful sources of complementarity between PVEST and my own work in Cultural Modeling. Figure 9.3 is a representation of the PVEST framework.

Each of these conceptual frameworks is complex. While they focus on different phenomena, they wrestle with the broad complexities of the cultural and ecological medium through which learning and development occur. To employ or adapt these frameworks can serve an important heuristic function in terms of focusing the researcher's attention on the dynamic and interrelated issues that influence human learning and development. Each in its own way takes an explicitly cultural perspective, attending to the role of beliefs, values, and intergenerational practices.

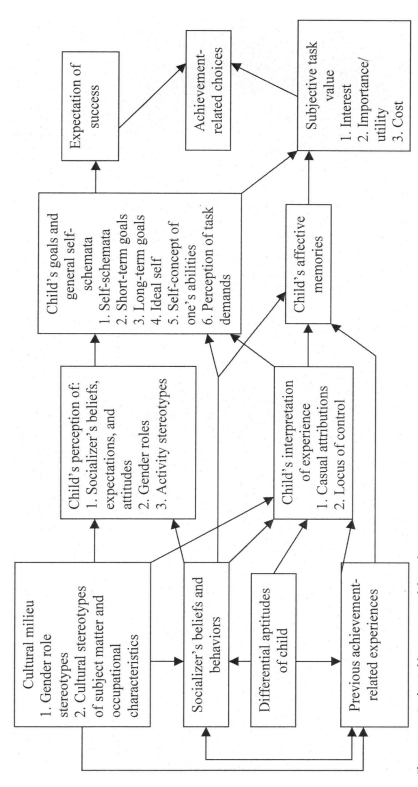

Figure 9.2.   Eccles Achievement Model (Eccles, 2005, p. 106)

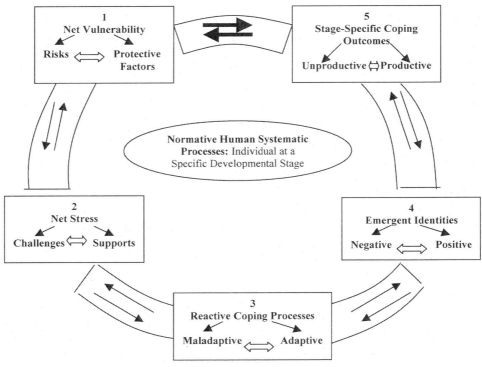

Figure 9.3.   Spencer's PVEST (Lee, Spencer, & Harpalani, 2003, p. 9)

METHODOLOGICAL CHALLENGES

Perhaps even more challenging is the question of what research designs and analytic methods are available to deal with such complex dynamic systems. Important is the ability to address issues of change across time, especially when the underlying mechanisms influencing such change involve dynamic rather than simple linear relationships; the reciprocal relationships across nested contexts; and influences on change at different levels of context, such as the influences of macro-level historical, political, and economic events on both group patterns but also individual variation in impact. In terms of quantitative approaches, we have methods such as hierarchical linear modeling, growth-curve modeling and event history analysis that can address issues of multiple context and influences on growth over time. However, in a practical sense, the kinds of questions that have more often than not been addressed by these sophisticated tools have not been of the complexity that I have been describing with regard to a cultural and ecological orientation to human learning and development. I think there are several reasons for this situation. First, the challenges to conducting research with this orientation are both conceptual and methodological, as I have described. If one is studying, for example, the joint influences of family and school on children's academic development, and one wishes to go beyond simple correlations between some measure of academic outcome and some input variables with regard to family and school characteristics or demographics, it is necessary to have a deep conceptual understanding of family processes and pedagogical processes. Typically, we do not find single individuals who bring the methodological training in these multilevel methods as well as deep conceptual understanding of domains of human development and learning. As a consequence, the kinds of research that I envision will likely require partnerships in which these multiple sources of expertise can be brought to bear.

These multilevel statistical models generally require large sample sizes. As a consequence, if one is interested in process as well as outcomes, collecting indicators of processes for a large sample can be challenging. Recent research by Deborah Ball, Brian Rowan, and colleagues at the University of Michigan has made progress in this area by developing observational protocols of classroom practices provided by both students and teachers in order to achieve the large sample size needed to study processes beyond direct observation (D. L. Ball & Rowan, 2004; Hill, Rowan, & Ball, 2005; Rowan, Correnti, & Miller, 2002). These protocols do not require direct observation and therefore allow for large-scale sampling. The design involving joint survey-like data from both students and teachers in the same classroom provide a validity check for the observations. The design is an important breakthrough because the survey items are repeated across time and focus on instructional processes, thus providing a useful bridge between what researchers are able to capture through direct observation and the potential generalizability with larger sample sizes.

Qualitative methods offer useful tools for examining processes in situ, within and across settings. However, such methods are labor intensive and as a consequence often involve small sample sizes. There are often challenges about the generalizability of findings involving small sample sizes. However, we need further discussion about how the accumulation of comparable findings across smaller qualitative studies can provide warrants for generalizability. For example, what does a research synthesis for qualitative studies as a parallel to meta-analysis in quantitative syntheses look like? In addition, it can be challenging using qualitative methods to examine changes over stretches of time; the use of cross-sectional designs is one method of accounting for developmental changes over time, and archival research where appropriate can help us understand changes over broader stretches of cultural-historical time.

Mixed methods offer a toolkit of options that can potentially address the limitations of the sole use of qualitative or quantitative methods. I will briefly discuss several long-term programs of research employing mixed methods that can illustrate how an explicitly cultural and ecological orientation can be robustly examined.

Geoffrey Saxe's study of the evolution of changes in the construct of Fu among the Oksapmin of Papua New Guinea, his work among Brazilian children candy sellers, and Barbara Rogoff's study of the functions and distribution of intent participation among Mayan and Mayan descent communities are interesting and powerful examples (Rogoff, Paradise, Mejía-Arauz, Correa-Chávez, & Angelillo, 2003; Saxe, 1991; Saxe & Esmonde, 2005). These programs of research involved extended ethnography in each community. On the basis of patterns of routine activity and analyses of how these routine activities are organized and the kinds of knowledge developed from such participation, they then moved to designing clinical tasks based on these observations. The design of these clinical tasks took up the challenge proffered by Bronfenbrenner (Bronfenbrenner & Morris, 1998) with regard to ecological validity. Through strategic sampling for the clinical interviews—members of the cultural community of different ages or with different levels of expertise to capture expert-novice differences, comparative samples of people with varying degrees of experience with the routine activity of interest (from both within and outside the target community)—they were able to systematically document both what and how people learned, including documenting how what was learned differed according to experience. The design of the tasks was based on the rich ethnographic observations they had made. The clinical interviews involved a quasi-experimental design and were subjected to quantitative analyses. The clinical interviews also allowed them to examine outcomes of learning that occur in the context of everyday activity but that would not be amenable to examining quantitatively through observations in situ.

Saxe's research regarding the construct of Fu is particularly innovative. Among the Oksapmin of Papua New Guinea, *Fu* is a lexical term used in relation to their traditional system of counting using body parts. The mathematical functions of the term changed radically from 1978 when Saxe first studied Oksapmin mathematical cognition. As Saxe and Esmonde (2005) note, "The word form *fu* has changed from its use as an intensive quantifier that means 'a complete group of plenty' to one that means double a numerical value" (p. 171). This change evolved over many decades through changes in cultural contacts and forms of economic exchange. Saxe and Esmonde achieved major methodological advances in creating representations that show the influences of macro-level historical/political and economic events on changes in the form and function of this idea of Fu and how such changes look over life course development (i.e., how children and adults of different ages have different understandings and representations of Fu based on what was going on at critical points in their development). It is very rare to find research that is able to connect macro-genetic, ontogenetic, and micro-genetic processes as co-occurring and mutually interdependent. While sociologists often use large-scale data sets to make inferences about macro-level events and policies and impacts on groups of people, such work does not typically address variation in impact nor help to explain the social processes through which people actually experience macro-level events.

In my own work, I have tried to address questions that reflect a cultural and ecological orientation to human learning and development. I have been interested in *how structures of knowledge constructed out of everyday experience* can be scaffolded to support academic learning. The target academic domain is literary reasoning embodied in the teaching of literature at the secondary school level. The population of interest is African American adolescents who are also speakers of African American English Vernacular (AAEV). The cultural issues at play in this program of research include shared norms about language play in AAEV communities and in youth popular culture. The cognitive issues involve the structure of knowledge deployed in the process of making meaning of literary texts. I am interested in youth's participation in two settings—routine activities in family life and peer social networks in which attention to language play is central to what people are doing, and literature classes in high schools, particularly schools with histories of underachievement. I am interested in processes because I seek to understand what in the social, material, and physical organization of secondary literature classrooms in the kinds of schools I have described facilitate the uptake and transformation of the knowledge, dispositions, and habits of mind that these youth embody in everyday practices for the purposes of interpreting canonical works of literature. I have used the construct from Saxe of a form-function shift as a lens for trying to understand how such everyday knowledge changes over time. In examining this process of transformation of knowledge over time, I have been interested in both what this means at the level of individual development as well as group level changes over time. And because the object of my inquiry is reading comprehension, I needed measures not only of outcomes (i.e., the ability to answer particular kinds of literary questions), but also of internal processes deployed by individual readers. This attention to internal processes of reasoning is important in order to understand the range of strategies and the range of what readers attend to in acts of literary reading. Thus in this ambitious program of research, I have tried to think about what is entailed in taking up learning in everyday settings to school-based settings, the role of cultural beliefs and practices in the construction of knowledge, the kinds of processes that can facilitate the transformation of everyday knowledge, and what this means in terms of time.

I have not spent the kind of time that Saxe and Rogoff have in a particular community. Instead, my strategy to examine the questions I have posed has required a program of research involving multiple studies over time. However, I would argue that there are some interesting parallels between their long-term ethnographic work in particular cultural communities and my multistudy approach. I did not have to conduct extensive ethnographic studies of the language practices of the AAEV speaking community because that research had already been conducted by extensive studies in sociolinguistics (A. Ball, 1999; Labov, 1972; Morgan, 2001; Smitherman, 1977). I did not have to conduct studies of the practices of popular youth culture around rap, for example, because much of that work has already been and continues to be done (Fisher, 2007; Mahiri, 2000/2001; Morrell & Duncan-Andrade, 2002; Rose, 1994).

There are a number of interesting studies that examine the structure of everyday knowledge and its relationship to disciplinary knowledge. These studies have largely been in the domains of mathematics and science. However, with the Algebra Project (Moses & Cobb, 2001) as a notable exception in mathematics and the Chèche Konnen Project in science (Rosebery, Warren, Ballenger, & Ogonowski, 2005), few studies have examined how features of classroom pedagogy scaffold the transformation of everyday knowledge to the acquisition of disciplinary knowledge, nor examined the developmental trajectories of such transformations. While there is clearly much more to be done, this has been one of the primary aims of my work in Cultural Modeling, attempting to document a pedagogical model whose features are designed specifically to facilitate such transformation.

I describe below the topics, research designs, and methods I have employed across multiple studies to address some of the challenges that a cultural and ecological framework invites:

• Structure of problem solving—Through interrogating literary theory and empirical studies of expert readers engaged in literary reasoning, I have extrapolated several models of processes entailed in tackling problems of symbolism and satire. An indirect assessment of the viability of these models has been their incorporation as teachable heuristics in literature classrooms with African American adolescents who are speakers of AAEV.

• Cultural or shared norms with regard to language play within AAEV—Here again existing research in sociolinguistics has well documented such cultural norms among AAEV speakers. In Cultural Modeling classrooms with AAEV speakers, we have used discourse analytic tools to document both the presence of such attention to language play (both in the focus of analysis of texts as well as in oral communication as students are engaged in literary problem solving with both everyday as well as canonical texts) as well as the functions that such oral language play served in facilitating literary problem solving.

• Processes through which transformations of everyday knowledge in the routine practices of CM classrooms occur over time—We have analyzed pedagogical moves and student uptake of strategies, attention to textual detail and modes of reasoning across time within Cultural Modeling classrooms.

• Outcomes—We have designed talk-aloud protocols administered to case-study students selected on the basis of the range of levels of engagement demonstrated in instruction to determine to what features of texts they attended, what strategies they employed in efforts to make meaning, and how both of these changed from a first to a second reading. In addition, we administered end-of-unit exams in both multiple choice and extended response formats, using Hillocks's (Hillocks & Ludlow, 1984) taxonomy of literary questions, to examine students' abilities to transfer what they had learned from scaffolded examinations of what we call cultural data sets (i.e., everyday texts, such as rap lyrics and signifying dialogues) and the application of heuristics derived from the cultural data sets to canonical texts that embodied the same broad interpretive problem.

- Relations between group processes and individual outcomes—With the combination of process and outcome data, we struggled to understand how group processes were taken up by individuals at different points in time and how macro- or group-level everyday cultural resources were taken up as both tools for problem solving and medium of communication. This question of how group ideas and norms are taken up by individuals and how they move across settings I think is an essential dilemma of research that is based on a cultural-ecological orientation.

In the next section of this chapter, I will try to illustrate how we tackled this last problem of how group ideas and norms are taken up by individuals and how they move across settings. This continues to be a work in progress, with many methodological issues remaining to be tackled.

HOW EVERYDAY REPERTOIRES ARE TAKEN UP
IN DISCIPLINARY LEARNING

The everyday repertoires in this phase of our Cultural Modeling research focused on the deployment of features of African American English as both a medium of communication and as analytic tools used by students. Smitherman (1977) discusses at least three kinds of features of African American English: worldviews, rhetorical qualities, and modes of discourse. In the arena of worldviews, Smitherman illustrates how, often through lexicon, stock phrases, and proverbs, historically held belief systems are both communicated and sustained. Rhetorical qualities include exaggerated language, use of proverbial and aphoristic phrasing, playing on words, use of indirection and tonal semantics. Tonal semantics refers to the ways that meaning and point of view are communicated through the manipulation of tonal qualities in oral speech. Tonal semantics within African American English include, but are not limited to, strategic use of repetition and alliteration. African American English discourse modes include call-and-response and narrative sequencing. We have documented how students used all of these features in their talk, and with what consequences.

The CM intervention took place over a 3-year period in a historically underachieving high school in Chicago. As part of the intervention I taught one class each year. While we video taped benchmark lessons from all members of the English Department, my class was videotaped every day for 3 years. The data reported here are taken from a senior class I taught the last year of the project. The unit of instruction focused on learning to identify and tackle problems of symbolism in literature. Cultural data sets included rap lyrics, R&B lyrics, and a short TV film (5 minutes in length) called *Sax Cantor Riff*, directed by the award-winning filmmaker Julie Dash. Instruction was in two phases, the first with cultural data sets and the second with canonical texts, the second of which was the very complex and difficult novel *Beloved* by Toni Morrison (1987).

In Figure 9.4, we selected and transcribed a discussion by a small group of students about the symbolism in the film *Sax Cantor Riff*. In order to make claims about the representativeness of this discussion, we had analyzed each day's discussion during the cultural data set phase of instruction to capture relationships between levels of participation as well as levels of literary reasoning by students and the level of scaffolding provided by the teacher. This analysis also allowed us to evaluate the differential effectiveness of different kinds of cultural data sets. From this analysis, we concluded that the process of selecting cultural data sets requires a careful analysis of the lived experience of students. R&B selections from decades

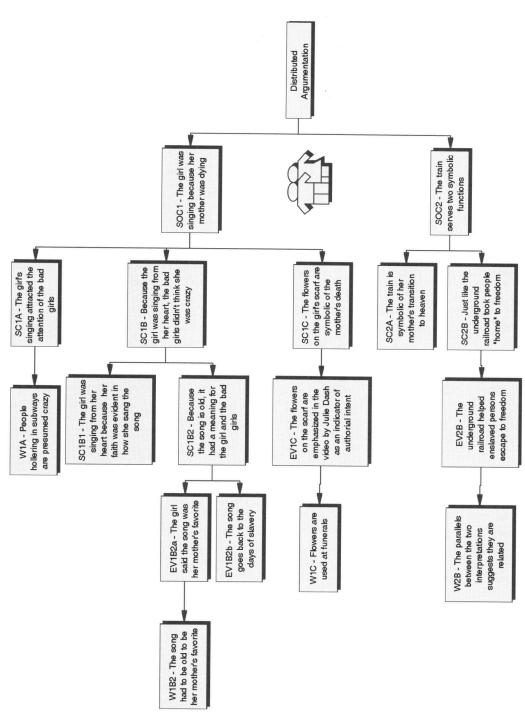

Figure 9.4. Nested Argumentation (reprinted from Lee, 2006)

before these young people were born did not elicit the same levels of engagement as more current rap lyrics and television media.

We were interested in this analysis in the sources of information that students used as evidence to support claims and as warrants to support evidence. We drew here on tools from sociolinguistics, specifically Goffman's (1974, 1981) construct of footing. Footing involves the way in which a speaker aligns himself or herself with regard to the content of discourse and toward others present and not present in the interactions. This construct of footing also helped us think about the distribution of ideas among students, including how and whether students took up one another's ideas in situ as they engaged in this collective problem solving. Saxe (1991) refers to this problem of the dispersion of ideas in micro-level face-to-face interactions as the sociogenesis of ideas.

In this analysis we drew on Toulmin's (Toulmin, Rieke, & Janik, 1984) taxonomy of argumentation, including the use of claims, evidence, and warrants; as well as his discussion of a very complex form of argumentation involving the use of nested claims. Nested arguments involve the use of superordinate claims under which a set of sub-claims are offered. It is the logic of relations across sub-claims that provides the evidence for the superordinate claim. We first identified claims, evidence, and warrants. We (C. D. Lee, 2006) created graphs of the logical relationships among claims, evidence, and warrants. It was through this analysis that we discovered the students used nested argumentation (see Figure 9.4). In the figure, SOC represents superordinate claim, SC sub-claims, W is warrants, and E is evidence. I have not taken the time to discuss the content of either the film or the argument because my goal here is to illustrate how this analytic method allowed us to document the structure of distributed argumentation, a phenomenon important to understanding how ideas emerge and are shared in interactions.

We then used the roles Goffman (Goffman, 1974) identified as lenses for understanding how interlocutors positioned themselves in relation to one another (i.e., footing): initiator, animator, author, principal, and primary recipient. Goffman illustrates these roles in the production of a single document, a presidential speech. The ideas in the speech are likely initiated by others than the president, who in Goffman's terms is the *animator* of the speech because he says the words. There may be more than one author of the speech, but the author is generally not the president; the *author* being the person who creates the words that embody the idea. The *principal* refers to the authorities that give credibility to the ideas, and may be equated with what Toulmin refers to as evidence and warrants to support claims. The *primary recipient* is the audience to whom the communication is directed, although Goffman notes that there can be secondary audiences. For example, the president may be giving a speech directly to reporters at a news conference as primary recipients, but craft his words in such a way as intended to influence a secondary audience in the House and Senate. Through this analysis we could see how students in the group took up one another's ideas. The analysis of what Goffman calls principal helped us think about the sources of knowledge upon which students drew in crafting their arguments. We found they drew primarily on community-based sources of shared knowledge and values as warrants to support claims they made about texts, both everyday and canonical. This analysis served as a proxy for examining how knowledge deployed in the everyday context was taken up in this academic context; and to what extent new sources of warranting based on the disciplinary norms being taught were also being deployed. What we found was that new hybrid practices began to emerge. This became particularly evident when the phase of instruction moved to canonical texts. The analysis of the distribution of ideas and the knowledge sources on which students drew is captured in Table 9.1. This is taken from a discussion of the T V film *Sax Cantor Riff*, one of the cultural data sets. The claims are interpretations students made of symbolism in

Table 9.1. Distributed Argumentation

Claim	Initiator	Animator	Author(s)	Principal	Primary Recipient	Shared Referent
The girl's singing attracted the attention of the bad girls	D	D	D SH	Community	Group	People hollering in subway presumed crazy
Because the girl was singing from her heart, the bad girls didn't think she was crazy	D	D	D CT	Community	Group	
The girl was singing from her heart because her faith was evident in how she sang	K	K	K SH	Community	Group	
Because the song is old, it had a meaning for the girl and the bad girls	Teacher	CT	CT K D	Community	Group	Families; appreciation of spirituals
The song goes back to the days of slavery	Teacher	CT	CT	Community	Teacher	
The train is symbolic of her mother's transition to heaven	Teacher	CT	CT SH K	Literary	Group	Church funerals; spiritual assumptions about death

the film. The letters represent students. We can see how students took up and expanded one another's ideas and drew upon shared community knowledge.

I want to continue to acknowledge that the use of these methods is a work in progress over a large corpus of data. While we have conducted similar analyses on discussions at other points in the instructional unit, we are not making any claims about the representativeness of this analysis across discussions of everyday and canonical texts. However, we do have representative data about growth in the use of textual evidence and warrants over time for the corpus of case study students we followed.

David Penner (2000) makes the following case about the role of prior knowledge in learning:

> An alternative to the argument that students' intuitive knowledge needs to be replaced is to con-sider how learners use their current understanding as they try to make sense of the world. . . . Consequently, subsequent knowledge refinement and reorganization, not replacement, are key characteristics of learning from a constructivist point of view. . . . Specifically, students' everyday thoughts are the foundation upon which scientific theory is built. (pp. 5–6)

Our work in Cultural Modeling shares much with this point of view articulated by Penner. However, it differs in that the constructivist framework is more focused on the internal reor-ganization in an individual's mind, but less so on the cultural foundations of the knowledge the learner brings and the ways in which such knowledge is situated in people's participation in an array of interrelated ecological settings. If we return to Rogoff's (1995) metaphor of the lens we take in examining experience, the lens of a cultural-ecological orientation takes a wide-angle view to account for influences from any of the following: participation in mul-tiple settings, participation across various stretches of time, and the perceptions and values that inform such participation, many of which will emanate out of group experiences. The reorganization of prior knowledge derived from participation in everyday routine activity, particularly when the everyday activities are associated with stigmatized membership in nondominant groups (e.g., race, class, immigrant status, disability, sexual orientation, etc.), is doubly challenging. This is because (1) our understanding of relations between everyday and disciplinary knowledge is not fully developed, and (2) because our attempts to examine such relationships are severely constrained by our stereotyped conceptions of cultural mem-bership and cultural processes.

CHALLENGES OF TRANSFORMING EVERYDAY FORMS OF REASONING TO DISCIPLINARY REASONING

In much later phases of our analysis of Cultural Modeling classrooms, we discovered an interesting dilemma that we think is very significant for this line of research for practice. It involves what I will call the problem of inscription. By inscription I refer to the formal models—typically graphical or symbolic—for representing constructs within disciplines and their use as modes of communication and reasoning (Larkin & Simon, 1987; Latour, 1987; Lynch & Woolgar, 1990). As Roth and McGinn (1998) indicate:

> The focus on inscriptions entails a concomitant focus on the establishment and maintenance of shared practices. Thus, whether an inscription is recognized within the community as a legitimate representation of a natural phenomenon depends on the degree to which the practices are ac-counted for and measure up to shared, legitimate, communal procedures. The degree an inscrip-tion is recognized depends on the extent to which the associated data transformation practices correspond to explicit and implicit communal norms. (p. 41)

The salience of inscriptions is perhaps most evident in mathematics and science. In mathematics and science, inscriptions are largely graphic or symbolic representations. Studies of cognition have addressed both the challenges of learning to use inscriptions among novices, including the existence and functions of intermediary forms of representation that novices will use in their transformations toward expert-like practice (Cobb, 2002). The Algebra Project (Moses & Cobb, 2001; Moses, Kamii, Swap, & Howard, 1989) directly addresses the question of moving from everyday to formal inscriptions in algebra. I have wrestled with this question in terms of the discipline of literary reasoning.

In response to literature, one can think of inscriptions in several ways. This field does not have formal symbols in the way that mathematicians and scientists employ. The problems presented are in natural language and the modes of communicating about texts are in natural language. However, in the academy, the modes of communicating about one's interpretation of a literary text involve specialized registers of language and speech genres (Bakhtin, 1986). These speech genres then have formal structural counterparts in written literary arguments. Certainly the written genres are required in school assessments of literary reasoning such as Advanced Placement exams and the essays and short-answer responses high school students are typically expected to construct in their English classes.

I began to think about this question of formal inscriptions in high school students' literary responses as I reexamined the logic of students' responses, both to the everyday and the canonical texts (Lee, 2007). We had transcribed arguments being made by individual students. Using models of literary reasoning drawn both from Toulmin (Toulmin et al., 1984) as well as literary theory, we were able to interpret the logic of students' arguments in ways we thought could be adequately warranted. However, we found we still had to make significant inferences. In fact, my research as well as that of colleagues (C. D. Lee, 2001, 2004, 2005a, 2005b, 2005c, 2006) has argued that central to the work of teachers is the ability to interpret what are often incomplete explanations by students as situated along a developmental trajectory toward expertise (D. L. Ball & Rundquist, 1993; Lampert, 2001; Rosebery et al., 2005; Warren, Ballenger, Ogonowski, Rosebery, & Hudicourt-Barnes, 2001). This is perhaps among the most difficult work of teaching. It is work that becomes all the more complex when the national languages, dialects, and social registers used by students are far removed either from the teacher's own linguistic repertoire or from the social languages, registers, and speech or written genres of the discipline (A. Ball, 2000, 2002, 2006). I think then this question of translation from the everyday to the disciplinary is an important issue not only for questions of transfer, but also for the world of practice. I choose to situate this question within a cultural-ecological framework because I am convinced that it is knowledge of the genesis and functions of everyday modes of communication and knowledge construction that is vital to strategic efforts to transform such knowledge to disciplinary forms and functions. Figure 9.5 captures the elements of everyday knowledge that I think need to be understood in design efforts to scaffold such knowledge for disciplinary purposes in the context of schooling. It is not unusual that each of these elements will be transformed in some way as novices build upon such knowledge to serve new functions in the contexts of learning in school.

I will illustrate the challenge of translating from what I will call everyday inscriptions of literary reasoning to disciplinary inscriptions. In the following example, Taquisha has responded to the opening of a chapter in *Beloved* in which we meet a woman who walks out of the water, sits on a tree stump, and then proceeds to the home of Sethe. *Beloved* is the story of an African woman who had been enslaved during the African Holocaust of Enslavement. When she tried to escape, she was brutally raped and beaten, while pregnant. After she finally escapes, the same men who beat and raped her return to try to take her

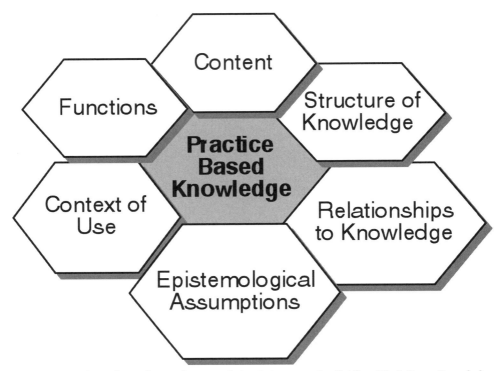

Figure 9.5.   Dimensions of Everyday Knowledge Relevant to Scaffolding Disciplinary Knowledge

and her children back into slavery. In a moment of sheer horror, Sethe kills her baby (the baby she had been carrying in her womb when she was raped and beaten). The novel is fundamentally about the consequences of that act for Sethe, her children, the baby who had been killed, and Paul D. who had also been enslaved with Sethe on the plantation ironically called Sweet Home. I will illustrate this challenge of everyday and disciplinary inscriptions in the study of literature with the case of a student named Taquisha. Taquisha responds to a chapter that begins with a thick description of a woman who walks out of the water and sits on a tree stump. We are not told who this woman is, but there are subtle unusual hints about her being extraordinarily thirsty, not being able to hold up her head, and "Her skin was flawless except for three vertical scratches on her forehead so fine and thin they seemed at first like hair, baby hair before it bloomed and roped into the masses of black yarn under her hat" (Morrison, 1987, p. 51).

Taquisha responds vehemently (literally) to this passage. She draws on her historical knowledge of the era—namely, that it was not uncommon where Sethe lived right off the Ohio River for persons escaping from slavery to show up at your door, unsolicited and un-known. However, such people would have typically just come through an arduous journey across the river and through the woods and as a consequence would not look as clean and pristine as this woman. Then, evidencing deeply literary reasoning, Taquisha hypothesizes that this woman is Sethe's baby, returned now as a ghost disguised as a woman. She further hypothesizes that evidence from the text has shown that the ghost is dangerous; and she does not understand why the characters at the house—namely, Sethe and Paul D.—don't recognize who this is; and implicitly she asks why the author, Toni Morrison, allowed such a deception to take place. Here is what Taquisha says:

Now wouldn't you want to know? You know! The questions—hair all straight like a baby, you know and stuff, drinking all this water? Okay! You know she said she ran away and stuff. You got some brand new shoes on yo' feet. You too clean to run away. Yo feet ain't swole. You ain't gonna expect nothing? You ain't gonna ask her no questions?

After a careful analysis of how Taquisha communicates her argument, I came to the following conclusions. She makes exactly the right claims and draws on exactly the right evidence and demonstrates exactly the kind of emotional attachment to the text world that is required for disciplinary literary reasoning. However, she does not make explicit the warrants that connect her claims and evidence, and she does not use the required academic language. Such literary language or what sociolinguists call a register would require that she situate her claims as connected to particular literary problems, such as authorial intent or irony, both of which I think are implicitly addressed in her argument. Thus, the next phase of Taquisha's academic transition needs to address the challenges of translating what is essentially an everyday register (in fact one that is doubly challenging in the academy because it is rooted in a dialect of English that the academy does not value, namely African American English Vernacular) to both an academic register and the structure of a formal literary argument. It is very unfortunate that the depth of her literary logic when expressed as it was would garner her no recognition on an Advanced Placement exam.

The problem is complicated in several ways. First, secondary literature classrooms rarely scaffold the skills, content knowledge, and dispositions toward language that the Taquishas of the world bring to the enterprise. Second, such classrooms typically address questions of form over underlying logic; so that most teachers would likely spend time trying to "correct" her syntax, rather than helping her further develop her literary logic and her attachment to engaging with such complex canonical texts.

In Table 9.2, I include Taquisha's argument and what I think a translation of that logic would look like inscribed in the structure of a formal literary argument. The emergent column contains Taquisha's words. The expert column is my extrapolation to an academic literary register.

The emergent column can be thought of as an intermediary representation or inscription of a logical literary argument. The fundamental logic of the argument is sound and the habits of mind she displays (e.g., her fundamental orientation and relationship to the problem) are also appropriate and highly desired. What is missing is her articulation of what warrants the evidence and the use of a literary linguistic register and syntax. I am arguing here that a fundamental problem of practice and a fundamental challenge of research on the transformation of everyday knowledge to disciplinary knowledge in the contexts of schooling is our ability to articulate what are the potential points of intersection as I have tried to identify them in Figure 9.5.

CONCLUSIONS

I have attempted in this chapter to argue for the importance of a cultural and ecological orientation to the study of human learning and development. I have argued that our most generative understandings of the range of pathways through which humans learn and develop over time, including the varied life course goals that individuals within and across various communities envision and embody in routine practices of socialization, come when we are able to examine multiple cultural communities. We know, of course, that fields studying various aspects of human learning and development (i.e., education, cognitive psychology,

Table 9.2. Comparing Expert and Emergent Representations of Disciplinary Argumentation

	Expert	Emergent
Overarching claim = theme	I am questioning authorial intent in terms of how Toni Morrison as author has crafted the reactions of characters to the woman.	"Now wouldn't you want to know? You know! The questions . . ."
Evidence Claim 1 (Textual)	The woman appears out of nowhere, hair straight like a baby, drinking a lot of water.	". . . hair all straight like a baby, you know and stuff, drinking all this water?"
Claim 1	These characteristics give the woman the attributes of a baby.	
Evidence Claim 1 (Textual & Logical)	Since the house was haunted and Sethe had killed her baby, it is reasonable to assume (1) that the house was haunted by the baby, and (2) this woman is the baby.	
Claim 2	If she has been haunting the house for years, her appearance now suggests possible danger for Sethe and those around her.	Implied
Evidence Claim 3 (Textual)	In addition, the woman appears and I see that her feet are not swollen; she has on brand new shoes; she has on clean clothing.	"You got some brand new shoes on yo feet. You too clean to run away. Yo feet ain't swole!" (Notice how she positions this as a real-world scenario—how she uses the referent "you" here to position her classmates inside the perspective of the characters of Sethe, Paul D., and Denver at the moment the woman arrives.)
Warrant Claim 3 (Historical)	We know that historically Africans escaping from enslavement would suddenly appear at someone's door, especially in this town just across from the river.	"Okay! You know she said she ran away and stuff."
Evidence Claim 3 (Logical)	This woman does not look like she just escaped from enslavement.	Implied
Claim 3	Thus it is not reasonable to assume that she is an escapee.	"You ain't gonna expect nothing?"
Summary of Claims 1, 2, 3	Therefore, I have serious questions about who she might be, and about whether she may be dangerous.	
Warrant Claims 1, 2, 3 (Logical)	If I can see this, why can't the characters see it?	"You ain't gonna ask her *no* questions?"
Summary of Overarching Claim as Critique of a Literary Problem	I see this as a critique of how Toni Morrison has crafted the characters in this scene.	

Source: Adapted from Lee, 2007, p. 152.

social psychology, human development, the learning sciences, sociology, even linguistics) have been limited historically by focusing investigations primarily on white, middle-class samples (Graham, 1992; Helms, 1992). As studies move across diverse populations, new conceptual challenges emerge with regard to ecological validity. In today's world, many people move across a variety of settings, including national borders as well as cultural communities defined by race/ethnicity, class, age cohort (e.g., youth culture), professions, and settings involving routine interests and areas of expertise (Hopson, Yeakey, & Boakari, 2008; Zakaria, 2008). This phenomenon further invites a cultural and ecological orientation, studying what people learn as a consequence of these varied forms of routine participation and what is involved in navigating across them (Magnusson & Stattin, 1998; Nasir et al., 2006; Nasir & Saxe, 2003; Spencer, 2006; Spencer, Fegley, & Dupree, 2006; Spencer, Harpalani, et al., 2006). This issue of navigating across settings is particularly pertinent, I think, to education, particularly with regard to youth from nondominant communities who in the United States (and many other industrialized countries) face persistent inequities in academic achievement. So for all these reasons I think it is important to draw attention to the role of culture and the full ecology of peoples' lives as in our research we think about the questions we will pose, the research designs we will use, the settings we will study, and the analytic methods we will employ (C.D. Lee, 2008; C. D. Lee, in press).

And while I do think many researchers across domains would not fundamentally argue with the above logic, the conceptual and methodological challenges of employing such an orientation in one's work are substantive. One of the goals of this chapter is to draw attention to such conceptual and methodological challenges. I have endeavored to illustrate how others have taken up these challenges in long-term programs of research, and then to conclude with brief examples from my own research in Cultural Modeling. My examples are in no way meant to be exhaustive or authoritative, but rather exploratory as I have wrestled with the complexities of such an orientation. My hope is to spark future sustained and institutionalized conversations and collaborations to further our understanding of how to address the dynamic and situated nature of human learning and development. This includes cross-disciplinary discussions and collaborations, which I am convinced are crucial to such efforts.

REFERENCES

Akbar, N. (1979). African roots of black personality. In W. D. Smith, K. H. Burlew, M. H. Mosley & W. M. Whitney (Eds.), *Reflections on Black Psychology* (pp. 79–98). Washington, DC: University Press of America.

Alvermann, D., & Hagood, M. C. (2000). Critical media literacy: Research, theory, and practice in "new times." *Journal of Educational Research, 93*, 193–205.

Alvermann, D., Hinchman, K. A., Moore, D., Phelps, S., & Waff, D. (2006). *Reconceptualizing the literacies in adolescents' lives* (2nd Ed.). Mahwah, NJ: Lawrence Erlbaum.

Asante, M. K., & Asante, K. W. (1990). *African culture: The rhythms of unity.* Trenton, NJ: Africa World Press.

Au, K. H. (1980). Participation structures in a reading lesson with Hawaiian children: Analysis of a culturally appropriate instructional event. *Anthropology and Education, 11*(2), 91–115.

Bakhtin, M. M. (1986). *Speech genres and other late essays* (V. W. McGee, Trans., C. Emerson & M. Holquist, Eds.). Austin: University of Texas Press.

Ball, A. (1995). Community based learning in an urban setting as a model for educational reform. *Applied Behavioral Science Review, 3*, 127–146.

Ball, A. (1999). Evaluating the writing of culturally and linguistically diverse students: The case of the African American English speaker. In C. R. Cooper & L. Odell (Eds.), *Evaluating Writing* (pp. 225–248). Urbana, IL: National Council of Teachers of English.

Ball, A. (2000). Teachers developing philosophies on literacy and their use in urban schools: A Vygotskian perspective on internal activity and teacher change. In C. D. Lee & P. Smagorinsky (Eds.), *Vygotskian perspectives on literacy research: Constructing meaning through collaborative inquiry* (pp. 226–255). New York, NY: Cambridge University Press.

Ball, A. (2002). Three decades of research on classroom life: Illuminating the classroom communicative lives of America's at-risk students. In W. Secada (Ed.), *Review of Research in Education* (Vol. 26, pp. 71–112). Washington, DC: American Educational Research Association.

Ball, A. (2006). *Multicultural strategies for education and social change: Carriers of the torch in the U.S. and South Africa.* New York, NY: Teachers College Press.

Ball, D. L., & Rowan, B. (2004). Introduction: Measuring Instruction. *The Elementary School Journal, 105*(1), 3–10.

Ball, D. L., & Rundquist, S. S. (1993). Collaboration as a context for joining teacher learning with learning about teaching. In D. K. Cohen, M. W. McLaughlin, & J. E. Talbert (Eds.), *Teaching for understanding: Challenges for policy and practice* (pp. 13–42). San Francisco, CA: Jossey-Bass.

Bereiter, C., & Engelmann, S. (1966). *Teaching disadvantaged children in pre-school.* Englewood Cliffs, NJ: Prentice Hall.

Bernstein, B. (1961). Social class and linguistic development: A theory of social learning. In A. Halsey, J. Floud, & C. Anderson (Eds.), *Education, economy, and society* (pp. 288–314). New York, NY: Free Press.

Boykin, A. W. (1986). The triple quandry and the schooling of Afro-American children. In U. Neisser (Ed.), *The school achievement of minority children* (pp. 57–92). Hillsdale, NJ: Lawrence Erlbaum.

Bronfenbrenner, U., & Morris, P. A. (1998). The ecology of developmental processes. In W. Damon & R. M. Lerner (Eds.), *Handbook of child psychology: Theoretical models of human development* (5th ed., Vol. 1, pp. 993–1028). New York, NY: Wiley & Sons.

Cazden, C., Michaels, S., & Tabors, P. (1985). Spontaneous repairs in sharing time narratives: The intersection of metalinguistic awareness, speech event and narrative style. In S. Freedman (Ed.), *The acquisition of written language: Revision and response.* Norwood, NJ: Ablex.

Champion, T. (1998). "Tell me somethin' good": A description of narrative structures among African-American children. *Linguistics and Education, 9*(3), 251–286.

Champion, T. (2003). *Understanding storytelling among African American children: A journey from Africa to America.* Mahwah, NJ: Lawrence Erlbaum Associates.

Champion, T., Seymour, H., & Camarata, S. (1995). Narrative discourse among African American children. *Journal of Narrative and Life History, 5*(4), 333–352.

Cobb, P. (2002). Reasoning with tools and inscriptions. *The Journal of the Learning Sciences, 11*(2–3), 187–215.

Cole, M. (1996). *Cultural psychology: A once and future discipline.* Cambridge, MA: The Belknap Press of Harvard University Press.

Cole, M. (2007). Phylogeny and cultural history in ontogeny. *Journal of Physiology, 101*, 236–246.

Coleman, J., et al. (1966). *Equality of educational opportunity.* Washington, DC: U.S. Department of Education.

Cross, W. (1991). *Shades of black: Diversity in African American identity.* Philadelphia, PA: Temple University Press.

Deutsch, M., & Brown, B. (1964). Social influences in Negro-White intelligence differences. *Journal of Social Issues, 20*, 24–35.

Dodoo, F. (1997). Assimilation differences among Africans in America. *Social Forces, 76*(2), 527–546.

Eccles, J. (2005). Subjective task values and the Eccles et al. model of achievement related choices. In A. Elliott & C. S. Dweck (Eds.), *Handbook of competence and motivation.* New York, NY: Guilford Press.

Eccles, J., & Midgley, C. (1989). Stage/environment fit: Developmentally appropriate classrooms for early adolescents. In R. Ames & C. Ames (Eds.), *Research on motivation in education* (Vol. 3, pp. 367–420). New York, NY: Academic Press.

Eccles, J., Midgley, C., Wigfield, A., Miller Buchanan, C. M., Reuman, D., & Flanagan, C. (1993). Development during adolescence: The impact of stage-environment fit on young adolescents' experiences in schools and families. *American Psychologist, 48*(2), 90–101.

Eccles, J., Wigfield, A., & Schiefele, U. (1998). Motivation to succeed. In W. Damon & N. Eisenberg (Eds.), *Handbook of child psychology* (5th ed., Vol. 3). New York, NY: Wiley.

Fisher, M. T. (2007). *Writing in rhythm: Spoken word poetry in urban classrooms.* New York, NY: Teachers College Press.

Fordham, S. (1996). *Blacked out: Dilemmas of race, identity and success at Capital High.* Chicago, IL: University of Chicago Press.

Furstenberg, F., & Hughes, M. (1995). Social capital and sucessful development among at-risk youth. *Journal of Marriage and the Family, 57*(3), 580–592.

Gee, J. P. (1989). The narrativization of experience in the oral style. *Journal of Education, 171*(1), 75–96.

Goffman, E. (1974). *Frame analysis: An essay on the organization of experience.* New York, NY: Harper and Row.

Goffman, E. (1981). *Forms of talk.* Philadelphia: University of Pennsylvania Press.

Graham, S. (1992). "Most of the subjects were White and middle class": Trends in published research on African Americans in selected APA journals, 1970–1989. *American Psychologist, 47*(5), 629–639.

Graham, S., & Hudley, C. (2005). Race and ethnicity in the study of motivation and competence. In A. J. Elliot & C. S. Dweck (Eds.), *Handbook of competence and motivation* (pp. 392–413). New York, NY: The Guilford Press.

Greenfield, P. (2004). *Weaving generations together: Evolving creativity in the Maya of Chiapas.* Santa Fe, NM: School of American Research Press.

Gutiérrez, K., Baquedano-Lopez, P., & Tejeda, C. (1999). Rethinking diversity: Hybridity and hybrid language practices in the Third Space. *Mind, Culture, and Activity, 6*(4), 286–303.

Gutiérrez, K., & Rogoff, B. (2003). Cultural ways of learning: Individual traits or repertoires of practice. *Educational Researcher, 32*(5), 19–25.

Hall, S., & Moats, L. (Eds.). (1999). *Straight talk about reading: How parents can make a difference during the early years.* Lincolnwood, IL: Contemporary Books.

Hart, B., & Risley, R. T. (1995). *Meaningful differences in the everyday experience of young American children.* Baltimore, MD: Paul H. Brookes.

Hatchett, S., & Jackson, J. S. (1999). African American extended kin systems: An empirical assessment in the national survey of Black Americans. In H. P. McAdoo (Ed.), *Family ethnicity: Strength in diversity.* Thousand Oaks, CA: Sage.

Heath, S. B. (2004). Risks, rules, and roles: Youth perspectives on the work of learning for community development. In A. N. Perret-Clemont, C. Pontecorvo, L. B. Resnick, T. Zittoun & B. Burge (Eds.), *Joining society: Social interaction and learning in adolescence and youth.* New York, NY: Cambridge University Press.

Heath, S. B., & McLaughlin, M. (1994). The best of both worlds: Connecting schools and community organizations for all-day, all-year learning. *Educational Administration Quarterly, 30*(3), 278–300.

Helms, J. E. (1992). Why is there no study of cultural equivalence in standardized cognitive ability testing? *American Psychologist, 47*(9), 1083–1101.

Hill, H., Rowan, B., & Ball, D. L. (2005). Effects of teachers' mathematical knowledge for teaching on student achievement. *American Educational Research Journal, 42*(2), 371–406.

Hilliard, A. G. (1998). *SBA: The reawakening of the African mind.* Gainsville, FL: Makare Publishing Company.

Hillocks, G., & Ludlow, L. (1984). A taxonomy of skills in reading and interpreting fiction. *American Educational Research Journal, 21*, 7–24.

Holloway, J. E. (1990). *Africanisms in American culture.* Bloomington: Indiana University Press.

Hopson, R. K., Yeakey, C. C., & Boakari, F. M. (Eds.). (2008). *Power, voice and the public good: Schooling and education in global societies.* Wagon Lane, England: JAI Press.

Jencks, C. (1972). *Inequality: A reassessment of the efffect of family and schooling in America.* New York, NY: Basic Books.

Labov, W. (1972). *Language in the inner city: Studies in the Black English vernacular.* Philadelphia: University of Pennsylvania Press.

Ladson-Billings, G., & Tate, W. (1995). Toward a critical race theory of education. *Teachers College Record, 97*(1), 47–68.

Lampert, M. (2001). *Teaching problems and the problems of teaching.* New Haven, CT: Yale University Press.

Lareau, A., & Horvat, E. M. (1999). Moments of social inclusion and exclusion: Race, class and cultural capital in family-school relationships. *Sociology of Education, 72*, 37–53.

Larkin, J., & Simon, H. (1987). Why a diagram is (sometimes) worth ten thousand words. *Cognitive Science, 11*, 65–99.

Latour, B. (1987). *Science in action: How to follow scientists and engineers through society.* Cambridge, MA: Harvard University Press.

Lave, J. (1988). *Cognition in practice: Mind, mathematics and culture in everyday life.* Cambridge, England: Cambridge University Press.

Lee, C. D. (1993). *Signifying as a scaffold for literary interpretation: The pedagogical implications of an African American discourse genre.* Urbana, IL: National Council of Teachers of English.

Lee, C. D. (1995a). A culturally based cognitive apprenticeship: Teaching African American high school students skills in literary interpretation. *Reading Research Quarterly, 30*(4), 608–631.

Lee, C. D. (1995b). Signifying as a scaffold for literary interpretation. *Journal of Black Psychology, 21*(4), 357–381.

Lee, C. D. (1997). Bridging home and school literacies: A model of culturally responsive teaching. In J. Flood, S. B. Heath & D. Lapp (Eds.), *A handbook for literacy educators: Research on teaching the communicative and visual arts* (pp. 330–341). New York, NY: Macmillan Publishing Company.

Lee, C. D. (2001). Is October Brown Chinese: A cultural modeling activity system for underachieving students. *American Educational Research Journal, 38*(1), 97–142.

Lee, C. D. (2004). African American students and literacy. In D. Alvermann & D. Stickland (Eds.), *Bridging the gap: Improving literacy learning for pre-adolescent and adolescent learners, grades 4–12.* New York, NY: Teachers College Press.

Lee, C. D. (2005a). Culture and language: Bi-dialectical issues in literacy. In P. L. Anders & J. Flood (Eds.), *Culture and language: Bi-dialectical issues in literacy*. Newark, DE: International Reading Association.

Lee, C. D. (2005b). Taking culture into account: Intervention research based on current views of cognition and learning. In J. King (Ed.), *Black education: A transformative research and action agenda for the new century* (pp. 73–114). Mahwah, NJ: Lawrence Erlbaum and American Educational Research Association.

Lee, C. D. (2005c). The state of knowledge about the education of African Americans. In J. King (Ed.), *Black education: A transformative research and action agenda for the new century* (pp. 45–72). Mahwah, NJ: Lawrence Erlbaum and American Educational Research Association.

Lee, C. D. (2006). Every good-bye ain't gone: Analyzing the cultural underpinnings of classroom talk. *Qualitative Studies in Education, 19*(3), 305–327.

Lee, C. D. (2007). *Culture, literacy and learning: Taking bloom in the midst of the whirlwind*. New York, NY: Teachers College Press.

Lee, C. D. (2008). The centrality of culture to the scientific study of learning and development: How an ecological framework in educational research facilitates civic responsibility. *Educational Researcher, 37*(5), 267–279.

Lee, C. D. (in press). Soaring above the clouds, delving the ocean's depths: Understanding the ecologies of human learning and the challenge for education science. *Educational Researcher*.

Lee, C. D., Spencer, M. B., & Harpalani, V. (2003). Every shut eye ain't sleep: Studying how people live culturally. *Educational Researcher, 32*(5), 6–13.

Lee, V., & Burkham, D. (2002). *Inequality at the starting gate: Social background differences in achievement as children begin school*. Washington, DC: Economic Policy Institute.

Lynch, M., & Woolgar, S. (1990). *Representation in scientific practice*. Cambridge, MA: MIT Press.

Magnusson, D., & Stattin, H. (1998). Person-context interaction theories. In W. Damon & R. M. Lerner (Eds.), *Handbook of child psychology: Theoretical models of human development* (5th ed., Vol. 1, pp. 685–760). New York, NY: Wiley & Sons.

Mahiri, J. (2000/2001). Pop culture pedagogy and the end(s) of school. *Journal of Adolescent & Adult Literacy, 44*(4), 382–386.

Maslow, A. H. (1954). *Motivation and personality*. New York, NY: Harper.

Massey, D., & Denton, N. (1993). *American apartheid: Segregation and the making of the underclass*. Cambridge, MA: Harvard University Press.

McKinsey & Company Social Sector Office. (2009). *The economic impact of the achievement gap in America's schools*. McKinsey & Company. Retrieved from http://www.mckinsey.com/app_media/images/page_images/offices/socialsector/pdf/achievement_gap_report.pdf

McLaughlin, M., Irby, M. A., & Langman, J. (1994). *Urban sanctuaries: Neighborhood organizations in the lives and futures of inner-city youth*. San Francisco, CA: Jossey-Bass.

Michaels, S. (1981). "Sharing time": Children's narrative styles and differential access to literacy. *Language in Society, 10*, 423–442.

Mills, C. W. (1997). *The racial contract*. Ithaca, NY: Cornell University Press.

Morgan, M. (2001). The African-American speech community: Reality and sociolinguistics. In A. Duranti (Ed.), *Linguistic anthropology: A reader* (pp. 74–94). Malden, MA: Blackwell Publishers.

Morrell, E., & Duncan-Andrade, J. (2002). Promoting academic literacy with urban youth through engaging hip-hop culture. *English Journal, 91*(6), 88–93.

Morrison, T. (1987). *Beloved*. New York, NY: Alfred A. Knopf.

Moses, R. P., & Cobb, C. E. (2001). *Radical Equations: Math Literacy and Civil Rights*. Boston, MA: Beacon Press.

Moses, R. P., Kamii, M., Swap, S. M., & Howard, J. (1989). The algebra project: Organizing in the spirit of Ella. *Harvard Educational Review, 59*(4), 423–443.

Nasir, N. (2000). "Points ain't everything": Emergent goals and average and percent understandings in the play of basketball among African American students. *Anthropology and Education, 31*(1), 283–305.

Nasir, N. (2002). Identity, goals, and learning: Mathematics in cultural practice. *Mathematical Thinking and Learning, 4*(2–3), 211–247.

Nasir, N. (2005). Individual cognitive structuring and the sociocultural context: Strategy shifts in the game of dominoes. *Journal of the Learning Sciences, 14*, 5–34.

Nasir, N., Hand, V., & Taylor, E. (2008). Culture and mathematics in school: Boundaries between "cultural" and "domain" knowledge in the mathematics classroom and beyond. *Review of Research in Education, 32*, 187–240.

Nasir, N., Rosebery, A. S., Warren, B., & Lee, C. D. (2006). Learning as a cultural process: Achieving equity through diversity. In K. Sawyer (Ed.), *Handbook of the learning sciences*. New York, NY: Cambridge University Press.

Nasir, N., & Saxe, G. (2003). Emerging tensions and their management in the lives of minority students. *Educational Researcher, 32*(5), 14–18.

Ogbu, J. U. (1981). Origins of human competence: A cultural-ecological perspective. *Child Development, 52*, 413–429.

Orellana, M. (2009). *Translating immigrant childhoods: Children's work as culture and language brokers*. New Brunswick, NJ: Rutgers University Press.

Orellana, M., & Bowman, P. (2003). Cultural diversity research on learning and development: Conceptual, methodological and strategic considerations. *Educational Researcher, 32*(5), 26–32.

Orellana, M., Reynolds, J., Dorner, L., & Meza, M. (2003). In other words: Translating or "para-phrasing" as a family literacy practice in immigrant households. *Reading Research Quarterly, 38*(1), 12–34.

Patillo, M. (1999). *Black picket fences: Privilege and peril among the black middle class*. Chicago, IL: University of Chicago Press.

Penner, D. (2000). Cognition, computers, and synthetic science: Building knowledge and meaning through modeling. *Review of Research in Education, 25*, 1–35.

Phillips, M., Brooks-Gunn, J., Duncan, G., Klebanov, P., & Crane, J. (1998). Family background parenting practices and the Black-White test score gap. In C. Jencks & M. Phillips (Eds.), *The Black-White test score gap* (pp. 103–145). Washington, DC: Brookings Institution Press.

Quartz, S. R., & Sejnowski, T. J. (2002). *Liars, lovers, and heroes: What the new brain science reveals about how we become who we are*. New York, NY: William Morrow.

Ramani, A. K., Gilbertson, L., & Fox, M. A. (2007). *Status and trends in the education of racial and ethnic minorities*. Washington, DC: Institute of Education Sciences National Center for Education Statistics.

Resnick, D., & Resnick, L. (1977). The nature of literacy: An historical exploration. *Harvard Educational Review, 43*, 370–385.

Rogoff, B. (1995). Observing sociocultural activity and three planes: Participatory appropriation, guided participation, and apprenticeship. In J. Wertsch, P. del Rio, & A. Alvarez (Eds.), *Sociocultural studies of mind* (pp. 139–164). New York, NY: Cambridge University Press.

Rogoff, B. (2003). *The cultural nature of human development*. New York, NY: Oxford University Press.

Rogoff, B. (Ed.). (2002). *How can we study cultural aspects of human development* (Special Issue). *Human Development, 45*(4).

Rogoff, B., & Chavajay, P. (1995). What's become of research on the cultural basis of cognitive development. *American Psychologist, 50*(10), 859–877.

Rogoff, B., Paradise, R., Mejía-Arauz, R., Correa-Chávez, M., & Angelillo, C. (2003). Firsthand learning through intent participation. *Annual Review of Psychology, 54*, 175–204.

Rong, X. L., & Brown, F. (2001). The effects of immigrant generation and ethnicity on educational attainment among young African and Caribbean blacks in the United States. *Harvard Educational Review, 7*(3), 536–565.

Rose, T. (1994). *Black noise: Rap music and black culture in contemporary America*. Hanover, NH: Wesleyan University Press.

Rosebery, A. S., Warren, B., Ballenger, C., & Ogonowski, M. (2005). The generative potential of students' everyday knowledge in learning science. In T. Romberg, T. Carpenter, & D. Fae (Eds.), *Understanding mathematics and science matters*. Mahwah, NJ: Erlbaum.

Roth, W.-M., & McGinn, M. K. (1998). Inscriptions: Toward a theory of representing as social practice. *Review of Educational Research, 68*(1), 35–59.

Rowan, B., Correnti, R., & Miller, R. J. (2002). What large-scale survey research tells us about teacher effects on student achievement: Insights from the Prospects Study of elementary schools. *Teachers College Record, 104*(8), 1525–1567.

Saxe, G. (1991). *Culture and cognitive development: Studies in mathematical understanding*. Hillsdale, NJ: Lawrence Erlbaum Associates.

Saxe, G. (1999). Cognition, development and cultural practices. In E. Turiel (Ed.), *Culture and development: New directions in child psychology*. San Francisco, CA: Jossey Bass.

Saxe, G., & Esmonde, I. (2005). Studying cognition in the flux: A historical treatment of Fu in the shifting structure of Oksapmin mathematics. *Mind, Culture and Activity, 12*(3–4), 171–225.

Scribner, S., & Cole, M. (1981). *The psychology of literacy*. Cambridge, MA: Harvard University Press.

Sellers, R., Shelton, N., Cooke, D., Chavous, T., Rowley, S. J., & Smith, M. (1998). A multidimensional model of racial identity: Assumptions, findings, and future directions. In R. Jones (Ed.), *African American identity development* (pp. 275–303). Hampton, VA: Cobb & Henry Publishers.

Smitherman, G. (1977). *Talkin and testifyin: The language of Black America*. Boston, MA: Houghton Mifflin.

Smitherman, G. (2000). *Talk that talk: Language, culture and education in African America*. New York, NY: Routledge.

Spencer, M. B. (1985). Cultural cognition and social cognition as identity factors in black children's personal-social growth. In M. Spencer, G. K. Brookins & W. Allen (Eds.), *Beginnings: The social and affective development of black children* (pp. 59–72). Hillsdale, NJ: Lawrence Erlbaum.

Spencer, M. B. (1987). Black children's ethnic identity formation: Risk and resilience in castelike minorities. In J. Phinney & M. Rotheram (Eds.), *Children's ethnic socialization: Pluralism and development* (pp. 103–116). Newbury Park, CA: Sage.

Spencer, M. B. (1995). Old issues and new theorizing about African American youth: A phenomenological variant of ecological systems theory. In R. L. Taylor (Ed.), *Black youth: Perspectives on their status in the United States* (pp. 37–70). Westport, CT: Praeger.

Spencer, M. B. (1999). Social and cultural influences on school adjustment: The application of an identity-focused cultural ecological perspective. *Educational Psychologist, 34*(1), 43–57.

Spencer, M. B. (2001). Identity, achievement orientation and race: "Lessons learned" about the normative, developmental experience of African American males. In W. H. Watkins, J. H. Lewis, & V. Chou (Eds.), *Race and education: The role of history and society in educating African American students*. Needham Heights, MA: Allyn & Bacon.

Spencer, M. B. (2006). Phenomenology and ecological systems theory: Development of diverse groups. In W. Damon & R. M. Lerner (Eds.), *Handbook of child psychology* (6th ed., Vol. 1, pp. 829–893). New York, NY: Wiley.

Spencer, M. B. (2008). Lessons learned and opportunities ignored since *Brown v. Board of Education*: Youth development and the myth of a color-blind society. *Educational Researcher, 37*(5), 253–266.

Spencer, M. B., Fegley, S., & Dupree, D. (2006). Investigating and linking social conditions of African-American children and adolescents with emotional well-being. *Ethnicity and Disease, 16*(2), 63–67.

Spencer, M. B., Harpalani, V., Cassidy, E., Jacobs, C., Donde, S., & Goss, T. N. (2006). Understanding vulnerability and resilience from a normative development perspective: Implications for racially and ethnically diverse youth. In D. Chicchetti & E. Cohen (Eds.), *Handbook of developmental psychopathology* (Vol. 1). Hoboken, NJ: Wiley.

Steele, C. M. (2004). A threat in the air: How stereotypes shape intellectual identity and performance. In J. Banks & C. Banks (Eds.), *Handbook of research on multicultural education* (2nd ed., pp. 682–698). San Francisco, CA: Jossey-Bass.

Super, C., & Harkness, S. (1986). The developmental niche: A conceptualization at the interface of child and culture. *International Journal of Behavioral Development, 9*, 545–569.

Tharp, R., & Gallimore, R. (1988). *Rousing minds to life: Teaching, learning, and schooling in social context*. New York, NY: Cambridge University Press.

Toulmin, S., Rieke, R., & Janik, A. (1984). *An introduction to reasoning*. New York, NY: Macmillan Publishing Company.

Valdes, G. (1996). *Con respeto: Bridging the distances between culturally diverse families and schools*. New York, NY: Teachers College Press.

Valdes, G. (2001). *Learning and not learning English: Latino students in American schools*. New York, NY: Teachers College Press.

Valdes, G. (2002). *Expanding the definitions of giftedness: The case of young interpreters from immigrant countries*. Mahwah, NJ: Lawrence Erlbaum.

Vygotsky, L. (1978). *Mind in society: The development of higher psychological processes*. In M. Cole, V. John-Steiner, S. Scribner, & E. Souberman (Eds.). Cambridge, MA: Harvard University Press.

Vygotsky, L. (1981). The genesis of higher mental functions. In J. Wertsch (Ed.), *The concept of activity in Soviet psychology*. Armonk, NY: M. E. Sharpe.

Warren, B., Ballenger, C., Ogonowski, M., Rosebery, A. S., & Hudicourt-Barnes, J. (2001). Rethinking diversity in learning science: The logic of everyday sense-making. *Journal of Research in Science Teaching, 38*, 529–552.

Weiner, B. (1985). An attributional theory of achievement motivation and emotion. *Psychological Review, 92*, 548–573.

Wertsch, J. (1985). *Vygotsky and the social formation of mind*. Cambridge, MA: Harvard University Press.

Wilson, W. J. (1987). *The truly disadvantaged: The inner city, the underclass, and public policy*. Chicago, IL: University of Chicago Press.

Zakaria, F. (2008). *The post-American world*. New York, NY: W. W. Norton.

10

An Ecological and Activity Theoretic Approach to Studying Diasporic and Nondominant Communities

Kris D. Gutiérrez and Angela E. Arzubiaga

The concept of community is a commonplace notion in everyday discourse that is often associated with things positive. Indeed, as Raymond Williams (1985) once wrote,

> Community can be the warmly persuasive word to describe an existing set of relationships, or the warmly persuasive word to describe an alternative set of relationships. What is most important, perhaps, is that unlike all other terms of social organization (state, nation, society, etc.) it seems never to be used unfavourably, and never to be given any possible opposing or distinguishing term. (p. 76)

In the same vein, Zygmunt Bauman's (2001) extended definition of community explores how the construct of community has come to be associated with positive experiences—promising pleasures, especially pleasures we would like to experience and seem to miss. To paraphrase Bauman, community is a "warm" place, a cozy, and a comfortable place in which we are safe. In a community, we are never strangers; we understand one another well and if we quarrel, they are friendly quarrels as we can count on each other's good will. What the word community evokes is everything we miss and what we lack to be secure, confident, and trusting (see Bauman, pp. 1–2).

In this sense, the idea of community is always an imagined community (Anderson, 1991) that is always in the future, a world that is regrettably not available to us (Williams, as cited in Bauman, 2001). Such conceptualizations of imagined communities, however, take a different turn when referring to cultural communities, especially nondominant communities.[1] In this chapter, we examine how narrow conceptions of community and methodological approaches that do not seek to capture the full range of human activity can perpetuate deficit understandings of cultural communities.[2]

This latter point is particularly important, as the concept of community is also a ubiquitous unit of analysis in the social science literature. Scholars across disciplines use the term liberally to refer to *diverse communities*, *Latino communities*, *linguistic* and *urban communities*, *immigrant communities*, and *communities at risk*, for example—often without consideration of the resources and constraints of the community's ecology or the internal logic or social fabric of the community's practices, including the range and variation of those practices and participants' motivation to participate therein. Or, conversely, idealized, romantic and imagined conceptualizations are proffered in which the practices of the dominant group are normative and counter-practices, disruptions, and contradictions are overlooked, dismissed, or pathologized. In either case, community is presented as a monolithic, static, and uncomplicated rendering of a collection of people and their practices; however, as we will argue, addressing the regularity and variance in communities would help reveal that culture is not shared uniformly: members of communities do not necessarily participate in the same social practices, in the same way, or with the same meaning (Gutiérrez, 2004; Gutiérrez & Rogoff, 2003).

In this chapter we address how current empirical studies of nondominant communities may perpetuate deficit and one-dimensional portraits of cultural groups and their practices. Drawing on work from cultural studies, historical analyses of labor unions in the U.S. South, and our own empirical work, we focus on how contemporary theorizations of and approaches to studying nondominant communities often work hand in glove to construct problematic renderings of individuals and their practices. The challenge we raise here is how to do empirical work that captures the complexity—the full range—of community activity toward deeper analyses of the community's ecology, the available affordances and constraints, and the influences on everyday practices. This task becomes more complicated when we layer on race and ethnicity, when we try to address issues of racism and other forms of inequality, and when we attempt to account for local, distal, and historical influences that mediate human activity.

We address these dilemmas in this piece and propose several approaches that help address the conceptual and methodological challenges encountered in conducting thoughtful empirical work in nondominant communities. In general, we argue that a cultural-historical activity theoretical approach (CHAT) can make visible the limitations of current conceptions of community in empirical work. First, we propose an instrumental view of culture within the cultural-historical tradition that challenges reductive notions of culture that are often at work in analyses of cultural communities, their participants, and practices. While remaining in this theoretical tradition, we then discuss the affordances of third-generation activity theory, a particular uptake of a CHAT approach, as a means for producing more expansive and dynamic understandings of nondominant and emergent diasporic communities and about what is learned in the movement of people and practices.

CHAT's defining principle—one that distinguishes this view from other understandings of learning and development—is its attention to the culturally mediated nature of human psychological activity. As Michael Cole (1996) puts it, culture is squarely in the middle of human psychological functions. Understanding the central role of cultural artifacts in mediating human activity helps us avoid analyses that separate the individual from her cultural means; as Engeström (1999) has argued, this view "resolves the Cartesian individual and societal divide" (p. 1); it makes visible what Linehan and McCarthy (2001) refer to as "the processes of the production" of communities through which we can document how culture and the individual are both transformed.[3]

Rethinking culture in this way takes us beyond deficit and essentialist views about cultural communities and provides a way to understand what is cultural about learning across the activities of people's lives within identifiable cultural communities. Culture, then, is not a single variable or something that can be identified directly by a person's appearance, race, ethnicity, or national origin, for example. Instead, culture is lived dynamically and reflected in people's participation in their community's practices, traditions, and institutions and is transformed as people and practices change as well.

We believe a cultural historical perspective proposes a way to understand human activity, which could otherwise be missed by static markers, trait-based thinking, or reified classifications that render invisible crucial aspects of human activity. At the same time, as we will also discuss, a dynamic view of culture does not mean that we stop looking for regularities in the ways members of cultural communities participate in everyday practices. We view the regularities in communities and the relatively stable characteristics of particular cultural environments as being in constant tension with the emergent goals and practices that participants construct in ways that contribute to the variation and ongoing change in an individual's and a community's practices (Gutiérrez, 2002).

THIRD-GENERATION ACTIVITY THEORY WITHIN A CULTURAL-HISTORICAL APPROACH

Our interest in the cultural mediation of people's activity is part of the movement toward compatible approaches that expand current conceptions of the constitution of individuals' practices across activity systems with interest in what takes hold—that is, what is learned as people and practices travel across activity systems. Toward this end, we believe that third-generation activity theory within a cultural-historical approach provides the theoretical and methodological tools to capture the local and distal influences on a community's practices, including nondominant and emergent diasporic communities—the focus of this chapter.

While holding to the central tenets of a cultural-historical approach, third-generation activity theory has important features that distinguish it from preceding generations of the theory. Theories are dynamic and evolve. As Engeström (2009) has theorized, understanding activity theory's evolution in terms of how it defines the unit of analysis helps us distinguish important affordances and limitations of a cultural-historical approach. First-generation activity theory, associated with Vygotsky (1978), focused on the notion of mediated action, while second-generation iterations of activity theory informed by Leon'tev were organized around activity as the central unit of analysis of human practice. In contrast and of relevance to this chapter, third-generation activity theory focuses on the idea that people are part of multiple activity systems, and that the relations among and contradictions that exist between activity systems are central to the analysis of human activity. Further, the conceptual tools provided by third-generation activity theory help us understand "dialogue, multiple perspectives, and networks of interacting systems" (Yamazumi, 2009, p. 214).

However, despite our own use of this approach, we also caution that even a cultural-historical activity theoretic framework will not mitigate the effects of using theoretical constructs that carry a history of preserving the dominance of some communities and their practices.

THE PROBLEM OF COMMUNITY

Portraying communities as unchanging and homogenous has had particular social, political, and educational consequences for people from nondominant groups. What are the consequences of such renditions of community? As we have written elsewhere (see Arzubiaga, Artiles, King, & Murri, 2008; Gutiérrez, 2006), theorizing and studying communities—especially those different from our own—requires us to examine the ideological positions at work in the constructs we employ, their history of use, as well as the frameworks and fields in which they operate—with attention to what has been naturalized and what has been ignored. For example, we would examine what has been normalized in commonplace educational terms such as disadvantaged, at-risk, underclass, community, diversity, urban, rural, immigrant, refugee, migrant, English Learner, and code-switching. In other words, what has already been taken for granted or assumed in these conceptions and their use?

To illustrate this point, let us consider the concept of the *underclass community* as an orienting construct in the study of work-related issues in urban communities. As historian Robin Kelley, in *Yo' Mama's Disfunktional!* (1997), points out, "the pervasive imagery of [an] 'underclass' [community] makes the very idea of a contemporary urban working class seem obsolete" (p. 127). Instead of hardworking urban residents, many from nondominant groups, Kelley argues, the dominant image of the U.S. "ghetto" is of idle young Black men,[4] drug dealers, and unwed mothers. Within this construction of community, "the ghetto is the last place to find the American worker" (p. 127).

Kelley's account is illuminating because it opens a window on the ways that flattened notions of community lead us away from understanding the complexity and diversity of human activity. Of relevance to this chapter, even our theories and methods, however robust, can be inadequate in documenting complex ecologies if our starting point is organized around weak understandings of the regularity and variance that are a part of all constellations of human living. For example, if we are only interested in main effects, we might be less disposed to using mixed methods, multileveled analyses, or hierarchical linear modeling that, like good ethnography, assume nestedness, multiple effects, and a need to tease out or unpack what mediates and organizes a community's practices. If our answer lies only in the local, even discourse analysis and critical ethnography can constrain our potential to seek alternative explanations to phenomena, to the effects of both proximal and distal influences, to multiple activity systems at work (Brandt & Clinton, 2002; Street, 2003). Similarly, a robust unit of analysis can fall flat if organized around understandings of communities without their sociocultural and historical contexts, without the interplay of the local and the global.

How might this narrowing conception of community unfold in a study of work in nondominant communities that utilizes the notion of *work as leading activity* as a focus of analysis? The idea of leading activity, first advanced by Leont'ev (1981) and later elaborated by Griffin and Cole (1984), was proposed as a means of separating those activities that are most related to an individual's development from those that are less important (Griffin & Cole, p. 50). According to Leont'ev,

> Some [activities] play the main role in development and others a subsidiary one. We can say, accordingly, that each stage of psychic development is characterized by a definite relation of the child to reality that is the leading one at that stage and by a definite, leading type of activity. (Leont'ev, 1981, p. 395, as cited in Griffin and Cole, 1984, p. 50)

Work within a cultural-historical activity theoretical framework is considered a leading developmental activity in Western society (Griffin & Cole, 1984). Within this perspective, we might expect work as a leading activity to be a productive object of analysis for individual development. In the United States, we also attach a moral valence to the kind and amount of work we do. Following Kelley's (1997) argument, however, if our notions of work in nondominant communities do not allow us to see work and workers when we make sense of activity in urban communities, we are left with a stereotypical description of the urban community, or we focus our gaze on the exotic, the sensational—for example, the drug dealer or prostitute on the corner. Thus, even if we use a robust theory such as cultural-historical activity theory and we view work as a leading developmental activity, how would we explain how people are developing and learning if we begin with the assumption that there is no work or worker in today's urban communities or if economic disparity limits opportunities to engage in work as a sustainable practice in the community?

ATTENDING TO CULTURE

We turn to our earlier conversation on culture to argue that some working metaphors of community in empirical studies are constrained by reductive notions of culture that often lead to overly general statements about the cultural practices of communities, especially in relation to cultural communities. In our scholarship we have argued the importance of attending to the diversity in the kinds of practices in which individuals and groups participate, while also focusing on the unifying elements that constitute a community (Arzubiaga, Ceja, & Artiles, 2000; Arzubiaga, Rueda, & Monzó, 2002; Gutiérrez & Correa-Chavez, 2006). Capturing this complexity, we argue, requires attending to the cultural dimensions of people's everyday lives: that is, what is actually cultural about people's practices. In this way, we build on this body of research and propose that the study of cultural communities should capture various foci of analysis of community life: regularity in community life and in the ways families organize everyday life, leverage their resources, and negotiate the constraints of the various activity systems of which they are a part (Rogoff, 1995).

Arzubiaga et al. (2000), for example, utilize an ecocultural approach to account for the complexity of the daily routines of Latino families. This focus is of particular importance, as the practices of cultural communities often are represented as static and homogenous, or are under-theorized in terms of local and distal influences. The word *ecoculture* (Weisner, 1984) combines the concepts of *eco*logy, that is, resources and constraints, with the word *culture*: values, beliefs, and schemata. Thus, an ecocultural methodological approach— with its focus on stable scripts or routines that families develop to negotiate the demands of quotidian activity—helps to unpack the sociocultural context, including the variation therein. Based on a local rational-action theory—that is, the decisions about practices that people make, and their understandings of the consequences of particular courses of actions within specific contexts (e.g., the situatedness of specific locales)—an ecocultural approach assumes all families have the universal task of organizing a sustainable daily routine (Weisner, 1984; Arzubiaga et al., 2000). From this perspective, family adaptation involves balancing the ecological affordances and constraints of their niche, their culture or values, beliefs, and schemata, and the needs and abilities of family members in the organization of daily routines.

In this sense, the activity system of the family can be conceived of as one system working toward the sustainability of the family's daily routine. However, each individual family member's participation is not always aligned with the family's leading activity, the sustenance of its daily routine; rather, family activities are often in the process of both being constituted and contested—that is, in the process of resolving contradictions that emerge in the family's activity systems. Of significance to the dynamic and processual notion of culture we advance, each family must continually resolve the demands and contradictions of creating a sustainable routine within a given set of ecological affordances and constraints. In this way, we expect to document differences in the ways families organize the routines of daily life.

We present an example of a daily routine in the Gomez family to help illustrate the processes discussed above.[5] The Gomez family, a nuclear family of seven who had migrated to Tennessee from Texas, arranged a daily routine around homework for their children such that knowledge and assistance are distributed across family members. As we learn in the following interview, in this family routine, all the children sit together around the kitchen table to do their homework. The social organization of this routine, explains Dalia, the mother, is arranged so that the youngest child can ask the sibling who is older than her for needed assistance, while that older sibling can ask the next oldest, and so forth. However, the eldest child, as the mother points out, has no one to ask but at times asks her for help and eventually asks the father if need be.

From the perspective of the family as the unit of analysis, this routine, with its assigned roles, tasks, personnel, and scripts, works at a sustainable pace for the family to help them accomplish the necessary tasks needed to meet the demands of school, and, at the same time, leaves time for the mother to prepare meals or tend to other household chores. In the excerpt below, Dalia (D) describes to the researchers (P and M) the routine she has organized for her children[6]:

D: [The children] go get Giuliana and they arrive with her and that way, if the kitchen is dirty, well they pick it up and then they all sit to do homework.

P: You mean the eldest?

D: Yes, the eldest, yes Sandra. As soon as they arrive from school, everybody to do homework.

P: Where, they do it here?

D: Ah, at the table, yes.

P: Ah.

D: Yes, they do it all together, so that if one doesn't know, they ask the eldest. Well, she doesn't have anyone to ask [she laughs]. Giuliana asks Javier and that way, between the three they help each other.

M: And from what time to what time more or less? [do they do homework]

D: Homework?

M: Yes.

D: I think that from around 4 to 6 because they are slow to do their homework. Since they turn on the TV, they study a little and there, they study and that way, but [One of the children says something to his mother]

D: Ok, if they are there from 4 onward, more or less they do their homework.

P: And what happens when you say that they help each other when there is someone that doesn't know something, what happens if—

D: Let's say, when Sandra doesn't know, she almost always knows how to help them both. But when she doesn't know she asks me. And we look it up; we look until we find it, since what she asks sometimes is mathematics, almost always.

P: Ahh.

D: We look for it, and if not, we ask her father [she laughs]. If we don't know between the two of us, and if we don't know, she talks to a friend of hers.

P: The eldest, Sandra, talks to a friend of hers?

D: Yes.

Dalia organizes family resources in ways she believes best support her children's learning. However, there are contradictions that arise in the accomplishment of this routine. Not all members benefit equally from this practice. For example, participating in the family routines means that the oldest daughter is missing out on attending an advanced after-school program or meeting her girlfriends at the park.

In this sense, the family's leading activity to create a sustainable daily routine to accomplish everyday life might be in contestation with competing activity systems of other family members. In this case, the oldest daughter's beliefs about preparing to go to college and her desire to participate in a community of friends might compete or be in contestation with the family's routine.

Or we might find that the routine requires the mother to take care of the children instead of being able to enroll in the English classes she wants to take. In other words, what works for the maintenance of the daily routine of the family is not necessarily in the "best" interest of each individual family member or beneficial in the same way. Here we begin to understand the enabling and constraining nature of cultural practices, the material and nonmaterial affordances and limitations of the ecocultural context, and the importance of examining how households within ecological niches construct family life. This sociocultural approach pushes us to think differently about communities and families within those communities.

MOVING BEYOND THE BOUNDED AND
IMAGINED CONCEPTIONS OF COMMUNITY

One of the enduring criticisms of past anthropological work on communities has centered on enduring conceptions of communities as bounded and impermeable entities; such views do not account for the dynamic constitution of communities or the ongoing movement and flow occurring especially in communities experiencing migration and transmigration (Gutiérrez, 2007, 2008; Hage, 2005; Marcus, 1998). The increased interest in studying the effects of rapid globalization, immigration, diasporic communities, and cultural communities in general, makes rethinking the ways we theorize and study communities a compelling issue to address. These new areas of scholarship both push us toward complexity and also make visible the ethical demands and contradictions inherent in conducting such research.

One response to the limitations of studying the bounded community has been the development of the multi-sited ethnography (Marcus, 1998) that requires what Marcus (2005) calls the valorization of methodological bricolage. Rephrasing Marcus's notion, the methodologist functions as a kind of bricoleur. The bricoleur makes use of things at hand to accomplish functions needed in the moment—things not designed to perform that new function. In other words, bricolage involves the use of a tool designed for one function to perform a different function. The creativity of the bricoleur, then, involves being able to imagine new uses of existing tools for new functions (Erickson, 2010). In the context of this discussion, the bricoleur's use of tools is contingent on the problem at hand, rather than relying on a single tool or specific tool designed for a single or specific task or functioning within a kind of presumed methodological orthodoxy that can limit or constrain studying communities and practices in flux.

Tools should be recruited to help address the problems at hand. In this vein, we are proffering the need for a robust methodological toolkit that works hand in glove with a rich framework for human development to conduct empirical work in communities that helps better account for the changing nature of communities and their practices; this is particularly useful in accounting for the intercultural dimensions that are a part of new communities, including immigrant and diasporic communities.

This view helps us understand the affordance of approaches like the multi-sited ethnography, which, as writes Marcus, "is at its best, most interesting and creative when it examines distributed knowledge systems and focuses on process and connections" (p. 7), especially since

> the habit or impulse of the multi-sited research is to see subjects as differently constituted, as not products of essential units of difference only, but to see them in development—displaced, recombined, hybrid in the once popular idiom, alternatively imagined. (p. 7)

Seeing participants developmentally, such as understanding immigrant families' practices across time and space, should help us better understand how the practices of migration, transmigration, and living interculturally, for example, influence the everyday practices of immigrant families under examination. Attending to the flow and diffusion of people across settings moves us away from static and bounded notions of culture and cultural communities, including those conceptions at work around immigrant families. In this methodological approach, the ethnographer is "an ethnographer of movement rather than stillness" (Hage, 2005, p. 467) who focuses on what Hall (2004) specifies as the "circulation of discourse, the production of social imaginaries, and the forging of transnational networks across levels of scale and connecting people across time and space" (p. 109).

While traditional ethnography focuses on localized everyday practices, understanding the experience of immigrant and diasporic communities involves the "interplay of transnational, national, and local processes" [to study the] 'cultural flows' that move across time, space, or levels of social scale" (Hall, 2004, p. 109). This point is particularly crucial in the documentation of recent immigrants' practices, particularly those from Central America—communities that are marked by transnational flow.

NEW TOOLS FOR UNDERSTANDING NEW COMMUNITIES

Activity theory, we believe, extends the fundamental principles of the multi-sited ethnographic approach and deepens our understanding of new immigrant and diasporic communities by examining how cultural activity is influenced both by people's interpretive processes, as well as local and more distal sociohistorical and sociopolitical demands. An activity theoretic approach can help us see the social world as a multilayered network of interconnected activity systems rather than, as Engeström (1999) has argued, "a hierarchy of rigid institutions and structures with a single center of power" (p. 36).

For those of us interested in documenting both individual and community learning, cultural-historical activity theory serves as a theoretical tool for studying social practices and interpreting human behavior in ways that make visible the "relations between the collective and the individual, and the collective within the individual" (Smolka, 1995, p. 365). An exclusive focus on how knowledge and understandings are transferred thus shifts to an understanding of how people appropriate different aspects of practices to use in and across various activities. Here the notion of nonlinear development is instrumental in understanding the interaction between individuals and a community's affordances and constraints.

STUDYING MULTIPLE ACTIVITY SYSTEMS

Our interest in diasporic Mexican communities has motivated us to advance a method encouraged by third-generation activity theory in which we examine "a minimum of two interacting activity systems" (Engeström, 2005, p. 62), with a focus on people's movement across activity settings and their learning through participation in those settings (Gutiérrez,

2008). Documenting what takes hold as people move across the various activity systems helps us understand how individuals' repertoires of practice are constituted (Gutiérrez & Rogoff, 2003).

We return to the case of the Gomez family discussed earlier to highlight the importance of understanding individual and family practices across multiple activity systems. Recall that the Gomez family had organized a daily homework routine in which the younger children relied on the older children for assistance. While the family routine is designed to make use of the available resources, the family's constraints and the abilities and needs of family members together play a role in how the Gomez family promotes their children's learning. We would expect differences in the social organization of family activity depending on the available resources and constraints. For example, families with more income, nuclear families with a single child, or families with different social networks might arrange home routines differently or utilize outside assistance from tutors or after-school programs.

To learn more about the developmental pathways of the Gomez children, we would want to know more about their participation in a range of practices both in the home and beyond, as well as the resources and constraints therein. We focus on the literacy practices of one of the children, Giuliana, to illustrate the various influences on her literacy learning.

Members of ethnic groups and microcultures within societies organize the education needed for their children's futures, as Dalia does for her children (Levinson & Holland, 1996). In one documented discussion of the family's literacy practices, Giuliana's mother discusses her daughter's reading practices. We learn that while her mother believed she fell short in her reading at home, she meets her teacher's expectations at school, and is lauded for her rapid progression in reading ability. Her teacher stated, "and then I have Giuliana, who probably will be exited from ELL 'cause she reads well and, you know, attempts almost all the things that I do in my regular classroom."

However, the literacy practices Dalia organizes for her children are vastly different from Giuliana's reading practices at school in which narrower dimensions of reading such as speed-reading are emphasized and individual assessments of how fast a student can read are valued. Reading at home is a collaborative effort where family members discuss meaning and negotiate their understandings about text. One such salient literacy event involved a collective sense-making discussion about Helen Keller's biography in which Dalia, her eldest daughter Sandra, and the family's younger children negotiated the meaning of this well-known text. In contrast to the children's school literacy practices, this family routine organized literacy learning as a distributed activity, where each family member brought something to bear on the text's meaning and factual points and individual interpretations were openly challenged in the service of reading for meaning and understanding. What can be learned from an analysis of this family's literacy practices? Of significance, without examining literacy practices across multiple activity systems, it might be easier to assume deficiencies in the Gomez's family routines and thus expect their literacy practices to be less robust than school-based literacy learning.

At the same time, we learn that the tensions between the two activity systems of home and school have material effects on the children's learning. Consider that Giuliana's practices at home and school both shape and constrain her reading strategies, as the activity systems of home and school are in contention with one another. This, of course, poses a problem for her mother, Dalia, who contrasts her daughter's progress and reading ability with her prior experience with her children's participation in different reading practices in the Texas schools they attended before moving to Tennessee. Her older children had learned to read in Texas schools in which their teaching and learning communities utilized both Spanish and English and Dalia's participation in school and in reading practices was welcomed.

Of consequence, understanding the various activity systems of which Dalia has been a part also helps us understand what gave rise to Dalia's educational repertoire. Similarly, by documenting Giuliana's practices across multiple activity systems, we can observe what new understandings of literacy she appropriates across systems of meaning, as well as what contradictions emerge as she traverses the various activity systems that constitute her life. In this sense, Giuliana's literacy community is not bounded in one community of practice. More to the point of this chapter, our task in studying cultural communities entails accounting for regularity in a community's practices, as well as the variance among its members to move away from facile conclusions based on overly general analyses of participants' practices. Close analysis of families' routines and the scripts they develop to organize and sustain family life, such as we saw in the Gomez family, involves attention to an additional unit of analysis. Thus, constructing more accurate accounts and fuller representations of families' practices is enhanced by documenting individuals across multiple activity systems.

STUDYING MOVEMENT ACROSS ACTIVITY SYSTEMS

Traditional approaches to the study of nondominant communities and families too often focus on the analysis of families in one activity system or center around binary contrasts of home and school or school and community in ways that reinforce dichotomous views of home and school, rather than focusing on the repertoires of practice that are constituted through participation across activity settings. Paraphrasing Hage (2005), we emphasize that what is significant is not just that people move across activity settings, but rather what individuals find significant about the movement, what is learned, and what kinds of expertise develop.

What kind of toolkit is needed to *see* learning as movement and to capture the repertoires of practice people develop across activity? We argue for a robust theoretical framework of learning and development that relies on interdisciplinarity and multiple methods to help meet this challenge in our scholarship. A CHAT approach supports problem-oriented research and draws on a range of methodological tools to study the phenomenon at hand. For example, we could use qualitative methods to study processes and practices, microanalysis of talk and interaction to make visible conflict and contradiction within and across activity systems, as well as an examination of the efficacy of tools that mediate individual and collective practice. In short, it is important to understand the instrumental aspects of activity.

Within a CHAT perspective (Vygotsky, 1978), *activity* is the explanatory principle in psychological theory: that is, mind is influenced by labor-mediated and productive activity, thus highlighting the relationship between practical activity and psychological phenomena. Third-generation activity theory encourages us to also widen the lens to examine individuals' practices both within and across activity systems with attention to what takes hold as people move across the contexts and activity systems of their everyday lives.

We draw from our work to illustrate how a cultural-historical approach view helps us conceive of the literacy practices as part of a toolkit that is socially and culturally shaped as individuals participate in a range of practices across familiar, new, and hybrid contexts and tasks. In this way, we begin to understand that literacy learning is not an individual accomplishment and instead is built on a history of relationships and influences, both local and distal. For example, if we are interested in understanding the literacy practices of migrant students in California or immigrant families in Tennessee, a cultural-historical activity theoretic view pushes us to consider both an ecological view of students' learning to understand how repertoires of practice develop (Gutiérrez & Rogoff, 2003), as well as how students' environments and practices also are the consequence of globalization, transmigration, and the intercultural experiences of their everyday lives. In this way, rather than focusing on immigrant students' "linguistic deficiencies" we would focus on the sociohistorical influences on their language and literacy practices, as well as on their social, economic, and educational realities, as Scribner (1990) observed, things mediated by the social, both proximally and concretely, as well as distally and abstractly (Gutiérrez, 2007).

Further, we would want to examine students' language and literacy practices across at least two activity settings and a range of practices (Engeström, 2003; 2005); in doing so, we would be less inclined to rely on analyses that dichotomize home and school or in and out of school practices or to oversimplify what counts as literacy for these youth. Instead we would focus our analyses on what takes hold as youth move within and across tasks; contexts; and spatial, linguistic, and sociocultural borders. Such an analysis would also encourage us to attend to successful pathways and contextual supports that promote youth's literacy learning. And we would attribute observed regularities in students' practices to their history of participation in familiar cultural practices, to public schooling experiences in California, for example, that restrict engagement and limit the use of cultural resources that are part of their repertoires. Such regularities would also be understood, in part, as a historical consequence of colonizing practices of which they have been a part. We also would document individuals' movement within and across activity systems and how individuals' repertoires of practice help them negotiate movement within and across a range of developmental tasks and contexts. For example, we would want to know more about what is learned in border crossing, which practices travel in that movement, or about the consequences of participation in intercultural exchange and hybrid practices (Gutiérrez, 2008).

Indeed, our identity toolkit is filled with contradictions, as the communities of practice in which we participate are filled with inconsistency, ambiguity, conflict, tension, and competing objects and motives—practices that are at odds with one another. We use the following excerpt from Michael Keith Honey's insightful book, *Black Workers Remember: An Oral History of Segregation, Unionism, and the Freedom Struggle* (1999), to illustrate how communities of practice are anything but benign and to illustrate the importance of attending to the people's movement across the multiple activity systems of their lives, as well as the local and historical constraints at work.

In recounting the oral histories of Black factory workers in Memphis, Tennessee, in the 1930s and 1940s, Honey documents how being part of a union both improved the economic conditions and also preserved the racist practices under which Blacks had been under slavery and later as sharecroppers under Jim Crow laws of racial separation. Jim Crow practices influenced all aspects of public and private life, as there were formal and informal rules of the social organization of Black/White relations or "social etiquette" at work under Jim Crow laws. As Honey writes,

> While conditions in the city were an improvement over sharecropping or day labor in the countryside, Jim Crow at work and in the society around them limited the progress of black workers in a multitude of ways. During the height of segregation, as one worker, Mr. Holloway observed, despite blacks' hatred of white supremacy, they could not confront it directly. Most of the time they adopted a pragmatic and realistic recognition of their situation; they had to accommodate whites to survive. . . . On the other hand, if you seemed too assertive or proud, trouble could follow. A fine line existed between resistance and abject accommodation, and black workers in interracial factory settings walked that fine line every day. (p. 46)

Under Jim Crow, factory environments were particularly hard; separate but equal extended not only to bathrooms, locker rooms, and water fountains, but also to wage and job assignment and working relations in and outside the factory.

Honey's documentation provides an opportunity to deepen our analysis about the everyday lives of Black workers in the unionized factories, to push on our notions of resistance, and to document how the object of achieving a better life as a member of the workforce in a unionized factory—mediated by a history of separate and unequal practices—was only a partially shared practice among Black and White factory workers; thus, becoming a union member alone could not provide the same full work and civic participation in the era of Jim Crow. However, as Honey reports, none of the official union and city documents or accounts from the White union workers revealed radically different conceptions of the workplace community from the oral histories of union life recounted by Black workers. How could this be the case?

The varied stances that Black workers took in this highly racialized work environment, including their seemingly nonresistant responses and narrative accounts, make visible the contradictions in the various activity systems these workers traversed and, thus, highlight the importance of attending to the multiple activity systems in which the workers participated to learn how the persistence of racist practices under Jim Crow affected the everyday lives of the Black workers, both collectively and as individuals in the factory and community, as well to see the affordances of participating in a new workforce. First, consider that both Black and White workers sought the same goal of achieving a better life for themselves and their families. The union was instrumental in helping to achieve that goal. However, with Jim Crow practices and ideologies at work, life both in the factory and in the city was necessarily different for members of the two racial groups. If we understand the everyday lives of the Black and White workers across at least two activity systems—with the union in the factory as one activity system and Memphis under Jim Crow being another—we can understand how all participants could benefit from the union's practices and could participate in the shared practice of working under better and more stable economic conditions than they did as sharecroppers or farmers. At the same time, the workplace, like city life, was also mediated by Jim Crow's racist practices and ideologies, making work and living conditions inequitable and difficult. Thus, unions both helped improve the economic conditions of Black factory workers, as well as perpetuated separate but equal practices.

Attending to conflict and contradictions within and across the two activity systems helps us understand the affordances and constraints of the unionized factory, the lack of variance in the responses, as well as the amount of agency afforded each group to speak up—responses and behaviors mediated by local and historical constraints. We use this historical case to illustrate the affordances of understanding human activity across multiple activity systems. Consider what is lost when we focus solely on the factory as a workplace, without attending to social and historical practices, ideologies, and sensibilities at work at this historical moment.

RE-MEDIATING OUR WORK IN COMMUNITIES

Across the various examples we have presented, we have argued against the narrow conceptions of community at work in the study of nondominant and diasporic communities and reductive notions of culture in such conceptions. We have proposed the use of third-generation activity theory to develop more robust theories of communities and methods to help capture complexity, as well as regularity, variation, and contradiction. Like Marcus (1998), we work against the macro-micro dichotomy and call for a multi-locale, system-directed ethnography of complex connections that are "places-, rather than place-focused" (p. 50). We also argue that activity theory helps us resolve the individual and societal divide by focusing on the mediating role of culture and cultural artifacts. And finally, we argue for the importance of studying individuals' movement across a minimum of two activity systems to begin the process of re-mediating (Cole & Griffin, 1983; Gutiérrez, Morales, & Martinez, 2009) current conceptions of cultural communities in our empirical work.

NOTES

1. We use the term *nondominant* to refer to communities or individuals who have less power, historically as well as in the present, vis-à-vis the dominant community—for example, economically, sociopolitically, educationally. We believe that a focus on power differential is more accurate than using descriptors such as *minority* or *communities/persons of color*, for example.

2. By *cultural community* we mean a coordinated group of people with some traditions and understandings in common, extending across several generations, with varied roles and practices and continual change among participants, as well as transformation in the community's practices (see Gutiérrez & Correa-Chavez, 2006; Rogoff, 2003).

3. See Barton and Tusting, 2005; Engeström, 2005; Gee, 2005; and Gutiérrez, 2004, for elaboration of this notion.

4. We prefer to capitalize the terms *Black* and *White* to emphasize and reflect the contrast between their everyday use and our intended meaning, as well as the racial social construction.

5. The Learning Sciences Institute of Vanderbilt University funded the study for two years. The study involved the following individuals in principal investigator roles: Alfredo Artiles, David Bloome, Vicki Risko, and Angela Arzubiaga. In addition, Paula Rampulla and Mauricio Altamonte, both bilingual and bicultural Spanish-speaking doctoral candidates, participated in data collection and analysis.

6. This is a translation of the actual Spanish transcript.

REFERENCES

Anderson, B. (1991). *Imagined communities: Reflections on the origin and spread of nationalism.* New York, NY: Verso.

Arzubiaga, A., Artiles, A., King, K., & Murri, N. (2008). Beyond culturally responsive research: Challenges and implications of research as situated cultural practice. *Exceptional Children, 74*(3), 309–327.

Arzubiaga, A., Ceja, M., & Artiles, A. J. (2000). Transcending deficit thinking about Latinos' parenting styles: Toward an ecocultural view of family life. In C. Tejeda, C. Martinez, Z. Leonardo, & P. McLaren (Eds.), *Charting new terrains of Chicana(o)/Latina(o) education* (pp. 93–106). Cresskill, NY: Hampton Press.

Arzubiaga, A., Rueda, R., & Monzó, L. (2002). Family matters related to the reading engagement of Latino children. *Journal of Latinos and Education, 1*(4), 231–243.

Barton, D., & Tusting, K. (Eds.) (2005). *Beyond communities of practice: Language, power, and social context.* Cambridge, England: Cambridge University Press.

Bauman, Z. (2001). *Community: Seeking safety in an insecure world.* Malden: MA, Blackwell Publishers.

Brandt, D., & Clinton, K. (2002). Limits of the local: Expanding perspectives on literacy as a social practice. *Journal of Literacy Research, 34*(3), 337–356.

Cole, M. (1996). *Cultural psychology: A once and future discipline.* Cambridge, MA: Harvard University Press.

Cole, M., & Griffin, P. (1983). A socio-historical approach to re-mediation. *The Quarterly Newsletter of the Laboratory of Comparative Human Cognition, 5*(4), 69–74.

Engeström, Y. (1999). Activity theory and individual and social transformation. In Y. Engeström, R. Miettinen, & R. Punamaki (Eds.), *Perspectives on activity theory* (pp. 19–38). New York, NY: Cambridge University Press.

Engeström, Y. (2003). The horizontal dimension of expansive learning: Weaving as texture of cognitive trails in the terrain of health care in Helsinki. In F. Achtenhagen & E. G. John (Eds.), *Milestones of vocational and occupational education and training. Volume I: The teaching-learning perspective* (pp. 153–180). Bielefeld, Germany: Bertelsmann Verlag.

Engeström, Y. (Ed.). (2005). *Developmental work research: Expanding activity theory in practice, 12.* Berlin, Germany: International Cultural-Historical Human Sciences, Lehmanns Media.

Engeström, Y. (2009). The future of activity theory: A rough draft. In A. Sannino, H. Daniels, & K. Gutiérrez (Eds.), *Learning and expanding with activity theory* (pp. 303–328). New York, NY: Cambridge University Press.

Erickson, F. (2010). Personal communication. June 9, 2010.

Gee, J. (2005). Semiotic social spaces and affinity spaces from the age of mythology to today's schools. In D. Barton & K. Tusting (Eds.), *Beyond communities of practice: Language, power, and social context* (pp. 214–232). Cambridge, England: Cambridge University Press.

Griffin, P., & Cole, M. (1984). Current activity for the future: The zo-ped. In B. Rogoff & J. V. Wertsch (Eds.), *Children's learning in the zone of proximal development*. San Francisco, CA: Jossey-Bass.

Gutiérrez, K. (2002). Studying cultural practices in urban learning communities. *Human Development, 45*(4), 312–321.

Gutiérrez, K. (2004). *Rethinking community: Implications for research*. Paper presented at the 17th Annual Conference on Interdisciplinary Qualitative Studies. University of Georgia, Athens, GA, January 9–11.

Gutiérrez, K. (2006). White innocence: A framework and methodology for rethinking educational discourse and inquiry. *International Journal of Learning, 12*(10), 223–229.

Gutiérrez, K. (2007). Commentary on a sociocritical approach to literacy. In C. Lewis, P. Enciso, & E. Moje (Eds.), *Identity, agency, and power: Reframing sociocultural research on literacy* (pp. 115–210). Mahwah, NJ: Lawrence Erlbaum Associates.

Gutiérrez, K. (2008). Developing a sociocritical literacy in the third space. *Reading Research Quarterly, 43*(2), 148–164.

Gutiérrez, K., & Correa-Chavez, M. (2006). What to do about culture? *Journal of Lifelong Learning in Europe, 3*, 152–159.

Gutiérrez, K., Morales, P. L., & Martinez, D. (2009). Re-mediating literacy: Culture, difference, and learning for students from non-dominant communities. *Review of Research in Educational Research, 33*, 212–245.

Gutiérrez, K., & Rogoff, B. (2003). Cultural ways of learning: Individual traits or repertoires of practice. *Educational Researcher, 32*(5), 19–25.

Hage, G. (2005). A not so multi-sited ethnography of a not so imagined community. *Anthropological Theory, 5*(4), 463–475.

Hall, K. (2004). The ethnography of imagined communities: The cultural production of Sikh ethnicity in Britain. *Annals, AAPSS, 595*, 108–120

Honey, M. K. (1999). *Black workers remember: An oral history of segregation, unionism, and the freedom struggle*. Berkeley: University of California Press.

Kelley, R. D. G. (1997). *Yo' mama's disfunktional! Fighting the culture wars in urban America*. Boston, MA: Beacon Press.

Leont'ev, A. N. (1981). The problem of activity in psychology. In J. V. Wertsch (Ed.), *The concept of activity in Soviet psychology*. White Plains, NY: Sharpe.

Levinson, B. A., & Holland, D. (1996). The cultural production of the educated person: An introduction. In B. A. Levinson, D. Foley, & D. Holland (Eds.), *The cultural production of the educated person: Critical ethnographies of schooling and local practice* (pp. 1–54). Albany: State University of New York Press.

Linehan, C., & McCarthy, J. (2001). Reviewing the "Community of Practice" metaphor: An analysis of control relations in a primary school classroom. *Mind, Culture, and Activity, 8*(2), 129–147.

Marcus, G. E. (2005) *Multi-sited ethnography: Five or six things I know about it now*. Presented at Problems and Possibilities in Multi-Sited Ethnography Workshop, June 27–28, University of Sussex (unpublished).

Marcus, G. E. (1998). *Ethnography through thick and thin*. Princeton, NJ: Princeton University Press.

Rogoff, B. (1995) Observing sociocultural activity on three planes: Participatory appropriation, guided participation, and apprenticeships. In J. V. Wertsch, P. Del Rio, & A. Alvarez (Eds.), *Sociocultural studies of mind* (pp. 139–164). Cambridge, England: Cambridge University Press.

Rogoff, B. (2003). *The cultural nature of human development*. New York, NY: Oxford University Press.

Scribner, S. (1990). Reflections on a model. *Quarterly Newsletter of the Laboratory of Comparative Human Cognition, 12*(2), 90–94.

Smolka, A. (1995). The constitution of the subject: A persistent question. In J. V. Wertsch, P. Del Rio, A. Alvarez (Eds.), *Sociocultural studies of mind* (pp. 165–186). Cambridge, England: Cambridge University Press.

Street, B. (2003). What's "new" in New Literacy Studies? Critical approaches to literacy in theory and practice. *Current Issues in Comparative Education, 5*(2), 77–91.

Vygotsky, L. S. (1978). *Mind in society: The development of higher psychological processes*. Cambridge, MA: Harvard University Press.

Weisner, T. S. (1984). Ecocultural niches of middle childhood: A cross-cultural perspective. In W. A. Collins (Ed.), *Development during childhood: The years from six to twelve* (pp. 335–369). Washington, DC: National Academy of Science Press.

Williams, R. (1985) *Keywords: A vocabulary of culture and society*. New York, NY: Oxford University Press.

Yamazumi, K. (2009). Expansive agency in multi-activity collaboration. In A. Sannino, H. Daniels, & K. Gutiérrez (Eds.), *Learning and expanding with activity theory* (pp. 212–227). Cambridge, England: Cambridge University Press.

11

Reconstructing Education in America

Henry M. Levin

Normally when the topic of infrastructure arises in America, it conjures images of bridges, airports, highways, levees, water supplies, communications networks, pipelines, and energy grids, primarily works of steel, concrete, asphalt, cable, and satellites. Infrastructure is viewed as the connective tissue that links and serves the population and has a long life, but must be constantly maintained, rehabilitated, and modernized because of persistent deterioration in form and function. It is the skeletal structure of a productive nation.

Although education is not normally thought of as infrastructure, its elevation to the status of human capital in the 1960s (Schultz, 1961) made it analogous to physical capital. Education represents one investment in a human population that contributes to its productivity and well-being. It must be constantly maintained and improved to avoid deterioration of a productive and democratic society. Although families reproduce the human population, its capabilities are augmented by schools and communities. If the educational preparation of the workforce is insufficient or allowed to deteriorate over time, the negative consequences for the nation as a whole are likely to be even larger than the impact of deterioration in physical infrastructure. Historically, the input of human labor has accounted for about two-thirds of the output of the U.S. economy.

This chapter addresses the potential deterioration of the human infrastructure of the United States and its consequences as well as how to reconstruct it. In the first section I present demographic and educational changes that represent a threat to the existing infrastructure of the future workforce. In the second section, I use the present knowledge base to develop a set of interventions that can resurrect and improve human capital development infrastructure while also ensuring greater equity across the population in opportunity and productivity. Finally, I suggest that these interventions should be coordinated to have a systematic and maximal impact and that the economic returns to the taxpayer on such a public investment are likely to be high.

DETERIORATION IN HUMAN INFRASTRUCTURE

Historically, successive generations of Americans have been better educated than the previous one. Parents worked to make sure that their children advanced educationally as education was perceived as vital to social and economic mobility. Moreover, school systems expanded to accommodate the growth in enrollments. For the population 25 years and older, the percentage of high school graduates more than doubled between 1960 and 2007, from about 41 percent to 86 percent according to the U.S. Census (2009). During this period, the percentage of college graduates quadrupled from about 8 percent to 29 percent. Although minorities such as blacks and Hispanics did less well overall, even their high school and college completions rose extraordinarily. In 1960 about 20 percent of the black population 25 years and older had a high school degree, and only 3 percent were college graduates; by 2007 more than 80 percent were high school graduates and almost 19 percent were college graduates. Among Mexican-Americans 25 years and older in 1970 (no figures are available earlier), about 24 percent were high school graduates and less than 3 percent were college graduates; by 2007 these figures had risen to 53 percent and 9 percent respectively.

With respect to educational attainment, the pattern of dramatic progress has slowed in recent years. In part, it has been affected by demographic shifts as groups who had historically attained less education—that is, racial minorities, immigrants, and the poor—are a rapidly increasing share of the overall population. As those segments of the population that have historically attained less education become larger shares of the total population, we can expect to see a decline in the education of the overall labor force unless we provide powerful interventions that reverse the trend (Tienda & Alon, 2007).

Kelly (2005) used U.S. Census data to project educational attainment levels from 2000 to 2020 (less than a decade from now). He estimated that during this period, as a result of projected changes in race and ethnicity of the labor force among 25- to 64-year-olds, those with less than high school would actually increase while high school graduates and those with some college would decline. College graduates, both two-year and four-year, would also decline as would graduate and professional degree holders. That is, there would be a rise for those with less education and a fall for those with more education, and this would just be in the near term. As more and more undereducated persons join the labor force and older members retire, the downward education trend will become even more pronounced unless we intervene powerfully and effectively to revamp our human capital infrastructure. In contrast, virtually every other industrialized country will be enjoying a trend of substantial improvements in their educational attainments with results that already exceed the educational outcomes for the United States.

By 2007 some 18 countries of the OECD had higher secondary graduation rates than the United States, including such countries as Greece, Slovenia, Slovak Republic, Hungary, and Poland (OECD, 2009). In the same year, nine countries exceeded the United States in entry rates into four-year postsecondary institutions, with others gaining and expected to pass the United States in the next years (OECD, 2009). Worse yet is the poor completion rate of college entrants in absolute terms and relative to other countries (Dynarski, 2007). In the United States it is estimated that only about half of students in four-year institutions complete their degrees over six years, and the completion rates for blacks and Hispanics are considerably below those of whites (Bailey, 2007).

There are two clear implications of the foregoing discussion. The first is that we must dramatically raise the educational accomplishments of the U.S. population and labor force if we are to maintain our economic vitality, standard of living, and competitive position in the international economy. A recent OECD report asserts that raising average cognitive achievement of the U.S. workforce will result in a substantial increase in economic growth rates and hundreds of trillions of dollars in additional economic outcomes over the lifetimes of a population cohort with higher achievement (Hanushek & Woessmann, 2010).

The second is that any improvement in overall educational outcomes will require a substantial improvement in the equity of educational opportunities and outcomes for ethnic and racial minorities and the poor. As the latter become a larger and larger share of the population, it is their educational accomplishments that will carry a heavier and heavier influence on the overall educational level of the United States. The principle theme of this chapter is that improving substantially the education of the overall population and labor force means improving dramatically the education of those portions of the population who have experienced the poorest educational outcomes in the past. A higher quality of education of the population and the labor force is inextricably tied to improving equity in educational outcomes.

A POTENTIAL PROGRAM OF INVESTMENT

In order to set out a plan for improving the educational infrastructure of the nation, one ought to be clear about goals. The most important principle in doing this is to equalize educational opportunities and success for all segments of the population. More specifically, this needs to be done by

1. increasing dramatically high school completion and college readiness;
2. increasing college enrollments; and
3. increasing college completions at both two-year and four-year institutions.

How this might be done is certainly the subject of debate and discussion, but I will suggest a range of activities that might accomplish these goals.

Focus on All Students

In the past we have left student educational outcomes largely to the fortunes of families and the communities in which they are located. Differences in family income, residence, and other measures of socioeconomic status (SES) have largely determined where individuals and groups in the population ended up educationally (Bailey, 2007). Those from the highest socioeconomic background achieved more years of schooling and higher-quality education than those from lower socioeconomic backgrounds. For example, the U.S. Department of Education reports that among students in the bottom 20 percent of SES, the rate of students who do not complete a high school diploma is estimated to be about six times higher than for the top 20 percent of student SES (Wirt et al., 2004). These differences are directly connected with differences in the educational opportunities that families and communities have had for their children. Lower-income and less educated families and those without two parents have had fewer educational resources to provide directly to their children in terms of educational support and assistance. They have been less likely to afford and provide the educational experiences outside of school that are an important part of the overall education of a child and the extra educational advantages that reinforce school learning. Beyond this, school funding has been based heavily on the income or wealth of the states and their local school districts, leaving the poor and minorities in jurisdictions with inferior schools. The result is that systems of state and local educational finance—although fairer than they were historically—still discriminate against those in less wealthy communities and states (Evans, Murray, & Schwab, 1997). Neighborhood concentrations of children in poverty and from minority communities also attract fewer highly qualified staff to their schools and have reduced exposure to other students with high educational achievements and aspirations (Clotfelter, Ladd, Vigdor, & Wheeler, 2007).

This means that refurbishing the educational infrastructure must overturn many of the unequal consequences of relying so heavily on family differences and financing and channeling large portions of students from low-income, minority, and immigrant families into schools that are underfunded and segregated. We must begin to think of an overall educational system that prepares all students in ways that enable them to lead productive personal, civic, and economic lives that contribute to their own well-being and society as a whole, rather than relying so heavily on family or neighborhood circumstances that determine educational outcomes. How this might be done is the focus of what follows.

The Ecology of Education

When one thinks of upgrading the educational infrastructure, one normally thinks of improving schools. Without a doubt it is necessary to raise school effectiveness, especially for children from low-income, minority, and immigrant families, and that is an important focus of this chapter. But, education takes place in a far larger context than schools. Most of the waking hours of a child between the ages of 0 and 18 are accounted for by out-of-school experiences. Children are subjected to influences outside of schools that can either promote or blunt productive learning and that can either support or undermine the efforts of schools. In almost every dimension, families with greater socioeconomic resources are able to obtain better schooling and provide more productive learning experiences for their children.

For these reasons it is important to think of improvements in the overall context in which children live, and especially for the poorest families in our society. Rothstein (2004) has set out this challenge in its boldest terms, demonstrating inequalities in nutrition, health status, housing, and many other dimensions of life that affect the human and educational development of children. It is this broad view of renewing the educational infrastructure of society that is at the heart of the view expressed here, even though much of the focus will be on educational institutions. A summary of this approach can be found in the organization A Broader, Bolder Approach to Education (BBA),[1] which comprises a broad strategy to improve the education of low-SES children by improving all of the institutional influences that affect their educational success, not just schools. Their agenda is designed to address the following:

- contextual factors of family, community, social, and economic influences (e.g., housing, neighborhoods, employment, income);
- quality preschool and health care;
- school improvement;
- out-of-school learning opportunities;
- child and adolescent development; and
- immigrant transition.

All of these dimensions are important for vastly upgrading our educational infrastructure. However, in this chapter I will focus primarily on the school and out-of-school learning components of this agenda. I wish to be clear that refurbishment of the educational infrastructure requires attention to all of its dimensions as emphasized by the BBA, which had its origin in the work of Rothstein (2004).

Quality Preschool and Health Care

Even prior to reaching school age, a large gap opens between the achievement and school readiness skills of children of different family income. On average, kindergarten entrants in the bottom 20 percent of SES show academic achievement that is 60 percent below the top quintile (Barnett & Belfield, 2006; Lee & Burkam, 2002). Nor is this difference mysterious. A highly regarded study of language and vocabulary based upon observations among families of different SES found that children of welfare families were exposed to far less vocabulary and less rich vocabulary than children of either working-class or professional families (Hart & Risley, 1995). The former were exposed to only about one-third of the vocabulary per unit of time relative to children from the latter. A summary of the literature has also found that disparities in early health care affect school readiness (Currie, 2005). Longer-term evidence suggests that access to early health care had a substantial positive impact on later student achievement among black students and explains, in part, the racial gap in achievement (Chay, Guryan, & Mazumdar, 2009).

It is clear that early deficiencies in health care and exposure to skills required for success in school can be compensated for by quality preschools and health services. Camilli, Vargas, Ryan, and Barnett (2010) reviewed 123 studies of early-childhood interventions, both quasi-experimental and experimental studies. Although the largest effects were found for the interventions improving cognitive skills, preschool education was also found to impact children's social skills and later school progress. Especially important in terms of quality of instruction was the emphasis on small-group instruction and teacher-directed instruction. Strong preschool programs of high quality have substantial positive impacts on later student performance, and especially for families from minority, immigrant, and low-SES backgrounds (Magnuson, Ruhm, & Waldfogel, 2007).

What Has Happened to School Improvement?

Over recent decades there have been many attempts to find ways to improve education with a particular focus on student achievement. There also have been vast refinements in evaluation methodologies and in the training and sophistication of researchers in applying these methodologies (Shadish, Cook, & Campbell, 2002). The federal government has established the What Works Clearinghouse, which is dedicated to sifting through evaluations of different educational interventions to ascertain which ones have the strongest evidence of effectiveness.[2] Relatively few of the many attempts to improve educational outcomes are buttressed by credible evidence, in part because the costs of rigorous evaluation are substantial, so most interventions lack evaluative studies that meet scientific criteria.

Nevertheless, there are a large and increasing number of different approaches that have garnered evidential support of effectiveness, although no silver bullets in the sense of large effects at minimal cost. These include reductions in class size, computer instruction, some types of teacher training, and higher salaries to attract better teachers (Loeb & McEwan, 2009). While each of these may be worth considering, differences in implementation and school capacity may provide very different results from school to school rather than a guarantee of effects.

Certainly, it is important to consider the specific interventions that the What Works Clearinghouse and other systematic evaluations have found to be effective. However, as a way of drastically improving our educational infrastructure, such approaches are limited by two factors. The first is that even when they are found to have statistically significant effects on achievement, the overall effect is modest, rarely more than one-fifth of the gap in racial achievement between the higher-achieving white and Asian students and the lower-achieving black and Hispanic students. Moreover, there is almost no evidence that the benefits are cumulative over time. The second is that the results are limited to specific subjects and grades rather than being generalizable across school subjects and duration of schooling. That is, at best the evidence suggests that for a specific subject and grade, a statistically identifiable impact has been found, usually of modest size.

Because of the difficulties of identifying a large range of reforms that will improve academic achievements in different subjects and at all grade levels and implementing them effectively as a unified effort, attempts have been made to consider larger-scale reforms that will transform entire schools. Early efforts at this transformation entailed adopting school policies that seemed to be associated with success, the effective schools movement (Edmonds, 1979; Purkey & Smith, 1983). However, it was found that identifying apparently successful schools and their practices was not equivalent to knowing how to implant those practices with comparable accomplishments in ineffective schools. So-called whole school reform also produced disappointing results in both the longevity of the changes and their academic impacts.

In response to these disappointments, some have blamed government and bureaucratic rigidity of schools as thwarting change. Such critiques have brought forth movements to improve education through adoption of different forms of ownership and control of schools on the premise that direct government operation of schools limits school performance (Belfield & Levin, 2009). The largest movement in this direction has been that of public charter schools with more than 4,000 such schools having been established since 1992. Such schools are premised on creating autonomy through release from many of the laws and regulations that apply to traditional public schools to provide school choice to families and competition among schools for students (Bulkley & Wohlstetter, 2004).[3] An even more extensive departure from traditional public schools is that of educational vouchers, which have been applied in Milwaukee, Cleveland, Florida, and Washington, D.C. Parents are provided with a publicly funded certificate that can be used for tuition at private schools of their choice. The idea behind educational vouchers is to create an educational marketplace that will promote competition and choice. Although the arguments for choice may have their own merits, there is little evidence that these approaches have improved educational achievement relative to traditional public schools with similar students (Barrow & Rouse, 2009; Bifulco & Bulkley, 2009; CREDO, 2009; Loeb & McEwan, 2009; Zimmer & Bettinger, 2009). Indeed, much of the evidence is in the opposite direction.

TRANSFORMATION OF TEACHING AND INSTRUCTION

Given this background it seems clear that replacing and advancing the educational infrastructure will require major improvements in the content of schooling, instruction, and leadership. Based upon diverse forms of evidence, it seems useful to consider three major reforms that seem to show promise: Accelerated Schools, Leadership and Teacher Effectiveness, and Reduction of Student Segregation. All three have both empirical support and are designed to change the entire direction of the educational system rather than being restricted to marginal changes in a curriculum or teacher training or class size. What I am suggesting is that a major change in school instruction and academic content is needed, not minor changes in process; that a higher quality of teaching personnel and leadership must be attracted and retained to implement the change in school direction; and that both quality and equality will be expanded considerably by greater student heterogeneity in schools and classrooms. Each of these will be taken up briefly.

Accelerated Schools

Reviewing the challenge to the school, the demography of our nation is changing in a direction where higher proportions of the population will be drawn from groups that have not done well in school for reasons of inadequate access to the necessary resources and to other conditions for success. In order to improve the average educational outcome for the population, special attention must be devoted to ameliorating these conditions. At a minimum, substantial improvements in health, nutritional, and preschool educational services are preconditions for school success. But, once arriving at school, we must replace the present practices that leave such students farther behind the academic mainstream and provide conditions that will accelerate their progress.

Traditionally, the schools have accommodated differences in student preparedness by incorporating them into a highly stratified system where the social origins of a child were matched to schools and classrooms that reflected these origins (Oakes, 2005). Students from wealthier backgrounds went to better-financed schools where the challenge and pace of instruction was accelerated relative to those from poorer and minority origins. Within schools, students were assigned to tracks and classrooms that reflected their academic readiness, a reflection of family SES. Even within classrooms, students were placed in groups that were expected to progress at different rates of learning according to their previous accomplishments. Such a system worked to sustain and even increase gaps in achievement (Levin, 2007; Oakes, 2005). Although many of the practices that reinforced academic differences have been reduced, what we have not seen is a strong movement to more nearly equalize and accelerate academic progress for all students, although the No Child Left Behind legislation has emphasized measuring such gaps.

In my view this ambitious undertaking can be accomplished only by dedicating the entire school to accelerating the academic progress of all students, not just those who are behind. Rather, the entire school must be marshaled to raise achievement for all students by devoting the entire school to the most effective forms of instruction with the goal of raising all students to a very high level. There are many forms of academic acceleration, but the most effective strategies typically enlist enriched approaches usually reserved for "gifted and talented" students (Renzulli & Reis, 2002). These replace the tracking systems by creating a "high opportunity school" for all students (Burris & Garrity, 2008). The slow-paced and less challenging instruction used for remediation is abandoned in favor of a more dynamic instructional approach that permeates the school and embeds the learning of basic skills into highly engaging projects and other student learning activities at both classroom and school levels. Such activities motivate and engage students by building directly on their talents, experiences, cultures, and curiosities (Finnan & Swanson, 2000; Hopfenberg, Levin, et al., 1993; Levin & Finnan, 2006).

At all levels of elementary and secondary education, the following general principles are used in the accelerated instructional process. Clearly, they will be applied differently depending upon the educational level, but they are virtually the opposite of the traditional drill-and-repetition approach of remediation and teaching toward the test, and they still obtain improved results even on traditional tests (Bloom, Ham, Melton, & O'Brien, 2001):

Motivation: building on the interests and goals of the students.
Substance: building skills within a substantive or real-world context as opposed to a more abstract approach.
Inquiry: developing students' inquiry and research skills to help them learn about other subjects and areas about which they might be curious.

Independence: encouraging students to do independent meandering within the course structure to develop their own ideas, applications, and understandings.

Multiple Approaches: using collaboration and teamwork, technology, tutoring, and independent investigation as suited to student needs.

High Standards: setting high standards and expectations that all students will meet if they make adequate efforts and are given appropriate resources to support their learning.

Problem Solving: Viewing learning less as an encyclopedic endeavor and more as a way of determining what needs to be learned and how, and then implementing "the how."

Connectiveness: emphasizing the links among different subjects and experiences and how they can contribute to learning rather than seeing each subject and learning experience as isolated and independent.

Supportive Context: recognizing that to a high degree, learning is a social activity that thrives on healthy social interaction, encouragement, and support.

I do not wish to understate the major effort it will take to vastly change and "rebuild" the educational system. Past experience shows the challenges of replacing traditional instruction and the slowed-down pace and challenge of instruction typically provided to minorities and lower-SES students under the rubric of remediation. New school leadership, teacher talent, and a very different way of preparing teachers and making classroom and school decisions is required to move away from the present school culture of routinization promoted by remedial approaches. Research has shown that the traditional school approach of guiding the educational process through providing teachers and students with standardized "scripts" can be implemented far more easily than the radical changes required for accelerated schooling (Rowan & Miller, 2007). For the latter, teachers must develop accelerated applications and instructional strategies according to the principles set out above. But effective implementation of acceleration has the potential to lift student academic performance for all students far above the scripted results.

Rockville Centre, New York

For example, in a suburban community with considerable diversity, Rockville Centre, New York, the schools have achieved a high level of achievement for all groups. Although this school district is largely middle class, about one-quarter of the enrollment is comprised of African Americans and Hispanics (most from low-SES households). By using an accelerated approach, all groups of students benefited, and the achievement gap among groups was narrowed dramatically. Initially the focus was on mathematics, and for students from all groups—minorities, low-SES, genders, and initial achievement levels—middle school acceleration doubled the number of advanced high school mathematics courses undertaken by students relative to the early, more traditional approach (Burris, Heubert, & Levin, 2006).

Following the middle school success, the high school's multitrack system with its remedial and less challenging tracks was replaced by a high-content track and an honors track with IB (International Baccalaureate) and AP (Advanced Placement) courses. All low-content and remedial courses were eliminated. High school graduation rates, Regents Diploma (the highest-level diploma) awardees, and International Baccalaureate participation soared as the gap between minority and white students narrowed rapidly, with all students enrolled in the equivalent of a "high track" (Burris, Wiley, Welner, & Murphy, 2008). In 1996, prior to this change only about one-third of the minorities obtained the Regents Diploma in contrast with 88 percent of whites; by 2009 the respective percentages were 95 percent and 99 percent. Equally dramatic improvements took place in students taking the rigorous IB courses, from only about 24 percent of minorities and 72 percent of whites taking at least one IB course to about 90 percent of both groups in 2009.

Roseland School District, Santa Rosa, California

At the other end of the country in Santa Rosa, California, the Roseland School District had been established many years ago to contain mostly children of migrant farm workers who were not desired by the Santa Rosa City School District. Even today the district serves primarily poor Hispanic/Latino families with almost all meeting the criteria for free or reduced-cost lunches. But, for almost 20 years the district has been using an accelerated schools strategy of powerful learning for all of its students (Hopfenberg, Levin, et al., 1993). As a result, its schools outperform schools in the surrounding area with similar students. For example, two-thirds of its students scored at advanced or proficient levels in mathematics in 2009 in the elementary grades, and its overall performance levels across all subjects was considerably higher. Only 3 percent of its students had unexcused absences or tardies for 3 or more days compared to a range of 15–60 percent among the five comparison high schools. At the high school, the pass rate for the California High School Exit Examination was more than 82 percent in mathematics and 74 percent in English, relative to pass rates at comparison schools averaging about 60 percent in mathematics and about 50 percent in English for Latinos.

Half of the Roseland high school students met the requirements for the University of California or California State University entry, double that of the comparison schools. Although Santa Rosa City district has about ten times as many Hispanic/Latino males in its five high schools, Roseland produced as many Hispanic/Latino males who met this important eligibility criterion for further study at public, four-year institutions. Roseland had a grade 9–12 dropout rate of less than 4 percent in comparison with 16 percent among Hispanic/Latino enrollments in comparison high schools.[4]

Leadership and Teacher Effectiveness

The greatest challenge to the establishment of accelerated schools is the difficulty of implementing a profoundly different instructional strategy that requires considerable leadership, capable teachers, and a transformation of school culture (Levin & Finnan, 2006). In particular, it will take more capable teachers and school leaders to provide articulation and cohesion across grades and a high level of curriculum and instructional strategies required of accelerated schools. Both Rockville Centre and Roseland adopted accelerated instruction and curriculum across all of the schools in their districts, building articulation and a common philosophy for all school staff, parents, and students. This commitment has been sustained for a decade or more by visionary long-term leadership at both district and school levels with careful selection of teachers as well as considerable professional development opportunities and strong peer support. Support of high-quality peer learning for teachers seems to improve teacher effectiveness as measured by student achievement (Jackson & Bruegmann, 2009).

Perhaps by coincidence, these are exactly the mechanisms that have emerged from more general research on teacher policy and school leadership. In the past it was assumed that if teachers were trained according to the certification requirements of the state, then they were qualified to teach. Further, it was assumed that additional education beyond the bachelor's degree and teaching experience improved teaching success and student achievement. But recent research has shown some startling results. The first is that there are large differences in effectiveness among individual teachers. But differences in teacher training and certification do not seem to be able to explain these differences. And even additional degrees seem to show little impact along with experience beyond the first few years. Although it appears that different teachers can have remarkably different levels of effectiveness, we are unable to predict these differences from the formal preparation of teachers (Aaronson, Barrow, & Sander, 2007; Boyd, Grossman, Lankford, Loeb, & Wyckoff, 2006). The only formal measures of teachers that seem to be at least slightly related to student achievement are the pertinence of their college major in the case of mathematics teachers, the first few years of teaching experience, quality of the undergraduate institution, and teacher test scores (Wayne & Youngs, 2003).

Improving dramatically the teacher infrastructure will require substantial changes from existing teacher policies (Goldhaber & Hannaway, 2009). Although we cannot readily predict teacher productivity from the initial information available on the qualifications of teacher applicants, most states provide only limited time before a district must decide to give a teacher a permanent appointment. For example, in California the decision must be made by winter of the second year in order to provide mandated notices by March 1 of the tenure decision. Further, negotiated contracts with teachers often limit the structure, duration, and frequency of evaluations. To raise the quality and effectiveness of the teacher force, I would suggest the following changes.

1. Teacher salaries should be raised and supplemented with performance bonuses and working conditions that make a teaching career competitive with other professional careers sought by the most talented individuals. In response to this change it would be expected that a larger and more talented pool of applicants would seek to join the profession.

2. Teacher training programs, whether in schools of education or through alternative routes, need to be revamped along lines that are presently emerging from research. These changes should be closely informed by what is being learned on teacher effectiveness (Goldhaber & Hannaway, 2009).

3. Based upon the results of the general research on teacher effectiveness as well as feedback from experience of the schools on this topic, hiring for even the probationary period of employment should be highly selective, including evaluations of the quality of the prospective teacher's educational experience, potential testing, multiple interviews, and sample lessons. In contrast, it appears that much teacher hiring at present is more cursory and dependent upon traditional use of teacher credentials and pedestrian recommendations from their training programs.

4. Upon hiring, teachers should be provided with considerable training, mentoring support, and coaching in conjunction with periodic evaluations of their progress. That is, teaching prowess should be viewed as heavily developmental in which observation of teaching and student results guide feedback and assistance in areas needing improvement.

5. Provision of "permanent" or tenured appointments should not take place for four or five years, allowing time for adequate teacher development and evaluation. Tenure should be granted only to teachers who reach the highest level of performance in this period.

6. Evaluations for tenure and salary bonuses should be based upon both the improvements in student performance of the teacher's students as well as other contributions that the teacher manifests, including special learning projects, development of an innovative curriculum, progress with "difficult" students, and school leadership. It should not be based only on student achievement gains as suggested by some policymakers, because the evidence suggests that decisions beyond the control of the teacher can influence such gains, even when observable differences in student characteristics are considered (Harris, 2009; Downs & Goldhaber, 2009).

7. Even less is known about how to prepare effective principals, although considerable research is underway (e.g., Clark, Martorell, & Rockoff, 2009; Horng & Loeb, 2010). There is evidence suggesting school principals are capable of making performance distinctions in identifying effective and ineffective teachers with regard to student achievement (Harris & Sass, 2009; Jacob & Lefgren, 2008). And school policy is moving in the direction of placing greater responsibility on principals to make these distinctions in terms of hiring, tenure, and remuneration of teachers. Stability in school leadership is called for so that schools can make long-term transformation a reality rather than adopting different reforms on a frequent basis as leadership and school governance revolves.

Greater Student Diversity in Schools and Classrooms

Adoption of high-content and accelerated instructional approaches will require considerably stronger teachers and leaders, and this school infrastructure must be upgraded massively over time to improve the educational infrastructure of the nation. In addition, changes must also take place in the composition of schools and classrooms. There is a growing research literature that suggests when lower-performing students from immigrant, poverty, and minority backgrounds are concentrated in schools and classrooms with similar students, their educational results are lower than when the same students are placed in schools with higher performers. Segregation by poverty and race is the norm in the United States, largely because of housing patterns, but also because of tracking within schools (Oakes, 2005), and the situation is getting more extreme over time (Orfield & Lee, 2005). In an extensive statistical analysis, Rumberger (2007) found that attending schools with a low concentration of students in poverty, a situation that overlaps with race, as few minorities are typically found in such schools, provided a general boost in student achievement or more specifically a peer effect. Research evidence on peer effects suggests that increasing the racial and income diversity of student enrollments induces higher achievement results for low-income and minority students relative to their placement in more segregated schools and classrooms (Card & Rothstein, 2007; Hanushek, Kain, Markman, & Rivkin, 2003; Hoxby, 2000). The impact of increasing the number of higher-achieving peers on the performance of other students has become a consistent finding in the literature as school enrollments have become more stratified. Peer effects are viewed as stemming not only from positive peer influences but also from the ability of low-poverty schools to attract better teachers and principals (Clotfelter et al., 2007), and to set more demanding curriculum for their students (Levin, 2007).

The imperative for creating schools and classrooms (Burris & Garrity, 2008) that reflect the broad diversity of our country is consistent with a democracy that requires social interaction across individuals of different races and social class backgrounds (Wells, 2009). It is also an ingredient for improving educational achievement and attainments, particularly of those students most in need of effective schools, who will ultimately comprise an increasing share of the adult population and labor force. To reduce student segregation will require a strong social commitment along with the formation and implementation of imaginative and effective strategies. One promising strategy is the structuring of approaches to school choice that increase diversity, and especially the expansion of high-quality magnet schools that will attract students from all backgrounds as well as collaboration between urban and suburban schools (Kahlenberg, 2003; Wells & Crain, 1997). A major social movement will be required to promote this challenge, one that promulgates a societal awareness that advances associated with the education infrastructure of the future labor force and citizens of a democracy necessitates the dismantling of separate schools by race and socioeconomic status.

SUPPORTING CAST

At the heart of upgrading the educational infrastructure is the transformation of instruction and curricula to increase academic challenge and content along with the instructional resources to meet those challenges. Such accelerated approaches will require a capable force of teachers and school leaders who will be attracted and sustained by greater financial rewards for demonstrated success as well as the provision of mentoring and coaching assistance and opportunities to grow in their careers. In addition, it will be necessary to mount successful efforts to increase the demographic diversity of schools and classrooms to replace the present academic segregation of students. This goal will be more feasible by setting high standards for attainment by all students so that schools are not characterized or stigmatized by the demographic status of their enrollments.

Earlier in this chapter I argued that school reforms in isolation are not enough to propel an educated population and labor force. More than 90 percent of a child's waking hours from birth to the age of eighteen are spent outside of school in an environment that is heavily conditioned by experiences in the family and community. As stressed above, even prior to school attendance there must be an effort to provide quality preschools and adequate nutrition, health status, and housing as preconditions to school success. But, in addition, there are two other aspects of the learning experience that must be addressed both prior to arrival in kindergarten and during the school years—parenting approaches and out-of-school learning opportunities.

Parenting

Learning opportunities in the home are closely linked with parent education and resources as well as parenting styles. Clearly the knowledge and motivation of parents to help their children succeed educationally is important. Further, parents' education and income are resources that can enhance their child's educational progress and complement school efforts. Often these resources are viewed as stemming from a parent's socioeconomic status, which is shorthand for a parent's education, occupation, and income. But, viewing parent capability as inextricably linked to SES ignores the fact that this measure is just an indicator of parental resources, not a measure of what parents can actually do to improve the learning outcomes for their students.

Studies of the relationships between parental SES and parent behaviors that are linked to student learning have revealed many dimensions of knowledge and activity that can be taught to parents (Belfield & Levin, 2002). For example, simple behaviors such as discussing school activities on a regular basis with children have been linked to greater academic achievement (Ho & Willms, 1996). Schools, social welfare agencies, community-based organizations and faith-based entities can work with parents to teach parenting approaches that will reinforce learning and school success (Epstein, 2001; Ferguson, 2007). I submit we need to make parenting education and assistance a regular feature of the programs offered to families as part of school- and community-based outreach. In immigrant communities these programs must be culturally and linguistically aligned with the needs of local populations.

Supplementary Education

Full educational preparation requires much more than just productive school and home experiences. Students who are most successful educationally in our society have generally been exposed to many learning opportunities outside of schools such as participation in sports, music lessons, artistic performances, travel, art classes, summer camps, part-time work, and internships. In families of adequate means, the family is able to pay for many of these experiences. But for immigrants, minorities, English-language learners, and low-income families, appropriate opportunities might not be affordable. Although some of these opportunities are sponsored as co-curricular or extracurricular activities in schools, and others are found in community-based organizations such as Boys and Girls Clubs, YMCAs, athletic leagues, and faith-based institutions (Heath & McLaughlin 1993), a strong expansion of such opportunities is needed for those not presently served. Substantial attention to supplementary educational opportunities shows not only their potential, but the prospect that in the absence of their expansion it will not be possible to give less advantaged populations the types of educational experiences that will prepare them for the future (Gordon, Bridglall, & Saa Meroe 2005). Some of these options can be provided through enriched after-school programs and summer schools. This approach is consistent with research findings that indicate students from less advantaged communities experience a loss of achievement during the summer months (Alexander, Entwistle, & Olson, 2001).

RETURNS TO INVESTMENT IN EDUCATIONAL INFRASTRUCTURE

Restoring and upgrading the educational infrastructure of the nation will require more than just spot repairs. It must marshal a comprehensive and systematic program that will include

- revamping and expanding preschool programs to improve their quality and to encompass the children of the most needy families;
- establishing provisions for nutrition, health services, and housing that promote well-being and learning;
- transforming schools by replacing remediation with high-level academic content and accelerated instruction;
- attracting, cultivating, and maintaining the teacher and leadership talent that will be required;
- desegregating schools and classrooms to create more diverse peer cultures and interactions;
- upgrading parenting skills; and
- providing learning opportunities for all students through abundant supplementary educational options throughout communities.

Clearly, this is an ambitious framework that will require deep social commitment, and the question might be raised legitimately of how much it will cost. But cost represents only one side of the equation. As an investment, there are also benefits that may even exceed the cost. In that case, the investment will generate a surplus for society which can be further invested or returned to the taxpayer.

Recent studies of the economics of investment in the most educationally at-risk portions of the population have shown that the returns to the public or the taxpayer far exceed the costs. When individuals are inadequately educated, they are more likely to be unemployed or to be employed at less productive jobs. Meager income translates into low tax revenues and requires additional taxpayer burdens for public assistance, public health, and the crime and criminal processing of populations with inadequate education and poor employment opportunities. Many of these costs can be reduced dramatically by increasing educational success, and thus providing benefits to the taxpayer that offset the costs of investment in educational revitalization.

For example, a study of five dropout prevention programs that have shown rigorous evidence of effectiveness found that for every dollar of cost there was a return of from about one and a half to three dollars of benefits to the taxpayer. The median intervention in terms of benefits relative to costs showed net benefits after costs were taken into account of the equivalent of a gain to the taxpayer of $127,000 in value over a lifetime for each new graduate who would otherwise have dropped out (Levin & Belfield, 2007). Since this was calculated as a present value, it is equivalent to the additional high school graduate walking across the stage and receiving a diploma and then depositing a certificate of deposit as a gift to the taxpayer of $127,000 (the surplus generated after the cost of investment has been accounted for) along with an expression of his or her gratitude. For one of the groups most impacted by high dropouts, black males, the net returns to the taxpayer are even higher (Levin, Belfield, Muennig, & Rouse, 2007).

Overall, the rebuilding of educational infrastructure as the population demography and labor force change is more than just good public investment policy with high monetary returns. A society that provides fairer access to opportunities; that is more productive; and that has higher employment, better health, less crime, and lower dependency on government is a better society in itself. That the attainment of such a society is also profoundly good economics is simply an added incentive. The challenge of rebuilding the educational infrastructure is enormous, but so are the rewards to the nation.

NOTES

1. See http://www.boldapproach.org/index.php?id=01
2. See http://ies.ed.gov/ncee/wwc/
3. Also see www.USCharterschools.org
4. These results were obtained from the Roseland School District, Santa Rosa, California, and are taken from data of the California State Department of Education.

REFERENCES

Aaronson, D., Barrow, L., & Sander, W. (2007). Teachers and student achievement in the Chicago Public Schools, *Journal of Labor Economics, 25*, 95–135.

Alexander, K. L., Entwisle, D. R., & Olson, L. S. (2001). Schools, achievement, and inequality: A seasonal perspective, *Educational Evaluation and Policy Analysis, 23*(2), 171–191.

Bailey, T. (2007). Implications of educational inequality in a global economy, In C. R. Belfield & H. M. Levin (Eds.), *The price we pay: Economic and social consequences of inadequate education* (pp. 74-95). Washington, DC: Brookings Institution Press.

Barnett, S., & Belfield, C. (2006). Early childhood development and social mobility. *Future of Children, 6*(2), 73–98.

Barrow, L., & Rouse, C. E. (2009). School vouchers and student achievement: Recent evidence, remaining questions. *Annual Review of Economics, 1*, 17–42.

Belfield, C. R., & Levin, H. M. (2002). Families as contractual partners in education. *UCLA Law Review, 49*, 1799–1830.

Belfield, C. R. & Levin, H. M. (2009). Market reforms in education. In G. Sykes, B. Schneider, & D. Plank (Eds.), *Handbook of educational policy research* (pp. 513–527). New York, NY: Routledge.

Bifulco R., & Bulkley, K. (2009). Charter schools. In H. Ladd and E. Fiske (Eds.), *Handbook of research in education finance and policy*. New York, NY: Routledge.

Bloom, H. S., Ham, S., Melton, L., & O'Brien, J. (2001). *Evaluating the accelerated schools approach: A look at early implementation*. New York, NY: MDRC.

Boyd, D., Grossman, P., Lankford, H., Loeb, S., & Wyckoff, J. (2006). How changes in entry requirements alter the teacher workforce and affect student achievement. *Education Finance and Policy, 1*(2), 176–216.

Bulkley, K., & Wohlstetter, P. (2004). *Taking account of charter schools: What's happened and what's next.* New York, NY: Teachers College Press.

Burris, C., & Garrity, D. (2008). *Detracking for excellence and equity.* Alexandria, VA: ASCD.

Burris, C., Heubert, J., & Levin, H. (2006). Accelerating mathematics achievement using heterogeneous grouping. *American Educational Research Journal, 43*(1), 137–154.

Burris, C. C., Wiley, E., Welner, K. G. & Murphy, J. (2008). Accountability, rigor, and detracking: Achievement effects of embracing a challenging curriculum as a universal good for all students. *Teachers College Record, 110*(3), 571–608.

Camilli, G., Vargas, S., Ryan, S., & Barnett, W. S. (2010). Meta-analysis of the effects of early education interventions on cognitive and social development. *Teachers College Record, 112*(3), 579–620.

Card, D., & Rothstein, J. (2007). Racial segregation and the black-white test score gap. *Journal of Public Economics, 91*(11–12), 2158–2184.

Chay, K., Guryan, J., & Mazumdar, B. (2009). *Birth cohort and the black-white achievement gap: The roles of access and health soon after birth* (NBER Working Paper 15078). (Cambridge, MA: National Bureau of Economic Research).

Clark, D., Martorell, P., & Rockoff, J. E. (2009). *School principals and school performance* (Working Paper 38). Washington, DC: CALDER, The Urban Institute.

Clotfelter, C., Ladd, H. F., Vigdor, J., & Wheeler, J. (2007). High-poverty schools and the distribution of teachers and principals. *North Carolina Law Review, 85,* 1346–1380.

CREDO. (2009). *Multiple choice: Charter school performance in 16 states.* Stanford, CA: Hoover Institution, Stanford University.

Currie, J. (2005). Health disparities and gaps in school readiness. *The Future of Children, 15*(1), 117–138.

Downs, T. A., & Goldhaber, D. (2009). Key issues in value-added modeling (Special Issue). *Education Finance and Policy, 4*(4).

Dynarski, S. (2007). Building the stock of college-educated labor. *Journal of Human Resources, 43*(3), 576–610.

Edmonds, R. (1979). Effective schools for the urban poor. *Educational Leadership, 37*(1), 15–18, 20–24.

Epstein, J. (2001). *School, family, and community partnerships.* Boulder, CO: Westview.

Evans, W. N., Murray, S. E., & Schwab, R. M. (1997). Schoolhouses, courthouses, and statehouses after Serrano. *Journal of Policy Analysis and Management, 16*(1), 10–31.

Ferguson, R. (2007). Toward excellence with equity: The role of parenting and transformative school reform. In C. R. Belfield & H. M. Levin (Eds.), *The price we pay: Economic and social consequences of inadequate education.* Washington, DC: Brookings Institution Press, 225–254.

Finnan, C., & Swanson, J. (2000). *Accelerating the learning of all students: Cultivating culture change in schools, classrooms, and individuals.* Boulder, CO: Westview.

Goldhaber, D., & Hannaway, J. (Eds.). (2009). *Creating a new teaching profession.* Washington, DC: Urban Institute Press.

Gordon, W. W., Bridglall, B. L., & Saa Meroe, A. (Eds.). (2005). *Supplementary education: The hidden curriculum of high academic achievement.* Boulder, CO: Rowman & Littlefield.

Hanushek, E. A., Kain, J. F., Markman, J. M., & Rivkin, S. G. (2003). Does peer ability affect student achievement? *Journal of Applied Econometrics, 18*(5), 527–544.

Hanushek, E., & Woessmann, L. (2010). *The high cost of low educational performance.* Paris: OECD.

Harris, D. N. (2009). Would accountability based on teacher value added be smart policy? An examination of the statistical properties and policy alternatives. *Education Finance and Policy, 4*(4), 319–380.

Harris, D. N., & Sass, T. R. (2009). *What makes for a good teacher and who can tell?* (Working Paper 30). Washington, DC: CALDER, The Urban Institute.

Hart, B., & Risley, T. R. (1995). *Meaningful differences in the everyday experience of young American children.* Baltimore, MD: Brookes.

Heath, S. B., & McLaughlin, M. W. (1993). *Identity and inner city youth: Beyond ethnicity and gender.* New York, NY: Teachers College Press.

Ho, E., & Willms, J. D. (1996). Effects of parental involvement on eighth grade achievement. *Sociology of Education, 69*(2), 126–141.

Hopfenberg, W., Levin, H., & Associates. (1993). *The accelerated schools resource guide.* San Francisco, CA: Jossey-Bass.

Horng, E., & Loeb, S. (2010) New thinking about instructional leadership. *Phi Delta Kappan, 93*(3), 66–69.

Hoxby, C. (2000). *Peer effects in the classroom: Learning from gender and race variation* (NBER Working Paper 7867). Cambridge, MA: National Bureau of Economic Research.

Jackson, C. K., & Bruegmann, E. (2009). Teaching students and teaching each other: The importance of peer learning for teachers. *American Economics Journal: Applied Economics, 1*(4), 1–27.

Jacob, B., and Lefgren, L. (2008). Can principals identify effective teachers? Evidence on subjective performance evaluation in education. *Journal of Labor Economics, 25*(1), 101–136.

Kahlenberg, R. D. (2003). *All together now.* Washington, DC: Brookings Institution Press.

Kelly, P. (2005). *As America becomes more diverse: The impact of state higher education inequality.* Boulder, CO: National Center for Higher Education Management Systems. Retrieved from http://www.nchems.org/pubs/docs/Inequality%20Paper%20Jan2006.pdf

Lee, V. E., & Burkam, D.T. (2002). *Inequality at the starting gate.* Washington, DC: Economic Policy Institute.

Levin, H. M. (2007). On the relationship between poverty and curriculum. *North Carolina Law Review, 85*(5), 1381–1418.

Levin, H. M., & Belfield, C. E. (2007). Educational interventions to raise high school graduate rates. In C. E. Belfield & H. M. Levin (Eds.), *The price we pay: Economic and social consequences of inadequate education* (pp. 177–199). Washington, DC: Brookings Institution Press.

Levin, H. M., Belfield, C.E., Muennig, P., & Rouse, C. (2007). The public returns to public educational investments in African-American males. *Economics of Education Review, 26*(6), 699–708.

Levin H. M., & Finnan, C. (2006). Accelerated schools and the obstacles to school reform. In M. Constas & R. Sternberg (Eds.), *Translating theory and research into educational practice.* (pp. 127–150). Mahwah, NJ: Lawrence Erlbaum.

Loeb, S., & McEwan, P. (2009). Educational reforms. In P. B. Levine and D. J. Zimmerman (Eds.), *Targeting investments in children: Fighting poverty when resources are limited* (pp. 145–180). Chicago, IL: University of Chicago Press.

Magnuson, K., Ruhm, C., & Waldfogel, J. (2007). Does prekindergarten improve school preparation and performance? *Economics of Education Review, 26*: 33–51.

Oakes, J. (2005). *Keeping track: How schools structure inequality* (2nd ed.). New Haven, CT: Yale University Press.

Orfield, G., & Lee, C. (2005). *Why segregation matters: Poverty and educational inequality.* Cambridge, MA: Harvard University, The Civil Rights Project.

Purkey, S. C., & Smith, M. S. (1983). Effective schools: A review. *Elementary School Journal, 83*(4), 426–452.

OECD. (2009). *Education at a glance.* Paris: OECD Indicators. Retrieved from http://www.oecd.org/document/24/0,3343,en_2649_39263238_43586328_1_1_1_1,00.html

Renzulli, J., & Reis, S. (2002). What is schoolwide enrichment? How gifted programs relate to total school improvement. *Gifted Child Today, 25*(4), pp. 18–25.

Rothstein, R. (2004). *Class and schools: Using social, economic and educational reform to close the black-white achievement gap.* New York, NY: Teachers College Press.

Rowan, B., & Miller, R. J. (2007). Organizational strategies for promoting instructional change: Implementation dynamics in schools working with comprehensive school reform providers. *American Educational Research Journal, 44*(2), 252–297.

Rumberger, R. (2007). Parsing the data on student achievement in high poverty schools. *North Carolina Law Review, 85*(5), 1293–1314.

Schultz, T. W. (1961). Investment in human capital. *American Economic Review, 51*(1), 1–17.

Shadish, W., Cook, T., & Campbell, D. (2002). *Experimental and quasi-experimental designs for generalized causal inference.* Boston, MA: Houghton Mifflin.

Tienda, M., & Alon, S. (2007). Diversity and demographic dividend: Achieving educational equity in an aging white society. In C. E. Belfield & H. M. Levin (Eds.), *The price we pay: Economic and social consequences of inadequate education* (pp. 48–73). Washington, DC: Brookings Institution Press.

U.S. Census. (2009). *The 2009 statistical abstract.* Table 221. Washington, DC: Government Printing Office. Retrieved from www.census.gov/compendia/statab/cats/education/educational_attainment.html

Wayne, A. J., & Youngs, P. (2003). Teacher characteristics and student achievement gains: A review. *Review of Education Research, 73*(1), 89–122.

Wells, A. S. (2009). *Both sides now: The story of school desegregation graduates.* Berkeley: University of California Press.

Wells, A. S., & Crain, R. L. (1997). *Stepping over the color line: African-American students in white suburban schools.* New Haven, CT: Yale University Press.

Wirt, J., et al. (2004). *The condition of education, 2004.* Washington, DC: National Center for Educational Statistics, U. S. Department of Education. Retrieved from http://nces.ed.gov/pubs2004/2004077.pdf

Zimmer, R., & Bettinger, E. (2009.) Getting beyond the rhetoric: Surveying the evidence of vouchers and tax credits. In H. F. Ladd & E. B. Fiske (Eds.), *Handbook of research in education finance and policy.* New York, NY: Routledge.

12

Can School Improvement Reduce Racial Inequality?

Stephen W. Raudenbush

From the end of World War II until about 1990, racial inequality in educational attainment declined dramatically. Collins and Margo (2003), Allen and Farley (1986), and Neal (2006) tell the history of black-white gaps in educational attainment from 1900 to the present.

Consider two men, one white, one black, both 30 years old in 1950. We would expect the white man to have attained almost 2.5 years more of schooling than the black man. Now consider two men of the same age in 1995. We would expect the gap between black and white males to be .8 year—still intolerably large, but one-third of what it had been (Neal, 2006). For women, the story is similar. The black-white gap was almost 2 years in 1950. By 1995, the gap was just over half a year. College graduation rates tell a similar story. In 1960, white males were almost four times more likely to receive a 4-year college degree than were black males. By 1990, white males were about twice as likely to do so. So, although a large gap in college graduation rates persisted from 1960 to 1990, the gap was dramatically reduced. The gap in college graduation for females was never as large as for males, but it too became narrower during those years.

Neal (2006) traces a similarly remarkable reduction in the achievement gaps as measured by standardized test scores. His analysis, based on the National Assessment of Educational Progress, shows a very large black-white achievement gap, more than a full standard deviation, in reading for 13-year-olds tested in 1971: A typical African American child would score below 82 percent of all white children. For children tested 17 years later, in 1988, this gap was reduced almost by half. Data on math achievement show a similar trend, although not quite so dramatic. And Donohue and Heckman (1991) make a strong case that the dramatic changes in civil rights law and policy had large impacts on reducing racial inequality in the workplace.

GOOD NEWS AND BAD

So the good news is that, during the postwar period until 1990, there was a dramatic reduction in the gap between blacks and whites in educational attainment and academic achievement, with strong implications for labor market success. The bad news is that, by all accounts, the process of convergence stopped around 1990. And there is even some evidence that the gap has widened since 1990. For children of the same age tested in 1999, the black-white gap in reading had increased to about two thirds of its original size (Neal, 2006). Results for math were similar. Analyses of other nationally representative samples using other tests show strikingly similar results.

In this chapter, I first ask why the progress in reducing racial inequality stopped. To answer this question, one must understand powerful social forces largely beyond the control of educators. A second question then emerges: if these social forces have generated the current crisis, is it reasonable to expect school reform alone to substantially reduce racial inequality? My answer, based on a reading of research on the amount, quality, and distribution of schooling opportunities, is affirmative. However, to capitalize on this research will apparently require significant changes in school organization.

WHY DID PROGRESS IN REDUCING INEQUALITY STOP?

Social scientists have offered several explanations for the halt in the march toward educational equality.[1] In my view the most powerful explanation comes from William Julius Wilson's (1987) seminal book *The Truly Disadvantaged.* Despite critics, the broad outlines of Wilson's argument have stood the test of time.

At the time that landmark civil rights decisions were beginning to take hold, many African American workers had begun to enjoy unprecedented access to the American dream through employment in comparatively high-paid jobs in U.S. cities. Those jobs were concentrated in big industrial cities like Chicago, Detroit, Cleveland, St. Louis, and Buffalo. The hours were long and the work hard, but the pay was often good enough to buy a modest home and car and—important for our current discussion—to pay the next generation's tuition at a local public college. African Americans lived in racially segregated sections of these great cities, but the cities were economically strong and some had respectable public school systems. Black and white workers lived apart, but they often worked side by side, and some of their children were beginning to attend college side by side.

For these cities and especially for low-income African Americans, the next decades were disastrous. Wilson describes the massive decline in industrial jobs and, with it, dramatic increases in unemployment, loss of income, disruption of families, and the decline of schools in central cities. Ironically, Wilson claims that the equal opportunity emanating from the civil rights era, while benefiting many, had a perverse and unexpected effect on many in black communities in the nation's largest cities.

Recall the great suburban migration of the 1960s and 1970s. Though sometimes labeled the era of white flight, Wilson cited research showing that many black families, taking advantage of new opportunities for upward mobility and desegregated housing markets, also moved from the central city. He labeled those left behind as "the truly disadvantaged." Several factors undermined the educational opportunities of their children: loss of income, reducing the investments parents could make in their children; delays in family formation, leading to dramatic increases in the numbers of children growing up in single-parent families; social isolation of poor black children growing up in sections of cities that were hypersegregated, not only by race but now also by social class; and decline in school quality.

Neal (2006) provides evidence that loss of income and changes in family formation help account for racial inequality in educational outcomes. Social isolation deprived poor children and their families of contact with others who had benefited from education and separated these children from sources of information about schools, jobs, and routes to upward mobility. Social isolation separated the poorest African Americans from contact with people who used academic English—the language of instruction in schools—likely making it more difficult for such children to benefit from instruction when they got to school.

The difficulties of growing up poor in a single-parent family were likely multiplied by the fact that such children were concentrated in resource-deprived sections of cities where virtually all of their neighbors were also members of poor, single-parent families. The collective capacity of such a community to monitor and supervise children and to generate what sociologists call "informal social control" or "collective efficacy" (Sampson, Raudenbush, & Earls, 1997) were low, creating a climate that supported the rapid escalation of gang activity, drug abuse, and crime. These negative forces generated further incentives to move out, but of course, only those with means could do so, further intensifying the social isolation and concentration of disadvantage among those who remained. Finally, school improvement efforts in these areas, where schools were greatly disadvantaged, encountered an array of challenges, discussed in detail by Bryk, Sebring, Allensworth, Luppescu, and Easton (2009).

The cumulative effect of the concentration of disadvantage among those living in the poorest neighborhoods—including lost income, family disruption, social isolation, criminal victimization, and the erosion of school quality—appears to have substantially reduced opportunities for growth in academic learning, educational attainment, and upward mobility.

A recent study (Sampson, Sharkey, & Raudenbush, 2008) presents evidence that living in a neighborhood characterized by severe concentrations of disadvantage—high poverty, high unemployment, high levels of welfare receipt, and single parenthood—substantially reduces the verbal abilities needed for academic advancement and good jobs. The study found that, in its Chicago sample, only African American children were at risk of living in such neighborhoods—and most African American children had some substantial risk of doing so.

CAN SCHOOLS REDUCE INEQUALITY?

One interpretation of the history sketched above is that broad changes in political, legal, and economic structures have driven trends—the good and the bad—affecting inequality in educational outcomes. In this view, school quality follows in the wake of broad social change rather than promoting it. If that is true, then perhaps school improvement by itself can have little effect on racial inequality.

In contradiction to such a notion, my claim here is that school improvement by itself has the potential to make an enormous difference in the lives of children even if broader social change is slow in coming. The children who depend most on good schooling for academic growth are the least likely to receive it. If school improvement begins early in life and is sustained, the most disadvantaged children stand to benefit most. This reasoning suggests that increasing the amount, quality, and equity of schooling can substantially reduce inequality in academic achievement.

One set of studies I review below shows that attending school dramatically increases children's academic achievement. The simplest explanation for these findings is that most children receive more effective academic instruction when they are in school than when they are not in school. This finding may seem so obvious that it is hardly worth mentioning, but it is essential for understanding why schools have great potential to reduce inequality.

For any child at any moment in time, we can conceptualize the schooling effect on academic achievement as the difference between what a child would learn if in school and what that child would learn if at home (or in some other nonschool environment, such as home day care). It follows that, for any child, the schooling effect will be greatest when the contrast between the effectiveness of the academic instruction in school and in the home is greatest.

Decades of research show that the effectiveness of the academic instruction parents provide at home, particularly instruction in academic English, varies enormously from family to family. To some considerable extent, this variation is associated with variation in parent use of academic language at home (Huttenlocher, Haight, Bryk, & Seltzer, 1991), parent teaching of reading, and parent provision of school-related general knowledge (McLloyd, 1998). Such differences are strongly correlated with socioeconomic status (SES)—particularly maternal education—as well as with ethnicity, and in particular, with race (Heath, 1983).

In contrast, schools, while far from equal in their instructional effectiveness, are much less variable in effectiveness than are homes. The seminal work of James Coleman et al. (1966) brought this fact to light, which came as a shock to those who believed that variation in children's academic achievement resulted primarily from variation in school quality.[2] However, every assessment of educational attainment since 1966 has replicated this finding.

If school instructional quality varies less than home instructional quality, and if home instructional quality is strongly associated with social background, it follows that, for children of low SES, the contrast between the quality of instruction they receive in school and the quality of instruction they receive at home is, on average, larger than the same contrast for high-SES children. This would imply that low-SES children stand to gain more from schooling than do high-SES children, particularly if educational policy removes the correlation between student SES and school quality.

However, our reasoning assumes that low- and high-SES children have equal capacity to benefit from a given "dose" of instruction (defined as a given contrast between instructional quality in school and at home). Carneiro and Heckman (2003) hypothesize that, as children's academic ability grows early in life, their capacity to benefit from instruction expands. It follows that if high-SES parents are especially effective in teaching academic skills to very young children, and if their young children's academic skills therefore grow more rapidly, these children will benefit more, on average, than low-SES children from the same "dose" of instruction they receive at school. It might then be that social and racial inequality in academic learning opportunities early in life create a basis for increasing inequality later on. This reasoning supports an argument for especially intense schooling interventions early in life. It follows that one of the most important ways to increase the amount and quality of schooling is to provide more and better schooling for very young children, and, in particular, for low-SES children.

Yet continued exposure to high-quality instruction during the K–12 years would be required to sustain any gains achieved through early childhood intervention. This is partly because high-SES children would tend to experience more favorable academic instruction at home—especially during the summer recess—while in Grades K–12. Such reasoning may help explain the "fade out" of the effects of early intervention on low-SES children's cognitive skills after those children enter elementary school (McCarton et al., 1997; Schweinert, Barnes, & Weickart, 1993).

This reasoning lays the basis for education policy that aims quite dramatically to improve the amount, quality, and equity of schooling to which low-SES students have access as a strategy for reducing inequality in academic skills. There is strong reason to believe that doing so would disproportionately benefit African American children, who are far more often exposed to severe socioeconomic disadvantage than are white children.[3]

In addition, we know that low-income children, who are disproportionately minority, encounter more lower-quality schooling experiences than do high-income children. Eliminating these inequities can be expected to reduce social inequality in outcomes, which would tend also to close black-white gaps in outcomes.

In the next two sections, I review recent research suggesting that increases in the amount, quality, and equity of schooling can reduce social and racial inequality. The review suggests potential for school reform, but it also reveals that current conceptions of teaching and school organization create barriers opposed to school improvement. The final section of this chapter sketches an alternative view of schooling, in which the schoolhouse is organized to motivate and support ambitious and effective instruction for the children who need it most.

INCREASING THE AMOUNT OF SCHOOLING

Three recent sets of studies reveal powerful effects of schooling: studies that use the "age-cut-off" method to identify the impact of attending school; early childhood intervention studies; and studies of academic-year versus summer learning. In each case we see that schools have large effects, especially for low-SES students, with the suggestion that expanding schooling would reduce inequality.

Age-Cutoff Studies

Powerful evidence about schooling effects comes from studies that exploit the cutoff age for enrollment. Fred Morrison (2000) has pioneered this method and replicated it on a number of samples. Morrison compares children who are legally too young to enter kindergarten with those who just barely meet the legal cutoff age for attending school. He then follows these two samples over the first few years of school. The two groups appear identical except for a trivial difference in age. These studies reveal dramatic effects of schooling on literacy skills. It is clear from the results that many children who were regarded as too young for compulsory schooling and therefore stayed home would have benefited from schooling.[4] The benefits presumably would be larger for the children whose home environments are least conducive to literacy acquisition. This simple insight helps us understand why early childhood education, discussed briefly below, has been found so important for low-income children.

Early Childhood Schooling

Perhaps the most dramatic evidence of the potential long-term impact of formal schooling comes from research on early childhood schooling (see review by Carneiro & Heckman, 2003). The most famous study is the Perry Preschool Study, in which children were randomly assigned to receive an intensive program of instruction in school readiness skills (Schweinert et al., 1993). Exposure to the intervention produced immediate effects on children's cognitive test scores, although the effects faded during the early elementary years. The long-term results were remarkable: Children assigned to the preschool intervention were found to have higher educational achievement, lower rates of special education placement, lower propensities to commit crimes, and higher earnings as adults. Encouraging as these results are, generalizations from a single, small-sample study are unwarranted. However, since then, several additional randomized studies have essentially replicated the results.

Academic Year Versus Summer Learning

Striking evidence of the impact of attending elementary schools comes from a series of studies that test children in the fall near the beginning of the school year and in the spring, at the end of the school year (see review by Krueger, 2003). Such studies allow us to compare children's learning rates during the summer and the academic year. Growth rates are dramatically higher during the school year than during the summer, especially in math, for which summer growth rates are effectively nil. In reading, children do make gains during the summer, not surprisingly, because they encounter text at home from a variety of sources. However, growth rates in reading comprehension are far greater during the academic year than during the summer.

Moreover, there is growing evidence that low-income children benefit more from schooling than do other children. High-income children gain more (or lose less) in the summer than do low-income children, especially in literacy skills (Bryk & Raudenbush, 1988). In contrast, academic-year growth rates are similar. So if we define the school effect as the difference between the growth rate while in school and the growth rate during the summer, we see that school effects are greatest for the lowest income children. And this is true despite the current ineffectiveness of schools serving low-income and minority children.

Policy Implications

One obvious strategy for reducing inequality is to provide more schooling, particularly to children who need it more (Krueger, 2003). We can ensure that far more children receive more pre-K instruction. And we can ensure that more children, particularly low-income children and children who demonstrate a need for more instruction, have access to good instruction during the summer months.

INCREASING SCHOOL QUALITY AND EQUITY

The proposition that investments in schools can substantially increase student learning has been surprisingly controversial in social science. This skepticism is rooted in almost 50 years of research showing mostly weak effects of improving conventional resources such as per-pupil spending, school facilities, and teacher credentials (Cohen, Raudenbush, & Ball, 2003). Recent new evidence, however, demonstrates that teachers vary substantially in their effectiveness. Moreover, there is new evidence that three kinds of conventional resources make a difference: small class sizes, teacher experience, and teacher knowledge. Taken as a whole, a reasonably coherent picture emerges: The conventional resources that appear to matter most are those that are most proximally linked to instructional quality. Low-income children have less access to these resources than do high-income children, so increasing the equity of distribution of these resources can be expected to reduce social inequality in outcomes. Finally, recent research on subject-matter instruction reveals specific ways in which changing instruction can reliably increase student learning, particularly for low-income children.

In reviewing this evidence, we find encouragement that increasing the quality of schooling overall and equalizing access to high-quality schooling can reduce social and therefore racial inequality in outcomes. However, we shall also find that, although instructional quality matters, schools are not currently organized well to mobilize effective instruction. This insight leads me to propose in the final section of this chapter ways in which changes in school organization might be reframed to support ambitious instruction.

Value-Added Studies

We now have good evidence that teachers vary dramatically in their effectiveness. Many "value-added" studies work as follows: Identify children who look similar at the beginning of a study in terms of prior outcomes and social origins, and take note of which teachers they are assigned to; next, follow those children for a year, test the children again, and compute, for each teacher, the average gain. The average gain is called the *value added* for that teacher, after correcting for the inevitable errors of measurement and sampling. If value added varies a lot, then the impact of teacher assignments must be substantial. And that is just what researchers from a variety of disciplines using a variety of tests have found. The approach can be made more efficient by following children over multiple years and multiple teachers and comparing multiple cohorts.

A criticism of this method is that children are not assigned to teachers at random, and it may well be that controlling for prior test scores and social background is not adequate to remove what statisticians call unobserved selection bias. For example, it may be that highly motivated parents work especially hard to ensure that their children are assigned to the best teachers and that parent motivation is actually driving part or even most of the apparent teacher effect. It's hard for researchers to measure and control for such motivation, so the results of value-added studies may be biased.

To overcome this problem, Nye, Hedges, and Konstantopoulos (2004) reanalyzed data from the Tennessee class-size study, where teachers were assigned at random to large or small classes, and children were assigned at random to teachers. The researchers compared the value added of teachers, controlling for the assignment to large or small classes. Because the children were randomly assigned to teachers, concerns about selection bias were eliminated. These researchers found very large differences in teacher effects—differences, in fact, that were very similar in size to those found in the earlier, nonrandomized value-added studies.

So value-added studies clearly reveal that the classroom to which a child is assigned matters a great deal. But these studies tell us little or nothing about how to ensure that children get excellent instruction. There is an irony here. Value-added studies show dramatic differences in teacher effectiveness, and we know from careful surveys of instruction (Hong & Hong, 2009) that elementary teachers vary remarkably in such basic features of their work as the amount of time they devote to literacy instruction, the amount of time they devote to math instruction, whether they group children for instruction, and whether and how they use diagnostic assessments to gauge their children's progress. But with some exceptions that I will mention, we have precious little knowledge about how these core elements of instructional practice are linked to outcomes—or, more important, how these core elements can be combined to produce a coherent instructional system that we can train teachers to enact reliably in order to optimize the impact of schooling.

Why do educators tolerate dramatic, unexplained differences in the effectiveness of teaching practice while physicians insist that medical practice be subject to rigorous research and conform to common standards? In part, the difference reflects differences in the knowledge base that underlies practice. Vastly more is spent to study cell biology, disease transmission, and trials of the efficacy of new drugs and surgical procedures than is spent to understand how children learn, how they respond to instruction, or how well new models of instruction work.

Perhaps for this reason, contradictory notions of professionalism have evolved in the two domains. In medical practice, professionalism requires that practitioners know the science underlying practice and that their decisions are guided by shared, explicit notions of best practice. Autonomy is not the highest virtue: Attending physicians scrutinize the practice of residents, and decisions are open to professional and legal challenge.

In contrast, teachers find their work subject to frequent interventions—shall I say disruptions—that typically are not based on credible knowledge of student learning and classroom organization. Teachers then understandably assert autonomy to protect their work from these intrusions and to ensure that they can respond flexibly to the high levels of uncertainty they face every day. This response is quite rational at the level of the individual. However, the collective effect of such autonomous, privatized, and idiosyncratic practice is largely unexplained variation in teaching effectiveness, leading to amplified inequality in student outcomes.

Class-Size Reduction

The late Fred Mosteller, a revered statistician and a leader in the invention of the modern clinical trial in medicine, regarded the Tennessee class-size experiment (Finn & Achilles, 1990; Krueger & Whitmore, 2001) as the most important study in the history of education research. Teachers and children in 79 school districts in Tennessee were assigned at random to small or large classes. The results settled one of the most enduring questions in education: Can the reduction of classroom sizes in elementary schools significantly improve educational achievement? The answer was a definitive "Yes." The effects on test scores appeared modest in magnitude, but they were sustained and led to significant long-term differences in college attendance. Moreover, African American children especially benefited. Indeed, a sophisticated analysis by Krueger and Whitmore (2001) suggested that class-size reduction can significantly reduce the black-white gap in college attendance.

Perhaps even more remarkable, this result was achieved with no deliberate attempt to modify instruction to capitalize on the reduced class size. Presumably, the impact could have been much larger if teaching practice had fully capitalized on the smaller classes (Cohen et al., 2003).

The major limitation of the Tennessee study is that, without knowing anything about how class size influenced instructional practice (or how to tailor instructional practice to benefit from reduced class size), it is hard to know whether the benefits of class size reduction found in Tennessee would be reproduced elsewhere. When California invested massive amounts of money in class-size reduction, school districts competed for a limited pool of teachers, and many perceived a rather substantial deterioration of teacher quality, particularly in hard-pressed districts. Observers concluded that California failed to reap the benefits of reduced class size achieved in Tennessee, perhaps because of this reduction in teacher quality.

Class-size reduction can work only if it leads to better interactions between teachers and students surrounding the subject matter. Without knowing the other resources required to make better interactions occur (e.g., teacher knowledge), and without in fact ensuring that these instructional changes do happen, it is simply an educated guess as to whether reducing class size will boost achievement in any particular setting.

In a schooling system that emphasizes teacher autonomy, each teacher uses a small class size to do what that teacher thinks is best. Class-size reduction is an innovation without a known technology, and therefore without a strategy for quality control. Moreover, it's a rather expensive innovation. To make such an expensive innovation without any handle on quality control risks wasting the investment.

Teacher Experience

There is growing evidence that teachers with 2 or more years of experience are, on average, more effective than teachers with 1 year of experience or less (Clotfelter, Ladd, & Vigdor, 2007). Moreover, low-income children are less likely than high-income children to have access to such experienced teachers, as experienced teachers frequently use their seniority to transfer out of challenging schools. Taken together, these findings suggest that creating incentives for experienced teachers to stay in high-poverty schools would reduce social and ethnic inequality in outcomes.

Obtaining an equitable social distribution of teacher experience is fair and just. But if inexperienced teachers are ineffective, perhaps no children should simply be left alone with them! Changes in school organization would plausibly reduce the inequality in student learning generated by variation in teacher experience. An emphasis on a common system of instruction, mutual observation and feedback, along with on-the-job training in the use of assessment and instruction, would presumably compensate for teacher inexperience and advance the rate at which teachers learn. The aim would be to reduce or even eliminate the statistical association between teacher inexperience and poor teaching rather than to distribute inexperience and poor teaching more equitably.

Teacher Knowledge

There is evidence that teacher knowledge affects achievement, especially in mathematics (Brewer, 1997; Hill, Rowan, & Ball, 2005), and that low-income children are less likely than high-income children to have access to teachers with high levels of knowledge (Raudenbush, Fotiu, & Cheong, 1998). The implication is that a policy that creates incentives for well-prepared teachers to take jobs in high-poverty schools will increase equity in outcomes. So it makes great sense to recruit knowledgeable teachers and to ensure that low-income children have equal access to such teachers. Once again, however, how schools are organized would plausibly modify the association between teacher knowledge and student outcomes.

Consider an extreme example of teacher autonomy in which every elementary school teacher is required to invent his or her textbook, assessments, and instructional strategies. Clearly, only the most knowledgeable teachers would be able to produce decent instruction. The association between teacher subject-matter knowledge and student achievement would be extraordinarily high; and given the current level of mathematical thinking of most elementary school teachers in the United States, most students would suffer a terrible mathematical fate.

In contrast, consider Liping Ma's (1999) study of elementary mathematics instruction in China. The teachers she studied did not have 4-year college degrees, but they had a good working knowledge of the mathematics they needed to teach, and somewhat beyond. They had a common curriculum, common assessments, common instructional strategies—a shared, systematic instructional system. They collaborated closely, sharing knowledge, expertise, and teaching plans. They tested their students frequently and generated common strategies to overcome student misconceptions and to drive instruction to the next level. Their students displayed uniformly high levels of achievement. Access to expert teachers supported the least expert teachers and developed the leadership capacities of the most expert.

Studies of Instruction

Studies of instruction reveal enormous potential to improve school quality because they focus on the proximal cause of student learning in schools. Moreover, there have been major advances in research on instruction in recent years. However, schools are not currently organized well to capitalize on this work, as is clear in a brief review of studies of instruction in reading, science, and mathematics.

Early Reading Instruction

For years researchers battled over whether to emphasize phonics versus "whole language" in elementary school reading instruction. However, a series of careful studies in the 1990s, many funded by the National Institute of Child Health and Human Development (2000), have led to a consensus. The consensus is that explicit instruction in phonemic awareness and word decoding is essential to achieve high levels of reading literacy, especially for disadvantaged children. The operative word "essential," however, does not imply sufficiency. We have known for many years that the ability to decode familiar text (in Grades 1 and 2) is foundational for learning to read new text (Chall, 1983). We also know, however, that children with parents of modest educational attainment generally come to school behind in terms of skills in academic English vocabulary and syntax. These language skills, along with a high level of culturally valued knowledge, combine with word-decoding skills to enable children by Grades 3 and 4 to read new text with high comprehension. The implication is that early elementary instruction must aspire much higher than simply to teach decoding skills. Thus much more instructional time in literacy is required than is generally observed in U.S. elementary schools, particularly if the most disadvantaged children are to read with high comprehension by Grade 3.

Age-Cutoff Studies Once More

I mentioned earlier the findings of Fred Morrison (2000). Using the age-cutoff method, he has repeatedly found that although children typically learn a great deal about word decoding during the early elementary years, they appear to learn very little vocabulary. This finding is consistent with the inference that early elementary instruction teaches the decoding of familiar text, one of the foundations of successful reading instruction. However, these findings suggest that current teaching practice does not sufficiently emphasize the acquisition of oral language, which would drive the acquisition of vocabulary, an essential component of reading comprehension that is often lacking among the most disadvantaged children.

Early Elementary Science Instruction

A series of studies suggests that effective science instruction not only enhances children's knowledge about science content but also can drive large gains in the vocabulary and the syntax of academic discourse, with positive spillover effects on reading comprehension (Guthrie, Wigfield, & Percenevich, 2004; Romance & Vitale, 2001; Stein, Anggoro, & Hernandez, in press). The logic is straightforward: Good science teaching is remarkably effective in engaging young children's interest. If well structured, such instruction encourages children to use causal reasoning and causal language, to state explicit predictions, to evaluate new evidence, and to consider alternative explanations. In short, it gives children a compelling reason to use the language of critical thinking and academic discourse, undergirding advances in reading comprehension and vocabulary development.

To make this happen, it is essential that all key concepts and the relations among them be made explicit, and that the instructional system meticulously uncover and correct children's misconceptions. As a result, a highly systematic and explicit approach to instruction is required, one that uses frequent assessments of student misconceptions followed by correct, targeted feedback. This is an instructional regime of the type rarely implemented in a world of privatized, idiosyncratic practice. Moreover, the approach is most likely to be powerful when explicitly linked to language arts instruction, a task that requires close collaboration among teachers.

Finally, results indicate that this approach enables children to learn high-level subject matter (such as Newtonian mechanics and thermodynamics) at much younger ages than is typical, and that the approach is successful for children who vary greatly in socioeconomic background. In contrast, science instruction based on incomplete representation of subject matter or inexplicit connections between concepts requires that children fall back on their background knowledge to make sense of the instruction. Because older children and children of highly educated families tend to have more background knowledge to fall back upon, the less explicit approaches to science instruction will presumably exacerbate rather than overcome inequalities in age and social background.

Early Mathematics Instruction

There are fewer rigorous studies of mathematics instruction than of reading instruction. Nevertheless, a National Academy of Sciences report (National Research Council, 2004) summarizes reasonably convincing evidence, based on a series of rigorous studies, that new, conceptually driven early mathematics curricula developed by the University of Chicago School Mathematics Project produces, on average, better math learning than do more traditional curricula. A limitation of this research is that it provides a curriculum alone rather than a systematic approach to instruction. Such an approach would include not only a curriculum but also formative assessments and shared approaches for using the assessments in instruction (Ma, 1999). In short, the approach was developed for dissemination within a paradigm of privatized, idiosyncratic instruction, constraining the potential power of the approach.

In the next and final section of this chapter, I shall sketch an attempt to refashion the organization of the elementary school to ensure that every child will have access to ambitious instruction capable of supporting ambitious intellectual work. The idea is to transform school organization to capitalize on research suggesting that school improvement can substantially reduce social and racial inequality in educational outcomes.

HYPOTHESIS: MOBILIZING SCHOOLS IN THE SERVICE OF AMBITIOUS INSTRUCTION CAN TRANSFORM OUTCOMES FOR LOW-INCOME MINORITY CHILDREN

Broad questions about instruction and school organization come sharply into view when one attempts to use the best available research to create an outstanding school. I believe that experience in doing so in Chicago offers fresh insights that can be useful elsewhere.

In the early 1990s Anthony Bryk, Sharon Greenberg, and Sara Spurlark launched the Center for Urban School Improvement—better known as CSI—at the University of Chicago. Their aim was to work closely with a small network of South Side schools to improve literacy instruction. The work was inspiring and frustrating: inspiring because of what it revealed about children's intellectual energy and potential for dramatic growth, frustrating because school norms and bureaucratic rules seemed constantly to get in the way of the ambitious instruction the children needed.

In 1998 therefore, Bryk and colleagues adopted a new strategy for school improvement by starting a new elementary charter school, the North Kenwood Oakland School (NKO). This was a Chicago public school, chartered by the city's school district. Because charter schools have relaxed rules, USI had pretty much free rein in designing and running NKO, although within quite limited resources. The school leaders were free to shape teacher recruitment, curriculum design, and—particularly important—instructional time, to pursue ambitious intellectual goals for the student body, which was nearly all African American and about 75 percent low income.

An Instructional Regime to Enhance Literacy

Over the next couple of years, Bryk, Greenberg, and their CSI colleagues, working closely with a number of outstanding practitioners and researchers, built NKO's literacy instruction around a school-wide formative assessment system known as STEP (Strategic Teaching and Evaluation of Progress). Every child was assessed every 10 weeks on a broad array of literacy skills, hierarchically arranged. Associated with each level was one or more required books for children to read, calibrated for difficulty. And associated with each level of STEP was a series of instructional strategies designed to get to the next level.

Specifically, a student who is at STEP 12 by the end of third grade is believed capable of serious critical engagement with texts that are actually beyond what we commonly regard as "grade-level reading." Such a student is well on the way to being capable of ambitious intellectual work in secondary schools and beyond. Every student in the school is expected to be at least at STEP 12 by end of third grade. Working backward, every second grader should be at STEP 9, every first grader at STEP 6, every kindergartner at STEP 3 by the end of each year.

It is the collective responsibility of the faculty to ensure that the children reach these benchmarks. If children show signs of getting off track, teachers tailor instruction to ensure that they get back on track and achieve the desired STEP. This may involve an extended day or summer school.

Implications for the Teachers' Work

In the central office at NKO is a "STEP wall" where the progress of every child and the history of every instructional intervention is recorded. The STEP wall reveals to the principal and staff how well every child is doing in every class and pinpoints the need for intervention not only at the level of the child but also at the level of the teacher.

The development of STEP and its routine application revealed that instruction could not be left to chance or to the judgment of the singular teacher. Of course, some teachers would do well under such a loose system, but such a system could not ensure quality control for all children. Some children in every class would thrive, but not every child would receive the high level of explicit instruction needed. So, gradually, NKO developed a shared, systematic approach, replacing instructional autonomy with collective staff responsibility for child outcomes.

Central to this approach is that teachers vary in their expertise in using it. At the most elementary level, teacher expertise involves an understanding of STEP assessment and how its results should be linked to instruction. At a more advanced level, teachers more deeply master the developmental theory behind the assessments so that they can skillfully "assess and instruct" moment by moment. At a still more advanced level, teachers whose students reliably progress to high levels will have gained expertise about how to help other teachers improve their practice. They then become instructional leaders, with formalized leadership roles and appropriate increases in compensation

School leaders are accountable for evidence of academic progress school-wide. This accountability motivates them to identify and promote the most expert teachers as instructional leaders. Because the STEP results of every child in every classroom are known to staff, teaching results are open to inspection, and each teacher is motivated to promote high levels of student learning—and to seek assistance if some children are not doing well. Variation in teacher expertise is public knowledge, and teachers have an interest in having their most expert colleagues as mentors. The system rewards advances in expertise as it accords more responsibility to the more expert teachers.

Teacher expertise is not a generic quality but rather a set of attainable skills and knowledge embedded in a well-defined instructional system. To be expert is to understand that system, to demonstrate skill in enacting it, and to develop the capacity to help other teachers enact the system effectively.

Extending Time and Engaging Parents

In 2004 Timothy Knowles, who had been the chief academic officer in the Boston Public Schools, became the executive director of CSI. The next year, Knowles and his team opened the Donoghue School, located, like NKO, on the South Side of Chicago. Donoghue, also a charter school, drew students who were similar to those at NKO, all African American but nearly 85 percent low income. It was farther from the university than NKO was, in an area with many vacant lots and a fairly high crime rate.

Nicole Iliev, the principal of Donoghue, was shocked when she saw the literacy assessment results for the incoming students. The school started as a K–3 school, with the aim of adding a grade each year. The initial results for the third graders, whose experiences in Grades K–2 had apparently been quite unsatisfactory, were especially worrisome. Iliev took several steps.

First, she dramatically expanded instruction time—in three ways. She insisted that 3–5 hours per day be allocated to literacy instruction—a mixture of explicit word decoding, directed reading, teacher read-aloud with discussion, and writing, ensuring that vocabulary and syntax were woven in to supplement explicit decoding work. She implemented an extended day with tutoring for those who needed it and required summer school for those who needed more help to make their STEP.

At the same time, she launched an ambitious parent outreach program. One aim was to make sure parents understood the STEP tool, what STEP their child was on, what the next STEP would be, what the school was doing to achieve it, and what the parents' role would be in helping their child reach the next goal. Parent responses were heartening. Even parents who themselves had very limited education made sure to participate actively and became convinced that they could play a powerful role in their children's learning. However, not every family had the resources to participate. For the children of those families, the school set up a within-school support network of staff to take up the slack.

The parent outreach aspect of this work was sufficiently ambitious that it required a shift in school organization. The position normally called "vice principal" became "director of parent and community engagement." Todd Barnett took this job. Barnett was intimately familiar with STEP and with how the instructional system worked. He knew all the parents, met them at the door in the morning, frequently reached out to them for help, and organized myriad events. He knew the children's older siblings—all of whom were encouraged to come for the after-school program, and many of whom helped with tutoring.

Summary

The shared assumption in these schools is that college success is a natural outcome of continuous engagement in ambitious intellectual work from early preschool school through secondary school. The central premise is that nearly all children will thrive intellectually if exposed to ambitious instruction carefully tailored to frequent, objective assessments of student progress throughout the schooling years. Such instruction requires that the current conceptions of autonomous teaching practice that characterizes U.S. schools give way to a shared, systematic approach that emphasizes teacher accountability and school-wide collaboration. In such a system, teacher expertise in using the system will vary, and schools will be organized to motivate and support advances in expertise. This conception of the effective school has broad implications for school leadership, parent engagement, social services, and teacher preparation. Clarifying how such an approach can be conceived, implemented, tested, and broadly shared requires a novel sense of how practitioners and researchers should interact, with implications for how universities should best organize themselves to support powerful urban schooling.

We don't yet know whether the approach to school organization and instruction that I have discussed in this section will produce dramatic improvement in student learning. What does seem clear is we must reframe current conceptions of teaching and school organization if we are to capitalize on compelling evidence suggesting that increases in the amount, quality, and equity of schooling can improve academic achievement overall and reduce social and racial inequality.

NOTES

1. One explanation emphasizes continued discrimination in the labor market. Neal (2006) does not deny the existence of discrimination in the labor market. But he shows that the labor market provides strong incentives to obtain degrees—and these incentives are even stronger for minority youth than for white youth. Hernstein and Murray (1994) argued that once civil rights laws eliminated legal barriers to educational access, the remaining gaps between racial and ethnic groups then reflected real differences in intellectual ability and that these differences are inherited. Three kinds of evidence refute this argument. First, as Dickens and Flynn (2006) show, black-white gaps in IQ test scores have substantially diminished over time, "faster than genes can travel." Second, studies show that black-white gaps in IQ are small to negligible when black children raised by white parents are compared with white children raised by white parents (Nisbett, 1998). This finding gives interesting new support to the claim that IQ tests measure cultural capital rather than some kind of culture-free, innate intelligence. Third, the passage of civil rights laws did not eliminate barriers to equal opportunity. A large body of social science evidence refutes this assumption (see Loury, 2002).

2. It is likely that unequal school quality has contributed enormously to inequality in outcomes through an intergenerational mechanism whereby parents transmit inequality in their benefits from schooling to their children, who then pass down to their own children the unequal benefits of the instruction they received at home. Such an intergenerational accumulation of inequality would be most pronounced when school quality and home instructional quality are positively correlated, as all research suggests they are. However, for any given generation, variation in cognitive skills is explained far more by variation in home environments than by variation in schooling environments.

3. A similar argument can be made with respect to other ethnic gaps, such as the gap between Hispanics and whites. However, given the focus here on black-white inequality since the *Brown* decision, this chapter will confine itself to black-white inequality.

4. Oreopoulous (2006) provides parallel evidence about the powerful impact of compulsory schooling during adolescence.

REFERENCES

Allen, W. R., & Farley, R. (1986). The shifting social and economic tides of black America, 1950–1980. *Annual Review of Sociology, 12*, 277–306.
Brewer, D. (1997). Why don't schools and teachers seem to matter? Assessing the impact of unobservables on educational productivity. *Journal of Human Resources, 32*(3), 505–523.

Bryk, A. S., & Raudenbush, S. W. (1988). Toward a more appropriate conceptualization of research on school effects: A three-level hierarchical linear model. *American Journal of Education, 97*(1), 65-108.

Bryk, A. S., Sebring, P. B., Allensworth, E., Luppescu, S., & Easton, J. Q. (2009). *Organizing schools for improvement.* Chicago, IL: University of Chicago Press.

Carneiro, P., & Heckman, J. (2003). Human capital policy. In A. Krueger & J. Heckman (Eds.), *Inequality in America: What role for human capital policies?* (pp. 77–239). Cambridge, MA: MIT Press.

Chall, J. (1983). *Learning to read: The great debate.* New York, NY: John Wiley.

Clotfelter, C. T., Ladd, H. F., & Vigdor, J. (2007). Who teaches whom? Race and the distribution of novice teachers. *Economics of Education Review, 24*(4), 377–392.

Cohen, D. K., Raudenbush, S. W., & Ball, D. L. (2003). Resources, instruction, and research. *Educational Evaluation and Policy Analysis, 25*(2), 1–24.

Coleman, J., Campbell, E. Q., Hobson, C. J., McPartland, J., Mood, A. M., Weinfeld, F. D., et al. (1966). *Equality of educational opportunity.* Washington, DC: U.S. Department of Health, Education, and Welfare.

Collins, W. J., & Margo, R. A. (2003). *Historical perspectives on racial differences in schooling* (NBER Working Paper No. 9770). Cambridge, MA: National Bureau of Economic Research.

Dickens, W. T., & Flynn, J. R. (2006). Black Americans reduce the racial IQ gap. *Psychological Science, 17*(10), 913–920.

Donohue, J. J., III, & Heckman, J. J. (1991). Continuous versus episodic change: The impact of civil rights policy on the economic status of blacks. *Journal of Economic Literature, 29,* 1603–1643.

Finn, J. D., & Achilles, C. M. (1990). Answers and questions about class size: A statewide experiment. *American Educational Research Journal, 27*(3), 557–577.

Guthrie, J. T., Wigfield, A., & Percenevich, K. C. (2004). *Motivating reading comprehension: Concept-oriented reading instruction.* Mahwah, NJ: Lawrence Erlbaum.

Heath, S. B. (1983). *Ways with words: Language, life, and work in communities and schools.* Cambridge, England: Cambridge University Press.

Hernstein, R. J., & Murray, C. (1994). *The bell curve: Intelligence and class structure in American life.* New York, NY: Free Press.

Hill, H. C., Rowan, B., & Ball, D. B. (2005). Effects of teachers' mathematical knowledge for teaching on student achievement. *American Educational Research Journal, 42*(2), 371–406.

Hong, G., & Hong, Y. (2009). Reading instruction time and homogeneous grouping in kindergarten: An application of the marginal mean weighting method. *Educational Evaluation and Policy Analysis, 31*(1), 54–81.

Huttenlocher, J. E., Haight, W., Bryk, A. S., & Seltzer, M. (1991). Early vocabulary growth: Relation to language input and gender. *Developmental Psychology, 27*(2), 236–249.

Krueger, A. B. (2003). Inequality: Too much of a good thing. In A. Krueger & J. Heckman (Eds.), *Inequality in America: What role for human capital policies?* (pp. 1–75). Cambridge, MA: MIT Press.

Krueger, A. B., & Whitmore, D. M. (2001). The effect of attending a small class in the early grades on college test-taking and middle school results: Evidence from Project STAR. *Economic Journal, 111,* 1–28.

Loury, G. (2002). *The anatomy of racial inequality.* Cambridge, MA: Harvard University Press.

Ma, Liping. (1999). *Knowing and teaching elementary mathematics: Teachers' understanding of fundamental mathematics in China and the United States.* Mahwah, NJ: Lawrence Erlbaum.

McCarton, C. M., Brooks-Gunn, J., Wallace, I. F., Bauer, C. R., Bennett, F. C., Bernbaum, J. C., et al. (1997). Results at age 8 years of early intervention for low-birth-weight premature infants: The Infant Health and Development Program. *Obstetrical & Gynecological Survey, 52*(6), 341–342.

McLloyd, V. C. (1998). Socioeconomic disadvantage and child development. *American Psychologist, 53*(2), 185–204.

Morrison, F. (2000). Specificity in the nature and timing of cognitive growth in kindergarten and first grade. *Journal of Cognitive Development, 1*(4), 429–448.

National Institute of Child Health and Human Development. (2000). *Teaching children to read: An evidence-based assessment of the scientific research literature on reading and its implications for reading instruction* (Report of the National Reading Panel. NIH Publication No. 00-4769). Washington, DC: U.S. Government Printing Office.

National Research Council. (2004). *On evaluating curricular effectiveness: Judging the quality of K–12 mathematics evaluations.* Washington, DC: National Academy Press.

Neal, D. (2006). Why has black-white skill convergence stopped? In E. Hanushek & F. Welch (Eds.), *Handbook of economics of education* (chap. 9). Amsterdam, The Netherlands: Elsevier.

Nisbett, R. (1998). Race, genetics and IQ. In C. Jencks & M. Phillips (Eds.), *The black-white test score gap* (pp. 86–102). Washington, DC: Brookings Institution Press.

Nye, B., Hedges, L. V., & Konstantopoulos, S. (2004). How large are teacher effects? *Educational Evaluation and Policy Analysis, 26,* 237–257.

Oreopoulous, P. (2006). Estimating average and local average treatment effects of education when compulsory schooling laws really matter. *American Economic Review, 96*(1), 152–175.

Raudenbush, S. W., Fotiu, R. P., & Cheong, Y. F. (1998). Inequality of access to educational resources: A national report card for eighth-grade math. *Educational Evaluation and Policy Analysis, 20*(4), 253–267.

Romance, N. R., & Vitale, M. R. (2001). Implementing an in-depth, expanded science model in elementary schools: Multiyear findings, research issues, and policy implications. *International Journal of Science Education, 23*, 373–404.

Sampson, R. J., Raudenbush, S. W., & Earls, F. (1997). Neighborhoods and violent crime: A multilevel study of collective efficacy. *Science, 277*, 918–924.

Sampson, R. J., Sharkey, P., & Raudenbush, S. W. (2008). Durable effects of concentrated disadvantage on verbal ability of African-American children. *Proceedings of the National Academy of Science, 105*, 845–852.

Schweinert, L., Barnes, H., & Weickart, D. (1993). *Significant benefits: The High Scope Perry Pre-School Study through age 27*. Ypsilanti, MI: Hiscope Press.

Stein, N. L., Anggoro, F. K., & Hernandez, M. W. (in press). Making the invisible visible: Conditions for the early learning of science. In N. L. Stein & S. Raudenbush (Eds.), *Developmental science goes to school*. New York, NY: Taylor and Francis.

Wilson, W. J. (1987). *The truly disadvantaged*. Chicago, IL: University of Chicago Press.

13

Seeing Our Way Into Learning Science in Informal Environments

Shirley Brice Heath

Collin, a 7-year-old caterpillar enthusiast, spied a caterpillar while he and Marko, his 5-year-old playmate were playing catch. Collin ran to grab a loose board from the side yard, created a short ramp between the top two steps of the back porch, collected the creature, and placed it at the bottom end of the board. Marko watched from a distance until Collin called him over to see how the legs of the caterpillar worked on the incline of the ramp.

"How many legs do you think he's got?" Collin asked. Marko peered closely: "Where?" Collin pulled a twig from a nearby branch and pointed to the underbelly of the caterpillar: "See, here, right there—the legs—you can count 'em." Marko looked for an instant before running off to collect the ball that had rolled out of the yard.

Collin shouted in exasperation, "If you don't see it, you don't get it!" His futile shout to his young friend captures the current state of what we know about visuospatial attention in learning science. "Seeing it" matters. Indeed, it is becoming increasingly clear that "if you don't see it, you don't get it." Looking closely and imagining new possibilities—such as putting the caterpillar on an incline in order to inspect (and count) the legs in movement—constitute fundamental ways of taking in information and shaping future scenarios of what can or might happen. Teams of scientists move their projects forward through just the kind of joint looking, gesturing, and envisioning of possibilities Collin tried to put in place. This budding young scientist intuitively tried to "distribute" intelligence though mutual visual attention, gesture, and the language of demonstration and explication.

From backyards to museums and community organizations, informal learning environments offer abundant opportunities for careful and sustained observation (National Research Council, 2009). The public media tell citizens about changes and connections citizens can observe in climate, insect life, plant growth, local bird populations, and soil erosion. Newsletters on health remind citizens that prevention of many health problems depends on the willingness of patients to learn from and respond to reports from medical research. Media reports on scientific research related to landfills, air pollution, water and air quality, climate change, disease control, pharmaceutical research, and the need for energy efficiency invariably include a message of civic and personal responsibilities to scientific understanding. Television news programs feature neighborhoods and industries that have taken meaningful steps toward identifying and solving problems based on information from scientific research that citizens have used to make changes in local practices and policies.

Museums and youth-oriented community organizations, well aware of the need to keep young people in school and to interest them in careers in science, enlist teens in community gardening and other social enterprises that require practice and knowledge acquisition related to the study of science in school. All of these moves in social engagement with civic responsibilities that depend on scientific information and method result from deliberation within informal environments, such as neighborhood meetings, family conversations during vacations in different ecozones, and community youth groups starting environmental awareness campaigns.

This chapter considers the potential of these informal learning environments for inciting curiosity in the sciences, often with help from imagination, the arts, props, and voluntary and credentialed experts. Laid out here is a vision of research that is needed on the learning of science within these informal environments. Offered here as a basis for this research are current learning theories that account for (1) the interdependence of visual and gestural representation, (2) identity alignment with what being a scientist means, (3) coordinated attention to visual detail, and (4) distribution of specific functions of language chunks within deliberative discourse. These theories have had little application or consideration in the study of learning science in informal environments. In combination, visual perception, verbal explication, and embodiment of role appear to increase the likelihood that specific interests, skills, and facts about science will have portability across environments—formal and informal—in learners' lives.

This chapter opens by considering primary findings from research on visuospatial, gestural, and embodied learning in science. Of key focus in the next section is the nature of the language of deliberative discourse—that which gives voice to different positions, raises questions, and offers new information that allows a range of alternative possibilities for action. Explained here are three features of such discourse and their relationship to the modes of learning noted in the chapter's opening section. The chapter closes by urging scholars in education to consider the potential of informal learning environments for further research on ways that conceptual understanding develops in collaborative distribution of information in the procedural and critical enterprise of science. The premise here is that citizens thinking with and acting from principles of science in deliberative democracy must be key players in bringing about policy changes and improved governmental regulation on matters that range from environmental preservation and conservation to waste management, climate change, and health policy.

SEEING SCIENCE LEARNING

Researchers in science education, as well as neuro- and cognitive science, show the benefits of visual and spatial modes to creativity, memory, and linguistic fluency in scientific language (Ramadas, 2009). Visual thinking, mental modeling, and envisionment of act and consequence in future scenarios work in coordination with language-based forms of reasoning (Roskos-Ewoldsen, Intons-Peterson, & Anderson, 1993). The high overlap in neural networks between visual perception of details and imagery suggests that modal layering makes possible the simultaneity of cognitive operations (Struiksma, Noordzij, & Postma, 2009). Visuospatial thinking serves as a mnemonic for verbal material and as an aid to reasoning with mental models (Anderson, 1998; Schnotz, 2002). Role enactment—that is, taking on the identity of scientist in gesture and body posture to deliver accounts of scientific thinking behind experiments and explanations within demonstrations—depends on visuospatial and gestural representations, thereby layering the benefits of each of these modes.

Visuospatial Learning

Learning that originates in or relies on seeing what is taking place begins in infancy. Visual input stimulates mental modeling of objects in space and scenarios of act and consequence to come. For infants and toddlers, visual cues set off anticipation and expectation. Something quite similar goes on in the heads of older children and adolescents learning science as well as in the minds and collaborative tasks of professional scientists. Visual imagery, often aided by strategies such as drawing in the air, animating visual props, using gesture, and expressing image-rich verbal narrative, stands out in developmental learning.

Children usually understand joint visual attention well before eighteen months of age. As they mature, they gain an understanding of visual perception in terms of what they can see and what and how the visual perspectives of others might work (Gopnik & Slaughter, 1991). Such neural and cognitive work underlying what it means to "see" and the early development of joint visual gaze and "tuning in" are well established before children appear to grasp mental states of "knowing" or "thinking." Thus "seeing it" does indeed precede "getting it."

Psychologists in early child development have posited "scientist in the crib" or "the scientist as child" to indicate the keenly perceptive nature of very young children and their propensity for constructing theories based on what they see (Gopnik & Meltzoff, 1998; Gopnik, Meltzoff, & Kuhl, 1999). Children view the world and re-create it in their internal representations, dramatic reenactments, and often their drawings. As they do so, they devise mental rules to accompany their representations. Accounts of children explaining their drawings are filled with linguistic evidence that their drawing is part of a larger scene or situation—a whole world in their head. This world is "child-centered" and ordered through the rule-making of the child. Kindergarten teacher Vivian Gussin Paley spread this message to a wide readership through her account of child-artist Reeny, who combined her passion for drawing with the narrative art of author Leo Lionni to lead an entire classroom to create multimodal worlds of wonder (Paley, 1997). Numerous studies document the histories of individual children finding and ordering their own worlds through their sketches and drawings. These children explore points of view and symbolism, create metaphors, and work out denotational values to assign to their lines and shapes (Matthews, 1999, 2003). Realizing they are often ignored or deluded by adults, children "correct" this reality of the way the world works through visual images they draw and enact (Lindstrom, 1957).

Scientists parallel children's creation and use of visual images in their work. They observe, take part in, and represent their world, often showing rearrangement of givens, creating rule-governed systems, and laying out abstract ideas to explain what they "see." Vision is highly efficient. It sets into play the brain's capacity for convergence of multiple perceptual systems through which learners perform mental operations, such as recognizing, comparing, and contrasting (LeDoux, 2002; Newcombe & Learmonth, 2005). Cognitive scientists have long pointed out that research on how vision works as initiating force for convergence must be fundamental in our attempts to grasp the nature of how the mind works. Metaphors reliant on activities associated with what the eye does convey the extent to which cognitive work amounts to "seeing it," "getting a glimpse," and "reflecting" (Kosslyn, 1995).

Once visually perceived, details can transform as depictive and abstracted in working and long-term memory. However, the reverse is not necessarily the case: purely verbal information may not call upon other representational modes or mental imagery and their correlated depictive and abstracting symbolic notations (Ramachandran & Hubbard, 2001; Roskos-Ewoldsen et al., 1993).

In a longitudinal study of early elementary children learning to use science concepts (e.g., horizontal/vertical) while painting, modeling, and sketching architectural designs, researchers found that children showed gains in problem-solving skills related to mathematics in their first year and added gains in language development (especially in their use of meta-phor) in the next two years (Heath & Wolf, 2004). Taking part in a design experiment that integrated creation and interpretation of visual arts into literacy development, the children developed fluency in the use of scientific terms and means of inquiry (e.g., questions seeking explanation of process, exploring contrast, and describing positional perspectives).

A similar design experiment within a secondary school positioned Robert Jarvis, a musi-cian and composer, within the school environment as a resource for projects the students chose to design. Initially curious and distrustful, students described by their classroom teachers as "rowdy," "troublesome," or "disruptive" sought out the musician. Simultane-ously, these students "volunteered" to take part in a research study that asked them to collect data on specific kinds of language they encountered in school, home, and neighborhood (e.g., compliments that did more than place a single label of evaluation on them and their actions). Requests of the students by Jarvis and the research directors required the students to listen and look intently and repeatedly before they recorded data and contexts.

Within a year, these students undertook several research projects within their school, studying space allocation on the school grounds and uses of these spaces by students. When they learned that the school administration was drawing up plans for a structure in the cen-ter of the school grounds, the students stepped forward to survey the student body, prepare a report of their findings, and represent these ideas in conference with the school administra-tion. Within the next year, the students, working in close coordination with administrators and faculty, helped reshape the curricular choices available for first-year students. The school moved to a multitrack, age-flexible curriculum that rearranged scheduling to give students more time for talk among themselves to bring their school science studies to bear in the creation of garden-based social enterprises for their community. Their first-year curriculum included "The Global Food Project," bringing citizenship and enterprise education together in project-based learning that centered on creating large vegetable and flower gardens. The students undertook activities to create farmers' markets whose proceeds went to charities supporting Third World needs (Lyng, 2007).

In both the elementary and secondary design experiments described above, observation of details of behavior, physical space, and expert-novice interactions centered the students' data collection and analysis. Working with the secondary students, Jarvis consistently responded to the students as they worked through their creative projects by demonstrating and giving them prompts such as "Look, and then show me what you see. After you do that, we can talk about what you hear and can imagine you might do."

This method of inquiry toward creation of a project also marked a musical project that brought three schools together and involved adolescents of mixed abilities, race, and age (12–16). On walks through the local hills and forests with Jarvis, the students were asked to be completely silent: "Just listen and look." He then asked them to use what they heard to inspire them to compose a piece of music, combining instruments and voice, and reflecting what their heightened sensibilities led them to learn about themselves and their local surroundings. Over one full school term, the students had the task of creating a professional-quality sound instal-lation to last exactly as long as it took the Eurotrain to make the Channel Tunnel journey from Folkston, England, to Calais, France. At an appointed time near the end of the term, members of the Treasury came from London to Folkston to join local and regional stakeholders on a designated rail car on the Channel Tunnel trip to Calais. The dignitaries were outfitted with earphones for listening to the students' composition during the one-way portion of the trip from Folkston to Calais. Silence was requested for this part of the journey.

Entitled "Europhonix," the piece was based on the theme of place and identity. The year was 2004, when asylum seekers and immigrants were increasingly being located by the British government in small towns unaccustomed to the diversities of urban areas. On the return trip, the young people led the adults in discussion about how they had created the piece and what the theme meant to them as they thought about the balance between looking at their local place and themselves and also looking outward to their newcomer international neighbors. The CD, produced by the students with composer Robert Jarvis, was shortlisted for The British Composer of the Year Award that year (Cutler, 2007). In follow-up interviews at the end of 2004, the students repeatedly talked about their sharp realization of what looking and listening closely in the absence of talk and other intrusive sounds had meant for their creativity and insight on which they drew when they realized the risks were high and the audience real (Heath, Paul-Boehncke, & Wolf, 2007).

This project and other highly effective longitudinal work bringing together art and science for civic engagement makes direct use of hands—sketching, drawing, shaping, strumming the guitar, playing the piano, and building gardens. This manual work stimulates mental imagery that envisions steps along the way toward achieving a highly complex goal that depends on listening, looking, imagining, creating—and only later—explaining. Learners see ahead to what has to be done, and they restructure ideas as needed. Sketching, trying a melody in the head out on the piano, or building a model of a greenhouse: all of these manual try-outs provide "perceptual interface" through which learners discover underlying nonvisual functional relations (Suwa & Tversky, 1997). Thus though novice learners may not be able to express verbally the hypothetical or *what-if* reasoning behind problems or plans, they have "memories of the future" that involve variables, conditions, and possible interactions and consequences (Ingvar, 1985).

Gestural Representation

Scholars have long noted the universality of conveying meaning through gesture. The hand and body create and complement meaning transmitted in other modes, doing so with props such as drawings, graphs, charts, film, or dramatic narrative. The effectiveness, and indeed the necessity, of iconic gestures is now well supported through both experiments in Western cultures and long-term ethnographic study of gestural representation in societies around the world (Gentner & Goldin-Meadow, 2003; Goldin-Meadow, 2003; Kendon, 2004). When learners embody through gesture and enactment/demonstration what they have envisioned, memory is reinforced and sustained (Gigerenzer, 2000; Ingvar, 1985; Jeannerod, 1997; Libet, 2004; Pfeifer & Bongard, 2007; Wilson, 1998). Studies of the role of gesture by experienced scientists and novices learning science come from university laboratories and other research settings and also from elementary and secondary classrooms.

In a long-term study of a university physics laboratory, a team of linguistic anthropologists examined the extensive use of gesture by physicists who set up entire visual domains through their gestures. The scientists used talk, graphic representations, and gesture to convey their work and to achieve mutual understanding and a working consensus around experimental findings (Ochs, Gonzales, & Jacoby, 1996). The study reinforced the importance within deliberative discourse of speakers' gestural work, use of props, and framing of complex activities (such as ongoing experiments).

In such talk, speakers set out ideas that accumulate content along with negations, amendments, and negotiation of fine points of detail. Deliberative talk enables participants both to test and build propositions as the talk goes forward. Visuospatial resources, whether as diagrams, graphs, charts, models, or schematic representations, come into the deliberation as props, additive material, and locus of visual attention to detail. Gestural moves to reinforce verbal deictics (e.g., *here, there*) and create narrative worlds stimulate interlocutors to create mental images of the work represented—whether from past experiments or toward performances projected. Physicists documented in this ethnographic study pulled one another into joint consideration of inanimate objects as well as membership in an imagined physical world made up of physicists. In many statements, the referent of pronominal references such as *I* or *you* amounted to the blended identity of physicist and arena of inquiry. The *I* in statements such as *"When I come down I'm in the domain state"* captures the essence of this blended identity "composed of both the animate physicist and the inanimate physical entity undergoing some change of state" (Ochs et al., 1996, p. 348).

Other studies of science laboratories focus much more on the vocal activities of participants than on their uses of gesture (Latour, 1986, 1987; Latour & Woolgar, 1986). However, implicit in all these studies is the fact that talk surrounds and often depends on "artifact" either currently present or referenced from past experiments (Lynch, 1985). Gestures and deictic references attune visual focus to props that interlocutors use to support and extend their verbal work. Moreover, as noted above, scientists join with the actual physical objects involved in their research, blending their identity as actor or agent into the object world that functions as stage or setting. This merger ensures that gestures, many of which heighten affect and draw audience members into the same scene, often involve not just hand movements and head turns, but full-body engagement or reorientation. These moves allow the actor/scientist to reenact aspects of past events or to turn away from the audience in order to draw, sketch, or adjust a piece of equipment in current use for demonstration.

This interdependence of spatial alignment, deixis, and gesture has long been attested to by linguists and anthropologists studying laboratories as well as the collaborative work of professionals using their knowledge of science to navigate their everyday worlds—often both with and without reliance on face-to-face vocal interaction (Gladwin, 1970; Haviland, 1993; Widlok, 1997). Pilots and air traffic controllers simultaneously "read" similar instrument panels and communicate verbally, though often with some lag time between reading and speaking. Much of the "expertise" on which they depend comes from inanimate objects (robots, computer transmissions, etc.) that provide channels of communication along with human experts in verbal interaction. These combined technological and human interpreters of scientific knowledge and skills make possible the navigation of ships entering a harbor or the take-off and landing of a plane or space capsule on earth, in space, or on the moon or Mars (Goodwin, 1994; Goodwin & Goodwin, 1995; Hutchins, 1995; Hutchins & Klausen, 1995).

Research on the use of gesture in settings where experienced scientists are at work either within the same physical locale or in far-flung locations differs in emphasis from studies carried out in science classrooms. These latter studies generally consider the "effectiveness" of particular variables, such as gesture, use of visuospatial activities, or spectator events such as videos and films. The degree of influence of any of these variables is determined in some cases through clinical trials with control and treatment groups and in other instances through single-case and often short-term qualitative studies. Assessment of the influence on student learning of more or less gesture and in which contexts within classrooms generally comes through before-and-after standardized assessments, randomized pull-out of students who take part in customized situations designed to test conceptual understanding, and self-report evaluations from students. The majority of studies of the influence of gestures on learners in middle childhood and adolescence show the cointerpretability of vocal and gestural interpretation and the benefits that result from instructors' use of gesture to highlight conceptual points or to stop the flow of talk to focus on metacognitive processes or mnemonic strategies (Roth, 1996, 1999, 2000). However, longitudinal research on novice learners gaining experience with multiple modes and locations of input is rare and generally comes from anecdotal self-reports of "special cases," such as winners of the Intel Science awards for secondary students (Dutton, 2011).

Of critical importance are studies that examine opportunities in which young learners step into roles other than that of "student." Research that has examined the effects of uses of mime and role play with younger children in general science studies suggest why role expansion is important. A few studies of adolescents in classes of chemistry, biology, and physics indicate the readiness with which these learners act the scientist, skeptic, reporter, or roving reporter in frames that give them these dramatic possibilities. Inevitably, drama enlists and demonstrates a host of modes beyond the gestural and vocal (Kress, Jewitt, & Ogborn, 2001). Well-known drama productions, such as *Copenhagen* by Michael Frayn, brought to the public stage the scientist engaged with not only the question of science at hand, but also the public positioning of scientists. Highlighted in plays such as this one and also in television programs such as *Nova* have been the dilemmas that result from the clash of scientists' public and private worlds, folk beliefs and the "truth" of scientific facts and methods, and science facing off against ethical and religious beliefs. In the anniversary celebrations in 2009 surrounding Charles Darwin, his personal life history and the dilemmas presented by evolution appeared everywhere in the media of economically advanced nations. Highly publicized readings and debates among scientists, ethicists, and religious leaders left little doubt about the imperative force behind arguments that every citizen should take into account responsibility for what could be "the world without us" (Weisman, 2007). Students have a wide range of provocative roles and engaging models related to science to draw from as they think about their own futures.

Drama enables children to take on the mantle of expert and thereby to enact or "play out" a "theory of mind" approach to how scientists think (Heath & Wolf, 2005; Heathcote, 1980; Wolf, 2006, 2009). Much has been made of the empathy developed by children engaged in literature-based drama, but the sense of what it means to question and to be questioned as an expert comes with equal measure to learners who are given the opportunity to think and act as a scientist in dramatic roles. Moreover, such work helps to develop students' interpretation of visuospatial modes as well as their facility in producing visual materials and using metaphors. The cyclical nature of group-devising, trying out, adapting, rehearsing, and performing naturally brings students repeatedly to reconsiderations of technical information—its forms and interpretations. Learners and experts have to return often to "check out" or "check on" ideas remembered or represented in illustrations, charts, graphs, and photographs as well as written texts (Dorion, 2009).

The norm for scientists is to be within an "as if" world. This state is also, of course, the essence of improvisational drama that places novice learners *within* the hypothetical rather than *outside* as spectator to hypotheses put forward by others. Research shows that through role play learners experience directly analogical modeling and grasp through their own embodiment processes of metaphor and analogy in science (Aubusson, Harrison, & Ritchie, 2006). Studies have shown that involvement in drama enhances students' facility with metacognitive understanding of concepts that benefit from contrastive analysis and the relational bases of analogical reasoning (Gentner, Holyoak, & Kokinov, 2001; Goswami, 1992). A further benefit to students' understanding of methods in the sciences is the need for repositioning and perspective change that both dramatic performance and collaborative work in science demand (Edmiston & Wilhelm, 1998). Early education practitioners intuitively put into practice these neuro- and cognitive science findings by having young children draw, paint, block-build, map, sing with gestural enactment, and create dramatic play. They usually do so, however, to enhance linguistic skills—oral and written—rather than to build understanding of science concepts (Fleer, 2009; Heath & Wolf, 2005). However, the same principles of cognitive growth toward grasping analogical reasoning and a theory of mind about how others think result from intensive work in drama regardless of subject matter of focus.

Within improvisation drama, players have to attend visually on a constant basis not only to one another but also to any audience that might be present. This kind of sustained attentive focus and search for clues and cues enables novice learners to practice overcoming inattentional blindness—a state of attending to only that which has been tagged as significant or has become entirely predictable and expected in the environment (Mack & Rock, 2000). Within improvisation work, players have to take in as many cues as possible in order to bring about the next set of actions. Like scientists, they "hope for accidents" or the unexpected shift in current circumstances that open up new possibilities (Heath & Wolf, 2004). Catching these "grand openers" requires simultaneous attention to the immediate moment and spontaneous imagination of a future scenario. Serendipity amounts to the kind of "accidents" scientists (and artists) hope for. In a time of puzzlement, stagnation, or just the ordinary flow of the laboratory or set of experiments, something comes along that inspires a flash of illumination (Roberts, 1989). To improvise well, science learners have to be "like a man [*sic*] walking backwards"—remembering content and scenes from the past while incorporating these into future moves that propel the demonstration, scene, or improvised drama underway (Johnstone, 1989, p. 116).

IDENTITY ALIGNMENT

Well established is the importance of coordinated identity possibilities for young learners. When novices see themselves and their interests reflected and represented in their models and expert guides, they have less disjuncture to overcome before their curiosity, trust, and willingness lead them to learn something new. Though definitions differ, most ideas of identity center on self-identity and include the three dimensions of "how a person understands his or her relationship to the world, how that relationship is constructed across time and space, and how the person understands possibilities for the future" (Norton, 2000, p. 5).

The shifting and multi-layered nature of self-identity for an individual in any given moment relies not only on past personal history but also on socialization into intimate groupings—family, friendship circles, and workplace. The quantity of nodes of interaction—and the density of each of these nodes—constitutes the social networks of individuals in their face-to-face and virtual worlds. Social network analyses that portray density or frequency and intensity of interaction with others centered in common interests and activities offer the best evidence of identity development through participation in both proscribed nodes (such as those of family and legal status within a state system) and voluntarily joined nodes. As individuals mature, they may usually opt out of former ways of participating within proscribed nodes and enrich the density of their interactions within voluntary memberships. Individuals may choose either temporarily or long-term to enact the adage that "friends are God's apology for relatives" and seek deep identity within specific social networks that differ significantly from the proscribed node of family. For both individuals and groups, identity is fluid and dynamic, and change comes across the life span as environments of learning and working disappear or alter in character.

Construction of group identity works in ways that differ from the paths that individuals take to their self-identity. In large part, group identity around or in science depends not only on joint interest and shared goals, but also on the need for distribution of different talents within the group. University laboratories, commercial ventures, health facilities, and national science projects prize diversity in the background experiences of employees and participants and often ground their identity in such diversity. Specialized fields of science, such as biomechanical engineering, have come about as a result of the creative thinking possible when highly trained professionals from different fields of preparation come together to work on a set of issues or a single problem and recognize the need for a "break-away" identity or new group identity outside the original group.

Group identity figures centrally not only for experts in science, but also for novices who often find science through "real" projects that need their particular talents and interests. Though "relevance" is often touted as critical for enticing the young into science, research has shown that "real" projects enlist learners far more easily than projects that are only "realistic." Herein lies the problem of "relevance" and its relationship to "real" as distinct from "realistic." Just as diverse levels and kinds of knowledge and skills create groups of expert scientists, so group projects that deeply engage novices must include a range of expertise and interests and ideally access to "real" experts or models. Directly watching and interacting with scientists at work enables young learners to see the collective mind of scientists at work. As scientists across the ages have noted, repeated instances of observation, trial and error, and comparative investigation preface their discoveries and inventions. Contrarian thinking marks achievement in the sciences. Fluency in specialized lexicons, along with an easy relationship with certain syntactic structures and genres, marks scientists' ways of talking and writing. Yet beyond the expected use of exceptional and specialized vocabulary, scientists see future scenarios for themselves and their projects and do so with the aid of particular functions of language. When these scientists do their "real" work with novices as apprentices, the young see into the workings of the mindfulness that makes science happen.

Differences in background experience among novice learners mean that "real" projects have to involve diversity of levels and types of experiences. Such diversity will distribute roles, thereby giving individuals the chance to play more than one role across the span of a project's life. These projects also benefit when they meet a felt need on the part of novices.

Formal learning environments cannot easily give groups of young learners either truly meaningful roles or opportunities for participation in longitudinal projects. The schedules, curricula, and assessment of elementary and secondary schools preclude sustained enactment of critical features of informal environments. In science classes of schools, even when "open" questions and project-development have engendered highly creative thinking and questioning, the ultimate identity of young learners as "students" will rise to the forefront when standardized authorities such as textbooks enter the picture (Viechnicki & Kuipers, 2008).

Museums and community organizations have wider possibilities, especially when art and science come together to create performance, exhibition, and production (Boehncke & Heath, 2004; Heath & Smyth, 1999). Voluntary involvement in such opportunities of the young—especially teens today—benefits from a "cool quotient" as well as peer collaboration appropriate for age and gender norms. In addition, young people's ease and facility with external representations, such as drawing, building models, and enacting through gesture and role as demonstrator and collaborator depend in part on cultural practices. Background socialization experiences in families also influence interpretation of patterning and creation of symbols, as well as ways of describing, narrating, or projecting the self under labels such as "museum devotee," scientist" or "nerd" (cf. Greer, Mukhopadhyay, Powell, & Nelson-Barber, 2009; Saxe, 1991).

All learners have intuitive notions (sometimes called "folk theories) about the natural world as well as "practical intelligence" (Sternberg & Wagner, 1986). Scholars point out that contemporary young learners who engage with visuospatial and enacted representation undergo conceptual change that relies on coordination class (diSessa & Sherin, 1998). This view includes intuitive understanding and experience as productive base from which the learner integrates systematic and interlaced knowledge. The "funds of knowledge" of learners thus remain to be reorganized (instead of replaced) and amplified, modified, and theorized as learning advances (Gonzales, Moll, & Amanti, 2005; Vygotsky, 1978).

Mental imagery around the question of "who am I now and who can I be?" helps discovery, creativity, and understanding in science learning. Young people who envision futures in science and see themselves ending up in science careers tend to be those who follow through in their academic study. Researcher Robert Tai and colleagues have shown the importance to the continuation of science study of young students' early self-identity as "scientist," now and in the future. Students in middle school who were "expecting" to go on in science were 3.4 times more likely to go forward than their peers who did not express such a future vision for themselves (Tai, Liu, Maltese, & Fan, 2006).

The ability to envision the self in a future role as scientist brings about meaningful learning in subsequent years. Successful scientists through the centuries repeatedly attest to the precedence of visuospatial conceptualizations and their propensities for "tinkering" and "trying it out" in the evolution of their careers (Latour, 1987; Stafford, 1990, 2007). Renown physicists and biologists have repeatedly reported that they think in mental images, to be sure, but they could not do their creative work without techniques that make these images accessible to them and others for alterations and interpretation (Root-Bernstein, 1989; Shepard, 1978, 1988). Noted historian of science and art Barbara Stafford has firmly admonished scholars who care about science learning to study "visual education." She notes:

> Those of us with knowledge about the techniques for making and understanding images and their constructive, *cognitive* role throughout history had better speak up now or be content to vanish into disciplinary extinction. The notion that the typeset text forms the rule and highest principle of interpretation must finally be put to rest for a democratic hermeneutics of pattern recognition and visual design to be created. (Stafford, 1990, pp. 310–311, italics in the original)

Though views differ on how this radical repositioning of research on science learning might come about, agreement on the value of producing and interpreting external representations is solid (Ramadas, 2009; Stafford, 2007). Equally solid is agreement that drawing, sketching, and modeling facilitate putting knowledge into action or practice, especially for problem recognition and problem solving. Some scholars refer to the combination of envisionment, enactment, and representation as "understanding by building," while others resist this notion as appearing to overemphasize learning facts and givens from the past while undervaluing discovery and creativity (Austin, 2003; Gibbs, 2006; Gigerenzer, 2000). This either-or argument overlooks the point that both retrieval and creative thinking have to take place during learning, and both can be enhanced in circumstances where social returns are high. In other words, if the question, issue, and audience for the external representation and/or embodiment of knowledge depend on young learners' involvement in real roles, then motivation for gaining more science skills and knowledge and being creative while doing so will be sure to increase (Greer, Mukhopadhyay, Powell, & Nelson-Barber, 2009).

THE LANGUAGE BEHIND SEEING AND DOING

Yet visual learning is not enough. It draws upon and needs support from the language that makes possible the collaborative work of the deliberative discourse that is vital to thinking as a scientist or seeing the world through the lens of scientific findings.

Examined here is the nature of the procedural enterprise of deliberative language—that which characterizes much of what goes on within experimental work and project development in science laboratories. Yet we must remember that this same kind of language happens in informal learning environments in which novices and experts work together in citizen science, family projects based in inquiry and experimentation, or youth-focused designed environments (such as museums) whose activities center in science-related projects (Heath, 2011; Heath & Smyth, 1999). Though deliberative discourse, like conversation, meanders and takes its own course, certain functional features stand out in extended stretches of deliberative talk that support the work of gaining and holding mutual focus of group members on future action.

Aristotle, in *Rhetoric*, Book 1, argued the vital role of deliberative discourse in sustaining democracy and ensuring the flourishing of freedom (cf. Gutmann & Thompson, 2004). Since the 1990s, "deliberative democracy" has been a much debated topic, with numerous studies arguing that citizens living in democracies owe one another mutually acceptable reasons for laws and policies. Reciprocity, openness, and reliable informed judgments characterize deliberation, a dynamic joint linguistic process that aims to bring forth decisions that will bind group members to conjoined action and to caring about what happens in the participation that must follow deliberation (Bohman & Rehg, 1997; Dryzek, 2000; Elster, 1998; Mutz, 2006).

Deliberative discourse relies on gestural attention-pointing as well as sustained visual attentiveness to distribution of participant opportunities and also to objects and visual representations. Simply put, the idea is that "we are looking and thinking together toward the future, and we must depend on one another as we talk now as well as in the work ahead." Three kinds of language chunks have functions specific to the extended stretches of here-and-now talk that moves group members toward making the work of the future possible. These functions are *relational*, *referential*, and *extensional*. All three kinds of language chunks help speakers "see together" and achieve joint long-term planning, consideration of consequences, and agency of individuals and the group as a whole.

Relational Language

Bringing interlocutors into deliberations and sustaining their participation calls for joint recall of shared information and asks for and offers clarification through acknowledgment of the contributions of others within the group.

The simplest means of getting those working together to relate to one another's ideas— the essence of deliberation—is to use the *vocative call-up*. Here, one speaker uses the name of another within the group and generally simultaneously gestures toward the individual and/or looks in his or her direction. Vocative call-ups come as direct vocative (e.g., *Janet* in Example 1 below) or as attributed source of an idea or experience that needs clarification (e.g., *Riley* in Example 2 below).

1. *Janet, back awhile, you were in this situation in your lab, right? Do you mind bringing us up to date on what happened?*
2. *What . . . let's see, Riley, when you brought that project on board, Richard was still here, as I recall.*

In both these instances, the attention of the named individual who is being addressed is asked for, and the group is reminded that this specific individual has made a prior contribution to the conversation at hand or to past shared experiences familiar to group members.

A second means of bringing about relational interaction is through the use of the *attributional call-in*. In Example 3, *Rodney* is being asked to respond in a confirming or expanding way in order to build upon the idea that the current speaker has stated. In Example 4 *Hazel* is noted as the author of an idea and implicitly given the conversational floor to explain, deny, or expand on the idea being attributed to her. At this point, attention of the group is directed toward a common object for viewing (the computer screen) as well as an idea under consideration. Hence, the focus in relational language is not merely on a specific person; it is also on this individual as creator of an idea that will be attributed to this individual throughout the deliberation.

> 3. *And when Rodney figured this spacing . . . you* [nodding the head toward Rodney] *used this* [pointing to a set of calculations on the computer screen]; *have I got that right?*
> 4. *Hazel's idea is that we get this ball rolling and worry about paying for it later. . . . OK by me!*

In Example 5, the speaker calls on the collective attention or recall of an idea being noted. Therefore, a common experience is attributed to any and all members of the group who may see the conversational floor as cleared for any one of the group to contribute further or expand on the point being referenced.

> 5. *Before that paper came out, we had a briefing . . . anyone remember that? Better yet, anyone got those slides?*

An additional role of relational language is to call on the self as speaker in the present moment and note the need for an accounting of prior mental states or internal dialogues and also to note the possible need for correction and clarification. In Example 6, the speaker asks for both specific information and explication of the mental processes that may have gone on to bring about the current action (usually a visual representation of some sort).

> 6. *What did I do here?* [looking at detail of drawing] *Hmmm, I'm not sure, now that I think of it. Let me see if I can remember.*

This request for verbal contributions from other members in response to the articulated mental processes of the speaker is termed *accountability call-in*.

Such a call-in need not be centered in the individual speaker; it may also invoke all members of the current deliberations as in Example 7:

> 7. *We've not made this step clear* [pointing to a particular feature of the operational chart placed before the members]; *as part of this whole sequence, it isn't standing out, so we've got to rethink this, don't you think? Or is anyone else having trouble here?*

Here the pronoun *we* plus the use of *anyone else* makes clear the need for the group to relate to one another and to the visual before them.

Relational language does not always include only those members who are within the immediate scene. As Example 2 above indicates, members of a group that at some previous point in time included an individual (e.g., *Richard*) not currently present may also be called up in the joint memory of the group. Relational language also indicates that a speaker is "inside" the head of another member of the group and anticipating the need to account for actions and representational forms currently under review (Examples 6 and 7). Relational language depends heavily on first-, second-, and third-person pronouns to sustain a sense of the shared identity and responsibility of the group. Deictics, such as *here, there*, call upon the visual attention of all those in immediate physical contact or jointly attending through video conferencing. Gestural narratives in relation to schematics, models, or other visual materials lay out progress from a current state toward a future or intended set of moves.

Referential Language

Here members of a collaborative team cite verifiable retrievable evidence and often use specialized language of the field or the current group project in doing so. Primary within such language is reference to a source that will be retrievable for all beyond the present moment and that can be referenced and accessed by individuals not linked to the current deliberative interlocutors. Such language often includes acronyms and vocabulary items or given names expected to be known by members of the science community.

The most easily recognized type of referential language is the naming of a shared known "authority" as in Examples 8, 9, and 10. Note that the authority may be a generic form of sourcing, such as a list of research projects previously funded or regulations issued by an acknowledged power that holds some influence and control over the actions of the current group (e.g., the National Science Foundation or state or city regulators). Most common as authorities are individuals, university laboratory groups, or commercial research and development laboratories identified by proper nouns, such as those indicated in Example 10.

8. *With an entry like that* [pointing to a listing of research projects in view of all members], *they've got to have . . . some kind of expectation that equipment is gonna be available.*
9. *Those regs* [regulations], *the new ones from city hall, are sure to affect the budget for that water project. Has anyone had a chance to look at 'em yet?*
10. *Did you* [addressed to the group as a whole] *catch Ferlon's talk this week? Interesting stuff, and he's got that new post-doc, the one who coauthored the paper in* Science *this year.*

As Example 10 illustrates, it is quite common in any chunk of referential language to include several names and kinds of authorities (e.g., publication outlets, specific schools of research, or particular conferences). The primary function of referential language beyond giving the group a shared knowledge base is establishment of a platform of information from which the work of scientific investigation can move forward.

Extensional Language

An additional form of platform determination comes through language that moves the group from past expressed ideas (which may have been based only in the relations known to group members or in the common reference base of all) forward into a future beyond the current group. Such language intentionally calls attention to the future thrust of the group's work and extends current deliberation toward achievements to come. Extensional language includes the naming of a range of variables that may affect the path of action and likelihood of success (Examples 11 and 12).

11. *And if we could get this reviewed . . . what's the general lead time here? . . . Then we would be able to take advantage of the NSF site visit before the next deadline when we can expect new RFPs?*
12. *What about pulling in those post-docs right before we get this ready to go out the door? Would that work? Otherwise, we'll be forced to see if we can bring in some senior grad students to help out.*

By implication as well as by highly specific mandating language, the chunks of extensional language within deliberative discourse state what must or should be done. Therefore, the language used generally includes modals (e.g., *will, would, can, could, should, must, ought to, have to*) and verbs with imperative intent (e.g., *force, compel, direct, redirect*).

Critical within extensional language is the laying out of variables or conditions related to temporal and causal considerations. Thus extensional language chunks include conjunctions and prepositions that mark time as well as act and sequence (*when, then, because, since*), lay out hypothetical propositions, and raise questions of *What if* or *What then*. Such language indicates the interdependence and complexity of variables that may affect outcomes or the future projections of tasks.

A further function of extensional language relates to the long-standing axiom of scientific language that centers in the role of hypotheses—projections of possible events or outcomes in relation to given conditions. Relational and referential language chunks enable the work of extensional talk. Relational language provides the social and mental glue of group focus and interactional history, while referential language ensures a common informational base for the team.

Throughout both functions, the group prepares not only to commit and consider the future expressed in extensional language, but also to do the comparative and contrastive case analysis on which the future work depends. The point of such analyses often rests in specific cases or instances, but emotive and opinionated responses also figure here. Prior cases or instances need not be within the given knowledge base of all group members, but they may be introduced, described, and explained by individuals in relation to the focal task of the group. Doing so allows the group to consider not only how they place themselves in relation to other teams, projects, or tasks, but also to relate or compare additional instances or cases, along with affective evaluation of their own situation and planning.

The work of contrast and compare within extensional chunks may also include individual idiosyncratic contributions through emotive wrapping of points that affirm, contradict, deny, or supplement issues currently under consideration by the deliberative group and within the discussion frame as in Example 13:

> 13. *I'm just not seeing where this is going. I'm sensing the way we're heading now as a stretch too far in order to meet funding guidelines.*

Implicit in such statements is a contrast between what currently seems to be "where this is going" and what the guidelines of the RFP (a referenced common authority in the group) indicate about possibilities of direction. In many instances, speakers who set forward such a comparison single out their own experiences or specific knowledge of other cases as in Example 14:

> 14. *I remember one other time when I felt like this. . . . We were working on a Woods Hole project, and this new guy came in and . . . well, we all tried to redirect what we were doing to hook up with his project in Finland. Some of us said then that we weren't ready for that move. I feel that way now as I listen to where we think we may be headed.*

Emotive responses and value judgments, offered by a single speaker and stated as generalizations or opinions, often open the discourse floor for other speakers to join in the comparative and contrastive work of analyzing the present in relation to feelings as well as to past individual experiences. The full group can thus be led by such comments to back away from or amend the direction of deliberations in order to think more clearly and work more effectively toward the future.

What is often termed *comparison* in such cases is more often than not *contrast*. The distinction here is in the degree of detail regarding differences and similarities likely to appear when the work of contrasting is going on. Comparison, more often than not, relies on general or broad-based assessment. Contrastive analysis lays out specific points of distinction—similar and different.

THE ETHNOGRAPHER'S RESPONSIBILITY IN
INFORMAL SCIENCE LEARNING

As ethnography and qualitative research have become more and more accepted within the research of professionals in education, many of these scholars have looked at language uses in relation to learning. However, almost no attention has gone to how language works in informal learning environments, aside from those involving play and friendship circles of young children and adolescents (Corsaro, 2003; Eder, 1995). Most of this work stresses affective and cognitive dimensions of these informal settings over language socialization (but see Goodwin, 1990, for an exception). Relatively little attention has gone to the visual attentional demands of membership within informal learning situations.

This chapter, through its review of research literature on visuospatial and gestural contributions to science learning and specific linguistic functions within the deliberative work of collaborative groups learning science, is intended to encourage research on science learning within civic-oriented informal environments. Environmentally dedicated citizen groups, mutual self-help groups in health sciences, and community gardeners dedicated to organic farming represent the face of science in local communities. These groups see themselves dedicated to using what science can tell them about the course of action to take on specific issues, such as what it will take to bring about a clean-energy economy. In such settings, the acquisition of the language of science by novices goes on in ways that parallel in many ways the deliberative discourse that takes place among professional scientists.

We know enough about the lexical and syntactic features of the language of science classrooms to be able to track these features quantitatively and contextually in informal learning environments. This chapter argues the need to track also language chunks that carry specific functions. Quantitative records of these, in relation to the number and variation of speaker turns in deliberative discourse, can be correlated with the growth of mental coherence of group members. Such coherence is linguistically indexed by the kinds of overlaps and interruptions of interlocutors as well as by the relative proportionality of types of language chunks of different functions. In other words, when, as in Examples 15 and 16, speakers' overlaps and interruptions are grammatically cohesive, the sense of "togetherness in our thinking" is high among members.

15. [Overlap indicated by //] Speaker a: *Right at the outset // in this proposal, we've got to establish how we'll deal with the work that Marshall did before he joined us.*
    Speaker b: *// yes, right up front.*
16. [Interruption indicated by =] Speaker a: *We'll need to get the custodial staff lined up to =*
    Speaker b: *= monitor temperature readings.*

The number and frequency of similar kinds of coherence in thinking among group members can be established and compared with self-ratings by members of the group both following each deliberative session and across several sessions.

As Barbara Stafford notes in the quotation provided above, "disciplinary extinction" is a distinct possibility. She calls for interdisciplinary research that takes seriously the competing domains of visual representation and the multiplicities of visual cultures. Thus researchers in education, including ethnographers in particular, since these scholars are often those who undertake longitudinal work, must create teams that include members from disciplines outside education departments and schools. Learning science in informal environments calls on scholars who study visual cognition as well as anthropologists and linguists accustomed to documenting multiple modes of learning. Social theory related to identity has to be brought to bear on what we can learn about the informal learning of citizen science groupings, museum projects involving young people, and community-based projects in the environmental sciences. Such research will, ideally, involve a scientist whose interests include the practice of science and the learning of science by citizens untrained in the sciences.

The range of roles likely in such groups will reflect varieties of stances or personae. At different points and often within the same role, individuals are sure to move among stances (e.g., oppositional, supportive, skeptical, etc.), ideally when doing so will advance deliberations around the project in process. Theorists who examine the role of both planning and play in learning (Baker-Sennett, Matusov, & Rogoff, 2007; Lave & Wenger, 1991; Rogoff, Baker-Sennett, & Matusov, 1994; Rogoff, Gauvain, & Gardner, 1987; Sutton-Smith, 1997) have written for two decades about the importance of visual observation, an impending sense of participation, and looking ahead toward "pitching in." Such research underscores the vital role that collaborative planning—envisionment of possible scenarios with variables along the way—takes on for moving joint thinking for a project forward successfully.

The coming together of experts and novices around the meaning of science around us took a big step forward through the publicity surrounding the film and volume from Al Gore on global climate change (Gore, 2006). Community organizations previously dedicated primarily to specific realms of activity, such as the arts or community gardening, began to think more about the role of the sciences in their mission and activities. Many of these efforts brought adolescents together as planners for the future of community organizations as "social enterprises" in which the young would earn money and create social good for their communities. These initiatives also enlisted professional adults in the sciences and other fields as consistent mentors and advisors as well as clients (see, for example, the websites of Artists for Humanity, The Food Project, and Fresh Roots for descriptions of the joint work of teen novices and professional experts in the service of urban ecology, food systems, environmental sciences, and the arts). Informal learning environments dedicated to enlisting young people and improving familiarity between novices and experts in art and science now have little research representing their processes and projects longitudinally.

Education researchers working in interdisciplinary teams have an obligation to draw on theories and methods from visual cognition, linguistics, and performance studies to show the cumulative contributions of informal learning environments to civic responsibility. As economically advanced nations increasingly depend on citizens to extend and deepen understanding of science throughout the general public and to assess and shape policies informed by research, informal community groups will, undoubtedly, increase in number and vibrancy. In addition, as youth-oriented community organizations respond more to youth interests and concerns around environmental issues, education researchers cannot continue to ignore this kind of knowledge and action growth. However, as they turn their attention to informal learning environments centered in science, these researchers have a special responsibility to do so through the use of multiple research methods and interdisciplinary teams.

REFERENCES

Anderson, R. E. (1998). Imagery and spatial representation. In W. Bechtel & G. Graham (Eds.), *A companion to cognitive science* (pp. 201–211). Malden, MA: Blackwell.

Aubusson, P. J., Harrison, A. G., & Ritchie, S. M. (Eds.). (2006). *Metaphor and analogy in science education*. Dordrecht, Germany: Springer.

Austin, J. H. (2003). *Chase, chance, and creativity: The lucky art of novelty*. Cambridge, MA: MIT Press.

Baker-Sennett, J., Matusov, E., & Rogoff, B. (2007). Children's planning of classroom plays with adult or child direction. *Social Development, 17*(4), 998–1018.

Boehncke, E., & Heath, S. B. (2004). Platforms for youth responsibility: Ways of studying learning between the lines. In A. Bron & A. Gustavsson (Eds.), *En vänbok till Birgitta Qvarsell. Pedagogik som vetenskap* (pp. 190–213). Stockholm, Sweden: Stockholm University.

Bohman, J., & Rehg, W. (Eds.). (1997). *Deliberative democracy.* Cambridge, MA: MIT Press.

Corsaro, W. A. (2003). *We're friends, right? Inside kids' culture.* Washington, DC: Joseph Henry Press.

Cutler, A. (2007). Foreword. In S. B. Heath, E. Paul-Boehncke, & S. Wolf. *Made for each other: Creative sciences and arts in the secondary school* (pp. vii–ix). London, England: Creative Partnerships.

diSessa, A. A., & Sherin, B. (1998). What change in conceptual change? *International Journal of Science Education, 10*(10), 1155–1191.

Dorion, K. R. (2009). Science through drama: A multiple case exploration of the characteristics of drama activities used in secondary science lessons. *International Journal of Science Education, 31,* 1–24.

Dryzek, J. (2000). *Deliberative democracy and beyond.* Oxford, England: Oxford University Press.

Dutton, J. (2011). *Science fair season: Twelve kids, a robot named Scorch . . . and what it takes to win.* New York, NY: Hyperion.

Eder, D. (1995). *School talk: Gender and adolescent school culture.* New Brunswick, NJ: Rutgers University Press.

Edmiston, B., & Wilhelm, J. D. (1998). Repositioning views/reviewing positions. In B. J. Wagner (Ed.), *Educational drama and language arts: What research shows* (pp. 90–117). Chicago, IL. Heinemann.

Elster, J. (1998). *Deliberative democracy.* Cambridge, England: Cambridge University Press.

Fleer, M. (2009). Supporting scientific conceptual consciousness or learning in "a roundabout way" in play-based contexts. *International Journal of Science Education, 31*(8), 1069–1089.

Gentner, D., & Goldin-Meadow, S. (Eds.). (2003). *Language in mind: Advances in the study of language and thought.* Cambridge, MA: MIT Press.

Gentner, D., Holyoak, K. J., & Kokinov, B. N. (2001). *The analogical mind: Perspectives from cognitive science.* Cambridge, MA: MIT Press.

Gibbs, R. (2006). *Embodiment and cognitive science.* Cambridge, England: Cambridge University Press.

Gigerenzer, G. (2000). *Adaptive thinking: Rationality in the real world.* Oxford, England: Oxford University Press.

Gladwin, T. (1970). *East is a big bird: Navigation and logic on Puluwat Atoll.* Cambridge, MA: Harvard University Press.

Goldin-Meadow, S. (2003). *Hearing gesture: How our hands help us think.* Cambridge, MA: Harvard University Press.

Gonzales, N., Moll, L. C., & Amanti, C. (Eds.). (2005). *Funds of knowledge: Theorizing practices in households, communities, and classrooms.* Mahwah, NJ: Erlbaum.

Goodwin, C. (1994). Professional vision. *American Anthropologist, 96,* 606–633.

Goodwin, C. (1995). Seeing in depth. *Social Studies of Science, 25,* 237–274.

Goodwin, C., & Goodwin, M. H. (1995). Seeing as situated activity: Formulating planes. In D. Middleton & Y. Engestrom (Eds.), *Cognition and communication at work* (pp. 61–95). Cambridge, England: Cambridge University Press.

Goodwin, M. (1990). *He-said she-said.* Bloomington: Indiana University Press.

Gopnik, A., & Meltzoff, A. (1998). *Words, thoughts, and theories.* Cambridge, MA: MIT Press.

Gopnik, A., Meltzoff, A. N., & Kuhl, P. K. (1999). *The scientist in the crib.* New York, NY: Perennial.

Gopnik, A., & Slaughter, V. (1991) Young children's understanding of changes in their mental states. *Child Development, 62,* 98–110.

Gore, A. (2006). *An inconvenient truth.* New York, NY: Rodale.

Goswami, U. (1992). *Analogical reasoning in children.* Hove, England: Psychology Press.

Greer, B., Mukhopadhyay, S., Powell, A. B., & Nelson-Barber, S. (Eds.). (2009). *Culturally responsive mathematics education.* New York, NY: Routledge.

Gutmann, A., & Thompson, D. (2004). *Why deliberative democracy?* Princeton, NJ: Princeton University Press.

Haviland, J. (1993). Anchoring, iconicity, and orientation in Guugu Yimithirr pointing gestures. *Journal of Linguistic Anthropology, 3,* 3–45.

Heath, S. B. (2011). Language socialization in art and science. In A. Duranti, E. Ochs, & B. Schieffelin (Eds.), *Handbook of language socialization* (pp. 425–442). London, England: Blackwell.

Heath, S. B., Paul-Boehncke, E., & Wolf, S. A. (2007). *Made for each other: Creative sciences and arts in the secondary school.* London, England: Creative Partnerships.

Heath, S. B., & Smyth, L. (1999). *Artshow: Youth and community development.* Washington, DC: Partners for Livable Communities.

Heath, S. B., & Wolf, S. A. (2004). *Visual learning in the community school.* London, England: Creative Partnerships.

Heath, S. B., & Wolf, S. A. (2005). *Dramatic learning in the primary school.* London, England: Creative Partnerships.

Heathcote, D. (1980). *Drama as context.* Aberdeen, Scotland: Aberdeen University Press.

Hutchins, E. (1995). *Cognition in the wild.* Cambridge, MA: MIT Press.

Hutchins, E., & Klausen, T. (1995). Distributed cognition in an airline cockpit. In D. Middleton & Y. Engestrom (Eds.), *Cognition and communication at work* (pp. 15–34). Cambridge, England: Cambridge University Press.

Ingvar, D. (1985). Memory of the future: An essay on the temporal organization of conscious awareness. *Human Neurology, 4*(3), 127–136.

Jeannerod, M. (1997). *The cognitive neuroscience of action*. Oxford, England: Blackwell.

Johnstone, K. (1989). *Impro: Improvisation and the theatre*. New York, NY: Routledge.

Kendon, A. (2004). *Gesture: Visible action as utterance*. Cambridge, England: Cambridge University Press.

Kosslyn, S. M. (1995). Visual cognition: Introduction. In S. M. Kosslyn & D. N. Osherson (Eds.), *Visual cognition* (Vol. 2, pp. xi–xiii). Cambridge, MA: MIT Press.

Kress, G., Jewitt, C., & Ogborn, J. (2001). *The rhetorics of the science classroom: A multimodal approach*. London, England: Cassell.

Latour, B. (1986) Visualization and cognition: Thinking with eyes and hands. *Knowledge and society, 6*, 1–40.

Latour, B. (1987). *Science in action*. Cambridge, MA: Harvard University Press.

Latour, B., & Woolgar, S. (1986). *Laboratory life: The construction of scientific facts*. Beverly Hills, CA: Sage.

Lave, J., & Wenger, E. (1991). *Situated learning: Legitimate peripheral participation*. Cambridge, England: Cambridge University Press.

LeDoux, J. (2002). *Synaptic self*. New York, NY: Penguin.

Libet, B. (2004). *Mind time: The temporal factor in consciousness*. Cambridge, MA: Harvard University Press.

Lindstrom, M. (1957). *Children's art*. Berkeley: University of California Press.

Lynch, M. (1985). *Art and artifact in laboratory science*. London, England: Routledge.

Lyng, A. (2007). Afterword. In S. B. Heath, E. Paul-Boehncke, & S. Wolf, *Made for each other: Creative sciences and arts in the secondary school* (pp. 111–115). London, England: Creative Partnerships.

Mack, A., & Rock, I. (2000). *Inattention blindness*. Cambridge, MA: MIT Press.

Matthews, J. (1999). *The art of childhood and adolescence: The construction of meaning*. London, England: Falmer Press.

Matthews, J. (2003). *Drawing and painting: Children and visual representation* (2nd ed.). London, England: Paul Chapman.

Mutz, D. (2006). *Hearing the other side: Deliberative versus participatory democracy*. Cambridge, England: Cambridge University Press.

National Research Council. (2009). *Learning science in informal environments: People, places, and pursuits*. Washington, DC: The National Academies Press.

Newcombe, N., & Learmonth, A. (2005). Development of spatial competence. In P. Shah & A. Miyake (Eds.), *Handbook of visuospatial reasoning* (pp. 213–256). New York, NY: Cambridge University Press.

Norton, B. (2000). *Identity and language learning: Gender, ethnicity and educational change*. London, England: Longman.

Ochs, E., Gonzales, P., & Jacoby, S. (1996). "When I come down I'm in the domain state": Grammar and graphic representation in the interpretive activity of physicists. In E. Ochs, E. Schegloff, & S. Thompson (Eds.), *Interaction and grammar* (pp. 328–369). Cambridge, England: Cambridge University Press.

Paley, V. (1997). *The girl with the brown crayon: How children use stories to shape their lives*. Cambridge, MA: Harvard University Press.

Pfeifer, R., & Bongard, J. (2007). *How the body shapes the way we think: A new view of intelligence*. Cambridge, MA: MIT Press.

Ramachandran, V. S., & Hubbard, E. M. (2001). Synaesthesia: A window into perception, thought, and language. *Journal of Consciousness Studies, 8*(12), 3–24.

Ramadas, J. (2009). Visual and spatial modes in science learning. *International Journal of Science Education, 31*(3), 301–318.

Roberts, R. (1989). *Serendipity: Accidental discoveries in science*. New York, NY: Wiley.

Rogoff, B., Baker-Sennett, J., & Matusov, E. (1994). Considering the concept of planning. In M. M. Haith, J.B. Benson, R. J. Roberts Jr., & B. F. Pennington (Eds.), *The development of future-oriented processes* (pp. 353–373). Chicago, IL: University of Chicago Press.

Rogoff, B., Gauvain, M. & Gardner, W. (1987). The development of children's skills in adjusting plans to circumstances. In S. L. Friedman, E. K. Scholnick, & R. R. Cocking (Eds.), *Blueprints for thinking: The role of planning in cognitive development* (pp. 303–320). Cambridge, England: Cambridge University Press.

Root-Bernstein, R. (1989). *Discovering*. Cambridge, MA; Harvard University Press.

Roskos-Ewoldsen, B., Intons-Peterson, J. J., & Anderson, R. E. (1993). *Imagery, creativity, and discovery: A cognitive perspective*. Amsterdam, The Netherlands: Elsevier.

Roth, W. M. (1996). Art and artifact of children's designing: A situated cognition perspective. *Journal of Learning Sciences, 5*, 129–166.

Roth, W. M. (1999). Discourse and agency in school science laboratories. *Discourse Processes, 28*, 27–60.

Roth, W. M. (2000). From gesture to scientific language. *Journal of Pragmatics, 32*, 1683–1714.

Saxe, G. (1991). *Culture and cognitive development: Studies in mathematical understanding*. Mahwah, NJ: Erlbaum.

Schnotz, W. (2002). Towards an integrated view of learning from text and visual displays. *Educational Psychology Review, 14*(1), 101–119.

Shepard, R. N. (1978). Externalization of mental images and the act of creation. In B. Randhawa & W. E. Coffman (Eds.), *Visual learning, thinking and communication* (pp. 133–189). New York, NY: Academic Press.

Shepard, R. N. (1988). The imagination of the scientist. In K. Egan & D. Nadaner (Eds.), *Imagination and education* (pp. 153–185). New York, NY: Teachers College Press.

Stafford, B. (1990). *Artful science: Enlightenment entertainment and the eclipse of visual education.* Cambridge, MA: MIT Press.

Stafford, B. (2007). *Echo objects: The cognitive work of images.* Chicago, IL: University of Chicago Press.

Sternberg, R., & Wagner, R. K. (Eds.). (1986). *Practical intelligence.* New York, NY: Cambridge University Press.

Struiksma, M. E., Noordzij, M. L., & Postma, A. (2009). What is the link between language and spatial images? *Acta Pyschologica.*

Sutton-Smith, B. (1997). *The ambiguity of play.* Cambridge, MA: Harvard University Press.

Suwa, M., & Tverksy, B. (1997). What architects and students perceive in their sketches: A protocol analysis. *Design Studies,* 18:385–403.

Tai, R. H., Liu, C. Q., Maltese, A. V., & Fan, X. (2006). Planning early for careers in science. *Science, 312*(5777), 1143–1144.

Viechnicki, G., & Kuipers, J. (2008). Objectification and the inscription of knowledge in science classrooms. *Linguistics and Education, 19,* 203–318.

Vygotsky, L. S. (1978). *Mind in society.* Cambridge, MA: Harvard University Press.

Weisman, A. (2007). *The world without us.* New York, NY: St. Martin's Press.

Widlok, T. (1997). Orientation in the wild: The shared cognition of Haillom bush people. *Journal of the Royal Anthropological Institute, 3,* 317–332.

Wilson, F. R. (1998). *The hand.* New York, NY: Vintage Press.

Wolf, S. A. (2006). *A playwright's life for me! Young children's language and learning through drama.* London, England: Creative Partnerships.

Wolf, S. A. (2009). *From the "mantle" to expertise: The arc of creative partnerships.* London, England: Creative Partnerships.

14

No Color Necessary

High School Students' Discourse on College Support Systems and College Readiness

Evellyn Elizondo, Walter R. Allen, and Miguel Ceja

For over three decades, achievement gaps have stubbornly persisted between poor Latino and black children across America and their more affluent white counterparts. Gaps between low-income minorities and higher-income whites were narrowed temporarily between 1970 and the early 1980s, only to gain momentum once again in the late 1980s, and they have steadily broadened (Haycock, 2001). Achievement trends show by the fourth grade, Latino and black students were 2 years behind their counterparts with gaps widening to twice as much by the beginning of twelfth grade (Robelen, 2002). Furthermore, it was found that Latinos and blacks were exiting high school with reading and math skills comparable to that of white eighth-grade students (Haycock, 2001). Given the growing demand for a college education in today's workforce, children of color are at a vast disadvantage in competing for high-paying jobs and contributing fully to the nation's economy.

It has been well documented by the college choice literature that various circumstances factor into different experiences in students' access to higher education (e.g., Chapman, 1981; Hossler, Braxton, & Coopersmith, 1989; Litten, 1982; Ready, Lee, & Welner, 2004). Students who have college-educated parents are more likely to participate in higher education and develop a college roadmap, conavigated by family who possess the expertise to aid successfully in their college preparation (e.g., Gándara, 2002; McDonough et al., 2000; Plank & Jordan, 2001). Such students benefit from having parents who are able to serve effectively as liaisons between their school and home life. These students are provided with a large and sophisticated network of resources, strategic academic options, access to costly college test-taking courses and perhaps equally important, parental testimonies of successful college experiences (Carpenter & Fleishman, 1987; Hossler, Schmit, & Vesper, 1999; McDonough, 1994). This privileged wealth of information shapes students' understanding of their role in higher education, perceiving college to be a natural progression and a rite of passage afforded them by their parents (e.g., Bateman & Hossler, 1996; Yang, 1981).

On the other hand, students who have parents with little or no college history often face the daunting task of navigating their academic endeavors and college choice process by themselves (e.g., Ceja, 2004, 2006; Gonzalez, Stoner, & Jovel, 2003; Lareau & Shumar, 1996; Hossler & Gallagher, 1987; Hoover-Dempsey & Sandler, 1997). The decision to attend college is too often a pioneering effort, one that deviates from traditional family and cultural trends. Many of these students are not well informed about accessing higher education and they also lack the instrumental knowledge, mentorship, and social support network necessary to negotiate their academic preparation and college options (e.g., Ceja, 2004; Cooper, Jackson, Azmitia, & Lopez, 1998; McDonough, 1994; Phelan, Davidson, & Yu, 1991). Unfortunately, it has long been established that such students have not had an equal opportunity to develop the necessary help-seeking skills or academic support systems that lead to successful college preparation (e.g., Fordham & Ogbu, 1986; Karabel & Astin, 1975). In fact, research has shown disadvantaged students, such as ethnic minorities, have received poor and conflicting academic mentorship from institutional agents, such as high school guidance counselors, resulting in gatekeeping of college resources (Carter, 2004; Stanton-Salazar, 2004). Minority students are vulnerable to developing an inadequate frame of reference from which to base their college expectations without open access to information and resources.

Social capital theory suggests disadvantaged students can seek instrumental relationships at school that carry the potential to gain access to resources (Stanton-Salazar, 1997). Such relationships developed with teachers, coaches, academic counselors, and other school personnel play the important role of "institutional agent" and transmit to students the knowledge, experiences, and opportunities that lead to a successful college transition (Blumberg, Venegas, Oliverez, & Colyar, 2004; Coleman, 1988; Saunders & Serna, 2004). In essence, these relationships can function as vehicles of social mobility and fill the gap normally satisfied by resources available to families of high socioeconomic status. For this reason, we examine the nature of privileged and disadvantaged students' college support networks as a means to understanding their college preparation and access to higher education. Through focus group discussions, this study seeks to grasp the processes by which ethnic minority and majority students construct meaning, and describe in their own words, their high school experience and academic preparation. The goal of this investigation is to understand more fully the dynamic relationship between social support systems and student outcomes.

METHODOLOGY

Study Design

This study is part of a larger research project aimed at addressing educational access, equity, and diversity issues in higher education. The main goal of the project is to identify factors related to educational successes among African American and Latino students residing in Southern California. This research carried out a cross-sectional, mixed-method design. Quantitative and qualitative data were collected from teachers, parents, counselors, and students at 10 Los Angeles Basin high schools varying in school characteristics and demographics (Allen, Kimura-Walsh, & Griffin, 2009).

For the purposes of this study, we selected one school site, Cove High School (CHS) (institutional name is fictitious) because of its unique school environment. The student population is not only the most racially and socioeconomically diverse of all our schools but also among the highest academically credentialed public schools in the state of California. In this present study, we focus on quantitative and qualitative data from Latino and white students.

Data Collection Procedures

Approval from University of California Los Angeles Human Subjects Review Committee was obtained prior to data collection. In coordination with school staff and administrators, university researchers recruited 10 high schools in Los Angeles County to participate in this study. The primary investigator arranged meetings with school principals and/or staff to discuss the possibility of their participation. Schools agreed to participate in exchange for a full disclosure of their school's statistical findings. Participation was voluntary and students who consented to join our study were given two movie passes as a small gratuity. Prior to data collection, parental consent forms were collected for each student respondent under 18 years of age.

Most students were either recruited from an Advanced Placement (AP) course or from the Advancement via Individual Determination (AVID) program. Briefly, AVID is an in-school educational support program for Grades 5–12 that prepares traditionally disadvantaged students for college eligibility. AVID takes academically average-performing students and places them in advanced classes while providing the academic support to succeed. Data were collected on the high school campus from September 2001 through June 2002 in compliance with standards for ethical research.

Group interviews varied from 1 to 2 hours and were conducted by the primary research investigator, coprincipal investigators, or a graduate student researcher. Each focus group was audio recorded, transcribed by a professional agency, and coded by project student researchers. Group interviews were broadly structured, using open-ended questions designed to tap into college readiness, social expectations to attend college, availability of resources, as well as school-related support networks and barriers to higher education.

Data Analyses

Survey data were used to contextualize students' qualitative responses broadly. Incorporating students' demographic information and general impressions of their quality of education allows for a point of reference from which to interpret students' unique experiences. Focus group transcripts were reviewed by individual research team members for the purposes of identifying recurring themes in the data. Group discussions were facilitated to develop coding categories for use in ATLAS to analyze the data. SPSS software was used to analyze survey data collected in this study. Combining both forms of data provides a more complete view of the similarities and differences in minority and majority students' school experiences.

School Description: Cove High School Profile

Cove High School is an academically above-average-performing school located in a large coastal community with a population of approximately 90,000. The community is largely comprised of college-educated (50 percent), white-collar professionals (75 percent). Of these residents, 78 percent are white, 13 percent Latino, and 4 percent African American. During the 2001–2002 academic year, Cove enrolled over 3,000 students. Given that Cove High buses Latino and black students from lower-income neighborhoods, the student body represents a diverse ethnic and socioeconomic community comprising 51 percent white, 34 percent Latino, and 11 percent African American. The families at Cove range from affluent to low income. The distribution of wealth and parental education among minority and majority students depicts a bimodal trend with Latino and black students reporting considerably lower income and parental education than white and Asian students.

Academically, Cove considers itself a college-going community, producing college-going rates for blacks and Latinos higher than the state average. During the 2001–2002 academic year, slightly over half (58 percent) of the senior class were UC/CSU eligible. Compared to average statewide college eligibility rates (68 percent Asian, 34 percent white, 19 percent black, and 16 percent Latino), Cove high eligibility rates across most groups were greater (73 percent white, 66 percent Asian, 37 percent black, and 36 percent Latino) (California Postsecondary Education Commission, 2002). On average, 2002 Cove graduates scored higher SAT I math (550) and verbal (518) scores than both the statewide (517 math/498 verbal) and nationwide (514 math/506 verbal) averages. The school offers the largest number of Advanced Placement classes across all of our 10 participating schools, including those serving larger student populations. Cove offers 40 AP courses whereas larger participating schools offer 30 AP courses. However, the representation of Latino and black students enrolled in AP courses remains disproportionately low compared to their Asian and white counterparts.

Cove is accredited by the Western Association of Schools and Colleges (WASC) with teachers who ranked higher than 91 percent of high schools in the country based on the proportion with earned master's degrees or higher. The school employs a balance of younger and more experienced teachers. The student-teacher ratio is 25:1 and the average class size is approximately 31. Compared to student enrollment, the faculty is less diverse by race/ethnicity: 68 percent white, 16 percent Latino, 9 percent African American, 4 percent Asian, and 2 percent American Indian. Of these teachers, 88 percent are fully credentialed.

During the 2001–2002 academic year, eight counselors served the total student population. Students were assigned to two counselors by grade level and were then divided in half alphabetically. Unique to Cove High, a Summer Freshman Bridge Program has been developed for all incoming freshmen. Although this program is not mandatory, it provides students the opportunity to learn about their graduation and college eligibility requirements.

Sample Description

Students: In this study, we present data from our Latino and white Cove High student volunteers. A total of 70 students participated in focus group discussions: 35 identified as Latinos and 35 as whites. The majority were females (62 percent) enrolled in Advanced Placement high school courses (57 percent). White students (97 percent) reported the highest percentage for having at least one parent with college experience while Latinos (26 percent) reported the lowest percentage of college-educated parents. Similarly, white students reported the highest average annual income ($70,000–$74,000) and Latinos ($30,000–$39,000) the lowest annual income.

When students were asked to indicate their highest educational goal, Latinos on average aspired to master's degrees, whereas whites on average aspired to doctorate degrees. Although both groups aimed for an advanced college degree, not all were equally prepared for college. A one-way analysis of variance revealed a reliable difference in students' grade point average (GPA) across groups, $F(2, 95) = 4.70$, $p < .001$. Based on the significant F test, a Scheffe Post Hock analysis showed whites' GPA ($M = 3.29$) was reliably higher than Latinos' ($M = 2.91$). Furthermore, a larger proportion of whites (89 percent SAT I; 71 percent SAT II) had completed their college entrance exams compared to Latinos (67 percent SAT I; 37 percent SAT II). Lastly, our survey showed white and Latino students rely most heavily on different school agents. The popular response for important college resource among white students was counselors, while Latino students reported teachers as their most important college resource.

QUALITATIVE DATA

School Agents

Overall, two different perceptions of campus support emerged from these data across groups. White students reported Cove High was an encouraging and supportive campus that fostered a strong sense of student commitment and high academic expectations. Whites expressed that both teachers and college counselors were motivational and consistent about offering information regarding college. One white male commented that his teacher made sure the class understood what to expect on a college campus by sharing personal college experiences:

My history teacher really talked a lot about college. He was a young guy right out of Santa Barbara and so he knew what was going on. He was a really cool guy to talk to us about education. He talked about the differences between high school and college and making the transition so we know what to do. This teacher really impacted my decisions. He was pretty helpful.

Another student discussed how college counselors kept them focused on higher education by ensuring they were well informed about the college process:

They're always on top of us. They never left us alone. During the year, they're really on top of us, coming in classes and telling us about dates and like what needs to be done and they wouldn't get off your back about college. They just did a great job.

On the contrary, Latinos generally expressed that school staff were pessimistic about their academic potential and reported often being discouraged from attending competitive colleges. For Latinos, it was not easy communicating to school staff higher aspirations than those established by negative racial stereotypes, and students often found themselves debating with school staff about their intellectual credibility. A Latina student recounted a confrontation with an administrator concerning her academic potential and ambitions:

He was saying to me that I should have taken not a college prep course but a prep course for a class I wanted to take, other than a class I needed to go to college. For like 45 minutes, we were having the argument, and he was saying that I wasn't going to go to college, and it was basically based on my race, that since I was a Latina, I wasn't going to be able to succeed in college.

Although Latinos generally perceived marginal support from general school staff, they did find refuge in the AVID program. AVID was seen as a positive learning space where Latino students were expected to have high academic goals, encouraged to attend 4-year universities, and validated in their potential for college success:

I've gotten the support through the AVID program in the school. It's a group of students who are first-generation and going to college. AVID gives us the support that maybe our parents don't know exactly how to because they haven't gone to college. Knowing that [in AVID] there are other people in the same place as you is very supportive. My AVID teacher has been very amazing. Because of him, he's actually opened the doorway for me to think about getting my master's and also my Ph.D.

Similarly, a Latina female reported AVID helped her consider the possibility of attending a 4-year institution rather than a community college:

I was encouraged [by the school counselor] to attend a community college because we lived right across the street from it. Everyone that lives around us would go there or drop out to work. So I always had the mentality that I would go to a community college. But it was through AVID that it really hit me that there are other colleges than community college. Four-year colleges are competitive and you have to challenge yourself. Through AVID, I saw that UCLA is an opportunity other than community college.

Latinos also reported school staff were not as forthcoming with college information and they were relatively unaware of the various college resources available at Cove High. This lack of information directly impacted their understanding of the college process. However, Latinos again turned to AVID for support and guidance. In many cases, Latinos commented that AVID was the catalyst for gearing them toward a 4-year college. One Latino student found himself understanding the college process only through the AVID program:

If it weren't for AVID, we honestly wouldn't know anything about our PSATs. We wouldn't be having the goals we have now, you know, to shoot higher than community college. You know, to actually try and do good on our SATs. I know that if it weren't for AVID, I wouldn't have been taking the SATs. I would have probably been like, what's that, you know.

College Readiness and Access

The college preparation process of white students was vastly different than that for Latino students. Whites were predominately enrolled in AP and/or honors courses and reported having open access to high school counselors and college information:

It just depends on how many times you want to go in there [counseling center]. It's a center and you go, you write in your name and they'll call you out of class within like those couple of days and they'll come talk to you. So if you need to go to talk to them every couple days or every week, you just sign your name and they'll call you out. Some people don't ever use that as a resource and it is a really good resource.

Students reported college information was readily available to anyone who simply was proactive in their inquiry:

Well, there really isn't a place . . . not that I know of that you can just go to and find out everything about college. But as long as you talk to people, you'll find out enough information. You've always got the Internet. And you can access it through the school or at home. You can find out anything you want to know.

Furthermore, white students insisted race played no role in access to college and that counselors and teachers were willing and supportive of all students. One white male tried to explain how school staff do not make hasty judgments based on race:

I think a bigger part [of getting help] is the impression you give people. I know plenty of white people who are not that smart and they don't have to be in order to be encouraged to go to college or whatever. But I mean, when you meet someone and the first impression you give him or her when you start talking is that you are smart, they would see how intelligent you are and like right away, they would encourage you. They'd say something like, "You're smart and you should be this and that."

White students were also relatively unaware of personal or circumstantial obstacles involved in college access. In fact, their experiences with school agents were so positive that they were convinced all students had the same opportunities to improve their preparation for college:

Mr. Yoler [teacher], for example, really pushed me to be my best. That helped me get into college because I definitely did better than I would have otherwise. And I think he does that for all students.

Although the majority of white students did not acknowledge race as a factor in college preparation, one white male did state he was encouraged to excel academically because of his race: "I found I have more encouragement because of my race. I'm pushed to strive harder and to succeed in life. I'm expected to be a guide for others of the same race as me to strive to do well."

On the other hand, Latino students explained they had witnessed or personally experienced numerous racial barriers to access. Many of these students framed their exclusion in the context of college-preparatory AP classes. One Latino student discussed how a teacher shared that more AP classes could not be offered because this would require the school to racially integrate advanced courses and "Their parents don't want that. They really don't want the integration with colored students 'cause it will bring down their child's level of education. And that shocked me." Another student gave his account of a counselor who discouraged him from enrolling in AP classes and going into a 4-year university simply because he was Latino:

> But I think all of us can agree that even teachers and counselors are kind of biased to certain kids. Even if they see you have like a 3.0 and taking all AP classes, they still encourage you to go to community college. If you're a student of color and you want to take an honors or AP course, they always have an excuse not to let you in even though at this school, you can waive into the AP class. I personally feel that this school is not fair or equal with the access they're giving students. And I think that's because of the tracking system. But I still feel that counselors are kind of biased towards students of color. And they always just judge you beforehand.

Latino students reported that because school agents had lower expectations of them compared to their white counterparts, it created a hostile learning environment for students of color. Many minorities in AP classes felt a sense of isolation as a result of the social divisions between them and their white peers:

> And it's like all the white people in those AP classes, they all know each other. They're friends and take all these classes together. They know how to work around the system and work with the teachers. They make it work for them. So they have better benefits like higher grades.

One Latina commented that AP classes had a distinctive atmosphere that was uncomfortable for minorities:

> The thing at this school is that we have what we call a two-school phenomenon. Basically, you have people who are in AP courses and people who are not. If you walk into a class, you can basically tell the differences between the two classes. You can tell if you're in an AP class or a regular class. When you walk into the AP classes, you can feel the vibes. You can feel that sometimes people just look at you like you're not supposed to be in there. You know, "How did you get in this class?" And it's intimidating. There's probably two or three Latinos. There's no African Americans. And the rest are Asians and Caucasians.

Another Latino student expressed that it was the system, not the teachers, that was responsible for the clear division among whites and minorities:

> I think that teachers try to be supportive and understand students. But the system has structured these other kids, the privileged kids, to make them feel like they have power, and they can speak

over everyone in the class. So, most of the time, when one of us tries to say something, you know, the other kids try to speak over us or make us feel stupid. And the teacher doesn't like really calling them out. So the students of color in those AP classes have no support. Even if the teacher says that he is supporting you, you don't really feel the support because of those students. And I don't blame him. That's just how the system has worked for them. And that's why us students that want to go to class and succeed, we can't really succeed because of how the class is structured.

DISCUSSIONS AND CONCLUSIONS

In his work on social capital, Stanton-Salazar (1997) talked about the inconsistent and often contradictory role fulfilled by school agents such as counselors. Stanton-Salazar suggested that while school agents have the potential to act as important sources of information and support, they can also act as gatekeepers and controllers of scarce resources. Moreover, he argued that when school agents act as gatekeepers of information, there exists a "practice of shifting institutional support toward high performers" (Stanton-Salazar, 1997, p. 18). Ultimately, what results from such practices is the alienation of those students in most need of institutional support from school agents who are in the position to provide such support. The experiences of Latino and white students at Cove High School provide evidence of the dual functionality of institutional agents Stanton-Salazar describes.

Indeed, our study has shown college information and opportunities for college readiness are experienced and accessed vastly differently by Latino and white students at Cove High School. For instance, our findings suggest that, generally, white students held a positive perception of the school culture with regard to accessibility of counselors and college preparatory courses. In contrast, Latino students consistently indicated that access to these same types of courses was often restricted or discouraged by school officials. In fact, Latino students were explicit about the role race played in restricting and hampering their access to and interactions with school agents. White students, on the other hand, felt race was a nonfactor in accessing college information and felt all students, if proactive, had an equal opportunity to interact productively and positively with counselors and other school agents.

Research tells us most students who plan to apply to college normally rely on high school counselors for college guidance (Bemark & Chung, 2005; Blumberg et al., 2004). Yet the findings from this study suggest that for Latino students, counselors assumed a gatekeeping role not only to the types of courses that would support a college pathway but also to information about different aspects of the college choice process. The fact that college counseling was not evenly distributed to all students by Cove High School counselors meant access to college guidance and information did not exist equally for all students despite the perception among white students. The negative ramifications for student success are clear when the learning environment within a school and the opportunities it confers to its students are not democratic.

For many first-generation Latino students, the networks of individuals that exist within the school setting are usually the primary sources of college information. Research on the college choice process of Latino students has found that for many of these students, access to college knowledge and information may not always be readily available at home, therefore making their interactions with school agents much more crucial (Ceja, 2006; Gonzalez et al., 2003). In contrast, for many white students, access to college information and opportunities at school usually supplements the knowledge base these students are able to access at home. Fortunately for the Latino students in this study, the presence of the AVID program helped expand the pool of institutional agents they were able to access for college information. In fact time and time again, Latino students indicated the importance of the AVID program with respect to developing college aspirations, expanding the pool of colleges they were considering attending, and providing information on college requirements and qualifications.

The experience of Latino students at Cove High School compared to their white peers forces us to engage the following questions: How does the campus climate of high schools enrolling diverse students become a racialized environment that marginalizes students of color? How does the campus racial climate shape the learning experiences and educational opportunities of students of color? These two questions take on a greater significance given the fact that Latinos, more than any other ethnic/racial group, have experienced increasing segregation in public education enrollment (Frankenberg & Lee, 2002), resulting in a less diverse learning environment. Indeed, students of color and low-income students continue to experience substandard educational opportunities throughout our nation's schools. The findings from this study suggest that if left alone, the racialized learning environments of our schools will continue to benefit certain students at the expense of others. As researchers, practitioners, and policymakers, we must reaffirm our commitment to equity in educational opportunities for all students. Not doing so will have negative implications for our schools and society at large.

REFERENCES

Allen, W. R., Kimura-Walsh, E., & Griffin, K. (2009). *Towards a brighter tomorrow: College barriers, hopes and plans of black, Latino/a, and Asian American students in California*. Charlotte, NC: Information Age Publishing.

Bateman, M., & Hossler, D. (1996). Exploring the development of postsecondary education plans among African American and white students. *College and University, 72*(1), 2–9.

Bemark, F., & Chung, R. (2005). Advocacy as a critical role for urban school counselors: Working towards equity and social justice. *Professional School Counseling, 8*(3), 196.

Blumberg, C. Z., Venegas, K. M., Oliverez, P. M., & Colyar, J. E. (2004). School counsel: How appropriate guidance affects educational equity. *Urban Education, 39*(4), 442–457.

California Postsecondary Education Commission. (2002). *University eligibility study for the class of 2001*. Sacramento: State of California.

Carpenter, P. G., & Fleishman, J. A. (1987). Linking intentions and behavior: Australian students' college plans and college attendance. *American Educational Research Journal, 24*(1), 79–105.

Carter, P. (2004). Beyond ascription: Racial identity, culture, schools, and academic achievement. *DuBois Review, 1*, 377–388.

Ceja, M. (2004). Chicana college aspirations and the role of parents: Developing educational resiliency. *Journal of Hispanic Higher Education, 3*(4), 1–25.

Ceja, M. (2006). Understanding the role of parents and siblings as information sources in the college choice process of Chicana students. *Journal of College Student Development, 47*(1), 87–104.

Chapman, D. W. (1981). A model of student college choice. *Journal of Higher Education, 52*, 490–505.

Coleman, J. S. (1988). Social capital in the creation of human capital. *American Journal of Sociology, 94*(Supplement), 95–120.

Cooper, C. R., Jackson, J. F., Azmitia, M., & Lopez, E. M. (1998). Multiple selves, multiple worlds: Three useful strategies for research with ethnic minority youth on identity, relationships, and opportunity structures. In V. C. McLoyd & L. Steinberg (Eds.), *Studying minority adolescents: Conceptual, methodological, and theoretical issues* (pp. 111–125). Mahwah, NJ: Lawrence Erlbaum Associates.

Frankenberg, E., & Lee, C. (2002). *Race in American public schools: Rapidly resegregating school districts*. Cambridge, MA: The Civil Rights Project, Harvard University.

Fordham, S., & Ogbu, J. U. (1986). Black students' school success: Coping with the "burden of acting white." *Urban Review, 18*(3), 176–206.

Gándara, P. (2002). A study of high school Puente: What we have learned about preparing Latino youth for postsecondary education. *Educational Policy, 16*(4), 474–495.

Gonzalez, K. P., Stoner, C., & Jovel, J. (2003). Examining the role of social capital in access to college for Latinas: Toward a college opportunity framework. *Journal of Hispanic Higher Education, 2*, 146–170.

Haycock, K. (2001). Closing the achievement gap. *Educational Leadership, 58*(6), 6–11.

Hoover-Dempsey, K. V., & Sandler, H. M. (1997). Why do parents become involved in their children's education? *Review of Education Research, 67*(1), 3–42.

Hossler, D., Braxton, J., & Coopersmith, G. (1989). Understanding student college choice. In J. C. Smart (Ed.), *Higher education: Handbook of theory and research* (pp. 231–288). New York, NY: Agathon Press.

Hossler, D., & Gallagher, K. S. (1987). Studying student college choice. A three phase model and the implications for policy makers. *College and University, 2*(3), 207–221.

Hossler, D., Schmit, J. S., & Vesper, N. (Eds.). (1999). *Going to college: How social, economic, and educational factors influence the decisions students make.* Baltimore, MD: Johns Hopkins University Press.

Karabel, J., & Astin, A. W. (1975). Social class, academic ability, and college quality. *Social Forces, 53*(3), 381–398.

Lareau, A., & Shumar, W. (1996). The problem of individualism in family-school polices. *Sociology of Education, 69*, 24–39.

Litten, L. H. (1982). Different strokes in the applicant pool: Some refinements in a model of student college choice. *Journal of Higher Education, 53*(4), 383–402.

McDonough, P. (1994). Buying and selling higher education: The social construction of the college applicant. *Journal of Higher Education, 65*(4), 427–446.

McDonough, P., Perez, L., Fann, A., Tobolowsky, B., Smith, M., Teranishi, R., et al. (2000). *Parent involvement program in education: Best research and practices.* Los Angeles: University of California, Los Angeles, GEAR-UP State Support Systems for Families Implementation Committee.

Phelan, P., Davidson, A. L., & Yu, H. C. (1991). Students' multiple worlds: Navigating the borders of family, peer, and school cultures. In P. Phelan & A. L. Davidson (Eds.), *Cultural diversity: Implications for education* (pp. 52–88). New York, NY: Teachers' College Press.

Plank, S. B., & Jordan, W. J. (2001). Effects of information, guidance, and actions on postsecondary destinations: A study of talent loss. *American Educational Research Journal, 38*(4), 947–980.

Ready, D. D., Lee, V. E., & Welner, K. G. (2004). Educational equity and school structure: School size, overcrowding, and schools-within-schools. *Teachers College Record, 106*(10), 1989–2014.

Robelen, E. W. (2002). Taking on the achievement gap. Retrieved July 26, 2004, from http://www.ncrel.org/gap/takeon/toc.htm

Saunders, M., & Serna, I. (2004). Making college happen: The college experiences of first-generation Latino students. *Journal of Hispanic Higher Education, 3*(2), 146–163.

Stanton-Salazar, R. D. (1997). A social capital framework for understanding the socialization of racial minority children and youths. *Harvard Educational Review, 67*, 1-40.

Stanton-Salazar, R. D. (2004). *Manufacturing hope and despair: The school and kin support networks of U.S.-Mexican youth.* New York, NY: Teachers College Press.

Yang, S. W. (1981, August). *Rural youth's decision to attend college: Aspirations and realizations.* Paper presented at the annual meeting of the Rural Sociological Society, Guelph, Ontario.

15

Taking Math and Science to Black Parents

Promises and Challenges of a Community-Based Intervention for Educational Change

Roslyn Arlin Mickelson, Linwood Cousins,
Anne Velasco, and Brian Williams

Race disparities in academic achievement remain intractable and perplexing puzzles facing educators, parents, and students. Such disparities across the curricula are not random; rather, they are the products of social processes involving educators (teachers, counselors, and administrators); parents; and students interacting with school structures, policies, and practices, all of which exist within the context of a social system that remains stratified by race and social class (Jencks & Phillips, 1998; Mickelson, 2003a). Curricular tracking is a striking example of a social process that contributes to racial and social class disparities in academic achievement.

The research described in this chapter examines attempts to address the black-white gap in mathematics and science in the Charlotte-Mecklenburg Schools (CMS). CMS constitutes an important set of sites to examine the gap because from 1971 through 2002 the district operated under court-ordered desegregation, a policy intended to close racial gaps in achievement. Although mathematics and science gaps have narrowed since 1971, they still exist. Mickelson (2001) established that a significant contributing factor to the gaps in CMS has been curricular tracking in secondary schools. She also found that black students were more likely than their comparably able white counterparts to be in lower academic tracks and less advanced classes.

This chapter presents the origins, theoretical frameworks, organization and design, and general findings from the Math/Science Equity Program (MSEP), an intervention intended to reduce racial disparities in students' math and science achievement.[1] MSEP was built around community workshops designed to enhance the involvement of black parents in their adolescent children's mathematics and science course placement and academic track. The underlying logic of the intervention links greater parental knowledge about the operations of the school system, parents' educational rights, mathematics and science concepts, and the course selection process to greater parental involvement. Informed, assertive black parents are expected to push their children to enroll in more rigorous science and mathematics classes, which will help close the achievement gap as enrollments of black students in these courses increase. Figure 15.1 presents a schematic diagram of MSEP's logic model.

CMS's black/white race gap in mathematics and science is far from unique. Results from the National Assessment of Education Progress (NAEP) indicate that test scores have been increasing for all American students, but gains in NAEP scores have not closed the race gaps

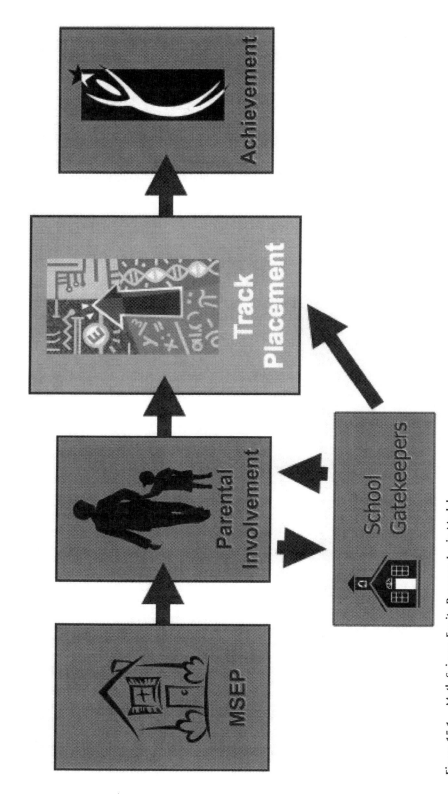

Figure 15.1. Math Science Equity Program Logic Model

in either mathematics or science achievement (Lee, Grigg, & Dion, 2005, 2007; National Research Council, 1999). While overall scores indicate some narrowing of the 25-point gap found in 1978, at higher skill levels blacks are not catching up with whites, because both groups' scores are rising similarly. During the last 15 years or so, the rate at which the gap is closing has slowed (Hedges & Nowell, 1995; Jencks & Phillips, 1998), and in some grades, it has halted (Magnuson & Waldfogel, 2008). The gap is especially problematic in mathematics and science achievement (Lee et al., 2005, 2007).

Scholars investigating the sources of the gaps have identified a host of likely contributing factors (Jencks & Phillips, 1998; Mickelson, 2001, 2003b; Thompson & O'Quinn, 2001), including teacher quality and instructional styles (Ingersoll, 1999); class size (Molnar, 2001); curricula, tracking, and grouping practices (Lucas, 1999; Oakes, Muir, & Joseph, 2000); segregation and desegregation (Mickelson, 2001); and family background factors (Coleman et al., 1966; DuBois cited in Gordon, 2001; Suter, 2000). Family background factors include the influences of parental cultural, social, and human capital resources (Baker & Stevenson, 1986; Bourdieu & Passeron, 1977; Gordon, 2001; Lareau, 2003; Muller, 1998) and parental involvement in children's education both in and out of school (Epstein, 1995, 2002; Lareau, 2003).

National race gap patterns are similar to those found in North Carolina and CMS. Independent reports on the race gap in North Carolina show that despite decades of high-profile school reforms (Clotfelter, Ladd, & Vigdor, 2009; Darity, Castellino, & Tyson, 2001), serious race gaps in top-level class enrollment remain across grades and subject areas in CMS. The failure to eliminate these gaps is the result of many factors, including the uneven implementation of various reform initiatives attempted since 1992 (Smith & Mickelson, 2000), and the general inability of whole-school systemic reforms to generate fundamental shifts in race and class inequities in achievement and attainment (Berends, 2005).

MSEP's reforms focused on parental involvement because it intersects with the social organization of schooling, specifically tracking, and how tracking affects the race gap in math and science achievement. In this chapter, we describe MSEP and examine the program's accomplishments and struggles. After a brief review of the literature that informed MSEP's development, we present the background for MSEP and describe the program in detail. We present the program's organizational structure, the research design of the study, and findings. We conclude by drawing implications for future research, policy, and practice.

RELATIONSHIP OF TRACKING AND PARENTAL INVOLVEMENT TO RACIAL INEQUALITY IN EDUCATIONAL PROCESSES AND OUTCOMES

Because of the pervasive practice of curricular differentiation (tracking and ability grouping), students are sorted into educational trajectories soon after they enter school (Kornhaber, 1997; Lucas, 1999; Oakes, 2005). As early as elementary school, children are placed into ability groups for instruction. The process of identifying students for placement in gifted and special educational programs also begins at this time (Eitle, 2002; Kornhaber, 1997). Ideally, tracks or ability groups match students' abilities with differentiated curricula and instruction (Hallinan, 1992; Kulik & Kulik, 1987; Loveless, 1999). Within any given track, however, students have a wide range of student abilities. Teachers often recommend placing students in particular ability groups based on their perceptions about each student's potential ability, a perception that may be influenced by stereotypes, teacher beliefs about different racial and class groups, or racist ideologies (Mickelson, 2001, 2003b; Oakes et al., 2000; Welner, 2001).

Once students are identified and placed into any program, ability group, or level—whether gifted, regular, or special education—the instruction, curricula, and content to which they are exposed begin to differ. Compared to their peers in lower tracks, students in higher tracks tend to cover more of the formal curriculum each semester, are exposed to more challenging curricula, and are taught in ways that encourage more higher-order thinking. As students proceed along a given educational trajectory, the effects of the previous years' differentiated curriculum influence their transitions to subsequent courses and schools. The cumulative effects of these differences result in varying educational experiences over the course of students' educational careers and differential access to opportunities after they complete their schooling (Kornhaber, 1997; Oakes, 2005). Tracking tends to reinforce the learning problems of educationally disadvantaged students: These students are provided with less effective instructors, who use teaching methods least likely to challenge children to learn (Finley, 1984; Ingersoll, 1999; Loveless, 1999; Lucas, 1999; Mickelson, 2001; Oakes, 2005).

The relationship of tracking to racial equality in education often is discussed in terms of first- and second-generation segregation (Meier, Stewart, & England, 1989; Wells & Crain, 1994). First-generation segregation refers to racial segregation among schools within a school district and has been the focus of national reform efforts since *Brown v. Board of Education* (1954). Second-generation segregation refers to the racially correlated allocation of educational opportunities within schools, typically caused by curricular grouping or tracking of core academic classes in English, mathematics, social studies, and science. A growing body of research has suggested that tracking practices result in unjustifiable and disproportionate assignment of minority students to lower tracks and their relatively rare assignment to accelerated tracks; they offer them inferior opportunities to learn and are responsible, in part, for their lower achievement. In these ways, racially stratified tracks create a discriminatory cycle of restricted educational opportunities for minorities, irrespective of their academic abilities (Lucas, 1999; Lucas & Berends, 2002; Mickelson, 2001; Oakes 1990; Oakes et al., 2000; Welner, 2001).

Parental involvement is an important remedy to challenges associated with racially stratified tracking. Parental involvement refers to active participation in educational decision making, course selection, assisting and monitoring homework, or volunteering in the school. Such involvement is critically important if students are to excel in a rigorous college preparatory trajectory in secondary school (Baker & Stevenson, 1986; Catsambis, 1994; Epstein, 2002; Muller, 1998; Useem, 1992, Yonazawa, 1997). Race, ethnicity, and social class shape the likelihood and nature of parents' involvement in course selection. Research has indicated, for example, that middle-class parents are more likely to be involved in their children's education, both at home and in school, than lower-class parents (Chazen, 2000; Epstein, 2002; Lareau, 1987; Moses & Cobb, 2001; Yonazawa, 1997).

Perhaps one reason that even the best school reforms typically do not eliminate the association between social origins and school outcomes is that they do not affect the way family background influences school outcomes. Results from the Third International Mathematics and Science Study (TIMMS) confirm a persistent association between family background and mathematics and science achievement (Schiller, 2000; Schmidt et al., 1997; Suter, 2000). A host of studies has shown that parental involvement in the course selection and placement process is one key avenue through which differences in family background (socioeconomic status and culture) operate (Epstein, 2002; Ho & Willms, 1996; Lareau, 1987, 2003). Parents of color and working-class parents are less likely than white and middle-class parents to have access to the official information, informal social networks, and lived experiences needed to guide their children's educational choices. MSEP sought to address these differences among parents by enhancing their extant knowledge and networks with new information and additional skills.

BACKGROUND OF THE MATH/SCIENCE EQUITY PROGRAM (MSEP)

MSEP was located on the campus of the University of North Carolina at Charlotte. Charlotte is known for its landmark *Swann v. Charlotte-Mecklenburg Schools* (1971) decision, in which the Supreme Court upheld the use of within-district mandatory busing as a remedy for segregated schooling. For almost 30 years, CMS was regarded as a model of how a school system could provide seemingly equitable, high-quality, desegregated public education through busing and other means. While CMS was successfully desegregating at the building level (responding to first-generation segregation), systematic tracking of academic classes re-segregated students within schools (second-generation segregation). During the 1998–1999 school year, for example, 54.5 percent of whites compared to 20.7 percent of blacks completed at least one Advanced Placement (AP) or International Baccalaureate (IB) course, producing a 33.8 percent race gap in highest-level track enrollments. In the 2000–2001 school year, 59.4 percent of whites but only 24.4 percent of blacks completed at least one AP or IB course. Thus, although more black students enrolled in top courses, so did more whites, and the race gap grew to 35 percent.[2]

Previous survey research on CMS (Mickelson, 2001, 2003a) indicated that while CMS was desegregating its schools from 1975 to 1992, within the schools students were resegregating. Racially correlated tracking in almost all secondary-school core academic classes resegregated students irrespective of the school's overall racial composition. Figures 15.2 and 15.3 show the race differences in the probabilities of English course enrollment among CMS students in the four tracks, even after controlling for prior achievement. The figures demonstrate how

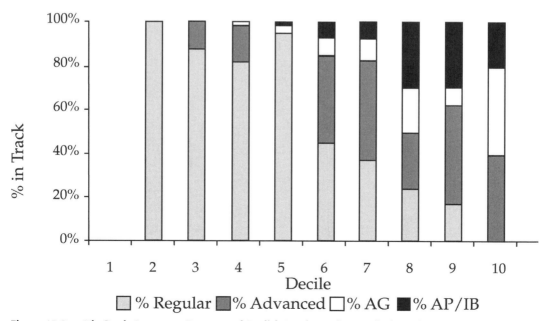

Figure 15.2.   6th Grade Language Battery and English Track Grade 12: Black Students

comparably able blacks and whites were in very different tracks, with whites more likely to be assigned to top tracks and blacks more likely to be assigned to lower tracks. Given the strong relationships between (a) exposure to rigorous curricula and achievement, and (b) higher track placement and opportunities to learn rigorous curricula, the racially correlated gap in mathematics and science course placement contributes to the racial gaps in mathematics and science preparation.

Three years prior to the beginning of the MSEP project, Mickelson and Velasco (2006) conducted approximately 140 in-depth interviews with black and white adolescents, their parents, counselors, teachers, and school administrators in order to identify the underlying reasons for the race gap in higher-level course enrollments. Using a combination of snowball and purposive sampling strategies, the researchers obtained a sample of respondents who could illuminate how race and social class differences in family, school, and peer dynamics undergird the course selection and placement processes.

Despite the limitations of the self-selected sample, the interviews offered important insights into the dynamics of course selection, indicating that students, parents, and educators (counselors and teachers) all participated in this process. Interviews with parents confirmed prior research findings demonstrating that middle-class parents—irrespective of their ethnic background—tend to have knowledge, networks, and interpersonal skill sets useful for managing their children's educational careers.[3] Interviews with counselors, teachers, and administrators confirmed that working-class and ethnic-minority parents were less likely to be involved in the course selection process than their middle-class or white counterparts.

In addition to earlier research on CMS, prior research on black family dynamics and education provided a foundation for MSEP. Cousins's research on black communities and education has focused on identifying sociocultural norms and practices that influence the interactions of African Americans in such mainstream institutions as schools and social service agencies (Cousins, 1997, 1998, 1999, 2001, 2008; Cousins et al., 2004). Cousins's recent

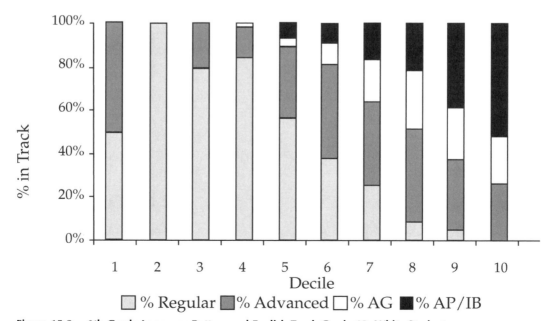

Figure 15.3.   6th Grade Language Battery and English Track Grade 12: White Students

work with Mickelson, Williams, and Velasco (2008) has identified principles and practices for developing effective community-based partnerships between parents and schools to increase parental participation in the schooling of black students.

Combining his work with other scholarship on community organizing and development (Fisher, 1994; Fisher & Karger, 1997; Gutiérrez, 1997; McKnight, 1995; Rivera & Erlich, 1995), Cousins concluded:

1. School reform efforts must transcend community development barriers that limit meaningful and effective parental and community participation.
2. Program planning and change activities must include parents' and community members' cultural beliefs, values, and perceptions about the source of problems and their solutions.
3. Racial and cultural uniqueness should be used as an organizing strategy in the community.
4. School reform efforts must respect African American culture by beginning with a focus on the interests of the community and an understanding of the complexity of group identity for African Americans.
5. Reform organizers must challenge the mistrust of outside "professional mainstream helpers" who are perceived as selfishly "using" (read: "abusing") African American communities by attempting to develop a base of community resources and services beyond the life of a project.

Adding to what Cousins asserts as an empirical foundation of MSEP is Williams's (2003) research on community factors associated with academic success in mathematics and science among black youth. Williams found that family support and encouragement were significant factors in the achievement of students of color in science, engineering, and mathematics (also see Garrison, 1987; Harper, 1989; Hilton, Hsia, Solorzano, & Benton, 1989; Huang, Taddese, Walter, & Peng, 2000; Levine & Nidiffer, 1996; Maton, Hrabowski, & Schnitt, 2000; Yonazawa, 1997). More than teachers or counselors, members of the students' families mediated their early experiences in science, engineering, and mathematics. These family members continued to support students as they moved through the science, engineering, and mathematics pipeline.

Some parents delegate complete authority to school officials to direct the trajectories of their children's careers, because they do not know how to support their children's interest in science, engineering, or mathematics. Williams's (2003) study suggests, however, that school officials often obstruct these trajectories through tracking. To address this problem, researchers hypothesized that parents educated to act as advocates for their children, particularly in their mathematics and science education, would lead to higher enrollments in college preparatory math and science courses compared to youths whose parents did not participate in MSEP workshops.

In response to the results from the North Carolina interviews, their own prior research, and the scholarly literature in the field, MSEP leadership team[4] reasoned that if black parents could enhance their knowledge and networks with the kinds of valuable formal and informal information networks, and official knowledge that many middle-class white families share, then black parents could manage their children's educational careers more successfully and more black adolescents would enroll in and complete higher-level mathematics and science courses. Drawing upon Williams's expertise as a mathematics and science educator, MSEP's leadership team designed community-based parent enrichment workshops to enhance and strengthen black parents' social, cultural, and human capital regarding their adolescent children's academic course selection and placements. MSEP's workshops empowered parents to be assertive, knowledgeable advocates on behalf of their children's educational careers; specifically, parents learned to advocate for their children, so that their academically able sons and daughters could enroll in higher track courses in mathematics and science.

MSEP'S HOME WORKSHOPS AND TEEN SUMMITS

MSEP presented two versions of its program. The first version, the HOME Workshop (Helping Ourselves Mold Education) consisted of 2-hour meetings held on six consecutive Monday, Wednesday, or Thursday evenings. The second version, the Teen Summit, delivered the parent enrichment curriculum in 4-hour sessions held on two consecutive Saturdays. The HOME Workshops and Teen Summits were conducted in both community venues (e.g., churches, recreation centers, and libraries) and on the university campus. One of the Teen Summits was held on a CMS middle school campus.

Variations in formats and sites were introduced in an effort to adapt to the needs of the parents expected to attend the workshops. Each variation represents MSEP's struggle to maintain a delicate balance between the time required for the workshops to be effective and the time parents could practically afford to sacrifice from their busy schedules. Early in the program's implementation, MSEP coordinators realized that many parents would find it difficult to commit to the extensive, 6-week (12-hour) HOME workshop schedule. To address this limitation, MSEP distilled the most pertinent information from the original HOME version into one workshop of 5 hours and 30 minutes, the Teen Summit.

The day-long Teen Summit also represented MSEP's first attempt to connect with parents specifically through their children, because teens who wished to attend the Teen Summit needed a parent to attend the workshops. A two-session version of Teen Summit was a compromise between the 6-week HOME workshops and the 1-day Teen Summit. The 2-day version was designed to reduce the time commitment required of parents and their children, while providing enough time for critical discussions of core topics. Evaluations of this version of Teen Summit indicated that parents retained more of the information than they did with the 1-day workshop. During the 2 years of workshop implementation, MSEP conducted three 6-week (2 hours each week) HOME workshops, a one-session (5.5-hour) Teen Summit, and four two-session (4-hour) Teen Summits.

The parent enrichment curriculum presented at both the 6-week HOME and the 1- and 2-week Teen Summits consisted of the following:

1. Information about mathematics and science courses and their value in a student's educational career.
2. Hands-on mathematics and science experiences in four of the six gateway courses (algebra, geometry, physics, biology, earth science, and chemistry).
3. Curricular tracking, Courses of Study,[5] and parental involvement in the related decision-making processes.
4. Parental educational rights, including North Carolina's constitutional guarantee for a sound basic education for all children.
5. Strategies for effective parent-educator communications, including the difference between assertive and aggressive communication.

6. Strategies for effective parent-child communications.
7. Networking skills building on existing parental and community networks.

Both the HOME workshops and Teen Summits were designed to be convenient and flexible for parents. Consequently, all participants and their children were provided with lunch or dinner, as well as transportation to and from the workshop if needed. A set of youth workshops (one for students in Grades K–6 and another for students in Grades 7–12) was designed to run concurrently with each parent workshop. The youth workshops focused on developing valuable life skills (i.e., goal setting and college planning), introduced students to topics in mathematics and science through engaging and culturally relevant experiences, and provided students with opportunities to discuss subjects pertinent to their lives (i.e., hip hop music's influence on youth).

In addition to the workshops, MSEP employed other strategies to remain connected to parents and provide them with additional resources that would reinforce the initial workshop dynamics. A program newsletter, Letters from HOME, was mailed to parents, schools, and community members every two months. The newsletter included articles of specific interest to parents of children in CMS, accessible articles about mathematics and science topics, educational resources in the Charlotte-Mecklenburg community, updates on mathematics- and science-related events geared to families in the Charlotte area, and information about this program. MSEP also established a website (http://www.msep.uncc.edu, which remains an archive of the project), where the newsletters were posted, along with extensive information about MSEP and links to other mathematics and science educational sites.

During the last year of the program's implementation, MSEP hosted a program reunion/holiday celebration to provide every workshop participant, community member, school official, and MSEP program organizer with an opportunity to network with the others. The final parent/community event sponsored by MSEP was an event called "Special Edition," to remind parents of the course selection advice they had received in their original HOME workshops or Teen Summit. Special Edition was scheduled strategically by MSEP before parents were to guide their children's course selection for the following school year. This event offered parents who had completed either a Teen Summit or a HOME workshop an opportunity to revisit key topics and reconnect with other parents from throughout the Charlotte-Mecklenburg community.

MSEP ORGANIZATIONAL STRUCTURE

The program team was highly diverse in terms of discipline (sociology, anthropology, social work, and education), gender, and ethnicity. Between 2002 and 2005, approximately 17 graduate and undergraduate students were trained as researchers and supported by the program: five black males, five black females, two white males, four white females, and one Indian female served as student research assistants for the program. There was a conscious effort to create a diverse team that would reflect the diversity of the community MSEP served.

Community Advisory Council (CAC)

The CAC, composed of community activists, parents, and educators from the neighborhoods feeding into the three treatment-site high schools, gave feedback to the leadership team regarding the direction and content of the workshops.

Academic Advisory Board (AAB)

Several scholars with specific expertise relevant to the program served on an AAB. The AAB met in January 2003 and in December 2004. Each one-and-a-half-day meeting presented members with updates on the program's activities, success, and challenges. The AAB offered guidance relative to overcoming the challenges and better meeting the goals and objectives of the program.

Workshop Staff

MSEP hired several CMS educators and community members as consultants when the program staff's expertise was inadequate. For example, MSEP used the expertise of a high school counselor to develop and teach the course selection and placement curriculum. A CMS physics teacher instructed adolescents in the physics of music during the Teen Summits, and an attorney with expertise in North Carolina educational rights developed the parents' rights curriculum.

RESEARCH DESIGN, METHODS, AND DATA

MSEP was a National Science Foundation–funded research project, designed as a quasi-experiment involving three sets of matched CMS high schools. One school in each set served as the treatment site, while the other school in the pair served as the control site. Parents of academically able black students in the three treatment high schools were eligible to attend the enrichment program. MSEP staff recruited parents using outreach through churches, community organizations, and school personnel who identified appropriate families; still, parent participants were a self-selected group.

After its first year operating the parent enhancement workshops, MSEP held a 2-day AAB meeting. Based on the advisors' feedback, MSEP made three key refinements in the program's design:

1. It expanded the sampling frame to include parents of academically able students from 6th through 10th grade, not merely 9th- and 10th-grade high school students, as originally planned.
2. In addition to the three treatment high schools, MSEP also recruited in middle schools that feed into these high schools.
3. To address disappointing parent turnout at HOME workshops during April, May, and June 2004, MSEP leaders condensed the delivery of the workshop's core material as outlined previously. The shorter, renamed workshop incorporated the AAB's advice to appeal to parents' central concerns. The enrichment information offered to parents was basically the same; however, fewer activities on parent networking, parent-child communication skills, and hands-on mathematics and science for parents were provided to attendees. The change in format did not improve turnout. In the seven months of Teen Summits, an average of 10–15 parents participated in Day 1 of each Teen Summit, and about 7–10 returned for Day 2. The advantage of the 2-week format was that more parents cycled through the treatments in 2 weeks compared to 6 weeks.

Recruitment of parents proved to be one of the most difficult challenges that MSEP faced. Recruitment efforts were complicated by program requirements. Specifically, parents were required to have guardianship of a black student classified as academically able who was also enrolled in one of the three target high schools or a feeder middle school. Identifying the students and their parents required information about students not publicly available. Recruitment and outreach efforts included appearances at school Parent-Teacher Association (PTA) meetings, announcements in PTA newsletters, recruitment tables at school events, and a luncheon for school leadership and counseling staffs who, in turn, agreed to mail MSEP brochures to target parents. Program staff attended church services, community meetings, and other events that our target parents might attend. The most fruitful method of recruiting parents for the workshops, however, was an invitational letter sent to them by school counselors.[6] Counselors identified students who could perform better but did not take challenging classes, and then sent MSEP's invitation to their parents.[7]

Sample

From 2003 through 2005, 98 adults[8] (79 female, 19 male) attended at least one MSEP workshop. However, most of this discussion focuses on the 75 adults (61 female, 14 male) who *graduated* from HOME or Teen Summit. Graduation is defined as completing at least four sessions of the 6-week HOME program or both days of the Teen Summit. Approximately 65 children age 13 and over and 34 children age 12 and under participated in the youth programs offered by HOME and Teen Summit.

Data

MSEP collected qualitative and quantitative data throughout the program. The researchers took ethnographic notes during the workshop and community advisory council meetings. Student research assistants and the leadership team kept field journals. Parent participants completed a pretest; then after each workshop they completed a brief assessment of each component of the curriculum, and at the end of the final workshop session, participants completed a posttest so that the program team could assess whether individuals had met program objectives.

The research design originally proposed a Disparity Index as a key outcome variable. The Disparity Index calculates the percent of black students in higher-level mathematics and science courses as a proportion of the total enrollment of blacks in the school. MSEP expected the Disparity Index to narrow more sharply in treatment schools than in their matched control schools. Calculating the Disparity Index required course enrollment data by school, subject, and track level, disaggregated by race. However, the project leaders concluded that for a number of reasons, the Disparity Index most likely would not reveal that the workshops had any impact on the proportion of blacks enrolled in higher-level courses in treatment schools. One reason for this expectation was that fewer parents participated in MSEP workshops than anticipated. Another reason was the nontrivial amount of student mobility among the schools. For example, a student who attended a treatment middle school ended up not attending a treatment high school. Also, upon realizing the importance of getting their children in higher-level classes with quality instructors, some parents who attended the workshops decided to transfer their children to schools that they considered as having more of an "academic press" than their home schools, which were the actual treatment schools where the Disparity Index would have been calculated. Consequently, a number of MSEP families did not participate in the phase of the study that assessed the effects of the intervention. Finally, some attendees provided inaccurate school enrollment information so that they could participate in the program.[9] Thus, while these last two types of parental behavior may indicate a degree of success for MSEP, they obviously did not contribute to an increase in black students taking higher-level mathematics and science course at treatment schools.

Follow-up interviews with parent participants were conducted during the 2005–2006 academic year. MSEP staff interviewed parents who participated in the workshops. MSEP developed three interview protocols with varying amounts of detail. The research team collected only 23 follow-up interviews because of (a) the mobility of the participants—MSEP's contact information had become outdated and the staff of interviewers could not contact them; and (b) parents' burnout—parents who had been excited about the program immediately after the workshops seemed to lose interest by the time they were asked to participate in follow-up interviews.

FINDINGS

These MSEP findings present a mixed picture. Based on the pre- and posttests parent participants completed and field notes collected during the workshops, the research team concluded that the parent workshops tapped into a previously unmet need and filled it.[10] Parents' responses to the various assessments they completed indicated that they left the workshops more informed, motivated, and inspired to act on behalf of their children than when they began, and several expressed anger (or sorrow) that the school system had failed to inform them of critical information about tracking, Courses of Study, parent rights, and other topics they learned about at the workshops. Several parents—primarily women—expressed amazement and satisfaction that they had succeeded in the hands-on mathematics and science activities. Most parents who participated were dedicated to completing the HOME or Teen Summit series. One parent of several children worked full-time and was 7 months pregnant, yet completed a 6-week workshop. Several husband/wife couples also completed the workshops.

What began as child care and educational enrichment activities for participants' children became a parallel children's mathematics and science program with simultaneously implemented versions for elementary and secondary students. The student version of the mathematics and science workshop was a response to students' requests to do the same kinds of "fun" hands-on mathematics and science activities that their parents were doing. The children's program became so popular that some parents attended the workshops primarily because their children wanted to attend the children's program and could not do so unless their parent also attended. MSEP also midwifed a new parent leadership group, the PEP (Parents Empowering Parents) Squad. Drawing from the pool of graduates of HOME and Teen Summit, MSEP leaders identified parents who had expressed an interest in developing a community-based organization that would continue MSEP's work. Program leaders served as mentors, attended initial planning meetings, and made program resources available to PEP Squad members.

Previous experience and familiarity with research on community-based interventions convinced program leaders that they needed to develop a reputation as a trustworthy program before community groups and individuals would participate in the workshops. As a new, untested program, MSEP had little credibility when it was launched in the target communities. The leadership team sought to overcome its initial lack of credibility by partnering with other established agencies. Program leaders hoped that these other agencies would trust and value UNCC's reputation and that their support would encourage target parents' acceptance. However, MSEP found that having an association with a large research institution became a "double-edged sword." Gaining access to parents through existing community organizations was challenging because of the black community's occasional bitter memories of poor relations with previous university-based researchers. On numerous occasions, MSEP staff heard accounts of researchers riding in on the proverbial white horse, providing little of worth to the community, getting their data, and never being heard from again. Understandably, community members were unenthusiastic about committing to a new "solution" to their community's woes, with the thought that they would be exploited again for the sake of another outsider's research agenda. These views existed even though MSEP's leadership and team were visibly diverse in gender and ethnicity.[11]

At times, even if an existing agency or parent advocacy group valued what MSEP offered, there seemed to be "turf" conflicts. These organizations feared that MSEP might "steal" some of their clients, so they were reluctant to advertise and recruit for the program. Indeed, had MSEP "stolen" their clients, this would have been a great boon to the project because parent recruitment proved to be a difficult, labor-intensive, time-consuming, and ultimately less-than-satisfying endeavor. MSEP eventually found established agencies and parental support groups that were willing to support its efforts and further its mission.

Another unanticipated challenge that MSEP faced was dealing with a large school system's bureaucracy. Even though the leadership team obtained informal approval from the superintendent, key school board members, and various principals for their staff to assist the program, the leadership team occasionally experienced official obstacles. Administrators at certain schools were reluctant to participate even if members of their faculty and the central office approved the program. In addition, because of uncertain lines of communication between the central office and the "front lines," administrators and teachers who did not trust that they had permission to work with MSEP were hesitant to exercise their site-based prerogatives. Navigating these barriers drained MSEP staff's time and resources away from recruiting participants.

Sample attrition and corruption were major concerns for MSEP, and various incidents contributed to both. To adhere to the quasi-experimental design, parents from target schools received the workshops, and at the end of the treatment, MSEP expected to compare the Disparity Index of the experimental school with that of its "control." Ultimately, the Disparity Index was not calculated because it became clear to the research team that a program effect likely would not be found because of (a) low numbers of participants in the workshops, (b) sample corruption (participants' children did not actually attend treatment schools), and (c) sample attrition (parents who received the treatment left the study for new schools or new cities).

DISCUSSIONS AND CONCLUSIONS

Whether by design or unintended consequence, academic tracking and ability grouping result in children of color and lower income students learning in lower tracks compared to their white and middle-class peers. Because tracks and ability groups are integral organizational features of public education, such patterns of racially correlated access to opportunities to learn represent structural aspects of everyday racism in education. To the extent that greater parental involvement can increase the numbers of academically able blacks in higher tracks, educational racism can be reduced. Access to higher-level math and science is critical for students who must eventually enter the high-tech world of the information age.

Yet not all parents are equally equipped—in terms of experience, knowledge, willingness, and sense of empowerment—to engage effectively with school personnel on either course selection or placement processes. Prior research has indicated that certain parents—typically middle-class whites—are more likely to have negotiation skills, education, and network con-nections that mesh with school practices and policies. These parents utilize their assets in ways that contribute to middle-class white students disproportionately accessing top ability groups and tracks. Minority parents are more likely than middle-class white parents to defer to educators' decisions about their children's course placement. They do so because minor-ity parents often assume that educators' professional expertise trumps their own knowledge and experiences, and that they should not—or cannot—advocate a higher track placement for their children. Working-class parents of color—especially those with limited English-language proficiency—are the least likely of all parents to have the relevant knowledge, language skills, or sense of empowerment necessary to effectively become involved in school decisions or to question school personnel. Powerful, well-educated school administrators and teachers intimidate parents whose own educational experiences were unsatisfactory.

MSEP leadership reasoned that if black parents could enhance their knowledge and net-works with valuable informal and formal knowledge of schooling, they would be prepared to challenge practices that hamper their children academically—particularly in areas related to mathematics and science. As a result, more black adolescents would enroll in and complete advanced mathematics and science courses. In an effort to facilitate this behavior, MSEP de-signed and implemented a set of community-based parent workshops aimed at providing a space for black parents to better understand and develop the necessary social, cultural, and human capital, as well as the formal knowledge related to their children's education. MSEP's workshops attempted to empower parents to be assertive, knowledgeable advocates for their children's educational careers—specifically, by advocating that their sons and daughters en-roll in college preparatory tracks and advanced courses in mathematics and science.

MSEP's approach centered on parental workshops where participants received informa-tion about high school mathematics and science course sequences and their relationship to postsecondary education and professional careers. Parents also learned about their educational rights under the North Carolina constitution; they engaged in hands-on math-ematics and science activities, and participated in role-playing activities designed to equip them for effectively managing their children's educational careers. MSEP offered critical informational support about secondary course-tracking practices, strategies for effectively engaging school officials, and informal network supports to black CMS parents. For many black parents, MSEP's workshops leveled a very uneven playing field because workshops provided them with the information, networks, and negotiation skills they typically did not possess, but that many white, middle-class parents already had and often used to their children's advantage.

From 2002 through 2006,[12] MSEP offered parents, educators, and community activists a concrete intervention to eliminate racially correlated access to opportunities to learn in the Charlotte-Mecklenburg Schools. Despite the strengths and initial accomplishments of MSEP, it remains unclear as to what effects, if any, MSEP has had and will have on the core dilemma that prompted the program in the first place—the race gap in mathematics and science track placements.

Some critics might say that making tracking work better for minority students misses the point: Tracking hurts all students, while it fosters white, middle-class educational privilege by excluding many working-class and most students of color from rigorous college-prep classes. Therefore, tracking and ability grouping need to be eliminated, not made to oper-ate more fairly. Such arguments have merit. So long as tracking remains an almost univer-sal feature of schooling, MSEP's parent workshops hold the potential to be one valuable component of a larger effort to reform public education so that it operates more equitably while improving outcomes for all students. Findings suggest that MSEP offered parents information and strategies, and altered the balance of power in the school-home-community sphere for those who were involved. MSEP attempted to empower black parents to directly challenge racially disparate educational outcomes rooted in the race gaps in higher-level track enrollments. Although much remains to be done before the race gaps in science and mathematics are closed, MSEP's contribution was far from trivial, at least for the families in Charlotte, North Carolina, that participated in it.

NOTES

1. All descriptions of MSEP's organizational structure are presented later in this chapter.

2. In the late 1980s, the multiracial social and political coalitions sustaining desegregation in Charlotte began to weaken as more and more Northerners moved to Mecklenburg County. In 1997, a white suburban family sued CMS to end all race-based policies and practices, including desegregation. The lower court declared CMS unitary in 1999. The district appealed the ruling and, in the spring of 2002, the U.S. Supreme Court ultimately refused to review the unitary decision. Consequently, in the 2002–2003 school year, a newly unitary CMS began a neighborhood schools–based pupil assignment plan that has resulted in substantial resegregation of the district by race and social class.

3. The self-selected samples of parent and student interviewees were disproportionately middle-class, making it difficult to ascertain from the interviews how social class and race shaped parental involvement.

4. MSEP's leadership team consisted of the PIs (Cousins and Mickelson) who were university professors, a science educator postdoctoral fellow who served as project coordinator (Williams), the full-time program manager (Velasco), and several graduate students.

5. In 2000, the North Carolina Department of Public Instruction adopted a rigid four-track high school curriculum called Courses of Study (COS). Students entering ninth grade must choose one of four curricular pathways that determine the courses they take and strongly influence the post–high school direction they follow. These curricular pathways or Courses of Study are Career Preparation, College/Tech Prep, College/University Prep, and Occupations (for learning-disabled students). Although in principle a person may switch from one COS to another, in practice it is very difficult because graduation requirements within COS differ, and switching means a student is unlikely to meet the requirements of the new pathway without spending additional time in school (North Carolina Department of Public Instruction, 2000).

6. Relations with the CMS District constrained the program's design. Given the sensitive relationship between the researchers and CMS, the leadership team, Mickelson, Cousins, and Williams, met with most CMS board members and the new CMS superintendent during the summer and fall of 2003. They introduced MSEP not as a collaboration with CMS but as a university research initiative that paralleled CMS's own efforts to close the race gap in higher-level mathematics and science enrollment. They obtained oral support for MSEP's work from the superintendent and from several board members.

A member of the leadership team obtained the oral approval to recruit parents at CMS schools from the assistant superintendent for assessment. Her approval was important because any opposition from her office could make collaborating with individual schools more difficult. She subsequently withdrew her informal approval and requested that we apply for formal permission to conduct research in CMS because the use of any CMS personnel (to recruit parents, etc.) constituted grounds for requiring permission. In September 2004, MSEP received formal approval to use CMS school personnel to identify parents who might benefit from the workshops. However, MSEP delivered the final workshop in April 2005.

7. Track placement decisions involve teachers, counselors, students, and in many cases parents. A counselor may recommend a high-track placement but the student may decline in order to be with friends, avoid more challenging courses (sometimes because of a fear of failure), or avoid scheduling conflicts. Alternatively, because of stereotypes and low expectations, a counselor may not see a child as competitive for higher tracks.

8. Two female participant/graduates attended both a HOME workshop series and a Teen Summit.

9. Participants openly provided information about the inaccuracies during follow-up interviews after the workshops.

10. After the completion of MSEP, the Charlotte-Mecklenburg Schools instituted a program called Parent University. It sought to educate parents about many of the issues that MSEP covered. The researchers were not consulted by CMS Parent University's development or implementation.

11. Early in the process of gaining credibility with the community, an African American graduate assistant reported that some community activists expressed their concerns that the African American Co-PI and graduate students were agents only serving as camouflage for the actual leaders who were the white Co-PI and graduate students.

12. These dates cover the entire span of the MSEP project.

REFERENCES

Baker, D., & Stevenson, D. (1986). Mothers' strategies for children's school achievement: Managing the transition to high school. *Sociology of Education, 59*(3), 156–167.

Berends, M. (2005). An assessment of NASDC whole school reforms. In A. Wells, & J. Petrovich (Eds.), *Putting equity back in: School reform and educational equity* (pp. 83–99). New York, NY: Teachers College Press.

Bourdieu, P., & Passeron, J. (1977). *Reproduction in education, society, and culture.* Beverly Hills, CA: Sage.

Brown v. Board of Education. (1954). 347 U.S. 483.

Catsambis, S. (1994). The path to math: Gender and racial-ethnic differences in mathematics participation from middle school to high school. *Sociology of Education, 67,* 199–215.

Chazen, D. (2000). *Beyond formulas in mathematics and teaching: Dynamics of the high school algebra classroom.* New York, NY: Teachers College Press.

Clotfelter, C., Ladd, H. F., & Vigdor, J. L. (2009). *School segregation under color-blind jurisprudence: The case of North Carolina* (Working Paper Series, SAN08-02). Durham, NC: Duke University, Terry Sanford Institute of Public Policy.

Coleman, J., Campbell, E. Q., Hobson, C., McPartland, J., Mood, A., Weinfeld, F., et al. (1966). *Equality of educational opportunity.* Washington, DC: U.S. Government Printing Office.

Cousins, L. (1997). Toward a sociocultural context for understanding violence and disruption in black urban schools and communities. *Journal of Sociology & Social Welfare, 24*(2), 41–64.

Cousins, L. (1998). Partnerships for vitalizing communities and neighborhoods: Celebrating a "return!" *Journal of Sociology & Social Welfare, 25*(1), 61–69.

Cousins, L. (1999). Playing between classes: America's troubles with class, race and gender in a black high school & community. *Anthropology & Education Quarterly, 30*(3), 294–316.

Cousins, L. (2001). Moral markets for troubling youths: A disruption! *Childhood, 8*(2), 193–212.

Cousins, L. (2008). Black students' identity and "acting black and white." In J. U. Ogbu (Ed.), *Minority status, oppositional culture and schooling* (pp.167–189). New York, NY: Routledge.

Cousins, L., Mickelson, R., Williams, B., & Velasco, A. (2008). Class and race challenges to community collaboration for educational change. *School/Community Journal, 18*(2), 29–52.

Cousins, L., Todman, L., Hyter, Y., Fails-Nelson, R., Bee, A., Cooper, R., et al. (2004). Social and academic relationships in the lives of black children: Transdisciplinary research and practice. *Journal of Human Behavior in the Social Environment, 9*(3), 57–82.

Darity, W., Castellino, D., & Tyson, K. (2001, May). *Increasing opportunity to learn via access to rigorous courses and programs: One strategy for closing the achievement gap for at risk and ethnic minority students.* Raleigh, NC: State Board of Education, Evaluation Section Division of Accountability Services, Instructional and Accountability Services.

Eitle, T. M. (2002). Special education or racial segregation: Understanding variation in the representation of black students in educable mentally handicapped programs. *Sociological Quarterly, 43,* 575–605.

Epstein, J. L. (1995). School/family/community partnerships: Caring for the children we share. *Phi Delta Kappan, 79*(9), 701–712.

Epstein, J. L. (2002). *School, family, and community partnerships: Your handbook for action* (2nd ed.). Thousand Oaks, CA: Corwin.

Finley, M. (1984). Teachers and tracking in a comprehensive high school. *Sociology of Education, 57,* 233–243.

Fisher, R. (1994). *Let the people decide: Neighborhood organizing in America.* New York, NY: Twayne Publishers.

Fisher, R., & Karger, H. (1997). *Social work and community in a private world: Getting out in public.* New York, NY: Longman.

Garrison, H. H. (1987). Undergraduate science and engineering education for blacks and Native Americans. In L. S. Dix (Ed.), *Minorities: Their underrepresentation and career differentials in science and engineering: Proceedings of a workshop* (pp. 234–255). Washington, DC: National Academy Press.

Gordon, E. W. (2001, September). Affirmative development of academic abilities. *Pedagogical Inquiry and Praxis, 2,* 1–4.

Gutiérrez, L. (1997). Multicultural community organizing. In M. Reisch & E. Gambrill (Eds.), *Social work in the 21st century* (pp. 249-259). Thousand Oaks, CA: Pine Forge Press.

Hallinan, M. T. (1992). The organization of students for instruction in the middle school. *Sociology of Education, 65*, 114–127.

Harper, C. (1989). *The impact of societal and institutional factors on the production of black graduate students in the sciences* (Unpublished master's thesis). Atlanta-Clark University, Atlanta, GA.

Hedges, L. V., & Nowell, A. (1995). Changes in black-white gap in achievement tests. *Sociology of Education, 72*, 111–133.

Hilton, T. L., Hsia, J., Solorzano, D. G., & Benton, N. L. (1989). Persistence in science of high-ability minority students. Princeton, NJ: Educational Testing Service.

Ho, S. E., & Willms, J. D. (1996). Effects of parental involvement on eighth-grade achievement. *Sociology of Education, 69*, 126–141.

Huang, G., Taddese, N., Walter, E., & Peng, S. S. (2000). *Entry and persistence of women and minorities in college science and engineering education* (NCES 2000-601). Washington, DC: National Center for Educational Statistics.

Ingersoll, R. (1999). The problem of underqualified teachers in American secondary schools. *Educational Researcher, 28*, 26–37.

Jencks, C., & Phillips, M. (1998). *The black-white test score gap*. Washington, DC: Brookings Institution Press.

Kornhaber, M. L. (1997). *Seeking strengths: Equitable identification for gifted education and the theory of multiple intelligences* (Unpublished doctoral dissertation). Harvard University, Cambridge, MA.

Kulik, C. L., & Kulik, J. (1987). Effects of ability grouping on student achievement. *Equity and Excellence, 23*, 22–30.

Lareau, A. (1987). *Home advantage*. New York, NY: Falmer.

Lareau, A. (2003). *Unequal childhoods*. Berkeley: University of California Press.

Lee, J., Grigg, W., & Dion, G. (2005). *The nation's report card, 12th-grade reading and mathematics 2005*. Institute for Educational Sciences, National Center for Educational Statistics. Retrieved from http://nces.ed.gov/Pubsearch/pubsinfo.asp?pubid=2007468

Lee, J., Grigg, W., & Dion, G. (2007). *The nation's report card, mathematics 2007: NAEP progress at Grades 4 & 8*. Institute for Educational Sciences, National Center for Educational Statistics. Retrieved from http://nces.ed.gov/nationsreportcard/mathematics/

Levine, A., & Nidiffer, J. (1996). *Beating the odds: How the poor get to college*. San Francisco: Jossey-Bass.

Loveless, T. (1999). *The tracking wars*. Washington, DC: Brookings Institution Press.

Lucas, S. R. (1999). *Tracking inequality*. New York, NY: Teachers College Press.

Lucas, S. R., & Berends, M. (2002). Sociodemographic diversity, correlated achievement, and de facto tracking. *Sociology of Education, 75*, 34–55.

Magnuson, K., & Waldfogel, J. (Eds.). (2008). *Steady gains and stalled progress*. New York, NY: Russell Sage .

Maton, K. I., Hrabowski, F. A., & Schnitt, C. L. (2000). African American college students excelling in the sciences: College and postcollege outcomes in the Meyerhoff Scholars Program. *Journal of Research in Science Teaching, 37*(7), 629–654.

McKnight, J. (1995). *The careless society: Community and its counterfeits*. New York, NY: Basic Books.

Meier, K. J., Stewart, J. J., & England, R. E. (1989). *Race, class, and education: The politics of second-generation discrimination*. Madison: University of Wisconsin Press.

Mickelson, R. A. (2001). Subverting Swann: First- and second-generation segregation in the Charlotte-Mecklenburg Schools. *American Educational Research Journal, 38*, 215–252.

Mickelson, R. A. (2003a). Achieving equality of educational opportunity in the wake of the judicial retreat from race-sensitive remedies: Lessons from North Carolina. *American University Law Review, 52*(6), 152–184.

Mickelson, R. A. (2003b). When are racial disparities in education the result of discrimination? A social science perspective. *Teachers College Record, 105*(6), 1052–1086.

Mickelson, R. A., & Velasco, A. (2006). Bring it on: Diverse responses to "acting white" among academically able African Americans. In E. M. Horvat & C. O'Connor (Eds.), *Beyond acting white: Reassessments and new directions in research on black students and school success* (pp. 4–27). New York, NY: Teachers College Press.

Molnar, A. (2001). *Vouchers, class size reductions, and student achievement: Considering the evidence*. Bloomington, IN: Phi Delta Kappa Education Fund.

Moses, R., & Cobb, E. C. (2001). *Radical equations: Math literacy and civil rights*. Boston, MA: Beacon Press.

Muller, C. (1998). Gender differences in parental involvement and adolescents' mathematics achievement. *Sociology of Education, 71*, 336–356.

National Research Council. (1999). *High stakes: Testing for tracking, graduation, and promotion*. Washington, DC: Author.

North Carolina Department of Public Instruction. (2000). *NC course of study graduation requirements*. Retrieved September 12, 2003, from http://www.iss.k12.nc.us/curriculum/cos_requirements.pdf

Oakes, J. (1990). *Multiplying inequalities: The effects of race, social class, and tracking on opportunities to learn mathematics and science*. Santa Monica, CA: Rand.

Oakes, J. (2005). *Keeping track* (2nd ed.). New Haven, CT: Yale University Press.

Oakes, J., Muir, K., & Joseph, R. (2000, May). *Course taking and achievement in math and science: Inequalities that endure and change*. Paper presented at the National Institute for Science Education Conference, Detroit, MI.

Rivera, F., & Erlich, J. (1995). *Community organizing in a diverse society*. Boston, MA: Allyn and Bacon.

Schiller, K. S. (2000). Beyond the "one best system": Using TIMSS to explore educational policy and practice. *International Journal of Educational Policy, Research, and Practice, 1*, 129–132.

Schmidt, W. H., McKnight, C. C., Raizen, S. A., Jakwerth, P. M., Valverde, G. A., Wolfe, R. G., et al. (1997). *A splintered vision: An investigation of U.S. science and mathematics education*. Dordrecht, The Netherlands: Kluwer Academic Publishers.

Smith, S., & Mickelson, R. A. (2000). All that glitters is not gold: School reform in Charlotte-Mecklenburg. *Educational Evaluation and Policy Analysis, 101*, 111–117.

Suter, L. E. (2000). Is student achievement immutable? Evidence from international studies on schooling and student achievement. *Review of Educational Research, 70*, 529–545.

Swann v. Charlotte-Mecklenburg. (1971). 402 U.S. 1, 15.

Thompson, C., & O'Quinn, S. D. (2001, June). *Eliminating the black-white achievement gap: A summary of research*. Raleigh: North Carolina Education Research Council.

Useem, E. (1992). Middle schools and math groups: Parents' involvement in children's placement. *Sociology of Education, 65*, 263–279.

Wells, A. S., & Crain, R. L. (1994). Perpetuation theory and the long-term effects of school desegregation. *Review of Educational Research, 64*, 531–556.

Welner, K. G. (2001). *Legal rights, local wrongs: When community control collides with educational equity*. Albany: State University of New York Press.

Williams, B. (2003). *Charting the pipeline: Exploring the critical factors in the development of successful African American scientists, engineers, and mathematics* (Unpublished doctoral dissertation). Emory University, Atlanta, GA.

Yonazawa, S. S. (1997). *Making decisions about students' lives: An interactive study of secondary students' academic program selection* (Unpublished doctoral dissertation). University of California, Los Angeles.

IV

RESEARCH ON HUMAN DEVELOPMENT, HEALTH, AND HUMAN SERVICE PROVIDERS IN SOCIAL CONTEXT

16

Maximizing Culturally and Contextually Sensitive Assessment Strategies in Developmental and Educational Research

Margaret Beale Spencer, Brian Tinsley,
Davido Dupree, and Suzanne Fegley

W. E. B. DuBois (1935) concluded that "Negro children need neither segregated nor mixed schools. What they need is education" (cited in Gunnar Myrdal [1944], p. 90). Today, almost 75 years following DuBois's stridently framed conclusion, and virtually 50 years after the U.S. Supreme Court's *Brown v. Board of Education* ruling (1954), his views remain poignant. DuBois's perspective resonates with many and suggests authenticity and consistency given the current social conditions in many urban centers. His conclusion affords cogent insights concerning the achievement gap since, particularly for males and too frequently across social class demarcations, Black children still *need an education*. However, youths' perceptions and experiences vary with the expressed societal beliefs concerning the foundational salience of education.

Perceptions are important for behavior. Phenomenology refers to the ways in which people make meaning of their lives (i.e., their perceptions as they contemplate "next steps"). It aptly describes the continuing 21st-century dilemma concerning the inadequate representation of youths' everyday American experiences as depicted in the social science marketplace. Neither the privileges enjoyed by some citizens nor the persistency and character of broad inequalities experienced by others is generally represented in the questions pursued in the social sciences. Specifically—and as represented by the "gold standard" (i.e., best practices perspective) marketed for evaluating the adequacy of social, educational, and developmental research studies conducted; practices implemented through programmatic training (i.e., for teaching, service providers and medical services); as well as mandated policies—the noted disparate contextual conditions are ignored. At the same time, fiscal assistance for science and practice is provided either by tax dollars emanating directly from federal or state-supported initiatives or indirectly through tax-exempted private foundations. Unfortunately, tax dollar dispersion (e.g., through philanthropic or federal initiative options) may unintentionally abet uninformed analyses, problematic core beliefs and perspectives, and misrepresented and implemented "gold standard" criteria for research and its evaluation. Accordingly, assumptions about the latter (i.e., gold standard status) serve as the baseline perspective directing policy, training content and practice character. In general and too frequently, "gold standard" assumptions do not include insights concerning a group's cultural traditions and contextual experiences (both physical and psychological), including everyday inequalities such as the inaccessibility of supports as well as their quality. That is, they may not necessarily represent "targeted" individuals' actual real-life perceptions and everyday contextual experiences (i.e., persons who are daily challenged by the particular social situation of concern). Ultimately, the failure to capture this contextual information may negatively influence the authenticity of research findings.

In fact, even though representing an adult exemplar of the social dilemma, the recent experience of Dr. Henry Louis Gates of Harvard University (one of the nation's leading public intellectuals) with a uniformed Cambridge, Massachusetts, officer of the law as reported as a *New York Times* Op-Ed by Brown University Professor, Glenn C. Loury, provides a good illustration of perceptual differences between police officers and citizens of color. Loury (2009) indicated that even the nation's first African American president saw fit to make a comment during an unrelated but recent national forum.

Most important, the unacknowledged latter situation may contribute to stereotypes and the media-assisted social belief that the particular "seminal problem" of focus (e.g., in the case of Professor Gates, disorderly behavior) lies solely within the individual (e.g., assumptions that racial disparities for achievement outcomes, incarceration rates, or health status differences emanate from minority or economically impoverished youths themselves). Equally salient, the perspectives communicated by the media frequently imply that the patterned character of untoward outcomes demonstrates imperviousness to change or an assumed lack of potential responsiveness to intervention (e.g., high unemployment, highly vulnerable health status, achievement outcomes, and incarceration rate patterns). Accordingly, whether explicitly framed published literature as a philosophical and foundational assumption about group membership outcome (e.g., Kardiner & Ovesey's perspective about blacks described in *The Mark of Oppression*, 1951) or framed more subtly in the developmental science literature as consistent untoward themes, both connote individual decision making or efforts as the source of the social concern highlighted (e.g., underachievement or untoward incarceration rates). That is, the interpretations made suggest that individuals create their own adverse contexts (e.g., impoverishment) or outcome (e.g., teen pregnancy). *Thus, the stereotype-reinforcing view both communicated and taught is that individuals are responsible for creating their own situations.* Inadvertently, the noted "line of reasoning" provides credibility to socially constructed sets of conditions that contribute to persistent inequality and gap findings (e.g., health gaps, achievement gaps, school completion-rate differences, disproportionate incarceration rates, and asset and income gaps). The unstated and meritocracy-associated social analysis and conclusion, if acknowledged at all, is that *privilege is earned and disadvantage is volitional*. The latter means that a social status is attributable primarily to individual responsibility for creating one's own physical context, psychological environment, and social situation.

In addition and as suggested, nationally promulgated "gold standards" infrequently embody institutionalized disparate conditions vis-à-vis a status of privilege. Accordingly, implemented policies may be inadequate, at best, which then undermine the effective use of social and human capitol. We suggest that perspectives taken, too frequently, have questionable validity. Consequently, policy-dependent practices "intended" to provide supports, instead function inadequately as systems, which result in *unintended systems injury*.

The conceptual dilemma alluded to is different from our point of view questioning both the adequacy of an assumed "gold standard" research tradition as well as the authenticity of a narrowly conceptualized policy orientation (i.e., one that omits the perspectives of individuals for whom the policy is intended to support). Of course, it may be that a change in the foundational premise of funded research will be needed. More specifically, an *identity shift* may be required for those designing and implementing research. The suggested change would assist in questioning generally unacknowledged perspectives about the authenticity of one point of view (i.e., that of the recipient or focus of programming) versus the current trend, which emphasizes the *primacy of the point of reference provided by the researcher* (particularly given established working assumptions concerning the objectivity of science).

BACKGROUND AND INTRODUCTION: THE NEED FOR ALTERNATIVE CONCEPTUAL FRAMEWORKS FOR RESEARCH AND PRACTICE

We believe that new conceptual frames and culturally sensitive, context-linked assessment strategies are needed to fully analyze and inform the needed direction of collaborative efforts intended to improve policy (especially for education research and training-dependent practices). Nothing less strident is needed for radically reversing a steady and worsening achievement gap, particularly for America's youth of color as well as impoverished young people more generally. In keeping with the concerns noted by DuBois and aired by subsequent scholars, the context-focused perspective we encourage encompasses an appreciation of the many facets of the social ecology important for human outcomes as well as a cognizance of the diverse pathways leading to these outcomes. .

Approximately 30 years following DuBois's (1935) pronouncement (as cited by Gunnar Myrdal, 1944) concerning the education of black youth in the United States, another provocative statement published by Leon Chestang (1972) titled *Character Development in a Hostile Environment* also resonates and affords a perspective about the salience of social ecology. This deceptively powerful statement, published while Chestang was an assistant professor at the University of Chicago (School of Social Service Administration) as an Occasional Paper in the University of Chicago Series, posited that hostile environments function *antithetically to good outcomes*. Chestang's powerful psychological context-acknowledging point of view underscored the importance of considering the nature of context character for understanding youth development and positive life outcomes, including school engagement and achievement.

Given several decades' hindsight, and at least 3 decades of developmental and education research and social science efforts conducted with youth of color, conceptual shortcomings are evident and remain inadequately analyzed. In fact, it can be concluded that the legal strategy of integration embodied as the *Brown v. Board of Education* decision to affect equal educational opportunity and equity, in and of itself, was inadequate to overcome the enduring psychological risks and identity challenges prompted by America's brand of slavery (see Cross, 1991). In addition, ongoing black segregation, implemented as "red-lining" strategies and restrictive loan practices as well as various sources of economic inequality, continue to undermine efforts to eliminate the achievement gap (see Darity & Myers, 1998). Legal scholars have been particularly vocal in suggesting significant flaws in the underlying assumptions of *Brown v. Board of Education* and offering alternative conceptual strategies (e.g., see Balkin, 2001). The deep and long-term effects of psychologically hostile environments for some (e.g., peoples of African and Hispanic descent) examined concurrently with the socially constructed and unacknowledged privileging character of contexts for others (i.e., America's whites) (e.g., see Luthar & Becker, 2002; Luthar & Lattendresse, 2002; McIntosh, 1989) have been consistently *under-examined* in the social sciences. And when these divergent contexts have been considered, the pattern of research findings has been infrequently examined from a human development–sensitive perspective (see Spencer, 1985, for a review). The program of research demonstrates why children's reports of their "beliefs" and "attitudes" cannot be interpreted as suggesting the same meaning-making process and outcome as, in fact, parallel questions asked of middle-childhood youngsters, adolescents, and young adults (e.g., see Spencer, 1985, 2006, 2008b; Spencer & Dornbusch, 1998; Spencer & Markstrom-Adams, 1990).

Consequently, when integrating and applying social science and education research findings to policies salient for America's students, teachers, and administrators (given what has been conceptually overlooked in research traditions) as a "trickle-down outcome," gap findings are not unexpected. However, the published literature determines policy decisions for students' schooling content and design; designates administrator training; and, at multiple levels, influences teachers' everyday practices (e.g., teacher training, content knowledge, pedagogy, and reinforced cultural practice). Thus, patterns of misinterpretations can be deleterious.

Accordingly, cultural and context-sensitive perspectives that integrate themes including race, cultural traditions, social class differences, gender, developmental status, skin color, and interactions among these themes in diverse social contexts continue to be salient factors and suggest important considerations for education research and child study (see Spencer, Brookins, & Allen, 1985; Swanson, Edwards, & Spencer, 2010). Unfortunately, these perspectives are frequently considered as separate and distinct entities rather than as themes that interact with each other in ways that change the underlying assumptions made when examining them out of context. It is these interactional themes, such as the interaction between race and gender, that are in need of critical attention for the teaching of pedagogy and enacted practice by teachers if true change aligned with policies based on findings from funded research studies is to occur. As such, the persistent and worsening achievement gap findings, particularly for African American male students, is not surprising given poverty and gender themes along with under-examined race-based practices (see Lee, Spencer, & Harpalani, 2003). The broadly communicated gender-by-race interaction findings are in keeping with the oft-reported statistic that African American male adolescents have the lowest secondary school graduation rate when compared with other gender-by-race groups. Similarly, and not surprisingly, only 20 percent of African American males enroll in colleges (see Harper, Patton, & Wooden, 2009) and are disproportionately represented in the criminal justice system. The nation's history of broad inequalities associated with communities of color has been infrequently addressed in developmental and education research as a necessary emphasis for understanding how to maximize youths' achievement. The value of the findings would emanate from their ability to inform the character of educational innovations and social service training, programming, and service delivery designs needed for offsetting and neutralizing the high-risk character of their most high-need clients. Thus, the information would assist in decision making concerning pedagogy and the implementation of policies and practices for obtaining desired social status improvements and educational outcomes (e.g., decreasing the achievement gap especially evident for black and Hispanic males). As suggested, the perspective has been especially desirable given the nation's history, divergent treatment, and support of its diverse citizens. A consideration of each group's societal treatment and life course experiences as translated into constructs for determining best practices for programs of research and teaching application remains important. In fact, developmental and education research findings are critical inputs needed for (1) understanding cultural traditions of the broader society (both facilitative and injury-causing); (2) interpreting the evolved and multilayered context character of underserved youth in order to identify and maximize the needed level of supports required; and (3) designing and implementing meaningful programming, strategies, and training models (i.e., of assistance to staff) for obtaining the best youth outcomes.

Ideally, programming allegedly designed for diverse individuals who share a national context should have their respective perspectives and meaning-making processes represented, especially those in need of significant and accessible supports. This is different from the traditional strategy. The standard approach structures input from one group (e.g., the researcher and/or designer of client-focused supports) to define—often without valid input of the "end user"—the "targeted group's reality." In fact, if the targeted group's perspective is present, too frequently it is provided from the powerless position of graduate assistant input.

The point we've tried to emphasize is that multiple perspectives are needed for obtaining the best climate and achievement outcomes. Youths' developmental status determines perceptions, meaning-making processes, and social experiences. At the same time, the every-day feelings and practices (both as reactive and more stable [identity] coping processes) of *teachers and other youth-serving adults who work with and interact with young people on a regular basis* (e.g., transit police, school personnel, and school security) also require consideration. Thus, perspectives, developmental status, and normative processes of those representing both the targeted audience as well as those delivering the services need to be acknowledged. The acknowledgment and careful consideration of both points of view should be integrated into the planning and design of research and evaluation as well as the structuring of adult training (e.g., the curriculum content of teacher education programs and strategies for im-proving pedagogy, the core content of graduate training of administrators, and the quality of ongoing teacher and social service provider workshops made available to teacher and social welfare–providing professionals).

For example, practicing teachers themselves have significant need of support from their principals; lacking quality support has consequences for student learning (see Dell'Angelo, 2009). In like fashion, Hafiz (2009) suggests another generally ignored factor; she reports that many teachers have significant fear of their students (e.g., assumptions of youth violence or discomfort with the underresourced character of many urban neighborhood schools). Thus, as everyday practices at the student, teacher, and administrator levels, critical resources and supports may be withheld for particular groups (e.g., teachers may not receive the specific supports actually needed from principals and No Child Left Behind–type poli-cies); at the same time, risks and challenges may be multiplied for others. Examples of the latter might include, as suggested, teachers' fear because of where their schools are located, students' feelings of being disrespected because they infer their teachers' devaluation of their communities and families, and parents' discomfort and feelings of devaluation when summoned to school settings that may represent their own experiences of miseducation. As suggested, potential differences in experiences either within or between groups have sig-nificant salience for teaching, learning, and parental responses. Of course, at the same time, unacknowledged privileges are made available to some and denied to others, although all strive for a variety of competencies and effectance motivation.

The noted perspectives and the introduction of other contributing and interfering practices are important. They bring attention to generally under-recognized assumptions about and perceptions of a group's inferred humanity, their socially acceptable (or not) treatment, and their ease of access to social protections under the law, including resource accessibility. Of course, the latter are in addition to the baseline human dignity that members of all groups are privy to and need, although *the fact is frequently not shared*. The view that all humans require human dignity and respect has been used in historical analyses as a strategy for understanding the context and source of child treatment (and maltreatment) (see Aries, 1962, for a review). The acknowledgment of a person's collective status as a human being having normative hu-man development processes and also being burdened by unavoidable vulnerability (i.e., the needed consideration of each person's risk level *and* protective factor presence) is a relatively new and *infrequent* consideration for interpreting the daily experiences and contemporary life of youth of color and young people more generally (see Spencer, 2006; 2008b; Spencer, Cross, Harpalani, & Goss, 2003).

Accordingly, this chapter serves three purposes, given the thematic issues described. Thus, building upon the framing function of the introduction, the first section describes a collaborative research group that, as is its tradition, tackles these issues as part of its implemented program of context-focused developmental science (e.g., neighborhood assessment). The second section specifically reviews research on neighborhood contexts and the continuing challenges confronted by this necessary line of work. The third section provides a context-sensitive approach to achievement findings as an illustration of a culturally sensitive and context-linked mixed-methods strategy. The fourth, and final, section of the chapter makes use of an identity-focused cultural ecological framework to interpret the school data, neighborhood assessment strategy, and achievement outcome findings described briefly in the third section. Use of the phenomenological variant of ecological systems theoretical framework (i.e., PVEST: Spencer, 1995, 2006, 2008a, 2008b) serves a specific purpose. It takes into account the meaning-making processes of the respective respondents. This is a quite different tactic from the more traditional strategies that more often than not ignore or fail to represent respondents' normative meaning-making efforts.

THE COLLABORATION FOR HEALTH, ACHIEVEMENT, NEIGHBORHOODS, GROWTH, AND ETHNIC STUDIES: A DEMONSTRATION OF A CULTURE- AND CONTEXT-SENSITIVE PROGRAMMATIC RESEARCH EFFORT

The CHANGES Research Project at Chicago (Collaboration for Health, Achievement, Neighborhoods, Growth, and Ethnic Studies [*acronym* CHANGES]) continues a long-term programmatic research effort, which stresses the salience of culture and context for developmental science and education research. The acronym CHANGES was initially used at the University of Pennsylvania (Center for Health, Achievement, Neighborhoods, Growth, and Ethnic Studies) and the work continues as the CHANGES Project at Chicago. As an organized effort with the focus noted, CHANGES is unique and does not exist elsewhere. Also making it unique, as inspired by the perspective of W. E. B. DuBois, its basic research and application orientation emphasizes DuBois's premise that scholarship is to be used to improve the human condition. Accordingly, the CHANGES Project at Chicago operates on the premise of *universal human vulnerability* (i.e., that all humans both confront risks and benefit from protective factors of one sort or another as each individual navigates the world). Importantly, its foundational assumption of universal human vulnerability does not reflect most traditional research perspectives. More often than not, situations of privilege (and implicit benefits) are communicated as if they were the norm for all. That is, some of a society's citizens are viewed as the norm. Their disproportionate possession of protective factors enjoyed as significant support is infrequently acknowledged or is represented as an ever-present knapsack of benefits and privileges accompanied by few burdens due to "everyday challenges" (McIntosh, 1989). The fact of inequity in the distribution of resources and citizens' access to supports is infrequently noted. Moreover, beliefs concerning meritocracy, emanating from assumed commensurate work, effort, and intrinsic motivation, further reinforce a sense of privilege as the "norm" for particular individuals.

In contrast, a view of universal human vulnerability seeks to account for challenges linked to risks and supports, which are associated with protective factors. Our view is that culturally specific and shared protective factors, strengths, and supports (e.g., religious beliefs, spirituality, family traditions, emotional interdependence, active faith, social connectedness, and cultural socialization) are infrequently acknowledged. At the same time, the socially constructed sources of a group's heightened vulnerability due to the concomitant risks (i.e., poor health or low achievement) more often than not are ignored.

Thus, there are two views and sets of values upon which programs of research are implemented and findings interpreted. The *first* view considers mainly protective factors for certain youth and groups while, at the same time, primarily assuming that others are inherently inferior (i.e., possessing mainly risk factors without acknowledging the availability of protective factors and strengths). Accordingly, this perspective is associated with assumptions of meritocracy for some as well as presumptions that high-risk-status individuals are devoid of strengths and supports. On the other hand, the *second* perspective, promulgated by CHANGES, suggests a universal human vulnerability perspective. That is, it operates on the assumption that all humans possess *both risks and protective factors*. Functioning at the same historical moment in research communities, these two sets of research values and their fundamental conceptual imbalance create significant dissonance.

There continue to be media-emphasized assumptions of earned status and a narrow focus on strengths for some (i.e., a privileged status) and, at the same time, a heightened focus on risk factors and untoward outcomes for others (i.e., assumptions of "self-determinative" disadvantage), including a pattern of not acknowledging the group's strengths, endogenous protective factors, or exogenous sourced and earned supports. These conceptual shortcomings—given the media and frequent social science text presentations of status differences—introduce underacknowledged complexities. That is, construing citizens as representing either the status-earned norm (i.e., actually those having unacknowledged privileges that protect against high risk) or portraying them as disadvantaged (i.e., assumed self-determining underproductivity), in fact, represents a virtual conceptual and social conundrum.

In sum, and as an aspect of the invisible social riddle alluded to, presenting individuals as either embodying mainly risks (i.e., "earned disadvantage") or possessing mainly earned strengths (i.e., "meritocracy beliefs-based privileges" enjoyed) engenders problematic reasoning. As a research unit and representing a conceptual response, CHANGES both questions and confronts the flawed reasoning, shortsighted assumptions, and patterns of disparate findings that emanate as an outcome. Representing a program of research and conceptual strategy, the CHANGES program of research, among other emphases, explores the role of context in human development for diverse groups, particularly youth.

Accordingly—as linked with the conundrum described, and on the one hand—the dilemma described keeps privileged individuals from acknowledging the *condition of shared human vulnerability. As noted, and unfortunately, vulnerability is most frequently operationalized as risk*; this is different from a point of view professed by CHANGES and enacted as a program of research. Specifically, the conceptual and programmatic strategy of the research unit acknowledges that human life, in and of itself including its various developmental expressions, represents a *normative and unavoidable state of vulnerability for all humans*. CHANGES' evolved identity, programmatic research strategies, patterned findings, and theory-driven analysis, considered collectively, constitutes a particular orientation. That is, the foundational and patterned efforts described along with the *normative vulnerability stance* alluded to (i.e., the view that all humans are vulnerable and possess both risks and protective factors) makes the orientation of the research collaboration—in general—conceptually unique.

CHANGES grew as a basic research and collaborative application unit. It remains committed to exploring and integrating contextually oriented and culturally sensitive perspectives as applied to the human condition of diverse communities of youth and families. Given the research, policy, and practice orientation generally taken in regard to people of color and poor families, the collaborative research unit includes a particular focus. Specifically, along with foundational interests in human development across the life course, CHANGES continues to include an emphasis on individuals of diverse resources as well as those of ethnically and racially diverse backgrounds although mainly those living in the United States. Thus, the culturally inclusive orientation continues as an especially salient aspect of the programmatic studies conducted.

The 1994 objective to institutionalize the multi-method research strategy, which considered and integrated a developmental perspective with considerations of culture and context, in fact, afforded a two-pronged purpose. The goal of CHANGES was to maximize the findings yielded through the Center's theory-driven programming and human development research tradition as well as to increase the applicability of findings to collaborative programming opportunities. The ultimate vision of the CHANGES program of research was to improve the efficacy, general developmental character, cultural authenticity, and ecological validity (including an acknowledgment of the embedded nature of the contexts of human development) of subsequent policy outcomes as a function of ongoing development-sensitive and collaborative programming applications.

Thus, the conceptual perspectives adopted by CHANGES, both as a basic research approach and as a collaborative application orientation, recognize their *frequent absence in the social sciences* generally and in developmental science specifically. As suggested, a working assumption of the research unit's approach is that a *human vulnerability perspective* (i.e., individuals possess both risks and protective factors) has been differentially applied. Specifically, the experiences of particular groups (black and Hispanic children and poor youth, more generally) have been predominantly portrayed in the literature as solely representing conditions of high risk. On the other hand, the experiences of other groups (e.g., white children, wealthy youth), have been depicted as not having risks. For the latter group, however, more important than the absence of risk considerations is that their general privileged life course experiences have been largely ignored in the literature. Thus, poor people, blacks and Hispanics have been examined as a function of their membership in a devalued group and its attendant and unavoidable risk status. For whites human development and social status is absent the consideration of risks; further, their intergenerational inherited protective factors, which are often experienced as privileges, most frequently are ignored. Without question, the human vulnerability perspective espoused by CHANGES, then, varies from that espoused by other researchers and research teams (Spencer, 2006, 2008a, 2008b).

The conceptual approach described is decidedly different but consistent with the perspective of James Anthony and others (Anthony, 1974) in that it appreciates and conceptually integrates the working assumption that *all humans are vulnerable*. As described, vulnerability is shared by all humans and *is not synonymous* with risk. As part of our humanity, everyone is burdened by some level of vulnerability, having both a level of risk and protective factor presence. The combinatory effect of risk level and protective factor presence has different implications when experienced at different periods of the life course. Vulnerability is unavoidable and exists independent of, for example, group membership, position in the life course, gender, physical features (e.g., skin color, height, weight), and social status. As each individual tackles a life stage's particular developmental tasks (e.g., sphincter control, language acquisition, and overcoming early egocentrism as hurdles in the first few years of life), risk factors are experienced as challenges (see Spencer, 2006, 2008b). Each has the potential of complicating the successful achievement of stage-specific outcomes. The ability to achieve success appears to be associated with the level of protective factors present (i.e., the degree of supports available) for clearing the hurdles normatively confronted or expected at that particular life stage (see Havighurst, 1953). In addition, the individual's personal attributes, temperament, and experience with parallel tasks, to name but a few factors, also matter. Thus, the question is whether an individual is able *to embrace the opportunity* for growth given the particular normative hurdle confronted or is left merely to struggle and cope with the developmental transition at hand. Obviously, the task of teaching (and outcomes expected) will be different if teachers expect that students are uniformly arriving at school with "an embracing orientation" toward learning than it would be if they expect a "coping with hurdles" state of readiness. Undoubtedly, the level of protective factor presence or the character of supports available clearly matter.

Protective factors such as cultural socialization, competent and calming parenting practices, quality and character of housing and home supports, and a history of school achievement assist the smooth transition and productive embracing of or enhanced coping with life's unavoidable hurdles. The successes or failures of a developmental period have implications for the level of risks to be encountered in the subsequent developmental period in addition to that period's anticipated and unique tasks. For example, an unusually difficult infant-to-toddlerhood transition may require more protective factors to be used as significant supports during the subsequent stage of development in ages 2 through 7. Our point is that risks are mitigated as a function of having equivalent protective factors available. The protective factor presence and accrued benefits (experienced as individual strengths) available and used for offsetting the emotional reactions associated with the challenges confronted at a particular period of the life course (e.g., developmental tasks) matters tremendously. This perspective may also be legitimately applied to the experiences of groups; that is, individual members inherit risks or protective factors as a function of group status or how the group is treated and supported.

Accordingly, we can once more link the ideas concerning vulnerability with the general social science literature used in support of *Brown v. Board of Education* (1954). Specifically, when considering the Court's deliberation, only risks were acknowledged, as opposed to an appreciation of the black community's strengths and protective factors as well. In fact, it might have been beneficial to acknowledge a common state of *human vulnerability* for Americans more generally. However, at the same time, conceding varied sources of vulnerability for blacks and whites would have suggested the need, potentially, for different supports. That said, the remedies proposed by the Court might have been *customized for encouraging the same outcome* (i.e., achieved resiliency or the acquisition of a good education) for all citizens, although by different implemented strategies. For some whites, resiliency might have included overcoming both their stereotypic a priori assessments of blacks as well as their persistent and unquestioned beliefs concerning the superiority of whites.

For some blacks, on the other hand, resiliency might have included galvanizing and sustaining the love of education, knowledge, and the interconnectedness of family and fictive kin irrespective of the interminable forms of oppression confronted (see Spencer et al., 2003). Thus, the actual supports designed for and accessible by each group—given varying confronted risks—would need to be different. That is, each would have to represent a specific level of support and be of a particular character for confronting particular challenges (i.e., the realized and manifested risk factors).

That view was not evident either in the insights provided by the consultants or research findings presented to the Court when *Brown v. Board of Education* was argued. In fact, consistent with historical perspectives, practices, and extant research assumptions (see Spencer et al., 2003), blacks were viewed as possessing mainly risk factors; on the other hand and as suggested, whites continue to be associated singularly with innate strengths (i.e., inherent protective factors). Unfortunately, an inclusive social science emphasis that includes examination of how diverse people live, what challenges regularly confront them, and how they make meaning of their situations as America's black, yellow, white, and brown citizens, in fact, was not represented and continues to be virtually absent from the literature.

Given each group's uneven access to resources and the attendant intergenerational economic status and social situations associated with each, disparate outcomes have not been unexpected. In fact, we posit that disparities in health, education, and economic situation, as well as the heightened vulnerability of adolescents and young adults, have been virtually unavoidable and should have been anticipated before the media's emphasis contributed to their framing as stereotypes. We believe that both the intergenerational transmission of economic resources that continues to be enjoyed by some whites due to the economic benefits of 200-plus years of slavery as well as the underacknowledged color-linked burdens placed on blacks mattered then and they continue to matter today. The disparities in conditions of groups are acknowledged in historical accounts but continue to be underrepresented *as conceptual themes and representative measurement strategies* integrated into the social sciences. We believe this shortcoming contributes to policy failings and "unintended systems injury" (Spencer, 2006). On the other hand, and as described by Spencer et al. (2003), the protective factors and supports blacks utilized before enslavement, during the Middle Passage, and subsequently throughout slavery in North America continue to be underacknowledged, remain unattended to, and are not built upon as factors of salience for policy and practice. This inability to recognize and build upon available protective factors and culturally linked supportive traditions represents a significant *missed opportunity*.

The program of research and practice (e.g., collaborative evaluation and training) emanating from CHANGES suggests other desirable perspectives needed for determining contemporary policy-associated remedies. The point of view that all humans live *as cultural beings* (see Lee et al., 2003) utilized by CHANGES continues to be especially pertinent given groups' social status, hierarchical organization, unavoidable human "meaning making," and consequent coping practices in culturally influenced contexts. Accordingly, the research efforts maintain an integration and examination of the interaction between historically dependent cultural traditions, human developmental life course tasks, varying social conditions (e.g., long-standing inequities), and physical and psychological contexts. The developmental perspective emphasized explores how the interactions noted come to be understood and experienced by children and youth as they navigate communities and cope with stage-specific developmental tasks.

As described, CHANGES was formally launched in the mid-1990s at the University of Pennsylvania and continues as CHANGES Research Project at Chicago today. However, the foundational and thematic research efforts and perspectives utilized actually began fifteen years prior to its formal launching at Penn. Its contemporary legacy includes a continuing effort to address the aftermath of America's integration-relevant issues engendered by *Brown v. Board of Education* (e.g., identity questions, cultural socialization influences, skin color salience research). The collaborative research unit's emphasis is in keeping with the view that the *Brown* decision continues to have an impact on teacher and social-service training, policy priorities, and a broad range of practices into the current century. Footnote 11 of *Brown v. Board of Education* (1954) cited social science evidence used to make the case to end America's school segregation. Kenneth and Mamie Clark's doll studies' findings, which demonstrated white preference in black and white children, were a part of the social science evidence submitted (see Cross, 1991; Spencer, 1985; Spencer & Markstrom-Adams, 1990, for an overview). More general reference group orientation studies (i.e., the content and focus of children's social identifications), however, continue as a theme for theory and scholarship produced at CHANGES (e.g., see Markstrom-Adams & Spencer, 1994; Spencer 1985; Spencer & Markstrom-Adams, 1990). Utilizing programmatic strategies, the conceptual branching of the work has included an extensive and ongoing exploration of the role of identity processes more generally (Markstrom-Adams & Spencer, 1994; Spencer 1999; Spencer, Swanson, & Cunningham, 1991). Ultimately the "self" emphasis was further broadened and evolved into a particular theoretical orientation (Spencer, 1995, 2006, 2008a, 2008b; Spencer, Dupree, & Hartmann, 1997).

At the same time, collaborations with consulting scholars have facilitated assimilating other perspectives and generating conceptual cautions consistent with those frequently found in legal scholarship. For example, legal scholar Derrick Bell (as cited by Trei) believes that while the rhetoric of integration promised significant results, in fact, "court orders to ensure that Black youngsters received the education they needed to progress would have achieved more," and thus, a different outcome would have emerged. Bell surmises that counter to settling the nation's racial difficulties, in fact, the *Brown* decision actually increased the situation's complexity. More to the point and as reported by Lisa Trei (2004), Bell laments:

> Racial disparities, wide and widening in every measure of well-being, overshadow the gains in status achieved by those of us black Americans who by varying combinations of hard work and good fortune are viewed as having made it. (para 9)

Importantly, as suggested over 35 years earlier by Chestang (1972), Bell's conclusions as a legal scholar forefront the role and impact of daily context-linked micro-aggressions experienced by adults and children—and frequently perpetuated by those expected to function as sources of support (e.g., teachers, school administrators, service providers, and medical personnel).

Over the years, CHANGES' collaborative relationships with a variety of scholars have provided opportunities to integrate diverse conceptual insights as well as suggest cautions about the "missed opportunities" of *Brown*. For example, Edwards (2008) sees the nation's educational dilemma as associated with assumptions concerning the "integrationist ideal" that obfuscates an accurate portrayal of "the fact" of youths' and families' everyday lived experiences. Jones's (2008) conceptual perspective, more specifically, focuses attention on school reform efforts and, like the *Brown v. Board* decision, Jones posits that there is a continuing *inadequacy of social science documentation* that supports the school reform industry. Jones postulates that short-sighted perspectives funnel billions of dollars from the government, philanthropic communities, and business sectors into inadequately conceptualized reform efforts. O'Connor's (2008) conceptual strategy emphasizes that the problem of the *Brown v. Board* decision was its inability to address the continuing problem of majority-held beliefs concerning white supremacy while, at the same time, persisting in fomenting assumptions about black inferiority. She provides a focus on the implications for teachers by specifying how teachers and systems of teacher training inadvertently contribute to the black-white achievement gap, given their responsibility to educate students, including youth of color. Her perspective acknowledges the problematic content and conceptual holes in much of teacher-training content. Also underacknowledged is that achievement themes are not independent of health status.

Collaborative input from health-focused investigators such as T. R. Spencer (2008) provides yet another emphasis, as she provides a lens for considering how the restricted character of conceptual themes of the *Brown* decision limits youths' well-being and health status. Her perspective illustrates systems-relevant limitations of student-reported attendance data and adverse schooling outcomes by linking health status with student competence, effectance motivation, and academic resiliency. Students living in underresourced communities and lacking adequate health supports (e.g., the dearth of health centers, acute care services, and hospitals) not surprisingly would be expected to miss more days of school. As illustrated in the next section's review of neighborhood literature, context is an important consideration in matters of assessment and methodology.

NEIGHBORHOOD QUALITY AND INDIVIDUAL BEHAVIOR

As one illustration of a particular response to shortcomings, research issues shared about context character and neighborhoods, as published by CHANGES collaborations in general, have been inconsistently emphasized in publication outlets. Development of quantitative social indicators has been the subject of scholarly study for more than 30 years (e.g., Campbell & Converse, 1972). The geographic unit of analysis for indicators has typically been nations, metropolitan areas, or cities. Until recently, virtually all indicator analyses at the neighborhood scale depended on census data collected only every 10 years. This limited the benefit of these tools to community leaders, local planners, and policymakers, who typically seek more up-to-date information that can portray richer dynamic processes than decennial snapshots (Sawicki & Flynn, 1996).

There are sparse studies that expressly focus on the logistics of how neighborhood assessments should or could be evaluated. Few researchers specify their strategy for operationalizing and defining quality/character outside of socioeconomic status (SES). Many neighborhood assessments incorporate population density as a "key" neighborhood indicator. Of course, the reports generally do not note that high-income people who live in urban condo enclaves reside under highly dense conditions. Ignored, of course, is that such neighborhoods possess significant community resources such as food markets and quality medical supports. Not surprisingly, an examination of articles that touch on "neighborhood quality" suggests that SES represents the default variable for many researchers to designate neighborhood quality. Low-income neighborhoods (as assessed by measuring parent/household income) are essentially grouped together (in essence stereotyped) as having shared characteristics. Assessing neighborhoods based on other factors such as physical buildings (green space, abandoned, hospitals, schools per capita, etc.) infrequently appear in the published studies. In fact, there appears to be a virtual disconnect between the measures that are formulated for the purposes of collecting policy-relevant information (i.e., census measures) and the research methods used by those in the actual field of research (i.e., academia). A concern that arises here is that census tracts are inherently flawed neighborhood approximations due to the boundaries that they statistically impose.

Before moving to a literature review, several observations are apparent. First, ethnographic work on the subject is severely lacking. In our opinion, mixed methods as part of systematic inquiry is underrepresented. In addition, a few articles have been published in other fields, focusing primarily on the impact of neighborhoods on mental health (Aneshensel & Sucoff, 1996; Leventhal & Brooks-Gunn, 2000) and perception of neighborhood safety (Aisenberg & Herrenkohl, 2008; Burton, 1997; Emory, Caughy, Harris, & Franzini, 2008).

Some research focuses not on quality-of-life outcomes from a child well-being standpoint, but instead narrowly from a financial perspective; in other words, neighborhood assessments are sometimes driven by and used as a means of gathering information best used by those interested in financial investments in a particular neighborhood or for those inquiring about the general economic well-being of a community. Lacking is an equivalent concern for safe, nurturing, and healthy contexts for child development to be enjoyed by all young people. Thus, as opposed to a high valuation placed on needed contextual changes required for youth resiliency, the assessment strategy is primarily concerned with financial gain as an outcome of investment priorities. Not unrelated is an interesting and not surprising observation. Those designing and conducting the research implement much of it in African American communities. For some of the well-known research on small areas, researchers assert that the context provided by inner-city enclaves and the geographic concentration of poverty are themselves factors harming people and families living there (Wilson, 1987, 1992). The situation lends itself to the following point raised in the literature, which touches on the issue of neighborhood perceptions.

With few exceptions, historical analyses have rarely attempted to develop neighborhood-level indicators. However, Sawicki & Flynn (1996) convey five lessons for neighborhood indicators, which stand out from the limited literature. The first is that the numbers communicate a specific policy purpose. Second, geographic indicators play a special role more important than that of subject area indicators, because policy is administered through geographic units and neighborhoods and cities themselves affect the quality of people's lives. The third lesson is that it is critical to ascertain from the outset a distinction between indicators that measure *neighborhood well-being* and those that measure the well-being of *neighborhood residents*. A fourth "lesson learned" is that to be useful, unique component contributors to overall indicators must be provided. The specificity also contributes to the design of supports and interventions. Finally, the movement to use geographic indicators, especially on a neighborhood scale, is in its formative years. In the mid-1990s, neighborhood-level indicators were just beginning to be used to make and evaluate policy and to search for the causes of change in neighborhoods and in the lives of their residents.

In general, much of the efforts dedicated to neighborhood research efforts have been on larger "units of analysis" (i.e., cities, states, and nations). However, Sawicki & Flynn (1996) acknowledged that two factors have evolved to promote the use of neighborhood indicators: (1) microcomputing, including desktop geographic information systems (GIS) software and (2) the shift of responsibilities for social and economic welfare from the federal to the state and local levels, and the simultaneous emphasis on public-private partnerships and neighborhood empowerment (Wallis, 1994). These approaches are the latest attempt to forge new alliances for small-area improvement.

In order to develop a set of responsive and effective neighborhood indicators of both institutional and social performance, it appears critical to first specify the intended client. Who will use these indicators and for what purpose? A number of possible objectives exist that revolve around the ultimate goal of making neighborhood concerns more visible at the national level. A second allows for generating statistics that measure meaningful change in neighborhoods. Another option would be for building capacity to systematically collect and disseminate indicators that inform and support local initiative taking. A final, and also a helpful, goal is for developing dynamic models of neighborhood change. The latter would be used for evaluating the likely impact of existing and/or proposed policies on neighborhoods and/or their residents, as well as measuring inequality over space and time both within and between regions. The strategy noted would also assist in setting goals for neighborhood and resident status improvements, and for developing surrogate census-like measures for intercensal years. Finally, the noted suggestions would contribute toward understanding the role that the geographic mobility of residents plays in their own welfare and the welfare of their (new and old) neighborhoods.

A useful question posed is whether any single system of neighborhood indicators might address the range and depth of insights required to inform policy for a diverse group of residents. More than likely, no one system could do that. A more productive strategy would be to encourage localities to adopt standard area-size delineations and statistical indicators by substantive area. This strategy is best illustrated by a case study. One carried out by the

Urban Institute (Sawicki & Flynn, 1996) that served as part of the National Neighborhood Indicators Project (NNIP) effectively serves the purpose and follows.

The Providence Plan, part of the National Neighborhood Indicators Project or NNIP, was established and funded by the city of Providence and the state of Rhode Island with the goal of informing public policy. The principal goals of the plan were to put people to work, retain the city's middle class, make the neighborhoods safe, improve the public school system, provide quality affordable housing, and revitalize the downtown area of the city. The Providence Plan began working with faculty at the Taubman Center at Brown University in 1992 to develop a set of indicators as part of a comprehensive Geographic Information System (GIS) database. This information is used in policymaking and planning (i.e., targeting the locations of neighborhood-based family health, education, and child development centers). The Providence Plan used its GIS maps to identify the city's most distressed neighborhoods, which then became target areas for National Park Service planning. The GIS system was also used to identify the locations of students with need of additional attention (e.g., dropouts, special needs). Thus, the Providence Plan indicators project has had a significant bearing on the allocation of vital public funding.

As a whole, the NNIP projects were designed to provide information on social and economic conditions in their respective cities, focusing specifically on poverty and neighborhood decline. In turn, data are available that are easily accessible by a variety of entities.

As a byproduct of the Providence Plan, Sawicki and Flynn (1996) were able to offer beneficial points, which should be seriously considered upon completion of neighborhood studies. Promulgated ideas include the issues of measuring causality, data availability and timing, and interfacing between researchers and residents. Sawicki and Flynn (1996) also support the notion that the timing and the availability of geographic data are also problems and, thus, critical themes needing to be addressed. Researchers may be concerned with current achievement outcomes for schools situated in neighborhoods where current changes are not represented by available census data. In sum and when considered together, the researchers and policy analysts concluded that a context-considering perspective allows clear links and insights concerning the salience of diverse contexts for development and performance outcomes for a community's youth. In other words, both physical and cultural contexts matter.

NEIGHBORHOOD CONTEXT AS A
FACTOR IN ADOLESCENT OUTCOMES

Neighborhoods and Achievement

Some studies have been produced that focus on the relationship between neighborhood quality and educational performance as well as school completion rates of adolescents (Bowen & Bowen, 1999; Crane, 1991; Duncan, 1994; Leventhal & Brooks-Gunn, 2000). Research also suggests that neighborhood quality is associated with educational and occupational expectations (Ceballo, McLoyd, & Toyokawa, 2004; Hope, 1995). In this section, multiple subthemes related to neighborhood context as a factor in adolescent outcomes will be described. The first subtheme provides a general description of socialization and social outcomes more generally. It includes a consideration of neighborhood effects with socioeconomic status influences and education. Following this overarching description, other linked subthemes consider (a) racial composition and social outcomes, (b) relocation and social outcomes, and (c) school reform and social outcomes.

Socialization and Social Outcomes

A still growing body of research has documented that youth living in poor neighborhoods have less favorable developmental outcomes compared to their counterparts from more privileged neighborhoods (Leventhal & Brooks-Gunn, 2000). Neighborhood socioeconomic status has been consistently positively associated with academic outcomes (Harding, 2003) and has been linked with adolescent expectations via socialization (Sampson, 1997; Sampson, Raudenbush, & Earls, 1997; Wilson, 1987). Research shows a significant association between levels of collective socialization and delinquency among children (Sampson, 1997). Subsequent research suggests that neighborhood adults collectively socialize neighborhood children through adult supervising, monitoring, and role modeling (see Spencer et al. 2006). Thus, neighborhood adults may act as collective role models for adolescent residents. Collective socialization was inversely associated with conduct problems in a study of African American children 10–12 years old residing in small towns and cities (Simons, Simons, Conger, & Brody, 2004).

Prior research indicates the existence of a positive relationship between neighborhood socioeconomic status and educational attainment as well as occupational expectations (Ceballo et al., 2004; Hope, 1995). Crane's (1991) research suggested that neighborhood effects may influence educational outcomes solely under the worst environmental conditions. Neighborhoods were categorized by census tract areas, and the percentage of workers in professional or managerial jobs served as an index of neighborhood quality. Neighborhood effects were far from linear, and the influence of neighborhood factors on dropping out of school was dramatically greater in what was referred to as "urban ghetto neighborhoods" versus the situation in other communities. Neighborhood quality was 50 times more likely to influence dropout rate of African Americans (living with their parents) in the lowest-quality neighborhoods than those neighborhoods with higher income levels.

Racial Composition and Social Outcomes

There have been a number of neighborhood studies that have examined the neighborhood racial composition and other demographic factors in an attempt to better understand adolescent social outcomes. Among African American adolescents, low neighborhood socioeconomic levels have been associated with earlier onset of puberty and increased deviant behavior (Ge, Brody, Conger, Simons, & Murray, 2002) as well as parenting and conduct disorder (Brody et al., 2003).

Some studies report a beneficial impact of the percentage of middle-class residents on the likelihood of graduating from high school for African American male adolescents (Connell, Halpern-Felsher, Clifford, Crichlow, & Usinger, 1995; Ensminger, Lamkin, & Jacobson, 1996). In a study of 262 single African American mothers and their children (seventh and eighth grade), results indicated that neighborhood conditions shape early adolescents' beliefs and attitudes about their education, potentially years before they actually proceed with dropping out of school (i.e., an important finding demonstrating that academic self-efficacy predicts educational values and effort).

The literature describes notably different results for African American female versus male adolescents. Several studies focus on the impact of neighborhood conditions on school retention. According to Crane (1991), African American male teenagers are the most vulnerable to dropping out of high school because of neighborhood influences. Using different indicators of neighborhood quality, Duncan (1994) reported results that similarly underscore Crane's earlier findings on the greater vulnerability of African American males. Duncan found that affluent neighbors positively influence the total years of schooling completed by groups of both African American and white adolescents with the exception of African American males.

Prior research indicates that neighborhoods are differentially associated with academic outcomes across gender, with many studies suggesting that male adolescents are more sensitive to neighborhood effects than their female counterparts. In a study of African American and European American primary and secondary school students, neighborhood income had a stronger effect on math achievement for male adolescents than female adolescents (Entwisle, Alexander, & Olson, 1994). Furthermore, when residing in low-income neighborhoods, African American male adolescents had a substantially higher probability of dropping out of high school compared with female adolescents (Halpern-Felsher et al., 1997).

Hope (1995) illustrated that middle-class African American adolescents living in lower-income neighborhoods were less likely to aspire or plan to attend college than those in higher-income neighborhoods. When maternal education, per capita household income, and the school attended by the adolescent were controlled for among African American adolescents, having a higher amount of affluent neighbors has been associated with a higher valuing of education (Ceballo et al., 2004). In addition, those adolescents in higher-income communities tend to view education as more important and more useful. Thus, greater effort was put forth by students. In contrast, some research has shown that female adolescents are more sensitive to neighborhood income levels than males. Ceballo et al. (2004) found that the educational values of African American female adolescents were positively associated with neighborhood SES, but this was not the case for male adolescents. The results resemble Duncan's (1994) findings, demonstrating that the presence of affluent neighbors does not beneficially affect African American males, which may have implications for relocation experiments.

Relocation Studies and Social Outcomes

There is a literature related to neighborhood context that examines the influence of family relocation on adolescent social outcomes. A critical study that highlights the issue at hand is the Moving to Opportunity for Fair Housing Demonstration (Feins, Holin, & Phipps, 1996). Conducted in several cities (Baltimore, Boston, Chicago, Los Angeles, and New York City), this randomized study looked specifically at whether or not moving from high- to low-poverty neighborhoods was associated with low-income minority children's achievement, grade retention, and suspensions/expulsions. The study focused on 583 children who were between 6 and 18 years old at follow-up. Results demonstrated that moving to low-poverty neighborhoods had positive effects on achievement scores for adolescent boys above the age of 11 as compared with their low-income neighborhood counterparts. Findings concluded that male adolescents' scores were comparable to females' scores in higher income areas, whereas male adolescents in low-income neighborhoods fared worse than female peers (Leventhal, Brooks-Leventhal, & Brooks-Gunn, 2004).

Another unusual study, conducted by Sanbonmatsu, Kling, Duncan, and Brooks-Gunn (2006), focused on families originally living in public housing who were assigned housing vouchers by lottery, thus encouraging relocation to neighborhoods with lower poverty rates. Although it was hypothesized that reading and math test scores would be higher among children in families offered vouchers (with larger effects among younger children), the results show no significant effects on test scores for any age group among more than 5,000 children aged 6 to 20 years. In addition, there was no evidence of improvements in reading scores, math scores, behavior or school problems, or school engagement, overall or for any age group. Developmental theory suggests more rapid cognitive development among younger children and greater ability to adapt to new social environments.

The relocation studies suggest that transitioning to a new neighborhood, while important to adolescent development, is not a sufficient intervention if the goal is to positively influence important social outcomes. Although there are effective resources for students in general, many adolescents coming from different neighborhoods may need more; specifically, youth may require additional support over and above the traditional level. In addition, the studies did not take into account students' perceptions. Students may feel inadequate and/or intimidated upon moving to new locations in which they are (or are perceived as being) behind their peers.

School Reform and Social Outcomes

There is at least one study that has examined recent school reform efforts as part of neighborhood studies literature. The study examined whether performance on standardized tests mandated by No Child Left Behind (NCLB) legislation differs based on neighborhood characteristics in which a child's school is located. The project utilized data from two sources: The Hispanic Paradox Project (HPP) and the Houston Independent School District (HISD) during and between 2001 and 2002, two academic years (Emory et al., 2008). In this heavily minority sample (52.3 percent Hispanic and 46.7 percent African American), the majority of the students were considered "economically disadvantaged" as 84.2 percent of students were eligible for free or reduced lunch. The study found that students eligible for the free/reduced-lunch program had lower reading rates than those not eligible. Also, students living in neighborhoods with higher educational attainment expectations had higher mathematics and reading passing rates. Students living in high collective socialization and/or high collective efficacy neighborhoods had higher reading pass rates. The study also found that mathematics completion rates were higher in neighborhoods with high economic impoverishment, high educational expectations for children, high levels of collective efficacy, low levels of fear of retaliation, and low levels of fear of victimization (Emory et al., 2008).

Although analysis may appear to be rich across studies on the topic, causality is often difficult to establish. For example, though Ceballo et al. (2004) indicate that "although they found that adolescents whose mothers worry about their academic futures report less willingness to work hard in school, there is no evidence of a causal relation. Worrisome mothers may lead to academically disenchanted adolescents, or the reverse may be true, such that students who do not work hard at school cause their mothers greater concern" (p. 735). Thus, this finding calls into question past findings that indicate linear as opposed to recursive relationships (Dweck, 1978; Eccles et al., 1983). An additional limitation of many of the studies conducted is that they rely heavily on self-reported data. For some adolescents, there may be a large discrepancy between self-reported assessments of school-related effort or ability and more direct measures of actual school-related behavior. An important inference taken from this work is that multiple perspectives and assessment strategies are required for understanding how individuals make sense of their contextual experiences, given performance expectations.

NEIGHBORHOOD CONTEXT AND ADOLESCENT OUTCOMES: A MIXED-METHODS DESCRIPTIVE CASE STUDY

The purpose of this section is to provide a brief overview of a study that exemplifies the type of theoretical perspective and sensitivity to cultural context that is called for in the introductory remarks of this chapter and in the discussions of the review of the neighborhood studies litera-ture. This exemplar study used CHANGES archival data from a longitudinal study, which exam-ined the impact of incentives on achievement (see Spencer, Noll, & Cassidy, 2005). CHANGES colleagues designed a study that examined the relationships among school community char-acteristics on urban adolescents' school performance, behavior, and psychological well-being.

The project designed by CHANGES proposed two research questions:

1. Are characteristics of the neighborhood surrounding high schools related to the behav-ior and academic performance of students attending those high schools?
2. Are the characteristics of neighborhoods surrounding high schools related to the per-ceptions and psychological well-being of the students attending those high schools?

Sample Adolescent Participants

The samples of ethnically diverse 9th-, 10th-, and 11th-grade adolescents were academi-cally high- or marginally performing participants of a 3-year longitudinal study. Students attended one of 41 public high schools in a large, northeast urban region. Similarly, the school neighborhoods were represented by 41 neighborhoods proximal to the high school attended by the sample's 889 students.

Measures Used in the Study

Both drive-through observations and system-level assessment reports are included as well as student self-reports.

- NACC observational instrument (Neighborhood Assessment of Community Character-istics [Spencer, McDermott, Burton, & Kochman, 1997]) provided options for catego-rizing dimensions of neighborhoods. It is a drive-through instrument, which included approximately 130 descriptors of neighborhoods (e.g., housing character, density, and neighborhood content including green spaces)
- School characteristics data (1999–2000) were system assessment information that was converted from interval data to categorical data (School District of Philadelphia)
- Fear of Calamity/Environmental Risks youth completed measure (Riechard & McGar-rity, 1994)
- Negative Teacher Perception adolescent self-assessment measure (Abbott Adjective Checklist [Abbott, 1981])

Conceptual Underpinnings

The PVEST theoretical framework (Phenomenological Variant of Ecological Systems The-ory) (Spencer, 1995, 2006, 2008; Spencer et al., 1997; Spencer & Harpalani, 2004) informed the measures chosen and study design (see Figure 16.1). As described (Spencer, 1995, 2006, 2008b), PVEST represents a framework that explores human vulnerability as linked to cop-ing processes and life course outcomes. It is a recursive model; thus, outcomes at a particular developmental period have implications for level of protective factors available in addition to consequent risk level and, as a consequence, is cyclically manifested as lives unfold across the life course. That is, it is ontogenetic in that one level of development and the character of coping have implications for subsequent stages of life.

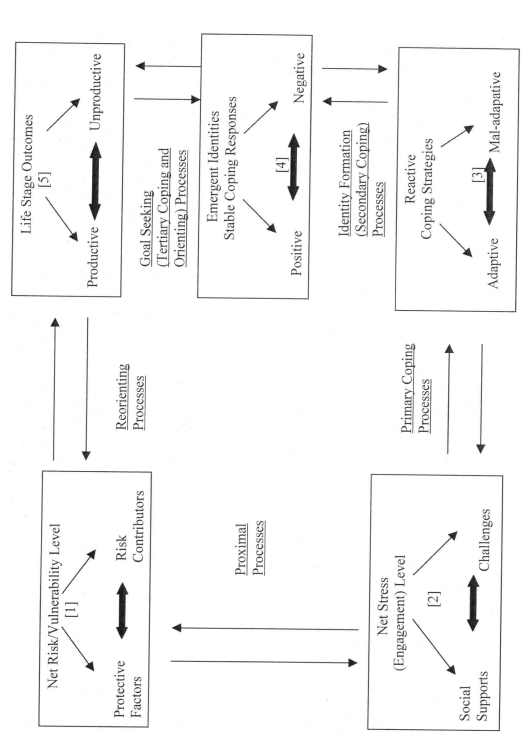

Figure 16.1. Spencer's (1995) Phenomenological Variant of Ecological Systems Theory (PVEST)

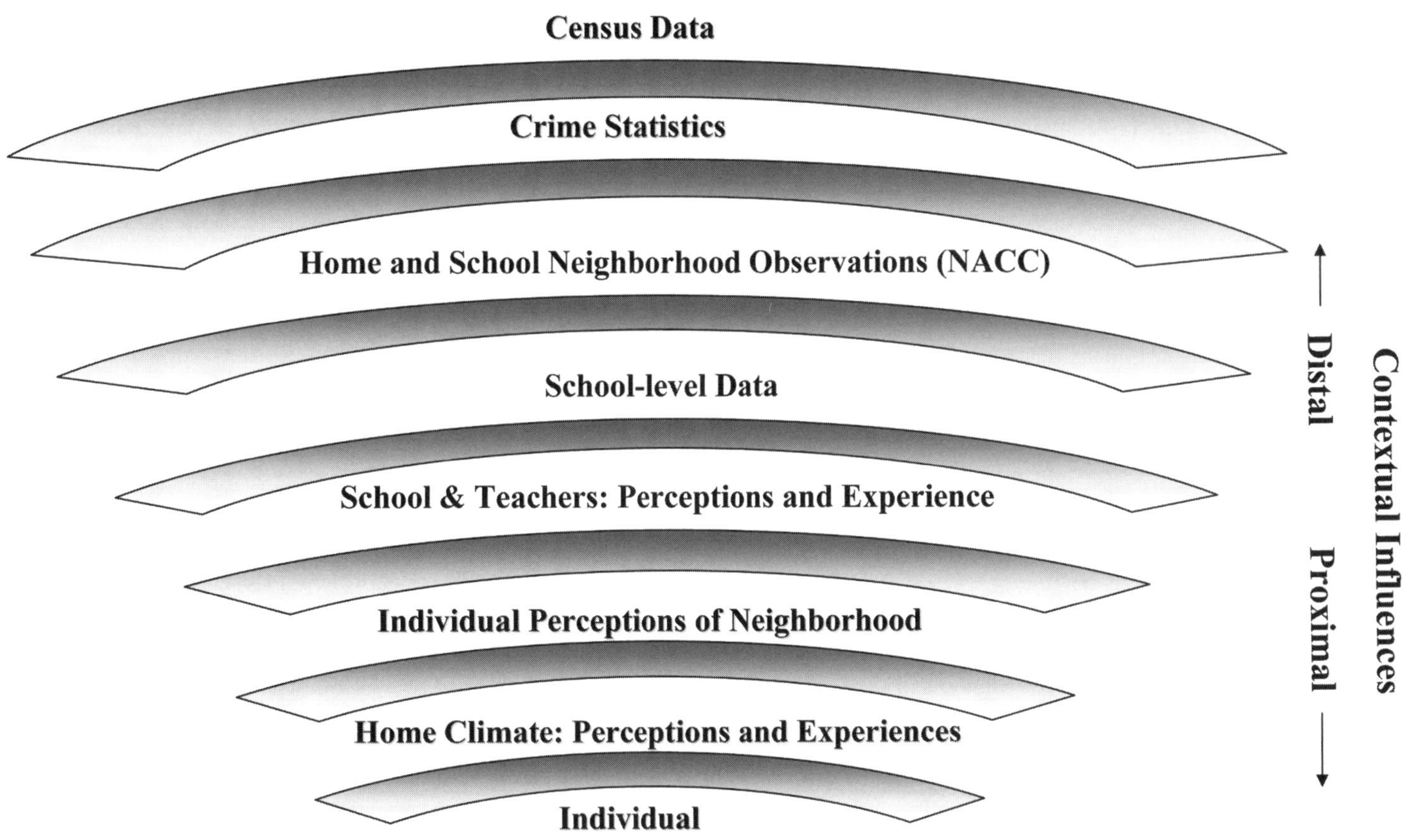

Contextual Influences

← Distal   Proximal →

Census Data

Crime Statistics

Home and School Neighborhood Observations (NACC)

School-level Data

School & Teachers: Perceptions and Experience

Individual Perceptions of Neighborhood

Home Climate: Perceptions and Experiences

Individual

Figure 16.2.   Nested Context Assessment Strategy

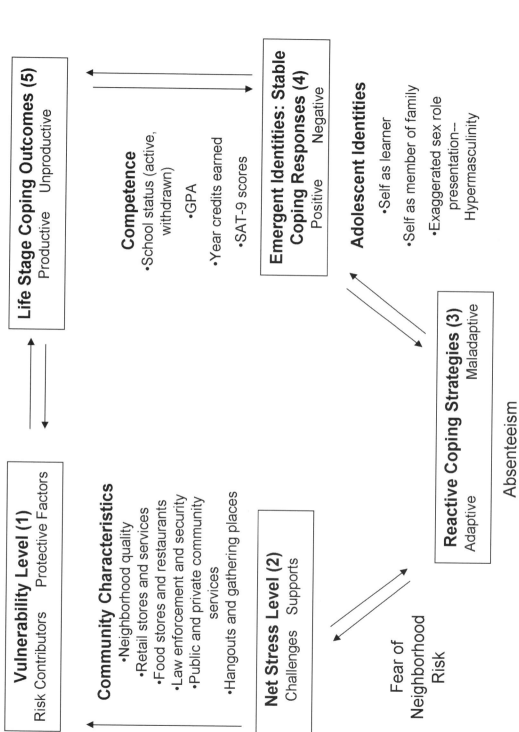

Figure 16.3.   Using PVEST to Consider the Effects of Neighborhoods and Community Characteristics on Adolescent Academic Outcomes

Study Design

As described in Figure 16.2, the design represented a nested approach. That is, levels of context (e.g., broader neighborhood descriptors and school system–collected school-level data) were considered and viewed as having implications for children's ways of thinking (e.g., adolescents' perceptions of fear and their inferences concerning teachers' evaluations of them [i.e., negative teacher perceptions]). Thus, the conceptually embedded neighborhood assessment framework is presented as Figure 16.2. The constructs described are linked to the theoretical framework to represent either the cause of support (i.e., protective factors) or as sources of challenge (i.e., risk factors). Thus, the representative constructs were linked with the research questions representing the PVEST framework and are inserted and presented as Figure 16.3. The descriptors for the 41 schools participating in the study are included as Figure 16.4. The school characteristics for the 41 northeast-region urban public high schools were for the 1999–2000 year. As indicated in Figure 16.4, school characteristics include three types of enrollment level (i.e., fewer than 1,000; 1,000–2,000; and more than 2,000). Also included are the dropout rates; proportion of low-income students; number of student assaults; average daily attendance, students below basic achievement; percent minority (39 percent to 100 percent); and number of violent incidents.

Findings

The findings were organized to answer each of two general questions. *The first question asked whether characteristics of the neighborhoods surrounding high schools related to the behavior and academic performance of students attending those high schools.*

- Schools with the highest numbers of within-school assaults were located within communities that were higher in quality and upkeep [$F(2,34) = 4.43$, $p = 0.02$].
- Students attending schools located in neighborhoods characterized as being of good quality have fewer days absent than students attending schools in poor-quality neighborhoods.

School Characteristics	%	School Characteristics	%
Enrollment		Average Daily Attendance	
Fewer than 1,000	28.9	Less than 75%	43.2
1,000–2,000	39.5	75–84%	27.0
More than 2,000	31.6	85–95%	29.7
Dropout Rate		Students Below Basic Achievement	
0–10%	63.2	Fewer than 50%	16.2
11–15%	21.1	50–79%	21.6
16–30%	15.8	Greater than 80%	62.2
Low-Income Students		% Minority (39.0–100%)	
Fewer than 50%	21.1	<50%	15.4
50–74%	31.6	50–75%	28.2
75–91%	47.4	Greater than 75%	56.4
Number of Student Assaults		Number of Violent Incidents	
None	16.2	0–10	32.4
10 or fewer	51.4	11–30	27.0
More than 10	32.4	More than 30	40.5

Figure 16.4. Selected School Characteristics for 41 Philadelphia Public High Schools, 1999–2000

- Among males in the sample, being a marginally performing student and living in poor-quality neighborhoods were significant contributors to absenteeism. Being Hispanic was associated with decreased likelihood of absenteeism.
- Among females, significant predictors of being absent were being Hispanic, being white, and being a marginally performing student.

Other general findings were impressive and are described briefly.

For the poorest group of students, the NACC factor indicating higher presence of law enforcement predicted greater absenteeism from school. Poverty status also mattered and demonstrated interesting patterns. Income eligibility for inclusion in the study was contingent on having a family income that was no more than 10 percent above the income limit for the Federal Free Lunch program. In this sense, the variability in economic status is limited. However, the welfare reform literature has demonstrated the differential challenges facing the "poor" versus the "'poorest of the poor" (see Spencer et al., 2005); the latter group consistently show mean family income scores that are significantly lower than the demarcation for poverty. Accordingly, we divided the analysis sample into two groups: those whose family income was more than 50 percent *below* the Federal Free Lunch guidelines (35 percent of the sample), and those whose family income was between 50 percent below and 10 percent above the guideline (65 percent of the sample).

Consequently, the second question linked neighborhood factors to well-being. *Are the characteristics of neighborhoods surrounding high schools related to the perceptions and psychological well-being of the students attending those high schools?*

- Students attending schools in neighborhoods characterized as being of poor quality expressed more fear of neighborhood risk than students attending schools in better quality neighborhoods.
- Females expressed significantly more fear than males (on average, the score for females was 2.62 points higher than the mean for males), and white students expressed significantly less fear when compared with students of other ethnicities (5.4 points lower on average than the mean for other ethnicities).
- Students attending schools in high-quality neighborhoods perceived their teachers as having higher opinions of them than students living in poor-quality neighborhoods.
- Males and females were equally as likely to think their teachers held them *in low esteem*. However, marginally performing students were more likely to perceive lower teacher evaluations (as inferred by an average of 9.5 points difference) than the high-performing students ($p < .001$). We found no direct or moderating effect of ethnicity or student poverty status on negative teacher perception.

Conclusions Drawn from the Data

Utilizing a variety of data types in the theory-driven research described, the study design appeared helpful in obtaining a richer appreciation of the links between multiple component context variables and youths' meaning making.

- The level of upkeep and vigilance necessary to maintain *the appearance* of a community may be necessary but not sufficient to drive violence out of a community.
- Students' marginal school performance may in part be due to their fearfulness of the school neighborhood and thus concern for their personal safety. Such preoccupation may hinder their full academic engagement and performance.

- For students attending schools in poor-quality neighborhoods, their academic performance may be constrained by their perception that teachers hold them in low esteem.
- Low-quality neighborhoods may limit students' access to resources (e.g., responsible adults and community organizations) that reinforce prosocial norms, such as school attendance.

DISCUSSION AND IMPLICATIONS FOR FUTURE RESEARCH DIRECTIONS

As indicated in the description of CHANGES, theory-driven frameworks that strive toward obtaining sociocultural understanding of youths' meaning making are important. The experiences of adolescent learners, especially, take place in multiply layered contexts and should be inclusive of particular considerations (e.g., with caring or less caring adults and in physical settings). The findings of the exemplar study described suggest critical implications and have salience for future directions of research initiatives as well as introduce critical policy considerations. Accordingly, several cautions are suggested:

- Examine the link between school neighborhood characteristics and students' perceptions of teachers' perceptions of them.
- Investigate adolescents' coping responses to neighborhood fear.
- Examine the role of resiliency in producing high academic achievement despite poor-quality school neighborhoods and negative teacher perceptions.

The content and organization of this chapter aided a particular conceptual emphasis. The suggested approach serves to highlight the need and salience of theory-driven perspectives for research more generally although as especially facilitative of education research. The suggested conceptual strategy increases insights about human development frameworks of special salience for policy decisions needed for maximizing youth and family outcomes. Importantly, the approach also enhances one's power to understand and unpack the contributions of basic human development and coping processes as insights critical for the design and implementation of effective teacher and staff training. Finally, a conceptual orientation of the type noted also increases the probability of arriving at programming and policy supportive of competence outcomes and more general achievement outcomes for the nation's most vulnerable youth.

REFERENCES

Abbott, A.A. (1981). Factors related to third grade achievement: Self-perception, classroom composition, sex, and race. *Contemporary Educational Psychology, 6,* 167–179.

Aisenberg, E., & Herrenkohl, T. (2008). Community violence in context: Risk and resilience in children and families. *Journal of Interpersonal Violence, 23,* 296–315.

Aneshensel, C. S., & Sucoff, C. A. (1996). The neighborhood context of adolescent mental health. *Journal of Health and Social Behavior, 37*(4), 293–310.

Anthony, E. J. (1974). The syndrome of the psychologically invulnerable child. In E. J. Anthony & C. Koupernik (Eds.), *The child in his family: Vol. 3. Children at psychiatric risk* (pp. 529–544). New York, NY: Wiley.

Aries, P. (1962). Centuries of childhood: A social history of family life. New York, NY: Knopf.

Balkin, J. (Ed.). (2001). *What* Brown v. Board of Education *should have said: The Nation's top legal experts rewrite America's landmark civil rights decision.* New York: New York University Press.

Bowen, N. K., & Bowen, G. L. (1999). Effects of crime and violence in neighborhoods and schools on the school behavior and performance of adolescents. *Journal of Adolescent Research, 14*(3), 319–342.

Brody, G. H., Ge, X., Kim, S. Y., Murry, V. M., Simons, R. L., Gibbons, F. X., et al. (2003). Neighborhood disadvantage moderates associations of parenting and older sibling problem attitudes and behavior with conduct disorders in African American children. *Journal of Consulting and Clinical Psychology, 71*(2), 211–222.

Brown v. Board of Education. (1954). 347 U.S. 483.

Burton, L. M. (1997). Ethnography and the meaning of adolescence in high-risk neighborhoods. *Ethos, 25*(2), 208–217.

Campbell, A., & Converse, P. E. (Eds.). (1972). *The human meaning of social change.* New York, NY: Russell Sage Foundation.

Ceballo, R., McLoyd, V. C., & Toyokawa, T. (2004). The influence of neighborhood quality on adolescents' educational values and school effort. *Journal of Adolescent Research, 19*(6), 716–739.

Chestang, L. (1972). *Character development in a hostile environment.* Occasional paper No. 3. Chicago, IL, University of Chicago Press.

Connell, J. P., Halpern-Felsher, B. L., Clifford, E., Crichlow, W., & Usinger, P. (1995). Hanging in there: Behavioral, psychological, and contextual factors affecting whether African American adolescents stay in high school. *Journal of Adolescent Research, 10*(1), 41–63.

Crane, J. (1991). The epidemic theory of ghettos and neighborhood effects on dropping out and teenage childbearing. *American Journal of Sociology, 96*, 1226–1259.

Cross, W. E. (1991). *Shades of black: Diversity in African American identity.* Philadelphia, PA: Temple University Press.

Darity, W., & Myers, S., Jr. (1998). Persistent disparity: Race and economic inequality in the United States since 1945. Cheltenham, England: Edward Elgar.

Dell'Angelo, T. (2009). *Teacher trust and perceived obstacles as mediators of student achievement in Philadelphia high schools* (Unpublished doctoral dissertation). University of Pennsylvania, Philadelphia.

DuBois, W. E. B. (1935). Does the Negro need separate schools? *Journal of Negro Education, 4*, 329–335.

Duncan, G. J. (1994). Families and neighbors as sources of disadvantage in the schooling decisions of white and black adolescents. *American Journal of Education, 103*(1), 20–53.

Dweck, C. S. (1978). Achievement. In M. Lamb (Ed.), *Social and personality development* (pp. 114–130). New York, NY: Holt, Rinehart & Winston.

Eccles, J. S., Adler, T. F., Futterman, R., Goff, S. B., Kaczala, C., Meece, J. L., et al. (1983). Expectancies, values, and academic behaviors. In J. T. Spence (Ed.), *Achievement and achievement motives* (pp. 75–146). New York, NY: Freeman.

Edwards, M. (2008, March). *Effects of school community characteristics on urban adolescents.* Panel presentation at the Annual Meeting of the American Education Research Association. New York, NY.

Emory, R., Caughy, M., Harris, R., & Franzini, L. (2008). Neighborhood social processes and academic achievement in elementary school. *Journal of Community Psychology, 36*(7), 885–898.

Ensminger, M. E., Lamkin, R. P., & Jacobson, N. (1996). School leaving: A longitudinal perspective including neighborhood effects. *Child Development, 67*, 2400–2416.

Entwisle, D. R., Alexander, K. L., & Olson, L. S. (1994). The gender gap in math: Its possible origins in neighborhood effects. *American Sociological Review, 59*, 822–838.

Feins, J., Holin, M. J., & Phipps, A. (1996). *Moving to Opportunity for Fair Housing Program operations manual.* Cambridge, MA: Abt Associates.

Ge, X., Brody, G. H., Conger, R. D., Simons, R. L., & Murray, V. M. (2002). Contextual amplification of pubertal transition effects on deviant peer affiliation and externalizing behavior among African American children. *Developmental Psychology, 38*, 42–54.

Hafiz, W. F. (2009). *Fear and the pedagogy of care: An exploratory study of veteran white female teachers' emotional resilience in urban schools* (Unpublished doctoral dissertation). Temple University, Philadelphia.

Halpern-Felsher, B. L., Connell, J. P., Spencer, M. B., Aber, J. L., Duncan, G. P., Clifford, E., et al. (1997). Neighborhood and family factors predicting educational risk and attainment in African American and white children and adolescents. In J. Brooks-Gunn, G. Duncan, & J. L. Aber (Eds.), *Neighborhood poverty, Vol. 1: Context and consequences for children* (pp. 146–173). New York: Russell Sage Foundation.

Harding, D. J. (2003). Counterfactual models of neighborhood effects: The effect of neighborhood poverty on dropping out and teenage pregnancy. *American Journal of Sociology, 3*, 676–719.

Harper, S. R., Patton, L. D., & Wooden, O. S. (2009). Access and equity for African American students in higher education: A critical race historical analysis of policy efforts. *Journal of Higher Education, 80*(4), 389–414.

Havighurst, R. J. (1953). *Human development and education.* New York, NY: McKay.

Hope, J. (1995). The price they pay for the places they live: A case study of the association of educational achievement and aspirations with residential incongruence among middle-class black adolescents. In J. Cardell (Ed.), *American families: Issues in race and ethnicity* (Vol. 1015, pp. 407–427). New York, NY: Garland.

Jones, B. A. (March, 2008). Policy, profit and the private sector: The ongoing structural failure of voice, representation, and success in the U.S. school reform industry. In M. B. Spencer (Chair), *Kenneth and Mamie Clark Revisited: Unfinished Business of 21st-Century Disparities and Policy Inadequacies*. Annual Meeting of the American Educational Research Association, New York, NY.

Kardiner, A., & Ovesey, L. (1951) *The mark of oppression: A psychosocial study of the American Negro*. New York, NY: Norton.

Lee, C., Spencer, M. B., & Harpalani, V. (2003). Every shut eye ain't sleep: Studying how people live culturally. *Educational Researcher, 32*(5), 6–13.

Leventhal, T., & Brooks-Gunn, J. (2000). The neighborhoods they live in: The effects of neighborhood residence on child and adolescent outcomes. *Psychological Bulletin, 126*(2), 309–337.

Leventhal, T., Brooks-Leventhal, T., & Brooks-Gunn, J. (2004). A randomized study of neighborhood effects on low-income children's educational outcomes. *Developmental Psychology, 40*, 488–507.

Loury, G. C. (2009, July 25). Obama, Gates and the American black man. *New York Times.*

Luthar, S. S., & Becker, B. (2002). Privileged but pressured? A study of affluent youth. *Child Development, 73*, 1593–1610.

Luthar, S. S., & Lattendresse, S. J. (2002). Adolescent risk: The cost of affluence. *New Directions in Youth Development, 95*, 101–121.

Markstrom-Adams, C., & Spencer, M. B. (1994). A model for identity intervention with minority adolescents. In S. Archer (Ed.), *Interventions for adolescent identity development* (pp. 84–102). Thousand Oaks, CA: Sage.

McIntosh, P. (1989, July–August). White privilege: Unpacking the invisible knapsack. *Peace and Freedom*, 10–12.

Myrdal, Gunnar (1944). *An American dilemma: The Negro problem and modern democracy*. New York, NY: Harper & Bros.

O'Connor, C. (March, 2008). Black pathology in academic, popular, and professional discourse: Marring educational opportunity and social policy 50 years post *Brown*. In M. B. Spencer (Chair), *Kenneth and Mamie Clark Revisited: Unfinished Business of 21st-Century Disparities and Policy Inadequacies*. Annual Meeting of American Educational Research Association, New York, NY.

Riechard, D. E., & McGarrity, J. (1994). Early adolescents' perceptions of relative risk from 10 societal and environmental hazards. *Journal of Environmental Education, 26*, 16–23.

Sampson, R. J. (1997). Collective regulation of adolescent misbehavior: Validation results from eighty Chicago neighborhoods. *Journal of Adolescent Research, 12*, 227–244.

Sampson, R. J., Raudenbush, S. W., & Earls, F. (1997). Neighborhoods and violent crime: A multilevel study of collective efficacy. *Science, 277*, 918–924.

Sanbonmatsu, L., Kling, J. R., Duncan, G. J., Brooks-Gunn, J. (2006). Neighborhoods and academic achievement: Results from the Moving to Opportunity experiment. *The Journal of Human Resources, 41*(4), 649–691.

Sawicki, D. S., & Flynn, P. (1996). Neighborhood indicators. *Journal of the American Planning Association, 62*(2), 165–184.

Simons, L. G., Simons, R. L., Conger, R. D., & Brody, G. H. (2004). Collective socialization and child conduct problems: A multilevel analysis with an African American sample. *Youth and Society, 35*(3), 267–292.

Spencer, M. B. (1985). Self-concept development. In D. T. Slaughter (Ed.), *Perspectives on black child development: New directions for child development* (pp. 59–72). San Francisco, CA: Jossey Bass.

Spencer, M. B. (1990). Parental values transmission: Implications for black child development. In J. B. Stewart & H. Cheatham (Eds.), *Interdisciplinary perspectives on black families* (pp. 111–130). New Brunswick, NJ: Transactions.

Spencer, M. B. (1995). Old issues and new theorizing about African American youth: A phenomenological variant of ecological systems theory. In R. L. Taylor (Ed.), *Black youth: Perspectives on their status in the United States* (pp. 37–69). Westport, CT: Praeger.

Spencer, M. B. (1999). Transitions and continuities in cultural values: Kenneth Clark revisited. In R. L. Jones (Ed.), *African American children, youth and parenting* (pp. 183–208). Hampton, VA: Cobb and Henry.

Spencer, M. B. (2006). Phenomenology and ecological systems theory: Development of diverse groups. In W. Damon & R. Lerner (Eds.), *Handbook of child psychology, Vol. 1. Theory* (6th ed., pp. 829–893). New York, NY: Wiley.

Spencer, M. B. (2008a). Lessons learned and opportunities ignored post-*Brown v. Board of Education*: Youth development and the myth of a colorblind society, *Educational Researcher, 37*(5), 253–266.

Spencer, M. B. (2008b). Phenomenology and ecological systems theory: Development of diverse groups. In W. Damon & R. Lerner (Eds.), *Child and adolescent development: An advanced course* (pp. 696–735). New York, NY: Wiley.

Spencer, M. B., Brookins, G. K., & Allen, W. R. (Eds.). (1985*). Beginnings: Social and affective development of black children*. Hillsdale, NJ: Erlbaum.

Spencer, M. B., Cross, W. E., Harpalani, V., & Goss, T. N. (2003). Historical and developmental perspectives on black academic achievement: Debunking the "acting white" myth and posing new directions for research. In

C. C. Yeakey & R.D. Henderson (Eds.), *Surmounting all odds: Education, opportunity and society in the new millennium* (pp. 273–304). Greenwich, CT: Information Age Publishers.

Spencer, M. B., & Dornbusch S. M. (1998). Challenges in studying minority youth. In R. E. Muuss & H. D. Portion (Eds.), *Adolescent behavior and society: A book of readings* (5th ed., pp. 316–330). Boston, MA: McGraw-Hill.

Spencer, M. B., Dupree, D., & Hartmann, T. (1997). A phenomenological variant of ecological systems theory (PVEST): A self-organization perspective in context. *Development and Psychopathology, 9*, 817–833.

Spencer, M. B., & Harpalani, V. (2004). Nature, nurture, and the question of "How?": A phenomenological variant of ecological systems theory. In C. Garcia-Coll, K. Kearer, & R. Lerner (Eds.) (Chap 3) *Nature and nurture: The complex interplay of genetic and environmental influences on human behavior and development* (pp.53–77). Mahwah, NJ: Lawrence Erlbaum Associates.

Spencer, M. B., Harpalani, V., Cassidy, E., Jacobs, C. Y., Donde, S., Goss, T. N., et al. (2006). Understanding vulnerability and resilience from a normative developmental perspective: Implications for racially and ethnically diverse youth. In D. Cicchetti and D. J. Cohen (Eds.), *Developmental psychopathology* (pp. 627–672). Hoboken, NJ: Wiley.

Spencer, M. B., & Markstrom-Adams, C. (1990). Identity processes among racial and ethnic minority children in America. *Child Development, 61*(2), 290–310.

Spencer, M. B., McDermott, P. A., Burton, L. M., & Kochman, T. J. (1997). An alternative approach to assessing neighborhood effects on early adolescent achievement and problem behavior. In J. Brooks-Gunn, G. Duncan, & J. Lawrence Aber (Eds.), *Neighborhood poverty: Context and consequences for children* (Vol. 2, pp. 145–163). New York, NY: Russell Sage Foundation.

Spencer, M. B., Noll, E., & Cassidy, E. (2005). Monetary incentives in support of academic achievement: Results of a randomized field trial involving high-achieving, low-resource, ethnically diverse urban adolescents, *Evaluation Research, 29*(3), 199–222.

Spencer, M. B., Swanson, D. P., & Cunningham, M. (1991). Ethnicity, ethnic identity and competence formation: Adolescent transition and identity transformation. *Journal of Negro Education, 60*(3), 366-387.

Spencer, T. R. (March, 2008). New directions: Cultural and developmental context considerations for research on health outcomes. In M. B. Spencer (Chair), *Kenneth and Mamie Clark Revisited: Unfinished Business of 21st-Century Disparities and Policy Inadequacies.* Annual Meeting of American Educational Research Association, New York, NY.

Swanson, D. P., Edwards, M., & Spencer, M. B. (2010). *Adolescence: Development in a global era.* Burlington, MA: Academic Press.

Trei, L. (2004). Black children might have been better off without *Brown v. Board*, Bell says. Retrieved from http://news.stanford.edu/news/2004/april21/brownbell-421.html

Wallis, W. (1994). The third wave: Current trends in regional governance. *National Civic Review 83*(3), 290–310.

Wilson, W. J. (1987). *The truly disadvantaged: The inner city, the underclass, and public policy.* Chicago, IL: University of Chicago Press.

Wilson, W. J. (1992). Another look at the truly disadvantaged. *Political Science Quarterly, 106*(4), 639–656.

17

Immigrant Children

Hiding in Plain Sight in the Margins of the Urban Infrastructure

Michael A. Olivas

If 1982's *Plyler v. Doe* is the true high-water mark of immigrant rights in the United States, then hectoring President Obama on the issue of immigrant rights during a presidential televised address on health care reform is the low-water mark (Hulse, 2009). In today's polity, it is easier to point to the denial of immigrant rights in localized conditions than it is to cite evidence of the extension of immigrant rights; in many respects, 30 years later, alien children would be unlikely to have prevailed. As one indicator, state legislatures are formally considering record levels of immigrant-related legislation. In the first 6 months of 2009, more than 1,400 bills have been considered in all 50 states; as of June 30, 2009, 144 laws and 115 resolutions had been enacted in 44 states, with bills sent to governors in two additional states. A total of 285 bills and resolutions have passed legislatures; 23 of these bills are pending governor's approval and three bills were vetoed. No bills have been enacted in Alaska, Massachusetts, Michigan, or Ohio, the only four states not to have done so (National Conference of State Legislatures, 2009).

These recent statutes run the gamut, from enacting, on the one hand, pro-immigrant state programs for college tuition to, on the other, a number of blatantly restrictionist and nativist statutes, including ones in Arizona, which for the undocumented and Mexican American population resembles 1950 and 1960-vintage Mississippi (Doty, 2009). Maricopa County, Arizona, has attempted to characterize alien entry into the country as a conspiracy to smuggle oneself, giving rise to enhanced criminal penalties (Berry, 2006; Immigration Policy Center, 2008). This extraordinary rise in such legislative interests is undoubtedly due to a poor national economy and overburdened states and locales, well-publicized and highly polarized federal attention to immigration, a sharp rise in conservative media regularly flogging the issue, and an undifferentiated fear of foreign and domestic terrorism, all of which have led to a leadership vacuum in the field. *Plyler v. Doe*, decided in 1982, settled the question of whether undocumented children could attend public K–12 education, or whether states such as Texas could restrict their attendance. In a 5–4 decision, the Court held that the state could not regulate immigration by denying these children attendance, a ruling that has not been challenged in the Supreme Court since (Olivas, 2005). It has been almost 25 years since the last national legalization reform of immigration, 1986's Immigration Reform and Control Act, signed into law by President Reagan. Various state, county, and local ordinances aimed at regulating general immigration functions are unconstitutional as a function of exclusive federal preemptory powers. If purely state, county, or local interests are governed and if federal preemptory powers are not triggered, such ordinances may be properly enacted, provided they are not subterfuges for replacing or substituting federal authority. Purely state benefits, as one example, can be extended to or withheld from undocumented college students, as tuition benefits and state residency determinations are properly designated as state classifications, which reference but do not determine immigration status (Olivas, 2004, 2008; Romero, 2003). However, a number of Supreme Court decisions and common law do not reserve a substantive role in immigration enforcement absent such delegation and carefully controlled, designated purposes (Kobach, 2005; Olivas, 2007; Pham, 2006; Wishnie, 2001).

In this chapter, I examine one settled area in detail, noting how *Plyler v. Doe* has morphed beyond its original K–12 public school tuition moorings. This attestation to an important feature of immigrant life and the U.S. polity demonstrates that even 25 years of immigrant children's rights have not been fully resolved and have required additional litigation and additional vigilance to secure the Supreme Court's rulings. I believe this thesis can be advanced by thick descriptions of a case where more of an equilibrium has been reached, the case of undocumented school children, where the record reveals substantial and long-standing accommodation to the 1982 development of *Plyler v. Doe*. However, even this settled case has been contested regularly in school board meetings and classroom buildings, and as this record will show, *Plyler* implementation issues have continued, sometimes necessitating additional litigation. Thus, the vigilance to secure these rights has stretched more than 30 years, since Texas enacted the state law in 1975 that enabled its public school districts to charge tuition to parents of undocumented school children. Although the underlying legislative history is unclear, and although no public hearings were ever held on the provision, certain border Texas school superintendents had urged the legislation, which was enacted without controversy as a small piece of larger, routine education statutes (Olivas, 2005). In 1982, the Mexican American Legal Defense and Educational Fund (MALDEF) attorneys prevailed in the U.S. Supreme Court, in a 5–4 opinion authored by Justice William Brennan.

Justice Brennan struck down the Texas statute, finding the state's theory to be "nothing more than the assertion that illegal entry . . . prevents a person from becoming a resident for purposes of enrolling his children in the public schools" (*Plyler*, p. 205). This holding has since driven restrictionist policy behavior and litigation, particularly in the auxiliary area of college tuition residency. Almost immediately after *Plyler*, a corollary issue was litigated, involving a U.S. citizen child of undocumented Mexican parents, who had left the child in the care of his adult sister in a Texas town. This time, the Court determined that his domicile was not in Texas, a precept of traditional family law, which holds that the domicile of unemancipated children is that of their parents; in this instance, he was not a legal charge of his sister, hence could not be considered a "resident" of the Texas school district. (This is a legal infirmity that could be remedied by several means.) *Martinez v. Bynum* did not limit the earlier *Plyler*, and no other K–12 residency-related immigration case has been decided by the U.S. Supreme Court since 1983. A postsecondary residency case involving nonimmigrant visa holders was decided in 1982 for the alien college students on preemption grounds (*Toll v. Moreno*), but *Plyler* has remained in force, undisturbed since 1982.

This is not to say that it has not been attacked, at a variety of levels, in the 25 years since it was decided. On the more quotidian level, MALDEF and other lawyers have had to file several dozen actions since the early 1980s to enforce *Plyler*'s clear holding, including school board actions to require Social Security numbers, school requests for drivers' licenses to identify parents, additional "registration" of immigrant children, "safety notification" for immigrant parents, separate schools for immigrant children, and other policies and practices designed to identify immigration status or single out undocumented children. This chapter examines the range of these *Plyler* implementation issues, analyzing direct and indirect challenges that have arisen in the intervening quarter century, both in legislative reactions and in the many school-based policies that have eroded the blanket enrollment permission accorded the children by the original case. Some of these policies affect children, Latino children disproportionately, but several of them have continued to single out children on immigration grounds and thus directly undermine their enrollment status. At the end of the day, it is difficult to ignore the petty nature and widespread harassment of the children, who, it must be remembered, have committed no crime of their own, and who are innocent victims of behavior that might have been committed by their parents. This original sin concept may have biblical roots, but it is difficult to square with *Plyler*'s clear holding. Justice Brennan's majority opinion accurately characterized this situation as one "imposing special disabilities upon groups disfavored by virtue of circumstances beyond their control [and which] suggests the kind of 'class or caste' treatment that the Fourteenth Amendment was designed to abolish" (*Plyler*, p. 218, footnote 14).

In the first part of this chapter, I examine the direct challenges to *Plyler*, both those that have been legislative efforts, including those that appeared to have settled the matter in the mid-1990s in California, and more current ones that have arisen, state ballot issues that were enacted to address issues of illegal immigration in 2006. Direct challenges to undocumented students have also included "helicopter children," those whose parents sent them to study in the United States without parental residence; a subset of this complex issue is parents who have legally entered the country but whose behavior has resulted in their being out of status, rendering even citizen children removable; campus policing policies; and nonlegislative, school-based initiatives such as the use of Social Security numbers and identification measures. The original case has proven quite resilient, fending off litigation and federal and state legislative efforts to overturn it, and nurturing efforts to extend its reach to college attendees who were allowed to stay in school by the original case. It has had to be reinforced by vigilant efforts, but it has proven more hardy than it appeared 25 years ago (Inniss, 1996). I also examine cases and school-district or state actions that indirectly implicate *Plyler*, and analyze the various means by which restrictionist policies have attempted to extirpate the practice allowed by *Plyler* and to overturn its holding. Indirect measures include a variety of language issues, including bilingual education and English as a Second Language (ESL); building, siting, and attendance zone concerns; undocumented students who become at risk when their achievements bring them into the spotlight or when they win national awards for academic prowess; the mean-spirited assault on programs that provide resources to undocumented children; separate immigrant schools and programs that concentrate the children in a special, circumscribed environment; college preparation issues; and even miscellaneous issues having to do with drivers' licenses and school transportation. There is a long list of such topics that disproportionately affect these children, who are marginalized even within the difficult world of public and private schooling in the modern United States (Pizarro, 2005; Valencia, 2008).

DIRECT CHALLENGES TO *PLYLER*

The most direct challenges have been legislative. In November, 1994, by nearly 60 percent, California's voters passed a popular state referendum, Proposition 187, which would have denied virtually all state-funded benefits (including public education) to undocumented Californians. Immigration scholars Kevin Johnson and Ruben Garcia have carefully cataloged the many public comments that constituted the discourse over the passage of the proposition, and while reasonable people were on both sides of the issue, many unreason-able remarks and racist commentary coarsened the exchange. Professor Johnson perceptively noted,

> Proposition 187 is the product of a deeply complex, perhaps unique, set of political forces in the United States. As the solid support for the measure amply demonstrates, its backing did not split along classic liberal-conservative lines. The limited political power of noncitizens made it easier for one powerful politician [Gov. Pete Wilson] to use Proposition 187 and anti-immigrant/anti-immigration sentiment to build a bipartisan coalition, ensuring his re-election and the initiative's passage. . . . Curiously enough, a much-debated aspect of the passage of Proposition 187—that it is nativistic and racist—in all probability will never be decided. (Johnson, 1995b, p. 672)

Professor Garcia has noted, after reviewing these strains in the U.S. immigration history, culminating in Proposition 187, that "immigration law and policy continue to be partially motivated by a drive for cultural and racial homogeneity" (Garcia, 1995, p. 119). The re-appearance of state and local ordinances calls Professor Johnson's "uniqueness" note into question, but he is surely correct when he notes the "deeply complex" nature of the issue, and he was writing years before the issue of terrorism and attack upon the U.S. and its allies raised this dimension as a wellspring of immigration policy.

Proposition 187 was clearly intended by its sponsors to rescind *Plyler*, restrict access to public benefits, and expel aliens from the state. The preamble in Section One, for example, indicated, "[Californian citizens] have suffered and are suffering economic hardship . . . personal injury and damage caused by the criminal conduct of illegal aliens in this state. [By enacting this legislation, Californians intend to] establish a system of required notification by and between such agencies to prevent illegal aliens in the United States from receiving benefits or public services in the State of California." The Proposition would have required law enforcement officials to ascertain the legal status of every person "suspected of being present in the United States" without proper immigration authorization and to notify fed-eral and state authorities of their suspicions. It would have extended the same affirmative notification obligation to state social service and health care workers if they "determined or reasonably suspected" that a client was out of proper status. While the details of these requirements were not fleshed out at the early stages, the overall scheme, if implemented, clearly would have placed certain obligations upon various state, county, and local public officials and administrators to effectuate apprehension or notification requirements. In a complex but authoritative opinion, the trial judge enjoined implementation and enforce-ment of sections 4, 5, 6, 7, and 9 of Proposition 187, and then subsequently struck down virtually all of the provisions, citing either preemption for the social service benefits or *Plyler* for the educational provisions. During the pendency of these actions, Congress passed the Personal Responsibility and Work Opportunity Reconciliation Act of 1996, after which the judge held that the provisions of PRWORA preempted any remaining provisions of the Cali-fornia Proposition, as Congress had clearly "occupied the field," squeezing out any such role for states to act (Inniss, 1996; Johnson, 1995a, 1995b; Olivas, 1994).

Had these proposition provisions been able to stand, they would have even gone further than had the original Texas statute, which had allowed, but not required, school districts to charge tuition, but had not banned students from attending Texas public schools. Proposi-tion 187 would have enacted an absolute ban, and would not have even allowed school districts to charge tuition for enrolling undocumented children. In addition, it would have required school authorities to report undocumented parents or guardians: "Each school district shall provide information to the State Superintendent of Public Instruction, the At-torney General of California, and [federal immigration authorities] regarding any enrollee or

pupil, or parent or guardian, [of children] attending a public elementary or secondary school
. . . determined or reasonably suspected to be in violation of federal immigration laws
within forty-five days after becoming aware of an apparent violation." The language even
would have arguably required authorities to report undocumented (or apparently undocumented) parents or guardians of enrolled citizen children. Careful scholars who examined
these provisions also raised a number of other problems with them, including the state's
constitutional right-to-education features, national origin and race discrimination, and the
obvious preemption issues (Brickman, 2006; Pabon Lopez, 2004, 2005; Ruiz-de-Velasco,
Fix, & Clewell, 2000).

In 1997, the federal court hearing this dispute put an end to virtually all the remaining
provisions of Proposition 187, its implementing regulations, and the interaction between
the federal PRWORA and the state statute, when the trial judge concluded:

> After the Court's November 20, 1995 Opinion, Congress enacted the PRA [PRWORA], a com-
> prehensive statutory scheme regulating alien eligibility for public benefits. The PRA states that it
> is the immigration policy of the United States to restrict alien access to substantially all public
> benefits. Further, the PRA ousts state power to legislate in the area of public benefits for aliens.
> When President Clinton signed the PRA, he effectively ended any further debate about what the
> states could do in this field. As the Court pointed out in its prior Opinion, California is powerless
> to enact its own legislative scheme to regulate immigration. It is likewise powerless to enact its
> own legislative scheme to regulate alien access to public benefits. It can do what the PRA permits,
> and nothing more. Federal power in these areas was always exclusive and the PRA only serves to
> reinforce the Court's prior conclusion that substantially all of the provisions of Proposition 187
> are preempted. (*LULAC v. Wilson*, 1997, p. 1259)

There were some mopping-up details remaining, and when Wilson's successor, Gray Davis,
came into office, he finally ended the matter by reaching a settlement with the litigants. *Plyler*'s supporters breathed a sigh of relief as they realized that they had dodged the bullet. By
the end of this protracted process, not only had a federal court comprehensively dealt with
the various features of Proposition 187 and the implementing regulations, but California
statutes had been amended to safeguard *Plyler*: Section 1643 of the California Education
Code reads, "Nothing in this chapter may be construed as addressing alien eligibility for
a basic public education as determined by the Supreme Court of the United States under
Plyler v. Doe."

The challenges to Proposition 187 had occurred predominantly in one court, that of
Judge Mariana R. Pfaelzer of the Central District of California, with some of the more
technical and procedural issues being decided on appeal to the Ninth Circuit, including
the consolidation of the many parties at interest and resolving the State's assertion that the
law of abstention had been misapplied and whether the district court had abused its discre-
tion in entering the original preliminary injunction (Baird, 2007; McDonnell, 1999). She
was upheld in the preliminary matters, and when Governor Davis conceded the issues and
reached a settlement, the substantive matter never returned to the Ninth Circuit, from where
an appeal might have gone to the United State Supreme Court. This meant that the original
supporters of the proposition and Governor Wilson never got what it was they really wanted,
an opportunity for the Supreme Court to accept *certiorari* and to overturn *Plyler*. Moreover,
any court taking up the issue would likely have held that 1996's PRWORA had preempted
any such State initiative, whether enacted by a legislature or ballot measure. In addition,
the California education statute itself had been amended to give ostensible authority to the
original holding of *Plyler*, which would have made it difficult to repeal the central holding
of the case through regulation or school board action.

During the pendency of the state legislative efforts, the year 1996 had seen the enactment of restrictionist federal legislation (IIRIRA and PRWORA), and the efforts of Representative Elton Gallegly (R-Cal.) to amend federal law by allowing states to enact the type of legislation that Texas had passed in 1975, which had led to *Plyler*. At the end of the process, the "Gallegly Amendment" was not added to the provisions that were signed into law. However, if it had been enacted, it would have allowed states "to deny public education benefits to certain aliens not lawfully present in the United States" or to charge these students tuition for public school enrollment, as Texas had done. It drew sufficient negative attention to force its withdrawal from the other legislative proposals, a number of which were enacted (Olivas, 2005; Schrag, 2000). But his hard line took on another, more symbolic role in the struggle between President Clinton, who genuinely wanted welfare reform, and the Republican Congress, which wanted to restrict immigrant rights and tighten up what many considered to be permissive loopholes in alien benefit eligibility.

In a fascinating and authoritative book by Professor Philip Schrag on the refugee and asylum provisions of the 1995–1996 congressional debates, he wrote of the Gallegly proposals:

> Agenda control worked for the Republican leadership in a more random way at a later stage of the process. Representative Gallegly was not able to make his public education amendment into law, but he was able to dominate the immigration agenda for months during the summer of 1996, so that other issues . . . were unable to break into most news stories. If the House had voted down the Gallegly amendment to begin with, Senator [Arlen] Spector or others might have had the attention or political capital available for other conflicts, and other sections of the final bill might have become more moderate. (Schrag, 2000, p. 311)

While the provisions that did pass were draconian in other respects, removing much of the play in the joints for federal enforcement purposes and restricting immigrant benefits generally, Congress did not move to exclude schoolchildren. Even the two Republican senators from Texas (Phil Gramm and Kay Bailey Hutchison) publicly signaled their opposition to repealing *Plyler*. Prior to the final draft of the comprehensive bill, President Clinton indicated he would veto any version that would overturn *Plyler*'s holding.

The Gallegly Amendment also did not appeal to the groups most closely identified with the issue, public school officials and teachers. By 1996, after more than a decade of living with *Plyler*, educators had made their peace with its requirements and had come to accept the decision. My own interaction with Houston-area school administrators, who had lost the original consolidated case and who had originally opposed the decision, revealed relief that they would not have to play immigration police or attempt to identify which of the 220,000 school children were in proper immigration status and which were not (Hood, 2003; Snyder, 2007; Zehr, 2004). In addition, 25 years after the case, the District has enacted special programs for non-English speakers, migrants, and refugee children, as well as a special high school for undocumented students. It also hired its first Mexican American School Superintendent, who retired in late 2009 after a successful term. Thus, the political process worked to remove any impediments to undocumented K–12 enrollments at the state and federal levels, even as severely tightened immigration restrictions were enacted into law; affirming *Plyler*'s holding as national policy exacted a high price in terms of immigration reform and for welfare reform.

The passage of comprehensive and restrictive state statutory schemes to regulate immigration shows how the grounds have shifted since 1994's Proposition 187, which singled out undocumented school children, even exceeding *Plyler*'s 1975 scheme (Watanabe, 2007). In the last dozen years, there has been a conscious effort by immigrant restrictionists not to touch the third rail of school children, at least not directly. After Proposition 187's failure and the doomed efforts of Representative Gallegly to overturn *Plyler* at the federal level, the blowback has caused those who wish to expel these children to do so by making it harder for their parents to remain in the United States. While there are regular and ongoing efforts to educate Congress about the detrimental effects of *Plyler* and birthright citizenship, restrictionists have taken a different tack by making the issue one of equity and fairness, and couching their rhetoric as school finance reform and school overcrowding issues (Federation for American Immigration Reform, 2010; Kasarda, 2009; Kobach, 2005). In addition, they have ratcheted up the postsecondary *Plyler* pressure, as was evident in several of the state efforts. While Arizona has a substantial number of potential undocumented students and a longtime policy that permitted them to establish resident status for purposes of paying lower tuition, it is inconceivable that Georgia or Connecticut have such a problem, or would over time.

It is clear that squeezing out undocumented adults has become a more viable and more widely employed stratagem, both by the local and state ordinances that restrict benefits generally and higher education residency status in particular, and by general efforts to enact omnibus nuisance measures. Even the traditional Americanizing efforts such as adult education programs and ESL classes are now being targeted in Arizona. Workplace raids and the other widespread harassment measures have become the centerpiece of efforts to locate and remove undocumented adults, who will have to take their children, even their citizen children, with them when they are removed (Byrne, 2008; Capps et al., 2009; Preston, 2007; Santos, 2007).

This has been a successful change of direction, as even the dissenters in *Plyler* indicated that they thought that removing innocent children was bad policy. Chief Justice Burger, as one example, wrote in his dissent, "Denying a free education to illegal alien children is not a choice I would make if I were a legislator. Apart from compassionate concerns, the long-range costs of excluding any children from the public schools may well outweigh the costs of educating them" (*Plyler*, p. 252). Moreover, while the children may have been innocent, restrictionists can claim, their parents surely have dirty hands. Although even this claim is problematic, it is a better sound bite, even as infants are being characterized as "anchor babies," conveying putative citizenship benefits to their illegal and lawbreaking alien parents who make illegal entries and foul our nest. The *New York Times Style Manual* requires its reporters to use "illegal immigrants" in news coverage and headlines, and bans "undocumented" or "unauthorized" as preferred adjectives; because the *Manual* is the widely employed arbiter for many other newspapers, these pejorative terms are regularly used and constitute the discourse even in the educated and literate population (Siegal & Connolly, 1999). This Lou Dobbs/Fox channel effect has had its intended purpose on public discourse about immigration, even if the taproot case has not been overturned or legislated away.

In reviewing the direct threats to *Plyler* and the enrollment of undocumented children, it is reassuring that the overall issue has become enshrined in law, practice, and politics. As was the case in the original litigation, where the combination of the facts, excellent lawyering, and some luck blew the way of the children, so it was with state threats such as the *LULAC* litigation, the timing of which found the more agreeable Governor Davis rather than the progenitor of the proposition, Pete Wilson, who never would have settled and would have likely appealed as far as the case would have allowed him. The case drew an exceptional federal judge who carefully reasoned her way through the exceedingly complex litigation: Judge Pfaelzer was appointed to the U.S. District Court for the Central District of California by President Jimmy Carter in 1978, and she assumed senior status later in the year she ruled on *LULAC*. All her rulings that were appealed were upheld by the Ninth Circuit, but it need not have gone this way. On the federal stage, the Gallegly amendment could have fallen on fertile ground, rather than facing a Congress that did not want to scapegoat children and a Democratic president who singled out that particular provision as the one he would not support and would veto if it made its way to his desk. As noted, immigrant rights advocates correctly felt that a great deal was lost in the exchange leading to IIRIRA and PRWORA, but there have been no serious legislative threats to undocumented schoolchildren at the Congressional level since 1996, or at the state level since *LULAC* was settled in 1997. California incorporated *Plyler*-language into its Education Code, while the Texas governor in 2007 indicated he would not support efforts to roll back the undocumented college student provisions he had signed into law earlier (Robison & Ratcliffe, 2007). To be sure, more states have singled out postsecondary *Plyler* issues, some adding and some restricting residency, but the DREAM Act may have traction in Congress, and, if enacted, would resolve this issue as a part of comprehensive immigration reform. Doing so would also allow immigrant advocates to concentrate upon other issues rather than having to fight college issues state legislature by state legislature—even having to protect statutes that were enacted that have had to be defended even after enactment. Of course, it would also mean not having to go to federal court or state court to defend state statutes, as was necessary in Kansas and California, or to sue states, as in Virginia (Cortez, 2008; Olivas, 2008).

The legislative and litigation issues have included direct attacks upon the enrollment of undocumented school children and college students, but in terms of sheer advocacy, much of the shoring up and preservation of that right has taken place in terms of *Plyler*'s school implementation; unequal treatment of the children or their parents; and a large array of collateral and supporting issues at the school board, school, and classroom levels. Three of the more evident manifestations of problems with local administration of *Plyler* have been the treatment of students whose parents do not have legitimate Social Security numbers, school chase and access policies, and students whose presence implicates extraordinary immigration status.

To most adults and a large number of children in the United States, holding a Social Security Number (SSN) is simply no big deal; I was issued an SSN card when I was four or five years old, when my parents established a bank account for me, after I received a savings bond from my grandparents as a birthday gift. It is a card issued to persons who work or who have work authorization, and to persons who claim dependents upon their income tax returns. Although undocumented persons who do not have proper papers or authorization to work are not eligible for an SSN, federal law requires everyone receiving income in the United States to file a tax return (Lipman, 2006, 2007; Loonin & Wu, 2002). An important feature is that anyone who is not a U.S. citizen is considered a "resident alien" under the U.S. tax code, and all resident aliens—including those without immigration status—have the same tax obligations as do U.S. citizens. As a result, three paths are available to the undocumented worker in this circumstance. She can get a Taxpayer Identification Number (TIN), secure an SSN not her own, or engage in the underground economy and go bareback without any number or documents. Further, while the undocumented are not able to secure a valid SSN, the TIN will not suffice for employment identification or authorization purposes. Thus, virtually all undocumented workers, while required to pay taxes and have withholding drawn from paychecks, engage in subterfuge and expose themselves to various fraud and tax-related problems. One thorough and useful analysis of this complex issue summarizes it as "the separate, unequal, and 'underrepresented' federal income tax treatment of undocumented aliens" (Singer & Dodd-Major, 2004) and "A Mismatch Made in Hell" (Lipman, 2006, p. 20). The details of tax law, an area as complex as immigration and nationality law itself, are beyond the scope of this chapter, but it is essential for observers to recognize that identifying numbers, paperwork details, and documentation are literally the linchpin, the quintessence of being "undocumented."

Any use of an SSN or TIN by school officials will cause undocumented parents to avoid the transaction, where possible, and children often suffer as a result, such as when schools innocently, casually, and routinely employ these numbers for their own uses, as simple registration or identification of schoolchildren. Persons who are subjects of identification fraud or ones who lose a credit card or change banks come to realize the pervasiveness of private identification numbers and credit information; this is the closest civilian parallel to the experience of being undocumented. The quotidian use of SSNs far exceeds their legitimate, narrow purpose of tax and Social Security identification and authentication, as when bank, credit card, membership, registration, and myriad consumer transactions require the use of an SSN. Schools and colleges have routinely, and improperly (mis)used SSNs for academic records, grade posting, and other inappropriate uses that violate federal or state laws ensuring privacy (Blum, 2007; Coyle, 2007; Lipman, 2006, 2007; Olivas, 2009). To be sure, such excesses are inconvenient and can implicate substantial credit risk and theft, but with undocumented parents and their children, the requirement that an SSN be used for school transactions puts the enrolled children at unnecessary risk and can force their parents to avoid school transactions or limit their children's participation in educational programs and activities.

Because this phenomenon has become so widespread, some states and school authorities have begun to exercise more care and caution in their requirements for identification and documentation in parent-school transactions. As one example, in 2003, Virginia amended its Education Code § 22.1-260, which had required that parents provide schools with an SSN for each student at the time of first enrollment; it was amended to permit school officials to use another individual identifying number or to waive the requirement if parents were unwilling to disclose an SSN for their children. Other states and school authorities have drafted policies for this issue, printed materials and pamphlets to inform parents and to train school officials, and maintained websites to provide information about these requirements. Some jurisdictions also use similar federal or state law provisions for homeless children, who will often lack such formal identifiers, including home addresses and permanent phone numbers, and for whom special accommodations must be made (Byrne, 2008; Capps et al., 2009). It is also evident that maintaining contact with parents becomes much more difficult and time consuming for regular parent-teacher transactions and school-community relations, which also means that support services and corollary informational interaction is diminished. And sometimes schools do not meet their obligations or do not properly take into account these features, even in programs designed and funded to address the special needs of such schoolchildren.

Even when schools want to do the right thing, the lack of proper documentation can cause problems, such as authenticating parents or relatives who are authorized to pick up children after school, proof of vaccinations and public health records, and proper contact with parents in the event of emergencies. The unavailability of drivers' licenses for the undocumented, uneven availability of "consular matricular" cards or foreign documents, and fear of the use of banking services or credit unavailability all combine to make these issues difficult, even when school officials are disposed to take the necessary precautions or to have the requisite cultural sensitivity (Pabon Lopez, 2004). When they are not so disposed, it renders these transactions even more problematic. Until Congress acts to provide comprehensive immigration reform, with realistic and efficacious provisions concerning identification, Social Security participation, and drivers' licenses, such issues will leach into the treatment of undocumented schoolchildren. In addition, issues of privacy, identity theft, data availability, and the proper balance between consumers and commercialized credit information will continue to affect the undocumented even more than they will the rest of U.S. society (Jordan, 2008; Preston, 2007).

In addition, the unavailability of proper documentation can extend to many other school-related attestations, such as proof of residence in the district. This is a complex matter, including constitutional concerns about domicile and custody. But it is also often a literal matter of documentation, as in the example of *Joel R. v. Mannheim Middle School Dist.*, a 1997 Illinois state court case where school authorities would not recognize the custody assertions in a matter of an undocumented child. The school would not acknowledge the notarized document executed by Joel's parents before a judge in Mexico, who had granted a relative residing in the school district custody over Joel, on the grounds that "the Mexican document was not sufficient to enroll Joel because it did not establish, through an American court, that [the relative] was Joel's legal guardian" (*Joel*, p. 653). The courts required the school district to admit the child and to accept the authenticated documents. Immigration authorities are conversant with the various forms of authentication and must deal with foreign documents as a matter of course, whereas campus officials may not have the expertise or experience in doing so, but failure to observe principles of comity and international law regularly implicates educational decision making, nowhere more commonly than in dealing with international children or the undocumented.

Maintaining safety on campus and making sure that no unauthorized persons enter school grounds is a common worry of educational officials and law enforcement authorities, and as a general rule, immigration authorities do not extend their dominion to schools, while school security personnel do not generally act as immigration enforcement officials, carrying out immigration raids or searches. However, there are occasions where the twain do meet, as in *Murillo v. Musegades*, a 1992 case in El Paso, where INS authorities kept a too-watchful eye upon the public high school on the U.S. side of the U.S.-Mexico border. In granting a request for a temporary restraining order against the INS, the federal judge noted:

> The El Paso Border Patrol has a regular, consistent, and prominent presence on the Bowie High School campus, whether their presence be by parking in the parking lots, speeding along the service roads, jumping across the curbs, or driving across concrete sidewalks and grassy areas. The El Paso Border Patrol's presence is further made known by their driving over the football practice field and baseball diamond, entering the football locker rooms, surveilling with binoculars from the football stadium, and using binoculars to watch flag girls practicing on campus. Bowie High School provides an oasis of safety and freedom for the students and staff who reside within the School District. The continued harassment of Bowie High School students and staff by the El Paso Border Patrol is both an invasion of their civil rights and the oasis. . . . The El Paso Border Patrol does not comply with the policy issued by [the District Director of the INS Service El Paso District], which states "that all law enforcement activities at all levels and types of schools is [*sic*] prohibited unless prior approval has been granted as provided. . . . Although the policy warns 'failure to comply with this policy will lead to appropriate disciplinary action,'" Defendants produced no evidence of disciplinary actions for policy violators. (*Murrillo*, p. 487)

Reviewing all the details in this complex case, including the school coach and students having been detained at gunpoint, the judge held:

> INS in this case discriminated against Plaintiffs in violation of their Fifth Amendment rights to equal protection. The INS has repeatedly and illegally stopped, questioned, detained, frisked, arrested, and searched Plaintiffs and numerous other students from the Bowie High School District. El Paso Border Patrol Agents have subjected Plaintiffs and others to indecent comments, obscene

gestures, and humiliation in the presence of their co-workers, friends, family, and relevant community. The proffered evidence strongly supports this Court in its conclusion that the illegal and abusive conduct of the El Paso Border Patrol was directed against Plaintiffs, staff, and residents in the Bowie High School District solely because of their mere immutable appearances as Hispanics. (*Murillo*, p. 501)

In addition, there had been a recent El Paso case concerning acceptable INS procedure, which the INS ignored in its Bowie police pursuit policies. Following this case, all the parties entered into a stipulated agreement where the INS agreed that it would not violate the "oasis" nature of the school and its students, irrespective of their immigration status.

In the Bowie High School instance, it was school authorities and both undocumented and citizen students who were affected by improper immigration authority behavior. In 2004, it was the school and police who initiated the inappropriate behavior, 300 miles north in Albuquerque, New Mexico. Albuquerque Public Schools found three students outside the chain link fence at Del Norte High School, adjacent to school property, and suspecting them of being out of status, turned them over to the Border Patrol (Miller, 2006). In federal court, the students filed suit, contending that Albuquerque Public School administrators, officers of the Albuquerque Police Department, and a Border Patrol Agent violated the students' constitutional rights, including the right to a public education when the boys were seized, interrogated, searched, and ultimately turned over to the Border Patrol. The children were sent back to Mexico, although they were allowed to return to New Mexico to testify in the legal proceedings.

In July 2006, all the claims against the school district defendants were dropped as a result of a settlement, which provided that the school district would implement new procedures and directives and conduct additional training of its personnel regarding the right of immigrant students to attend school, provide a district liaison for immigrant parents, and launch a public information campaign for immigrant parents to assure them that the district would not deny immigrant students an education (Miller, 2006). In addition, the school district defendants paid damages and attorney's fees. By 2008, the City of Albuquerque and the Albuquerque Police Department had settled, and the action against them was resolved for the damages and fees.

In both the El Paso and Albuquerque cases, there had not been clear immigration enforcement guidelines in place, even though there had been a recent case in El Paso, of which the INS authorities swore that they were unaware. For school districts located in states along the U.S.-Mexico border, it is conceivable and foreseeable that there would be undocumented immigration, and school districts would do well to have model plans in place, both to regulate immigration enforcement and to guide local police authorities. For example, there was evidence that the city's police officers would call in immigration authorities whenever there was a need for translation services, or when persons apprehended could not converse in what was considered acceptable English. At the time the children in Albuquerque were apprehended, they were students at the school, and their presence on the school grounds broke no civil law; there was no reason to have apprehended them and turned them over to anyone other than their parents or school authorities, other than their inchoate undocumented status, which police authorities are not in a position to determine. Simply having stereotypical "Mexican" features in a state as Mexican-dominant as New Mexico or even in rural Idaho cannot be an articulable reason for police authorities to apprehend students in or near a school, "solely because of their mere immutable appearances as Hispanics" (*Murillo*, p. 501).

In 2006, two new *Plyler* threats arose at the school level, both of which ultimately resolved themselves but revealed the complexities generally associated with noncitizen enrollments.

In March 2006, the school board in Elmwood Park, Illinois, refused to let an undocumented student enroll, on the grounds that she and her family had entered on B-2 tourist visas, long expired. The State Board of Education threatened to remove funds, and the local board blinked, revising its attendance policies (Long, 2006; Mastony & Redo, 2006). Even though persons can become undocumented either by surreptitious entry or by violating the terms of legal entry, no earlier decisions had turned on the means by which the original unauthorized status or entry had been effected; cases turned on undocumented status, not upon exactly how the alien had entered the country or the particular state. As in so many of the immigration-related cases, the Elmwood Park case turned on complex technical immigration categories. It is necessary for schools to recognize that these categories can be fluid and confusing, and that many noncitizen families are mixed, including some members who might be citizens or have permission to be in the country, while others might have entered surreptitiously or entered with proper permission, only to run afoul of visa requirements, intentionally or unintentionally (Walfish, 2003). At the time of *Plyler*, immigration legal expertise might not have been widespread, but in recent times, such expertise is much more widely available and accessible. There is simply no reason why school districts must, through action or inaction, make mistakes concerning the immigration status of school children or parents.

In the *Joel R.* case, cited earlier in discussing the technical issue of documentation, the state appeals court held, for purposes of determining residency:

> Applying the law to the facts of the instant case, we find the circuit court did not err. First, it is uncontroverted that Joel lives indefinitely on a full-time basis with [his relative]. Second, it is also clear that [she] exercises complete control over Joel and is fully responsible for his care to the exclusion of Joel's parents who reside in another country. Third, [she] is Joel's legal guardian. Fourth, there was ample evidence of other non-educational factors being a part of the reason Joel moved to Melrose Park: the abject poverty and lack of social and economic opportunities he faced in Mexico; the desire to learn more about the country of his birth; and the need to eventually aid his parents financially. All of these factors support the circuit court's legal conclusion that Joel was a bona fide resident of District 83 and that his move to the district was not solely for educational purposes. Thus, we find no error in the circuit court's decision. In closing, we note that defendants argued before the circuit court and this court that a deferential policy of *experto credite* should be adopted with regard to residency determinations made by school districts. To this end, defendants attempt, without citation to any relevant authority, to analogize school disciplinary cases, where courts have correctly afforded deference to a school's decision, to residency determinations. We find this argument to be wholly without merit and completely unsupported by the case law. (*Joel*, p. 656)

Since losing this case, Illinois has been required to train its educators about such residency requirement determinations, and it has posted these requirements online and made them publicly available.

In 1996, Congress acted to eliminate the ability of parents to "helicopter" their children into school districts by simply sending them to live with other families, such as informal or even formal sponsors or noncustodial relatives. These students are ineligible for F-1 nonimmigrant status on their own and may not attend a public school for more than a year, and must pay the actual cost of instruction for any such period of attendance. The provision does not affect private schools, although it could affect charter schools and other private schools that are established and funded by public appropriations. Although this provision was enacted to keep more advantaged foreign families from sending their children abroad at the U.S. school's expense, this provision has been interpreted by some public school districts as affecting undocumented student attendance (Long, 2006; Mastony & Redo, 2006). Other corollary rulings concerning resident and domicile have also affected this issue, as in Elmwood Park, and the overall complexity has occasionally caught undocumented students in the snare.

In 2006, in Austin, Texas, hundreds of miles away from the Mexican border, there was mixed evidence that ICE authorities were targeting schools and coming onto school grounds to apprehend children whose parents were arrested on the suspicion of being in the country without authorization. School officials felt that they had to notify parents that such ICE actions would take place, so they sent out notices, warning, "Tell the students they are safe. That they have rights to not answer questions and to request to speak to attorney [*sic*] if they are picked up. . . . Some parents have come and withdrawn their children (students) today. We can't stop a lawful investigation, but we can certainly inquire as to their credentials and to the existence of a lawful investigation. We must also abide by any court orders, such as warrants, they present" (KTBC, 2006). Of course, given such a notice, undocumented parents might withdraw their children out of a simple, undifferentiated fear of apprehension concerning their families. Such a situation places school districts in a similar conundrum: Do they inform parents about any such pending acts by immigration authorities, knowing how they might reasonably react, or do they not inform parents, on the chance that immigration authorities will only come onto a campus in the event a parent has been apprehended and ICE needs to notify and secure the children as well?

To observers who are familiar with the El Paso, Elmwood Park, and Albuquerque incidents, as well as other such occasions, it is not an idle or unreasonable fear on the part of undocumented adults, whose worst dreams include not only their own arrest or apprehension, but also fears of being separated from their children. And schools have an obligation to communicate with parents, particularly parents who would be at risk, so this information is being disseminated out of a sense of duty and professional responsibility, the way that a school would notify parents of a new vaccination requirement or school functions or other such routine announcements. If school officials act badly and raise false specters or cry wolf in order to not have to deal with these children, which certainly can happen, that is one thing, and unforgivable. As taxpaying parents with legal obligations to place their children in schools, even undocumented parents deserve respect and consideration, the same as would any more advantaged parent. But it is clear that school-community relations have to be treated and conducted differently when the parents are undocumented and likely non-English-speaking, poor, and poorly educated.

Recent cataclysmic events such as California's fires and Hurricane Katrina in New Orleans have also revealed the extent to which undocumented residents were caught up in even more fundamental service needs, in the complete breakdown of emergency services and flood evacuation (Johnson, 2008). The confusing signals sent by FEMA and other federal, state, and local officials, as well as Red Cross service providers during the fire and flood evacuations made it dangerous for undocumented families to seek and receive assistance. Although emergency assistance, including medical and other safety services are required to be provided without regard to immigration status, it was clear from these disasters that such services were not provided, and conflicting messages were sent that unauthorized immigrants would not only be ineligible but would be detained (Johnson, 2008; Shavers, 2008). In the confusion surrounding the complete collapse of the New Orleans public school system, it is unclear how *Plyler* children are being accommodated, as the entire system has become a "charter school" alternative regime, with uncertain legal status and obligations (Reyes, 2009).

In Florida, another example of a nonimmigrant student surfaced, and while it was correctly decided, it revealed the difficulty in determining the residency and domicile of persons who are not citizens or permanent residents. In this instance, it was a high school student who was the son of a treaty trader (a person with permission to engage in commerce under the terms of a treaty to which the United States is party), an E-2 nonimmigrant (Griffith, 2006). The issue of undocumented students has not been limited to K–12 public school students, as a number of cases before and since *Plyler* have dealt with the corollary issue of undocumented college students, and the extent to which college resident tuition and admissions benefits are to be extended to the postsecondary, post-compulsory schooling level. Since 2001, when Texas Governor Bush's successor signed legislation granting postsecondary residency for undocumented students into law, more than a dozen states have acted, ten allowing residency, and several denying it, and one state (Oklahoma) rescinding its resident tuition practice (Robison & Ratcliffe, 2007). In 2008's presidential politics, college immigration issues briefly surfaced as the focus of attention and debate, before receding into the welter of complex politics (Eckstein, 2009; Hebel, 2008; Kobach, 2006; Luo, 2007). In 2010, Congress has under consideration a federal version of the state statutes, the DREAM Act, which if enacted would also accord limited legalization benefits.

INDIRECT CHALLENGES:
THE IMPLEMENTATION OF *PLYLER V. DOE*

The evidence marshaled thus far has examined only the direct challenges to *Plyler*'s continued vitality, and has indicated that the holding is alive and well. But the last direct challenge at the state level was in 1996–1997's *LULAC* holding in the challenge to California's Proposition 187, and the last serious federal challenge was the ill-fated 1996 Gallegly amendment, which was traded away by its supporters in exchange for restricting alien benefits and tightening up refugee and immigration provisions generally. Viewed in this sense, there has not been a direct assault upon *Plyler* since these attempts failed over a decade ago. Even some conservative Republican senators were not willing to enlist in this effort—despite the issue being contained in the national party's presidential platform—and states appear to have resigned themselves to the policies derived from the case and found ways to accommodate the children (Brickman, 2006; Eckstein, 2009; Hebel, 2008). As additional evidence of acceptance, almost all the major receiver states and even other states have extended the reach of the case to the benefit of undocumented college students, permitted by the same 1996 legislation to which Representative Gallegly was trying to attach his restrictions.

But the real contests have shifted to the more quotidian, everyday, school level, and from this vantage point, every day is a calf scramble. In a variety of areas, it is the daily implementation of *Plyler* by school boards and school districts that poses the more potent threat, not only because this is the level at which individual children and families experience the policies, but because the national immigrants' rights groups and advocates form networks that guard against state and federal predations, and cannot always monitor or frame the issues at local flashpoints. When undocumented parents in Austin, Texas, pull their citizen children out of their school due to perceptions that school raids will be forthcoming, it is clear that *Plyler* as implemented requires constant monitoring and attention.

Here, I consider a number of these local issues, including a sampler to show the many that have arisen: general issues of language instruction, building and zoning policies, publicity that arises when students do exceptionally well and draw attention to themselves, involvement in extracurricular programs, housing and local ordinances, separate schools and racial isolation, and miscellaneous practices that will disproportionately affect undocumented school children and their parents. There are literally dozens of such cases in various stages of litigation in school districts across the country (National School Boards Association & National Education Association, 2009).

In addition to the legal and legislative issues, the media and the cultural discourse have thrown light into these corners. Undocumented students even have surfaced when they have had extraordinary academic success. Recent cases include four students from Hayden High School in Phoenix, who went to the Niagara Falls area for a class trip, after they won a prestigious national robotics competition (Carlson, 2005; Gonzalez, 2006). They were arrested as they crossed into Canada and returned with their class, and because Arizona no longer accords in-state tuition to undocumented college students, they have not been eligible to attend college in the state as residents. Another undocumented robotics student, this one from Senegal, was able to remain in the United States, due to enormous legal and politic pressure exerted on his behalf (Bernstein, 2006). In 2006, an undocumented Dominican student who had graduated with honors from Princeton surfaced when he won a scholarship to Oxford University (Jordan, 2006). In Farmers Branch, Texas, legislators attempted to zero out city funding for a "Summer Funshine" child care program, designed to keep young children from affiliating with gangs, because they suspected that some undocumented children were participating. The program, which serves 350 students each summer, has 110 places targeted for low-income children whose families pay less for the program in conjunction with eligibility for federal free and reduced lunches (Sandoval, 2006). Farmers Branch, a suburb of Dallas, was the first local jurisdiction in Texas to have passed comprehensive immigration reform provisions at the local level, which immediately were enjoined by the court and which were pending in 2010.

Plyler is essentially about residency requirements and who gets to go to school in what attendance zone. In the year after *Plyler*, the U.S. Supreme Court decided a companion case, *Martinez v. Bynum*, and held that parents or guardians of undocumented children (or for that matter, their children) were required to reside in a school district attendance zone. This was not a significant narrowing of *Plyler*, where the parents had actually lived in the school districts that their children attended, albeit in unauthorized status. The student in *Martinez* was a citizen child whose undocumented parents had left the country and left him in the care of his adult sister, which was not his legal guardian. The Court in *Martinez* sustained the state's determination that the child did not reside in the district and thus did not qualify for free public schooling there, ruling that *Plyler* did not bar application of an appropriately defined bona fide residence test. In its footnote 22, the *Plyler* case had indicated that the undocumented may establish domicile in the country, a much larger issue than that presented in *Martinez*, where the child's parents had not established the requisite residence in the school district. This holding also loops back to *Joel R. v. Mannheim Middle School Dist.*, the 1997 Illinois state court case mentioned earlier, where school authorities would not recognize the custody assertions in a matter of an undocumented child.

The Houston Independent School District, where one of the strands of *Plyler* arose, has begun a high school that concentrates upon immigrant students, in order to provide them with the additional counseling and services they need to navigate school (Hood, 2003; Snyder, 2007; Zehr, 2004). In 2000, the Urban Institute published a comprehensive review of the issue, *Overlooked & Underserved, Immigrant Students in U.S. Secondary Schools*, which investigated several such sites, and reached very critical conclusions about the lack of coordination among schools, the poor achievement of these students, and the structural problems that school districts face in educating such large numbers of immigrant children who have not progressed and who are non-English speakers (Ruiz-de-Velasco et al., 2000).

Other reports have found similar massive problems; other school districts have also tried unusual means to reach and educate these children (Passel & Cohn, 2009; Rabin, Combs, & Gonzalez, 2008).

CONCLUSION: *PLYLER'S* REACH

In the first part of this chapter, I examined the direct challenges to *Plyler*, both legislative efforts and state ballot issues as well as the issue of "helicopter children," whose parents have sent them to study in the United States without parental residence or whose parents have legally entered the country but their behavior has resulted in their being out of status. I also reviewed campus chase and policing policies and nonlegislative, school-based initiatives such as the use of Social Security numbers and identification measures. While the original case has proven quite resilient, it has had to be reinforced by vigilant efforts.

This chapter also reviewed cases and school district or state actions that have indirectly implicated *Plyler*, and analyzed the various means by which restrictionist policies have attempted to extirpate the practice allowed by *Plyler* and to overturn its holding. Indirect measures include a variety of language issues, including bilingual education and English as a Second Language (ESL); building, siting, and attendance zone concerns; undocumented students who become at risk when their achievements bring them into the spotlight; the assault on programs that provide resources to undocumented children; separate immigrant schools and programs that concentrate the children in a circumscribed environment; and other miscellaneous issues entangling immigration and public schooling. Recent community emergencies have also revealed the nether world in which undocumented families find themselves, even when services are allowed to be extended. In all likelihood, comprehensive immigration reform will occur, and should alleviate some of these problems, particularly in providing a form of legalization and extending some benefits. If reform does not occur, the racial hatred and scapegoating of immigrants will continue and will escalate (Buckley, 2008; Sacchetti, 2009). But the children and their parents will keep coming, drawn by the possibilities of work and improving their lives. Such immigration reform will undoubtedly be a contentious and uncertain project, but until it occurs, these issues will continue to fester and will drive the practices even deeper, and even more hidden in plain sight.

CASES CITED

Plyler v. Doe, 457 U.S. 202 (1982).
Toll v. Moreno, 458 U.S. 1 (1982).
Martinez v. Bynum, 461 U.S. 321 (1983).
Murillo v. Musegades, 809 F. Supp. 487 (W.D. Tex. 1992).
LULAC v. Wilson, 908 F. Supp. 755 (C.D. Cal. 1995); *Gregorio T. by and through Jose T. v. Wilson*, 59 F.3d 1002 (9th Cir. 1995); *LULAC v. Wilson*, 997 F. Supp. 1244 (C.D. Cal.1997).
Joel R. v. Manheim Middle Sch. Dist., 686 N.E.2d 650 (1997).

STATUTES CITED

Personal Responsibility and Work Opportunity Reconciliation Act of 1996 (PRWORA), 110 Stat. 2105 (1996).
Illegal Immigration Reform and Immigrant Responsibility Act of 1996 (IIRIRA), Pub. L. No. 104-208, 110 Stat. 3009 (1996).

REFERENCES

Baird, V. (2007). *Answering the call of the court.* Charlottesville, VA: University of Virginia Press.

Bernstein, N. (2006, July 19). Senegalese teenager wins right to study in the U.S. *New York Times*, p. A13.

Berry, J. (2006, December 6). Smuggling verdict tossed; Judge cites lack of evidence. *Arizona Republic*, p. A1.

Blum, C. (2007). Rethinking tax compliance of unauthorized workers after immigration reform. *Georgetown Immigration Law Journal, 21*, 595–620.

Brickman, J. (2006). Educating undocumented children in the United States: Codification of *Plyler v. Doe* through federal legislation. *Georgetown Immigration Law Journal, 20*, 385–405.

Buckley, C. (2008, November 21). 6 Long Island Teens Charged with Hate Crimes. *New York Times*, p. A26.

Byrne, O. (2008). *Unaccompanied children in the United States: A literature review.* New York, NY: Vera Institute of Justice.

Capps, R., Fix, M. E., Murray, J., Ost, J. Passel, J. S., & Hernandez, S. H. (2009). *The new demography of America's schools: Immigration and the No Child Left Behind Act.* Washington, DC: Urban Institute.

Carlson, P. (2005, March 29). Stinky the robot, four kids and a brief whiff of success. *Washington Post*, p. C1.

Cortez, N. G. (2008). The local dilemma: Preemption and the role of federal standards in state and local immigration laws. *SMU Law Review, 61*, 47–66.

Coyle, J. (2007). The legality of banking the undocumented. *Georgetown Immigration Law Journal, 22*, 21–55.

Doty, R. L. (2009). *The law into their own hands: Immigration and the politics of exceptionalism.* Tucson: University of Arizona Press.

Eckstein, M. (2009, May 8). In-state tuition for undocumented students: Not quite yet. *Chronicle of Higher Education*, p. A19.

Federation for American Immigration Reform (FAIR). (2010). Birthright citizenship. Retrieved from http://www .fairus.org/site/News2?page=NewsArticle&id=16535&security=1601&news_iv_ctrl=1007

Garcia, R. J. (1995). Critical race theory and proposition 187: The racial politics of immigration law. *Chicano-Latino Law Review, 17*, 118–148.

Gonzalez, D. (2006, December 12). "Wilson four" deportation case settled; panel says students wrongly targeted, *Arizona Republic*, p. 10A.

Griffith, K. (2006, September 10). Immigration rules bug Brits. *Orlando Sentinel*, p. J1.

Hebel, S. (2008, August 25). Higher-education platforms develop as convention season begins, *Chronicle of Higher Education*, p. A1.

Hood, L. (2003). *Immigrant students, urban high schools: The challenge continues.* New York, NY: Carnegie Corporation.

Hulse, C. (2009, September 10). In lawmaker's outburst, a rare breach of protocol. *New York Times*, p. A26.

Immigration Policy Center (2008). *E-Verify and Arizona: Early experiences for employers, employees, and the economy portend a rough road ahead.* Washington, DC: Author. Retrieved from http://www.immigrationpolicy.org/just -facts/e-verify-and-arizona-early-experiences-portend-rough-road-ahead

Inniss, L. K. B. (1996). California's proposition 187: Does it mean what it says? Does it say what it means? A textual and constitutional analysis. *Georgetown Immigration Law Journal, 10*, 577–617.

Johnson, K. R. (1995a). Public benefits and immigration: The intersection of immigration status, ethnicity, gender, and class. *UCLA Law Review, 42*, 1509–1575.

Johnson, K. R. (1995b). An essay on immigration politics, popular democracy, and California's proposition 187: The political relevance and legal irrelevance of race. *Washington Law Review, 70*, 629–673.

Johnson, K. R. (2008). Hurricane Katrina: Lessons about immigrants in the administrative state. *Houston Law Review, 45*, 11–71.

Jordan, M. (2006, September 14). Princeton's 2006 salutatorian heads to Oxford, still an illegal immigrant. *Wall Street Journal*, p. B1.

Jordan, M. (2008, October 22). Mortgage prospects dim for illegal immigrants. *Wall Street Journal*, p. A3.

KTBC Television Station Memo. (2006, April 4). *Email warns of illegal immigration crackdowns in classrooms.* Retrieved from www.texascivilrightsproject.org

Kasarda, R. W. (2009). Affirmative action gone haywire: Why state laws granting college tuition preferences to illegal aliens are preempted by federal law. *BYU Education and Law Journal, 2*, 197–244.

Kobach, K. W. (2005). The quintessential force multiplier: The inherent authority of local police to make immigration arrests. *Albany Law Review, 69*, 179–235.

Kobach, K. W. (2006, August 14). *The senate immigration bill rewards lawbreaking: Why the DREAM Act is a nightmare.* Washington, DC: Heritage Foundation [Backgrounder #1960].

Lipman, F. J. (2006). The taxation of undocumented immigrants: Separate, unequal, and without representation. *Harvard Latino Law Review, 9*, 19–58.

Lipman, F. J. (2007). Bearing witness to economic injustices of undocumented immigrant families: A new class of "undeserving poor." *Nevada Law Journal, 7*, 736–758.

Long, J. (2006, December 13). "Bully" contract leads to apology; District 26 denies Spanish speakers were targeted. *Chicago Tribune*, p. Metro-1.

Loonin, D., & Wu, C. C. (2002). *Consumer rights for immigrants.* Boston, MA: National Consumer Law Center.

Luo, M. (2007, December 2). Romney's words testify to threat from Huckabee, *New York Times*, p. YT 29.

Mastony, C., & Redo, D. (2006, February 28). Barred teen pleased as lawsuit is dropped: Elmwood Park district reluctantly ends fight. *Chicago Tribune*, p. Metro-1.

McDonnell, P. J. (1999, July 29). Davis won't appeal prop. 187 ruling, ending court battles. *Los Angeles Times*, p. A1.

Miller, A. (2006, June 2). APS safe for migrant students. *Albuquerque Journal*, p. A1.

National Conference of State Legislatures. (2009). *State laws related to immigrants and immigration.* Washington, DC: Author. Retrieved from http://www.ncsl.org/documents/immig/ImmigrationReport2009.pdf

National School Boards Association & National Education Association. (2009). *Legal issues for school districts related to the education of undocumented children.* Washington, DC: Author. Retrieved from http://www.nea.org/assets/docs/09undocumentedchildren.pdf

Olivas, M. A. (1994). Preempting preemption: Foreign affairs, state rights, and alienage classifications. *Virginia Journal of International Law, 73*, 217–236.

Olivas, M. A. (2004). IIRIRA, the DREAM Act, and undocumented college student residency. *Journal of College and University Law, 30*, 435–464.

Olivas, M. A. (2005). The Story of *Plyler v. Doe*, The education of undocumented children, and the polity. In D. Martin & P. Schuck (Eds.), *Immigration Stories* (pp.197–220). New York, NY: Foundation Press.

Olivas, M. A. (2007). Immigration-related state and local ordinances: Preemption, prejudice, and the proper role for enforcement. *University of Chicago Legal Forum, 2007*, 27–55.

Olivas, M. A. (2008). Lawmakers gone wild? College residency and the response to Professor Kobach. *SMU Law Review, 61*, 99–132.

Olivas, M. A. (2009). Undocumented college students, taxation, and financial aid: A technical note. *Review of Higher Education, 32*, 407–416.

Pabon Lopez, M. (2004). More than a license to drive: State restrictions on the use of driver's licenses. *Southern Illinois University Law Journal, 29*, 89–128.

Pabon Lopez, M. (2005). Reflections on educating Latino and Latina undocumented children: Beyond *Plyler v. Doe*. *Seton Hall Law Review, 35*, 1373–1406.

Passel, J. S., & Cohn, D. (2009). *A portrait of unauthorized immigrants in the United States.* Washington, DC: Pew Hispanic Center.

Pham, H. (2006). The constitutional right not to cooperate? Local sovereignty and the federal immigration power. *University of Cincinnati Law Review, 74*, 1373–1413.

Pizarro, M. (2005). *Chicanas and Chicanos in school: Racial profiling, identity battles, and empowerment.* Austin: University of Texas Press.

Preston, J. (2007, March 22). Illegal worker, troubled citizen and stolen name. *New York Times*, p. A1.

Rabin, N., Combs, M. C., & Gonzalez, N. (2008). Understanding *Plyler*'s Legacy: Voices from border schools. *Journal of Law & Education, 37*, 15–82.

Reyes, A. H. (2009). The right to an education for homeless students: The children of Katrina. In L. Oren, E. Marrus, & H. Davidson (Eds.), *Children, law, and disasters: What have we learned from the hurricanes of 2005?* (pp. 261–312). Washington, DC and Houston, TX: American Bar Association and the Center for Children, Law, & Policy.

Robison, C., & Ratcliffe, R. G. (2007, January 12). Perry to stick by law giving tuition breaks to illegal immigrants. *Houston Chronicle*, p. B4.

Romero, V. C. (2003). Noncitizen students and immigration policy post–9/11. *Georgetown Immigration Law Journal, 17*, 357–366.

Ruiz-de-Velasco, J., Fix, M. E., & Clewell, B. C. (2000). *Overlooked and underserved: Immigrant students in U.S. secondary schools.* Washington, DC: Urban Institute.

Sacchetti, M. (2009, September 25). Lynn's immigrants and police share a gulf. *Boston Globe*, p. Metro-1.

Sandoval, S. (2006, September 21). Funding intact for youth group. *Dallas Morning News*, p. 1B.

Santos, F. (2007, February 27). Demand for English lessons outstrips supply. *New York Times*, p. A1.

Schrag, P. S. (2000). *A well-founded fear: The congressional battle to save political asylum in America.* New York, NY: Routledge.

Shavers, A. W. (2008). The invisible others and immigrant rights: A commentary. *Houston Law Review, 45*, 99–151.

Siegal, A. M., & Connolly, W. G. (1999). *The New York Times manual of style and usage.* New York, NY: Three Rivers Press.

Singer, P. N., & Dodd-Major, L. (2004). Identification numbers and U.S. government compliance initiatives. *Tax Notes, 104*, 1429–1438.

Snyder, M. (2007, April 5). HISD's ESL enrollment belies census numbers on immigrants. *Houston Chronicle*, p. B1.

Valencia, R. R. (2008). *Chicano students and the courts: The Mexican American struggle for educational equality.* New York: New York University Press.

Walfish, D. (2003). Student visas and the illogic of the intent requirement. *Georgetown Immigration Law Journal, 17*, 473–503.

Watanabe, T. (2007, January 25). Illegal immigrant youths in a benefits twilight zone; State policies toward such children vary, reflecting sympathy for their situation and disapproval of their parents' behavior. *Los Angeles Times*, p. B1.

Wishnie, M. (2001). Laboratories of bigotry? Devolution of the immigration power, equal protection and federalism. *New York University Law Review, 76*, 493–569.

Zehr, M. A. (2004, September 22). Working immigrants get new school options. *Education Week*, p. 5.

18

Delivering High-Quality Public Services to Vulnerable Families and Children in America's Cities

The Lessons From Reforming Child Welfare

Olivia Golden

This chapter is about delivering change in large, troubled organizations that serve very vulnerable children and families. It is also about reform under difficult circumstances, including a history of failure, intense public scrutiny, and extremely limited resources. It draws on a specific example of such difficult reform: efforts to dramatically improve the performance of public child welfare agencies, which are the public agencies charged to respond to children in danger because their parents can't or won't care for them safely.[1] And it seeks to explore the particular implications of such reform efforts for America's cities, where the nation's most troubled and underfunded government agencies too often encounter its most vulnerable families and children.

Two stories from my first months as director of the District of Columbia's child welfare agency frame the complex challenges faced by these agencies and those who seek to reform them. In the summer of 2001, I had just been recruited by the District's then-mayor, Anthony Williams, to bring the Child and Family Services Agency (CFSA) back from court-appointed receivership.

At 10:00 one night, I sat in an office with two or three of the agency's senior program staff trying to figure out what to do about the 20 children on the first floor of our office building. The boys and girls of all ages had either been removed from their parents by the agency's social workers or had left, or been ejected from, foster homes or group care facilities, and they had no place else to stay that night. They were crowded into a space filled with cots and staffed by two or three aides. A few weeks earlier, when I was downstairs late at night, I had seen the terror of the younger children as an older boy screamed in anger. It was not a situation that I wanted to be responsible for, but I was.

Nothing about the situation, or any of the choices available to us at that moment, was consistent with what we knew about what was best for children. We all knew that the trauma of abuse and neglect was compounded by chaotic settings and abrupt moves, that children did best in families, that all transitions should be prepared for, and that crowded settings with children of all ages and both genders posed additional dangers for children, beyond those that brought them there. Yet we were not acting in accordance with any of those findings. Most likely, the children downstairs were going to spend the night either in the office building or in an emergency shelter. We just did not see any other choices at that moment.

Around the same time, one of our lawyers burst into my office at 6 p.m. on a Friday to say that a local superior court judge had just sent a social worker to jail for contempt because she had failed repeatedly to submit a report on time. (State and local judges in every state make the key decisions about children's removal from their homes and oversee children's care while they are in foster care, with child welfare agency social workers providing recommendations and reports.) The judge apparently believed that he had run out of options to get timely reports, and he thought he was doing the best thing for children. But the social worker was a single parent, unable to arrange for her own children's care on the weekend. And the decision represented the worst fear of the agency's social workers, who joked grimly about the need to carry a toothbrush for appearances before certain judges who were viewed as hostile.

As soon as I heard, I asked one of the mayor's most senior attorneys to join me and our agency attorney, and we rushed over to the court to talk to the judge before he left for the weekend. After we pleaded, he rescinded the decision, but by then, the social worker had already been processed at the jail. It took us until 10 p.m. to free her. When social workers heard the story Monday morning, they wanted to walk out in protest.

What happened? Interestingly, I could never have predicted at the time which problem would be easy to solve and which would be hard. In the case of the social worker sent to jail, we weren't able to get her out of jail until 10 that night, and on Monday, the social workers' union was understandably furious. But the crisis took a positive turn fairly quickly, as the judicial leadership realized that they needed to help calm this down if there was to be a hope for child welfare reform. So the most senior judges came over to our agency building—something that had never happened before—and met with a group of social workers. It was the beginning of a process that eventually led to real teamwork.

On the other hand, even though we tried many policy and practice changes, it took more than two years to completely eliminate the practice of children sleeping in the building. The problem turned out to have so many layers that each time we fixed one, we found another. For example, a foster parent who couldn't cope with a child's behavior might get so frustrated when a social worker wouldn't return her phone calls that she would drive the child to the agency building. The police contributed—they dropped children off at the building late at night. Even our contracting system contributed: our contracts with group homes (dormitory-like institutions that cared for children and youth referred by CFSA) allowed them to send a child back to us without notice if the child broke rules, so some of them routinely sent young people over to the office building during the night if they came back after curfew. We eventually fixed all the causes, but it took a long time.

These stories illustrate several themes that have shaped my approach to this research and to the problem of effective agency reform. First, the "problem" in troubled agencies is *not* one-dimensional. Whatever the public believes about the "one thing" that could be fixed in a troubled public agency, whether child welfare or mental health or schools, isn't the complete picture. No single solution—better staff or more money or a different policy—will solve this kind of multifaceted problem.

Second, as these stories also illustrate, the intertwined problems in failing agencies include both internal capacity and the external environment. The agency is unable to do its own work well at the same time that its outside partners, stakeholders, and political overseers fail in their roles, and the two kinds of failures play into each other. For example, social workers fail to meet judges' needs, judges react harshly, social worker recruitment and retention becomes impossible because of what social workers experience as harassment and disrespect, and judges become more convinced of the complete incompetence of individual workers and the agency as a whole.

Finally, the intertwined nature of the problems suggests that the solutions too will need to be complex and multifaceted. Given their complexity, the solutions will need to play out over time, yet still maintain momentum and not exhaust the patience of cynical stakeholders. These are the puzzles that I set out to explore in the research on reforming child welfare.

THE EVIDENCE AND THE METHODS

To conduct an inquiry that would make sense of this kind of multilayered problem and the strategies that work to fix it, I needed a research approach that would identify lessons useful for large organizations. Research on services and programs that work represents an evidentiary base about how to help children and families that is important and useful in its context.[2] But it falls short of this chapter's goal, which is to identify ideas that have been tested in large public child welfare agencies, not just small pilot projects. To find such ideas, researchers need to grapple with the agencies' real life environment and scale: delivering services through hundreds or thousands of stressed frontline workers in a tense public and political context; navigating complex relationships with a half dozen big public agencies and private service organizations; and struggling to get city- or statewide personnel, budget, and contracting systems to help rather than hinder progress. Consequently my interest was above all in ideas that have been tested in the worst large public systems, those with a history of persistent failure. I wanted to understand how to raise the bar for all child welfare systems—how to make improvement possible for the most vulnerable families, even those in the most troubled settings.

Given my goal, a core method of the research was to analyze examples where a large and deeply troubled public child welfare system turned around its services and results in measurable ways that outside observers can document. I look closely at three such examples in the research summarized here. The first example is a personal account of change in the District of Columbia's child welfare agency during three crucial turnaround years. I was the director during those years as the agency moved from court-ordered receivership to much better, though still flawed, performance. Writing from the inside makes it possible to analyze, in retrospect, what we thought we were doing, what it felt like, and what led us to good or bad choices. The advantage of a personal story is its richness, leading to insights about both setbacks and progress. At the same time, the lessons might not apply to other places: child welfare systems differ considerably by jurisdiction, and the District of Columbia, with its unique legal structure and history, might seem the most distinctive of all. In addition, the subjectivity of a personal story, the flip side of its richness, might mean that the lessons I draw are biased or just wrong.

So to complement the D.C. case study, I examine two other success stories in Alabama and Utah. These two additional case studies of child welfare turnarounds allow me to test my impressions and hypotheses in two different settings. I picked Alabama and Utah as the second and third examples after interviewing about a dozen national experts and reviewing court reports and other evidence. I was interested only in dramatic, documentable turnarounds: systems that had started off very bad and got better, not good systems that had enhanced the quality of their work. My criterion for a turnaround was evidence of great strides over time, not evidence that no problems remained, since even much-improved systems would still have problems to solve.

I initially chose three locations to study, mostly because information pointing to a turnaround was available and consistent. I narrowed the examples down to Alabama and Utah where I was able to interview 5 to 10 leaders and review media coverage, court filings, and published reports. In the third of the originally planned sites, New York City, I was able to interview only a handful of leaders, so I do not try to tell its full story.

I also draw on the national perspective I gained as the federal official overseeing child welfare policy in the Clinton administration,[3] on national data and research findings about child welfare and vulnerable children and families, and on research about management and leadership in public and private organizations. These broader perspectives help me frame and extend the site lessons, fill gaps, and distinguish between findings consistent with prior research and anomalies in need of additional exploration or interpretation. To address subjectivity, I used documentary evidence (court reports and newspaper articles) to supplement findings and interviews. I also tested my insights and lessons on colleagues from across the country, looking for hints about which findings had broad relevance and application. Most often, I found gasps of recognition, because while the specifics of the political and bureaucratic situation might be different, many failing agencies share underlying problems—such as the inability to generate or use accurate data despite a reasonably good technical information system—that I found in the District.

While I did not develop this research strategy in order to be able to comment on urban compared to nonurban settings, it has advantages for such an effort. Most obviously, the District is an urban setting, whereas Alabama and Utah include many nonurban areas, allowing for observation of both shared themes and differences. In Alabama in particular, those I interviewed spontaneously compared reform in the major cities, especially Birmingham, with reform in the rural counties. In addition, a few researchers have studied differences between urban and rural counties, large and small counties, or poor and nonpoor counties, providing a modest amount of additional data.

TWO MYTHS

Talking with many people about the themes of this research, I have encountered two kinds of skepticism. First, many people suspect the situation is hopeless. If it weren't, how could it so often happen that newspapers report a scandal or tragedy, an agency vows to reform, and yet another tragedy occurs a year or two later, under circumstances that suggest nothing has changed? And if it weren't hopeless, why would we see the same recurring problems—social worker turnover, high caseloads, and failed decision making, when children go home to dangerous parents or are removed from loving parents? Child welfare administrators can also come to feel success is impossible: they do their best, yet still find themselves failing and under attack.

The second kind of skepticism argues that success ought to be easy. Interestingly, the two views—that success is impossible and that a single obvious idea alone should save the day—sometimes co-exist: it is impossible now, but it would be easy if only we had the political will or spent enough money to support reform, or if we replaced bleeding-heart social workers with tough policemen who aren't fooled by parents' promises to change.

Neither claim is true. Success in child welfare is not impossible, as evidenced by important recent progress, both local and national. And success is not easy, for a whole host of reasons. Understanding the complexity of the task is necessary to design and deliver the right local, state, and national policy and system changes to make things better for children.

Success Is Possible

Over the past decade, successful child welfare reform strategies have emerged in both urban and rural systems that were once viewed as disastrous. While it is too soon to declare victory, these programs are much better than they were before, in significant ways that affect child welfare. Strong and credible evidence shows improvements in basic capacity, quality of services, and results for children and families. Improved capacity means, for example, lower caseloads for social workers and quicker investigations of abuse or neglect reports. Better quality means, for example, that families struggling to care for their children are more likely to find services and community support to help prevent abuse and neglect; social workers know children and families better, visit them often, and work with their extended families, teachers, and others active in their lives; and more children who cannot live safely at home live in nurturing foster families, not institutions. And in programs with better results, children who cannot live with their biological families are less likely to have to move among temporary foster homes and more likely to move quickly to a permanent home with a relative or adoptive family.

The three case studies offer specific examples of such positive changes in child welfare agencies that started out very troubled. After the reforms in all three sites, there were very large improvements compared to the starting points in basic measures of whether services were happening, in the quality of services, and on some results for children—yet in all the locations, there was a great deal still to do. For example, social workers in the District visited 50 or 60 percent of children every month compared to 5 percent before the reforms and cut in half the number of young children who lived in dormitory-like settings rather than foster families. The successes occurred in both urban and rural settings, though as I'll indicate in a moment, the Alabama evidence in particular suggests different diagnoses and different paces of change in the two types of settings.

For readers unfamiliar with child welfare services, an example may help illustrate how a child welfare agency that works better than it used to can make a positive difference for a child and family. Thirteen-year-old Lora[4] was one of several thousand children who were involved with Washington, D.C.'s public child welfare agency—the Child and Family Services Agency (CFSA)—in 2003:

"Lora," age thirteen, is the oldest child in a sibling group of four. . . . In April 2003, [community agency staff] reported physical abuse of Lora by her stepfather. . . . Lora was removed by CFSA. . . . In June of 2003, Lora reported sexual abuse by the stepfather during the time he still resided in the family home. [Her mother] currently is receiving treatment for a blood clot on her brain which resulted from a brutal incident of domestic violence by the stepfather. . . .

[After her mother received a protective order against the stepfather] Lora returned to live with her mother and three siblings in late August 2003. . . . Both mother and daughter feel very positive about their experience with CFSA. They report their current worker has much empathy and concern for the well-being of the family. She offers advice and has provided financial help with school clothing for the children. . . . In addition to almost weekly visits to the family home, [the mother] reports that their worker frequently calls to check on the situation in the home. . . .

Since the physical abuse incident in April 2003 many changes for the better have occurred for this family. Physical and financial stability have been achieved by their move to a Public Housing apartment and the beginning of TANF [Temporary Assistance for Needy Families] benefits and services. This mother has begun working on her GED and has clear plans to work toward employment, which will support her family without her having to work fourteen to sixteen hours a day. . . . A wide array of services are being provided to this family . . . [including] family therapy and individual counseling for Lora. . . . Lora's transfer to a new school seemingly has enabled her to start with a fresh slate as far as her past behavioral challenges are concerned.

So far, intervention by the child welfare system in this case seems to have helped turn things around for the child and the family. Lora got back on track academically and emotionally, and the restraining order against her stepfather stopped further abuse. Intervention also influenced her mother's decision to seek help and counseling to keep an abusive partner out of the home, and possibly contributed to the emotional well-being of Lora's three younger siblings, who now grow up in a safer environment. Even if the system has not eliminated the underlying difficulties faced by a mother with very limited education and skills, struggling to support her four children, and wrestling with her past dependence on a violent drug-abusing partner, it has changed the odds in her family's favor.

Nationally, the child welfare system's persistent failures have driven repeated waves of reform. But if reform sometimes seems to be a constant cycle yielding no results, children nationwide are better off in several ways than they were a decade ago.[5] For example, children have a better chance of living in a permanent family if they cannot go home to their biological family. Two important changes are the dramatic increase in adoptions of children from foster care—from about 25,000 in the mid-1990s to 50,000 or more each year from 2000 to 2006—and the expansion of subsidized guardianship programs, which now exist in more than 30 states and the District of Columbia (Children's Defense Fund, 2004) and have just been incorporated into federal law.[6] Subsidized guardianship allows relatives to receive financial support to care for a child permanently, without completely severing the child's legal ties with a biological parent, as an adoption would. For example, a grandmother can become her grandchild's legal guardian and receive help from the child welfare system without cutting the child's parent out of the picture. Like adoption, guardianship offers a child a permanent, lifelong family.

Yet It Will Never Be Easy

When I set out to research this topic, one of the central puzzles that motivated me was why each step along the way to reform was so painful and difficult, despite the agreement of agency staff and stakeholders with the broad goals (if not the specific steps) of reform in the District of Columbia's child welfare system. Just as it took two and a half years to end the practice of children sleeping in the office building even though no one wanted it to continue, the system's failures were so complicated and persistent that they defeated the good intentions of many individuals who wanted to do the right thing. The resulting cycle of good people burning out and drifting away because they couldn't "do what we came here to do" only made things worse.

As I began studying other successes, the theme of complex systems that defied simple solutions emerged. In Alabama, many of the same social workers and managers who drove the reform had been part of the old, failed system for years, always believing they were doing the best they could. What spurred the change if it wasn't new people? In Utah, major early steps by the state, including a sizable investment in hiring social workers and legal advocates for children, didn't help performance. What mysterious ingredient was added after 1997? Nationally, legislation that now pours hundreds of millions of dollars into subsidies for parents who adopt children from foster care was hardly used at all in its first decade. Again, what changed?

It is important to answer these questions, to better understand why changing failed child welfare systems is hard, and what pieces have to align to make success possible. If reform appears to rest on oversimplified solutions—the budget in one jurisdiction, the number of social workers in another, replacing the leaders in a third—yet never succeeds, then the public, the elected officials who oversee child welfare agencies, and the press are likely to become deeply cynical about whether anything can work. That risk makes it important to understand not only the individual components of success, but also how the pieces coalesce to change the patterns of failure.

URBAN CHILD WELFARE SYSTEMS IN THE NATIONAL CONTEXT

The job of the child welfare agencies at the heart of this research is summarized in federal law as "safety, permanence, and well-being" (U.S. Department of Health and Human Services [HHS], Administration for Children, Youth and Families [ACYF], 2000) To protect children's *safety*, agencies operate hotlines to receive reports of abuse or neglect, investigate the reports and assess the family situation in person, determine whether abuse or neglect occurred, and make judgments about what should happen next to protect the child. Services to protect children may be delivered in their own home, if possible, or through removing them from the home. If children are removed from their parents and placed in temporary homes, then agencies are responsible for developing a plan and coordinating services so children can have a *permanent* home and family as soon as possible, whether with their biological family or through adoption or guardianship. Agencies must also attend to the *well-being* of these vulnerable children and families—their physical and emotional health, children's education and development, and families' stability. Finally, some public agencies, working alone or with community agencies, try to prevent child abuse and neglect by offering support services to families under stress.

How are urban child welfare agencies similar to or different from the national context? This section places urban child welfare agencies in a national context, considering the agencies themselves, the children and families they serve, and the broader system of related organizations—such as other public agencies, state and local family court judges, and community services agencies—that together make up the child welfare system.

The Goals of Child Welfare

Child welfare agencies operate in a delicate zone, where national and state legislation authorizes intrusive government involvement in families only when children are seriously in danger. As a result, agencies may fail by taking too little action or too much. A Pulitzer Prize–winning *Washington Post* series in 2001 documented 8 years of child fatalities in the District, offering an indictment of failure to act that is often echoed around the country:

> From 1993 to 2000, 229 children died after they or their families came to the attention of the District's child protection system because of neglect or abuse complaints. In dozens of cases, police officers and social workers responsible for the safety of children failed to take the most basic steps to shield them from harm . . . at least nine D.C. children . . . perished after police officers and social workers conducted incomplete investigations or left the children to fend for themselves with violent, neglectful, or unstable parents or guardians. (Higham & Horowitz, 2001)

The same year, the *Salt Lake Tribune* described Utah state legislators angry about the opposite issue, excessive intrusiveness into families:

> More than 20 child welfare advocates, lawmakers, and attorneys are calling for sweeping changes in Utah's child welfare system. . . . "We have a problem in this state," said Rep. Tom Hatch. . . . "We have several parents raising legitimate concerns that DCFS is removing children from homes unjustifiably. . . . I've had constituents call me up with horror stories." Rep. Paul Ray, (R-Clearfield) . . . said, "When we have an organization that's breaking up families, and we have to pass laws to protect people . . . it's time to reorganize." (Estes, 2001)

The intense public attention reflects the potentially devastating effects of both kinds of failures—children's death or injury when public help is too little too late and family disruption and emotional devastation for children and parents when it is over-intrusive. One recent review of the national evidence argues that "It is hard to avoid the conclusion that the American child protective services system is investigating many families unnecessarily. . . . At the same time, however, CPS [child protective services] may be intervening too lightly, and providing too few services to some families" (Waldfogel, 1998, pp. 26–27).

This clash of goals and the high stakes for children are true both in urban and rural settings. A recent report on child deaths from abuse and neglect reports grim examples in every state, with the total from 2001–2008 ranging from 6 in Delaware and Vermont to 1,732 in Texas (Every Child Matters Education Fund, 2010). In all settings as well, many of the most public tragedies and failures cannot be laid at the feet of a single agency; drug abuse, family violence, and troubled neighborhoods have complex causes and no simple solutions.

Urban child welfare administrators often feel, however, that the clash of goals plays out in more public and devastating ways in big cities than in suburban and rural communities, with more castigation in the press, political turmoil, and likelihood that both agency heads and social workers will be fired whenever anything goes wrong. This had certainly been the District of Columbia's history. At the press conference where Mayor Williams appointed me, a longtime community activist asked the group to join him in bucking the District tradition of "looking for leaders and then destroying them." He was referring to a long-standing pattern throughout District government where when something went wrong the local newspaper would write a critical article, outside stakeholders would rush to distance themselves from the public agency, Congress or the District Council would hold oversight hearings, the agency would become further mired in responding to criticism rather than fixing problems, and eventually the agency's head would resign. In New York City, Nicholas Scopetta described the history of child welfare before the reforms that brought him on board as the first head of a new agency: "there would be a tragedy, the mayor would fire the commissioner, nothing changes—of course, nothing changes."[7]

By contrast, the history in Alabama and Utah before their reforms was of political neglect of and indifference to the child welfare system, not harshness or controversy. While no better for high performance, as we shall see in a moment, this climate was different from the harsh and punitive culture in New York and Washington. One longtime Alabama child welfare official summed up the climate before the reforms as "political neglect, budget neglect, indifference." The federal court monitor in Alabama saw it as a culture with no consequences at all for bad performance: "There were no clear expectations or accountability at all" and "counties performed as they performed" in a "laissez-faire" atmosphere.

Who Are the Children and Families?

The scale of child welfare involvement in the United States is surprisingly large. In 2006, state child welfare agencies received 3.3 million referrals involving 6 million children (HHS, ACYF, 2008a). After screening and investigation, the agencies found that 905,000 children had been abused or neglected, and removed about 22 percent of them from their homes for some period. The remaining 5 million-plus children, who were referred but not found to have been abused and neglected, are often in very precarious home situations, and seriously behind other children developmentally and behaviorally.

How do these numbers differ between urban and nonurban areas? The first important point is that child welfare services are shaped above all by state law and practice, and the characteristics of the system and the children and families who are involved with it vary hugely by state. Thus, cities located in different states could have very different reporting rates and patterns. For example, the share of children with a substantiated allegation of abuse or neglect in 2005 ranged from under 4 per 1,000 children (in Pennsylvania, New Hampshire, and Virginia) to 25 or more (in West Virginia, the District of Columbia, and Florida). The explanations suggested by HHS include different definitions of child maltreatment (set by state law), different levels of evidence required for a substantiated or indicated finding, and the choice to serve some families through alternative response systems (which do not lead to a decision about whether an allegation is substantiated) (HHS, ACYF, 2008b).

A few researchers, however, have looked for patterns at the county level, seeking systematic differences between urban and nonurban counties and between the poorest and the least poor counties. One such analysis (a special study of 296 counties in four states) suggests that poor cities may face elevated rates of maltreatment due to their poverty, but not just because they are urban (Wulczyn, Barth, Yuan, Harden, & Landsverk, 2005). According to this study, counties with high poverty rates have higher rates of maltreatment for children of all ages than counties with low poverty rates, with the greatest difference for infants. When counties are grouped into primary urban areas (a state's largest city), secondary urban areas (other cities), and nonurban areas, the primary urban counties have the highest maltreatment rates for infants and older children, but nonurban counties have the highest rates for toddlers and preschool-aged children. And when race is added, the results are again most striking for infants, with extremely high rates of maltreatment for African American infants in the poorest counties. These babies face a risk of maltreatment of 50 per 1,000 children, or 5 percent, compared to national incidence rates for all children of about 12 to 15 in 1,000 (Wulczyn et al., 2005).

These patterns suggest another interesting finding about urban child welfare systems. For all jurisdictions, children entering care are more likely to be very young or to be teenagers than to be children of 8 or 9. The risk of reported maltreatment is by far the greatest for infants, in all income and racial groups, with smaller peaks occurring for teenagers age 14 to 15 and for children just entering school—a peak often attributed to a "surveillance effect," when children are exposed to outsiders for the first time (Wulczyn et al., 2005). For urban areas and for poor areas, the extremely high rates for infants are even more pronounced. This could be because of "case-finding"—that is, cases of maltreatment are found earlier in crowded and service-rich urban areas but not until a child enters child care or kindergarten in nonurban areas. But it could also be because neighborhoods of concentrated poverty include young mothers whose own risks of experiencing homelessness, violence, substance abuse, and depression have the potential to endanger their babies.

These very high rates of infant maltreatment take on particular importance because of the vulnerability of all babies, and particularly babies reported to the system. Infants reported to the child welfare system are far more likely to be developmentally delayed than infants in the population as a whole, with more than half "at high risk for developmental delay or neurological impairment," based on a national sample (Wulczyn et al., 2005). Surprisingly, this very high rate of developmental risk is equally evident among children reported to the system whether or not they are found to be abused or neglected (Barth et al., 2008). While the full reason for this finding is not known, it could mean that such other features of a baby's home life as a chaotic or violent home or community are as damaging to development as actual incidents of abuse or neglect.

Turning to what is known about families involved with the child welfare system, there is no typical family, though many struggle with poverty, substance abuse, domestic violence, depression, and other mental and physical health problems. Poor families are disproportionately represented, but the reasons are complex (Macomber, 2006). Poor families face more stress, which can push them over the edge into child abuse or neglect, and have fewer resources to use in a family crisis, where health care or counseling is often needed. The direct consequences of extreme poverty, such as homelessness or insufficient food in the house, may be defined by an agency as neglect, even though poverty alone is not supposed to establish maltreatment. Underlying problems, such as substance abuse, can lead both to child maltreatment and to poverty. And, poor families are probably subject to more surveillance and critical assumptions about their behavior by doctors, teachers, and other professionals than better-off families.

Children and families in contact with the child welfare system nationally are disproportionately likely to be minority, particularly African American. The most recent summary of foster care children finds that in all but four states, a substantially higher proportion of children in foster care is black than in the general state population (HHS, ACYF, 2008a). African American children are more likely to come into contact with the system, more likely to be placed in out-of-home care, and likely to have longer stays in out-of-home care than white children. A review of the research concludes that "children of color and their families experience poorer outcomes and receive fewer services than their Caucasian counterparts" (Courtney et al., 1996, p. 99).

During the past decade, researchers have heightened their attention to these issues of disproportionate representation and disparate treatment of children of color in the child welfare system and have sought to untangle the reasons behind them (Hill, 2006; Barth, 2005). Among the many likely reasons are differences in the attitudes and assumptions of child welfare staff and others who interact with families, systematic differences in the resources available to white compared to African American families, and neighborhood-based differences in access to services, along with real differences in family circumstances. In the words of one child-welfare official: "When a family presents as more articulate and can gather resources easier . . . whether those resources are family or finances or provision of services, that changes the overall level of risk or the perceived level of risk."[8]

Besides poverty, many families in the child welfare system cope with such complex and often co-occurring challenges as family violence, substance abuse, and depression. For example, in the National Survey of Child and Adolescent Wellbeing (NSCAW) sample of families investigated by CPS, 44.8 percent of caregivers have some experience with physical violence by their spouse or partner.[9] Depression is also widespread among women involved with the child welfare system. The NSCAW sample of caregivers for children investigated by the child welfare agency finds that almost one-quarter have experienced a major depression in the past 12 months, almost twice the national percentage for all women (HHS, ACYF, 2005a). The proportion is even higher among women who have also been victims of domestic violence (Hazen, Connelly, Kelleher, Landsverk, & Barth, 2004).

For substance abuse, the range of estimates is considerable, but all sources suggest that the problem is widespread. According to a recent review of cases sampled for the states' Federal Child and Family Services Reviews, substance abuse brings the attention of the child protective services agency in 16 to 61 percent of cases (Young, Gardner, Whitaker, Yeh, & Otero, 2005). These estimates, however, are significantly lower than many other studies, possibly because child welfare workers have a difficult time identifying substance abuse during the rushed days of the initial investigation, and families have a strong incentive to conceal it. Another study of substance abusers in a child protective services caseload finds that 68 percent of the children have mothers who abuse alcohol or drugs (Jones, 2005).

Two important caveats qualify this bleak picture. First, families are not homogeneous: some who find themselves caught up in the system have none of these additional risk factors. In a sample of Boston families involved with child welfare, one researcher finds that despite the patterns of high risk that characterize some families, others are involved with the system for different reasons and are hard to classify (Waldfogel, 1998). Similarly, in my Washington, D.C., experience, the agency encountered parents who needed only specific and limited help, or who were suffering from a family tragedy—often a death or serious illness—that they could not cope with alone. For example, a mother with mild mental retardation could have cared for a healthy child but could not safely handle a chronically ill child's complex medical needs without help. And a father who had been caring for a deaf and mute child with the help of his own mother could no longer manage once the boy's grandmother died.

The second caveat is that even families whose lives are overrun by serious and chronic problems should not be narrowly defined by them. Parents' courage, resilience, and abiding love for their children can coexist with drug and alcohol problems, emotional instability, or severe depression. Telling the story of one mother's probably doomed battle to keep her children from being adopted after many years of trying to end her dependence on drugs, a journalist sums her up as "a terribly flawed but fiercely determined mother," whose young son says of her after a visit, "If that was your mommy, you would be lucky" (Bergner, 2006).

What can we glean about the specific features of families who interact with urban compared to rural child welfare systems? According to one overview, "Urban areas such as New York City, Chicago, Detroit, and Los Angeles are widely recognized as being difficult environments in which to operate child welfare programs, although why this is true is not understood fully" (Wulczyn et al. 2005, p. 95). More drug use, crime and violence in urban areas may contribute to the intensity of family problems (Barth, Wildfire, & Green, 2006). And concentrations of poor families in dangerous neighborhoods may increase the risks for children while also reducing access to services. A detailed study of practices and institutional features of child welfare in Michigan that disadvantage African American families highlighted differences in access by neighborhood. In one example, white families in rural areas of Saginaw County had access to housing vouchers, while African American families in urban areas of Saginaw County and in Wayne County faced shortages and waiting lists. In another example, providers that had contracts with Michigan's child welfare agency to provide home-based services to families did not allow their staff to visit the neighborhoods where many families lived, citing safety concerns (Center for the Study of Social Policy, 2009).

How do urban child welfare systems react when faced with these extremely difficult clusters of family and neighborhood challenges? One possibility, supported to some degree by the case studies, is that workers and systems tend to set a far higher bar for investigating and serving families in urban areas, because they are faced with so many distressing cases. And in the face of too few resources, they also are more likely than in rural areas to tip over into chaos—where reports pile up uninvestigated, children never see a caseworker, and overwhelmed workers depart soon after arriving.

For example, in Alabama before the reforms, longtime attorney James Tucker cited Alabamans' catch-phrase for the disparity between jurisdictions: in rural counties, a child would be removed for having lice, but in Birmingham, broken bones would get no attention. Children in the smaller communities suffered from a rush-to-judgment that broke apart families unnecessarily, while children in the state's large cities got little protection. The reason, Tucker thought, was that harsh assumptions about poor families particularly affected subjective child welfare judgments in some of the smaller, rural counties, where social workers had often grown up in more educated or well-off families in the same community where they worked. In those communities, it might take one complaint about lice in a child's hair to trigger long-held assumptions about poor families, such as that they would never change and the children would be better off if removed. On the other hand, in Birmingham, chaos rather than rigidity reigned, with 1,000 uninvestigated cases in the mid-1990s and piles of unassigned cases. Ivor Groves, the court monitor, reported that in 1995, as reform began in Birmingham, he was told, "See those cases there on that table? We don't know who they belong to."

Intuitively appealing as this picture of big cities compared to small rural communities may be, it is hard to determine how broadly it applies. A study of a nationally representative sample of local child welfare agencies found that poor counties investigated a *larger* proportion of reports relative to the number of poor families in the county than did nonpoor counties. This appears counter to the idea that poor counties are so overwhelmed they ignore some reports, but it is hard to be sure. After all, if the reports in the poor counties are far more serious than in the nonpoor counties, they could still have a higher bar even if they are numerically investigating a larger proportion. Consistent with the "chaos" finding, though, poor counties had lower child welfare expenditures per child and lower expenditures per investigation, suggesting that they were stretching their resources to deal with an overload of cases (HHS, ACYF, 2005a).

Both a result and a contributor to this overload, urban child welfare administrators would say, is their great difficulty recruiting and keeping caseworkers. Excessively high caseloads per worker, gaps in caseworker education and experience, meager on-the-job training, low salaries, and high turnover rates are frequent problems nationwide. One recent study found that child welfare workers typically have caseloads of 24 cases for investigation or 31 cases for ongoing case management—about twice the recommended number (Annie E. Casey Foundation, 2003). While none of the studies that I have reviewed compares urban and nonurban caseloads nationally, the resource findings just described are certainly consistent with the overwhelmed urban workers in the study sites. The concerns associated with inexperienced and overwhelmed staff nationwide were clearly a problem in these locations: bad decision making about children, too often driven by emergencies; little or no ongoing monitoring of children's circumstances or planning for their future; and plans made without family input and firsthand knowledge of parents' and children's circumstances.

Child Welfare and the Urban Infrastructure

Child welfare systems are complex not only because of the multiple and interlocking difficulties faced by children and families but also because of the extraordinary number of different people, organizations, branches of government, and levels of government involved in making decisions and delivering services. The federal and state governments split policy and funding responsibility, and the state in turn may split operational and funding responsibility with city or county governments or operate its own regional and local offices. The most recent detailed study of child welfare financing finds that in fiscal year 2006, just under half (48 percent) of the $25.7 billion spent on child welfare nationally was federal, 41 percent was state, and 11 percent was local. The local share of expenditures varied from none in 25 of 46 states responding to more than 20 percent in 5 (DeVooght, Allen, & Geen, 2008). Again, therefore, the implications for urban service delivery vary greatly depending on the state and its financing system.

The structure of local agencies also varies by state. In "state-supervised, county-administered" systems, the county government delivers services, overseen by the state. In state-administered systems, the state is responsible for service delivery, even though local or regional offices may be organized by county. While the federal government requires that systems be in one or the other category, some have hybrid features that recognize both state and county (or city) as important political stakeholders: for example, the county director may work for the state but be vetted by important county political figures.

The important players in child welfare go far beyond the executive branch. In particular, state or local judges have central responsibilities, as a result of the coercive power of the system. Because few Americans would want an agency to have the unfettered authority to take their child away, any more than we would want to empower police to send us to prison without a judge or jury hearing the case, federal and state laws require that judges make key decisions about children and families in the child welfare system. They determine that it is appropriate to remove a child from home, regularly review case plans, and if necessary terminate parental rights and create a new adoptive family. This judicial role reflects the grave decision to remove a child from his or her parents' home or to permanently terminate parental rights. A potential implication for urban child welfare systems is that overcrowded and underresourced courts, coping with the whole range of criminal and civil issues, may compound the problems of similarly overstretched and underresourced agencies.

Also central to child welfare systems are public and private agencies that provide such services as medical and mental health care, education, and family support. It seems likely that urban areas have a richer array of services than nonurban areas. For example, one study finds that child welfare agencies in urban counties subcontract for services more often than nonurban counties, perhaps reflecting a richer array of local services (HHS, ACYF, 2005a). However, the case studies and other research suggest that there may also be characteristic urban problems: for example, if the school system is overwhelmed and failing at the same time the child welfare system is struggling, then very vulnerable children in foster care are quite likely not to get the help they need in school. And even when a big city has many sophisticated mental health practitioners, they may not be located in the right neighborhoods, be willing to treat low-income young people or take Medicaid rates, or have the right professional training or experience to treat maltreated children and their families.

And finally, because of the complexity of recruiting staff and developing, paying for, targeting, and monitoring services, child welfare agencies depend critically on their administrative systems—budgeting, contracting, licensing, human resources, information systems—to coordinate and support the day-to-day work. These administrative systems may be part of the child welfare agency itself, located in some larger umbrella agency (for example, a human services cabinet agency), or located in a separate agency such as a civil service, personnel, or contracting office. I know of no evidence to indicate systematically whether urban or rural systems have more trouble with administrative supports, but the case studies certainly illustrated the huge challenges faced by urban systems when those administrative supports are weak. In both New York City and the District of Columbia, making administrative functions more accountable to the child welfare agency leadership and goals was central to the reform—but, at least in the District, the underlying weakness of personnel and contracting systems exerted a persistent drag on the speed of change.

A final dimension of complexity in urban child welfare was most evident in the District: the metropolitan setting. Child welfare agencies work with families, for whom jurisdictional boundaries may not be important. If an agency is working with a child who lives temporarily with an aunt in a suburban jurisdiction—which in the District and some other large metropolitan areas could easily be in another state—the agency must organize education, health care, and ongoing services to the child in one jurisdiction and the parents in another, with as little disruption to the child's life as possible. Low-income parents move frequently for a variety of reasons (Coulton, Theodos, & Turner, 2009); yet in some metropolitan areas, even moves to a nearby neighborhood may cross city, county, or state lines, forcing complex interjurisdictional negotiations to ensure children's safety, finance services, or that a child's education is not interrupted while they are under child welfare agency jurisdiction.

HOW CAN FAILING URBAN AGENCIES ACHIEVE SUCCESS?
REFLECTIONS ON THE CASE STUDY LESSONS

The research reported in *Reforming Child Welfare* identifies the elements of a multifaceted strategy that leads to turning around failing agencies. What aspects of that strategy are particularly important for reformers seeking to change urban systems and infrastructure? This section considers the *Reforming Child Welfare* findings in light of that question.

Vision and Diagnosis

In all the sites, leaders drew on a vision and priorities, a set of cross-cutting ideas that helped to explain their actions and communicate to others where they were going. Ira Burnim, the plaintiffs' attorney in Alabama's landmark child welfare case, *R.C. v. Wally*, was struck that when the new agency leader, Paul Vincent, began to articulate the vision embodied in the consent decree, "there was a lot of change in the system, even before staff came on board or money was spent." Richard Anderson, a longtime child welfare staffer who was first deputy and then director of Utah's system during reform, emphasized the importance of a coherent vision rather than a set of miscellaneous proposals: "People would talk about how to fix this and that. [But there were] a million philosophies in the agency. . . . Before we go out [to talk to people about good practice], we need to determine philosophy, principles."

This focus on vision is consistent with a much larger management literature arguing that successful leaders of change in public and private organizations draw on a vision and strategy, including clearly stated goals and priorities (Moore, 1995). But it is quite different from the way child welfare researchers and policy experts have often seen the steps to improvement. The implicit model for them is that leaders should identify problems and then find evidence-based practices to fit each problem, one by one.

Yet this step-wise approach was not in fact the one used by the leaders in the case study sites. As explored at more length in *Reforming Child Welfare*, in these complex organizations, a coherent vision is needed to communicate to the many inside and outside stakeholders who need to coordinate their actions to achieve change. At the same time, individual problems are so inter-linked, they often cannot be solved separately in the absence of a broader vision.

A second key finding is that no single vision works to achieve child welfare reform everywhere. Instead, while there are broad common themes, each of the leaders transform those themes into a specific vision that is anchored in a diagnosis of the particular system, its most urgent problems, and its greatest opportunities. For example, while all the leaders addressed in some way the nature of social workers' day-to-day work, Paul Vincent in Alabama saw rigidity as the major problem and focused on intensive retraining to teach a more individualized approach to responding for families, before he sought any resources to lower caseloads. In Utah, Richard Anderson (the first reform director) came on when many additional social workers had just been hired yet the lower caseloads had not improved results. He diagnosed a problem of new, raw caseworkers intimidated by lawyers and judges, and he focused both on training and on developing a "practice model" to lay out caseworkers' day-to-day jobs more specifically. In D.C., we started with hiring, because overwhelmingly high caseloads and the resulting emergency-driven approach to the work, along with chaos when even that approach broke down, were universally identified as most urgent.

Implications for Urban Reformers

The implication for leaders in urban systems is that they need to build a vision that is not copied from other cities. Instead, it needs to be grounded in a specific diagnosis of what is right and what is wrong in the individual city, drawing on the perspectives of staff, community leaders, families, political stakeholders, and other key partners. As we have seen, cities are likely to vary considerably depending on state laws, funding, policy, and practice, and on local history and political culture. The solutions for Birmingham, Salt Lake City, D.C., and New York were not identical, although they had important common themes.

This is important, because it can be tempting to shortcut the diagnosis and the involvement of individual stakeholders and to seek a cookie-cutter answer. Yet while others' experiences are helpful, they are best mined for hypotheses or questions: if this was a central problem in a similar setting, does it exist here too, are the underlying reasons the same, and could the same approaches work?

The earlier discussion has suggested several of these promising questions, by identifying some potential commonalities among cities. One that I would urge leaders to pay attention to is the evidence about the high proportion of babies reported to the system. In urban areas, as we have seen, the incidence of maltreatment among babies is strikingly high, and so is the proportion of reports handled by the agency that concern babies rather than older children. Given what we know about infant development, this has important implications for agency services. For example, placing babies in shelter or institutional care, rather than family care, is particularly damaging—yet big cities sometimes have a history of large shelters or group settings used even for young children. In the District, while a number of our early wins had to do with moving babies and young children from group to family care and our vision emphasized that children thrive best in families, we never focused especially on babies. In retrospect, such a focus might have helped us guide service delivery choices in helpful ways.

Information, Learning, and Performance Management

In all three sites, the leaders were deeply involved personally in creating and improving information, both quantitative and qualitative, so they could see how they were doing. Paul Vincent in Alabama noted that "You get what you measure" and invented a new approach to qualitative assessment in child welfare in order to measure the right things. Linda Gibbs in New York City, chief of staff during the child welfare agency's reform, said, "Unless you have the numbers and are telling people regularly where you are and where you are going, you can't get it done." And Richard Anderson in Utah articulated the role of data in changing practice: "The most important event in child welfare is when a social worker meets with a family. You can manage that event by training, data, and then getting outcomes."

One startling result in the District was that when we started measuring basics like visits and case plans, large improvements occurred even before we reduced social worker caseloads. Most likely, the reason was that measurement sent signals about priorities and at the same time helped organize the work. It made clear whose job it was to achieve which measurable results, a particularly important step in chaotic environments.

In child welfare and other programs affecting vulnerable people, of course, one worry is that numbers will capture only part of the reality. For that reason among others, all the jurisdictions used qualitative as well as quantitative measures systematically. Alabama created a whole new approach to qualitative review of cases, where interviewers talked to children, families, foster families, and social workers to assess the quality and outcomes of a case. That system has become one of the most lasting results of the reform, adapted by the federal government for use in reviewing states and used by many jurisdictions, including Utah and the District, in one form or another.

The leaders also all focused on using information for learning, not blame. While this was a challenge in these difficult political environments, where everyone expected that information would document problems and lead to punishment, it turned out that when information is regularly reported, it can actually help fight blame and improve motivation. The reason is that regular tracking of the same measures—required in these case studies by the courts—makes it possible to see performance improvement even when the starting point is weak. By contrast, the previous approach to information had been to look for it only when a tragedy forced intense public scrutiny. Thus, in the District, the regular tracking of agreed-on measures required by the court helped achieve rare positive recognition in the media, because when the court reported that we had achieved a required standard, that was news.

Implications for Urban Reformers

Measurement is an area where urban reformers may have an advantage over rural or nonurban jurisdictions, since many cities have pioneered both information technology and mayoral initiatives focused on measurement, such as Baltimore's CityStat (Behn, 2006). However, depending on the city's relationship to the state child welfare agency, city-specific information about child welfare cases may or may not be easily available. In the best case, the city is in a good position to consider both quantitative and qualitative information about child welfare and to juxtapose it with information about schools, neighborhoods, and other service provision. In the worst case, a city has no access to information or has to use an ill-fitting statewide system.

Thus, one key implication for urban reformers is to push for the data they need, including the inclusion of child welfare and other human services data elements in citywide information initiatives. However, one important caution is that citywide information systems and performance measurement staff, as well as the mayor's or city administrator's offices, need to gain sophistication in the measurement of programs for vulnerable people, to avoid unrealistic expectations about what can change, or pressure to use narrowly quantitative measures that miss important aspects of the problem. In cities that do not have major human services responsibilities, this might require a phased-in approach and considerable learning from other jurisdictions that use effective qualitative and quantitative assessments.

A second implication, certainly relevant to schools and quite likely to other urban systems, is that performance measurement that aims to turn around failing agencies needs a careful balance of support and accountability. The study sites used a wide range of skillful approaches to build up accountability of individuals, teams, and geographical areas (counties in these statewide examples, but potentially local offices in a city) while at the same time giving people the system-wide supports and tools they needed to succeed. Each time a new group of people—for example, contracted services agencies—were brought into the measurement framework, they had many complaints about the measures themselves and the flaws of technology and system support that made it impossible to meet them. It always turned out that they were partly right, and addressing those flaws directly was an important part of the solution—yet it was critical at the same time to move forward on the overall goal of accountability. The message above all from the study sites is that there are many ways to keep moving forward with a "both-and" approach that solves line staff's problems with measurement while continuing to expand it.

Politics of Performance Improvement

While agencies' internal steps to focus on performance mattered, leaders in all the study sites believed that they could not have changed agency performance just by measuring better and focusing on internal improvement. The political environment was crucial too. Damaging political environments had contributed to the agencies' history of failure, and improved environments were necessary to reform.

There turned out to be two kinds of political environments in the case studies that were damaging to agency performance prereform. In very harsh environments, described above with examples from the District and New York City (as well as Utah during one of its stages), everyone expected random punishment and firings and as a result wanted to stay under the radar and have no responsibility for anything. In completely negligent environments, like Alabama and Utah before the reforms, no one cared at all what the human services agency did; no performance, good or bad, could get political notice, reward, or resources. The negligent and harsh environments led to just the same passivity: the incentive for staff was to avoid notice and stay under the radar screen, not to attend to performance or results. Either way, bad systems were locked in.

How did the environments change? The full story as told in *Reforming Child Welfare* is long, but a couple of observations are important here. First, the reformers benefited from moments of opportunity—when political leaders were ready to try something new—but they also built their own opportunities. Sometimes in child welfare and other programs for vulnerable people, policy experts and activists talk about "political will" as either being there or not, but the case studies suggest that building political will is more a process than an on-off switch. Effective reformers find moments and build on them.

Second, the leaders had to understand the usual dynamics in their cities or states—the old, bad cycles—and then they had to act differently. For example, leaders might fight back when the usual expectation would be that their agency would be a passive victim. In the example at the beginning of this chapter, the decision by the court leadership to come to the child welfare agency for a meeting with social workers after a judge had sent a social worker to jail was a completely new, unexpected idea in the context of the District's history. Its originality made it a powerful symbol of the court's intention to show respect and improve the relationship. Choosing to act differently can be a strong catalyst for change.

Implications for Urban Reformers

We have already seen that the "harsh" variant of a failed political environment may be more likely to characterize urban settings, so successful reformers need to look for moments of opportunity when that environment can change. In the case study sites, federal court settlements offered such a moment, though not always at the beginning. In New York City, the opportunity came from the choice by a politically powerful mayor to respond to a tragedy not only with a new agency and new resources but also by empowering an agency head in whom he had great confidence.

While no generalization is certain, it also seems likely from the earlier discussion that urban settings are typically even more politically complex than child welfare settings in nonurban areas. Depending on whether the city contributes resources and operates the child welfare agency, both city and state elected officials will likely have a stake in the program, along with local media at least in the case of any tragedy. Local judges who oversee children's cases are important operational partners and they may also be important political players, whose judgment of the agency as effective or ineffective will be quoted in the media and taken seriously by elected officials. In many cities, metropolitan jurisdictions outside the city boundaries, possibly in other states, will also be important stakeholders not under the city's control. And federal overseers may in a few cases have a relationship with the city directly; in most cases, they will be part of the environment by way of the state.

With this complexity, local reform leaders need to be sophisticated about their political setting and skilled at defining a route to their child welfare reform vision that effectively moves the political as well as the bureaucratic setting. They also need support from and a close relationship with the local elected leadership, in particular, the mayor. In some of the case studies, a partnership between a largely "inside" leader and an "outside" leader with stronger relationships with elected officials, both executive and legislative, was very helpful. At the same time, even the "inside" leaders spent considerable time reaching out to stakeholders such as judges and community agencies even if they were not the lead in relationships with elected officials. This proactive outreach was quite different from the prereform history, where in most of the sites, agency heads did not interact with outside groups except around specific problems.

Reformers also need a strategy for working within the executive branch itself, given the importance of support from administrative agencies that govern budget, contracting, personnel, and information systems. In Alabama, a longtime agency staffer said to me about the reformers' efforts to retrain social workers that "you can teach people all day, but if the infrastructure doesn't work to support it, it won't change what they do." He was referring to what reformers had to do to break up the rigid statewide contracting system so individual counties and social workers could individualize services to families. In the District, one of many reasons that it took so long to fix the problem of children sleeping in the building was a failure of contracting capacity. As described earlier, one contributor to the problem was group homes' refusal to take children in when they returned at night after curfew or otherwise broke rules; some group homes would send them back to our office building instead. Allowing this seemed to us absurd, but it was in the homes' contracts, so we had to work through our overwhelmed contracting system to take back the authority to fix it.

What urban reformers need to understand from the sites is that making administrative systems support reform is very hard yet essential. The plaintiffs' attorney in Alabama said that he thought "changing hearts and minds" would be the hardest part and changing systems would be easy, but it turned out to be the reverse. In the sites, these administrative changes cannot typically be accomplished by child welfare leaders alone. Instead, chief elected officials—whether mayors or governors—play an important role in making the whole executive branch, including the administrative agencies, accountable for achieving the reform plan.

Taking Reform to the Front Lines

When a social worker talks to a mother and father about the plan for their child, when a nurse responds to a child's health crisis or a substance abuse counselor works with a parent, and when a grandparent or foster parent sits down to dinner with the children they are caring for, we are on the front lines of child welfare. Child development research demonstrates that all these interactions can affect children's development and family stability, for good or ill. So to change results for children, effective strategies for child welfare reform, whatever else they do, must have an influence on these front lines.

This conception of the front lines of child welfare, while drawn from child development research and the sites' experience, differs from much ordinary conversation and media coverage, which place the agency social worker there alone. Yet the sites illustrate that social workers are far from all-powerful when it comes to affecting children's lives and development.

They can't substitute for a loving family or a terrific early childhood educator, although they can certainly help or hurt a child's chances of connecting with either of those. Instead, front-line reform that truly affects children will need to improve all three dimensions: social worker practice, settings where children live, and services.

The sites offer a number of lessons about changing culture and practice on the front lines, explained more fully in chapter 9 of *Reforming Child Welfare*. Most important for this chapter, though, is the conclusion that the child welfare system's complexity means that culture change on the front lines often must reach far more people than the agency's social workers. Such colleagues in other systems as lawyers and judges, community agency staff, and substance abuse counselors need to change their values and practices in parallel to social workers, supported by systems changes and clear expectations consistent with those in the child welfare agency. Not surprisingly, such linked changes are difficult, and successes in the sites are partial and reflect intensive effort.

Implications for Urban Reformers

We've seen earlier that urban areas will likely encounter families with more complex and interlinked challenges, especially in high-poverty neighborhoods. At the same time, urban settings may be somewhat more service-rich than other jurisdictions, and they may (in the best case) have the ability to bring together data from different service systems to identify trends, track families, and find promising opportunities for collaborative strategies.

This combination of family challenge and service opportunities suggests that urban reformers may need and want to focus on the frontline linkages between child welfare and certain key partners. The selection of these partners is critical, because the site evidence illustrates vividly how incredibly complicated it is to change just one large, dysfunctional service system, let alone changing two in tandem. But reformers might start out looking for opportunities based on the evidence about family needs and the readiness of key partners to collaborate. Examples of collaborations that might be promising include the following:

- Early engagement of parents in mental health services, particularly treatment for maternal depression. This should be both a preventive strategy, before a child maltreatment report, and an easily accessible part of family services after a report, for mothers who would benefit. Recent health reform legislation has the potential to expand funding options focused on treating low-income parents.
- Partnerships between the city's substance abuse agency, the courts, and the child welfare agency, to identify and treat parents' substance abuse. Again, the goal would be to make services extensively available not only after parents enter the child welfare system but also before.
- Partnerships between the child welfare agency and intensive services for vulnerable mothers and babies, such as Early Head Start and home visit programs. Once again, the goal would be to build partnerships that included both prevention and services after a report.
- Neighborhood-based strategies, which could be a component of any of the partnerships just identified. Such a partnership would enrich more traditional community-based child welfare strategies, which risk failure if they target an already distressed neighborhood without adding services.

Choosing just a few targeted collaborations is important because the evidence from the study sites suggests the extraordinary complexity of making each one work. Child welfare agencies can be successful at reforms that stretch across organizational boundaries, but only with difficulty. Such cross-cutting reforms demand parallel culture change, supportive administrative systems, and clear and consistent expectations in two or more organizations. Adding to the difficulty is the extraordinary complexity of state and federal funding streams, budget rules, and the laws that govern each system. It is possible to resolve each one of these issues, but not for all potential collaborations at once. More promising is a strategy of starting with the top priorities, working through them systematically and persistently, and building momentum for future success.

CONCLUSION

This chapter has focused on lessons for leading child welfare reform in urban settings. Improving performance in these settings matters enormously, because of the large number of children, particularly young and poor children, who have contact with child welfare agencies and suffer disruption in their lives and development from maltreatment and its aftermath.

In contrast to many treatments of child policy issues, whether child welfare, education, early childhood education, or youth development, this chapter has not focused primarily on federal or state policy, on laws to be passed, or even on budgets. Rather, it has focused above all on the choices facing senior agency managers and executive branch officials who are interested not only in ideas, politics, and policy but also the hard work of leadership within organizations.

Even this brief discussion of the challenges suggests that nurturing public agency leaders who bring the complex mix of skills required to transform large, troubled organizations is not easy. Just as the education reform debate has brought into relief the need for superintendents and principals who have skills including but far beyond content expertise, a serious discussion of agencies that serve troubled families and children highlights not just resource and policy but also leadership gaps.

Nonetheless, at a moment when President Barack Obama's new administration has engendered a new interest in government among young people, the time should be right for attracting and developing the next generation of leaders. I hope this chapter, and the larger research project on which it draws, can contribute by highlighting the importance of their work and sketching the terrain ahead. As the nation and its cities come to realize the importance of effective investments in children, we need more than ever the effective agency leaders who can get the most from those investments—who can deliver repeated short-term improvements aligned with a long-term vision; attend to the complex intersections of policy, politics, and organizational culture; and support the capacity of agency staff to learn and improve. The best opportunity for children is a self-reinforcing cycle of good ideas, stronger performance, and a more supportive political setting.

NOTES

Conclusions and opinions expressed in this chapter are those of the author alone and do not reflect the views of the Urban Institute's staff, trustees, advisory groups, or any organizations that provide financial support to the Institute.

1. Most of the material in this chapter is adapted from my book *Reforming Child Welfare* (2009). The evidence and conclusions regarding the specific lessons for urban systems and jurisdictions are new.

2. Chapter 4 of *Reforming Child Welfare* provides a survey of relevant child welfare and child development research and evaluation.

3. As commissioner of the Administration on Children, Youth, and Families (ACYF) from 1993 to 1996 and then as assistant secretary for children and families from 1997 to January 2001, I oversaw the core child welfare programs, policies, and funding streams located in the Children's Bureau of ACYF.

4. Lora is not her real name. Her story is excerpted from the report of the Quality Services review team, outside experts who reviewed a randomly selected group of about 40 CFSA cases in fall 2003 (Center for the Study of Social Policy, 2004b, A30–A32).

5. A more detailed discussion of the evidence for national improvement, as well as remaining national challenges, can be found in chapters 1, 3, and 4 of *Reforming Child Welfare*.

6. The Fostering Connections to Success and Increasing Adoptions Act of 2008 (see HHS, ACYF, 2008c).

7. All quotations not otherwise sourced are from interviews I conducted as part of the research for *Reforming Child Welfare*.

8. Ken Mysogland, the director of the Stamford, Connecticut child welfare office, quoted in Bergner (2006, 53).

9. Caregivers in this sample were the current caregivers of children who had been reported for abuse or neglect. A small proportion (about one-ninth) were foster parents, but the rest were largely mothers, with a small number of fathers or others. In the most extreme situations, where children were removed from the home, their biological mothers were not in the sample. So this number and others reported for this caregiver sample are conservative, cautious estimates: the likely incidence of major problems among all mothers involved with child welfare is even higher (HHS, ACYF, 2005a).

REFERENCES

Annie E. Casey Foundation. (2003). The unsolved challenge of system reform: The condition of the frontline human services workforce. Baltimore, MD: Author.

Barth, R. P. (2005). Child welfare and race: Models of disproportionality. In D. M. Derezoles, J. Poertner, & M. F. Testa (Eds.), *Race matters in child welfare* (pp. 25–46). Washington, DC: CWLA Press.

Barth, R. P., Lloyd, E. C., Casanueva, C., Scarborough, A. A., Losby, J. L., & Mann, T. (2008). *Developmental status and early intervention service needs of maltreated children*. Washington, DC: U.S. Department of Health and Human Services, Office of the Assistant Secretary for Planning and Evaluation.

Barth, R. P., Wildfire, J., & Green, R. L. (2006). Placement into foster care and the interplay of urbanicity, child behavior problems, and poverty. *American Journal of Orthopsychiatry, 76*, 358–366.

Behn, R. (2006). *The theory behind Baltimore's CityStat*. Paper presented at the fall research conference of the Association of Public Policy Analysis and Management, Madison, WI.

Bergner, D. (2006, July 23). Her most difficult call. *New York Times Magazine*, 53–54.

Center for the Study of Social Policy. (2004a). *LaShawn A. v. Williams*: An assessment of the District of Columbia's progress as of September 30, 2003, in meeting the implementation and outcome benchmarks for child welfare reform. Washington, DC: Author.

Center for the Study of Social Policy. (2004b). *LaShawn A. v. Williams* qualitative review: Process, results, and recommendations. Washington, DC: Author.

Center for the Study of Social Policy. (2009). Race equity review: Findings from a qualitative analysis of racial disproportionality and disparity for African-American children and families in Michigan's child welfare system. Washington, DC: Author.

Children's Defense Fund. (2004). *States' subsidized guardianship laws at a glance*. Washington, DC: Author.

Coulton, C., Theodos, B., & Turner, M. A. (2009). Family mobility and neighborhood change: New evidence and implications for community initiatives. Washington, DC: The Urban Institute.

Courtney, M. E., Barth, R. P., Berrick, J. D., Brooks, D., Needell, B., & Park, L. (1996). Race and child welfare services: Past research and future directions. *Child Welfare, 75*(2), 99–137.

DeVooght, K., Allen, T., & Geen, R. (2008). Federal, state, and local spending to address child abuse and neglect in SFY 2006. Washington, DC: Child Trends.

Estes, A. (2001, April 26). Group seeks child welfare change; advocates, others ask Utah governor to investigate "illegal" removal of kids; DCFS response: Some changes are under way. *Salt Lake Tribune*, B1.

Every Child Matters Education Fund. (2010). *We can do better: Child abuse and neglect deaths in America*. Washington, DC: Author.

Golden, O. A. (2009) *Reforming child welfare*. Washington, DC: The Urban Institute Press.

Hazen, A. L., Connelly, C. D., Kelleher, K., Landsverk, J., & Barth, R. (2004). Intimate partner violence among female caregivers of children reported for maltreatment. *Child Abuse & Neglect, 28*, 301–319.

Higham, S., & Horowitz, S. (2001, September 12). A child endangered, without a lifeline: Mentally ill mother threatened her son, but D.C. police and Child Protection Agency failed to act. *Washington Post*, B1.

Hill, R. B. (2006). Synthesis of research on disproportionality in child welfare: An update. Baltimore, MD: Casey Family Programs.

Jones, L. (2005). The prevalence and characteristics of substance abusers in a Child Protective Services sample. *Journal of Social Work Practice in the Addictions, 4*(2), 33–50.

Macomber, J. (2006). An overview of selected data on children in vulnerable families. Washington, DC: The Urban Institute

Moore, M. H. (1995). *Creating public value: Strategic management in government.* Cambridge, MA: Harvard University Press.

U.S. Department of Health and Human Services, Administration on Children, Youth and Families, Children's Bureau. (2000, January 25). DHHS Child Welfare Final Rule Executive Summary, *Federal Register, 65*(16).

U.S. Department of Health and Human Services, Administration on Children, Youth, and Families, Children's Bureau. (2005a). *National Survey of Child and Adolescent Well-Being (NSCAW). CPS sample component, wave 1 data analysis report.* Washington, DC: U.S. Department of Health and Human Services.

U.S. Department of Health and Human Services, Administration on Children, Youth and Families, Children's Bureau. (2005b). *Synthesis of findings from the assisted guardianship child welfare waiver demonstrations.* Washington, DC: U.S. Government Printing Office.

U.S. Department of Health and Human Services, Administration on Children, Youth and Families, Children's Bureau. (2005c). *Synthesis of findings from the title iv-e flexible funding child welfare waiver demonstrations.* Washington, DC: U.S. Government Printing Office.

U.S. Department of Health and Human Services, Administration on Children, Youth and Families, Children's Bureau. (2008a). *Child welfare outcomes, 2002–2005.* Washington, DC: U.S. Department of Health and Human Services.

U.S. Department of Health and Human Services, Administration on Children, Youth and Families, Children's Bureau. (2008b). *Preliminary estimates for FY 2006 as of January 2008 (14).* Washington, DC: U.S. Department of Health and Human Services.

U.S. Department of Health and Human Services, Administration on Children, Youth and Families, Children's Bureau. (2008c). Program instruction: New legislation—The Fostering Connections to Success and Increasing Adoptions Act of 2008 (Public Law (P.L.) 110-351). Washington, DC: U.S. Department of Health and Human Services.

Waldfogel, J. (1998). The future of child protection: How to break the cycle of abuse and neglect. Cambridge, MA: Harvard University Press.

Wulczyn, F., Barth, R. P., Yuan, Y. T., Harden, B. J., & Landsverk, J. (2005). *Beyond common sense: Child welfare, child well-being, and the evidence for policy reform.* Piscataway, NJ: Transaction Publishers.

Young, N. K., Gardner, S. L., Whitaker, B., Yeh, S., & Otero, C. (2005). *A review of alcohol and other drug issues in the states' child and family services reviews and program improvement plans.* Version 20, updated November 2005. Irvine, CA: National Center on Substance Abuse and Child Welfare.

19

Health Disparities Among African Americans in Urban Populations

Sheri R. Notaro

Health disparities reflect differences in the quality and length of life that are experienced by members of certain groups (e.g., ethnic minorities, women, those of low socioeconomic status) in the United States (U.S. Department of Health and Human Services, 2001b). Health disparities also reflect the differential power, privilege, and resources that have a long and enduring legacy in our society. Those living in urban populations face some of the most severe health disparities in our nation because of the resource-poor environments in which they live, work, and raise their families (Schulz, Freudenberg, & Daniels, 2006). Urban populations experience continued disparities and inequities in health, as measured by a variety of indicators including health status and access to health care. In fact, although African Americans and whites living in rural and southern towns experienced economic conditions that were similar to or worse than those living in northern urban cities, the health status of the former was substantially better (Williams, 2002). Members of ethnic/minority groups, including African Americans, American Indians and Alaskan Natives, Latinos, and some Asian subgroups who inhabit these urban spaces experience greater morbidity, mortality, and inferior health care in comparison to the white majority (Geiger, 2006). Reducing health disparities is not only beneficial to these affected groups, but also offers the opportunity to improve the health of the entire U.S. population (Schulz, Williams, Israel, & Lempert, 2002).

African Americans experience the highest mortality rates of any U.S. racial group throughout the life span (except among the very old where black mortality rates are lower than white mortality rates) (LaVeist, 2005). Additionally, although all urban residents have a higher risk of mortality compared with that of the entire population, African Americas have higher mortality rates than do whites living in the same city (Freudenberg, 1998; Schulz et al., 2002). Moreover, the morbidity or disease burden of African Americans is typically higher than that of whites (Schulz et al., 2006).

In light of these serious disparities, this chapter will review the morbidity and mortality of African Americans living in urban spaces. Further, the chapter will frame these disparities in terms of family health because the well-being of families is crucial to the functioning and success of society's major institutions (e.g., communities, schools, and neighborhoods). Parents and children, arguably the main inhabitants of communities, schools, and neighborhoods, cannot participate in and contribute to the advancement of these cultural and physical structures if they are burdened by poor health outcomes. This chapter will narrow its focus further to review the health status of mothers, children, and adolescents, because the way in which society cares for its most vulnerable members is a strong and sensitive indicator of that society's civic and moral engagement with its citizens (Williams, 2002). This chapter will also describe research and interventions that strive to increase our understanding of the causes of these disparities as well as to help alleviate them.

AFRICAN AMERICAN DEMOGRAPHY

According to the 2000 United States Census, African Americans comprise 12.9 percent of the total U.S. population (36.4 million people). African Americans are the third largest racial group in the United States, behind whites and Latinos. As indicated in Table 19.1, in general, African American death rates are higher in comparison to American Indians/ Alaskan Natives, Asian/Pacific Islanders, Latinos, and whites (National Center for Health Statistics, 2003). Although their health has improved, minority populations continue to experience excess morbidity and mortality in comparison to the white population (Geiger, 2006). Excess morbidity and mortality are particularly severe for African Americans, whose mean life expectancy is 6 years shorter than that of whites (National Center for Health Statistics, 2003). It has been estimated that if African Americans had experienced the same age-adjusted mortality rates as whites during the decade of 1991–2000, as many as 866,000 black deaths (complications of pregnancy, HIV, cardiovascular disease, stroke, cancer, diabetes, pneumonia, and influenza) would have been avoided (Geiger, 2006; Woolf, 2004; National Center for Health Statistics, 2003).

Black men have higher death rates than whites for 11 of the 15 leading causes of death, and black women have higher death rates than white women for 12 of the 15 leading causes of death (National Center for Health Statistics, 2003). Compared to whites, rates for black men and women are at least twice as high for five causes of death (diabetes, nephritis, septicemia, hypertension, and homicide) (National Center for Health Statistics, 2003).

MATERNAL AND CHILD HEALTH

Maternal and child health status are commonly used indicators signifying the well-being of a population. The maternal mortality rate for African American women is more than three times the rate for white women and more than double the Latina rate (Centers for Disease Control and Prevention, 2007). As indicated in Table 19.2, African American women have the highest infant mortality rate of all ethnic groups in the United States (Centers for Disease Control and Prevention, 2007). In 2004, the African American infant mortality rate (13.6

Table 19.1. Age-Adjusted Death Rates for All Causes of Death by Race and Hispanic Origin: United States, 1950–1998

Race/Ethnicity	Death per 100,000 Residents
White	452.2
Black	690.9
American Indian or Alaska Native	458.1
Asian or Pacific Islander	264.6
Hispanic	342.8

Note: From "HHS Directory of Health and Human Services Data Resources," by U.S. Department of Health and Human Services, 2001a, http://aspe/hhs/gov/datacncl/datadir

Table 19.2.   Total Infant Mortality Rates by Race/Ethnicity of Mother: United States, 2004

Race/Ethnicity	Rate per 1,000 Live Births
White	5.66
Black	13.60
American Indian or Alaska Native	8.45
Asian or Pacific Islander	4.67
Mexican	5.47
Puerto Rican	7.82
Total	6.78

Note: From MacDorman, Callaghan, Matthews, Hoyert, & Kochanek (2007). Retrieved November 30, 2011, from http://www.cdc.gov/nchs/products/pubs/pubd/hestats/infantmort99-04/infantmort99-04.htm

infant deaths per 1,000 live births) was more than double the rate for Mexican Americans, whites, and Asians/Pacific Islanders, who had rates below 6 deaths per 1,000 live births (Centers for Disease Control and Prevention, 2007).

At each educational level the African American infant mortality rate greatly exceeds that of other groups. In fact, the African American infant mortality rate among women with the highest educational level is higher than the rate for all other ethnic groups at all educational levels, including the lowest (Centers for Disease Control and Prevention, 2007). White women who did not finish high school have a lower infant mortality rate than African American women with a college degree (Williams, 2002).

While the black-white differential in infant mortality has been linked to a complex interaction of biological, socioeconomic (e.g., access to neonatal technology), behavioral (e.g., diet), and psychosocial factors (e.g., racism) and lack of social support, recent research has attempted to explain this disparity using an intersectional approach (Jackson & Williams, 2006). Intersectional approaches explore the relationship among the political, structural, and societal arrangements that lead to the inequitable distribution of health-related resources such as health care services and the delivery of health care (Mullings & Schulz, 2006). It examines stereotypes and representations based on ethnicity, class, gender, and nationality that then influence health (Zambrana & Thornton-Dill, 2006).

Jackson and Williams (2006) attempted to explain the "paradox" that exists whereby the black-white differential in infant mortality becomes larger as maternal education increases using an intersectional approach. They hypothesized that differences in social class intersect with race and gender to account for health paradoxes (including infant mortality) facing some African American women. Their analyses focused on middle-class African American women who often work within organizations that are structured by racial and gender divisions (Jackson & Williams, 2006). Jackson and Williams (2006) hypothesized that middle-class black women's status is experienced in less beneficial ways as compared to any other group because they are not in a position to mobilize all of the resources that should be available to them given their social class standing.

Despite gains in professional opportunities for women over the past thirty years, many professional occupations remain male dominated. In 2002, women comprised 10 percent of engineers, 30 percent of doctors, and 29 percent of all lawyers (U.S. Department of Labor, 2003). Among middle-class women who are employed in managerial and professional occupations, the majority work in the government and nonprofit sector (e.g., employment, health, social services, and education) (Council of Economic Advisers, 1998). African American women are the most underrepresented subgroup in private-sector professional jobs and are likely to be a minority in professional workplace settings.

Some research suggests that African American women working in these settings experience added pressure to perform well, social isolation from colleagues, and stereotyping by colleagues as the woman who is a matriarch or the woman who spends too much time working away from home (Collins, 1997). Related research provides evidence that African American women face hostility and competition from African American men in the workplace (Bell & Nkomo, 2001). African American women have been shown to seek advice from colleagues about dealing with work problems less often than their male counterparts (Jackson & Williams, 2006). One study found that support of supervisors and coworkers did not reduce levels of depression among black professional women (Bailey, Wolfe, & Wolfe, 1996).

African American women earn lower wages at each educational level and realize less of a payoff for additional education than nonblack women and men (Bradbury, 2002). When income is scarce, people become vulnerable to negative events and psychological stress. At all levels of education, black and Hispanic men and women live in households with lower levels of income than whites (Williams & Collins, 1995). At the level of household economic resources, African American and Hispanic men and women are disadvantaged. Lower levels of household income for African American than for Latina women reflect the fact that African American women are more likely than Latina women to be the primary wage earner in the household. While women of all racial/ethnic groups earn less income at every educational level compared to men, the pattern is largest and most pronounced for African American women and persists for them at every level of education (DeNavas-Walt & Cleveland, 2002).

Another important factor that may help to explain health paradoxes for African American women is the finding that the benefits of receiving social support may not outweigh the costs of providing social support for African American women. Social support is generally given or received, but upwardly mobile African American women are twice as likely as their white peers to give support resources to family and friends than they are to receive support from these sources (Gray & Keith, 2003). This imbalance in social support may cause African American women to feel overwhelmed by support requests.

Marriage is a source of social support and predictor of health across racial groups in the United States and, on average, married persons live longer and enjoy better health than those who are not married (Jackson & Williams, 2006). African Americans have lower rates of marriage and higher rates of marriage dissolution than whites. These differences appear to be driven not by cultural preferences, but by social and economic conditions facing African Americans (Jackson & Williams, 2006). For both blacks and whites in the United States, rates of marriage are positively related to average male earnings and inversely to male unemployment rates (Bishop, 1980). African American women face challenges finding mates given high rates of unemployment, underemployment, and incarceration among black men.

Men have higher levels of college completion than women, but the pattern is not found among African Americans. Thus many professional black women marry mates who are lower in educational and occupational status than themselves. On average, white women receive larger economic benefits from marriage than black women. Added economic burdens faced by black women may be linked to poor health habits, less attention to personal health and well-being, and subsequent physical health problems, including those linked to birth outcomes (Jackson & Williams, 2006). Thus, the failure of African American women to reap the benefits of their middle-class status may contribute to factors (e.g., stress concerning economics, racism, lack of social support, and family life) that impact disparities in infant mortality.

The Harlem Birthright Project

In a similar vein to Jackson and Williams, the Harlem Birthright Project pursued an intersectional approach to understanding the relationship among the political, structural, and societal arrangements that lead to the inequitable distribution of health-related resources and ultimately poor maternal and child health for African American women (Mullings, 2006). Using an ethnographic approach, the Harlem Birthright project explored the meaning of inequality in the lives of women in Harlem by investigating how class, race, and gender interacted to produce these poor health outcomes. It was especially focused on understanding the "paradox" discussed by Jackson and Williams (2006)—that African American women have problematic birth outcomes regardless of socioeconomic position. The Harlem Birthright Project sought to challenge concepts of individual risk factors in relation to poor health status and to shift the emphasis from interventions focused on "behavioral change" (Mullings, 2006). This project instead attempted to understand the impact of structural constraints, employment, housing, and education on the birth outcomes of African American women in Harlem.

The Harlem Birthright Project was conducted in Harlem from 1993 to 1997, a time period that encompassed many negative effects of globalization (e.g., loss of domestic jobs, decreases in spending for social services, privatization of publicly funded institutions, decreased power of unions and resulting loss of benefits) (Mullings, 2006). In Harlem, job losses were reflected in unemployment rates of 16 percent in 1990, twice that of New York City (Mullings, 2006). At the time of the Harlem Birthright project, 60 percent of residents 16 and older were unemployed and more than 30 percent of all households had incomes below the federal poverty level (New York City Department of City Planning, 1990).

Low-income women in Harlem were especially vulnerable to unstable employment, which severely affected their income security and access to work-related benefits. Participants reported "piecing together" income from various sources, losing access to benefits, and struggling to maintain benefits and searching for jobs (Mullings, 2006). Low-income women used a variety of strategies to secure and maintain employment and job training (e.g., state subsidies and informal sectors—such as styling hair at home and using private food pantries and charities) (Mullings, 2006).

Middle-income participants also had problems maintaining employment since many of their jobs were concentrated in public sector and social service jobs, which are most affected by government disinvestment and spending cuts. In fact, 85 percent of professional African American women worked in health, social service, and education, all of which have been targets of state and federal budget cuts, downsizing, and privatization, making these women vulnerable to unemployment and loss of benefits (Burbridge, 1994; Mullings, 2006). Nearly three-quarters of middle-class respondents reported living from paycheck to paycheck; furthermore, they described working in stressful jobs with underfunded and underequipped facilities (e.g., working at hospitals with no hospital gowns or stretchers) (Mullings, 2006). All of these factors added to the stress of pregnancy.

During the study period, in addition to unemployment, there was also a critical shortage of affordable housing in Harlem. Between 1970 and 1990, the number of available housing units in Harlem had declined by 27 percent, as housing units were abandoned or neglected by city and private landlords (New York City Department of City Planning, 1990). At the same time, Harlem experienced increased investment in high-end housing and new retail establishments by the private sector. The need for housing affected low- and middle-income women in Harlem and intersected with many other areas of their lives, including health, exposing them to long-term stressors (Mullings, 2006). Women reported difficulty getting landlords to make repairs, and experiencing discrimination in obtaining and keeping rental properties. During the Harlem Birthright Project, approximately 50 percent of respondents were actively engaged in efforts to resolve housing problems (Mullings, 2006). For pregnant women, the need for extra space for children and the physical strain of dealing with housing problems (e.g., being forced to move from poorly maintained apartments, being evicted during pregnancy, negotiating over repairs, looking for a larger apartment) caused stress and strain (Mullings, 2006). Many of the respondents engaged in strategies to procure, maintain, and retain housing, including taking landlords to housing court to force them to complete repairs (Mullings, 2006). About 40 percent of respondents had been to housing court and over two-thirds had represented themselves without legal representation. Some respondents worked on these issues with block associations, tenant groups, and other community organizations.

Other aspects of the respondents' neighborhoods were also stressful (e.g., lack of quality retail and grocery stores, poorly maintained public parks, pollution from sewage treatment plants and bus depots). Airborne pollutants have been linked to lower birth weights and a higher prevalence of childhood asthma in Harlem as compared to the U.S. population (Nicholas et al., 2005; Perera et al., 2003). In fact the 29 percent prevalence rate of childhood asthma in Central Harlem, which is four times the national estimate of 7 percent, is one of the highest rates documented in any U.S. neighborhood (Nicholas et al., 2005). In response to these environmental hazards, many participants tried to improve the public spaces in Harlem by advocating for the removal of garbage and the installation of community gardens in vacant lots. Respondents reported little cooperation from city and state agencies in these efforts, which they believed was the result of discrimination.

The decrease in "marriageable" men was a final stressor identified by the women in the Harlem Birthright Project (Mullings, 2006; Jackson & Williams, 2006). This finding has been associated by many with the decrease in manufacturing and the industrial job sector that formerly provided employment for African American and other men of color as well as with the expansion of prisons, which house disproportionate numbers of African American men. This decrease in available men has led to an increase in women raising children without the economic support from men (Jackson & Williams, 2006). This finding affected women in the Harlem study, regardless of socioeconomic status. Nearly two-thirds of all households in Central Harlem at the time of the research project with children under age 18 were headed by women (Mullings, 2006).

Researchers proposed a short-term intervention for residents of Central Harlem, the Opportunity Zone, which sought to minimize barriers to employment, education, health, and housing and to increase the number and quality of community health centers, quality public schools, and affordable housing (Mullings, 2006). Long-term proposals included the establishment of a living wage, full employment, restoration of full civil rights for former prisoners, free quality public education, and universal health care. The Harlem Birthright Project emphasized the importance of understanding the connections between health and well-being of residents of Central Harlem as well as the rest of the United States.

ADOLESCENT HEALTH: HIV/AIDS

According to the Centers for Disease Control and Prevention (2008), at the end of 2003, an estimated 1,039,000 to 1,185,000 persons in the United States were living with HIV/AIDS. In 2006, 35,314 new cases of HIV/AIDS in adults, adolescents, and children were diagnosed in the 33 states with long-term, confidential name-based HIV reporting. Further, in 2006, persons aged 25–34 and persons aged 35–44 accounted for the largest proportions of newly diagnosed HIV/AIDS cases. Almost three-quarters of HIV/AIDS diagnoses among adolescents and adults were for males and the largest estimated proportion of HIV/AIDS diagnoses among adults and adolescents were for men who have sex with men, followed by persons infected through high-risk heterosexual contact (Centers for Disease Control and Prevention, 2008).

During the mid- to late 1990s, advances in HIV treatments slowed the progression of HIV infection to AIDS and led to dramatic decreases in deaths among persons with AIDS living in the 50 states and the District of Columbia (Centers for Disease Control and Prevention, 2008). In general, the trend in the estimated numbers of AIDS cases and deaths remained stable from 2002 through 2005. Estimates for 2006 suggest that the number of AIDS cases remained stable and that the number of deaths decreased; however, it is too early to determine whether this trend will hold. Better treatments have also led to an increase in the number of persons who are living with AIDS (Centers for Disease Control and Prevention, 2008).

As indicated in Table 19.3, although African Americans made up only 13 percent of the population in the 33 states with long-term, confidential HIV reporting, they accounted for almost half of the estimated number of HIV/AIDS diagnoses made during 2006 (Centers for Disease Control and Prevention, 2008).

The HIV/AIDS death rate for African Americans is more than seven times that for whites and is the 6th leading cause of death for African American men and the 10th leading cause of death among African American women, but is among the top 10 causes of death for only one other ethnic group—Hispanic men (National Center for Health Statistics, 2003; LaVeist, 2005). In fact, HIV/AIDS is the leading cause of death for African American men aged 25–44 years. The leading cause of HIV infection among African American women is heterosexual transmission, while for African American men, the leading cause of HIV infection is homosexual sex and injection drug use (National Center for Health Statistics, 2003).

The primary risk factors for HIV/AIDS infection are highly prevalent among African Americans (LaVeist, 2005; U.S. Department of Health and Human Services, 2001a). Poverty is the first risk factor, given that the African American poverty rate is 22 percent and those living below the poverty line have a higher risk of HIV infection due to reduced access to health care and less access to health education concerning HIV prevention (Diaz et al., 1994; LaVeist, 2005). The second risk factor is the high degree of stigmatization in the African American community for those with AIDS—especially for those infected through male-to-male sex. Black men are less likely to disclose homosexuality or bisexuality (Centers for Disease Control and Prevention, 2003). This reluctance may, in turn, cause them to be less receptive to HIV education messages targeted toward these populations and to be more likely to expose female partners to HIV/AIDS (Hader, Smith, Moore, & Holmberg, 2001; U.S. Department of Health and Human Services, 2001b). The third risk factor is the high

Table 19.3. Race/Ethnicity of Persons (Including Children) With HIV/AIDS Diagnosed During 2006

Race/Ethnicity	*Percentage Diagnosed*
White	30%
Black	49%
American Indian or Alaska Native	<1%
Asian or Pacific Islander	1%
Hispanic	18%

Note: "National HIV/AIDS Fact Sheet: HIV/AIDS in the United States, 2006," by U.S. Department of Health and Human Services, Centers for Disease Control and Prevention, 2008, Atlanta, Georgia, http://www.cdc.gov/hiv/resources/factsheets/us.htm

rates of incarceration among low-income black men. Incarceration is highly associated with HIV transmission due to the fact that in prison otherwise heterosexual men may have homosexual sex, causing increased risk of infection (Braithwaite & Arriola, 2003; LaVeist, 2005). The fourth risk factor is injection drug use—the second leading mode of HIV transmission for African American men and women—through needle sharing (LaVeist, 2005). Additionally, chronic drug users are more likely to engage in unsafe sexual practices including having multiple partners and not using condoms (Leigh & Stall, 1993).

REDUCING DISPARITIES IN HIV/AIDS

Health professionals and community members created REAL MEN (Returning Educated African American, Latino, and Low-Income Men to Enrich Neighborhoods) as a short-term health intervention for adolescent males leaving jail and returning to their neighborhoods in New York City (Schulz et al., 2006). Researchers involved in developing REAL MEN were attuned to the fact that over the past 30 years, criminal justice, poverty, and educational policies have greatly decreased the life opportunities available to young men living in urban environments (Schulz et al., 2006).

For example, problems in the public education system (e.g., decreased funding, larger class sizes, and poorly trained teachers) led to a situation whereby fewer than half of those entering high school in New York City graduate (Gootman, 2004). During the 1990s, New York state transferred nearly $1 billion from public education to build, expand, and staff prisons (Correctional Association of New York, 2004). Half a million African American adolescent males and older men are unemployed in New York City, largely due to the loss of manufacturing jobs and inadequate educational preparation, forcing many of them into the illegal pursuit of income, including selling drugs (Schulz et al., 2006).

New York City's zero tolerance for low-level crime and its practice of incarceration prior to sentencing increases the likelihood that young men who sell or use drugs will be arrested and incarcerated (Ayers, Ayers, Dorhn, & Jackson, 2001; Jacobson, 2001). It has been shown that black and Latino men are targeted through institutionalized racism (e.g., racial profiling) that disproportionately affects low-income communities of color (Miller, 1996). While African Americans and Latinos make up 30 percent of the population of New York State, they comprise 94 percent of the state prison population (New York State Division of Criminal Justice Services, 2004).

Higher rates of HIV and other STDS are found among adolescent males who have been in prison as compared to nonjailed populations, primarily due to unprotected heterosexual contact before and after incarceration (Malow, McMahon, Cremer, Lewis, & Alferi, 1997). Easy access to drugs and alcohol and the limited availability of effective prevention and treatment programs in these communities contribute to high rates of substance use, which is a risk factor for HIV infection (Schulz et al., 2006). HIV infection and drug use increase significantly between adolescence and early adulthood, among both incarcerated and general populations (Staton et al., 1999). Most young men leaving jail, prison, or juvenile detention have not participated in programs aimed at preventing HIV or increasing links to community services (Freudenberg, 2001). Within a year of release, most of these young men are rearrested, contributing to increases in HIV infection and drug use (LeBlanc, 2003).

The creators of REAL MEN (Schulz et al., 2006) acknowledge New York State's efforts to address some of these problems (e.g., increasing funding for public schools, decreasing class sizes, reforming drug laws, addressing police racial profiling, and increasing job opportunities). However, while these initiatives address inequities that increase risk, they do not address the needs of young men who are already part of the criminal justice system, or address specific physical and mental health concerns. REAL MEN incorporated the fact that young men who are released from jail often want to change their lives, but upon reentering the same environments which contributed to their incarceration (e.g., racism, poor education, family crises, negative peer influences), they become overwhelmed.

To combat these problems, REAL MEN partnered with community organizations to link adolescent males participating in the program to local health care providers specializing in substance abuse as well as physical and mental health services. They also provided connections to high school, general equivalency diploma, literacy, and job readiness programs (Schulz et al., 2006). Discussions were facilitated wherein the young men critically examined the ways in which concepts of masculinity and racial/ethnic identity impact health and health behaviors. The participants played important roles in helping to develop the format for these discussions. Much of the curriculum was based on research suggesting that views of "manhood"; conceptions of risk, trust, and power; and some components of racial identity, such as ethnic pride, may impact adolescents' mental health, self-esteem, academic achievement, and risk-taking behaviors (e.g., drug use and unprotected sex) (DiClemente et al., 2004; Harvey & Hill, 2004).

REAL MEN hypothesized pathways through which conceptions of masculinity may shape decisions made by young men as they are leaving jail. For example, a belief that manhood requires multiple sexual partners, having sex when high on drugs, and having unprotected sex may increase the risk of HIV infection and unintended pregnancies. Taking risks and showing no fear in face of risks is promoted through the media as normative and desirable behavior for men and may contribute to young men engaging in risky behaviors.

To address these issues, REAL MEN offered workshops in jail and after release to encourage young men to consider options related to drugs, relationships, sex, criminal activity, and jail (Schulz et al., 2006). Participants discussed media portrayals of manhood in terms of depictions in film and music. Through role plays, the participants developed and considered alternative responses to situations that were likely to arise with friends, sexual partners, employers, and family. The program also included activities designed to reinforce racial pride and solidarity, to promote community well-being, and to motivate young men to think about and plan for the future. After participants were released from jail, they were offered two additional days of group sessions, as well as educational and employment services in the community (Schulz et al., 2006).

Although all of the evaluation data is not yet available, preliminary evidence shows that young men were willing to discuss masculinity and ways that it impacted their behaviors. The REAL MEN project illustrates many of the challenges to offering programs to young men leaving jail. These challenges include an emphasis on security instead of rehabilitation, competition for young men's attention and time with family and peers upon release, the lure of illegal activities to earn money, tension between offering core message versus retaining flexibility, and sustainability of funding for educational and employment services. The REAL MEN project made an important effort to reduce the harmful effects of structural inequalities on the health of young men leaving the prison system. The next step is to address the underlying processes that create health inequalities in the first place (Schulz et al., 2006).

CONCLUSION

The focus of this chapter was to provide an overview of some of the most pressing disparities in health status facing African American families in urban populations. Specifically, disparities experienced by African American mothers, children, and adolescents were discussed, along with some of the most relevant research that attempts to explain and reduce these inequities.

In terms of maternal and child health, African American women have the highest infant mortality rate of all ethnic groups in the United States. The chapter summarized work by Jackson and Williams (2006) and by Mullings (2006), which both used an intersectional approach to explain the "paradox" that exists whereby the black-white differential in infant mortality becomes larger as maternal education increases. Intersectional approaches explore the relationship among the political, structural, and societal arrangements that lead to the inequitable distribution of health-related resources.

Jackson and Williams (2006) presented evidence that middle-class black women's status is experienced in less beneficial ways as compared to any other group because they are not in a position to mobilize all of the resources that should be available to them given their social class standing. Thus, the failure of African American women to reap the benefits of their middle-class status may contribute to factors (e.g., stress concerning economics, racism, lack of social support, and family life) that impact disparities in infant mortality.

The Harlem Birthright Project (Mullings, 2006) sought to challenge concepts of individual risk factors in relation to poor health status and to shift the emphasis from interventions focused on "behavioral change" (Mullings, 2006). This project instead attempted to understand the impact of structural constraints, employment, housing, and education on the birth outcomes of African American women in Harlem. Based on the findings from their ethnographic study, researchers proposed both short- and long-term interventions for residents of Central Harlem. They attempted to decrease barriers to employment, education, health, and housing and to increase the number and quality of community health centers, quality public schools, and affordable housing (Mullings, 2006). Over the long term, researchers envisioned the establishment of a living wage, full employment, restoration of full civil rights for former prisoners, free quality public education, and universal health care.

Regarding adolescent health, the ravages of HIV/AIDS are well documented among African Americans. In 2006, 35,314 new cases of HIV/AIDS in adults, adolescents, and children were diagnosed. HIV/AIDS is the leading cause of death for African American men aged 25–44 years. To address this health crisis, health professionals and community members created REAL MEN (Returning Educated African American, Latino, and Low-Income Men to Enrich Neighborhoods). REAL MEN was conceived of as a short-term health intervention for adolescent males leaving jail and returning to their neighborhoods in New York City (Schulz et al., 2006). REAL MEN partnered with community organizations to provide services including health care, substance abuse counseling, educational resources, and job readiness programs (Schulz et al., 2006). Discussions were facilitated wherein the young men critically examined the ways in which concepts of masculinity and racial/ethnic identity impact health and health behaviors. Preliminary evidence shows that young men were willing to discuss masculinity and ways that it impacted their behaviors. The REAL MEN project made an important effort to reduce the harmful effects of structural inequalities on the health of young men leaving the prison system.

In closing, one central theme emerges in the research discussed in this chapter. The health of African Americans and especially African American mothers, children, and adolescents, is connected to historical and current societal and political structures. The success of our communities, schools, and neighborhoods depends to a great extent on our ability to address the impact that these external structures have on health outcomes and health-related resources. Once we understand these connections, we must have the courage and vision to make the necessary changes in our society to provide health for all—not just health for some.

REFERENCES

Ayers, R., Ayers, W., Dorhn, B., & Jackson, J. (Eds.). (2001). *Zero tolerance: Resisting the drive for punishment*. New York, NY: New Press.

Bailey, D., Wolfe, D., & Wolfe, C. (1996). The contextual impact of social support across race and gender: Implications for African American women in the workplace. *Journal of Black Studies, 26*, 287–307.

Bell, E., & Nkomo, S. (2001). *Our separate ways*. Cambridge, MA: Harvard Business School Press.

Bishop, J. (1980). Jobs, cash transfers, and marital instability: A review of the evidence. *Journal of Human Resources, 15*, 301–334.

Bradbury, K. (2002, January–February). Education and wages in the 1980s and 1990s: Are all groups moving up together? *New England Economic Journal*, 19–46.

Braithwaite, R. L, & Arriola, R. J. (2003). Male prisoners and HIV prevention: A call for action ignored. *American Journal of Public Health, 93*(5), 759–763.

Burbridge, L. (1994). The reliance of African American women on government and third-sector employment. *American Economic review, 84*, 103–107.

Centers for Disease Control and Prevention. (2003). HIV/STD risks in young men who have sex with men who do not disclose their sexual orientation—six U.S. cities, 1994–2000. *Morbidity and Mortality Weekly Report, 52*(4), 81–100.

Centers for Disease Control and Prevention. (2007). *National infant mortality fact sheet: Trends in preterm mortality by race and ethnicity: United States, 1999–2004*. Atlanta, GA: Author. Retrieved September 10, 2008, from http://www.cdc.gov/nchs/products/pubs/pubd/hestats/infantmort99-04/infantmort99-04.htm

Centers for Disease Control and Prevention. (2008). *National HIV/AIDS fact sheet: HIV/AIDS in the United States, 2006*. Atlanta, GA: Author. Retrieved September 10, 2008, from www.cdc.gov/hiv/resources/factsheets/us.htm

Collins, S. (1997). Black mobility in white corporations: Up the corporate ladder but out on a limb. *Social Problems, 44*(1), 55–67.

Correctional Association of New York. (2004). *New York state of mind? Higher education vs. prison funding in the empire state, 1988–1998*. Retrieved September 15, 2008, from http://www.cjcj.org/pubs/ny/nysompr.html

Council of Economic Advisers for the President's Initiative on Race. (1998). *Changing America: Indicators of social and economic well-being by race and Hispanic origin*. Washington, DC: U.S. Government Printing Office.

DeNavas-Walt, C., & Cleveland, R. (2002). *Money income in the United States: 2000*. Washington, DC: U.S. Government Printing Office.

Diaz, T., Chu, S. Y., Buehler, J. W., Boyd, D., Checo, P. J., Conti, L. (1994). Socioeconomic differences among people with AIDS: Results from a multistate surveillance project. *American Journal of Preventive Medicine, 10*(4), 217–222.

DiClemente, R., Wingood, G., Harrington, K., Lang, D., Davies, S., Hook, E., et al. (2004). Efficacy of an HIV prevention intervention for African American adolescent girls: A randomized controlled trial. *Journal of the American Medical Association, 292*, 171–179.

Freudenberg, N. (1998). Community-based health education for urban populations: An overview. *Health Education and Behavior, 25*(1), 11–23.

Freudenberg, N. (2001). Jails, prisons, and the health of urban populations: Review of the impact of the correctional system on community health. *Journal of Urban Health, 78*, 214–240.

Geiger, H. J. (2006). Health disparities: What do we know? What do we need to know? What should we do? In A. J. Schulz & L. Mullings (Eds.), *Gender, race, class, and health: Intersectional approaches* (pp. 261–288). San Francisco, CA: Jossey-Bass.

Gootman, E. (2004, May 29). City creates new paths to a diploma. *New York Times*, B1.

Gray, B., & Keith, V. (2003). The benefits and costs of social support for African American women. In D. Brown and V. Keith (Eds.), *In and out of our right minds: The mental health of African American women* (pp. 242–257). New York, NY: Columbia University Press.

Hader, D., Smith, D., Moore, J., & Holmberg, S. (2001). HIV infection in women in the United States: Status at the millennium. *Journal of the American Medical Association, 285*(9), 1186–1192.

Harvey, A., & Hill, R. (2004). Africentric youth and family rites of passage program: Promoting resilience among at-risk African American youth. *Social Work, 49*(1), 65–74.

Jackson, P., & Williams, D. (2006). The intersection of race, gender, and SES: Health paradoxes. In A. J. Schulz & L. Mullings (Eds.), *Gender, race, class, and health: Intersectional approaches* (pp. 261–288). San Francisco, CA: Jossey-Bass.

Jacobson, M. (2001). From the back to the front: The changing character of punishment in New York City. In J. Mollenkopk & K. Emerson (Eds.), *Rethinking the urban agenda: Reinvigorating the liberal tradition in New York City and urban America*. New York, NY: Century Foundation Press.

LaVeist, T. A. (2005). *Minority populations and health: An introduction to health disparities in the United States*. San Francisco, CA: Jossey-Bass.

LeBlanc, A. (2003). *Random families: Love, drugs, trouble and coming of age in the Bronx*. New York, NY: Scribner.

Leigh, B., & Stall, R. (1993). Substance use and risky sexual behavior for exposure to HIV: Issues in methodology, interpretation, and prevention. *American Psychologist, 48*(10), 1035–1045.

MacDorman, M. F., Callaghan, W. M., Matthews, T. J., Hoyert, D. L., & Kochanek, K. D. (2007). Trends in preterm-related infant mortality by race and ethnicity: United States, 1994–2004. In *HCHS Health E-STAT*. Hyattsville, MD: National Center for Health Statistics.

Malow, R., McMahon, R., Cremer, D., Lewis, J., & Alferi, S. (1997). Psychosocial predictors of HIV risk among adolescent offenders who abuse drugs. *Psychiatric Services, 48*, 185–187.

Miller, J. (1996). *Search and destroy: African American males in the criminal justice system*. Cambridge, England: Cambridge University Press.

Mullings, L. (2006). Resistance and resilience: The sojourner syndrome and the social context of reproduction in central Harlem. In A. J. Schulz & L. Mullings (Eds.), *Gender, race, class, and health: Intersectional approaches* (pp. 345–370). San Francisco, CA: Jossey-Bass.

Mullings, L., & Schulz, A. J. (2006). Intersectionality and health: An introduction. In A. J. Schulz & L. Mullings (Eds.), *Gender, race, class, and health: Intersectional approaches* (pp. 3–17). San Francisco, CA: Jossey-Bass.

National Center for Health Statistics. (2003). *National Vital Statistics Reports, 52*(3).

New York City Department of City Planning (1990). *Persons 16 years and over by labor force status and sex, New York City, boroughs and community districts*. New York: Department of City Planning.

New York State Division of Criminal Justice Services. (2004). *Youth violence reduction strategy: Goals and guiding principles*. Retrieved September 10, 2008, from http://criminaljustice.state.ny.us/osp/downloads/guiding principlesfinalcombined2feb04.pdf

Nicholas, S., Jean-Louis, B., Ortiz, B., Northridge, M., Shoemaker, K., Vaughan, R., et al. (2005). Addressing the childhood asthma crisis in Harlem: The Harlem children's zone asthma initiative. *American Journal of Public Health, 95*(2), 245–249.

Perera, F., Raugh, V., Tsai, W, Kinney, P., Camann, D., Barr, D., et al. (2003). Effects of transplacental exposure to environmental pollutants on birth outcomes in a multiethnic population. *Environmental Health Perspectives, 111*(2), 201–205.

Schulz, A. J., Freudenberg, N., & Daniels, J. (2006). Intersections of race, class, and gender in public health interventions. In A. J. Schulz & L. Mullings (Eds.), *Gender, race, class, and health: Intersectional approaches* (pp. 371–393). San Francisco, CA: Jossey-Bass.

Schulz, A. J., Williams, D. R., Israel, B. A., & Lempert, L. B. (2002). Racial and spatial relations as fundamental determinants of health in Detroit. *Milbank Quarterly, 80*(4), 677–707.

Staton, M., Leukefeld, C., Logan, T., Zimmerman, R., Lynam, D., Milich, R., et al. (1999). Risky sex behavior and substance use among young adults. *Health and Social Work, 24*, 147–154.

U.S. Bureau of the Census. (2000). *Current population survey*. Washington, DC: Author.

U.S. Department of Health and Human Services. (2001a). HHS Directory of Health and Human Services Data Resources. Retrieved September 19, 2008, from http://aspe/hhs.gov/datacncl/datadir

U.S. Department of Health and Human Services. (2001b). *Healthy People 2010: Understanding and improving health*. Washington, DC: Government Printing Office.

U.S. Department of Labor, Bureau of Labor Statistics. (2003). *Employment and earnings*. Washington, DC: U.S. Government Printing Office.

Williams, D. (2002). Racial/ethnic variations in women's health: The social embeddedness of health. *American Journal of Public Health, 92*(4), 588–597.

Williams, D., & Collins, C. (1995). U.S. socioeconomic and racial differences in health. *Annual Review of Sociology, 21*, 349–386.

Woolf, S. (2004). Society's choice: The tradeoff between efficacy and equity and the lives at stake. *American Journal of Preventive Medicine, 27*, 49–56.

Zambrana, R., & Thornton-Dill, B. (2006). Disparities in Latina health: An intersectional analysis. In A. J. Schulz & L. Mullings (Eds.), *Gender, race, class, and health: Intersectional approaches* (pp. 192–227). San Francisco, CA: Jossey-Bass.

20

A "Tragic Dichotomy"

A Case Study of Industrial Lead Contamination and Management in a Company Town

Jill McNew-Birren

> The people of Herculaneum have mounted a Herculean effort to overcome the tragic dichotomy that has befallen this once idyllic community: a benevolent industry that has sustained the community for over one hundred years, whose product has harmed the most innocent—the children.
>
> —Herculaneum Master Plan (2006, p. 1)

What is the tragic dichotomy that has befallen the community of Herculaneum, Missouri? To answer this question one must understand that Herculaneum is a town founded upon and sustained by lead processing activities, based on its location near both the Missouri Lead Belt and the Mississippi River. The lead industry has concurrently constituted a source of economic vitality and of environmental contamination with one, the other, or both dominating community discourse at different times throughout the history of Herculaneum. As the town has evolved from a small settlement dominated by three towers for processing lead into shotgun ammunition (hereafter shot towers), into a company town owned and maintained by the local large lead processing plant, and ultimately to its modern state as a small community experiencing uneven patterns of both growth and decline, lead has remained central to the community's existence and identity.

The purpose of this chapter is to provide a nuanced account of the multiple, complex, and interwoven impacts lead has had on the Herculaneum community, its families, and its children. The first section of this chapter provides a background on environmental regulation and an overview of the historical controversy surrounding the management of lead in the United States, followed by a summary of research on the community impacts associated with the presence of lead industry facilities. The second section provides one historical account of the town of Herculaneum and its interaction with the lead industry. A third section provides additional insight into Herculaneum through an overview of the modern-day demographic and economic conditions there. This case study of lead regulation describes critical decisions and events that occurred in the first few years of the 21st century. A final section will examine how the situation in Herculaneum has impacted lead regulation nationally.

BACKGROUND ON LEAD IN HEALTH AND THE ENVIRONMENT

The Process of Environmental Regulation

Protection of human health is the driver for the majority of environmental regulatory efforts. Existing processes for protecting the public from exposure to environmental health threats involves a highly complex progression of defining negative health effects, tracing and quantifying the relationship between health effects and sources of exposure in the environment, identifying the origin of pollution in environmental media, setting limits and issuing permits for the amount of pollution allowable in various media, enforcing pollution limitations, and measuring reductions or changes in public health indicative of reduced exposure (see Figure 20.1). This process constitutes a feedback loop of sorts, in which scientific and political developments can act as inputs at any stage in the process, ultimately shaping environmental regulation efforts, health outcomes, and disease definitions.

Tracing exposure pathways, calculating dose-response relationships, setting standards for acceptable media-levels and guidelines for acceptable exposures involving a multisource, multimedia contaminant in a complex environment presents a difficult challenge for environmental regulators. Theoretically, the regulatory process should improve with the ad-

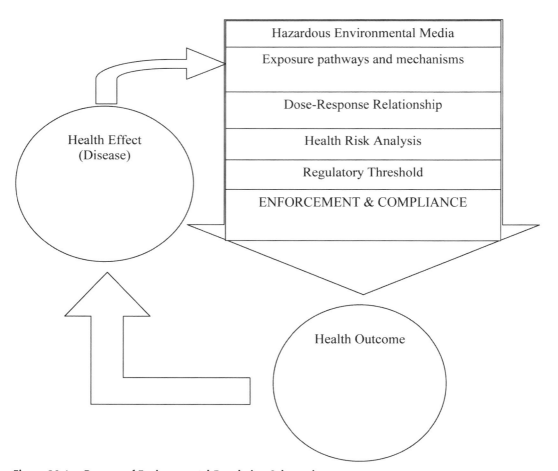

Figure 20.1.   Process of Environmental Regulation Schematic

vancement of environmental science, medical science, and epidemiology, and as a result of improved technologies for measuring lead in various media and cleaner processing mechanisms. Although lead is one of the longest recognized and most extensively researched environmental toxins, the complexity of its impacts on human health, particularly neurological development, and its multimedia, multipathway characteristics continue to fuel controversy over the ways that it is understood and regulated as an environmental contaminant. The next section presents a historical overview of scientific and regulatory controversies related to lead toxicity and exposure.

Environmental Regulation Through the 1960s: Industrial Self-Regulation

Although lead poisoning has been recognized throughout much of human history, it was not until the mid-1900s that perspectives on lead toxicity identified any health effects of lead exposure except the most severe cases of lead poisoning. In these cases clinical symptoms of abdominal, head, joint, and muscle pain; poor coordination; affected cognitive and perceptive functions; and changes in behavior to the point of psychosis were evident and linked to high levels of lead exposure, primarily from lead-related occupations. Lead exposures were also implicated in certain kidney diseases, spontaneous abortions, infertility, and early childhood mortality in the 19th and early 20th centuries (Hernberg, 2000). The health effects of severe, often fatal, lead exposures on children were initially recognized in the early 1900s (Needleman, 2004). Throughout the early 20th century concerns over the detrimental effects of lead were limited to these most severe forms of lead poisoning, which have been estimated to occur in children at blood lead levels around 60 µg/dL (micrograms per deciliter).[1]

Lead was primarily used as a paint pigment in the United States through the early 1900s. Although an international agreement called the White Lead Convention banned interior use of paint containing white lead in several countries due to concerns over potential lead poisoning, the lobbying activities of the politically powerful Lead Industries Association leadership contributed to the successful prevention of similar legislation in the United States, where white lead continued to be used as an additive in both interior and exterior paints throughout most of the 20th century (Hernberg, 2000).

In the 1920s, the American automobile industry began to recognize beneficial properties of tetraethyl lead (TEL) as an antiknock component in gasoline. In 1923, General Motors and DuPont began marketing TEL as a gasoline additive. The effects of high-dose lead exposure quickly became evident in factories producing TEL:

> Shortly after production began, workers in all three plants began to go crazy and die, often in straightjackets. . . . A moratorium on the use of TEL was called and the Surgeon General [Cummings] convened a meeting of industrialists, public health specialists, and academic physicians to determine if this new product was a serious enough threat to be banned or whether it should be sold to the general public. (Needleman, 1998, p. 79)

Surgeon General Cummings' meeting aimed to bring a scientific perspective to concerns over increasing lead pollution. The gathering proved pivotal in shaping criterion for evidence of harm as part of regulatory actions targeted to address environmental and health impacts of industrial activity.

The Surgeon General's 1925 meeting pitted environmental and labor protection representatives against business leaders promoting industrial advancement in debates over a possible ban on TEL production (Nriagu, 1998). The public health representatives presented a variety of foundational concerns over potential health hazards due to lead-enriched automobile emissions. They argued that lead "should be banned, until it is shown safe" (Moore, 2003, p. 17). The lead industry was primarily represented by Robert Kehoe, who over the course of the 20th century reigned as the country's leading authority on lead toxicity. Kehoe called for data that would demonstrate the detrimental effects of leaded gasoline on the human population, suggesting that industrial representatives were prepared to discontinue production in the face of such evidence. However, during this period research linking lead contamination and health effects was extremely limited; as a result, public health and environmental scientists were unable to provide the evidence demanded (Nriagu, 1998; Skolnick & Currie, 2007).

Concerns over the possible effects of TEL as a gasoline additive and the use of white lead as a paint additive on human health were tabled until actual proof of harm to the American public from a specific contaminant could be produced (Moore, 2003). Although public health scientists were generally in agreement about the potential dangers of large-scale lead exposures, since they were poorly resourced and lacking a unifying voice, they were unable to counter Kehoe's demand for evidence of actual harm. By controlling the definition and quantification of lead's health effects, the lead industry helped to establish and support a system of industrial self-regulation. The industry operated largely under the assumption that lead was safe until it was directly linked to particular negative health outcomes. As a result, lead poisoning from gasoline and paint additives exacted heavy health, environmental, and economic costs in the United States before detrimental effects of environmental lead were sufficiently quantified (Grosse, Matte, Schwartz, & Jackson, 2002; Landrigan, Schechter, Lipton, Fahs, & Schwartz, 2002; Moore, 2003). In addition, since lead industry researchers were primarily responsible for investigating and defining lead toxicity, the health effects of lead exposures continued to be identified only as instances of severe poisoning with very extreme symptoms.

Scientific, political, and ideological shifts in the population following World War II created conditions where industrial domination of disease definition was more effectively challenged. The political climate called for an expanded role of government in protecting the health of the American public.

The 1960s: Environmental Regulation in Transition

In the 1960s, procedures for measuring lead concentrations in extracted blood used colorimetry; then atomic absorption spectrophotometry emerged as the accepted technique to measure the concentration of a metal in a sample (Hernberg, 2000). Despite this more promising technology, procedures were poorly standardized and measurements were unreliable, so blood lead levels (BLLs) from the same blood samples could not be replicated in different laboratories (Hernberg, 2000). Despite the limitations however, these methodological refinements provided scientists with an emerging evidentiary base that linked lead exposures to quantities of lead in human tissues. Thus, this upgrade in method opened the possibility of examining health effects across a spectrum of exposure levels, allowing the field to move beyond the analysis of only the most extremely symptomatic cases.

New technologies did not eliminate debate related to lead and public health. Robert Kehoe now directed the Kettering Laboratory at the University of Cincinnati. The laboratory was supported by C. F. Kettering, Ethyl Corporation, DuPont, and other lead manufacturers. Despite Kehoe's continued insistence that measurements at his laboratories were uniquely valid, his dominance of lead research and reporting came under serious scrutiny in the late 1950s and 1960s. The challenges were ushered in by an ideological and political shift in the ways that many Americans viewed the environment and environmental regulation:

Before World War II, environmental attention had focused on conservation of resources in the service of an industrial economy. Living standards improved after the war ended, and people turned to outdoor recreation. Americans began to regard the environment as an asset with intrinsic value apart from utilitarian purposes. (Needleman, 2000, p. 21)

As they became more aware of their environment, Americans also became increasingly concerned about environmental pollution and aware of the possibility of health harms due to exposure to environmental contaminants. The breadth of these concerns was evident in the passing of the first federal legislative actions to begin researching and monitoring air pollution and its effects on human health. The Air Pollution Control Act of 1955 funded research to identify the extent and sources of air pollution problems in the United States; the original Clean Air Act of 1963 funded a program to research, manage, and minimize air pollution; and the Air Quality Act of 1967 set up a structure for states to establish and begin enforcement of air-quality standards (History of the Clean Air Act, 2008). These legislative actions served to expand support for environmental research that was not exclusively funded by the polluting industries, providing the foundation for the emergence of a more cohesive environmental perspective on lead regulation. Although they focused almost exclusively on information gathering and included virtually no federal enforcement, this collection of legislative acts initiated federal intervention in environmental management, and provided new research capacity charged to examine the effects of lead exposure on human health.

During this time Clair Patterson surfaced as a figurehead for the emerging environmental movement, a group of researchers concerned about high levels of toxins in the environment and the health implications of this pollution (Nriagu, 1998, p. 76). Patterson, a geochemist, compared lead levels in 1960s samples of air, soil, water, and tissues, which he established under fastidiously controlled sterile conditions, to levels in preindustrial mummy tissues, deep sea fish, and ice cores from Greenland. These procedures reflected Patterson's primary critique of past studies that failed to carefully control for widespread lead contamination in the environment. Specifically, he argued that industrialization introduced such a high baseline lead burden to air and water that previous experimental controls were highly contaminated by exposure to high levels of lead in ambient air and water. Patterson's research approach and related findings suggested that (1) "technological activity had raised modern human body lead burdens 100 times that of our pretechnologic ancients," (2) urban air lead concentrations had increased 2,000-fold due to industrial activity, and (3) historically increasing lead levels in the atmosphere reflected trends in industrial development (Needleman, 1998, p. 81). Based on his own research, Patterson argued that industrial sources contributed unnatural quantities of lead to the environment and that environmental lead caused illnesses, likely affecting the nervous system, in large portions of the population. He emphasized that any amount of lead in the human system was not "natural," although due to widespread environmental contamination and exposures, the general population had sustained a body burden of lead that could be seen as "typical." Patterson's estimation of effects of subclinical lead exposure differed dramatically from Kehoe's:

When you expose an organism to a toxic substance it responds in a continuum, to continuously changing levels of exposure to this toxic substance. There is no abrupt change between a response and no response. Classical poisoning is just one extreme of a whole continuum of responses of an organism, human organism, to this toxic metal. (quoted in Needleman, 1998, p. 83)

Patterson's research called into question whether the body of accumulated research on the health and environmental effects of industrial lead use met basic scientific standards, since the bulk of this research was supported by and in the interest of the lead industry. Patterson "pointed out that when public health agencies collaborate with pollution industries to decide whether public health is threatened by their products, the results are often absurd" (Needleman, 1998, p. 82).

Kehoe continued to position himself as the preeminent expert on lead contamination. Partnering with other industry-funded researchers, he maintained that poisoning was defined only as exposure to the extent that clinical symptoms of severe brain damage or death were observed, which occurred primarily in lead workers and children with pica at BLLs greater than 80–100 µg/dL in adults and 60 µg/dL in children (Hernberg, 2000; Needleman, 1998).[2] These conclusions were based on two main assumptions made by Kehoe: first, that Cincinnati's air lead levels had decreased since the inclusion of TEL in gasoline, and second, that a baseline level of lead occurs naturally in the human environment and is measurable in "normal" body tissues taken from individuals not exposed to TEL in their occupations. These two assumptions were foundational to 30 years of his laboratory's research, which measured lead in air, soil, food, the tissues of factory workers both with and without contact with TEL, and the tissues of residents of rural Mexico.[3] These assumptions were central targets in Patterson's critiques of Kehoe's work, and more generally of industry-supported health research.

Ultimately, scientists began thinking of the health effects of lead in terms of dose-response relationships, rather than the traditional poisoning threshold. The Kehoe-Patterson controversy was central in the history of lead regulation in the United States. Versions of the perspectives of these two men continue to be reflected in current debates over lead toxicity and contamination.

Milestones in Environmental Regulation: 1970s and 1980s

The early 1970s realized the culmination of shifting attitudes with regard to managing health and the environment. Several legislative acts substantiated this extensive change. First, the Clean Air amendments of 1970 provided the first large-scale, enforceable environmental policy to manage air pollution in the United States from both mobile and stationary sources. Several regulatory systems were enacted in these amendments, but central to the current discussion of lead, the National Ambient Air Quality Standards (NAAQS) were mandated. The NAAQS standards required that the federal government identify and establish safety guidelines for air pollutants. Congress mandated that these standards were to be reviewed every five years to ensure that they reflected the most current science related to the health impacts of environmental contaminant exposure. The 1970 amendments established that the primary enforcement of NAAQS would be managed through State Implementation Plans, in which each state would develop a plan to meet the individual standards. The scale of enforcement required at the federal level by this new clean air legislation made it evident that a federal environmental agency was needed and the National Environmental Policy Act was passed in 1971, establishing the Environmental Protection Agency (EPA) to enforce and implement clean air policy. The limits on automobile emissions in the 1970 Clean Air Act Amendments preceded the passing of federal laws in 1973 and 1975 that required the use of catalytic converters on new cars.[4] Implementation of this legislation required widespread availability of unleaded gasoline, and permitted the establishment of a timeline for the gradual phase-out of the use of TEL in gasoline, ultimately completed by 1996.

Opponents of the use of lead as a paint pigment also won a legislative victory in 1971 with the passage of the Lead-Based Paint Poisoning Prevention Act (LBPPPA), which provided federal funding for lead abatement in U.S. cities, and prohibited the use of leaded paint in federal housing projects (Warren, 2000). Successive amendments limiting the use of lead in paint were set in 1973, 1975, and 1977; which gradually reduced the allowable level of lead content in indoor paint to 0.06 percent (Markowitz & Rosner, 2002; Silbergeld, 1997; Warren, 2000). Unfortunately, the historically widespread use of lead-based paints continues to be the cause of lead exposures in areas where housing stocks predate lead-limiting legislation. Programs to remediate and abate lead-based paint in older housing stocks continue to operate primarily through the Department of Housing and Urban Development (HUD).

Throughout the history of environmental regulation, court cases have played an important role in the interpretation and implementation of legislation. The courts have certainly played an important role in lead regulation, as Melnick (1983) pointed out: "between 1972 and 1981 hardly a day went by when the EPA was not involved in litigation over regulation of airborne lead" (p. 269). The EPA did not initially list lead among the criteria pollutants designated to be included as part of the NAAQS under the Clean Air Act Amendments of 1970, choosing instead to manage lead indirectly through limitations on automobile emissions. The National Resources Defense Council (NRDC) brought suit against the EPA in 1975 to include lead as a criteria pollutant, an effort that the D.C. Circuit Court supported (Melnick, 1983). In 1976, lead was listed as a NAAQS criteria pollutant, the level set at 1.5 micrograms per cubic meter ($\mu g/m^3$) in 1978 (Martineau & Novello, 2004).[5] This limitation on air pollution was tied to EPA's development of plans to gradually remove lead from gasoline. In 1976 the lead industry legally objected to the removal of TEL from gasoline and in 1980 to the level of the lead NAAQS (Melnick, 1983). However, the courts supported the EPA in both of these precedent-setting cases, upholding the removal of TEL from gasoline and the EPA's assignment of the appropriate NAAQS level for lead. Historically, the courts have generally supported the EPA in limiting quantities of lead in the environment.

All of this regulatory activity had a profound impact on the way lead exposures were understood to impact human health. Before 1970, clinical symptoms of lead poisoning were considered the primary indicators of harm; today's measurement techniques indicate that these symptoms usually occur at blood lead levels (BLLs) above 60 µg/dL in adults. Thus, the maximum tolerated levels hovered around this level as long as clinically symptomatic poisoning was considered the threshold effect of lead exposure. Until the early 1970s, BLLs below 40 µg/dL were defined as safe for children, since declining hemoglobin levels (anemia) are observable at this level in youth. Responding to evidence that lead exposures below clinically observable poisoning had serious negative health effects, the Centers for Disease Control (CDC) assigned a maximum allowable BLL of 30 µg/dL in 1975, which acted as an action level for screening children exposed to lead-based paint. By the early 1970s it was known that lead impacts oxygen transport below this threshold:

> Research showed that lead begins to effect the production of hemoglobin (the part of the red blood cell that transports oxygen in a number of ways). At 10 micrograms lead inhibits the formation of a catalyst in the production of hemoglobin molecules. Somewhere between 15 and 20 micrograms, levels of free erythrocyte protoporphrin (FEP) in the mitochondria rise, indicating further disruption of hemoglobin production. Far from clarifying the health effects issue, however, these new findings raised two additional questions: first, where precisely does each of these changes begin; and second, which of these various physiological changes are adverse? (Melnick, 1983, p. 273)

However, in setting the lead NAAQS in 1976, it was the CDC's 30 µg/dL of blood lead threshold that the EPA ultimately used as the target level, below which 99.5 percent of the vulnerable population should fall, with a mean BLL of 15µg/dL, which it considered the onset level for FEP elevation (Melnick, 1983). This interaction between the CDC's threshold for identifying lead-exposed children, and the most current scientific data regarding the epidemiology of lead toxicity, when used as an indicator of public health, determined the regulatory threshold for air lead that would be enforced by the EPA and state environmental agencies. Subsequently, EPA reviewed the lead NAAQS between 1981 and 1986, but kept it at $1.5\mu g/m^3$ despite a recommendation from its Scientific Advisory Board (SAB) that the standard be reduced by at least half. The SAB's work in reviewing the lead NAAQS was used, however, to justify reductions in acceptable lead levels in drinking water in 1986, and the complete ban on leaded gasoline in 1995 following the 1990 Clean Air Act Amendments (Silbergeld, 1997). These most recent amendments served primarily to expand the EPA's authority with regard to managing a number of additional air pollutants and increased EPA's capacity for enforcing existing NAAQS (U.S. Environmental Protection Agency, 2008b).

Following the removal of lead from paint and gasoline and enforcement of the lead NAAQS, reductions in the nation's exposure to lead became perceptible in epidemiological studies, and baseline blood lead levels throughout the U.S. population declined. As the population's mean lead exposure declined, the effects of lower lead levels on children became perceptible. Thus, the CDC threshold BLL was adjusted to 25 µg/dL in 1985, and again to 10µg/dL in 1991 to reflect emerging understandings of the persistent hazards at lower levels of exposure:

> Each time the screening guideline was revised, new studies were initiated to determine whether the new level used to define *normal* provided children with an adequate margin of safety. Although it is common to see the current screening guideline of 10 µg/dL referred to as a "safety limit" . . . the CDC intended it to be interpreted as a risk management tool rather than a threshold for adverse effect. Research conducted since the last revision of the screening guideline has indeed confirmed the appropriateness of this interpretation, with some results even suggesting that the decline in children's IQ scores per unit increase in blood lead level is greater in the range of 0–10 µg/dL than it is above 10 µg/dL. (Bellinger & Bellinger, 2006, p. 853)

This cycle has continued as researchers have linked BLLs at or below 10µg/dL in early childhood to reduced IQ scores, increased school failure, reduced reading ability, lowered class standing, increased failure to graduate, and reduced fine motor function (Needleman, 2004; Richardson, 2002; Tong, 1998). Additionally, behavior problems such as increased attention deficit, aggression, and delinquency have been demonstrated to be associated with lead exposure in animal models and ecological investigations into human populations as well as bone lead levels (a less invasive measure of lead exposure) in school-aged children (Canfield, Kreher, Cornwell, & Henderson, 2003; Needleman, 2004). Thus, many researchers now conclude that no safe level of lead exposure exists and debates over current CDC guidelines for toxic lead exposure continue (Canfield et al., 2003; Gilbert & Weiss, 2006; Lanphear, Dietrich, Auinger, & Cox, 2000; Needleman & Bellinger, 2001). However, scientists now recognize that the relationship between lead exposures and health impacts is far more complicated than the dose-response relationship proposed by Claire Patterson in the 1960s. The health effects of lead exposure are impacted by an array of factors including timing of exposure in developmental trajectory, diet and nutrition, exposure to other environmental toxins, other health concerns, genetics, and body chemistry. Reductions in the CDC's threshold BLL have altered the definition of lead poisoning and the understood health effects associated with lead exposures.

The science and regulation of lead demonstrates the complexity involved with environmental policymaking due in part to the intricate epidemiology, exposure pathway, and multimodal character of lead as a toxin. Continuing controversies about the extent of health effects associated with lead exposures and appropriate regulation further complicated the process. Complexity was also introduced by the structure of the organizations that regulate lead at the federal, state, and local levels. The involvement of the various agencies and programs in lead regulation will be further discussed as it relates specifically to the case of lead in Herculaneum.

Research on Leaded Communities

The impacts of lead contamination have been examined specifically in terms of contaminated communities, which are home to industrial lead processes including mining, milling, and smelting. These industrial processes emit lead into the air and water, exacerbating many of the problems associated with lead present from gasoline emissions and from household paint. However, a major source of contamination in mining and smelting communities is soil and dust contamination resulting from air emissions settling in the soil and from lead concentrates in various forms being spilled as they are transported from one location to another. Since much of the regulatory focus with regard to lead has been around lead-laden paint and gasoline, lead regulations have failed to adequately address challenges in communities with industrial-source lead pollution. There is a federal guideline for soil remediation, but no enforceable standard, and no guideline for road or house dust. The majority of mine and smelter community studies focus on the quantities of lead in local soil and house dust, the uptake of these media by children, and the bioavailability of the forms of lead deposited in these areas. In this arena of public health research, two main controversies permeate the predominantly quantitative case studies of lead-contaminated sites: (1) whether or not the forms of lead released into the environment by various mining, milling, and smelting processes are absorbed by residents, termed "bioavailability"; and (2) the long-term health effects of lead exposure from living in "leaded" communities.

Before reviewing studies conducted in mining and smelting communities, it is necessary to provide an abbreviated summary of lead mining and processing. Lead is excavated from mines in the form of lead ore, or galena, which is a combination of lead sulfides and other rocks and minerals. A mill is usually in close proximity to the mines for initial processing of the lead ore. Here the ore is crushed or ground, then passed through a chemical bath, which binds lead and copper compounds to air bubbles, causing them to float and allowing them to be separated from the sediment waste (McHenry, 2006). Waste from the milling process is disposed of near the mill and is called mine tailings or chat. Large hills of lead chat dot the landscape throughout the lead belt. Milling products are then dried and shipped as concentrate to a lead smelter for further processing. The first process in lead smelting is termed roasting. Heat is used to drive off sulfur and other remaining minerals from the concentrate, resulting in an impure lead oxide material. After roasting, additional materials are added to the ore to make "sinter," which is then passed through blast furnaces where oxygen and any remaining sulphur are removed through heat-induced reactions with the sinter ingredients to create lead bullion. Products are further separated and lead bullion is isolated out. The lead bullion is then allowed to cool and a layer of impurities called dross is removed before it is cast into bars for distribution to companies that use lead in manufacturing. The many byproducts of the blast furnace processes are treated to harvest other useful minerals, recycled back into sinter materials, or disposed of as "slag." Lead slag is treated much like lead chat and disposed of in large piles near the plant. In Herculaneum, for instance a 24-acre slag pile is maintained on the smelter grounds, where waste continues to accumulate on the banks of the Mississippi River. Various processes are used to treat other by-products, isolating valuable minerals before waste is discarded according to the company's government permits. However, throughout the processing of ore into lead bullion, and transportation of concentrates, lead byproducts are released into the environments of surrounding communities.

Mine Communities

Several environmental health studies have argued that mining wastes containing relatively high concentrations of lead present minimal risk to proximal residents due to the low levels of lead absorbed from mineral-lead compounds (Danse, Garb, & Moore, 1995; Steele, Beck, Murphy, & Strauss, 1990). For instance, one argument is that lead in the form of galena is bound in such a way that human systems absorb very little of it even when heavily exposed. This argument has been contested by population studies that compare the blood lead levels of children in mining communities with those in communities without industrial lead facilities. These studies find significant differences in mean blood lead levels in children in mining communities from those located elsewhere, with BLLs in mining communities approximately twice those of children in control communities (Murgueytio, Evans, & Roberts, 1998; Murgueytio, Evans, Roberts, & Moehr, 1996; Murgueytio et al., 1998). This research as well as other studies link lead levels in soil, house dust, and paint to children's BLLs in these communities, finding that soil and house dust make significant and substantive contributions to children's BLLs (Gulson et al., 1994; Malcoe, Lynch, Kegler, & Skaggs, 2002; Murgueytio, Evans, & Roberts, 1998; Murgueytio et al., 1998). Since mine wastes and lead deposits from transport settle into soil and house dust, this research is used as evidence to argue that mining wastes, which are spread throughout these communities, contribute to elevated lead levels in local children. Thus, the studies indicated that lead in mining waste is absorbed by the human system and impacts human health, although this absorption may be at a lesser degree than other forms of industrial lead waste.

Smelter Communities

Communities surrounding lead smelters have also been studied by environmental science and public health researchers. Research in smelter communities has shown that children living near lead smelters absorb more lead from consumption of contaminated soil and house dust than through breathing lead-laden air and that lead concentrations in soil, dust, and children's blood are all highly correlated, increasing with proximity to the smelter facility (Albalak et al., 2003; Roels et al., 1980). A study of the impacts of soil contamination following the deactivation of the historical smelting plant in Trail, British Columbia, found a mean decrease in nearby children's BLLs of 18 to 22 percent per year, far greater than the 5 to 6 percent per year decreases observed there due to emission reductions prior to the closure of the smelter (Hilts, 2003). This finding emphasized the importance of limiting ongoing smelter emissions in managing local health impacts from operating smelters.

A longitudinal study conducted in the smelter city of Port Pirie, South Australia, began in 1979 and has documented a variety of health implications for residents of the surrounding community, as well as the implications of regulatory efforts begun in 1989 to manage smelter emissions and clean up existing contamination in an attempt to reduce local lead exposures. This series of studies has identified negative correlations between postnatal blood lead levels in the smelter community and performance on intelligence assessments, as well as emotional and behavioral development throughout childhood and into adolescence (Baghurst et al., 1992; Burns, Baghurst, Sawyer, McMichael, & Tong, 1999; Tong, Baghurst, McMichael, Sawyer, & Mudge, 1996). Many studies on mining and smelting communities by local health departments are ongoing and will continue to explore ways that lead industry facilities more or less negatively impact the public health of nearby communities.

A HISTORY OF HERCULANEUM, MISSOURI

The town of Herculaneum emerged rapidly in the early 1800s. The area was first settled by homesteader John Conner in 1799. A handful of other settlers and groups of Methodist and Baptist missionaries followed closely behind. In the early 1800s lead prospectors Moses Austin and Samuel Hammond began purchasing land from the earlier settlers at the intersection of Joachim Creek and the Mississippi River, which they organized into plots for the purpose of establishing a convenient port for processing and shipping the products of the nearby lead mines. Austin named the settlement Herculaneum since "the fumes from his own lead smelters reminded him of the smoke that once arose from Vesuvius and because to his imaginative eye the edges of the limestone strata along the Mississippi resembled the seats of the great amphitheatre so recently discovered in Italy" (Gardner, 1980, p. 107). In the fall of 1815, 120 lots in the settlement were sold at auction to formally establish Herculaneum as a town. By 1818 the area served as home to "twenty grist mills and twenty-five distilleries. . . . It also boasted four stores, a school, the post office, a jail, and from thirty to forty houses" (Gardner, 1980, p. 108). Around this time the area was also home to a hemp rope factory and three lead shot towers.

The local region bordering the Mississippi River was officially designated Jefferson County in 1819 and Herculaneum was named the county seat, a designation it subsequently lost in 1832 when the county seat was relocated to a more central location. Articles for incorporating the town of Herculaneum were filed in the early 1820s, but were never acted upon as the redesignation of the county seat marked the beginning of a period of decline in the area. In 1876 a depiction of the area formerly occupied by Herculaneum in a county atlas showed only one standing building in the original Herculaneum location (Herculaneum Master Plan, 2006).

Reemergence—a Company Town (1860s–1950s)

In 1864 New York City–based St. Joseph Lead Company was founded with a mission to tap the rich resources of the lead mines in the Missouri Lead Belt. Recognizing the valuable commodity of Herculaneum's location, both on the Mississippi river and near many mines, they procured 540 acres, spanning a mile of the river's edge. In 1892 the company, referred to locally as "St. Joe," established an advanced lead-processing facility on this property that included a refinery, blast furnaces, and facilities for converting energy from coal into both steam and electric power. The establishment of the lead plant in this location has been linked directly to the reemergence of Herculaneum as a thriving company town:

> As the St. Joe Lead Company prospered in the late 1800s and early 1900s, the town of Herculaneum prospered as well. The town truly became a "Company Town." The paternalistic company basically owned the town and provided every need for the residents free of charge. The towering 350 foot smokestack of the company's lead smelter was not only a symbol of jobs for the town's residents, but also meant that homes, lights, streets, sewers and fire protection would be provided free of charge. (Herculaneum Master Plan, 2006, p. 4)

At this time the only civic function left to the town was to support local education, which was done by subscription according to the number of students in attendance. All other infrastructure was owned, controlled, and maintained by the lead company, including homes, local commerce, sewage, water, electrical, and street lighting services.

Transition Toward Independence (1960s–1980s)

Close ties between St. Joe and the town of Herculaneum extended throughout the late 1800s and early 1900s until the Great Depression, which proved devastating to the local economy. Despite company efforts to keep as many of its employees working as possible, many local workers were laid off as the declining economy forced restricted operations at the lead plant. Ultimately all enterprise in the area was closed down with the exception of reduced operations at the lead smelter and activities of the Works Progress Administration.

As business picked back up in the years following the depression St. Joe gradually sought to reduce its financial obligations to Herculaneum, selling or closing all company stores by 1945 and selling most of the company-owned houses to employees and other residents. A grocery store owner and long-time resident reflected on downtown Herculaneum around the mid-1900s as follows; "In those days, there were all sorts of businesses downtown . . . we had three groceries, a shoe shop, clothing store, furniture store, hardware store, barber shop, tavern and many others. Now they're all closed" (Selbert, 1998, p. 1). Reductions of St. Joe–owned and managed business in the town created a void in the city of Herculaneum, forcing residents to frequent retailers and other businesses in nearby towns. Although the company gradually reduced its ownership of commerce in the town, St. Joe did retain responsibility for much of the infrastructure of Herculaneum through the early 1970s when a civic group, Citizens for the Improvement of Herculaneum, moved to act on the Herculaneum incorporation documents from the 1820s. The town was officially incorporated as a fourth-class city in 1972, and city government began functioning with the election of a board of aldermen, a city marshal, a city clerk, and a municipal judge (Herculaneum Master Plan, 2006). The late 1970s construction of Interstate 55 at the western edge of Herculaneum prompted growth and expansion away from the historic downtown and the lead plant. The city continued to grow increasingly independent from Doe Run Co. throughout the 1970s and 1980s; however, many plant workers continued to reside there, and locals generally treated the company as a valuable contributor to the local economy and community. One writer described Herculaneum's transition through the 20th century as the town began to openly recognize challenges related to their close association to the lead company:

> [Herculaneum was] a gritty town of 2,300 on the Mississippi River about 30 miles south of St. Louis. In such a company town, the plant manager was more important than the mayor. When someone needed a screen door fixed, a company carpenter did it. Before they had a water system, townspeople took baths at the plant's change room. [The mayor] . . . said particulate matter from the plant as recently as 25 years ago [1970] was so heavy that it blocked the sun at times—so people couldn't see across the street or what was happening on the field at a high school football game. Residents and employees of the smelter had been unwilling to criticize it openly. (Malone, 1995b)

The mayor's comments demonstrate the growing tensions between the community's close ties to the lead industry and its awareness and concern over the plant's pollution toward the end of the 20th century.

The 1970s also brought environmental regulation to town. Soon after the lead NAAQS was first set in 1978, EPA began monitoring air lead levels in the area due to the smelter's designation as a known source of pollution. Several Herculaneum monitoring stations consistently reported noncompliant values throughout the late 1970s and 1980s; however, since the company participated in the development of State Implementation Plans (SIPs) for attempting to improve regional air lead pollution, they were generally not cited ("Get the Lead Out," 2007). The lead company, reported compliance with the NAAQS for lead in the first quarter of 1989, and for most of 1992 based on the average of the quarterly values of the seven operating air monitors in the area. The EPA interpreted noncompliance in terms of the average of the quarterly (three-month) measurements at any one area monitoring station producing a value above 1.5ug/dL. However, in both of these time periods at least one monitor registered average quarterly values above the NAAQS, leading the EPA and the Missouri Department of Natural Resources (MDNR) to counter that the area remained noncompliant (Ahmed, 1991). The maximum and average air lead readings in the area since 1982, according to the MDNR, are plotted in Figure 20.2, demonstrating the differences between the two readings of the NAAQS lead standard. The thin line represents the average across the eight area lead monitors, the value the lead company reported as compliant. The thick black line represents the maximum recorded value from those eight monitors, the value that the EPA considers in determining compliance. This chart shows the very important differences in the two interpretations for determining compliance with pre-2008 NAAQS (the second to last straight line) in the area. The chart also demonstrates the impact a lowered lead standard will have on the company's compliance, as the bottom line represents the new lead NAAQS established in the fall of 2008 and taking full effect by 2017.

In 1986 the corporation in charge of the lead smelter in Herculaneum, St. Joseph Lead Co., was purchased by St. Louis–based Doe Run Corporation (hereafter Doe Run). Doe Run was quickly acquired by partnership between several entities, ownership of which was eventually transferred entirely to Fluor Corp. In 1990 Fluor Corp sold Doe Run to the Renco Group, Inc., who maintain ownership. The headquarters of the Doe Run subsidiary are still located in St. Louis with approximately 360 employees, of which approximately 70–90 contractors work at the Herculaneum lead plant. Ownership of the local lead plant by a large and increasingly unfamiliar conglomerate further reduced the Herculaneum community's close ties and loyalty to the plant and the lead industry.

Severed Alliances—Strike (1990s)

In July of 1992, over 300 Teamsters walked out over failed contract negotiations with Doe Run officials. A significant point of contention concerned seniority structures and potential wage reductions (Flannery, 1992). The strike ended two and a half years after it began when Doe Run severed the employment of strikers following the approval of a vote by replacement workers to dissolve the company's labor relationship with the Teamsters Union:

> About 300 striking members of Teamsters Local 688 have lost their jobs at the Doe Run Co.'s lead smelter in Herculaneum after replacement workers voted to decertify the union. The end of the bitter 2½-year strike came quietly when the National Labor Relations Board recently upheld a decision that workers who were replaced couldn't vote in a decertification election. Their replacements were eligible to vote. (Malone, 1995a)

Following the strike, less than 20 plant workers resided in Herculaneum and loyalty between residents and the company largely disintegrated. The community entered the twentieth century with an ambivalent attitude toward its largest economic entity. While the company continued to provide the majority of the town's revenue through property taxes and donations, it was perceived by many to have betrayed unionized employees, and in turn a large portion of the local community.

Up until the time of the strike, the attitudes of Herculaneum residents were publicly unified in support of the lead industry and its local operations. The occurrence of the strike and

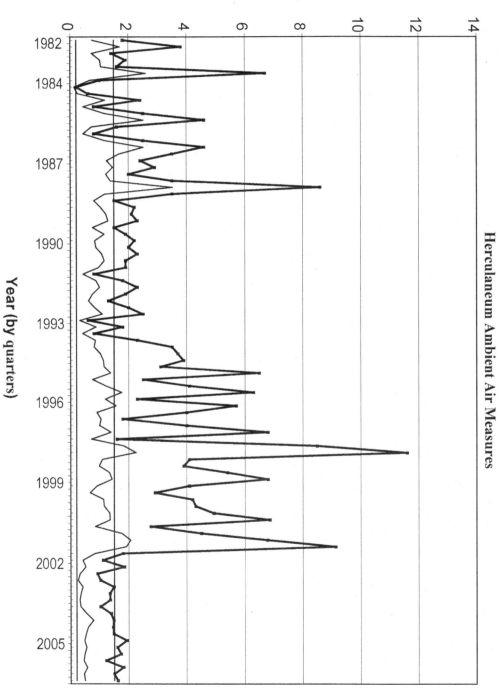

Air Lead Concentration in micrograms per cubic meter

Herculaneum Ambient Air Measures

Year (by quarters)

Figure 20.2.   Graph of Ambient Air Values in Herculaneum between 1982 and 2007 (data courtesy of Missouri Department of Natural Resources—Air Pollution Control Program, via Herculaneum Community Advisory Group)

the perceived mistreatment of local Doe Run employees by the large and distant company opened the door for public criticism and opposition to the company and its local activities. Moving forward from the strike, community members took up both sides of the issues; some defended and supported the company and its local activities while others became vocal critics of its record in terms of safety, pollution, and community participation.

THE MODERN-DAY HERCULANEUM CONTEXT

The physical boundaries and total population of Herculaneum have both expanded in recent decades as nonassigned areas near I-55 were incorporated into the city limits (U.S. Census Bureau, 2000). The total population of the city of Herculaneum declined slightly between 1980 and 1990 from 2,293 to 2,263. The town then grew 24.0 percent to a total population of 2,805 in 2000 (U.S. Census Bureau, 2000). Its growth is projected to have progressed at a gradually slowing rate to a peak of 3,183 in 2003 and then declined slightly to 3,172 in 2005. In perspective, Herculaneum's growth rate of 24.0 percent in the 1990s was more rapid than Jefferson County's growth rate of 15.6 percent, which was higher than the national average of 13.1 percent (Business Information Services LLC, 2007).

In the year 2000 the decennial census provided a snapshot of the demographic makeup of Herculaneum. The town of Herculaneum was predominantly white (96.6 percent) with a small percentage of black residents (2.6 percent) and less than 20 members of any other racial group. Of the 2,805 residents, 22.6 percent were under the age of 18 years, 21.8 percent were 65 years or older, and 55.6 percent were between the ages of 18 and 65, with a median age of 40.5 years (U.S. Census Bureau, 2000).

Herculaneum has been a town dominated by family households, with 736 of the 1,028 households (71.6 percent) being occupied by families in 2000, and 362 (35.2 percent) of these households were home to children under 18 years. The average household size was 2.52 and the average family size was 2.99. Of the 1,078 total housing units, only 50 were vacant as of the 2000 census, and 77.8 percent of the housing stock was owner occupied. The housing stock varies greatly in age, with 34.9 percent built since 1980, 19.7 percent between 1960 and 1979, 22.7 percent between 1940 and 1959, and 22.6 percent before 1939. In 2000, 99.7 percent of residents were native to the state of Missouri. Between 1995 and 2000 41.4 percent of the population had moved to a different home; 26.4 percent exchanged homes in Jefferson County (Business Information Services LLC, 2007).

Local Economy

Economically, Herculaneum faces several challenges in approaching the new millennium. In terms of employment, 58.8 percent of the population over 16 participated in the labor force in 2000, with 10.9 percent of the civilian labor force unemployed. The mean home-to-work travel time was 29.5 minutes, which indicates that most residents do not work in Herculaneum. Herculaneum is widely considered a working-class town with the majority of residents employed in the fields of manufacturing (22.9 percent), education, health or social services (17.9 percent), finance, insurance, real estate and rental leasing (8.3 percent), and retail (8.0 percent). The median earnings for full-time workers were $33,603 for male and $25,581 for female residents. In 2000 the median household income was $40,365 and the median family income was $50,615. Only 152 individuals (5.7 percent) and 18 families (2.4 percent) were assigned poverty status in 2000. For the sake of comparison, the median household income across Jefferson County was $46,338, and the median family income

$51,787, with 6.8 percent of individuals and 4.9 percent of families below the poverty level in 2000 (U.S. Census Bureau, 2000). Recently Herculaneum has been described as undergoing a period of transition. In the interest of promoting economic growth the city has proposed programs for (1) distributing grants as incentive for economic development that expand high-wage employment opportunities and increase the value of local properties, (2) extending infrastructure to newly developed areas, (3) assisting entrepreneurs in attaining skills and success, and (4) encouraging existing businesses to maintain Herculaneum locations (Herculaneum Master Plan, 2006).

Doe Run has contributed large sums to various civic and infrastructure projects. In addition, Doe Run contributes a large share of the city's tax revenue in property taxes. Today Doe Run is "a privately held natural resources company and the largest integrated lead producer in the Western Hemisphere and the third-largest total lead producer in the world" (Renco Group Inc., 2005). The company is highly profitable, having achieved $1 billion in sales in 2005 and $1.6 billion in 2006. Doe Run has earned many safety awards throughout its history and spends around $16 million each year "in keeping with the company's mission to consistently reduce environmental emissions and impact on the natural environment" according to the company website (Renco Group Inc., 2005).

Doe Run's Herculaneum operations constitute the only remaining functional primary lead smelter in the United States. Doe Run has continually made improvements to the smelter facilities; for instance, in 2007 the company spent $3.5 million to purchase a new furnace, and invested in improving pollution containment, increasing efficiency of lead production, and heightening cleanliness in transportation procedures.

Two news-making events signaled changes in local perceptions of Doe Run. The first occurred when the Occupational Safety and Health Administration (OSHA) fined Doe Run $2.78 million for 331 health and safety violations involving regulation and management of lead exposures to plant workers. The second involved a series of lawsuits filed by Herculaneum residents in the late 1990s against Doe Run. They held the company responsible for reductions in property values as well as negatively influencing the health of local residents due to environmental lead contamination. Doe Run's civic and fiscal contributions add complexity in local reactions to the company's persistent pollution problems as evidenced by the following description of public and industry reactions to the release of a SIP to attain NAAQS compliance in the early 1990s:

> Doe Run Co. is getting a "third shot" at cutting lead emissions at its smelter in Herculaneum to meet federal clean air rules. But city officials complain that the plan approved by the state is not strict enough. "This thing—to put it in layman's terms—stinks," said . . . an attorney for the city. "We understand that Doe Run is not an evil thing," [he] said. "But we also understand there are children in the city with lead in their blood." The Department of Natural Resources presented the plan Thursday for the approval of the Missouri Air Conservation Commission. [The] Commissioner . . . noted the jobs and taxes Doe Run brings to Herculaneum and asked [the attorney]: "Do you know what it's going to cost Doe Run—and your city—if we get too tough on them?" [The] Herculaneum Mayor . . . who was seated in the back of the meeting at the Doubletree Hotel Riverport, shouted: "What kind of price can you put on people's health?" [He] said later that Doe Run pays $120,000 in taxes annually to the city, and that only a few more than a dozen of the city's 2,300 residents work at the smelter. (Uhlenbrock, 1993, p. 9A)

Regulatory agencies were reluctant to address health and environmental concerns if action exacted too high a financial cost to the company, and ultimately to the community. This type of conflict is typical in discussions related to environmental regulation, as protection of health and the environment are constantly balanced with the need for profitability and commerce. Both concerns are important for local communities. Emerging findings about the extent of lead contamination in Herculaneum would soon shift the priorities in this balancing act in favor of public health, as will be demonstrated in the following sections.

REGULATING LEAD IN HERCULANEUM (2000–PRESENT)

Public meetings were held in Herculaneum beginning around 1999 to keep the community abreast of developments in lead contamination and management. A group of local citizens attended these meetings regularly and voiced concerns. One particular issue involved trucks hauling lead concentrates through local neighborhoods and spilling it onto roads and yards. The citizens felt they were ineffective in convincing regulators to alter existing enforcement strategies. Rather EPA, MDNR, Agency for Toxic Substances and Disease Registry (ATSDR) and Missouri Department of Health and Senior Services (MDHSS) representatives focused on reassuring the community of its continued safety and the role of the different regulatory agencies in protecting public health. However, behind the scenes in the late 1990s concerns over management of lead contamination in the area were mounting within regulatory agencies, particularly at the state level. One state agency representative explained several processes that contributed to this shift:

> John Carter[6]—[We] had done a lot of residential yard cleanups around the state based on lead mining and smelting, and Herculaneum was, kind of, sticking out as something that we hadn't looked at . . . and we knew that Doe Run was, kind of, doing things voluntarily, and I think we just started looking at it more closely. Oh, and there was another thing. We received . . . some data from US Fish and Wildlife Service that had a lot of bird toxicity data. Some studies done during the floods. A guy . . . motored right up under the slag pile and took a bunch of samples, and collected birds and fish, and it was pretty hot with lead, and I think that crossed our desk at, kind of, the same time. So we put together several things, decided to start negotiating, talking with the company about it. (personal communication February 19, 2009)

Ultimately, state regulatory agencies cooperating with the EPA began negotiating an Administrative Order on Consent (AOC) with Doe Run toward reduction and remediation of lead contamination in the area. AOCs are voluntary, but binding and enforceable, legal agreements between EPA, sometimes other agencies, and a party responsible for violating one of the laws or executive orders the agencies enforce. This particular AOC was entered into under provisions of the Resource Conservation and Recovery Act (RCRA) and of the Comprehensive Environmental Response Conservation and Liability Act (CERCLA, more commonly known as "Superfund"). It primarily demanded that Doe Run quantify lead pollution and replace contaminated soil throughout the Herculaneum community.

Community Reaction to Regulatory Change

Following negotiation of the terms of the AOC between Doe Run, EPA, and MDNR, the order was presented to the Herculaneum community for comment. State regulatory representative John Carter also described the community's reaction to this proposal:

> From my perspective we were, kind of, proud of it because it was way more comprehensive than anything we'd done before, but the community was not impressed [*laughter*] . . . it was like either we weren't doing enough, or "what are you doing in our town stirring things up?" (personal communication, February 2009)

Community members expressed anger and frustration that they had not been informed of existing exposure threats, and that their concerns had seemingly been ignored. At the same time, others feared and resented the implications of heightened regulatory activity in the area for the local reputation and economy, particularly with respect to a central economic entity, Doe Run. Public comments about lead management in Herculaneum contributed to revisions to the AOC, enhancing cleanup, health screening, and agency oversight of the various programs. The particular health concerns being considered as part of the health impact analyses were also adjusted to reflect local comments. Ultimately this AOC was signed and went into effect in May 2001.

A Pivotal Finding

Public meetings continued to occur regularly in Herculaneum. Regulatory representatives reported progress in implementing the plans in the AOC, while residents contended that the AOC was insufficient to address their concerns. At one of these meetings, a particularly vocal resident approached a state regulatory official, asking that he sample street dust in a particular part of town. The resident, Tom Burns, escorted the state regulator to a public street near Doe Run property on August 21, 2001, where he pointed out glittering dust reflecting in their headlights. A sample was taken, and it measured approximately 300,000 parts per million (ppm) lead, or one-third lead, 750 times the 400 ppm federal limit (Rowden, 2001). The influence that this sample had on environmental regulation in Herculaneum cannot be overstated. One concerned resident, Jane Irvin, described the importance of this discovery:

> Until the 300,000 parts per million lead concentration was found on the streets, that changed the ballgame for us because they hadn't addressed it in the AOC. So after that was done then I think the agencies—I don't know if they'd seen an opportunity or we had just shamed them into the fact that they hadn't looked at everything, and they should be looking at everything. (personal communication, October 2008)

Regulatory agents also considered this discovery pivotal because it provided them with justification to initiate a chain of regulatory actions that are considered appropriate only under extremely hazardous circumstances. After conducting additional soil and dust sampling throughout the town, MDNR reported its finding of unprecedented lead levels on Herculaneum streets to the EPA Region 7 office. They then approached the Missouri Department of Health and Senior Services (MDHSS), requesting a statement of the potential health impacts of such high lead levels. The director of the MDHSS complied, sending the MDNR director a letter stating that "due to the recent discovery of extremely elevated levels of lead contamination on some streets, yards, and play areas in Herculaneum, I believe risks to the public's health, especially women and children through age six, are clear and present and are an *imminent and substantial endangerment*" (Dempsey, 2001, italics mine).

Legal Action

By describing the situation in Herculaneum as an "imminent and substantial endangerment," the MDHSS dictated further action on the part of the MDNR: "We actually have the authority to declare an imminent and substantial health risk, and once we do that, DNR has to act. There is no choice other than act" (Barbara Jones, MDHSS, personal communication, April 2009). The MDNR proceeded to issue an Abatement Cease and Desist Order under Missouri's Hazardous Waste Management Law, Missouri's Air Conservation Law, and Missouri's Clean Water Law, demanding that Doe Run meet the requirements outlined in

The 2002 settlement agreement between Doe Run and MDNR ordered Doe Run to

- immediately cease all activities that cause fugitive dust to leave the facility;
- immediately upgrade their truck washing facility to include all vehicles leaving contaminated areas of the plant;
- complete all road and facility cleaning within seven days;
- ensure that all water from street and vehicle washing is contained and treated;
- repave any remaining contaminated roads within 60 days of the MDNR's notice to proceed;
- submit a detailed plan for discontinuing the use of open-backed trucks, either tarped or untarped, for hauling lead concentrate within 10 days;
- cease and desist the use of open-backed trucks for hauling lead concentrate within 45 days;
- complete all residential yard characterization and remediation outlined by EPA;
- fund MDNR or EPA to characterize and clean up indoor residential dust;
- cease and desist transport of lead concentrate along the streets of Herculaneum if any of the deadlines required in the order are not met (as summarized on DNR website http://www.dnr.mo.gov/env/herc/herc_abate.htm).

Figure 20.3. Conditions of 2002 Settlement Agreement Between Doe Run and Missouri Department of Natural Resources.
** Adapted from Missouri Department of Natural Resources, 2009. *Herculaneum lead contamination: Overview of actions.* Retrieved August 6, 2009, from http://www.dnr.mo.gov/env/herc/herc.htm

Figure 20.3. Failure to meet these conditions would result in severe fines. Doe Run appealed this order to several government authorities including the Missouri Hazardous Waste Management Commission, Missouri Air Conservation Commission, and Missouri Clean Water Commission as well as the governor's office. In relatively short order, most of the punitive financial provisions of the order were removed. However, pending appeals pressured the company to cooperate with the MDNR in clean up and management of lead in soil and dust locally, as well as participate in purchasing homes in the most affected areas.

Cleanup

The excessive lead levels discovered in 2001 brought about unprecedented remediation efforts in the Herculaneum area. In cooperation with the MDNR, Doe Run first moved families out of the neighborhood and attempted to professionally remove indoor lead dust and replace yard soil. However, the treated yards were showing signs of recontamination within several months. Regular use of vacuum street sweepers and the distribution of HEPA-filtered vacuum cleaners throughout the affected neighborhoods constituted further attempts to reduce public exposure to indoor and outdoor lead dust in the area (Herculaneum Master Plan, 2006). Emergency measures were taken to reduce children's exposure to extreme levels of lead in soil, including the posting of signs warning "Caution! High-Lead Levels on Streets: Do not allow children to play in the street or on curbs, have children play on solid grass cover or play at Crystal City park, remove shoes before entering your home, wash hands and face before eating, drinking and sleeping."

In addition to cleaning up existing pollution, a Community Advisory Group (CAG) was created under the auspices of a program supporting community involvement in resolving environmental threats. CAG participants worried about the health and environmental effects of lead approached environmental activist groups including the Missouri Coalition for the Environment (MCE), the Sierra Club, and the Washington University Environmental Law Clinic (later renamed the Interdisciplinary Environmental Clinic) for technical and legal support in understanding and defending their health interests. The involvement of environmental activists provided for more sophisticated argumentation in CAG meetings. The CAG was chaired by community members, who were closely allied with the environmental activist groups, and meetings became forums for these residents to confront regulatory representatives.

Risk Assessment

The DHSS and ASTDR cooperated with EPA and MDNR to initiate several health consultations. The first consultation, completed in February 2002 found that 28 percent of children in Herculaneum had BLLs over the 10μg/dL threshold. Further examination of this data showed that BLLs increased with residential proximity to the smelter, with 56 percent of children within one-quarter mile of the smelter having elevated BLLs (Missouri Department of Health and Senior Services & Agency for Toxic Substances and Disease Registry, 2001). Figure 20.4 provides the map that MDHSS released in association with this report demonstrating increasing BLLs in children with increasing proximity to the lead smelter. In April 2002 DHSS released its second health consultation, reporting that the lead cleanup and contamination management plans should reduce lead exposures in the community; however, the report expressed concern over management of lead in indoor dust (Missouri Department of Health and Senior Services & Agency for Toxic Substances and Disease Registry, 2002b). The Dunklin R-5 Schools Health Consultation released in June was a direct response to community members' concerns over the potential exposure from attending or working in area schools and established cleaning protocols for protecting the health of the school population (Missouri Department of Health and Senior Services & Agency for Toxic Substances and Disease Registry, 2002e). Fourth, a public health review of interior sampling methods was released in August 2002, which made specific recommendations for lead abatement in the interiors of residences, and for further testing of these locations for recontamination (Missouri Department of Health and Senior Services & Agency for Toxic Substances and Disease Registry, 2002c). Based on resident complaints two additional analyses were conducted during this period examining the possible health impacts from smelter emissions of sulphur dioxide, and of arsenic and cadmium (Missouri Department of Health and Senior Services & Agency for Toxic Substances and Disease Registry, 2002a, 2002d). A final exposure investigation tracked the specific sources of exposure of two local families with children measuring BLLs at or above 15 μg/dL. The study identified lead smelter emissions as a significant contributor to lead in house dust and the likely source of exposure for children in at least one of the households (Agency for Toxic Substances and Disease Registry, 2005). The MDNR also conducted data collection in the area as it continued to monitor air lead concentrations in accordance with the lead NAAQS and investigated pollution releases into the Mississippi River.

Settlement Agreement and Voluntary Purchase Plan

In April 2002 Doe Run and MDNR reached a settlement on the Abatement, Cease and Desist order. This agreement included specifications for materials handling and transportation, continued compliance with the 2001 AOC, a plan for rerouting concentrate hauling outside of residential areas, and, most dramatically, a large-scale Voluntary Purchase Plan, in which Doe Run agreed to purchase 160 homes surrounding the lead smelter (see Figure 20.5).

Homes not purchased in the buyout, but continuing to produce high scores on lead monitoring tests were provided repeated soil replacement and indoor cleaning and abatement services. In 2008 Doe Run constructed a fence to isolate the "contamination zone"

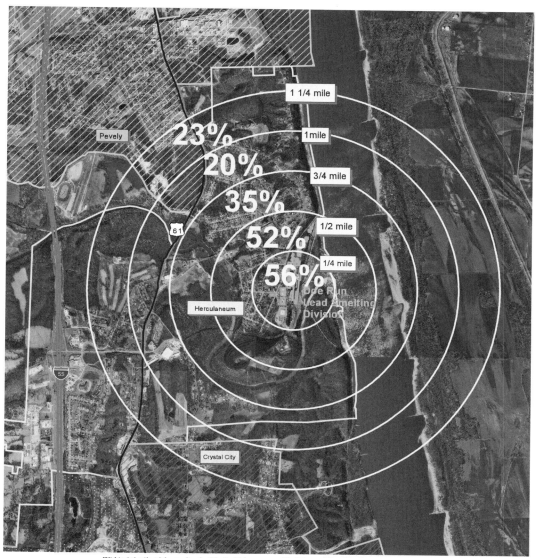

1 1/4 mile

1mile

3/4 mile

1/2 mile

1/4 mile

23%

20%

35%

52%

56%

Pevely

Herculaneum

Crystal City

Pea Run Lead Smelting Division

61

55

Within 1 4 mile of the smelter 5 of the 9 children screened had elevated blood lead levels. (56%)
Between 1 4 and 1 2 mile of the smelter 12 of the 23 children screened had elevated blood lead levels. (52%)
Between 1 2 and 3 4 mile of the smelter 10 of the 29 children screened had elevated blood lead levels.(35%)
Between 3 4 and 1 mile of the smelter 2 of the 10 children screened had elevated blood lead levels. (20%)
Between 1 mile and 1 4 mile of the smelter 3 of the 13 children screened had elevated blood lead levels. (23%)
Of 37 children screened beyond 1 1 4 mile of the smelter none had elevated blood lead levels.

Oos
TMS
hercul.apr
3/18/02

Source: 2001 Missouri CLPPP STELLAR data and August and October 2001 blood level screenings

0   0.25   0.5 Miles

Figure 20.4. Children's 2001 blood lead levels according to distance from lead smelter produced by Missouri Department of Health and Senior Services (2001). Herculaneum, Missouri—Elevated Blood Lead Levels in Children under 72 Months of Age. (Retrieved June 23, 2011, http://health.mo.gov/living/environment/hazsubstancesites/pdf/herc2001map.pdf)

Buy Out Zone

 Haul Road

Figure 20.5. Map of Herculaneum Voluntary Purchase Plan Area, courtesy of Missouri Department of Natural Resources—Air Quality Program (2002). Doe Run Herculaneum Smelter Buy Out Zone. (Retrieved June 23, 2011, http://dnr.mo.gov/env/herc/herc_buyoutmap.pdf)

and reduce its accountability for air lead levels in the areas surrounding the plant ("Doe Run builds fence around smelter," 2008).

The Voluntary Purchase Plan largely changed the landscape of Herculaneum, effectively emptying the historical core of the town. As this plan moved forward, some residents became concerned about the long-term implications of lead remediation and management for their community. The EPA responded by hiring a consultant to work with CAG. In conjunction with the EPA, a subgroup of the CAG worked on plans for the future use of the buyout zone. This group of citizens became very focused on community preservation and future growth. Eventually, a new civic organization emerged—Herculaneum Today & Tomorrow (HT&T)—out of community preservationist commitments. The efforts of this group in planning for the future use of the buy-out zone evolved and eventually led to the production of the Herculaneum Master Plan. The HT&T group tends to view the CAG group as alarmist and obsessive about lead concerns, which they view as largely in the past. Many CAG members, on the other hand, view HT&T members as more concerned about property values and community reputation than about the real and eminent health threats that they believe are perpetually present in Herculaneum as long as the lead smelter continues to function.

The CAG and HT&T have continued to function separately, and generally in opposition. CAG works closely with regulatory representatives and concerns itself with the protection of public health in light of the lead situation as well as informing the community of important developments and concerns. HT&T, with its focus on community sustainability, works with city government to attract residents and businesses to the area. Although their purposes are not in direct opposition, HT&T prefers to consider lead contamination problems resolved, and any further issues to be the purview of regulatory agencies. The CAG considers the lead concerns to be ongoing and expects the community to play a vital "watchdog" role in continuing regulatory enforcement and fastidiously defending public health protection.

THE IMPACT OF THE HERCULANEUM
CONTEXT ON NATIONAL LEAD REGULATION

The National Ambient Air Quality Standards (NAAQS) Revisited

In 2002 Herculaneum met the lead NAAQS for the first time, and continued to meet it in most quarters for the next several years. The CAG leadership remained unsatisfied that the company's borderline compliance with this standard was sufficient to prevent further consequential lead exposures in the area.

In May 2004, Herculaneum residents and the Missouri Coalition for the Environment, represented by the Washington University Environmental Law Clinic, filed a lawsuit demanding that the EPA review the NAAQS for lead according to the legislative requirement that such standards be regularly reexamined (*Missouri Coalition for the Environment et al., v. United States EPA*, 2005). In September 2005, the U.S. District Court Eastern District of Missouri ruled that the EPA had not met requirements for regular review of this standard and set a timeline for a thorough review of NAAQS to be completed by September 2008. As part of the review process the EPA considered a plan initiated by the lead industry in 2006 to revoke all standards for regulating lead in air due to prominent overall reductions in air lead levels following removal of lead from paint and gasoline ("Lost in the fine print," 2008). However, the final ruling released in November 2008 surprised almost everyone by detailing a 90 percent reduction in the lead NAAQS. The new standard of $0.15\mu g/m^3$ is not to be exceeded by any monitor reading averaged over a rolling three-month period (U.S. Environmental

Protection Agency, 2008a, 2008c). This standard requires a large-scale expansion of the air lead monitoring network throughout the United States. The EPA is requiring that states have monitoring plans in place by January 2011. In addition, designated noncompliant areas with established monitoring are charged to develop SIPS to bring them into compliance by July 2010. These areas are then expected to attain the standard by January 2016, with newly monitored areas following by January 2017.

The implications of the new lead NAAQS are extensive both throughout the country and for Herculaneum specifically. EPA expects over 200 monitoring sites to be created or relocated nationwide due to the monitoring requirements of the new standard. It is expected that additional monitoring will reveal many areas that are out of compliance with the new lead NAAQS and efforts to reduce lead emissions in these areas will have to be drastic to meet the 2017 deadline. In Herculaneum, the existing monitoring network is currently being reconsidered. Doe Run is examining its process to isolate sources of emissions where it can make adjustments, but it is not confident that lead can continue to be smelted at the Herculaneum facility when the new standard goes into effect. A Doe Run spokesman described the difficulty of managing the ever-smaller concentrations of emissions from the plant:

> As I mentioned, we didn't have any more big bites of the apple to take, we were just nibbling around the core to get this last SIP [Air Pollution Control Program (2007)]. . . . You know 1.5 is the limit. 1.2 is what we got at Broad Street and .2 is what we got at Sherman. . . . So I went [to] our lab. I said I want you to give me 1 milligram of lead concentrate; I want to see what it looks like. They said we can't do it but we can give you 2 milligrams for you. And it came back and I'm going to put this pencil on here and turn it and this dot right there that's about 2 milligrams. The air lead standard is in micrograms, which you have to divide a milligram by 1,000. So this dot right here you have to divide by 1,000 to get 2 micrograms right there and our limit is 1.5 micrograms to just kind of put it in perspective of what we're trying to capture on the monitors and what levels we're trying to meet in the air. And then coming soon to the area will be a new lead standard . . . so we'll do as we've done before, we'll strive to meet whatever standard we have. (statement at public meeting, September 2008)

Part of the company's striving includes a heightened investment in research and development on an alternative procedure for processing lead ore into bullion. The company is optimistic that this process will "revolutionize the industry globally, because this will be the new standard that everybody will need to hold themselves up to" (personal communication, May 2009). Whether or not this process will occur in Herculaneum, and how the shift will affect the local economy remains to be seen.

In the case of the lead NAAQS, environmental activists and Herculaneum residents were successful in using contemporary science to reframe the definition of health effects of lead exposure by using the community as an example of health harms occurring at existing levels. Between the 2004 lawsuit and the 2008 release of the final ruling, the EPA went through an extensive process of reconsidering health effects, dangerous media, exposure pathways, dose-response relationships and risk analysis (U.S. Environmental Protection Agency, 2007a, 2008a, 2008b, 2008c). Based on their analysis, the regulatory threshold was lowered substantially and enforcement agencies and lead producers are adjusting their practices to accommodate the new limit.

As a part of the research substantiating the revised lead NAAQS, the EPA considered the potential impacts of reduced lead exposure on child development in terms of lifetime earnings:

> EPA calculated the benefits of avoiding IQ loss for children under age seven that would result from a revised lead NAAQS. Because expected lifetime earnings are related to IQ, we describe

benefits as an expected increase in lifetime earnings at full implementation of the NAAQS in 2016. The estimate also includes co-benefits associated with other health improvements expected to occur as a result of fine particulate matter reductions resulting from controls applied to reduce lead levels. EPA estimates the revised standards will yield benefits between $3.8 billion to $6.9 billion. (U.S. Environmental Protection Agency, 2008a)

This is compared to an estimated cost of implementation of the new standard of $150 million to $2.8 billion. However, these aggregate costs and benefits fail to represent the improved quality of life for children in communities like Herculaneum, where lead exposures have been a daily reality. It also fails to represent the costs to this community where the lead industry is the central economic entity. The benefits to children, families, and the community will accrue over the generations of children who grow up in an environment that is exponentially less leaded than that experienced by residents past and present.

CONCLUSIONS: STILL A TRAGIC DICHOTOMY TODAY?

The Herculaneum Master Plan (2006) described the situation surrounding lead in Herculaneum as a "tragic dichotomy," and this case study has demonstrated how that dichotomy has operated as controversy over the appropriate roles and limitations for industry and environmental regulation, causing great community tensions. So where does Herculaneum stand with regard to the lead controversy and to the town's prospects for survival as of 2009? The physical environment in Herculaneum is demonstrably less lead laden than it was ten years ago, and the lead smelter has significantly limited emissions. Ongoing developments in accordance with the town's Master Plan (Herculaneum Master Plan, 2006) continue to enhance health protections and to improve the quality of life in Herculaneum. Far fewer children are experiencing lead exposures above the CDC's current threshold BLL. On the political front, a dedicated core of leadership has emerged, particularly within HT&T, with a unified vision for building a thriving, healthy, and sustainable community. This group is making important strides to ensure Herculaneum's survival and growth into the future. All of these developments indicate a positive future for Herculaneum.

From a community standpoint, the impacts of the last ten years are more ambiguous. The historical downtown area is now a fenced-off, well-landscaped field, isolating the smelter from remaining residences. Longtime residents complain that the town no longer feels the same since so many families have moved away, and former neighbors are less interconnected. Community structures, like the AMVETS, local churches, and clubs have suffered decreased participation. The town is now considered more of a bedroom community for St. Louis than a small town with its own separate identity. Uncertainty exists in the community with regard to the future of Herculaneum, particularly in terms of the continued presence of Doe Run as a central economic entity. Doe Run's operations in Herculaneum will be a technological and political challenge as the implementation of the new NAAQS lead standard moves forward.

The assertion that lead has shaped the town of Herculaneum is undisputed. Recent events surrounding the identification and management of widespread lead contamination have opened the future existence of the town and its identity to a great deal of uncertainty. Uncertainty and division within this community are ongoing and the dichotomy continues. Herculaneum's future depends primarily on its ability to adjust to the ever-present stresses that lead contamination and regulation place on the community and its economy. The introduction to the Herculaneum Master Plan (2006) closes with the following statement that summarizes the town's hopes and ambitions for the future:

In the 21st Century, Herculaneum has the opportunity to be the giant its name infers. That Herculean effort must continue and it must be done with one vision/one voice, so that Herculaneum will emerge triumphant in the end. This master plan is written for that purpose, to act as a guide when making decisions about the future of this fine City, whose history reverberates with the strength and vision of pioneers who met every challenge, never faltering, and established a City of trade and commerce on the mighty Mississippi River that helped to make possible the great country we know today as the United States of America. We can do no less today; we must move forward with the tenacity, determination and enthusiasm necessary to create the best Herculaneum ever known.

It is certain that the presence of the lead industry and lead contamination will continue to shape the town of Herculaneum well into the future. How the town will confront the challenges it faces remains to be seen.

NOTES

This chapter is based on research and development supported by the National Science Foundation under Award No. ESI0227619. Any opinions, findings, and conclusions or recommendations expressed here are those of the author and do not necessarily reflect the views of the National Science Foundation.

1. One mg (microgram) is equivalent to 0.000001 grams. It is used to measure extremely small quantities of mass. One dL (deciliter) is one-tenth of a liter, which is slightly less than half of a cup. Therefore, mg/dL is used here to measure and describe very small, but medically critical concentrations of lead in blood.

2. Pica describes a medical condition whereby individuals eat nondigestible materials. Here the term was likely misapplied to describe natural hand-to-mouth behaviors in young children.

3. Needleman (1998) retrospectively pointed out that Kehoe's investigations were "biased": for example, early air and soil measurements were taken in industrial sites, while fewer industrial sites were sampled in later measurements. He also asserted that in Kehoe's lab "their reagents, instruments, and the very air in their laboratories were freighted with lead. As a result the baseline measurements of all their samples were raised and their results blurred. In addition, the control subjects in Kehoe's studies, the workers in the Dayton plant who did not directly handle TEL, were nevertheless exposed to it. His second 'unexposed' group, the Mexican farmers, ate food that had been cooked in and served from lead-containing ceramic pots and plates" (p. 81). However, at the time the research was presented, these sources of contamination were not evident to the majority of scientists.

4. Small concentrations of lead in gasoline disable catalytic converters. Thus, in order to utilize this technology to limit automobile emissions, the gradual removal of lead from gasoline was required.

5. Micrograms (µg) are used here in the same manner as in measuring BLLs, to quantify very small amounts of mass. Since air-lead concentrations are mass per volume of a gas, the unit of volume used is cubic meters (m^3).

Also, controversy between industrial and environmental perspectives on lead regulation was primary in the determination of the appropriate level of the lead NAAQS as well. For a detailed description of this conflict, see Needleman, 2000, for a scientific perspective, or Melnick, 1983, for a legal perspective.

6. Names of individuals have been replaced with pseudonyms and efforts have been made to protect the anonymity of research participants.

REFERENCES

Agency for Toxic Substances and Disease Registry. (2005). *Health Consultation: Exposure investigation—Herculaneum lead smelter site, Jefferson County, Missouri.* Retrieved August 6, 2009, from http://www.atsdr.cdc.gov/HAC/pha/herculaneum2/her_toc.html

Ahmed, S. (1991, January 30). Official challenges significance of company's air-quality data. *St. Louis Post-Dispatch*, p. 4C.

Air Pollution Control Program. (2007). *2007 revision of the state implementation plan for the Herculaneum Lead Non-attainment Area*. Jefferson City Missouri: Department of Natural Resources, Division of Environmental Quality.

Albalak, R., McElroy, R. H., Noonan, G., Buchanan, S., Jones, R. L., Flanders, W. D., et al. (2003). Blood lead levels and risk factors for lead poisoning among children in a Mexican smelting community. *Archives of Environmental Health, 58*(3), 172–183.

Baghurst, P., Tong, S., McMichael, A. J., Robertson, E. F., Wigg, N. R., & Vimpani, G. (1992). Determinants of blood lead concentrations to age 5 years in a birth cohort study of children living in the lead smelting city of Port Pirie and surrounding areas. *Archives of Environmental Health, 47*(3), 203–210.

Bellinger, D. C., & Bellinger, A. M. (2006). Childhood lead poisoning: The torturous path from science to policy. *Journal of Clinical Investigation, 116*, 853–857.

Burns, J. M., Baghurst, P. A., Sawyer, M. G., McMichael, A. J., & Tong, S. (1999). Lifetime low-level exposure to environmental lead and children's emotional and behavioral development at ages 11–13 years: The Port Pirie Cohort Study. *American Journal of Epidemiology, 149*(8), 740–749.

Business Information Services LLC. (2007). Dunklin R-V School District: Demographics study. Retrieved January 28, 2008, from http://www.dunklin.k12.mo.us/images/District/Facilities%20Assessment%20Documents/Dunklin _Demographic_Report_071507.pdf

Canfield, R. L., Kreher, D. A., Cornwell, C., & Henderson, C. R. (2003). Low-level lead exposure, executive functioning, and learning in early childhood. *Child Neuropsychology, 9*(1), 35–53.

Danse, I. J. R., Garb, L. G., & Moore, R. H. (1995). Blood lead surveys of communities in proximity to lead-containing mill tailings. *American Industrial Hygiene Association, 56*(4), 384.

Dempsey, M. E. (2001, September 24). Missouri Department of Health and Senior Services letter—Herculaneum, Missouri, lead contamination public health risk. Retrieved August 6, 2009, from http://www.dnr.mo.gov/env/ herc/docs/dempsey-letter-dhss9-24-01.pdf

Doe Run builds fence around smelter. (2008, March 6). *Associated Press State & Local Wire*.

Flannery, W. (1992, July 31). 300 workers strike at Doe Run: Company imposed contract proposal. *St. Louis Post-Dispatch*, p. 10D.

Gardner, J. A. (1980). *Lead king: Moses Austin*. St. Louis, MO: Sunrise Publishing Co. Inc.

Get the lead out. (2007, March 5). *St. Louis Post-Dispatch*, p. B8.

Gilbert, S. G., & Weiss, B. (2006). A rationale for lowering the blood lead action level from 10 to 2 µg/dL. *Neuro-Toxicology, 27*, 693–701.

Grosse, S. D., Matte, T. D., Schwartz, J., & Jackson, R. J. (2002). Economic gains resulting from the reduction in children's exposure to lead in the United States. *Environmental Health Perspectives, 110*(6), 563–569.

Gulson, B. L., Davis, J. J., Mizon, K. J., Korsch, M. J., Law, A. J., & Howarth, D. (1994). Lead bioavailability in the environment of children: Blood lead levels in children can be elevated in a mining community. *Archives of Environmental Health, 49*(5), 326–331.

Herculaneum Master Plan. (2006). Retrieved May 9, 2008, from http://www.cityofherculaneum.com/services/ masterplan.html

Hernberg, S. (2000). Lead poisoning in a historical perspective. *American Journal of Industrial Medicine, 38*, 244–254.

Hilts, S. R. (2003). Effect of smelter emission reductions on children's blood lead levels. *Science of the Total Environment, 303*, 51–58.

History of the Clean Air Act. (2008). Retrieved August 6, 2009, from http://www.epa.gov/air/caa/caa_history.html

Landrigan, P. J., Schechter, C. B., Lipton, J. M., Fahs, M. C., & Schwartz, J. (2002). Environmental pollutants and disease in American children: Estimates of morbidity, mortality, and costs for lead poisoning, asthma, cancer, and developmental disabilities. *Environmental Health Perspectives, 110*(7), 721–728.

Lanphear, B. P., Dietrich, K., Auinger, P., & Cox, C. (2000). Cognitive deficits associated with blood lead concentrations < 10 microg/dL in US children and adolescents. *Public Health Report, 115*(6), 521–529.

Lost in the fine print. (2008, May 9). *St. Louis Post-Dispatch*, p. C10.

Malcoe, L. H., Lynch, R. A., Kegler, M. C., & Skaggs, V. J. (2002). Lead sources, behaviors, and socioeconomic factors in relation to blood lead of Native American and white children: A community-based assessment of a former mining area. *Environmental Health Perspectives, 110*(Supplement 2), 221–231.

Malone, R. (1995a, January 12). Doe Run strikers lose jobs at smelter: Replacement workers vote out Teamsters Local. *St. Louis Post-Dispatch*, p. 1C.

Malone, R. (1995b, October 8). Mood swing: Herculaneum shifts loyalty over plant's lead emissions. *St. Louis Post-Dispatch*, p. 1C.

Markowitz, G., & Rosner, D. (2002). *Deceit and denial: The deadly politics of industrial pollution*. Berkeley: University of California Press.

Martineau, R. J., & Novello, D. P. (2004). *The Clean Air Act handbook* (2nd ed.). Chicago, IL: American Bar Association.

McHenry, R. E. (Ed.). (2006). *Chat dumps of the Missouri Lead Belt, St. Francois County*. Park Hills, MO: Distributed by Missouri Mines State Historic Site and Museum.

Melnick, R. S. (1983). *Regulation and the courts: The case of the Clean Air Act.* Washington, DC: Brookings Institution Press.

Missouri Coalition for the Environment v. United States Environmental Protection Agency, Memorandum and Order, Case No. 4:04CV00660 ERW (E.D. Mo. Sept. 14, 2005).

Missouri Department of Health and Senior Services. (2001). *Herculaneum Missouri: Elevated blood lead levels in children under 72 months of age.* Retrieved August 6, 2009, from http://www.dhss.mo.gov/hazsubstancesites/herc2001map.pdf

Missouri Department of Health and Senior Services. *Pilot project—Herculaneum: Environmental public health tracking.* Retrieved June 29, 2010, from www.dhss.mo.gov/EPHT/Herc.html

Missouri Department of Health and Senior Services, & Agency for Toxic Substances and Disease Registry. (2001). *Health Consultation: Blood lead results for 2001 calendar year—Herculaneum lead smelter site, Herculaneum, Jefferson County, Missouri.* Retrieved August 6, 2009, from http://www.atsdr.cdc.gov/hac/PHA/herculaneum/hls_p1.html

Missouri Department of Health and Senior Services, & Agency for Toxic Substances and Disease Registry. (2002a). *Health consultation on sulphur dioxide monitors in Herculaneum—Herculaneum lead smelter site, Jefferson County, Missouri.* Retrieved July 7, 2007, from http://www.dhss.mo.gov/PreventionAndWellness/HercS02.pdf

Missouri Department of Health and Senior Services, & Agency for Toxic Substances and Disease Registry. (2002b). *Health consultation: Determination if remedial actions are protective of public health—Herculaneum lead smelter site, Herculaneum, Jefferson County, Missouri.* Retrieved August 5, 2009, from http://www.dhss.mo.gov/PreventionAndWellness/Hercprotectiveaction.pdf

Missouri Department of Health and Senior Services, & Agency for Toxic Substances and Disease Registry. (2002c). *Health consultation: Determination if site specific interior dust clean-up levels are protective of public health—Herculaneum lead smelter site, Jefferson County, Missouri.* Retrieved August 4, 2009, from http://www.dhss.mo.gov/PreventionAndWellness/Hercindoorsampling.pdf

Missouri Department of Health and Senior Services, & Agency for Toxic Substances and Disease Registry. (2002d). *Health consultation: Public health evaluation of arsenic and cadmium levels in air and residential soils—Herculaneum lead smelter site, Herculaneum, Jefferson County, Missouri.* Retrieved July 7, 2007, from http://www.dhss.mo.gov/PreventionAndWellness/HercCAS-CDfnlbe.pdf

Missouri Department of Health and Senior Services, & Agency for Toxic Substances and Disease Registry. (2002e). *Health consultation: Public health implications from attending or working at Herculaneum schools—Herculaneum lead smelter site, Herculaneum, Jefferson County, Missouri.* Retrieved July 2, 2007, from http://www.dhss.mo.gov/PreventionAndWellness/Hercschools.pdf

Missouri Department of Natural Resources. (2002). *Doe Run Herculaneum smelter buy out zone.* Retrieved August 6, 2009, from http://www.dnr.mo.gov/env/herc/herc_buyoutmap.pdf

Missouri Department of Natural Resources. (2009). *Herculaneum lead contamination: Overview of actions.* Retrieved August 6, 2009, from http://www.dnr.mo.gov/env/herc/herc.htm

Missouri Department of Natural Resources—Air Quality Program. (2002). *Doe Run Herculaneum smelter buy out zone.* Retrieved August 6, 2009, from http://www.dnr.mo.gov/enf/herc/herc_buyoutmap.pdf

Moore, C. F. (2003). *Silent scourge: Children, pollution, and why scientists disagree.* New York, NY: Oxford University Press.

Murgueytio, A. M., Evans, R. G., & Roberts, D. (1998). Relationship between soil and dust lead in a lead mining area and blood lead levels. *Journal of Exposure Analysis and Environmental Epidemiology, 8*(2), 173–186.

Murgueytio, A. M., Evans, R. G., Roberts, D., & Moehr, T. (1996). Prevalence of childhood lead poisoning in a lead mining area. *Journal of Environmental Health, 58*(10), 12–17.

Murgueytio, A. M., Evans, R. G., Sterling, D. A., Clardy, S. A., Shadel, B. N., & Clements, B. W. (1998). Relationship between lead mining and blood lead levels in children. *Archives of Environmental Health, 53*(6), 414–423.

Needleman, H. L. (1998). Clair Patterson and Robert Kehoe: Two views of lead toxicity. *Environmental Research, 78,* 79–85.

Needleman, H. L. (2000). The removal of lead from gasoline: Historical and personal reflections. *Environmental Research, 84,* A20–35.

Needleman, H. L. (2004). Lead poisoning. *Annual Review of Medicine, 55,* 209–222.

Needleman, H. L., & Bellinger, D. C. (2001). Studies of lead exposure and the developing central nervous system: A reply to Kaufman. *Archives of Clinical Neuropsychology, 16,* 359–374.

Nriagu, J. O. (1998). Clair Patterson and Robert Kehoe's paradigm of "Show me the data" on environmental lead poisoning. *Environmental Research, 78,* 71–78.

Renco Group Inc. (2005). The Doe Run Resources Corporation. Retrieved May 12, 2008, from http://www.rencogroup.net/companies/doerun.html

Richardson, J. W. (2002). Poor, powerless and poisoned: The social injustice of childhood lead poisoning. *Journal of Children & Poverty 8*(2), 141–157.

Roels, H. A., Buchet, J.-P., Lauwerys, R. R., Bruaux, P., Claeys-Thoreau, F., LaFontaine, A., et al. (1980). Exposure to lead by the oral and the pulmonary routes of children living in the vicinity of a primary lead smelter. *Environmental Research, 22,* 81–94.

Rowden, T. (2001, September 10). Lead test results prompt meeting in Herculaneum; public is invited Wednesday in gym. *St. Louis Post-Dispatch,* p. 1.

Selbert, P. (1998, September 3). Lead led to good and bad times for 190 years. *St. Louis Post-Dispatch,* p. 1.

Silbergeld, E. K. (1997). Preventing lead poisoning in children. *Annual Review of Public Health, 18,* 187–210.

Skolnick, J. H., & Currie, E. (Eds.). (2007). *Crisis in American institutions* (13th ed.). Boston, MA: Allyn & Bacon.

Steele, M. J., Beck, B. D., Murphy, B. L., & Strauss, H. S. (1990). Assessing the contribution from lead in mining wastes to blood lead. *Regulatory Toxicology and Pharmacology, 11,* 158–190.

Tong, S. (1998). Lead exposure and cognitive development: Persistence and a dynamic pattern. *Journal of Pediatric Child Health, 1998*(34), 114–118.

Tong, S., Baghurst, P., McMichael, A., Sawyer, M., & Mudge, J. (1996). Lifetime exposure to environmental lead and children's intelligence at 11–13 years: The Port Pirie cohort study. *British Medical Journal, 312,* 1569–1575.

Uhlenbrock, T. (1993, June 25). Herculaneum fights plan on Doe Run emissions. *St. Louis Post-Dispatch,* p. 9A.

U.S. Census Bureau. (2000). American fact finder: General demographic characteristics 2000. Retrieved January 28, 2008, from http://factfinder.census.gov

U.S. Environmental Protection Agency. (2007a). *Lead: Human exposure and health risk assessment for selected case studies.* Research Triangle Park, NC: Author.

U.S. Environmental Protection Agency. (2007b). Superfund community involvement: Community Advisory Group. Retrieved July 16, 2008, from http://www.epa.gov/superfund/community/cag/index.htm

U.S. Environmental Protection Agency. (2008a). *Fact sheet: Final revisions to the National Ambient Air Quality Standards for Lead.* Retrieved August 6, 2009, from http://www.epa.gov/air/lead/pdfs/20081015pbfactsheet.pdf

U.S. Environmental Protection Agency. (2008b). History of the Clean Air Act. Retrieved August 6, 2009, from http://www.epa.gov/air/caa/caa_history.html

U.S. Environmental Protection Agency. (2008c). *National Ambient Air Quality Standards for Lead: Final rule.* Retrieved August 6, 2009, from http://www.epa.gov/fedrgstr/EPA-AIR/2008/November/Day-12/a25654.pdf

Warren, C. (2000). *Brush with death: A social history of lead poisoning.* Baltimore, MD: Johns Hopkins University Press.

21

Pandemic Preparedness

Using Geospatial Modeling to Inform Policy in Systems of Education and Health in Metropolitan America

William F. Tate IV

Because college students and other young people are among the most susceptible to the H1N1 flu strain, university officials are taking a hard line to prevent the illness from spreading through dorm rooms and lecture halls. Public health experts caution that the combination of the new virus and the seasonal flu that hits each fall could disrupt classes at all levels of schooling.

—Malone (2009, para 6)

Local hospitals have long planned to use tents to treat massive numbers of patients after an earthquake or tornado. But the H1N1 flu virus struck first, and St. Louis Children's Hospital set up tents. . . . The hospital emergency room has recently experienced a 30 percent surge in patient volume attributed to flu, asthma, and allergies.

—Bernhard (2009, p. A5)

A century ago, the links between urban health and the built environment gave birth to the fields of public health and urban planning. After having drifted apart, researchers from both fields are now working to bridge the gap between the two fields. Much can be learned from integrating public health and planning research.

—Boarnet & Takahashi (2005, p. 399)

The first epigraph describes how the threat of a pandemic is a concern for educators. Today, institutions of higher education (IHE) as well as preK–12 education organizations across the United States and abroad are engaged in pandemic preparedness. The second epigraph describes the press experienced by health care providers in the St. Louis region charged with responding to H1N1 as well as other health concerns. The third epigraph makes an argument for a more integrated research and planning enterprise in the fields of public health and urban planning. I will argue in this chapter that the proposed integration of research and development in public health and urban planning should include scholars and professionals in the field of education. The preparation required to address the potential public health concerns related to the H1N1 virus is a case in point. Boarnet and Takahashi (2005) argued that geospatial science and related tools provide methodology to link scholars in public health and urban planning. In this chapter, it will be argued that geospatial tools have the potential to address questions of interest to educators, public health professionals, and urban planners. The threat of an H1N1 pandemic will serve as the social problem space for this discussion.

The purpose of this chapter is twofold. The first purpose of this chapter is to review selected social science and historical studies that provide insight into pandemics. A second purpose of this chapter is to examine the most recent pandemic threat—H1N1 virus—as part of a case study where a geospatial analysis of community, education institutions, and health care options are the primary factors of the inquiry. Metropolitan St. Louis will serve as the geographic region under study. Social scientists are uniquely positioned to inform the planning and analytical work of local governments. It has been argued elsewhere that this type of scholarship is part of the civic responsibility of education researchers (see the introduction of this book).

Why focus on the H1N1 virus in this book? The President's Council of Advisors on Science and Technology (PCAST, 2009) cautioned that one plausible scenario of H1N1 virus outbreak could potentially produce infection of 30–50 percent of the U.S. population in the fall of 2009 and winter of 2010. In addition, the advisors warned that approximately 20–40 percent of the population (60–120 million people) might produce symptoms, with more than half seeking medical attention. This scenario would lead to as many as 1.8 million U.S. hospital admissions during the epidemic. The hospitalizations of the very ill patients could occupy 50–100 percent of all intensive care unit (ICU) beds in affected regions of the nation at the peak of the epidemic. This would further stress ICU units that typically operate at close to capacity. The PCAST (2009) report stated that the influenza epidemic might cause between 30,000 to 90,000 deaths in the United States. The death projections indicated that disease-related mortality would be concentrated among children and young adults. In addition, there is research that suggests a past influenza pandemic negatively influenced educational attainment (Almond, 2006). The point is that an influenza pandemic is an important consideration for education leadership and researchers (Copeland, 2009).

Concentrated disease among children and young adults positions schools and institutions of higher education as important frontline organizations in this public health challenge. Further, federal officials have called for schools to serve as triage settings if H1N1 pandemic conditions resulted in patient volume that exceeded local health care service capacity. However, many school districts are ill-prepared to serve in this role. For example, one large school district called on central administrators to report for duty in local schools, as the H1N1 virus spread to students and teachers. During a professional development session for school leaders (largely central administrators), the school district's CEO used text messaging and e-mail to deliver reporting instructions for the next day. It should not be a surprise that many of the central administrators were reluctant to serve in buildings where the virus was spreading rapidly. The leaders were being deployed to schools in "H1N1 hot zones" to cover for infected personnel. Many of the leaders expressed concern for their families. None of the deployed administrators had any leadership training in managing triage environments.[1]

Historically, school nurses have been critical supports in public health challenges such as an H1N1 outbreak (Painter, 2009). The National Association of School Nurses and the Centers for Disease Control and Prevention recommended one school nurse be assigned for every 750 students. The role of the school nurse involves both the health of the school community and the care of students with illness. In addition, the school nurse's public health duties include vaccinations, screening for infectious disease, and alerting local officials when there is information suggesting infectious disease. Yet one-quarter of the United States public schools have no school nurse. On average, a school nurse in the United States is charged with oversight of 2.2 schools and 1,151 students (Toppo, 2009). The ratio of school nurses to students varies widely by state. States such as Vermont (1:275) and Kansas (1:552) have nurse-to-student ratios that align with recommended practice. In contrast, Michigan (1:4,204), Illinois (1:2,893), and California (1:2,240) far exceed the recommended school nurse to student ratio. In light of the risks associated with an H1N1 pandemic, the variation associated with the school nursing infrastructure suggests the need for further analysis of the health and education interface. While the nursing infrastructure is not the focus of this chapter, it is worth noting that many schools lack important personnel associated with H1N1 preparedness. This reality provides additional background for why the matter of H1N1 preparedness should be of concern to professionals in the field of education.

This chapter is organized into three major sections. The first section is a brief review of past pandemics with a specific focus on the influenza virus and related social outcomes. The second section is a discussion of health care access, as well as a related geospatial analysis of St. Louis City and St. Louis County, where issues of accessibility and H1N1 preparedness are central to the guiding questions and method. The final section is a call for researchers and professionals in the fields of education, health, and urban planning to more purposefully engage in interdisciplinary analytical efforts as part of a visual political literacy project. I will argue that GIS methodology provides a tool to support civic engagement related to important planning activities such as H1N1 preparedness.

PANDEMICS: LESSONS FROM THE PAST

What is a pandemic? A pandemic is a disease outbreak that is global in nature. Pandemics are well documented in the recorded history of humankind. The aim here is to provide a brief history of pandemics. A more specific focus of the review, discussed later, will be on influenza pandemics. The annals of history record how the pandemic of plague helped to end antiquity and escort in the Middle Ages (Little, 2007). Eight hundred years prior to the destructive force of the Black Death in the Middle Ages, a similar pandemic of plague spread throughout the regions surrounding the Mediterranean Sea and ultimately moving as far east as Persia and as far north as the British Isles. This pandemic persisted from AD 541 to 750, the time frame that witnessed the gradual growth of Christianity with Germanic and Celtic peoples, the early stages of Islam, as well as a new prominence of the Roman papacy and the emergence of a work ethic in the Latin West. The plague occurred during the reign of Emperor Justinian, and is at times referred to as the "Plague of Justinian." Literate observers offered precise descriptions of the plague symptoms. Little (2007) argued that lethal epidemics existed prior to the Plague of Justinian, but the diseases lacked agreed-upon diagnoses. Some of these epidemics were

> the "plague" at Athens in 430 BC described by Thucydides, in which Pericles died, the Antonine Plague in Galen's time that stretched over much of the Roman Empire between 169 and 194, in which Marcus Aurelius died, and that of a century later, between 250 and 270, in which another emperor, Claudius Gothicus, died. Smallpox, typhus, and measles were more likely the diseases involved in those epidemics. (p. 4)

Another documented pandemic, referred to as the Black Death, emerged in Central Asia in the 1330s (Little, 2007). It spread to ports all around the Mediterranean, and further inland than it had eight hundred years before—reaching Scandinavia and far into the Arabian Peninsula. It reoccurred for over 150 years, but then slowly faded to irregular outbreaks, disappearing in Europe in the 1770s and a few decades later in the Near East. A third pandemic occurred in China in the latter half of the 1800s. This nameless pandemic reached significant proportions as it devastated Canton and Hong Kong. The disease made its way to the rest of the world, excluding for the most part Europe and the polar regions, but including the United States (Little, 2007).

   The central concern of this review is influenza pandemics. According to Honingsbaum (2009), it is very difficult to pinpoint without intact viral genetic material retrospective diagnoses of past influenza epidemics. However, historical records suggest that highly contagious acute respiratory illnesses have existed since the start of civilization. Unfortunately, there has been a tendency by the public to treat influenza as if it were the virus associated with the common cold. This dangerous tendency is further reinforced in light of the fact that there are three types of influenza viruses posing different levels of threat. Type B viruses are responsible for the classic winter flu, while type C viruses usually do not cause disease in humans. Neither virus type is associated with pandemic threat. Type A viruses pose the pandemic threat (Centers for Disease Control and Prevention, 2009). Why is this the case? More information about the biology of viruses is required to answer this question. The influenza viruses have a helical shape. Influenza viruses (including type A viruses) consist of a central core of eight delicate strands of RNA (ribonucleic acid) surrounded by a coating of protein. The protein coating is the capsid. The core of the virus containing the genes is the genome. Honingsbaum (2009) described how the reproduction process of type A virus initiates the public health threat:

> RNA strands code for the proteins and enzymes of the surface of the virus and determine the particular configurations of the H's and N's. Unfortunately, RNA does not possess an accurate proofreading mechanism. During replication, when the virus invades and colonizes animal cells, manufacturing hundreds of thousands of copies of itself, the RNA makes small copying errors, resulting in genetic mutations to the surface antigens—the combination of H's and N's which dictate the production of antibodies and the body's immune response. These mutations are known as "antigenic drift." In addition, type A viruses can also "swap" or reassort genetic material with other viruses. This process, known as "antigenic shift," usually occurs when an avian or swine strain of influenza A exchanges genes with a human version of the virus, producing a completely new subtype. Inside the host, the eight RNA gene segments are shuffled randomly, like the symbols in the window of a slot machine. The result is a new virus that codes for proteins that may be new to the immune system and to which the body has no antibodies. It is these strains that historically have been the cause of pandemics.[2] (p. 11)

   In the modern era, there have been four major shifts in the genetic identity of type A influenza viruses. The first genetic identity, H1N1, is the name of the virus strain associated with the so-called Spanish flu pandemic of 1918 and is currently found only in pigs (Webster, 1998). According to PCAST (2009), the 1918–1919 pandemic was the worst natural catastrophe of the twentieth century, with an estimated mortality worldwide of 40–100 million. Webster (1998) reported that more than 200 million people were affected. H1N1 was the dominant strain found in humans until 1957 (Honingsbaum, 2009). H2N2 (Asian influenza) replaced H1N1 in 1957; it ignited a pandemic that killed an estimated one million people across the world. In 1968 a third type A virus shift appeared in Hong Kong as the H3N2 strain, which also resulted in approximately one million deaths worldwide. H3N2 is the strain presently spreading in human populations today. Finally, in 1977, the fourth shift was a reoccurrence of the H1N1 strain. The 2009 pandemic warnings are associated with H1N1. It is speculated that an H1N1 virus outbreak originated in an infected pig in Mexico, as an early case occurred within Veracruz where a large pig farm is located (Cohen, 2009). Another theory holds that the virus may have originated with a U.S.-based pig that was moved to Asia as part of the hog exchange. The virus may have infected a human there, who traveled back to the North American continent, where the virus gained the capacity to spread among humans. After perfecting human-to-human spread, the virus may have even moved from the United States to Mexico.

What is H1N1 virus and why is it a threat? According to Cohen (2009), a comparison to known influenza strains in different species using gene sequences of the H1N1 virus indicated that about one-third of the virus is from the classical North American swine influenza (HA, NP, NS), one-third is North American avian (PB2, PA), one-sixth is Eurasian swine (NA, MP), and one-sixth is human (PB1). The genetics of the H1N1 virus suggest there are no comparatively similar viruses. The genetic sequencing alone can't answer questions about why the virus transmits easily between humans. The prospect of dealing with another H1N1 pandemic suggests that additional discussion of the 1918 pandemic might be instructive. Further, in light of this chapter's aims, some discussion of St. Louis and the 1918 pandemic is in order.

The PCAST (2009) report argued that the most informative findings related to the 1918–1919 pandemic for the purposes of current preparation is its pattern of spread. A first wave started in March 1918 and spread sporadically in the United States, Europe, and Asia. Death rates in most regions were not significantly above seasonal influenza, while illness rates were high. The spring outbreak was sufficiently mild so that public health officials saw little cause for concern. However, a fall wave was global in nature, beginning in September through November 1918, with death rates about tenfold higher than the spring outbreak. During this period, cities that responded with emergency orders to restrict public gatherings by closing schools, churches, and theaters as well as discouraging social interaction appear to have had lower transmission and mortality while the policies were in effect. Most cities did not sustain the emergency policies restricting public gatherings and interaction, and many experienced the return of influenza. The 1918–1919 pandemic represents a case of the public health establishment failing in terms of the general lack of knowledge, contingency plans, and effective vaccines or treatment.

Who paid the price for this failure? Let's start with the unborn. Almond (2006) used the 1918 influenza pandemic as a natural experiment to test the fetal origins hypothesis. Specifically, he sought to understand whether or not chronic health conditions can be traced to the course of fetal development. Almond examined data from the 1960–1980 decennial U.S. Census, which indicated that cohorts in utero during the 1918 pandemic demonstrated reduced educational attainment, higher rates of physical disability, lower income and socioeconomic status, and higher transfer payments relative to other birth cohorts.

Garrett (2008) examined the effects of the 1918 influenza outbreak in a number of cities and states including the Eighth Federal Reserve District, which includes St. Louis. He found that the state size had no significant correlation with 1918 mortality rates, but state population density was correlated with 1918 mortality rates. This finding was muted since the correlation between mortality rates and density is less for 1918 mortalities than for the comparison year of 1915. In tandem, these two findings suggest that state size and population was less a factor in mortality during the 1918 influenza pandemic than in 1915, a non-pandemic year. In addition, the ratio of mortality rates had no significant relationship with state size, population, or population density.

Garrett's (2008) examination of cities produced different results than the state analysis. He reported that influenza mortalities in U.S. cities during the 1918 pandemic were three to five times higher on average than in the 1915 non-pandemic comparison year. St. Louis experienced three times the influenza mortality rate in 1918 as compared to 1915. Missouri's cities influenza mortality rate (1918) relative to the state mortality rate was 1.32. Since this ratio exceeds 1, it suggests that influenza deaths were on average greater in Missouri's cities than in the rural areas of the state. In a comparison of influenza mortality rates by race and city (1915 and 1918), Garrett demonstrated that nonwhite influenza mortalities were greater than white influenza mortalities in both pandemic and non-pandemic years in 13 of the 14 cities in his study—Birmingham, Atlanta, Indianapolis, Louisville, New Orleans, Baltimore, Memphis, Nashville, Dallas, Houston, Norfolk, Richmond, and Washington, D.C. The only exception was Kansas City (in 1918). The findings related to urban dwellers are very relevant for current influenza preparation. The nonwhite population in the United States is now more urban, 91 percent in 2000 compared to 27 percent in 1910. The white population also is more urban, 75 percent in 2000 compared to 49 percent in 1910. The positive shift in urban residential status suggests that population density will continue to be an important determinant factor of mortality in cities (see also, Massey, 2009).

Garrett (2008) argued that race and population density are not the only factors that are likely to influence mortality rates. He posited that access to health care is very important. Garrett reasoned that urban areas provide greater access to health care than rural areas: "Urban areas on average tend to have greater incomes, but this is an average and ignores . . . low incomes in urban areas. . . . The ability of free clinics and emergency rooms to remain open during a pandemic is critical" (Garrett, 2008, pp. 84–85). The next section of this chapter will expand on the topic of health care access, with metropolitan St. Louis as the focal point.

SPATIAL ACCESSIBILITY AND METROPOLITAN ST. LOUIS

Access to hospitals and pediatricians is an important public health concern during an H1N1 influenza pandemic. This is especially relevant as the H1N1 virus is predicted to more adversely impact adolescents. Guagliardo (2004) argued that the majority of research and policy effort to improve access and eliminate disparities in health care have involved costs. As a result there is a growing evidentiary base focused on the relationship between health care cost and utilization patterns. Constructs such as geographic availability and accessibility of health care providers are less well understood. Recent advances in geospatial analysis provide new methods to address this research and planning void. This section of the chapter provides some insight into basic concepts that can be used to examine access to hospitals and pediatrician offices as part of a brief case study of metropolitan St. Louis.[3] A specific focus will be on how the spatial arrangement of hospitals, pediatrician offices, schools, and universities are important considerations related to influenza preparedness and health care access.

What is health care access? Access to health care has a number of definitions. The conceptual challenge with the term *access* is that the definitions include both the potential for health care use and the act of using or receiving health care (Guagliardo, 2004). These definitions lead to a lack of clarity concerning the ability to get care, the act of looking for care, the actual delivery of care, and measures thereof. Greater clarity is achieved if access is viewed in terms of stages. One broad stage is the potential for health care delivery. A second broad stage is realized delivery of care. Potential is established when a population in need coexists geographically with a willing and able health care delivery system. Realized care follows when all obstacles to delivery are removed.

Penchansky and Thomas (1981) organized a set of obstacles into five dimensions: availability, accessibility, affordability, acceptability, and accommodation. The last three dimensions are largely aspatial, and reflect the financial parameters of health care and cultural factors. The first two dimensions are spatial in nature. Availability consists of the number of local health service points from which a patient can select. Accessibility is the distance or time between patient location and health service points. Guagliardo (2004) argued that the distinction between availability and accessibility is especially useful in the context of urban areas where multiple service locations are common. Further, he posited that the two dimensions should be considered simultaneously. The geography and social sciences commonly refer to this fusion as "spatial accessibility" (SA).

The analysis that follows builds on the SA concept in health care geography. Specifically, it is a spatial analysis that examines the potential for health care access. The aim is to present examples of promising planning tools for education, health, and civic leaders charged with preparing for an influenza pandemic.

Potential Access: A Spatial Presentation

There have been a number of studies that have examined the spatial arrangements associated with development and opportunity structures in metropolitan St. Louis (Baybeck & Jones, 2004; Gordon, 2008; Tate, 2008). A common concern in the literature on metropolitan St. Louis is the high degree of geopolitical fragmentation. A high degree of political fragmentation is an indicator that people who are in the financial position to afford housing outside the central city are leaving to secure suburban residency. This has been the trend in metropolitan St. Louis. According to Laslo (2004), in the period between 1950 and 2000, St. Louis City lost an average of 10,172 persons annually. During the first 30 years of this period, most of this out-migration moved to St. Louis County. This out-migration of high-income earners from the central city is potentially troubling for both the city and the county. According to Orfield (2002), despite the growing evidence of city and county interdependence, many regions are becoming more fragmented with growth and as a result cooperative planning has grown more difficult. Regional problems such as concentrated poverty, social and fiscal disparities, traffic congestion, and urban sprawl are just some of the problems that require collaboration and planning across jurisdictions.

Spatial accessibility to health care is another concern that requires regional planning. More specifically, according to the CDC, H1N1 preparedness requires the following agencies, organizations, and groups to be participants:

- State and/or local health officials
- State and/or local education officials
- State and/or local homeland security officials
- State and/or local governing officials (e.g., governor, mayors)
- Parent groups
- Churches and community organizations
- School nurses
- Health care providers and hospitals
- Teachers
- School food service directors
- Vendors that supply schools

This list is not exhaustive, yet as cataloged this recommended set of participants represents a massive communication network. Each of these participants must have a sound understanding of the spatial arrangement of schools, universities, and health care providers. The spatial analysis here is focused on two counties—St. Louis City (a county equivalent) and

St. Louis County. The city is treated as a county in the U.S. census. The spatial relationships presented represent an effort to respond to several guiding questions:

- Where are the hospitals and pediatrician offices located in St. Louis and St. Louis County?
- What areas of metropolitan St. Louis exceed a four-mile travel distance to a hospital?
- Are the hospitals in metropolitan St. Louis randomly distributed?
- Are the pediatrician offices in metropolitan St. Louis randomly distributed?
- What is the nature of the demographic distribution (age, race, and SES) in relation to the hospitals and pediatrician offices in metropolitan St. Louis?
- How are the educational institutions (public schools, private schools, charter schools, and IHEs) and hospitals arranged spatially?

Where are the hospitals and pediatrician offices located in St. Louis City and St. Louis County? According to Schuurman, Fiedler, Grzybowski, and Grund (2006), GIS offers numerous methods that can be used to describe the spatial dimensions of health care service delivery. Distance can be measured as a linear vector ("crow-flying distance") such as road travel or as time travel. The analytical challenge with both measures of distance is that a person leaving the same location headed to a hospital will experience different travel distances and times depending on whether they are driving or taking public transportation. Weather conditions also alter travel distance and time parameters. Meade and Emch (2010) argued that distance measures are so intercollinear that it usually does not matter which measure is used in statistical analysis. A simple and straightforward spatial-analytical method is called a buffer operation. Buffers are geometric shapes (i.e., circles or polygons) that are zones of a specific width around a point. In this case, a four-mile travel distance was selected as the radius of spherical shapes provided to help characterize the hospital distribution. The decision to use four miles as the radius of the spheres representing travel distance is largely normative. There is very little research on urban health care facilities to inform this decision (Guagliardo, 2004). The foundational challenge is that travel impedance to nearest provider and supply level within bordered areas lose validity in congested areas. Despite this challenge, the buffer zones provide a structure to visualize hospital recruitment areas.

Figure 21.1 provides the location of each hospital in St. Louis City and St. Louis County. In addition, major highways are included in the map to demonstrate automobile access to the hospital locations. All of the areas not covered by a spherical shape represent geographic areas beyond the four-mile travel distance to a hospital. Figure 21.2 provides the office location of pediatricians as well as the hospitals in St. Louis City and St. Louis County. This figure does not include the spherical shapes in order to better illustrate the spatial arrangements of both the hospitals and pediatrician offices.

Are the hospitals in metropolitan St. Louis randomly distributed? This question is directly related to H1N1 planning since emergency rooms as well as critical care services are central to spatial accessibility. To answer this question, our research team applied the nearest-neighbor index, a measure of clustering, to hospitals in metropolitan St. Louis (see Figure 21.3).

The 31 hospital locations were obtained from the 2008 version of ESRI Data & Maps 9.3. This data file is standard with ESRI ArcInfo 9.3 GIS software. The listings were checked against public records to confirm the addresses as well as remove any historical buildings not in full operation. The null hypothesis is that the hospitals are randomly located (distributed). The method calculated the distance between the site of each hospital and that of its nearest hospital neighbor. Next, the average of all of these nearest neighbor distances was computed. If the average distance is less than the average for a hypothetical random distribution, then

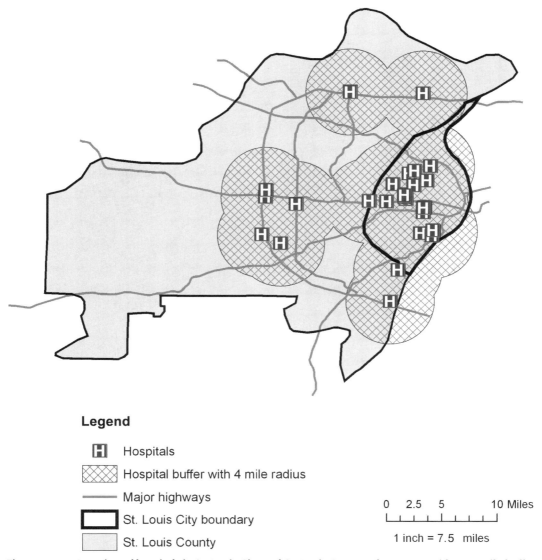

Legend

H Hospitals

Hospital buffer with 4 mile radius

Major highways

St. Louis City boundary

St. Louis County

0   2.5   5   10 Miles

1 inch = 7.5   miles

Figure 21.1.   Location of hospitals in St. Louis City and St. Louis County. The map provides a 4-mile buffer zone for each hospital.

the distribution of the metropolitan St. Louis hospitals is considered clustered. If the average distance is greater than a hypothetical random distribution, the hospitals are considered dispersed. The nearest-neighbor index is expressed as the ratio of the observed distance divided by the expected distance. The expected distance is based on a hypothetical random distribution with the same number of features covering the same total area. Thus, the numerical interpretation of the nearest-neighbor index is straightforward. If the index is less than 1, the pattern exhibits clustering. If the index is greater than 1, the pattern trend is toward dispersion. In this case, the nearest-neighborhood index measure was equal to .68 with a Z-score of -3.4 ($p < .01$). The null hypothesis is rejected, and the results suggest a statistically significant, high degree of clustering in St. Louis City and St. Louis County hospitals.

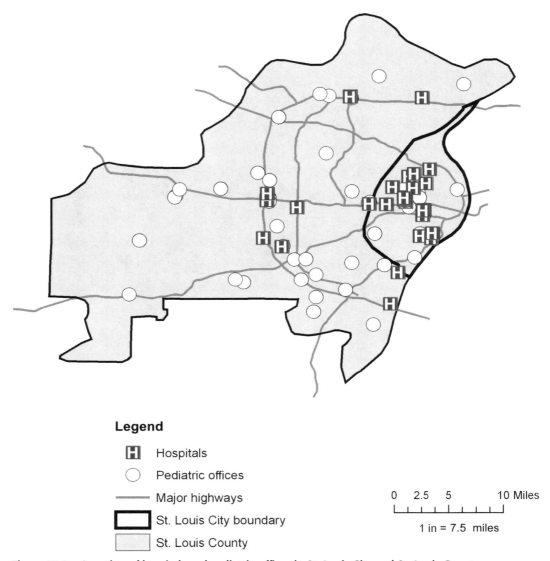

Legend

[H] Hospitals

◯ Pediatric offices

——— Major highways

▮▮ St. Louis City boundary

▢ St. Louis County

0   2.5   5   10 Miles

1 in = 7.5 miles

Figure 21.2.   Location of hospitals and pediatric offices in St. Louis City and St. Louis County.

Are the pediatrician offices in St. Louis City and St. Louis County randomly distributed? The H1N1 virus is predicted to have an adverse impact on children and adolescents. The negative impact includes lost opportunity to learn in schools. Thus, it is important to better understand the nature of the distribution of pediatrician offices in St. Louis City and St. Louis County. According to a data set acquired from Dun and Bradstreet Sales and Marketing Solutions 2009, there are 126 pediatrician offices combined in the city and county.[4] We applied the nearest-neighbor index, a measure of clustering, to pediatrician offices in metropolitan St. Louis. The calculation and method associated with this index was described in the discussion of the distribution of the hospitals. If the index is less than 1, the pattern exhibits clustering. If the index is greater than 1, the pattern trend is toward dispersion. The null hypothesis is that the pediatrician offices in St. Louis City and St. Louis County are randomly located (distributed). In the case of the pediatrician offices, the nearest neighbor-

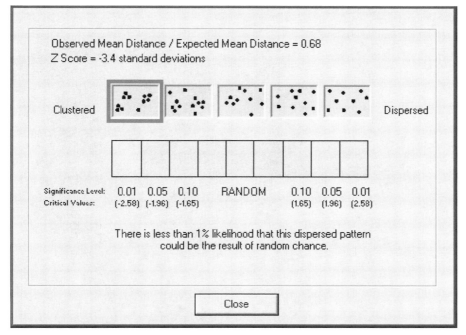

Figure 21.3. Nearest-Neighborhood Index (NNI). The NNI is computed by finding the distance between each hospital and the hospital closest to it, then calculating the average of these distances. The NNI measures how similar this mean distance is to the expected mean distance for a hypothetical random distribution. ESRI ArcInfo 9.3 GIS software produced the computation and graphic.

hood index measure was equal to .27 with a Z-score of -15.5 ($p < .01$). The null hypothesis is rejected, and the results indicate a statistically significant, high degree of clustering of pediatrician offices in St Louis City and St. Louis County. An examination of Figure 21.2 also reveals pictorially the high degree of clustering of pediatrician offices. The 126 pediatrician offices are represented by far fewer symbols in the figure. This reflects the fact that many of the pediatrician offices share the same mailing address.

What is the nature of the demographic distribution (i.e., age, SES, and race) in relation to the hospitals and pediatrician offices in metropolitan St. Louis? Figure 21.4 provides an illustration of the percentage of children ages 5–17 classified as living at or below federal poverty standards by census block groups in St. Louis City and St. Louis County. This figure also includes the hospitals and pediatrician offices. There is a high concentration of children classified as living in poverty within the boundaries of St. Louis City and particularly in north St. Louis City. The concentrated poverty in the northern sector of the city continues into north St. Louis County or more commonly referred to as "North County." It is not transparent on this particular map that the combined north St. Louis City and North County sectors are the most densely populated area in the region. However, this is the case. A high concentration of child poverty in the most densely populated area is an important H1N1 planning consideration.

A related study reported that there are approximately 25 physicians per 10,000 north St. Louis City residents, 70 percent fewer physicians per 10,000 residents than the rest of St. Louis City (Carter & Jackson, 2008). In addition, most areas in north St. Louis City have fewer than 8 physicians per 10,000 residents, and if community health centers are excluded, the ratio is fewer than 5 physicians per 10,000 residents. The limited distribution of primary

Legend

	0.0 - 5.0 %
	5.1 - 10.0 %
	10.1 - 15.0 %
	15.1 - 20.0 %
	20.1 - 80.0 %
H	Hospitals
○	Pediatric offices
—	Major highways
▭	St. Louis City boundary

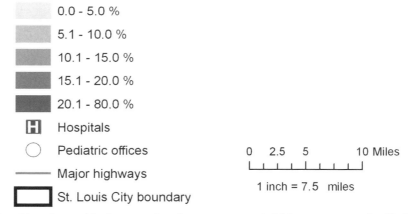

Figure 21.4. Year 2000 Census block groups showing percentage of children ages 5-17 classified as living below the poverty line. (data are from the 2000 U.S. Census, http://www.census.gov)

care physicians (i.e., family medicine, family practice, internal medicine, pediatrics, and women's health) is more pronounced in most areas of north St. Louis City with 4 primary care physicians per 10,000 residents (excluding clinic-based practitioners). The number and distribution of physicians may be related to the emergency room visits of residents of north St. Louis City. According to Carter and Jackson (2008), for many residents of north St. Louis City, the emergency room was the main source of primary health care.

According to the United States Census, over 95 percent of the population in St. Louis City and St. Louis County was classified as either white (77.4 percent) or black (18.2 percent). This demographic binary simplifies the mapping process as a map illustrating the residential distribution of either demographic group provides insight into both groups. Figure 21.5 is a map of the percentage black population by census block group in St. Louis City and St. Louis County. This map includes the hospital and pediatrician office distributions in both municipalities. A majority of St. Louis City is over 50 percent black with a higher concentration in the northern sector of the city. There is a contiguous area in St. Louis City and north St. Louis County where a predominately black residential pattern forms (over 75 percent). The northernmost areas of St. Louis County as well as areas in the county west of St. Louis City are predominately white in terms of residential patterns.

How are the educational institutions (public schools, private schools, charter schools, and IHEs) and hospitals arranged spatially in St. Louis City and St. Louis County? Figure 21.6 displays the location of schools as well as the hospitals and pediatrician offices in both municipalities. There are 567 schools distributed across the two municipal areas. Figure 21.7 is an illustration of the twenty colleges and universities in relation to the hospitals. There are no pediatrician offices listed in light of the age of college students.

Both Figure 21.6 and Figure 21.7 are important representations with respect to two key H1N1 planning considerations. First, the two figures provide a sense of where children and students across the education continuum will congregate as part of their academic experience. In past flu epidemics, closing education institutions was a part of the strategy to contain the virus. The figures provide insight into the scale and distribution associated with this kind of decision-making. Second, more recent planning considerations have included using schools as H1N1 triage sites. In St. Louis City, this consideration is extremely important as the northern sector of the city is less populated with primary care physicians, including pediatricians. Moreover, north St. Louis is densely populated with high percentages of residents using hospital emergency rooms. Thus, it follows that there should be planning related to the use of north St. Louis schools as H1N1 emergency care facilities.

Summary

The set of questions explored here was selected to stimulate a discussion about H1N1 preparedness where schools and universities are viewed as potential partners and resources as well as hosts to students and children at risk of H1N1 infection. Figure 21.8 shows the types of layers that were integrated in GIS as part of this analysis of the human-environmental contexts that are relevant to H1N1 planning. The idea is that political boundaries, specific land use arrangements (school and university settings), population characteristics, and health care locations will be relevant as H1N1 case points emerge. While actual H1N1 case points were not a part of this analysis, it is certainly feasible to add this layer to the type of spatial analysis conducted here.

This particular spatial analysis of the metro St. Louis region provided a few important points of emphasis for future planning. Clearly, hospital and pediatrician offices are clustered in a nonrandom fashion. There are a number of reasons that might explain the distribution

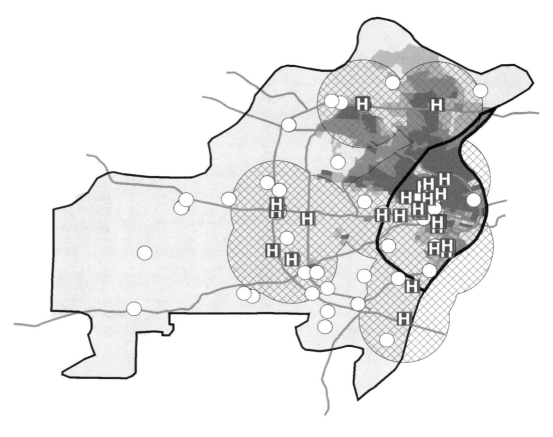

Legend

- 0.0 - 25.0 %
- 25.1 - 50.0 %
- 50.1 - 75.0 %
- 75.1 - 100.0 %
- **H** Hospitals
- ◯ Pediatric offices
- ▨ Hospital buffer with 4 mile radius
- ── Major highways
- ▭ St. Louis City boundary

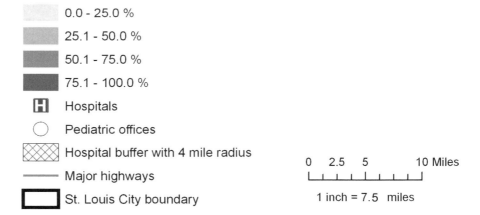

Figure 21.5.   Year 2000 Census block groups illustrating percentage of black population. (Data are from the 2000 U.S. Census, http://www.census.gov)

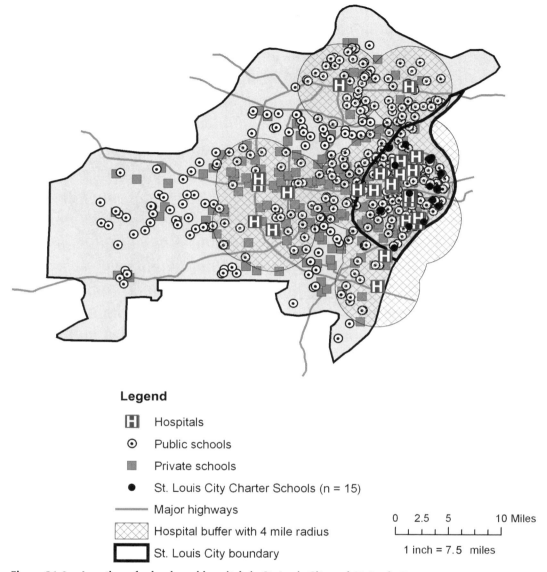

Legend

H	Hospitals
⊙	Public schools
▪	Private schools
●	St. Louis City Charter Schools (n = 15)
——	Major highways
▦	Hospital buffer with 4 mile radius
▭	St. Louis City boundary

0   2.5   5   10 Miles

1 inch = 7.5   miles

Figure 21.6.   Location of schools and hospitals in St. Louis City and St. Louis County.

patterns. The St. Louis City and St. Louis County hospitals are located near major highways in the region. This would partially explain the clustering of hospitals. Meade and Emch (2010) offered some insight into the question of where physicians locate their medical practices:

Many researchers started with the assumption that money was the main cause, but apparently it wasn't at the top of the list because physicians had a good living and community respect every-where. Money differentials mattered mostly at the state or city scales. Racial composition was not a factor for location at the state or city scale, but sometimes influenced location of offices within cities. The ability to pay and the needs of patients were both poor predictors of location. What mattered most were the social needs of the physicians: proximity to other professionals, place of training (which helped establish an information field), and amenities for relaxation from stress

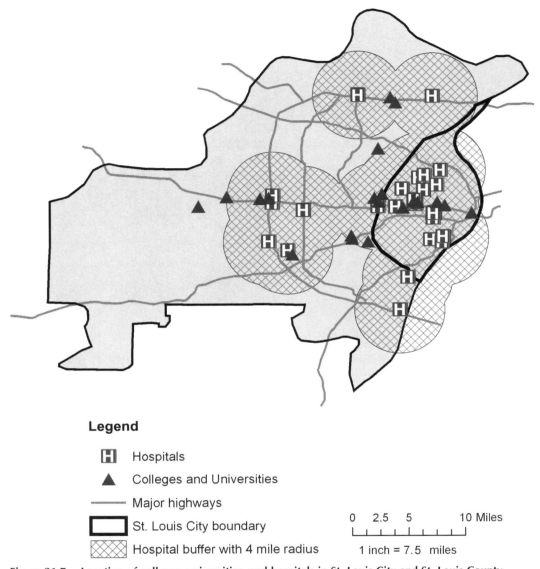

Legend

[H] Hospitals

▲ Colleges and Universities

—— Major highways

[▭] St. Louis City boundary

[▨] Hospital buffer with 4 mile radius

0   2.5   5   10 Miles

1 inch = 7.5 miles

Figure 21.7. Location of colleges, universities, and hospitals in St. Louis City and St. Louis County.

during leisure time. Physicians were concerned about the quality of the schools their children would attend, about their ability to stay up to date on medical developments, and (for those attracted to group practices) about the ability to obtain relief and share the 24-hour demands with at least one other physician. (p. 413)

Many of the influential factors listed above may be at work in metro St. Louis. Washington University Medical School and St. Louis University Medical School as well as their affiliate hospitals are located on or near Interstate 64/40. These medical centers are important training hubs for physicians. Many of the pediatrician offices are located near these medical education hubs or near hospitals. The lack of pediatrician offices in north St. Louis City as well as North County may be a function of a confluence of factors including race and hous-

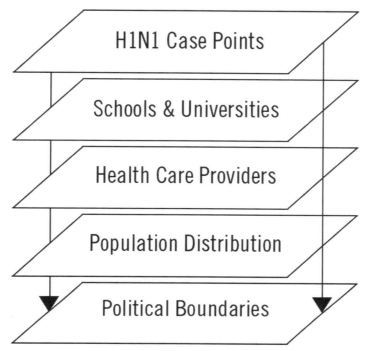

Figure 21.8. Human-environmental factors that can be overlaid with H1N1 virus locations.

ing patterns, school quality, and relatively limited leisure options (Gordon, 2008; Hogrebe, Kyei-Blankson, & Zou, 2008; Tate, 2008). Understanding the factors influencing pediatrician office location in the region is an important planning consideration.

Another consideration involves the use of schools as triage centers if pandemic conditions emerged. Some historical interpretations of past influenza pandemics suggest that school closings were linked to limiting the spread of the virus (PCAST, 2009). This history and other factors must be studied carefully to determine the right course of action by municipalities. The situation in north St. Louis City with respect to the limited number of primary care physicians (including pediatricians) located in the area, as well as the high volume of residents using emergency rooms as primary care facilities, suggests that triage centers in schools are worth considering. This will require regional planning as well as training for school staff at the designated triage school sites.

Visual Political Literacy: Health, Education and Urban Planning

It is extremely challenging to produce sustained civic engagement focused on problems that require a wide range of institutions and organizations. The challenge of H1N1 preparedness represents a problem space where persistent engagement and planning across political boundaries, health care providers, and educational institutions is required. The literature on urban regimes suggests that short-term civic engagement focused on capital projects such as the development of waterfronts, sports stadiums, and other clearly defined problems with specific time parameters are common in metropolitan America. However, matters of health, human services, and education that involve schools and other social institutions rarely remain part of the civic dialogue and related public-private alliances. Stone, Henig, Jones, and Pierannunzi (2001) contended that collective cognition matters on issues that require civic capacity and engagement. One strategy to inform collective cognition and related civic engagement is a visual political literacy project that links professionals and policymakers in the fields of education, public health, and urban planning. Geospatial tools provide a methodology to support a visual political literacy project involving multiple institutions and organizations.

Why is a visual political literary effort important? First, the spatial cognition and reasoning literature strongly suggests from childhood through adulthood that images, illustrations, and graphic representations have a positive effect on learning and reading. In particular, illustrated text supports delayed recall of information. Thus, visual literacy is a tool to support both elementary and complex reasoning processes linked to the different domains of human activity and knowledge development required for pandemic preparedness. If the challenges associated with this problem-solving task can be portrayed pictorially there is a greater likelihood of learning and retention than if presented as written text only.

Learning, reasoning, and retention are not the only benefits of visual modeling. Schwartz and Heiser (2006) argued that spatial representations capitalize on the perceptual system by enforcing and facilitating spatial computations. Two qualities of perception are relevant to this discussion of visual political literacy. One function of perception is to provide an integrated, stable experience. Colors, motion, brightness, shape, and location are processed in separate brain functions. Perception includes specialized abilities to more easily grasp the structure of complex arrangements such as the integration of population distributions, health care providers, political boundaries, education institutions, and H1N1 case points that are able to be represented in visual models. Another benefit to visual modeling is that perceptual structure is deterministic; at any one time, people only see one set of structures. Contrast the determinism associated with a visual model to language. If I say, "There are a few pediatrician offices near Washington Park School," the statement is somewhat vague about the pediatrician offices. Are the offices in front, behind, or to the right or left of the school? How many offices are next to the school? How far are the offices from the school? What travel routes are feasible from the pediatrician offices to the school? In contrast, a visual map of the situation can be very specific in terms of exact counts, placement, and travel options. The psychology literature focused on visual models suggests as a tool that graphic representations might help to inform planning associated with pandemic preparedness.

A second reason visual political literacy should be part of pandemic preparedness is that maps and related graphics have informed civic dialogue about other regional development issues. Orfield (2002) documented the key role that GIS mapping played as a tool to inform regional planning in the Minneapolis–St. Paul metroplex as well as other communities in the United States. Gordon's (2008) study of the St. Louis area used GIS mapping to illustrate how wealth shifted to the urban fringe while the central city experienced severe and negative trends in terms of resources to support human capital development. Using mappings to inform regional planning appears simplistic at first pass. However, when viewed in light of the psychological value of visual modeling—learning, reasoning, retention, and related perceptual benefits—GIS is a tool that at least hypothetically might support collective cognition about influenza preparedness.

Geospatial science and methodology exists to support an interagency and interdisciplinary planning response that is consistent with assuming civic responsibility for a threat to the social order. However, many graduate programs in the field of education do not require geospatial science as part of their methodological training. This curricular addition should be considered going forward. Colwell (2004) makes a case for integrating geospatial methods across the sciences and research enterprise:

I've spoken of a geographic "portal" onto this landscape of science. A portal can be a large and imposing entrance; it can be an organic conduit, such as a portal vein; and—the newest meaning—a website that serves as an entry point to new Web-scapes. Physical, biological, digital—the geographic portal is all of these. It frames three major vistas, all of which characterize the scientific landscape of today:

- First, there is the convergence of disciplines.
- Second, there is geography's tradition of crossing the scales, and linking the local with the global.
- Third, there are geography's deliberate efforts to connect to society. (p. 704)

Colwell's three vistas are directly related to the arguments of this chapter. First, there is a need to more purposefully link the research and development efforts of education, public health, and urban planning. The H1N1 case presented here is only one of many challenges that might be examined by interdisciplinary groups with expertise in education, public health, and urban planning. See, for example, the efforts of the National Center for Culturally Responsive Educational Systems,[5] which includes a system to map factors related to disability and special education placement as part of a geospatial project to help support opportunity to learn in several cities across the United States. Second, the ability to cross scales including political boundaries, educational systems, and health care delivery operations (hospitals and pediatrician offices) to examine the preparedness status related to a global concern (H1N1 pandemic) is one of the advantages of the geospatial approach. The ability to examine information across scales is very important to social scientists, including those in the field of education. GIS tools provide this capability. Finally, the geospatial approach described in this chapter was linked to civic concerns. As Sternberg (2009) reported, emergency rooms were flooded with children suffering from symptoms associated with the H1N1 virus. As previously stated, graduate programs in the field of education should seriously consider providing a geospatial learning portal. It is a matter of civic responsibility.

NOTES

This chapter is based on research and development supported by the National Science Foundation under Award No. ESI0227619. Any opinions, findings, and conclusions or recommendations expressed here are those of the author and do not necessarily reflect the views of the National Science Foundation.

1. I witnessed this occasion directly and followed up with questions to the leaders about their preparation to serve in this type of crisis. I am not attempting to generalize their preparation to other school leaders. This is an empirical question worth exploring.

2. According to Rajendiran (n.d.), influenza A has subtypes based on 16 surface antigens of Hemagglutinin (H1 to H16) and 9 distinct Neuraminidase (N) antigens (N1 to N9). Only H1, H2, H3, N1, and N2 have been linked to epidemics.

3. In this discussion, metropolitan St. Louis refers only to the city of St. Louis and St. Louis County. This is a limited geographic description of the region, which traditionally includes other surrounding counties.

4. This data file was acquired from http://www.zapdata.com.

5. http://nccrest.eddata.net/maps/index.php/

REFERENCES

Almond, D. (2006). Is the 1918 influenza pandemic over? Long-term effects of in utero influenza exposures in the post-1940 U.S. population. *Journal of Political Economy, 114*, 672–712.

Baybeck, B., & Jones, E. T. (Eds.). (2004). *St. Louis metromorphosis: Past trends and future directions*. St. Louis: Missouri Historical Society Press.

Bernhard, B. (2009, September 30). Bracing for swine flu. *St. Louis Post-Dispatch*, pp. A1, A5.

Boarnet, M. G., & Takahashi, L. M. (2005). Bridging the gap between urban health and urban planning. In G. Sandro & D. Vlahov (Eds.), *Handbook of urban health: Populations, methods, and practice* (pp. 379–402). New York, NY: Springer.

Carter, L. M., & Jackson, S. A. (2008). *North St. Louis health care access*. Alexandria, VA: Research and Evaluation Solutions.

Centers for Disease Control and Prevention. (2009). *ACIP recommendations: Introduction and biology of influenza*. Atlanta, GA: Author. Retrieved August 30, 2009, from http://www.cdc.gov/flu/professionals/acip/background.htm

Cohen, J. (2009, May 8). Out of Mexico? Scientists ponder swine flu's origins. *Science, 324*, 700–702.

Colwell, R. (2004). The new landscape of science: A geographic portal. *Annals of the Association of American Geographers, 94*, 703–708.

Copeland, L. (2009, August 3). Schools prep for spread of swine flu. *USA TODAY*, p. 3A

Garrett, T. A. (2008). Pandemic economics: The 1918 influenza and its modern-day implications. *Federal Bank of St. Louis Review, 90*(2), 75–93.

Gordon, C. (2008). *Mapping decline: St. Louis and the fate of the American city*. Philadelphia: University of Pennsylvania Press.

Guagliardo, M. F. (2004, February 26). Spatial accessibility of primary care: Concepts, methods and challenges. *International Journal of Health Geographics, 3*. Retrieved September 30, 2009, from http://www.ij-healthgeographics.com/content/3/1/3

Hogrebe, M. C., Kyei-Blankson, L., & Zou, L. (2008). Examining regional science attainment and school-teacher resources using GIS. *Education and Urban Society, 40*(5), 570–589.

Honingsbaum, M. (2009). *Living with enza: The forgotten story of Britain and the great flu pandemic of 1918*. London, England: Macmillan.

Laslo, D. (2004). The St. Louis region, 1950–2000: How we have changed. In B. Baybeck & E. T. Jones (Eds.), *St. Louis metromorphosis: Past trends and future directions* (pp. 1–23). St. Louis: Missouri Historical Society Press.

Little, L. K. (2007). Life and afterlife of the first plague pandemic. In L. K. Little (Ed.), *Plague and the end of antiquity* (pp. 3–32). Cambridge, England: Cambridge University Press.

Malone, T. (2009, August 18). College students get lessons on dealing with swine flu. *Chicago Tribune*. Retrieved August 24, 2009, from http://www.chicagotribune.com/news/local/chi-swine-college-side-18-aug18,0,3726593.story

Massey, D. S. (2009). The age of extremes: Concentrated affluence and poverty in the twenty-first century. In H. P. Hynes & R. Lopez (Eds.), *Urban health: Readings in the social, built, and physical environments of U. S. cities* (pp. 5–36). Sudbury, MA: Jones and Bartlett.

Meade, M. S., & Emch, M. (2010). *Medical geography* (3rd ed.). New York, NY: Guilford Press.

Orfield, M. (2002). *American metropolitics: The new suburban reality*. Washington, DC: Brookings Institution Press.

Painter, K. (2009, August 3). School nurses on flu front. *USA TODAY*, p. 4D.

Penchansky, R., & Thomas, J. W. (1981). The concept of access: Definition and relationship to consumer satisfaction. *Medical Care, 19*(2), 127–140.

President's Council of Advisors on Science and Technology (PCAST). (2009, August). *Report to the president on U.S. preparations for 2009—H1N1 influenza*. Washington, DC: Executive Office of the President of the United States.

Rajendiran, C. (n.d.). Swine flu: Clinical management and infection control measures. Unpublished manuscript. Retrieved August 30, 2009, from http://www.tn.gov.in/pressrelease/pr180809/pr180809_H1N1_Control_Measures.pdf

Schuurman, N., Fiedler, R. S., Grzybowski, S., & Grund, D. (2006, October 3). Defining rational hospital catchments for non-urban areas based on travel-time. *International Journal of Health Geographics, 5*. Retrieved September 30, 2009, from http://www.ij-healthgeographics.com/content/5/1/43

Schwartz, D. L., & Heiser, J. (2006). Spatial representations and imagery in learning. In R. K. Sawyer (Ed.), *The Cambridge handbook of the learning sciences* (pp. 283–298). Cambridge, England: Cambridge University Press.

Sternberg, S. (2009, October 27). Pushing hospitals to their limit: Emergency rooms flooded by waves of young patients. *USA TODAY*, p. 1A–2A.

Stone, C. N., Henig, J. R., Jones, B. D., & Pierannunzi, C. (2001). *Building civic capacity: The politics of reforming urban schools*. Lawrence: University of Kansas Press.

Tate, W. F. (2008). "Geography of opportunity": Poverty, place, and educational outcomes. *Educational Researcher, 37*, 397–411.

Toppo, G. (2009, August 8). School nurses in short supply. *USA TODAY*. Retrieved June 30, 2010, from http://www.usatoday.com/news/health/2009-08-10-school-nurses_N.htm

Webster, R. G. (1998). Influenza: An emerging disease. *Emerging Infectious Diseases, 4*, 436–441.

V

CASE STUDIES OF METROPOLITAN COMMUNITIES

22

Urban America in Distress

A Case Study Analysis of Gary, Indiana: 1968–1987

Gail E. Wolfe

> The city in America is in desperate straits. Its survival is by no means assured. The mobile flee our cities leaving behind the prospects of the meek inheriting not the earth, but congested concrete, decay and ugliness, foul air and fetid water. This unhappy prospect is the product of long years of profound indifference and neglect. Gary is no exception to this melancholy portrayal—it is a prototype.
>
> —Richard G. Hatcher (1969, p. 1)

Gary, Indiana's first African American mayor, Richard G. Hatcher, penned these prescient words in a letter to the citizens of his city, written in 1969. Hatcher's poignant message captures the plight of urban America in the second half of the 20th century. The principal features of this urban crisis, as it manifested itself particularly in industrial cities of the Northeast and Midwest, are well known. These features include the economic dislocations that accompanied the shift from an industrial to a postindustrial economy, the redistribution of populations within metropolitan areas (Kantor & Brenzel, 1992), persistent poverty and joblessness, declining urban fiscal capacity, and the provision and subsequent withdrawal of federal funding for urban renewal and revitalization. While the constituent elements of America's urban crisis may be well known, the ways in which these elements interacted on the ground to dramatically alter the economic, political, and social landscape of urban communities remain less visible.

This chapter represents an attempt to render visible the contours and content of urban distress through a case study of Gary, Indiana, from 1968 to 1987. As a monoindustrial city, built by the United States Steel Corporation at the turn of the 20th century, Gary provides a striking example of ways in which the decline of manufacturing in the United States in the second half of the 20th century dramatically altered the topography of America's industrial cities. The time period in question coincides with the mayoral tenure of Richard G. Hatcher. During the two decades in which Hatcher served as Gary's mayor, the city witnessed the collapse of its anchor industry, an economic shock that permeated and shaped all facets of life in Gary. In addition, between 1968 and 1987, Gary experienced the demographic shifts, employment shortfalls, poverty, crime, and fiscal crises that typify late 20th-century urban distress. Because of Richard Hatcher's successful pursuit of federal urban aid, Gary also bears the historical mark of the rise and fall of federal investment in America's declining cities.

The overarching objective of this case study is to paint as rich and detailed a portrait as possible of the complex and interwoven phenomena and institutions that coalesced to form Gary's identity during a period of accelerating urban crisis. The first section of the chapter provides a historical snapshot of Gary's beginnings, as well as a brief overview of demographic trends in Gary from 1910 to 1970. The second section of the chapter examines Gary's urban landscape from 1968 to 1987, with emphases on city politics, the collapse of U.S. Steel and its impact on the local economy, joblessness and poverty, metropolitan demographic shifts, housing, education, the environment, crime, and urban renewal. Through a detailed examination of the multiple and intersecting features of urban life that shaped Gary from 1968 to 1987, this chapter endeavors to craft a narrative that chronicles the precise meaning and consequences of urban distress for one Midwestern, industrial city.

HISTORICAL SNAPSHOT

The Genesis of Gary, Indiana

Historians Raymond Mohl and Neil Betten (1986) described the history of Gary, Indiana, as "the history of a company town, the largest ever planned and built by American private enterprise" (pp. 10–11). The private enterprise in question is former industrial giant United States Steel Corporation. In 1905, U.S. Steel's search for an ideal Midwestern industrial site led to an unpopulated tract of land along the southern shore of Lake Michigan, some thirty miles east of Chicago (Mohl & Betten, 1986, p. 11). As urban studies scholars point out, the presence of "low-cost, high-reliability fixed-path transport" (Rae, 2003, p. 56) was a central ingredient in late 19th- and early 20th-century urban development in the United States. In the case of Gary, although the land consisted primarily of swamps and sand dunes, the site provided ample water from Lake Michigan and the Calumet River for transportation and industrial purposes. In addition, existing rail connections, including the Elgin, Joliet & Eastern railroad, linked Gary to a web of major railroads that would facilitate access to external resource suppliers and steel markets (Mohl & Betten, 1986, pp. 12–13). U.S. Steel acquired the 9,000-acre site, complete with seven miles of shoreline along Lake Michigan, for the price of $7.2 million (Lane, 1978, p. 28). The site was named after prominent early 20th-century U.S. Steel president Elbert Henry Gary.

The initial planning of Gary, orchestrated by U.S. Steel, proved to be glaringly lopsided. Historian James Lane (1978) argued that U.S. Steel utilized "the most modern techniques in constructing its mill facilities but paid little heed to scientific methods of urban planning" (p. 29). An overwhelming 77 percent of the $78 million that U.S. Steel invested in the Gary project from 1906 to 1911 was funneled into the construction and development of Gary's steel mills (Greer, 1979, pp. 59–60). As a result of U.S. Steel's considerable financial and technological investment in its mills, Gary's steel mill complex would have the capacity to produce an astounding one-eighth of the nation's steel ingot (Greer, 1979, p. 58).[1] Within industrial circles, the innovation and scale of the Gary Works mills earned the complex such laudatory titles as "the eighth wonder of the world" (Mohl & Betten, 1986, p. 14).

In stark contrast to the meticulous planning involved in the Gary Works industrial site, U.S. Steel's town planning efforts can be described, at best, as utilitarian and shortsighted. U.S. Steel's vision of Gary as a "thriving city of homeowning workers" (Mohl & Betten, 1986, p. 19) was undermined by the scarcity and high cost of the housing that it built within its First Subdivision, just south of the Grand Calumet River, between Fifth and Ninth Avenues. While the First Subdivision provided quality housing for U.S. Steel's businessmen, management, and skilled workers, the housing needs of unskilled workers were virtually ignored by the Gary Land Company. As a result, U.S. Steel's unskilled workforce, comprised primarily of immigrants and people of color, was forced to take up residence in an area south of First Subdivision known as the Patch. Untouched by the governing hand of U.S. Steel, the Patch became "a slum of hovels, tarpaper shacks, and dingy boarding houses" (Lane, 1978, p. 37) controlled by real estate speculators and opportunistic landlords. The race and class segregation that characterized Gary's early residential patterns would prove to be a persistent and pernicious feature of the city.

Lane (2006) suggested that "successful city planning never became a reality [in Gary] because U.S. Steel put less emphasis on the welfare of the community than on efficiency and profitability" (p. 19). That U.S. Steel conceived of town planning as secondary to the construction of its Gary Works complex is evident in several major features of Gary's spatial layout. First, rather than adopt contemporaneous advances in city planning, such as diagonal streets, the Gary Land Company built the town using a rectangular gridiron design. Such a design proved to be both aesthetically and functionally inferior to the diagonal street pattern, which "added beauty and variety to street arrangements while speeding transportation" (Mohl & Betten, 1986, p. 20). Second, the virtual monopolization of the shoreline by the sprawling U.S. Steel industrial complex would prevent Gary residents from taking advantage of Lake Michigan's recreational opportunities. In addition, the close proximity of the steel mills to the town guaranteed significant air pollution in Gary. Furthermore, while U.S. Steel executives saw fit to donate land for the construction of public resources like schools, churches, and libraries, little to no consideration was given to addressing, let alone remedying, the housing shortage that relegated the majority of U.S. Steel's workforce to substandard, slum-like living conditions on the city's south side (Mohl & Betten, 1986, p. 21).

Demographic Trends, 1910–1970

In order to understand demographic changes in Gary between 1968 and 1987, it is necessary to widen the analytic lens and capture the broader contours of Gary's population over the course of the 20th century. Figure 22.1 illustrates the shifting composition of Gary's population between 1910 and 1970. Between 1910 and 1930, the major cleavage within Gary's working class was between native whites and immigrants. As Edward Greer noted in *Big Steel* (1979), Gary's immigrant population came primarily from Eastern and Southern Europe. Gary's foreign-born population, which peaked at 49 percent in 1910, declined steadily to a low of 6 percent in 1970. Gary's native white population swelled to a crest of 66 percent in 1940 before beginning its descent. In 1970, native-born whites comprised 41 percent of Gary's population. The downward trend in Gary's native white population occurred alongside steady growth in the city's African American population. While African Americans comprised a mere 2 percent of Gary's total population in 1910, that figure would increase to 53 percent by 1970.

THE CITY THAT RICHARD HATCHER BUILT: GARY, INDIANA, 1968–1987

Gary Politics: The Ascension of Mayor Richard G. Hatcher

Since its early days, Gary's political landscape had been characterized by entrenched party machine politics. From 1913 to 1934, the Republican Party retained control of the mayoralty of Gary and "worked in easy cooperation with the steel company" (Mohl & Betten, 1986, p. 84). In 1934, with the election of a Democratic mayor and six of nine

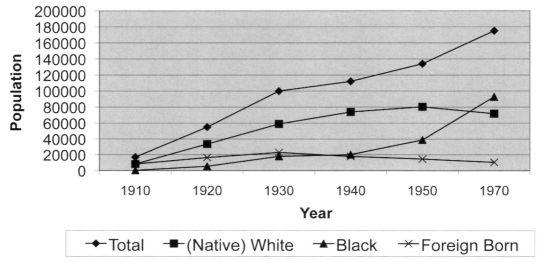

Figure 22.1. Gary Demographic Trends from 1910 to 1970. (Adapted from Greer, *Big Steel: Black Politics and Corporate Power in Gary, Indiana* [pp. 72 and 96]. Copyright 1979 by Edward Greer)

Democratic councilmen, the balance of local political power shifted from the Republicans to the Democrats. The next important political trend, within Gary's Democratic Party, involved the phenomenon of ethnic succession. Greer (1979) argued that the modus operandi of Gary's Democratic machine was to "rotate the mayoralty each term to a member of a different ethnic group, each of whom retired from office a millionaire" (p. 40). The Democratic machine's well-established pattern of corruption and control would remain in place until the 1967 election of Gary's first African American mayor.

Richard Hatcher, born on July 10, 1933, grew up in Michigan City, Indiana. After pursuing undergraduate studies at Indiana University and earning a JD from Valparaiso Law School in 1959, Hatcher took a job with Henry Walker, an attorney practicing in East Chicago, Indiana. In 1962, Hatcher began to make a name for himself in Gary by representing the plaintiffs in a discrimination suit against the Gary school board (Rich, 1996, p. 63). Hatcher transitioned into Gary politics through his involvement with a local organization called Muigwithania. Muigwithania, which signifies "we are together" in Swahili, began as a small, informal discussion group. As the organization evolved, it sponsored social events as a fund-raising vehicle for community projects. Eventually, Muigwithania's membership entered the arena of local politics (Lane, 1976). As Hatcher later told *Post-Tribune* staff reporter Vernon Williams, Muigwithania served as an "incubator of the leadership in this community" (Williams, 1984a, p. D2). In 1963, Hatcher was elected to an at-large seat on Gary's city council and named council president shortly thereafter. While serving on the city council, Hatcher increased his visibility through the leadership he exhibited in the struggle for open occupancy, increased access to municipal jobs for African Americans, and the eradication of police brutality (Catlin, 1997, pp. 135–136).

Richard Hatcher faced an uphill climb in his 1967 bid for mayor. First, he had to compete in the Democratic primary against incumbent Mayor A. Martin Katz and political outsider Bernard W. Konrady. After winning the primary by 3,000 votes, Hatcher encountered opposition from fellow (white) Democrats, under the auspices of the Lake County Democratic Party. Lake County Democratic Chairman John Krupa allegedly told Hatcher that in exchange for party support, Mayor-elect Hatcher would have to allow the party to select

Gary's police chief and controller. When Hatcher rejected Krupa's offer, Krupa withdrew the Lake County Democratic Party's support for Hatcher's campaign (Lane, 1978, p. 288). Despite the Democratic Party's decision to endorse Republican candidate Joseph Radigan, Hatcher emerged victorious on election day. Hatcher won the mayoral election by a narrow margin of 1,865 votes, capturing 96 percent of the African American vote and 12 percent of the white vote (Lane, 1978, p. 290). Hatcher remained in Gary's City Hall for nearly two decades, from 1968 to 1987. His mayoral tenure constitutes the time period of interest for this case study.

Gary's Economic Landscape: The Rise and Fall of U.S. Steel

Before exploring the impact of U.S. Steel's shifting fortunes on Gary's economic landscape, it is worthwhile to note some of the major trends across the U.S. steel industry from the early 1960s through the late 1980s. In the late 1950s, the U.S. steel industry occupied a position of global prominence, producing 27.7 percent of the world's steel, and equaling the combined steel production of Europe and Japan (Hall, 1997, p. 42). The global preeminence of the U.S. steel industry began to erode, however, in the 1960s due to increasing labor costs. Wage increases demanded by the United Steelworkers of America translated into higher prices for domestic steel. Soaring employment costs eventually translated into U.S. steel prices that exceeded those of their European and Japanese competitors. As a result, U.S. steel consumers began to turn increasingly to overseas producers for their steel needs. As Christopher Hall pointed out in *Steel Phoenix*, steel imports increased 73 percent between 1965 and 1968, from 10.38 to 17.96 million tons (p. 44). By the late 1960s, integrated steel mills like U.S. Steel's Gary Works complex, shown in Figure 22.2, were "slowly withdrawing from, or being pushed out of markets in which their production and freight costs now greatly exceeded those of overseas producers" (Hall, 1997, p. 48).

The period from 1972 to 1974 marked the "last great boom of the old steel industry" (Hall, 1997, p. 61). Hall argued that the end of the Vietnam War, the 1973 oil shock, and the termination of Voluntary Restraint Agreements limiting steel imports combined to wreak irreversible havoc on the U.S. steel industry. The outmoded equipment and processes utilized by U.S. integrated steel plants, most of which dated back to the early 20th century, further eroded U.S. steel's ability to compete in the mid-1970s global steel market. Moreover, U.S. steel producers were faced with additional challenges in the 1970s in the form of environmental regulations and new information-based markets that no longer relied heavily upon steel. Automation also played a role in the scale-back of employment in the U.S. steel industry. As historian Lance Trusty (1992) pointed out, 10.8 labor hours were required to produce

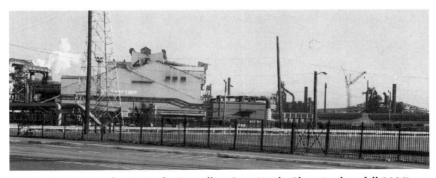

Figure 22.2.   Part of U.S. Steel's Sprawling Gary Works Plant (author, fall 2006)

a ton of steel in 1980. A decade later, this number had decreased to 3.5 labor hours per ton of steel (p. 3). While employment in the U.S. steel industry hovered between 500,000 and 600,000 employees between 1950 and 1974, employment levels dropped significantly beginning in the mid-1970s (Hall, 1997, p. 70). Between 1974 and 1989, for instance, integrated steel employment in the United States decreased by a devastating 67 percent, from 512,000 to 168,000 (Hall, 1997, p. 65).

The declining global position of the U.S. steel industry significantly impacted U.S. Steel's Gary Works complex. During periods of peak steel employment, the workforce at U.S. Steel's Gary Works swelled to nearly 30,000 employees. The end of the Korean War, however, marked the beginning of a steady decline in steel employment levels in Gary (Greer, 1979, p. 99). Employment levels at U.S. Steel's Gary Works site mirrored the dramatic layoffs that occurred industry-wide after 1974. As Richard Hatcher's mayoral tenure in Gary came to a close in 1987, the number of jobs at the Gary Works mills had decreased to fewer than 6,000 (Catlin, 1993, pp. 33–34). The 6,000-person workforce employed by U.S. Steel in the late 1980s represented a devastating 80 percent decrease from peak employment levels of 30,000. Because Gary was "essentially a one-industry company town dominated by U.S. Steel" (Catlin, 1997, p. 139), the shockwaves created by the steel industry downturn would violently reverberate throughout the local economy. The impact of the collapsing steel industry would prove to be even more acute in Gary as a result of U.S. Steel's reluctance, particularly during the 1920s and 1930s, to diversify Gary's manufacturing base in the interest of preventing local competition (Catlin, 1993, p. 33).

Gary Works and the Local Economy: The Ripple Effect

> Downtown Gary once enjoyed a fine reputation as the shopping "hub" of the Calumet. Still lined with anchor stores and a variety of large and small shops in 1970, Broadway lost everything in the 1980s, stores, banks, realtors, and insurance agencies. Where busy streetcars and buses once ferried shoppers to and fro was only desolation, as anchor stores, then the shops, tiptoed away. By 1990, even the second-hand stores had given up. The Gary National Bank fled even its name, and the *Gary Post-Tribune* became the *Post-Tribune* of someplace else.
>
> —Trusty (1992, p. 1)

When Richard Hatcher became Gary's first African American mayor, he declared in his 1967 victory speech that "[w]e shall prove that urban America need not wallow in decay, that our cities can be revived and their people rejuvenated" (Lane, 1978, p. 290). Halting the decay of Gary proved, however, to be a formidable task for the new mayor, particularly in the face of the sharp decline of the city's anchor industry. After all, as *Post-Tribune* staff reporter Lorraine McCarthy (1984) observed, Gary was "essentially a one-industry city in a one-industry region—and employment in that industry [was] shrinking" (p. D4).

In 1960, downtown Gary was a thriving commercial district, with 10,000 employees staffing some 500 business establishments. By 1979, only 5 years after the dramatic downturn in the U.S. steel industry, less than 40 businesses remained in downtown Gary. In addition to the staggering decrease in downtown businesses, the downtown retail workforce dropped from 10,000 to a mere 300 (Catlin, 1993, p. 27). The retail exodus from Gary was facilitated, in part, by the construction of two large shopping malls in the 1970s in Merrillville, a suburb located just 15 miles south of downtown Gary. By 1978, Gary's three anchor department stores, including Sears and J.C. Penney's, along with over 100 downtown retailers, had either closed altogether or relocated to the new suburban shopping districts (Catlin, 1993, p. 27).

Figure 22.3.   Gary's Downtown Shopping District (author, fall 2006)

Gary's two remaining downtown department stores, Goldblatt's and Hudson's, closed their doors in January of 1981 (Lane, 1992, p. 77). In a recollection of Gary in the 1980s, Carolyn East (1992) described the city's downtown shopping district as "a skeleton of its old self. The business area was all but gone. Only a handful of stores were open, and the rest were locked up and empty" (p. 56). Gary's beleaguered downtown shopping district is shown in Figure 22.3. The collapse of the downtown shopping district put Gary residents at a double disadvantage: not only did Gary's retail industry flee to the surrounding suburbs, but there was no public bus service connecting Gary to the new suburban shopping facilities (Catlin, 1993, p. 27).

Gary's business district also struggled to maintain other vital amenities. In 1975, visitors to downtown Gary would find its Holiday Inn closed and boarded up. Thanks to $2.5 million in Negotiated Investment Strategy money, provided by the U.S. Department of Housing and Urban Development (HUD), the Holiday Inn was rehabilitated and reopened as a Sheraton in 1981. Like its predecessor, the Sheraton was quickly beset with problems. From its opening in 1981, eight rooms at the Sheraton were used to provide emergency shelter for Gary's indigent population. In February of 1981, Gary's City Council voted to subsidize the Sheraton's utilities, which amounted to an annual cost of approximately $250,000 (Lane, 1992, p. 81). Even with this substantial subsidy, the Sheraton closed its doors in 1985 as a result of the same low occupancy problem that plagued the Holiday Inn (Catlin, 1993, p. 29). With the closing of the Sheraton, Gary was left with a single motel called the Interlude, which featured room rental by the hour, along with a selection of XXX-rated videos (Lane, 2001, p. 67).

The severe downturn of the local economy left Gary residents with few outlets for entertainment. Gary's Palace Theater, located on Broadway in the heart of the downtown shopping district, had regaled theatergoers with stage shows, vaudeville acts, and motion pictures since its opening in 1925. The historic theater (Figure 22.4) closed its doors in 1972. *Post-Tribune* movie critic Jim Gordon (1984) reported that "[r]umors of [the theater's] closing had spread long before but a stabbing death in the lobby seemed to seal the landmark establishment's fate. The violent incident reportedly was the result of one man's stepping on another man's shoe" (p. D9). The year 1983 witnessed the closing of Gary's last movie theater, the Dunes Twin Cinema (Catlin, 1993, p. 76). In a December 1984 article in the *Post-Tribune*, the head of the Greater Gary Arts Council described the city as "a cultural wasteland." The article's author, staff reporter Vernon Williams, noted that "[o]utside of

Figure 22.4.   Gary's Historic Palace Theater (author, fall 2006)

the schools, there is no ballet, opera, or live theater on an ongoing basis—only fraternities, sororities and other social groups that host once-a-year productions and spearhead trips to nearby Chicago for entertainment" (1984b, p. D9).

By 1983, Gary had also lost the majority of its chain supermarkets and fast food restaurants (Catlin, 1993, p. 61). In the words of Robert Catlin, Gary's economic distress had become so severe that "any type of new development was welcome regardless of its immediate esthetic effect, its short-term fiscal impact, its mid-range implications for the city's economic base and its long-term dynamics for land use" (Lane, 1992, p. 94). To illustrate the extent of Gary's economic plight in the 1980s, Catlin pointed to the fanfare that accompanied the opening of a Wendy's restaurant in Gary in 1986. The ribbon-cutting ceremony was a much celebrated event, featuring marching bands, local dignitaries, and the news media.

As downtown retailers abandoned Gary for the suburbs, other enterprises, including two large banks and a new hospital, followed suit. The new suburban hospital attracted 90 percent of Gary's white and Asian physicians from their practices in Gary out to the suburbs (Catlin, 1993, p. 27). The departure of medical personnel to the suburbs resulted in an inadequate presence of physicians to serve Gary residents. *Post-Tribune* staff reporter Fran Jeffries (1984) noted that Gary was home to only 29 general practitioners, 5 obstetricians, and 5 pediatricians in 1978. Given a population of over 155,000 in 1978, these low numbers of vital medical personnel fell below both the national average and the average for Lake County. The massive business and commercial flight from Gary in the 1970s and 1980s not only truncated the quality of life of Gary's residents, but also significantly diminished Gary's shrinking tax base. The erosion of Gary's tax base resulted in significant cutbacks in city services and personnel. In 1983, for instance, the city was unable to pay its utility bills. That same year, departmental budgets were cut by 10 percent and 384 municipal employees lost their jobs (Lane, 2006, p. 229).

Joblessness and Poverty

The downsizing of operations at U.S. Steel's Gary Works mills, along with the hemorrhaging of local businesses out to the suburbs, severely undercut economic opportunities available to Gary residents. The local economy offered little employment. In the words of historian Lance Trusty, employment prospects for former steelworkers were limited to "a McJob supervising a hamburger grill at a quarter of their former wages, clerking in a shop at Southlake mall, or telephone sales" (Lane, 2006, p. 235).

Figure 22.5 compares Gary's unemployment rate with that of the surrounding suburbs between 1970 and 1990 (as the closest approximation of the period of study in question).[2] Gary's unemployment rate, which started at a relatively low 5.5 percent in 1970, swelled to a devastating 16.6 percent by 1990. In stark contrast, the suburban unemployment rate remained below 5.5 percent throughout the 1970 to 1990 period. Figure 22.6 compares

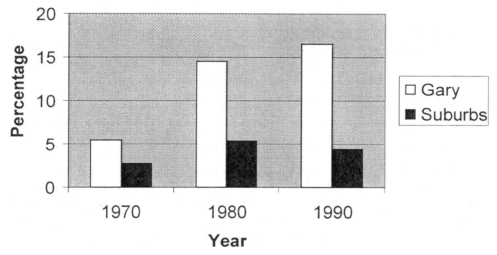

Figure 22.5. Unemployment Rate in Gary and the Surrounding Suburbs, 1970–1990. (Adapted from the U.S. Department of Housing and Urban Development, HUD USER Policy Development and Research Information Service [2005])

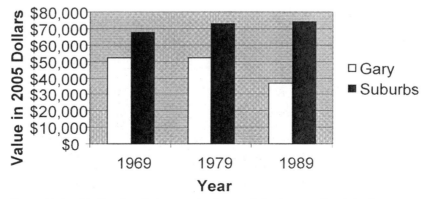

Figure 22.6. Median Family Income in Gary and the Surrounding Suburbs, 1969–1989. (Adapted from the U.S. Department of Housing and Urban Development, HUD USER Policy Development and Research Information Service [2005])

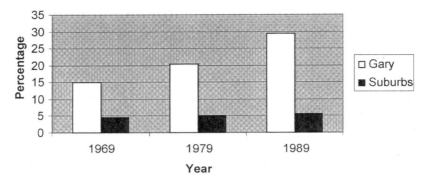

**Figure 22.7.   Poverty Rate in Gary and the Surrounding Suburbs, 1969–1989.
(Adapted from the U.S. Department of Housing and Urban Development, HUD
USER Policy Development and Research Information Service [2005])**

changes in median family income in Gary and the surrounding suburbs, measured in 2005 dollars, between 1969 and 1989. Gary residents fortunate enough to be employed saw their median family income decrease by 30 percent from $52,252 in 1969 to $36,497 in 1989. In contrast, the median family income for suburban dwellers increased by 9 percent, from $67,764 in 1969 to $73,798 in 1989.

The extent to which U.S. Steel's dramatically downsized workforce, along with the economic collapse of Gary's central business district, compromised the financial well-being of Gary's residents can be seen in Figure 22.7. Between 1969 and 1989, Gary's poverty rate skyrocketed from 15 percent to nearly 30 percent. In contrast, the poverty rate in the surrounding suburbs remained below 6 percent throughout the same period.

Demographic Shifts

The demographic shifts that occurred in Gary between 1970 and 1990 mirror the broader patterns observed for Gary over the course of the 20th century. Between 1970 and 1990, Gary's white population declined from 41 percent to 14 percent of the city's total population. In contrast, Gary's African American population increased from 53 percent in 1970 to 80 percent in 1990. It is significant to note that the dramatic changes in the composition of Gary's population coincided with the collapse of the U.S. steel industry, and its destructive impact on Gary's economic landscape. It is also noteworthy that Gary's total population decreased by 33.5 percent between 1970 and 1990, from 175,249 to 116,646. This overall loss of population is even more dramatic, given that the city of Gary gained approximately 13,000 residents through its 1972 annexation of Black Oak, a 6.75 square-mile area of unincorporated Calumet Township.

Figure 22.8, which illustrates the demographic trends for Gary's outlying suburbs between 1980 and 1990, presents an interesting counterpoint to the population trends indicated for the city of Gary. While Gary's population decreased by 23 percent between 1980 and 1990, the population of the surrounding suburbs increased by nearly 7 percent during the same period. In addition, while Gary's population was predominantly African American at the end of the 20th century, the suburbs were predominantly white. In fact, between 1980 and 1990, whites constituted over 84 percent of the total suburban population. During those same years, African Americans comprised less than 7 percent of the total suburban population.

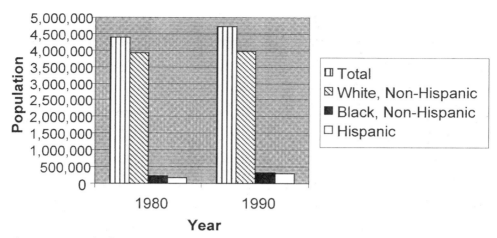

Figure 22.8. Suburban Demographic Trends, 1980–1990. (Adapted from the U.S. Department of Housing and Urban Development, HUD USER Policy Development and Research Information Service [2005])

Housing

> Because planners [in Gary] failed to include social factors in the planning equation, three generations of Gary residents have lived unnecessarily divided, unquestionably alienated and unspeakably embittered by the toxic poisons of nativism, racism and economic bigotry.
>
> —Richard Hatcher, address to the American Society of Planning Officials, May 14, 1974
> (Stundza, 1974, para 14)

Due to the shortsighted town planning engineered by U.S. Steel at the beginning of the 20th century, inadequate housing proved to be an intractable problem for Gary's residents. The burden of Gary's housing shortage initially fell almost exclusively to immigrants and people of color, who found themselves relegated to substandard housing on the city's south side. Beginning in the 1920s, a number of Gary's immigrants moved south of the Little Calumet River to the Glen Park section of the city. At the same time, the city's growing African American population became largely concentrated in Midtown, a neighborhood bordered by U.S. Steel's First Subdivision on the north and Glen Park on the south. By 1940, the spatial distribution of Gary's population constituted "one of the most racially segregated housing patterns in the entire country" (Greer, 1979, p. 84). Until 1950, the overwhelming majority of Gary's 40,000 African American residents lived in dilapidated housing in Midtown. As white flight to the suburbs took hold in the 1960s, Midtown residents began to move out of the central district in favor of neighborhoods vacated by fleeing whites. As Robert Catlin noted in *Racial Politics and Urban Planning*, Midtown's population decreased by approximately 43 percent between 1970 and 1980 (p. 95). When Richard Hatcher took office in 1968, while African Americans constituted over 50 percent of Gary's total population, they were confined to 25 percent of the city's housing units, and these units were undeniably substandard (Lane, 1978, p. 292).

When African Americans were able to purchase homes in white neighborhoods, in spite of the obstacles erected by realtors, insurance companies, and banks, they faced fierce resistance from their white neighbors. Lane (1978) recounted the experience of an African American teacher who purchased a home in 1963 in Gary's predominantly white Ryan subdivision. Upon moving in, she and her elderly mother were confronted by a group of men who threatened to fire-bomb their house. The following evening, in view of the police, a mob of 50 screaming demonstrators gathered in front of the women's home. Not surprisingly, the woman and her mother moved out of Ryan shortly thereafter. The growing racial tension in Gary culminated in the late 1960s with the ultimately unsuccessful attempt by Glen Park's 40,000 white residents to disannex from the city.

As Gary's economy began to falter in the 1960s, the number of new housing units built in Gary also declined. While 1,300 units of privately financed housing were constructed annually in Gary during the 1950s, this number dropped to under 300 units the following decade (Greer, 1979, p. 139). In addition, Gary's existing housing stock was falling into a state of disrepair. In a 1969 article in the *Chicago Sun-Times*, Bernard Nossiter reported that "[t]wo of every five houses in Gary are rated by the building commissioner as 'unsound' or riddled with 'major deficiencies'" (para 22). During his tenure as mayor, Richard Hatcher attempted to remedy Gary's bleak housing situation through the construction of low- to moderate-income housing units. Between 1968 and 1975, 3,000 units of housing were demolished in Gary's impoverished (and historically African American) central district. By 1983, these units had been replaced by 2,300 new subsidized housing units (Catlin, 1993, p. 54).

Figure 22.9 indicates housing trends in Gary from 1970 to 1990. Between 1970 and 1990, the percentage of housing units that were owner occupied versus renter occupied hovered around 60 percent and 40 percent, respectively. It is important to note that during Hatcher's twenty-year mayoral tenure, Gary boasted the nation's highest rate of African American home ownership (Lane, 1992, p. 72). This positive trend was offset by the percentage of vacant housing units in Gary, which swelled from 5 percent in 1970 to 13 percent in 1990. In her recollection of Gary in the 1980s, police officer Carolyn East offered a vivid description of the city's growing number of vacant homes. East (1992) explained that "[i]n the residential areas many of the homes were vacant. Some were boarded up, some had windows that were broken out, and some were completely vandalized inside and out. Some homes were burned completely to the ground" (p. 56). Median home value in Gary, measured in 2005 dollars, decreased from $75,704 in 1970 to $46,770 in 1990.

Figure 22.10 situates Gary's housing trends within the broader regional context. While 60 percent of Gary's housing units were owner occupied during the 20 years in question, this

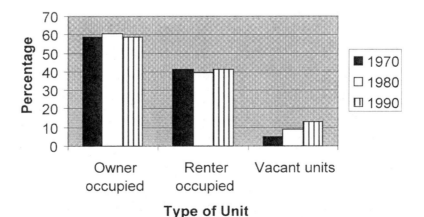

Figure 22.9. Homeownership, Rental, and Vacancy Rates in Gary, 1970–1990. (Adapted from the U.S. Department of Housing and Urban Development, HUD USER Policy Development and Research Information Service [2005])

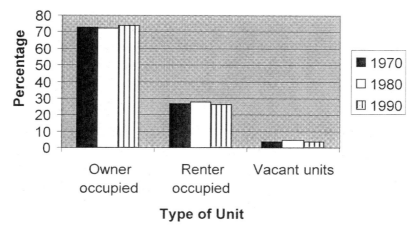

Figure 22.10. Homeownership, Rental, and Vacancy Rates in the Surrounding Suburbs, 1970–1990. (Adapted from the U.S. Department of Housing and Urban Development, HUD USER Policy Development and Research Information Service [2005])

figure remained steady at approximately 73 percent in the surrounding suburbs. Another striking comparison can be drawn between the two areas vis-à-vis vacancy figures. While the percentage of vacant units in Gary increased from 5 to 13 percent between 1970 and 1990, the percentage of vacant units in the suburbs peaked at 4.6 percent. In contrast with plummeting property value in Gary, the median home value in the suburbs surrounding Gary, measured in 2005 dollars, increased from $120,789 in 1970 to $159,593 in 1990.

Education

Segregation and inequity have a long history in Gary's educational system. Superintendent William A. Wirt, known for his renowned work-study-play educational philosophy, established segregated schools in Gary in 1908. Wirt argued that "it is only in justice to the Negro children that they be segregated" (Mohl & Betten, 1986, p. 55). By the 1920s, the city's only integrated school was the impoverished south side's Froebel School, attended by immigrant and African American children. Despite Froebel's allegedly integrated status, African American students were barred from participating in school-related extracurricular activities and social events (Mohl & Betten, 1986, pp. 55–57). Segregation continued to be official school board policy until 1945, when the school board voted to integrate Gary's schools. Although the board enacted a desegregation plan in 1947, de facto school segregation prevailed because of Gary's firmly entrenched pattern of residential segregation (Mohl & Betten, 1986, p. 59). In 1962, Richard Hatcher represented a group of local citizens in the lawsuit *Bell v. Schools, City of Gary*, in which the plaintiffs argued that the school board "deliberately fostered a de facto system" (Rich, 1996, p. 63). Despite the body of evidence marshaled by the plaintiffs, they ultimately lost the case.

During Hatcher's mayoral tenure, Gary's schools endured numerous shifts in leadership, as well as educational paradigm. When Hatcher came into office in 1968, although Gary's school population was 83 percent African American, the city's school board and school administrators were predominately white (Rich, 1996, p. 67). The first educational regime change came in 1968 on the heels of a massive school boycott, involving some 20,000 students. The boycott was organized by the Concerned Citizens for Quality Education to protest the segregationist policies of acting superintendent Clarence Swingley.

The school board quickly replaced Swingley with Dr. Gordon McAndrews, director of the Learning Institute of North Carolina and "an expert on the learning problems of under-achieving children" (Rich, 1996, p. 72). During his 11-year tenure as superintendent, McAndrews initiated a number of reforms, including (1) starting a community education program; (2) hiring a private curriculum development company to improve the reading and math scores of local elementary students; (3) adopting minimum competency requirements for high school graduation; and (4) providing high school students with the option to select a vocational, rather than academic, curriculum (Rich, 1996, pp. 72–77). The adoption of minimum competency requirements for high school graduation came about as a result of a 1974 study that found that Gary's graduating seniors were performing at an 8.6 grade level in reading and a 9.0 grade level in math (Rich, 1996, p. 76).

After terminating McAndrews in March of 1979, the Gary school board recruited Dr. Ernst Jones, a deputy superintendent from St. Louis. In January of 1980, Jones became Gary, Indiana's first African American superintendent. In assuming the position of superintendent, Jones inherited a financially troubled school district that was $8 million in debt (Rich, 1996, p. 80). In 1986, when the board voted not to extend Jones's contract, they cited lack of educational leadership and clashes with the teachers' union as their primary reasons (Rich, 1996, p. 81).

Trends in Gary's schools during Hatcher's mayoral tenure reflected broader municipal trends. Enrollment in Gary's schools contracted significantly in the 1970s and 1980s. *Post-Tribune* staff reporter Valli Herman (1984) pointed out that enrollment in Gary's schools peaked at 48,509 students in 1967–1968. By 1984, Gary's schools enrolled less than 30,000 pupils. Similarly, enrollment in Gary's Catholic schools decreased by roughly 50 percent, from 27,842 students in 1964–1965 to 13,724 students in 1984. In addition, the racial composition of Gary's student population changed significantly. While African Americans comprised 58 percent of Gary's student population in 1964, this proportion increased to 91 percent in 1984. Figure 22.11 provides a snapshot of changes in Gary residents' educational attainment during the Hatcher years.

Between 1970 and 1990, the level of education obtained by Gary residents increased. Gains made in the percentage of residents with a high school degree, as well as the percent-

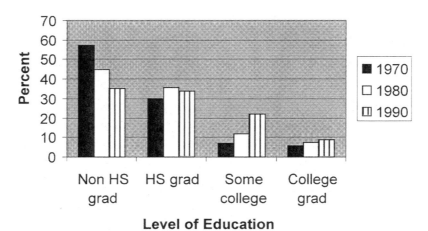

Figure 22.11. Gary Educational Attainment, 1970–1990. (Data indicate highest educational attainment of persons aged 25 or older. Adapted from the U.S. Department of Housing and Urban Development, HUD USER Policy Development and Research Information Service [2005])

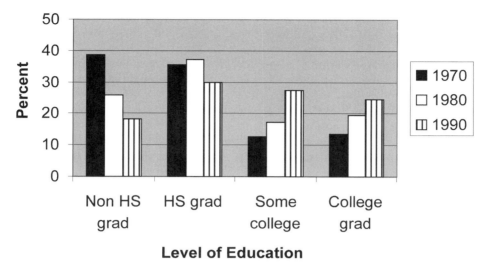

Figure 22.12. Suburban Educational Attainment, 1970–1990. (Data indicate highest educational attainment of persons aged 25 or older. Adapted from the U.S. Department of Housing and Urban Development, HUD USER Policy Development and Research Information Service [2005])

age of residents with a college degree, were relatively modest. In contrast, the percentage of residents with "some college" education rose from 7 to 22 percent.

In the interest of considering the educational attainment of Gary residents within a broader regional context, Figure 22.12 depicts the educational attainment of residents of Gary's outlying suburbs. The figures for Gary residents and their suburban counterparts with a high school diploma and "some college" are comparable. In contrast, the percentage of residents with a college degree in 1990 was nearly 25 percent in the suburbs, compared to less than 9 percent in Gary.

Environment: Big Steel and Big Pollution

> Every evening the mills presented viewers with a display of giant torches, erupting sparks, and massive factories engraved against a glowing red sky. Day and night, black and red smoke wafted through the atmosphere while oils, greases, and chemicals streaked across rivers and lakes. For those who lived and worked in Gary, pollution was inescapable.
>
> —Hurley (1995, p. 15)

In *Big Steel*, Edward Greer characterized U.S. Steel's Gary Works complex as the nation's worst water polluting steel mill, as well as "the single largest polluter of Lake Michigan" (1979, p. 197). Air pollution was another pernicious by-product of steel production at Gary Works. When Richard Hatcher became mayor in 1968, Gary's steel mills released nearly 70,000 tons of particulates into the air each year, in addition to significant quantities of noxious gases (Greer, 1979, pp. 183–184). Given that air pollution contributes to respiratory illness, cancer, heart disease, and birth defects, the pollutants spewed forth daily from the mills constituted a form of violence perpetrated against Gary residents. The Lake County Coroner alluded to the deadly consequences of this environmental violence when he remarked, in the March 7, 1967, issue of the *Post-Tribune*, that "[i]n the autopsies . . . I've seen lungs of people who've lived and worked here in Gary all their lives. These organs look like the inside of a coal mine" (Greer, 1979, p. 184). Pollution from the mills also undermined the health of Gary's children during Hatcher's tenure as mayor. Not only was Gary's childhood mortality rate two times higher than the national average, but over half of Gary's childhood deaths were due to respiratory illnesses (Greer, 1979, pp. 184–185). Due to the historically established pattern of residential segregation that concentrated Gary's African American population within the city's central district, African American children disproportionately suffered the effects of steel mill-generated pollutants. Even when income disparities were taken into account, the childhood mortality rate among African American children far exceeded that of Gary's white children (Greer, 1979, p. 185). Given that air pollution inside the mills could reach as high as 10 times the levels found in the city itself, the health of steelworkers was particularly at risk (Greer, 1979, p. 185).

U.S. Steel proved to be exceedingly intransigent in the face of local demands for compliance with environmental regulations. During his first term in office, Hatcher appointed activist Dr. Herschel Bornstein to the Gary Health Commission Board. With the support of the Environmental Protection Agency (EPA), Bornstein fought to amend a local air pollution ordinance, dating back to the mid-1960s, that exempted coke ovens from compliance with emission controls. Because coke ovens constituted the largest single source of pollutants in the Gary Works mills, they were an important target of environmental regulation. When Gary's city council repealed the coke oven exemption in 1970, U.S. Steel immediately applied for a one-year variance. In the legal battle that ensued, the Lake County Superior Court ruled that U.S. Steel would have to comply with the local ordinance concerning coke oven emissions. Unfortunately, however, ensuring compliance turned out to be nearly impossible for local authorities (Greer, 1979, pp. 190–193).

U.S. Steel was equally unyielding when federal agencies demanded that the corporation clean up its act at Gary Works. The EPA stepped in to regulate Gary's steel mills in 1973. As soon as the EPA issued a consent decree regarding air pollution at Gary Works, U.S. Steel initiated its strategy of demanding extensions. In a federal courtroom, U.S. Steel threatened to close down a portion of its facilities and lay off 2,500 workers unless the EPA granted the requested extension. Greer (1979) argued that U.S. Steel's tactics essentially amounted to unsubstantiated corporate bullying, given that there were, in reality, only 500 workers employed in the portion of the Gary Works complex under dispute (p. 194). U.S. Steel continued to fight the EPA's coke oven restrictions, until a settlement was ultimately reached in federal court in May of 1978. U.S. Steel's bitter resistance to coke oven regulation provides one example of the corporation's broader strategy of avoiding environmental regulation by threatening disastrous economic consequences. Greer (1979) asserted that "[i]n every community with steel plants, U.S. Steel has threatened cutbacks in investment and jobs if strict pollution control measures are enforced" (p. 204).

Crime: Cultivating a Culture of Fear in Gary

Crime and the perception of danger must be taken into account in a case study of Gary, Indiana, during the Hatcher years. When Hatcher ascended to the mayoralty in 1968, Gary's crime statistics indicated a homicide rate three times higher, and an auto theft rate seven times higher than the respective national averages (Greer, 1979, p. 125). In the early 1970s, during Hatcher's second term, the incidence of homicide increased in Gary due primarily to "drug-related crimes and well-publicized gang warfare among narcotics suppliers" (Lane, 1978, p. 303).

The specter of crime continued to haunt the Hatcher administration and Gary residents alike in the 1980s. Statistics in *Crime in America's Top-Rated Cities* indicate that the violent crime rate in Gary exceeded the national average throughout the 1980s. In *Crime in America's Top-Rated Cities*, the category of violent crimes includes murder, forcible rape, robbery, and aggravated assault. In 1980, the number of violent crimes per 100,000 people was 1,459.3 in Gary, compared to 596.6 in the nation as a whole. While the violent crime rate in Gary decreased to 973.3 per 100,000 people in 1987, this rate still far exceeded the year's national figure of 609.7. In 1982, with 86 murders, Gary earned the dubious distinction of registering the nation's second-highest homicide rate (Catlin, 1993, p. 53). That year, the number of murders per 100,000 people reached 59.8 in Gary, compared with 9.1 in the nation as a whole. Catlin (1993) suggested that the alarming homicide figures made sense in light of Gary's high rate of joblessness and poverty, which "produced alcoholism, drug addiction, despair, mental disorder, and other behaviors leading to violence" (p. 54). Nevertheless, Catlin faults the *Post-Tribune* for creating an inflated sense of fear among Gary residents through its unbalanced and sensationalized coverage of local crime.

Whether or not it was commensurate with reality, the fear of crime felt by Gary residents was a formidable force with which the city had to reckon. In a *U.S. News and World Report* article about Gary (White, 1982), former Gary resident Merle Cook explained that the fear of crime figured centrally in residents' decision to move out of Gary. In the same article, economist Gopal Pati argued that the fear of crime also provided a powerful disincentive for businesses that might otherwise consider setting up shop in Gary.

Urban Renewal in Gary: Projects or Planning?

Urban renewal was a rare phenomenon in Gary before Richard Hatcher moved into City Hall in 1968. Although Gary officially had an urban renewal agency before the Hatcher era, this agency was largely inactive, initiating only two projects between 1956 and 1962. One of these projects, carried out between 1957 and 1963, involved the demolition of 1,500 units of housing in the Pulaski neighborhood. Only 132 new units of housing were constructed in their place. According to Edward Greer (1979), 96 percent of the residents displaced by the Pulaski redevelopment project were African American. Only one-fourth of those displaced were able to relocate to Gary Housing Authority low-income units (p. 147).

In stark contrast with his predecessors, Hatcher would become nationally renowned for his tireless efforts to tap into federal dollars for urban renewal. Between 1968 and 1980, Hatcher's administration succeeded in securing $300 million in federal funds for a variety of programs, including urban renewal (Catlin, 1993, p. 31). In *U.S. News and World Report*, George White (1982) pointed out that Gary received twice as much federal aid as U.S. cities of comparable size between 1972 and 1982. In fact, during the last year of the Carter administration, 53.4 percent of Gary's general revenue came from the federal government. That same year, federal dollars accounted for less than 15 percent of general revenue for the average American city of Gary's size (Padley, 1984, p. D5).

Robert Catlin, who served as an adviser to the Hatcher administration between 1982 and 1987, argues that urban renewal efforts can proceed from either a project-based or a planning-based approach. At the behest of the local business community and its Committee of 100, a comprehensive development plan was drafted for Gary in the early 1960s. As Catlin points out, this plan, completed in 1964, would have displaced nearly 40 percent of Gary's African American residents. Instead of revising and working to implement the preexisting comprehensive plan, as his planning director Charles Allen repeatedly suggested, Hatcher opted for the method of urban renewal through individual projects.

Mayor Hatcher and his urban renewal agency turned their collective attention to several major downtown development projects. One of the largest undertakings was the Genesis

Convention Center, a 250,000-square-foot complex with a seating capacity of 8,500. Construction on the project began in December 1977. The $16 million convention center, funded by the Community Development Block Grant Program and the Economic Development Administration, opened its doors in December of 1981. However, because of cost overruns, the new convention center lacked kitchen facilities, directional placards for the restrooms, and public telephones (Lane, 1992, p. 80). Given Gary's crime rate and severely depressed central business district, it comes as no surprise that the Genesis Center, shown in Figure 22.13, did not prove to be an economic boon to the city. In fact, by 1987, the Genesis Center reported an annual deficit in excess of $1 million (Catlin, 1993, pp. 28–29). The $2.5 million Sheraton hotel redevelopment project turned out to be even more disastrous. The reader will recall that the grand opening of the downtown Sheraton in 1981 was followed, four short years later, by the hotel's closing due to low occupancy. Efforts to expand and improve Gary's airport also yielded disappointing results. Between 1977 and 1985, $40 million in federal aid was spent to extend the airport's runways and build a new terminal. Upon completion of the renovations in 1985, several corporations promised to support Gary-Indianapolis and Gary-Detroit airline service. In the summer of 1985, when the corporations failed to deliver on their pledges of support, air service out of the Gary airport was abruptly cancelled (Catlin, 1993, p. 39).

Alongside these urban renewal disappointments, Mayor Hatcher and his team engineered and executed numerous successful projects. In the late 1970s, the U.S. Department of Housing and Urban Development selected Gary; St. Paul, Minnesota; and Dayton, Ohio, to participate in a downtown redevelopment program called the Negotiated Investment Strategy (NIS). With the help of NIS money, the defunct Hotel Gary, located on Broadway in the heart of downtown, was transformed into a thriving senior citizens' housing complex. Low occupancy had forced the Hotel Gary, constructed in 1926, to close its doors in 1974. In 1981, the historic structure reopened as the Genesis Towers (Figure 22.14). Catlin (1993) noted that "the stable resident population has even provided a basis for renovation of an adjacent drug store and a small office complex" (p. 30). In the arena of housing, 3,000 units of substandard housing in Gary's historically African American central district were torn down between 1968 and 1975. By 1983, the demolished housing had been replaced by 2,300 units of new subsidized housing. In addition, the Hatcher team was instrumental in securing $10 million for the construction of a transportation center near the downtown Genesis Convention Center. Opened in 1985, the Adam Benjamin Metro Center serves as a hub for local rail and bus service.

Figure 22.13.   Genesis Convention Center, 1 Genesis Center Plaza (author, fall 2006)

Figure 22.14. Genesis Towers (Formerly the historic Hotel Gary), 578 Broadway (author, fall 2006)

Hatcher also harnessed federal funds for the improvement of local recreational facilities. During his mayoral tenure, Hatcher oversaw the building of seven new parks and five new public swimming pools. Under the auspices of the NIS program, the city also constructed a downtown headquarters for the Parks and Recreation Board. The building, which includes offices and a fitness center, opened in the summer of 1986. However, despite Hatcher's efforts to improve the city's recreational facilities, the overall condition of Gary's parks deteriorated over the course of his mayoral tenure. A 1983 survey of Gary's parks uncovered "swings, most with broken seats; broken playground equipment such as carousels and see-saws; fieldhouses with leaky roofs, peeling paint, and inoperable toilets; and baseball fields littered with weeds and broken glass" (Catlin, 1993, p. 79). A disastrous incident in 1985 provided yet another indication of Gary's declining capacity to maintain its municipal recreational facilities. Several children tragically died in an untended public swimming pool that was supposed to be empty.

Comprehensive planning became a factor in Gary's renewal efforts in 1983 when the city's planning department began work on the Gary Comprehensive Plan, Year 2000. Catlin (1993), a key member of the planning team, explained that one of the overarching aims of the plan was to reorient Gary "from thinking of itself as a central city . . . to the realization that its best hopes rested upon becoming a bedroom community for Chicago" (p. 98). The Gary Comprehensive Plan grew out of the following basic assumptions: (1) employment in the local steel mills was unlikely to increase; (2) attracting small-shop diversified manufacturing to the city was feasible; (3) Gary's airport would be a central feature in drawing businesses to Gary; (4) Gary's population would likely decrease until planning strategies were implemented; (5) Gary residents should train for service and technology jobs available in Chicago; (6) Gary should position itself as a viable housing market for upwardly mobile Chicagoans; and (7) federal and state aid would increase to mid-1970s levels after 1988 (Catlin, 1993, pp. 90–93). In December of 1986, just months before Richard Hatcher's defeat to Calumet Township Assessor Thomas Barnes, Gary's nine city council members voted unanimously to adopt the Gary Comprehensive Plan. Subsequent chapters in Gary's urban renewal story would depend largely on the leadership and vision of Mayor-elect Barnes.

CONCLUSION: GARY AT THE TURN OF THE 21ST CENTURY

This case study focused primarily on Gary during the two-decade mayoral tenure of Richard G. Hatcher. However, the story of Gary, Indiana, does not end with the inauguration of Mayor Barnes. In order to explore the long-term impact of the interlocking crises that befell the city between 1968 and 1987, it is worthwhile to fast-forward to Gary at the turn of the 21st century.

Gary, Indiana, greeted the 21st century with a number of auspicious developments. With the approval of the state legislature, granted in 1993, riverboat gambling arrived in Gary. While opponents feared the social ramifications of riverboat gambling, Gary's two new casinos created 2,500 jobs and generated $25 million in annual revenues for the city (Lane, 2006, p. 236). The national spotlight shined on Gary in March of 2001 when the city's beleaguered Genesis Convention Center hosted the Miss USA pageant. The Genesis Center also became home to a Continental Basketball Association team called the Gary Steelheads. During the summer of 2001, construction began on a 6,000-seat baseball stadium in downtown Gary. On May 26, 2003, the Gary SouthShore RailCats played their inaugural home opener at U.S. Steel Yard. In September of 2005, the RailCats earned the Northern League championship title. In addition, the Gary Housing Authority received nearly $20 million in Hope VI grant money from HUD in 1999 for the development of mixed-income, mixed-finance housing in Gary's Duneland Village and Horace Mann neighborhoods.

While the aforementioned developments represent an expansion of economic and cultural opportunities in Gary, statistics drawn from the U.S. Department of Housing and Urban Development's State of the Cities Data Systems (2005) paint a much bleaker picture of Gary's health at the turn of the 21st century. The trend of declining population, evident in the city since 1970, continued unabated into the 21st century. Between 1990 and 2005, Gary's population declined by nearly 17 percent, from 116,646 to 97,057. In addition to chronic loss of population, poverty proved to be a tenacious problem for the beleaguered city. In 1999, Gary's poverty rate registered at 25.8 percent, compared to 5.9 percent in the surrounding suburbs. The disproportionate share of metropolitan poverty concentrated in Gary reflects, in part, urban-suburban disparities in median family income. In 1999, Gary's median family income, measured in 2005 dollars, was $37,752, compared to $78,243 in the surrounding suburbs. Poverty in Gary also reflects the specter of unemployment that continued to haunt the city. In 2000, Gary's unemployment rate of 14.9 percent compared quite unfavorably to the suburban unemployment rate of 4.5 percent. Alongside the twin problems of poverty and unemployment, property values in Gary lagged far behind those in the suburbs. In 2000, Gary and the surrounding suburbs reported median home values, measured in 2005 dollars, of $60,563 and $184,318, respectively.

The 2000 edition of *Crime in America's Top-Rated Cities* (Garoogian, 2000) indicates that Gary also continued to be beset with crime at the close of the 20th century. The violent crime rate in Gary, a measure encompassing murder, forcible rape, robbery, and aggravated assault, reached a peak of 3,344.1 per 100,000 people in 1996. That year, the violent crime rate in Gary exceeded the national average of 636.5 violent crimes per 100,000 people by more than five times. By 1998, the last year for which data are available, Gary's violent crime rate had decreased considerably to 1,207.6 per 100,000 people. Nonetheless, even with this significant decrease, Gary's violent crime rate remained more than twice as high as that year's national average of 566.4 violent crimes per 100,000 people.

In an article appearing in November 1976 in the *Wall Street Journal*, Morris S. Thompson predicted that "[a] bright future [in Gary] wouldn't be much less dazzling than Atlantis rising out of Lake Michigan" (para 9). In light of the statistical profile of Gary outlined in the foregoing paragraphs, Thompson's words remain as relevant today as they were 35 years ago. As this case study has endeavored to demonstrate, the combined efforts of a dynamic leader and a concerned citizenry in Gary could not stem the rising tide of urban crisis sparked by the economic, demographic, and political transformations of the latter half of the 20th century. And as the statistical data indicate, the aftershocks of these transformations continue to be felt in Gary in the 21st century in the form of chronic unemployment, poverty, and crime. Indeed, Gary's ongoing struggles emblematize the contours, content, and consequences of distress in America's industrial cities. Stephen G. McShane, archivist-curator with the Calumet Regional Archives at Indiana University Northwest, captured the significance of Gary's fate in his observation that "Gary is American history in microcosm. You can see the twentieth century of America simply by looking at Gary" ("In Gary, Hope," 2006, para 11).

NOTES

1. Hall (1997) defined ingots as "solid blocks of steel that would be transported to a rolling mill for reheating and rolling into a finished shape" (p. 8).

2. In HUD's State of the Cities Data Systems (SOCDS), data for the suburbs surrounding Gary are calculated as the total for the Chicago-Naperville-Joliet, IL-IN-WI Metropolitan Statistical Area minus the sum of data for the following cities: Arlington Heights Village, IL; Chicago City, IL; Des Plaines City, IL; Elgin City, IL; Evanston City, IL; Hoffman Estates Village, IL; Joliet City, IL; Naperville City, IL; Schaumburg Village, IL; Skokie Village, IL; and Gary City, IN.

REFERENCES

Catlin, R. A. (1993). *Racial politics and urban planning: Gary, Indiana 1980–1989.* Lexington: University Press of Kentucky.

Catlin, R. A. (1997). Gary, Indiana: Planning, race, and ethnicity. In J. M. Thomas & M. Ritzdorf (Eds.), *Planning and the African American community: In the shadows* (pp. 126–142). Thousand Oaks, CA: Sage.

East, C. (1992). Police beat. *Steel Shavings, 21,* 56–57.

Garoogian, D. (Ed.). (2000). *Crime in America's top-rated cities: A statistical profile, 1979–1998* (3rd ed.). Lakeville, CT: Grey House Publishing.

In Gary, hope that a second century can reverse a decline. (2006, July 2). *New York Times.* Retrieved January 19, 2007, from http://select.nytimes.com/search/restricted/article?res=F50C1EFA3E540C718CDDAE0894DE404482

Gordon, J. (1984, December 16). Variety of factors send theaters reeling. *Post-Tribune,* p. D9.

Greer, E. (1979). *Big steel: Black politics and corporate power in Gary, Indiana.* New York, NY: Monthly Review Press.

Hall, C. G. L. (1997). *Steel phoenix: The fall and rise of the U.S. steel industry.* New York, NY: St. Martin's Press.

Hatcher, R. G. (1969). *The mayor's report to the people.* Gary, IN: City of Gary.

Herman, V. (1984, December 16). Dwindling school enrollment not harmful. *Post-Tribune,* p. D8.

Hurley, A. (1995). *Environmental inequalities: Class, race, and industrial pollution in Gary, Indiana, 1945–1980.* Chapel Hill: University of North Carolina Press.

Jeffries, F. (1984, December 16). Personal health care grows in importance. *Post-Tribune,* p. D8.

Kantor, H., & Brenzel, B. (1992). Urban education and the "truly disadvantaged": The historical roots of the contemporary crisis, 1945–1990. *Teachers College Record, 94*(2), 278–314.

Lane, J. B. (1976, July 25). Challenger from humble beginnings. *Post-Tribune.*

Lane, J. B. (1978). *"City of the century": A history of Gary, Indiana.* Bloomington: Indiana University Press.

Lane, J. B. (1992). An oral history of Mayor Richard G. Hatcher's administration, 1980–1987. *Steel Shavings, 21,* 69–104.

Lane, J. B. (2001). Black political power and its limits: Gary mayor Richard G. Hatcher's administration, 1968–1987. In D. R. Colburn & J. S. Adler (Eds.), *African American mayors: Race, politics, and the American city* (pp. 57–79). Urbana: University of Illinois Press.

Lane, J. B. (2006). Gary's first hundred years: A centennial history of Gary, Indiana, 1906–2006 [Special issue]. *Steel Shavings, 37.*

McCarthy, L. (1984, December 16). City's businesses suffer with steel industry. *Post-Tribune,* p. D4.

Mohl, R. A., & Betten, N. (1986). *Steel city: Urban and ethnic patterns in Gary, Indiana, 1906–1950.* New York, NY: Holmes & Meier.

Nossiter, B. D. (1969, March 9). A black mayor's struggle. *Chicago Sun-Times.*

Padley, K. (1984, December 16). Federal funding has failed to cure all of Gary's ailments. *Post-Tribune,* p. D5.

Rae, D. W. (2003). *City: Urbanism and its end.* New Haven, CT: Yale University Press.

Rich, W. C. (1996). *Black mayors and school politics: The failure of reform in Detroit, Gary, and Newark.* New York, NY: Garland Publishing.

Stundza, T. (1974, May 14). Hatcher: Basic scarcity is "shortage of concern." *Post-Tribune.*

Thompson, M. S. (1976, November 8). Black mayor urges new approach. *Wall Street Journal.*

Trusty, L. (1992). End of an era: The 1980s in the Calumet. *Steel Shavings, 21,* 1–7.

U.S. Department of Housing and Urban Development, HUD USER Policy Development and Research Information Service. (2005). *State of the cities data systems, 2005* [Data file]. Retrieved April 13, 2006, from http://socds .huduser.org/index.html

White, G. (1982, November 22). Gary, Indiana: A city federal millions haven't helped. *U.S. News & World Report, 93,* 79–80.

Williams, V. A. (1984a, December 16). Politicians' careers catapulted by Muigwithania. *Post-Tribune,* p. D2.

Williams, V. A. (1984b, December 16). Support limited for showcasing local talent. *Post-Tribune,* p. D9.

23

God's Will or Government Policy?

Katrina's Unveiling of History and the Mass Dispersion of Black People

Jerome E. Morris

From Africa, to America, new name?
Section 8, Hope VI, then Katrina came
Moved in, moved out, and moved away
Now back to the city and here to stay

Re-gentrify, redevelop, and renewal
Of bad hoods, bad people, and bad schools?
Once minority, now urban, no real change
It's all the same, but a different name

New Orleans, Nashville, or New York
Different city, same state, that's how it worked
Whether policy, promises, or a shovel
As James Baldwin said, it is still Negro Removal

—Jerome E. Morris

"GOD DID IT"? HOW THE LOWER NINTH WARD OF NEW ORLEANS CAME TO SUFFER THE GREATEST DEVASTATION FROM KATRINA

While Hurricane Katrina of August 2005 struck the entire Gulf Coast of the United States, including Texas, Louisiana, Mississippi, Alabama, and Florida, its greatest devastation was in the Lower Ninth Ward of New Orleans, Louisiana (American Society of Civil Engineers, 2007; "Elderly Appear," 2005). This result appears incompatible with the fact that Katrina first slammed into the Gulf Coast on August 29 near Buras-Triumph in Plaquemines Parish, Louisiana, nearly 70 miles southeast of New Orleans, its eye hovering over St. Tammany Parish and Hancock County, Mississippi (Knabb, Rhome, & Brown, 2005). Also, this outcome is at odds with the fact that St. Bernard Parish, which is predominantly white and contiguous to the Lower Ninth Ward, experienced equal flooding (National Black Programming Consortium, 2005). Indeed, of the nearly 2,000 deaths attributed to Katrina, 90 percent were from Louisiana, of which 73 percent were from Orleans Parish (New Orleans), the majority of whom were black people who died in eastern Orleans Parish—specifically, from the Lower Ninth Ward (Brunkard, Namulansa, & Ratard, 2008). Paradoxically, when Katrina struck, the population of the Lower Ninth Ward, at 14,000 people, represented less than 3 percent of New Orleans (Baum, 2006; Dessauer & Armstrong, 2006). One of the most segregated sections of the city at the time, the Lower Ninth Ward's population was over 98 percent black, approximately 36 percent of whom were poor (Dessauer & Armstrong, 2006).

The floodwater that overwhelmed and inundated the Lower Ninth in the wake of Katrina was the single greatest contributor to the loss of so much life (Jonkman, Maaskant, Boyd, & Levitan, 2009), and also resulted in the displacement of nearly all the people and the destruction of every home and institution there (Baum, 2006). The Lower Ninth Ward, where more than half the residents were designated as "not in the labor force" and around 22 percent worked in low-wage jobs, came to be obliterated (Baum, 2006; Dessauer & Armstrong, 2006). In the immediate aftermath, then-Congressman Richard H. Baker, a Republican from the state's capital, Baton Rouge, callously declared, "We finally cleaned up public housing in New Orleans. We couldn't do it, but God did" (Harwood, 2005). Baker later said he was misquoted, and corrected his statement with the following: "We have been trying for decades to clean up New Orleans public housing to provide decent housing for residents, and now it looks like God is finally making us do it" (Babington, 2005).

This attribution of the devastation of a poor, black community in the wake of Katrina to God or Nature is in conflict, however, with the fact that, while Katrina was the sixth-strongest hurricane in U.S. history, the disparate destruction of the Lower Ninth Ward has been construed as constituting "the largest *demolition* of a community in modern U.S. history [emphasis added]" (Connolly, 2005). Furthermore, this portrait of associating post-Katrina losses in the Lower Ninth to God is in conflict with the unnatural historical machinations of the U.S. government that effectuated the prevalence of oppressed blacks in New Orleans; the civic design around Jim Crow practices and policies of "benign neglect" that resulted in segregated black communities dispossessed of the essential resources to survive; the incompetent design and construction and substandard maintenance of New Orleans' levees, particularly surrounding the Lower Ninth, that resulted in its complete inundation and devastation; the gross malfeasance of government in the management of affairs in the Lower Ninth surrounding Hurricane Katrina; and the contemporary civic design to raze and reinvent this and other black communities in the city.

THE UNNATURAL HISTORICAL MACHINATIONS OF THE U.S. GOVERNMENT THAT EFFECTUATED THE PREVALENCE OF OPPRESSED BLACKS IN NEW ORLEANS

Once the colonizers of the French Mississippi Company overwhelmed and massacred nearly all the indigenous occupants of the land, particularly the Chitimacha people, they established *La Nouvelle-Orléans*, in May 1718. Avoiding the low-lying cypress swamps surrounding the area, including what would come to be New Orleans' Ninth Ward, they staked out their settlement on land along the east bank of the Mississippi River where sediment from the river had built up elevated areas. This site is now the famous French Quarter of New Orleans, or the Vieux Carré. Until 1763, the territory was controlled by France, as part of its burgeoning North American Empire, the center of which was its colony on the Caribbean Island of Saint-Domingue, with its lucrative sugar plantations. Under the 1762 Treaty of Fontainebleau, French king Louis XV had ceded New Orleans and the Louisiana territory west of the Mississippi River to his Bourbon cousin Charles III of Spain. The territorial colonizers continued to view themselves as French, however, and opposed Spanish rule. By 1769, approximately 14,000 people lived in the Louisiana territory, including around 3,500 in what would become New Orleans, the *majority* of whom—native people not being counted—were enslaved Africans (Louisiana State University Libraries, n.d.).

The Spanish continued to control the western part of the Louisiana territory throughout the War of the American Revolution until the 1783 Treaty of Paris, which ended the war. Under the treaty, the boundaries of the new country, the United States, were established, the western border stretching to the Mississippi River, with a grant of "perpetual" access to the river. Spain, however, contended that its boundary line included New Orleans and the entire Mississippi River. The Americans considered this claim problematic, as it impinged upon its trade and navigational needs (Louisiana State University Libraries, n.d.). Then, in 1795, Spain and the United States signed what is commonly referred to as Pinckney's Treaty, which allowed the Americans unfettered navigational use of the Mississippi River (Bemis, 1926; Encyclopedia Louisiana, 2004).[1]

In the meantime, the French were not content to have lost this stronghold of its empire, crucial as a supply depot for its Caribbean holdings, particularly Saint-Domingue. Saint-Domingue was the "pride of France," which, by the start of the French Revolution in 1789, was the world's most profitable colony, producing 40 percent of the world's sugar on plantations operated by hundreds of thousands of enslaved Africans (James, 1963; Metz, 2001; Rogozinski, 2000). In 1791, however, over 100,000 of the 500,000 enslaved Africans on the island colony rose up in rebellion. Within months, they had destroyed 180 sugar plantations and hundreds of coffee and indigo plantations (Babb, 1954; Censer & Hunt, 2001; H. Klein, 1999; Knight, 1990). At the time, Saint-Domingue had 800 sugar plantations, 800 cotton plantations, and 3,000 each of coffee and indigo plantations (Metz, 2001). The violence and high death rates among the enslaved forced French plantation owners to exit the island with their slaves. The exodus included thousands of others from the upper strata of the society, including members of the 5 percent of the population deemed free blacks, *gens de couleur* or mulattoes (Metz, 2001). In 1793 alone, over 10,000 left Saint-Domingue in daily voyages sailing out to any number of cities in the United States, such that, for example, in July of that year, 53 ships landed in Baltimore. Nowhere on the continent, though, was there a greater immigration from Saint-Domingue than to southern Louisiana.[2]

Although the alluvial soil in the New Orleans territory was ideal for growing sugar cane, the production of sugar had been unsuccessful until the uprising on Saint-Domingue. Until that time, men like French-born plantation owner Jean-Etienne de Boré, who owned a significant plantation property north of New Orleans, had organized his slaves to plant indigo (New Orleans Public Library, n.d.). Several years of drought, though, had brought de Boré and other planters to the verge of bankruptcy (New Orleans Public Library, n.d.; Payne, 1998; Schendel, 2008). In 1795, de Boré hired a sugar cane planter, a Saint-Domingue escapee working for a nearby plantation owner, who showed him how to construct a sugarhouse, which was completed by de Boré's 40 slaves at a cost of $4,000 (De Grummond, 1999). In that same year, de Boré produced a sugar crop that yielded him $12,000 (Stacey, 2004). Thereafter, a sugar industry exploded in Louisiana. By 1801, 75 sugar plantations in the Louisiana territory were producing five million pounds of sugar valued at $400,000 (McMillin, 2004); by 1802, the total value of the sugar crop of Louisiana was $25 million. The dramatic increase of sugar plantations along the Mississippi River drove sugar planters to import thousands upon thousands more African slaves to work the cane fields and process the sugar.

The French, by then under the leadership of Napoléon Bonaparte as First Consul of France, were being overwhelmed in Saint-Domingue. In 1801, Toussaint L'Ouverture, leader of the slave rebellion, had claimed victory, issuing a new constitution, abolishing slavery, and transforming Saint-Domingue into an autonomous department of France. However, Napoléon had just regained a base in North America, under the 1800 Treaty of San Ilde-fonso. In this Treaty, Spain had ceded the Louisiana territory back to France and Napoléon decided to retake Saint-Domingue (Chandler, 1973; Corbett, 1995; Kelly, n.d.). Napoleon's decision to retake Saint-Domingue emanated from the pressure that he received from the French sugar planters ousted from Saint-Domingue, the economic engine that had repre-sented one-third of the entire French economy prior to the revolt.

Napoléon's expansion plans made U.S. President Thomas Jefferson very anxious, given the loss of the agreement with Spain to use the Mississippi River. In 1801, then, Jefferson sent Robert R. Livingston to France to actually buy New Orleans (Kelly, n.d.).[3] In February 1802, Napoléon's brother-in-law, General Charles Leclerc, landed in Saint-Domingue with approximately 20,000 invading troops. By May, L'Ouverture had surrendered—and was sent to prison in France where he died the next year (Corbett, 1995). This invasion only further ignited the black revolutionaries, now under the leadership of Jean-Jacques Dessalines. By October, Leclerc begged Napoléon for more troops, but he was killed a month later. The black revolutionaries ultimately defeated the French troops, and in January 1804, General Dessalines declared Saint-Domingue the independent country of Haiti—derived from Ayiti from the native Arawak—the first free black republic in the world (Corbett, 1995; Encyclo-pedia Louisiana, 2004; Metz, 2001; Thomson, 2000).

Having realized many months before that the Saint-Domingue effort was a losing cause, Napoléon recognized that the continuing possession of the Louisiana territory represented a drain on France's resources. Instead his attention focused on the looming threat of war with Great Britain (Chandler, 1973). Napoléon then offered to sell the entire territory to the United States, his minister, Talleyrand, asking Jefferson's envoy, Livingston, how much he was willing to pay for the whole territory, not merely New Orleans. On April 30, 1803, France sold the United States the entire Louisiana territory, 828,000 square miles, including all of the present states of Arkansas, Iowa, Kansas, Missouri, Nebraska, and Oklahoma and parts of Colorado, Minnesota, Montana, New Mexico, North Dakota, South Dakota, Texas, and Wyoming, and, of course, Louisiana, the contentious land containing the city of New Orleans, that "single spot on the globe" that was so critical to the market interests of the United States. At the time, the Louisiana territory had 50,000 inhabitants, of whom 28,000 were black slaves (Louisiana State University Libraries, n.d.).

From 1800 to 1810, there was a rush of French and other immigrants, including slave masters and their black slaves, from Saint-Domingue to New Orleans. So many black slaves came to be imported into the Louisiana Territory from other states, the Caribbean, and Af-rica that, by 1810, Louisiana was home to some of the largest sugar plantations and concen-trations of black slaves on the entire continent of North America. Slaves in St. Charles parish comprised 70 percent of the total population in the Louisiana Territory (Louisiana State University Libraries, n.d.). Antebellum Louisiana would come to produce nearly one-half of all sugar consumed in the entire United States. The mass importation, and the subsequent exploitation, of Africans completely transformed the population of southern Louisiana, particularly along the Mississippi River above and below New Orleans (McMillin, 2004).

As the cultivation of sugar in Louisiana had exploded in the wake of the slave rebellion and establishment of Haiti, Anglo-American migrants from other states began flooding the new Louisiana territory with their enslaved blacks to seize the rich opportunities in sugar production (Blitzer & Simmons; 2009; Rothman, 2005). Even though the Louisiana Pur-chase Treaty had indirectly outlawed the *foreign* importation of enslaved blacks into the new territory, U.S. negotiator James Monroe had added language to the final document that allowed for the *domestic* importation of enslaved blacks into the vast territory (Antippas,

2003; Kennedy 2003). This was further clarified by the Governance Act of 1804, which not only divided the territory into upper (northern) and lower (southern) Louisiana, the District of Louisiana and Territory of Orleans respectively, but, while prohibiting *foreign* slave trade in Louisiana, also encouraged the *internal or domestic* slave trade (Avalon Project, 2008). Foreign slave importation continued, with African captives being brought in by smugglers and pirates through Lakes Borgne, Maurepas, and Ponchartrain and all the other inlets of the Gulf Coast (Kendall, 1922). These international slavers and the domestic slave-owners and slave traders from the other states brought what Jefferson described as "their hordes of Negroes" into New Orleans, inaugurating a deluge of slave auctions all over the city (Antippas, 2003; Kennedy, 2003).[4]

A territorial government was established that included only white male landowners with 200 acres of land (Louisiana State University Libraries, n.d.). Now armed with legal guarantees for free laborers, white planters and profiteers flocked to Louisiana's "sugar belt," and advanced a "sugar boom" in New Orleans and along the Mississippi River with a "compelling combination of sugar and slavery." Indeed, as the Louisiana Territory's first governor, Charles Cole Claiborne, had excitedly written President Jefferson in 1806, "The facility with which sugar Planters amass wealth is almost incredible" (Follett, 2007).

This wealth and the inundation of people into the Territory, particularly in and around the city of New Orleans and along the Mississippi, created the conditions for Louisiana's statehood. In anticipation, in 1807, the Territorial Legislature created 19 parishes as subdivisions for local governance. In addition, hordes of former Saint-Domingue planters and their slaves shifted their base of operation from Cuba to New Orleans. Expelled by the Spanish government from Cuba, it is estimated that nearly 10,000 migrated to the region in 1809 alone (Louisiana State Museum, n.d.). By 1810, 76,000 people lived in the Territory of Orleans (soon, the state of Louisiana), of which nearly 35,000 were slaves (Louisiana State University Libraries, n.d.; Rossiter, 1909).

By the end of 1811, Louisiana had attained statehood, with New Orleans as its capital (Encyclopedia Louisiana, 2004; Kastor, 2004; Louisiana State University Libraries, n.d.; Stacey, 2004). The Port of New Orleans exploded with commerce and the domestic slave trade (Clayton, 2002). Soon, New Orleans maintained one of the nation's largest slave markets, where over 100,000 slaves came to be bought and sold during the antebellum period, representing half a billion dollars in "property." By the 1830s, the population of New Orleans had doubled, and the state's slave population had gone from under 70,000 in 1820 to over 100,000 in 1830. Fed by 25 slave warehouses in and around the St. Charles Hotel—considered the first great American hotel and the centerpiece of commerce on St. Charles Street, which was known as the busiest street in America—slave auctions in every possible venue flourished in New Orleans. Indeed, New Orleans would become the South's "largest slave trading center" ("Hotel with a History," 1894; Kendall, 1922). By 1840, the Port of New Orleans was the fourth-largest in the world in volume of business, and New Orleans was the *wealthiest* city in the United States of America (Johnson, 1999; Lewis, 1976; Rossiter, 1909).

The rapid growth of New Orleans, its boundaries coextensive with that of Orleans Parish, sandwiched between Lake Pontchartrain, a salt lake 40 miles wide and 24 miles north to south, necessitated infrastructure improvements and adjustments. In 1838, the New Orleans Canal and Banking Company, capitalized by $14 million in tax dollars, funded the construction of the New Basin Canal, a shipping canal running through swampland to Lake Pontchartrain from the center of business in the booming area around St. Charles Street. This was fostered by Anglo-American businessmen to compete with the Carondolet Canal running from the lake to the downtown Créole sector of the city and to create a separate and independent "American sector" of New Orleans. As the use of slaves to build the canal grew in cost due to their rising purchase price, Irish immigrants were solicited and began arriving into New Orleans in shiploads to support the development. The canal allowed the city to develop "upriver," where affluent whites began settling (McNabb & Madère, 1983).

The fact that the Mississippi River coursed swiftly through the city toward discharge in the Gulf of Mexico compelled the municipal government to urgently address the ever-present threat of its overflow, a flood having overtaken the city in 1828. Under a new "bulwark-building campaign," ordinances regulating the size and maintenance of the levees were instituted. By 1852, the city's engineers had developed a plan to overcome the threat and control the river's flow by driving it down a single channel with large levees on each side, believing the river would naturally crush the earth and deepen the channel. While this policy would remain in place into the 20th century, it soon proved reckless, as the levees were regularly breached ("Storm That Drowned a City," 2005).

New Orleans' city government had become consolidated and wards were delineated by the mid-1850s. The Irish and other poor white immigrants and the small percentage of free blacks, including most Créoles of color, unable to afford to live in the new settlements, cleared swampland and settled in makeshift housing downriver, particularly in the area designated as the Ninth Ward (Buchanan, 2004; Baum, 2006; Landphair, 2007). The majority of blacks were slaves living outside New Orleans on the sugar and cotton plantations they worked; the black "city slaves," who were 16 percent of the population, lived in cabins behind their masters' homes (Blassingame, 1973).

By 1860, there were 331,726 slaves in Louisiana. While many city slaves had become skilled workers, leased out by their owners for hire, as engineers, bricklayers, carpenters, and the like, the majority were field hands on the surrounding cotton and, especially, sugar plantations (Blassingame, 1973). Even as tensions in the country were rising toward war, the profit-incentive of sugar production drove plantation owners to continue sugar production as usual, believing that whites could fight the war while faithful slaves maintained their plantations (Roland, 1997).

The U.S. Census of 1860 reported nearly four million enslaved blacks were in the United States. While most blacks lived in the South, the North was accommodating of slavery because of its economic benefits; New England, for example, shipped cotton to Europe, with cotton representing two-thirds of U.S. exports. At the same time, however, technological advances produced steamboats and the telegraph, and railroad development in the North was transforming and expanding business, leading to economic development and expansion of the nation, from the Atlantic to the Pacific (Haynes, 2006). This Northern modernization and free-labor capitalism was perceived as threatening to the South's "Slave Power," the wealthy planters who dominated the South and the nation, producing most of its presidents, Speakers of the House, and chief justices (McPherson, 2004). For the planters, the building of their wealth was the "driving force" for development of the new territories. As their products represented more than half the nation's exports, their role was foundational in the building of a "national market economy" (Stampp, 1993).

North-South tensions reached a boiling point with passage of the 1854 Kansas-Nebraska Act. Not only did the Kansas-Nebraska Act repeal the 1820 Missouri Compromise, an agreement that had restricted expansion of slavery, it also triggered an onslaught of the Kansas Territory by proponents and opponents of slavery to influence the vote on slavery. Soon, there were numerous outbreaks of mob violence in Kansas (McNamara, n.d.). Ultimately, the U.S. Supreme Court handed down the infamous Dred Scott Decision of 1857, effectively ruling slavery legal *nationally*.

The Republican presidential candidate, Abraham Lincoln, ultimately won the Electoral College vote in November 1860, although his name was not even on the Louisiana ballot. The vehement resistance to Lincoln in the South on account of his opposition to the extension of slavery into the new states was misguided. Lincoln supported aggressive enforcement of the Fugitive Slave Act. Moreover, Lincoln held beliefs about blacks consistent with proponents of slavery (Wills, 2009).[5] Still, as early as Christmas of 1860, only a month after Lincoln's election as president, Louisianians were forming local militias in anticipation of fighting a federal government bent against their interests (Hanger, 1996). South Carolina had voted to secede from the Union on December 20 (Avalon Project, 2008). In January 1861, the slave-holding state of Mississippi, followed by Florida, Alabama, Georgia, and Louisiana seceded. Mississippi's "Declaration of the Immediate Causes which Induce and Justify the Secession of the State of Mississippi from the Federal Union" plainly set forth the collective bases for secession:

> Our position is thoroughly identified with *the institution of slavery—the greatest material interest of the world. Its labor supplies the product which constitutes by far the largest and most important portions of commerce of the earth.* These products are peculiar to the climate verging on the tropical regions, and *by an imperious law of nature, none but the black race can bear exposure* to the tropical sun. These products have become necessities to the world, and *a blow at slavery is a blow at commerce and civilization.* That blow has been long aimed at the institution, and was at the point of reaching its consummation. There was no choice left us but submission to the mandates of abolition, or a dissolution of the Union, whose principles had been subverted to work out our ruin [emphasis added]. (Civil War Homepage, 2009)

In April 1861, New Orleans sugar planter P. G. T. Beauregard, the brigadier general in command of the provisional armed forces of the newly formed Confederate States of America, demanded the federal government quit its garrison at Fort Sumter, South Carolina. Upon the government's refusal, Beauregard ordered his men to open fire, thus commencing the U.S. Civil War, with a Confederate victory (National Park Service, n.d.). Once the Civil War had begun, Virginia, Arkansas, North Carolina, and Tennessee later joined the Confederacy. Then, on January 1, 1863, President Lincoln issued his Emancipation Proclamation as a "necessary war measure for suppressing [the] rebellion," declaring all slaves held in designated rebelling states and parts of states—*excluding* certain parts of Louisiana, including New Orleans—free, but admonishing those declared free "to abstain from all violence, unless in necessary self-defence . . . and labor faithfully for reasonable wages" (Lincoln, 1863). By then, the Confederacy was struggling to survive economically, borrowing $14.5 million from France and printing the rest of the money it needed (Smith, 2002).

Black slaves fled Southern plantations after Lincoln's issuing of the Emancipation Proclamation. By the summer of 1863, New Orleans was occupied by the Union army for over a year. In this particular year, over 10,000 black refugees poured into the city from surrounding plantations, destitute, starving, without clothing, diseased, and most walking the streets aimlessly. Major General Benjamin F. Butler, head of the Union's 12,000-strong Army of the Gulf occupying New Orleans, ordered make-shift shelters be built for the runaway slaves, "contraband" of war, and put hundreds to work to build up levees, widen drainage ditches, and perform other constructions in exchange for food and clothing (Blassingame, 1973; Hollandsworth, 1995).[6]

In the meantime, Lincoln had pressed his colonization idea for blacks. Gathering a delegation of Washington, D.C., black "leaders" to the White House in August 1862, he told them, "but for your race among us there could not be war," and, further, that they owed it to their people to make necessary sacrifices to leave the United States: "I think your race suffer very greatly, many of them by living among us, while ours suffer from your presence." This was an advancement of the plan promulgated by his hero, Henry Clay, a slaveholder, to colonize blacks in either Colombia, Haiti, or Liberia. Denounced by Frederick Douglass, it was rejected by blacks broadly (Jones, 1999).

Lincoln won reelection in November 1964. In January 1865, William Tecumseh Sherman, leading his force of 100,000 in its march from Atlanta to Savannah, issued Field Order No. 15, which ordered 400,000 acres of land along the coast of South Carolina, Georgia, and Florida be confiscated and redistributed to newly freed black families in 40-acre plots. This arose from (1) Sherman's military need to keep his army moving without being responsible to the thousands of blacks following, and (2) the desire to punish Confederate rice planters on the coast. Sherman's punishment of the rice planters emanated from a meeting earlier that month that Sherman and Secretary of War Edwin M. Stanton had with 20 black leaders, mostly Christian ministers, in Savannah regarding emancipation and the practical question of what was to be done with millions of newly-freed blacks.

Congress established the Bureau of Refugees, Freedmen, and Abandoned Lands, the "Freedmen's Bureau," in March 1865 to manage distribution of the 40-acre plots. Immediately, around 40,000 blacks in the Sea Islands were able to settle on their plots. In that same month, Sherman moved into North Carolina, just as Union forces under Grant entered Richmond. On April 7, Grant surrounded Robert E. Lee's forces and demanded surrender. Two days later, a truce was called. Less than a week later, Lincoln was assassinated.

Of the nearly 200,000 black troops who had served in the Union army and navy, about 24,000 were from Louisiana (Hanger, 1996). By the end of the war, the number of blacks in New Orleans had doubled since 1860, and the number of whites had decreased (Hanger, 1996). The New Orleans Freedmen's Aid Association had been formed among well-to-do blacks and some whites, and was attempting to assist freedmen by buying abandoned plantations to lease to freedmen. By August of 1865, it had rented a few plantations, made loans to freedmen, and furnished them horses and seeds and provisions to work the land. But, the postbellum immediate return of plantations to their "owners" thwarted and soon ended this effort (Blassingame, 1973). Moreover, the new president, Andrew Johnson, effectively revoked Field Order No. 15, as it applied to coastal South Carolina, Georgia, and Florida, by the fall of 1865, requiring the *return* of confiscated lands to former Confederate owners.[7]

Furthermore, early in the 1866 Congressional session, Andrew Johnson vetoed a bill to maintain the Freedmen's Bureau and guarantee freedmen civil rights, deriding the Bureau as an entity of "immense patronage," noting that no such law existed to provide land, schools or economic relief to his "own people" (Foner, 1988). After signing the Thirteenth Amendment to the Constitution, abolishing slavery, Johnson wanted to readmit the Confederate states, which he considered a "restoration" (Foner, 1988; Foner & Mahoney, 2003). Even though his veto was overruled, the Bureau had little funding and the question of black civil rights would go wanting for decades. Immediately thereafter, planters throughout New Orleans boldly organized to bar blacks from renting, much less buying land (Blassingame, 1973).

Louisiana's blacks resourcefully organized to obtain plots of land after the war. Antebellum free blacks in New Orleans already owned some property, much in the center of the city, some inherited from white fathers. Freedmen and their families crowded into center city districts, many in tenements near the river (Blassingame, 1973). The number of "indigent and destitute freedmen" in New Orleans rose, according to Freedmen's Bureau records, as did the number of "murders and outrages" committed against Freedmen (Blassingame, 1973; Freedmen's Bureau Online, n.d.).[8] Most of the black families lived in the districts de-

Table 23.1.   Population of New Orleans, 1870–1880

District	1870 White	1870 Negro	1875 White	1875 Negro	1880 White	1880 Negro
1	42,565	13,991	39,939	12,464	43,282	14,126
2	29,475	13,158	27,278	12,087	31,241	13,301
3	29,270	11,466	30,984	15,214	33,727	11,856
4	28,101	5,737	29,684	6,213	30,592	6,910
5	3,802	3,017	4,531	4,604	5,020	3,835
6	7,710	3,126	10,570	4,471	11,954	4,078
7	—	—	2,806	2,594	3,043	3,125
Total	140,923	50,495	145,792	57,647	158,859	57,647

Source: Adapted from John Blassingame (1973), *Black New Orleans*. Original data source is the Louisiana Board of Health, Annual Report, 1883.

lineated as Health Districts 1, 2, 3, and 4, the oldest, most dense sections of New Orleans, where there were large tenements, boarding houses and hotels. From the end of the Civil War up to 1880, these areas witnessed a drastic increase in the percentage of black people, many of them migrating from the rural plantations outside the city. In the central city, there was a large transient population of sailors and fishermen, steamboat men, and immigrants. Black families and transients alike had to move away when the Mississippi overflowed. The First and Second Health Districts would suffer disastrous overflows in 1870 and 1875, disproportionately forcing black people to move to other areas, but often returning once the overflow had subsided (see Table 23.1).

The opportunities for blacks to find employment and housing were severely restricted by Louisiana's Black Codes after the Civil War. While federal troops, along with passage of the Fourteenth and Fifteen Amendments to the Constitution, would act as mitigating factors, waves of white terrorist organizations carried out vicious attacks against blacks. In 1868, the Knights of the White Camelia formed in Louisiana; this group was succeeded by the White League (Hanger, 1996). Blacks organized to defend themselves, however, as indicated in an 1865 editorial in the first black daily newspaper in the country, the *New Orleans Tribune*:

> All over the state, the Freedmen are threatened in their lives, robbed of their liberties and deprived of the fruits of their toils and labor. . . . [A] system of terror has been inaugurated, to keep down the Freedmen; several have already been murdered and many more will be if we do not resist. The right of self-defense is a sacred right. . . . [A] few cases of self-defense followed by the punishment of the would-be murderers, would be sufficient to plunge into a solitary terror the slavocrats of the parishes. (C. Wilson, n.d.)

These waves of violence were also sanctioned by the passage of local vagrancy laws. And, pursuant to a compromise in the disputed 1876 presidential election of Rutherford B. Hayes, the remaining federal troops were withdrawn from the last two states in the South in 1877, South Carolina and Louisiana. In the Hayes-Tilden Compromise of 1877, Rutherford B. Hayes gave his endorsement in the disputed state gubernatorial election to former Confederate General Francis R. T. Nicholls; white supremacy was restored in Louisiana. The federal government then abandoned enforcement of the Fourteenth and Fifteenth Amendments to the Constitution and postbellum civil rights legislation (R. Davis, n.d.).

Louisiana, like every other former Confederate state, enacted "convict leasing" laws. By 1880, there were over 57,000 blacks in New Orleans and nearly 159,000 whites. Although many black men were skilled workers, including steamboat men, draymen, and carpenters, they were denied employment in their fields, and entrance into newly-formed, all-white labor unions, such as longshoremen and stevedore unions (Blassingame, 1973; R. Davis, n.d.). Unemployed black men in New Orleans, and sometimes women, arrested for "vagrancy," were entered into convict leasing arrangements, as the only way to avoid the brutality of the notorious prison chain gang. Under this arrangement, prisoners, 90 percent of whom were black, convicted of vagrancy or, perhaps, property crimes, were leased out by the city to work for planters, mines, lumber yards, railroads, and levee contractors, for free. Moreover, since the end of the Civil War, blacks had been subject to "debt peonage" and "crop lien" laws, binding black tenant farmers, sharecroppers, to white landowners to pay off debt incurred by the imposition of exorbitant charges for supplies, materials, and rent (Blassingame, 1973).

Black men faced great challenges in gaining employment, and most could not earn enough to bring their families above a subsistence level of living. Most black families in New Orleans were poor. On the other hand, despite overwhelming poverty, black families in 1880 were stable, records indicating few divorces and very few unwed mothers. Of the nearly 13,000 black families in New Orleans at the time, 78 percent were headed by males. The average black family size, though, was only 3.79 persons, due to the low birth and high infant mortality rates associated with poverty and prenatal care. However, the number of people living in the average black household was large, including extended and nonfamily members because of the high degree of transient males (Blassingame, 1973).

Nevertheless, these oppressive conditions were only exacerbated when, in addition to the series of laws denying blacks the right to *register* to vote, the last black elected to the legislature having been elected in 1876, black civil rights were all but completely abridged in 1883. In 1883, the U.S. Supreme Court ruled unconstitutional the Civil Rights Act of 1875, whereunder blacks were entitled to "full and equal enjoyment of [public] accommodations." Chief Justice Joseph Bradley wrote that the rights of the five plaintiffs, whose consolidated cases were before the court (*The Civil Rights Cases*, 1883), to "equal protection" under the Fourteenth Amendment had *not* been violated when they had been denied access to theaters, hotels, and public transportation, as the Amendment did not apply to "private businesses and individuals," but only to states. Louisiana passed a law in 1890, Act 111— known as the Separate Car Act—requiring blacks to sit in separate railroad cars from whites (Medley, 2003).

New Orleans would soon give full definition to what the great scholar W. E. B. DuBois asserted, that "the problem of the Twentieth Century is the problem of the color line" (DuBois, 1903/1994). To challenge the 1890 Separate Car Act, blacks formed an association and raised money to pay the famous white author and lawyer Albion Tourgée to be counsel for their court challenge; Tourgée refused to be paid for his legal services. Composed of prominent New Orleans blacks, including former lieutenant governor of Louisiana P. B. S. Pinchback, the Comité des Citoyens (Citizens' Committee) recruited Homer Plessy to conduct the test. Plessy was so light-skinned, deemed at the time an "octoroon," or a person with "one-eighth black blood," he could easily have passed for white. He was to board a segregated train, sit in the white section, identify himself as having a black ancestor, and get arrested. The Committee then hired a detective to board the train, to make sure he was arrested. On June 7, 1892, Plessy boarded an East Louisiana Railroad car in New Orleans, headed to Covington, Louisiana, took his seat in the whites-only section and advised the conductor he was "colored." When he refused to leave the white car as ordered, Plessy was arrested and jailed.

Homer Plessy declared that he had been denied his rights by the Railroad under the Thirteenth and Fourteenth Amendments, in the historic *Homer Adolph Plessy v. The State of Loui-*

siana court case. Judge Howard Ferguson rejected Plessy's claim, stating Louisiana had the right to regulate railroads operating within the state. The Louisiana Supreme Court upheld Ferguson. The appeal to the Supreme Court in *Plessy v. Ferguson* (1896) resulted in a ruling against Plessy, a ruling that would adversely affect the lives of blacks in America into the middle of the 20th century. Tourgée and his co-counsel, James C. Walker, argued not only that Plessy's constitutional rights had been violated but also that if Plessy looked white, he was entitled to the privileges enjoyed by whites (Medley, 2003). The ramifications of *Plessy*, the "color line," would indeed become the problem of the 20th century, as DuBois asserted. It would also represent what historians consider the "nadir of American race relations" for decades to come (Logan, 1997). After the ruling, the Comité des Citoyens declared: "We, as freemen, still believe that we were right and that our cause is sacred."

THE CIVIC DESIGN AROUND JIM CROW PRACTICES AND POLICIES THAT CREATED SEGREGATED HOUSING AND SCHOOLING IN 20TH-CENTURY NEW ORLEANS

In the midst of social, political, and legal restrictions such as *Plessy* and *Jim Crow*, black people still managed to acquire land and build homes, thereby laying the foundation for some of the historical black neighborhoods in New Orleans. One such community was Fazendeville, which was eventually razed during the middle of the twentieth century in the name of "civic progress." Founded during the Reconstruction Era in 1867, Fazendeville was a black community that was named for a freedman of color and a grocer who sold parcels of land that he inherited to newly emancipated blacks after the Civil War. To provide additional land for the National Historical Park to commemorate the Battle of New Orleans of 1815, city officials destroyed the Fazendeville Community in 1964 and displaced its black residents, most of whom were moved to the Lower Ninth Ward in New Orleans. A little more than four decades after their displacement from Fazendeville, Hurricane Katrina would continue the displacement of the Fazendeville residents living in the Lower Ninth Ward (Jackson, 2006).

Most of New Orleans' black population did not live in established neighborhoods such as Fazendeville, or Faubourg Tremé, one of the city's oldest black neighborhoods and where many of the free people of color lived. Instead, many of the poor black people lived in dilapidated and make-shift housing. For example, the infamous Story district of New Orleans, an area well known as a red-light district in the city from 1897–1917, had become a predominantly black and poor area by the 1930s and 1940s; many of its buildings were run-down. As a result of the U.S. Housing Act of 1937, a federal effort to rectify slum housing with the intentions of improving housing for poor and working-class families, the city of New Orleans declared 95 percent of the structures in the Story district as substandard, thereby clearing the way for a public housing project for whites in the 1940s, the Iberville Projects. In creating its first housing projects, city leaders in New Orleans were all the while reinforcing racial segregation; the city eventually created seven housing projects for blacks and three projects for whites (Mahoney, 1985). Iberville ultimately would house an overwhelming black and poor population at the time Katrina struck (Long, 2007).

The *Plessy* decision and Jim Crow practices and policies continued to shape not only the housing conditions of black people, but also the civic design of black schooling during the 19th and 20th centuries. For the vast majority of black people in New Orleans, schooling was prohibited up to the emancipation of slavery, although some free blacks in New Orleans established schools to educate their children (Hanger, 1996). Throughout the South, from the issuing of the Emancipation Proclamation up to the passage of the historic *Brown v. Board of Education* (1954) court decision, the schooling opportunities for black people were legally segregated (de jure) and inherently unequal (*Brown v. Board*, 1954; Morris & Monroe, 2009). Public school desegregation was not implemented in New Orleans until 1960, six years after *Brown*. And the manner in which this historic court case was implemented spoke volumes about civic leaders' willingness to ignore the judicial intent of supporting educational opportunity for blacks in order to align with the interests of whites, for example, subjecting black students who wanted to attend the all-white schools to admission tests and not admitting black male students at all. One of the most famous efforts to desegregate public schools was Ruby Bridges, a 6-year-old black female student who desegregated William Frantz Elementary School in New Orleans; a school located in the Ninth Ward section of the city. After carefully being selected as one of six black female students to attend all-white schools in the city (four went on to attend the white schools and two remained in their black school), Ruby Bridges faced taunts from white mobs while attending the elementary school. White families pulled their children out of these schools after the four black girls enrolled. Although the other three students attended one all-white school together, Ruby was the only one to attend William Frantz and was the only child physically located in her classroom because of whites' resistance to educating their children with black students (Rasheed, 2006).

As the school system's black student enrollment began to increase during the late 1960s, blacks outnumbering whites by 2 to 1, white families left the city for surrounding St. Bernard and Jefferson parishes or enrolled their children into private schools (Lavelle & Feagin, 2006; Lewis, 2003). Economic constraints and racial discrimination by white realtors prevented black people from moving into these predominantly white parishes (Lewis, 2003). By 1960, the New Orleans public school system had become predominantly black.

As was the case throughout the United States, the civil rights activism of the 1960s brought about a greater awareness of the inequalities, deprivation, and exclusion that black people experienced in New Orleans. Pressured by African American civil rights organizations such as SCLC, CORE, the NAACP, and SNCC, major legislation was passed to protect black people's rights in employment and public accommodations (Civil Rights Act of 1964), voting (Voting Rights Act of 1965), and the sale and rental of housing (Civil Rights Act of 1968). In essence, this civil rights legislation restored basic civil rights for black people in the United States, which had come to an abrupt stop with the ending of Reconstruction in 1876.

A sense of fervor swept urban areas as the Civil Rights Movement and the Black Freedom movement (which involved leaders at national and local levels) pressed for greater black representation in local, state, and federal government, as well as economic and community control. In New Orleans, a number of neighborhood-based political organizations emerged and were able to use the resources from the War on Poverty programs to effect change at the local level (Germany, 2007). The Ninth Ward's Southern Organization for Unified Leadership (SOUL), the Seventh Ward's Community Organization for Urban Politics (COUP), and Central City's Black Organization for Leadership Development (BOLD), were instrumental in effecting the outcomes of local and statewide elections, as well as ensuring that the War on Poverty's resources targeted black neighborhoods. Introduced by President Lyndon B. Johnson in 1965, the War on Poverty programs included initiatives such as Head Start and Job Corps and expanded the government's role in social welfare programs from education to health care. New Orleans, unlike many other urban areas such as Detroit and Newark, did not experience the race riots as a result of black discontent; black organizations and leaders in New Orleans were instrumental in promoting a sense of progress.

New Orleans' economic structure was hampered by the failure of the oil market during the 1980s, and New Orleans, like other major cities, was impacted by President Ronald

Reagan's decision to cut federal support to cities by 50 percent and other social welfare programs by 80 percent. Moreover, public support for these programs waned, particularly during the economic hard times of the late 1970s—many feeling that black people were the primary beneficiaries. New Orleans, a city that was then predominantly black with a significant percentage of its residents living at or below the poverty level, was extremely vulnerable to these shifts in priorities by the federal government. Furthermore, while a succession of black mayors from 1976 to 2009 may have represented black political progress, New Orleans' infrastructure further suffered from the lack of economic support.[9] As a result of white flight, the tax base of the city eroded while corporate support in the downtown area dwindled, resulting in major losses of revenue for the city. The white business elite's withdrawal of support from urban areas, especially when these cities became predominantly black and began to elect black mayors, superintendents, and predominantly black school boards (Henig, Hula, Orr, & Pedescleaux, 1999), and the decline in jobs for low-skilled black workers (Royster, 2003; Wilson, 1996), would exacerbate the social and economic conditions of the urban poor, and their children. Consequently, African American education leaders throughout urban areas like New Orleans inherited myriad social and financial concerns (Morris, 2009).

Rather than continuing to address the plight of the poor, New Orleans, like other cities, basically abandoned the push to effect change for the poor. In essence, civic efforts, now with black political leaders at the helm, merely focused on containing poverty rather than eliminating it. Civic leaders were further handicapped by the federal government's abandonment of urban areas and programs targeting the poor. Political and economic leaders in New Orleans and the rest of the United States had made "peace with poverty" (Germany, 2007). Katrina would bring the poor in New Orleans back into the national spotlight.

In August 2005, New Orleans' public school system was overwhelmingly black, low-income, and de facto segregated, segregated based on housing patterns and school attendance zones. At the dawn of the 21st century, New Orleans' public schools comprised more than 62,000 students; of this number, black students made up more than 90 percent of the children. And, more than three-fourths of these children received free and reduced lunch. According to the 2004 U.S. Census, while the overall poverty rate in the United States was 12.7 percent, 38.1 percent of New Orleans children lived below the poverty level (U.S. Census, 2004). Furthermore, the black infant mortality rate in New Orleans was 10.4 per 1,000 live births, in comparison to a white infant mortality rate in the city of 6.4 per 1,000 live births (Fass & Cauthen, 2005). Education, housing, and health factors at the time of Katrina reflected the harsh historical realities of New Orleans' political economy.

CIVIC DISASTER BY DESIGN? NEW ORLEANS' FLAWED HURRICANE PROTECTION SYSTEM

When Katrina hit New Orleans, catastrophic flooding of the city was the result of breaches in the levee system, and not solely because of the flooding from the storm. Nowhere was the flooding and devastation greater than in the Lower Ninth. Ironically, the Lower Ninth is not as low-lying as neighboring St. Bernard Parish, which sat four or more feet below sea level, compared to one and a half feet for the Lower Ninth. The Lower Ninth was doomed by its position near the junction of the Industrial Canal and the Mississippi River Gulf Outlet. Water flowed in from St. Bernard and also from two main breaches along Industrial Canal, and inundated Claiborne and Florida Avenues, thereby, emptying water directly into Lower Ninth neighborhoods (American Society of Civil Engineers, 2007). Many of the residents, particularly those who had no car or money to leave, drowned, or were stranded for days on rooftops.

In New Orleans, and now outside the city, many of these former Lower Ninth residents are still struggling to recover from the storm's onslaught (Morris, 2008). In 2006, the Center for Social Inclusion (2006) released a report card that illustrates the challenges that New Orleans' residents faced in rebuilding. The report card includes New Orleans' 13 planning districts. As the report highlights, many of the districts that had significant populations of low-income and persons of color were experiencing the greatest difficulty. While wealthier districts also struggled, these areas also have greater capacity to rebuild because their pre-Katrina conditions were not as deleterious as the low-income areas. For instance, after three years since Katrina, the Lower Ninth Ward received a C+ in terms of basic utilities being restored, whereas every other area received an A (Center for Social Inclusion, 2006).

An external review by the American Society of Civil Engineers (ASCE) (2007), details how the flawed engineering design, which resulted from decades of neglect and political leaders' lack of support for a comprehensive and scientifically sound hurricane protection system, devastated New Orleans in general, and the Ninth Ward in particular. According to ASCE's external review, design flaws in the engineering of the levees failed to account for factors such as the eroding of soil and levees, as well as the subsiding (the sinking of New Orleans) over time. The Industrial Canal structures were over 35 years old and had lost their capacity to protect due to the subsiding over the years, which caused the structures to be more than two feet below their intended design elevations. There were ruptures in approximately 50 locations in the levee system; 169 miles of the 284 miles of federal levees and floodwalls were damaged. The Lake Ponchartrain and Vicinity Hurricane Project experienced the most damage and resulted in the most serious consequences to New Orleans and its people.

The New Orleans Hurricane Protection System was really a disjointed agglomeration fashioned together in a make-do manner, rather than a comprehensive, well-budgeted, maintained, constructed, and operating system. The levees were funded on a project-by-project basis over many years, resulting in some parts of the levee system being better built than others. Moreover, the federal government, the state of Louisiana, and the city of New Orleans lacked an interagency and intergovernmental unit that would assume ultimate responsibility in handling the possibility of a hurricane. The scientists from the ASCE report concluded that had the levees been sound and the pumping stations working properly, then approximately two-thirds of the deaths could have been avoided, and half of the property losses would not have occurred.

THE CONTEMPORARY CIVIC DESIGN TO RAZE AND REINVENT POOR AND BLACK COMMUNITIES AND SCHOOLS

As a result of the devastation from Hurricane Katrina, at least 700,000 people along the Gulf Coast lost their homes, and a significant number of these people (approximately 300,000) were low-income according to federal poverty standards. A September 2005 analysis by the National Low Income Housing Coalition (2005) revealed that New Orleans accounted for about 47 percent (142,130) of the total housing units lost. Further analysis reveals that a majority of these lost or damaged units in New Orleans were rental units (55 percent). Whereas Hurricane Katrina was a naturally occurring storm, the breaking of the levees and the government's response to those who were displaced signaled the *second storm* (Morris, 2008).

After Katrina and the subsequent breaking of the levees, approximately 35 percent of the buildings in the public school system suffered significant damage. Other school buildings were operable but were not used. Nevertheless, the city and state delayed the reopening of the schools for months. Consequently, the United Teachers of New Orleans (UTNO)—a teachers' union that was eventually rendered voiceless—filed a lawsuit demanding the reopening of the schools, which, they argued, was essential to displaced residents' return to the city (Goodman & Gonzalez, 2006). In January 2006, decisions were made to terminate 4,000 teachers and 3,500 employees of the New Orleans public school system. The teachers' union, UTNO, no longer would have collective bargaining rights. Representatives of UTNO accused the city and state of delaying the opening of the schools so that private ventures such as organizations providing charter school services could eventually move in to take over some of the schools. The state took control of all but 15 of the 117 schools (Saltman, 2007). Several schools applied for charter school status and opened in early 2006. New Orleans now has the highest percent of public school students in the United States enrolled in charter schools.

Critics have raised deep concerns about the takeover of New Orleans' public schools and the largely charter school operation in the city (Lipman & Haines, 2007; Saltman, 2007), particularly after Katrina disrupted the educational system. Naomi Klein (2007) describes such actions as an example of *Shock Doctrine*, the tactic of taking advantage of a crisis or disaster in order to effect a radical change in public policy. While they are being embraced by the Obama administration because of their ability to provide educational options for low-income and minority children, the proliferation of charter schools in New Orleans and elsewhere may prove paradoxical for residents of low-income and minority communities, and contradictory to the development of a school as a communal institution that serves the nearby neighborhood and its students (Morris, 2009). Moreover, charter schools are increasingly being used as gentrifying tools in urban and low-income areas, resulting in the closing of local schools that may have had strong ties to the nearby communities and families (Morris, 2010). However, the positive and negative influences of this strategy in New Orleans have not been fully examined by empirical projects where education and other social outcomes are central to the investigation.

Katrina provided a new pathway for economic planning in New Orleans not seen since the antebellum period, as support for creative industries and tourism, rejuvenation of maritime industry, and residency of a better-educated, wealthier population were perceived as feasible regional goals. New Orleans' real estate investor James J. Reiss, a member of Mayor Ray Nagin's administration at the time and chair of the Regional Transit Authority, stated that Katrina had provided an opportunity to build a new city, "with better services and fewer poor people" (Cooper, 2005). More pointedly, Nagin financial backer and civic leader Joseph Canizaro, a property developer and former president of the powerful Urban Land Institute, declared that the post-Katrina civic design had to incorporate the "practical matter" that "poor folks don't have the resources to go back to our city. . . . So we won't get all those folks back. That's just a fact" (M. Davis, 2006).

Taking advantage of the human and material devastation caused by Hurricane Katrina, a concerted effort by government and the private economic sectors has focused on "rebuilding" New Orleans' public schools and housing communities in radically different ways from that which existed before the storm (Crowley, 2006; Gunewardena & Schuller, 2008; Saltman, 2007; Schuller, 2008). Once the cleanup from Katrina began, rebuilding efforts by conservatives and neoliberals reflected a more intense push for privately managed ventures such as charter schools, and the replacement of the city's public housing with so-called "mixed-income" communities. For many of the proponents of these new reforms, Hurricane

Katrina was the perfect storm because it fueled the "natural" dispersion of thousands of the city's low-income (and overwhelmingly black) residents without any individual directly to blame. According to these reformers, the devastation and displacement caused by Katrina eliminated the inertia around urban educational reform because it allowed the city to start anew. This sentiment was expressed by President Barack Obama's appointee for Secretary of Education, Arne Duncan:

> I've spent a lot of time in New Orleans and this is a tough thing to say but I'm going to be really honest. The best thing that happened to the education system in New Orleans was Hurricane Katrina. That education system was a disaster. And it took Hurricane Katrina to wake up the community to say that we have to do better. And the progress that they've made in four years since the hurricane is unbelievable. They have a chance to create a phenomenal school district. Long way to go, but that—that city was not serious about its education. Those children were being desperately underserved prior, and the amount of progress and the amount of reform we've seen in a short amount of time has been absolutely amazing. (News One, 2010)

Some interpreted Duncan's comments as callous and insensitive, which implied that poor black people in that city had to experience a catastrophic situation in order to pave the way for educational reform and rebuilding. Others, such as Paul G. Vallas, the former superintendent of the Recovery School District in New Orleans and the former superintendent in Chicago's public school and Duncan's former boss, stated that he had no problem with Duncan's comments about the impact of Hurricane Katrina on education reform in the city (Zehr, 2010). Secretary of Education Duncan, shortly afterward, apologized for his remarks: "It was a dumb thing to say. . . . [M]y point was a simple one, that despite a devastating, devastating tragedy, [I've observed] phenomenal progress in a short amount of time" (Zehr, 2010). However he meant it, Duncan, as do so many others, often discusses the contemporary social, economic, and educational conditions *devoid* of a thorough sociohistorical understanding of black and poor people's experiences in New Orleans—particularly its public housing communities and schools and how they came to be so segregated and so unequal for its majority poor black student population.[10]

New Orleans' public housing residents were already being displaced to other areas of the city years before Hurricane Katrina touched land; Katrina merely escalated the displacement and provided further rationale for using now coveted urban spaces for means besides housing the poor. As a result of HOPE VI—a housing program developed during the Clinton administration that favored mixed-income development—almost 7,000 public housing residents were moved out of New Orleans' public housing units between 1996 and 2005 (Goodman, Smith, Gonzalez, & Wright, 2005).[11] One particular public housing project was St. Thomas, which was located on prime real estate. St. Thomas would eventually be demolished as a result of HOPE VI in order to make room for a new mixed-income neighborhood, named River Garden. In this particular case, the Housing Authority of New Orleans received a HUD HOPE VI grant to relocate the nearly 3,000 residents to other parts of the city. The mixed income area would eventually feature a Wal-Mart superstore as well as condominiums. The fate of the black poor in housing projects such as St. Thomas paralleled black people's displacement from public housing communities in other cities throughout the United States such as Birmingham's Metropolitan Gardens (renamed Park Place) (Connerly, 2005), Atlanta's Techwood Homes (renamed Olympic Village) (Keating, 2001), and various communities in Chicago (Lipman, 2008; Lipman & Haines, 2007). Very few of the former residents would be re-housed in the renovated and mixed-income neighborhoods, and the local predominantly black schools would be closed or transformed into theme or magnet schools.

After Katrina hit and residents were eventually evacuated, the New Orleans Public Housing Authority closed all of the city's public housing; armed guards prevented anyone from attempting to return to collect personal belongings. Government agencies employed the notion of a "natural catastrophe" to rationalize the removal of poor blacks from prime real estate such as the St. Bernard Housing Projects in New Orleans (not to be confused with St. Bernard Parish) even though this area did not endure the same damage levels as seen in the Lower Ninth Ward (Saltman, 2007). Not only did the residents from New Orleans' public housing (almost 100 percent African American) face the abrupt loss of their communities, they were also maligned by white and black elected and public officials at the state and local levels. Amid the most devastating catastrophe in the United States, this low regard for public housing residents was exemplified by Representative Richard Baker's (R-LA) comments regarding "God's removal" of black poor people from public housing. In describing the rebuilding effort and the future demographic landscape of New Orleans, Oliver Thomas, who is an African American and the president of the New Orleans City Council, stated, "We don't need soap opera watchers right now. . . . We're going to target those who are going to work. It's not that I'm fed up, but that at some point there has to be a whole new level of motivation, and people have got to stop blaming the government for something they ought to do" (Berger, 2006).[12]

Once the black residents were locked out of public housing, HUD demolished several thousand public housing units after the storm. On June 14, 2006, HUD announced a plan to demolish more than 5,000 public housing units. HUD eventually would replace these units with a much smaller number of mixed-income units. According to Judith Browne-Dianis, the co-coordinator of the Advancement Project—a national civil rights group that serves as the acting counsel to New Orleans' public housing residents—the egregious part of this plan is that it was financed by money and tax breaks that were originally meant for those who qualified for hurricane relief money: "What this all means is that HUD plans to spend hundreds of millions of Katrina assistance funds to create far fewer affordable homes" (Dymi, 2007). For example, HUD Secretary Alphonso Jackson, as reported in the *Houston Chronicle*, said, "Whether we like it or not, New Orleans is not going to be 500,000 people for a long time . . . . New Orleans is not going to be as black as it was for a long time, if ever again" (Rodriguez & Minaya, 2005).[13] Contrary to the assertion that God had something to do with it, black and white key officials at every level of government consciously made decisions to disperse the poor from coveted urban areas of the city. Through force or through policies, poor black people continue to be disproportionately dispersed, all in the name of restoring the downtown areas and luring middle-class residents and tourists into the city.

DISCUSSION: TOWARD CIVIC RESPONSIBILITY, ACCOUNTABILITY, AND SCHOLARSHIP

A critical analysis of educational and housing policy in urban schools and communities, within and beyond New Orleans, is imperative in the larger quest to build civic capacity and encourage civic responsibility and accountability. Shortly before Katrina struck, there were some serious issues in terms of poverty and crime throughout the city, as well as corruption and mismanagement in New Orleans' city government, public housing, and schools. Too often, however, the framing of New Orleans' public housing and schooling conditions in the contemporary context has been devoid of a sociohistorical framework and analysis. Such an omission ignores the significance of race and place in shaping the opportunities and outcomes for black people across a range of areas (Morris & Monroe, 2009). The onslaught of

Katrina merely *unveiled* the historical and political forces that gave rise to the contemporary social, economic, educational, and housing conditions that were facing many of the city's black residents.

In my opinion, urban planning in New Orleans and related efforts to generate civic capacity must be inclusive of all of the members of the community, whether rich or poor, black or white, in deciding the future of a city, its communities, and its schools. This is particularly important given black people's deep sacrifice and contributions to New Orleans' existence. The exploited slave labor of black people contributed substantially to New Orleans' growth and culture during the 18th, 19th, and 20th centuries. African captives built levees, dug drainage ditches, and cleared forests. If it had not been for the institution of slavery, "New Orleans would not exist, since only force could keep these workers at their labor, while European contract farmers and workers arriving in the city moved on to more hospitable territory further inland" (Campanella, 2006; Fussell, 2007; Usner, 1979). Scholarly and policy conversations on fostering civic capacity and civic responsibility must *look back in order to move forward*, and interrogate the confluence of historical and contemporary forces that resulted in urban areas becoming overwhelmingly black and poor, and simultaneously, question how governmental actions and policies, *and not* God or Nature, are leading to the banishment of the black poor from cities across the United States.

The mass dispersion of black people has been ongoing, beginning when countless enslaved Africans were forcibly uprooted from their homes and placed in the holds of slave ships that set sail for the Americas. This dispersion continued with the internal slave trade throughout the United States, and persisted *after* Hurricane Katrina battered the Gulf Coast of the United States in late August 2005 (Morris, 2008). The hand of man (i.e., economic leaders and federal, state, and local government officials), rather than God or Nature, as some have suggested, was the culprit that caused the dispersion of poor black people in New Orleans. But this ongoing mass dispersion is not limited to New Orleans. New Orleans and Hurricane Katrina merely serve as metaphors for critiquing the ongoing mass dispersion of poor people in other parts of the United States. As Marc Morial, a former mayor of New Orleans whose father was the first African American mayor of the city, noted, "Many of the problems people see are not peculiar to New Orleans. There is a Ninth Ward in every major American city. And with joblessness and the economy, we are seeing a Katrina like impact beyond New Orleans" (Morial, 2009).

NOTES

1. Named after President Washington's negotiator, Thomas Pinckney, Pinckney's Treaty was officially called the Treaty of San Lorenzo, or the "Treaty of Friendship, Limits, and Navigation Between Spain and the United States."

2. See Schomburg Center for Research in Black Culture, New York Public Library (n.d.).

3. In an 1802 letter to Livingston, Jefferson pointed out the urgency of the prospective sale: "The cession of Louisiana and the Floridas by Spain to France works most sorely on the U.S. . . . There is on the globe one single spot, the possessor of which is our natural and habitual enemy. It is New Orleans, through which the produce of three-eighths of our territory must pass to market."

4. Moreover, to guarantee the interests of plantation owners and profiteers, Black Codes were passed in both the District of Louisiana and Territory of Orleans regulating the enslavement and behavior of blacks, including "free" blacks, outlining a series of harsh punishments for Code violations, including death, under which the only "right" of black slaves arose under the authority of their slave owners (Encyclopedia of Arkansas History & Culture, n.d.; Encyclopedia Louisiana, 2004; Shambaugh, 1913).

5. In his famous debates with Stephen Douglas during their contest for U.S. Senator from Illinois only a few years prior, he had made that clear: "I will say then that I am not nor ever have been in favor of bringing about in any way the social and political equity of the white and black races. . . . I as much as any other man am in favor of having the superior position assigned to the white race." He consistently argued that slavery violated the interests

of white workers, such that, even after his death, the great black abolitionist Frederick Douglass could say, "[Lincoln] was preeminently the white man's President, entirely devoted to the welfare of white men. . . . He came into the Presidential chair upon one principle alone, namely, opposition to the extension of slavery. His arguments in furtherance of this policy had their motive and mainspring in his patriotic devotion to the interests of his own race" (Lincoln, 1858; Wills, 2009).

6. Despite Lincoln's refusal to allow blacks into the Union army, Butler organized a 1,000-man black fighting force into the First Louisiana Native Guard, both free men of color and runaway slaves. It was the first black regiment in the Union Army. By November 1862, so many runaway slaves wanted to enlist that Second and Third Native Guard regiments were formed.

7. General Orders 145, October 9, 1865. See http://www.presidency.ucsb.edu/ws/?pid=72345

8. At the same time, there was a surge in the number of black marriages, despite the dearth of black men, who had a high death rate and the burden of former slave women who had been subjected to brutal rapes. While some former slaves searched far and wide for former mates, a large percentage settled into the patriarchal marriage tradition of whites, a marriage license having come to be an important "badge of freedom," marking the end of the white man's control of the black man's family (Blassingame, 1973).

9. On February 6, 2010, New Orleans elected Mitch Landrieu, its first white mayor in more than three decades. Mitch's father, Moon Landrieu, was the last elected white mayor when his term ended in 1978.

10. The devastating earthquake that shook Haiti on January 12, 2010, and killed more than 200,000 people elicited similar comments, particularly the notion that the earthquake may be good in terms of bringing about policies and proposals that would reform Haiti's society for the better. However, these proposals ignore the history of Haiti and those external forces that contributed to the impoverished conditions in the country.

11. For a detailed discussion of Hope VI, please see the document, False Hope: A Critical Assessment of the HOPE VI Public Housing Redevelopment Program, prepared by the National Housing Law Project in June 2002. This document can be accessed at http://www.nhlp.org/html/pubhsg/FalseHOPE.pdf

12. Rebuked by the *Houston Chronicle* for his uncompassionate attitude toward New Orleans' poor, Thomas later plead guilty to taking $20,000 in bribes and kickbacks from a businessman who wanted to retain a public parking garage contract. He began serving a three-year prison sentence in January 2008.

13. Alphonso Jackson later came under fire for providing contracts based on politics. He eventually resigned.

REFERENCES

Africans in America. (1998). Resource bank: The Compromise of 1850 and the Fugitive Slave Act. Retrieved from www.pbs.org/wgbh/aia/part4/4p2951.html

American Society of Civil Engineers. (2007). *The New Orleans hurricane protection system: What went wrong and why*. A report by the American Society of Civil Engineers Hurricane Katrina External Review Panel. Reston, VA: American Society of Civil Engineers.

Antippas, A. (2003). *A history of the Louisiana Purchase*. Retrieved November 12, 2009, from www.barristersgallery.com

Avalon Project. (2008). Confederate States of America—Declaration of the immediate causes which induce and justify the secession of South Carolina from the federal Union. Retrieved from http://avalon.law.yale.edu/19th_century/csa_scarsec.asp

Babb, W. C. (1954). *French refugees from Saint-Domingue to the Southern United States: 1791–1810* (Unpublished PhD dissertation). University of Virginia, Charlottesville.

Babington, C. (2005, September 10). Some GOP legislators hit jarring notes in addressing Katrina. *Washington Post*.

Baum, D. (2006, August 21). The lost year (New Orleans one year after Hurricane Katrina). *New Yorker*.

Bemis, S. F. (1926). *Pinckney's Treaty: A study of America's advantage from Europe's distress*. Baltimore, MD: Johns Hopkins University Press. Retrieved November 25, 2009, from Encyclopedia Louisiana http://www.enlou.com/documents/pinckneystreaty.htm

Berger, E. (2006, February 22). New Orleans says it won't give free ride: 3 City Council members' words to poor trouble Houston officials, some evacuees. *Houston Chronicle*.

Blassingame, J. W. (1973). *Black New Orleans: 1860–1880*. Chicago, IL: University of Chicago Press.

Blitzer, C. A., & Simmons, T. (2009, October 29). "Sugar is king in La." *Advocate eEdition*, www.2theadvocate.com

Brown v. Board of Education of Topeka, Kansas, 347 U.S. 483 (1954).

Brunkard, J., Namulanda, G., & Ratard, R. (2008). Hurricane Katrina deaths, Louisiana, 2005. *Disaster Medicine and Hurricane Preparedness, 2*(4), 215–223.

Buchanan, T. C. (2004). *Black life on the Mississippi: Slaves, free blacks and the western steamboat world*. Chapel Hill: University of North Carolina Press.

Campanella, R. (2006). *Geographies of New Orleans: Urban fabrics before the storm*. Lafayette: Center for Louisiana Studies.

Censer, J., & Hunt, L. (2001). *Liberty, equality, and fraternity: Exploring the French Revolution*. Retrieved November 25, 2009, from http://chnm.gmu.edu/revolution

Center for Social Inclusion. (2006). Race to rebuild: The color of opportunity and the future of New Orleans. Retrieved February 11, 2010, from http://www.centerforsocialinclusion.org/publications/?url=race-to-rebuild

Chandler, D. G. (1973). *The campaigns of Napoleon*. New York, NY: Simon & Schuster.

The Civil Rights Cases, 109 U.S. 3 (1883).

Civil War Homepage. (2009). Mississippi declaration of secession. Retrieved February 6, 2010, from http://www.civil-war.net/pages/mississippi_declaration.asp

Clayton, R. (2002). *Cash for blood: The Baltimore to New Orleans domestic slave trade*. Bowie, MD: Heritage Books.

Connerly, C. (2005). *The most segregated city in America: City planning and civil rights in Birmingham, 1920–1980*. Charlottesville: University of Virginia Press.

Connolly, C. (2005, October 3). 9th Ward: History, yes, but a future? *Washington Post*.

Cooper, C. (2005, September 8). Old-line families escape worst of flood and plot the future. *Wall Street Journal*.

Corbett, B. (1995). *The History of Haiti*. The Haitian Revolution, Part III: Toussaint and independence. Retrieved November 11, 2009, from http://www.hartford-hwp.com/archives/43a/105.html

Crowley, S. 2006. Where is home? Housing for low-income people after the 2005 hurricanes. In C. Hartman & G. D. Squires (Eds.), *There is no such thing as a natural disaster: Race, class, and Hurricane Katrina* (pp. 121–166). New York, NY: Routledge.

Davis, M. (2006, March 23). Who is killing New Orleans? *Nation*.

Davis, R. L. F. (n.d.). Creating Jim Crow. Retrieved November 25, 2009, from http://www.jimcrowhistory.org/history/creating.htm

De Grummond, J. L. (1999). *Renato Beluce: Smuggler, privateer and patriot 1780–1860*. Baton Rouge: Louisiana State University Press.

Dessauer, J. M., & Armstrong, A. (2006, January 18). Physical, economic, and social attributes of the New Orleans Ninth Ward. New Orleans Planning Initiative, Cornell University.

DuBois, W. E. B. (1903/1994). *The souls of black folk*. New York, NY: Dover.

Dymi, A. (2007, January 29). Quantity vs. quality in NO. *National Mortgage News*. Retrieved December 5, 2009, from http://www.nationalmortgagenews.com/premium/archive/?id=154528

Elderly appear to have borne brunt. (2005, October 23). *Times-Picayune*, p. A-15.

Encyclopedia Louisiana. (2004). Documents. Retrieved November 13, 2009, from http://enlou.com

Encyclopedia of Arkansas History & Culture. (n.d.) Slave codes. Retrieved November 14, 2009, from http://www.encyclopediaofarkansas.net/encyclopedia/entry-detail.aspx?search=1&entryID=5054

Fass, S., & Cauthen, N. K. (2005). *Child poverty in states hit hardest by Hurricane Katrina*. National Center for Children in Poverty. Retrieved December 4, 2007, from http://www.nccp.org/publications/pub_622.html

Follett, R. (2007). *The sugar masters: Planters and slaves in Louisiana's cane world, 1820–1860*. Baton Rouge: Louisiana State University Press.

Foner, E. (1988). *Reconstruction, America's Unfinished Revolution, 1863–1877*. New York, NY: Harper and Row.

Foner, E., & Mahoney, O. (2003). Rights and power: The politics of Reconstruction. In *America's Reconstruction: People and politics after the Civil War*. Retrieved on November 18, 2009, from http://www.digitalhistory.uh.edu/reconstruction/section4/section4_intro.html

Freedmen's Bureau Online. (n.d.) Records of the assistant commissioner for the State of Louisiana Bureau of Refugees, Freedmen, and Abandoned Lands, 1865–1869. Freedmen's Bureau Online. Retrieved from http://freedmensbureau.com/louisiana/index.htm

Fussell, E. (2007). Constructing New Orleans, constructing race: A population history of New Orleans. *Journal of American History, 94*, 846–855.

Germany, F. B. (2007). The politics of poverty and history: Racial inequality and the long prelude to Katrina. *Journal of American History, 94*, 743–751.

Goodman, A., & Gonzalez, J. (2006, June 20). All New Orleans public school teachers fired: Millions in federal aid channeled to private charter schools. *Democracy Now!* Retrieved February 9, 2010, from http://www.democracynow.org/2006/6/20/all_new_orleans_public_school_teachers

Goodman, A., Smith, D., Gonzalez, J., & Wright, B. (2005, September). Race in New Orleans: Shaping the response to Katrina. *Democracy Now!* Retrieved January 24, 2008, from http://www.democracynow.org/2005/9/2

Gunewardena, N., & Schuller, M. (Eds.). (2008). *Capitalizing on catastrophe: Neoliberal strategies in disaster reconstruction*. Lanham, MD: Altamira Press.

Hanger, K. S. (1996). A medley of cultures: Louisiana history at the Cabildo, Louisiana Museum Foundation. Retrieved from http://www.jimcrowhistory.org/resources/pdf/creating2.pdf

Harwood, J. (2005, September 9). Louisiana lawmakers aim to cope with political fallout. *Wall Street Journal*.

Haynes, S. W. (2006). Prelude to war: Manifest Destiny. Retrieved November 12, 2009, from http://www.pbs.org/kera/usmexicanwar/prelude/md_manifest_destiny.html

Henig, J. R., Hula, R. C., Orr, M., & Pedescleaux, D. S. (1999). *Race, politics, and the challenge of urban education.* Princeton, NJ: Princeton University Press.

Hollandsworth, J. G., Jr. (1995). *The Louisiana native guards: The black military experience during the Civil War.* Baton Rouge: Louisiana State University Press.

Hotel with a history. (1894, April 30). *New York Times.*

Jackson, J. M. (2006). Declaration of taking twice: The Fazendeville community of the Lower Ninth Ward. *American Anthropologist, 108*(4) 765–780.

James, C. L. R. (1963). *The black Jacobins: Toussaint L'Ouverture and the San Domingo revolution.* New York, NY: Random House.

Johnson, W. (1999). *Soul by soul: Life inside the antebellum slave market.* Cambridge, MA: Harvard University Press.

Jones, H. (1999). *Abraham Lincoln and a new birth of freedom: The Union and slavery in the diplomacy of the Civil War.* Lincoln: University of Nebraska Press.

Jonkman, S. N., Maaskant, B., Boyd, E., & Levitan, M. L. (2009). Loss of life caused by the flooding of New Orleans after Hurricane Katrina: Analysis of the relationship between flood characteristics and mortality. *Risk Analysis, 29*(5), 676–698.

Kastor, P. J. (2004). *The nation's crucible: The Louisiana Purchase and the creation of America.* New Haven, CT: Yale University Press

Keating, L. (2001). *Atlanta: Race, class, and urban expansion.* Philadelphia, PA: Temple University Press.

Kelly, M. (n.d.). *Jefferson and the Louisiana Purchase: Jefferson compromises his beliefs for a huge achievement.* Retrieved November 12, 2009, from http://americanhistory.about.com/od/thomasjefferson/a/tj_lapurchase.htm

Kendall, J. (1922). *History of New Orleans.* Chicago, IL: Lewis Publishing.

Kennedy, R. G. (2003). The Louisiana Purchase. *Common-place: The Interactive Journal of Early American Life 3*(3) Retrieved November 10, 2009, from www.common-place.org

Klein, H. (1999). *The Atlantic slave trade.* Cambridge, England: Cambridge University Press.

Klein, N. (2007). *The shock doctrine: The rise of disaster capitalism.* New York, NY: Metropolitan Books.

Knabb, R. D., Rhome, J. R., & Brown, D. P. (2005, December). *Tropical cyclone report: Hurricane Katrina, 23–30 August 2005.* Miami, FL: National Hurricane Center.

Knight, F. (1990). *The Caribbean: The genesis of a fragmented nationalism* (3rd ed.). New York, NY: Oxford University Press.

Landphair, J. (2007). The forgotten people of New Orleans: Community, vulnerability, and the Lower Ninth Ward. *Journal of American History, 94*(3), 837–845.

Lavelle, K., & Feagin, J. (2006). Hurricane Katrina: The race and class debate. *Monthly Review, 58*(3). Retrieved March 26, 2007, from http://www.monthlyreview.org/0706lavelle.htm

Lewis, P. F. (1976). *New Orleans: The making of an urban landscape.* Cambridge, England: Cambridge University Press.

Lewis, P. F. (2003). *New Orleans: The making of an urban landscape* (2nd ed.). Santa Fe, NM: Center for American Places.

Lincoln, A. (1858). Fourth Debate with Stephen A. Douglas at Charleston, Illinois, September 18, 1858. In *Collected Works of Abraham Lincoln* (Vol. 3). University of Michigan Digital Library Collection. Retrieved from http://quod.lib.umich.edu/l/lincoln/

Lincoln, A. (1863). The Emancipation Proclamation. Retrieved from http://www.archives.gov/exhibits/featured_documents/emancipation_proclamation/transcript.html

Lipman, P. (2008). Mixed-income schools and housing: Advancing the neoliberal urban agenda. *Journal of Education Policy, 23*(2), 119–134.

Lipman, P., & Haines, N. (2007). From education accountability to privatization and African American exclusion: Chicago public schools' "Renaissance 2010." *Educational Policy, 21*(3), 471–502.

Logan, R. W. (1997). *The betrayal of the Negro, from Rutherford B. Hayes to Woodrow Wilson.* New York, NY: Da Capo Press.

Long, A. P. (2007). Poverty is the new prostitution: Race, poverty, and public housing in post-Katrina New Orleans. *Journal of American History, 94,* 795–803.

Louisiana State Museum. (n.d.). Antebellum Louisiana: Agrarian life. Retrieved November 18, 2009, from http://lsm.crt.state.la.us/cabildo

Louisiana State University Libraries. (n.d.) Louisiana Purchase: A heritage explored: Historical perspectives, 1682–1815. Retrieved from www.lib.lsu.edu/special/purchase/history

Mahoney, M. R. (1985). *The changing nature of public housing in New Orleans, 1930–1974* (Master's thesis). Tulane University, New Orleans, LA.

McMillin, J. A. (2004). *The final victims: Foreign slave trade to North America, 1783–1810.* Columbia: University of South Carolina Press.

McNabb, D., & Madère, L. E. L., Jr. (1983). *A history of New Orleans.* Retrieved November 15, 2009, from www .madere.com/history

McNamara, R. (n.d.). The Kansas-Nebraska Act: Legislation intended as a compromise backfired and led to civil war. Retrieved from http://history1800s.about.com/od/slaveryinamerica/a/Kansasebraska.htm

McPherson, J. M. (2004, December 1). Antebellum Southern exceptionalism: A new look at an old question. *Civil War History, 50*(4), 418–433.

Medley, K. W. (2003). *We as freemen: Plessy v. Ferguson.* New York, NY: Pelican.

Metz, H. C. (Ed.). (2001). *Dominican Republic and Haiti: Country studies.* Washington, DC: Federal Research Division, Library of Congress.

Morial, M. (2009, November 20). *Morning Joe* television show interview. MSNBC Cable Television. Retrieved from http://www.msnbc.msn.com/id/3036789/vp/34060075#34060075

Morris, J. E. (2008). Out of New Orleans: Race, class, and researching the Katrina diaspora. *Urban Education, 43*(4), 463–487.

Morris, J. E. (2009). *Troubling the waters: Fulfilling the promise of quality public schooling for black children.* New York, NY: Teachers College Press.

Morris, J. E. (2010). Communally-bonded schools and the new localism: Implications for African American schooling and a democratic future. In R. L. Crowson & E. B. Goldring (Eds.), *The new localism in American education* (104–122). New York, NY: Wiley.

Morris, J. E., & Monroe, C. R. (2009). Why study the U.S. South? The nexus of race and place in investigating black student achievement. *Educational Researcher, 38*(1), 21–36.

National Black Programming Consortium. (2005). *The rebuilding of Saint Bernard Parish and the Lower Ninth Ward.* Retrieved November 25, 2009, from http://www.nbpc.tv/webcasts/katrina/index.php?entry=24&show=all

National Low Income Housing Coalition. (2005). Hurricane Katrina's impact on low income housing units: Estimated 302,000 units lost or damaged, 17% low income. Research Note #05-02. NLIHC, Washington, DC. September 22. Retrieved September 29, 2009, from http://www.scribd.com/doc/265294/Hurricane-Katrinas -Impact-on-Low-Income-Housing-Units

National Park Service. (n.d.). CWSAC battle summaries: The American battlefield protection program. Retrieved from www.nps.gov/history/hps/abpp/battles/scoo1.htm

New Orleans Public Library. (n.d.). Administrations of the mayors of New Orleans: Jean Etienne de Bore (1740– 1820). Retrieved November 25, 2009, from http://nutrias.org/info/louinfo/admins/bore.htm

News One. (2010). U.S. sec. of education: "Katrina was best thing to happen to education in New Orleans." Retrieved February 8, 2010, from http://newsone.com/nation/news-one-staff/u-s-sec-of-education-katrina-was -best-thing-to-happen-to-education-in-new-orleans

Payne, J. (1998, August 24). Rice, indigo, and fever in colonial South Carolina. Retrieved November 12, 2009, from http://www.geocities.com/Athens/Aegean/7023/indigo.html

Plessy v. Ferguson, 163 U.S. 537 (1896).

Rasheed, A. (2006). Education in New Orleans: Some background. *High School Journal, 90*(2), 4–8.

Rodriguex, L., & Minaya, Z. (2005, September 29). New Orleans' racial makeup up in the air: Some black areas may not be rebuilt, HUD chief says. *Houston Chronicle.*

Rogozinski, J. (2000). *A brief history of the Caribbean: From the Arawak and Carib to the present* (Revised ed.). New York, NY: Plume.

Roland, C. P. (1997). *Louisiana sugar plantations during the Civil War.* Baton Rouge: Louisiana State University Press.

Rossiter, W. S. (1909). *A century of population growth from the first census of the United States, to the twelfth, 1790–1900.* Washington, DC: U.S. Bureau of the Census.

Rothman, R. (2005). *Slave country: American expansion and the origins of the Deep South.* Cambridge, MA: Harvard University Press.

Royster, D. (2003). *Race and the invisible hand: How white networks exclude black men from blue-collar jobs.* Berkeley: University of California Press.

Saltman, K. J. (2007). *Capitalizing on disaster: Taking and breaking public schools.* Boulder, CO: Paradigm.

Schendel, W. V. (2008). The Asianization of indigo: Rapid change in a global trade around 1800. In P. Boomgaard, D. Kooiman, & H. S. Nordholt (Eds.), *Linking destinies: Trade, towns and kin in Asian history.* Leiden, The Netherlands: KITLV Press.

Schomburg Center for Research in Black Culture, New York Public Library. (n.d.). Haitian immigration: 18th & 19th centuries: The black republic and Louisiana. *In Motion: The African-American Migration Experience.* Retrieved from http://www.inmotionaame.org/migrations/topic.cfm?migration=5&topic=3

Schuller, M. (2008). Deconstructing the disaster after the disaster: Conceptualizing disaster capitalism. In N. Gunewardena & M. Schuller (Eds.), *Capitalizing on catastrophe: Neoliberal strategies in disaster reconstruction* (pp. 17–27). Lanham, MD. Altamira Press.

Shambaugh, B. F. (Ed.). (1913). *Proceedings of the Mississippi Valley Historical Association, Vol. 6.* Cedar Rapids, IA: The Torch Press.

Smith, F. E. (2002). *Ante-bellum and Civil War in the United States.* Macro History and World Report. Retrieved November 18, 2009, from http://www.fsmitha.com/h3/h42-cw.html

Stacey, T. (2004). *Notable men and women of Louisiana.* Southwest Louisiana Historical Association. Retrieved November 18, 2009, from http://www.swlahistory.org/bore.htm

Stampp, K. M. (1993). (Ed.). Introduction: Records of ante-bellum Southern plantations from the Revolution through the Civil War. A Microfilm Project of University Publications of America (pp. 5–6). Retrieved November 18, 2009, from www.lexisnexis.com/documents/academic/upa_cis/2405_AnteBellSouthPlanSerFPt4.pdf

Storm That Drowned a City. (2005). *A 300 Year Struggle.* NOVA Science Documentary Series. Retrieved November 13, 2009, from http://www.pbs.org/wgbh/nova/orleans/struggle.html

Thomson, T. (2000). The Haitian revolution and the forging of America. *History Teacher, 34*(1). Retrieved February 7, 2010, from http://www.historycooperative.org/journals/ht/34.1/thomson.html.

U.S. Bureau of the Census. (2004). Census Report. Washington DC: Author.

Usner, D. H., Jr. (1979). From African captivity to American slavery: The introduction of black laborers to colonial Louisiana, *Louisiana History, 20,* 25–48.

Wills, G. (2009). Lincoln's black history. [Review of the book *Lincoln on race and slavery,* by Henry Lewis Gates and Donald Yacovone], *New York Review of Books, 56*(10).

Wilson, C. (n.d.). First black newspaper founded. (Excerpt from the *Tribune,* New Orleans, July 18, 1865). Retrieved February 6, 2010, from www.blackpressusa.com/history/archive_essay.asp?NewsID=913

Wilson, W. J. (1996). *When work disappears: The world of the new urban poor.* New York, NY: Knopf.

Zehr, M. A. (2010). Duncan's remarks spark debate in New Orleans. *Education Week.* Retrieved February 10, 2010, from http://www.edweek.org/ew/articles/2010/02/10/21nola-2.h29.html

EPILOGUE

24

Research Infrastructure for Improving Urban Education

Larry V. Hedges and Nathan Jones

An inescapable reality of American urban education is that the output of urban schools is far below what is needed to support prosperity for all groups in American cities. State and local assessment programs have long suggested educational achievement gaps that were substantial and persistent. The National Assessment of Educational Progress (NAEP) also supported these conclusions albeit at a grain size that left open many questions. Better assessment evidence from the NAEP trial urban district assessments has tended to confirm the findings of state and local assessments (see http://nationsreportcard.gov). Indeed much of the impetus for the No Child Left Behind Act (NCLB) was the increasing awareness of large gaps in academic achievement between societal groups. For all its many flaws, NCLB was a courageous effort to focus attention on the plight of educationally disadvantaged children, and *require* schools to address the problem. NCLB along with the Education Sciences Reform Act enshrined in legislation the idea that scientific research on education was an essential element in meeting the challenges we face in closing education gaps and improving education for all students.

This chapter is based on the premise that scientific research is in fact an essential element in improving urban education. We take seriously the idea that improvements are possible, but we take the position of many economists that there is proportionality between causes and effects. All too often, expectations for social programs are astonishingly disproportional to their magnitude, scale, and cost. To put it simply, we propose programs of a scale that there is political will to fund (regardless of the scale of the problem) and expect them to solve a problem that is completely disproportionate. The experience with job training programs is an instructive example. Many of the programs funded cost at most a few thousand dollars per person, yet were expected to lift participants out of poverty by increasing their incomes by many thousands of dollars per year, forever. The expected return on this investment is, quite simply, unbelievable. Not surprisingly, it was unattainable. This did not mean that the programs were failures or that some were not cost effective (yielding more benefits than they cost), just that the expectations for them were unrealistic. If we are serious about improving urban education, we believe that we must consider remedies that are on a scale that is proportional to the magnitude of the problem. The fact that the problem is large has been extensively documented elsewhere. Considerable programmatic resources will have to be devoted to improving urban education. However, we take issue with the fact that we know everything we need to do this now, even if the resources were available.

Unfortunately, the No Child Left Behind Act (NCLB) and related legislation did not provide funding for programmatic changes necessary to meet its ambitious goals. While the funding for education research increased somewhat, the level of funding seems to have been predicated on an unrealistic optimism about the current state of knowledge to improve education research. An ambitious effort to collect and synthesize knowledge about the effects of education programs, practices, and interventions, the *What Works Clearinghouse*, revealed how little high-quality research there was to draw on in crafting education reform.

We focus here on the role that research should play in improving urban education and particularly on the research infrastructure that will be needed to make that possible. Many of us in the education research community have complained for years that the resources we have are inadequate to the task. We consider the question of what scale of research enterprise might be needed to realistically address the problems of urban education in America and how it might be organized. Then we consider the human capital resource requirements of such a research enterprise and how they could be met. Finally, we consider some of the implications for the composition of the urban education research community and how that might change education research itself.

MODELS FOR EDUCATION RESEARCH INFRASTRUCTURE

Before considering specific models for education research infrastructure, it may be advisable to consider how social research (including education research) can improve society. An important distinction was offered by Morris Janowitz (1969), who noted that social research can serve one of two functions. One function is what he called an *engineering* function. Social research can tell us which interventions are likely to have effects and what those effects are likely to be. This engineering function of social research is consistent with the kind of large-scale education research encouraged by the United States Institute of Education Sciences (IES) in the last few years. The engineering function of educational research would focus on generalizable findings from studies that are necessarily large in scale (though not necessarily *experimental* in the sense of randomized field trials). As the name implies, the engineering function of social research provides specific guidance about what effects we might expect certain policies to have.

A second function of social research is what Janowitz called *enlightenment*. This function of social research leads us to think about problems differently. It would not give specific guidance to the precise outcomes to expect, but might tell a policymaker what considerations to take into account (including ones that might not have been obvious) when making policies. The enlightenment function is important in shaping wise policymaking in situations where the research is not sufficiently detailed or results consistent enough to warrant very specific claims about the likely effects of specific policies. Much of the statistical research carried out though the National Center for Education Statistics has served an enlightenment function. For example, such research is responsible for telling us that there are substantial achievement gaps in American schools, that these gaps are associated with schools that have certain kinds of characteristics, and that while some have closed over time, others have stopped closing in recent years.

Note that these two uses of research are not mutually exclusive and to some extent there may be something of a continuum between them, but the concepts are useful to distinguish because research (and the research enterprise) needed for one purpose may be quite different from that of the other. Research for engineering purposes usually requires more extensive, specific, and expensive research projects. The nature of those projects requires certain kinds of expertise used in carrying out large scale studies. Studies carried out for enlightenment purposes may be of any type ranging from a large-scale statistical study to a small-scale case study. For example, observational studies of classrooms in the United States and other countries have enlightened us about the differences in instruction. Yet these range from very expensive studies involving videotaping many classrooms (the TIMSS video studies) to small-scale ethnographic studies of one or a few classrooms.

We argue that no one really knows exactly what research is needed to achieve the goals of NCLB or even more modest goals that might be more realistic in the next decade or two. Therefore we will not attempt to prescribe a needed urban education research infrastructure in detail. We will however draw on two visions for an education research infrastructure. One is a vision based largely on the public rhetoric embraced by the Obama administration. This particular vision is quite expansive. The second vision is based on the research and practice experiences of certain key players in the Obama administration and guesses as to their predilections. This second scenario is considerably more modest, but still would involve a substantial expansion of the education research infrastructure.

Vision I: Major National Commitment to Large-Scale Education Research

One vision of how we might approach urban education needs as a nation is based on the premise that there are widely generalizable facts that can be discovered, and if discovered, they can be used to improve urban education broadly. The premise is not that the details of specific educational contexts are irrelevant. Instead the idea is that some of the effects of context can be understood and even manipulated to improve achievement, and that the effects of other aspects of context are sufficiently small that they will not obscure systematic relations among variables that can be manipulated to improve urban education systems.

In this vision, improvement of urban education is (loosely) akin to the war on cancer. The major federal institution devoted to cancer research is the National Cancer Institute. The National Cancer Institute was established as one of the National Institutes of Health, but it has a special status as the only institute dedicated to a single disease. More importantly, the National Cancer Act of 1971 broadened its authority and allowed it to submit a budget request directly to the president of the United States (bypassing the process used by other institutes) with comment only by the NIH and the Department of Health and Human Services. The NCI has its own in-house research program and a substantial grants program funding research at Universities, hospitals, and research institutes. In 2007 NCI had approximately 4,000 direct employees.

A major research enterprise aimed at urban education could be organized along the lines of the NCI. Such a research enterprise might conduct the kinds of research that NCI does. It could involve very basic research on teaching and learning, applied research in field settings, education of practitioners, public outreach, partnering with complementary organizations both inside and outside of government, and large-scale field experiments using schools as sites much as the NCI uses hospitals as sites. The balance of these activities need not be the same in the education enterprise as it is in the NCI, but one can imagine many of the same functions would be represented to some degree. It is plausible that much more of the research activity in an education enterprise (than in NCI) would occur in satellite urban research centers throughout the country, because that is where the subjects of the research are (much like clinical trials are conducted in medical centers where there is a concentration of patients).

Infrastructure Requirements

The scale of such an enterprise has been suggested by a commitment of a fraction of the total education budget to research and development. The fraction used would obviously be a source of contention, but one figure that has been mentioned is 0.5 percent. The total amount of expenditures for K–12 education in 2007/8 was about $626 billion, so this fraction would lead to a total expenditure of about $3.15 billion. As a comparison, the 2009 budget for NCI is over $6 billion and was over $2 billion (in 2009 dollars) when it submitted its first bypass budget in 1973. Thus an effort of this scale to address an issue of major national importance is neither impossible nor unprecedented. The NCI involves a larger effort, concentrated entirely within one administrative unit. Moreover the war on cancer has many parallels to an all-out effort to improve urban schools. The problem is very complex, some of the causes are clear, but many of them are not entirely clear. It is not even clear that the labels applied to the phenomena are appropriate. Much as cancer appears to be not one disease but many related diseases, it is not clear that it is helpful to characterize problems of urban education as having the same etiology or the same potential solutions.

Even the most optimistic reading of state and federal budgets suggests that education research funding is less than $1 billion and perhaps not much more than half of that. Thus a research enterprise of the magnitude suggested here would require at least tripling, but more likely increasing the size of the education research community by a factor of four or five. Specifically, it would involve at least an additional $2.15 billion in research spending per year. The preponderance of this spending would be for personnel. Assuming PhD researchers with an average salary of only $100,000 per year, plus 25 percent benefits plus overhead of 60 percent (all figures on the low side of actual costs in research operations), this means that the average researcher costs at least $200,000 per year. Of course, research staff require support staff for administrative, technical, and clerical help, and so on. The National Cancer Institute budget allocates approximately one-sixth of its budget ($1 billion in 2008 of its $6 billion budget) to administration, or 20 percent of its research budget. It is not clear how much technical support this figure includes, but presumably much of the technical support is included in the research budget. Assuming that the equipment needs in education research are considerably smaller than those of biomedical research but the human support staff needs are somewhat larger, it seems reasonable to allocate 50 percent of research staff salaries to support and administration. Adding support staff at a ratio of one to two (one support staff member for every two researchers) at 50 percent of the salary of each researcher (a net cost of $100,000), we see that a reasonable cost figure is a total of $300,000 per year per researcher. Thus the additional $2.15 billion in research spending per year translates into a requirement for over 7,000 additional education researchers and 3,500 additional support personnel. By way of comparison, the National Cancer Institute claimed a staff of just over 4,000 in 2007 (including training fellows).

As a point of reference, the NCI is situated within a much larger biomedical research establishment that supported its growth, but the NCI budget has not quite tripled in 36 years since 1973. Arguably, urban education research is situated within a larger education research community and a much larger social research community that would support its growth. We will consider some possible consequences for urban education research of drawing substantially on that support in a later section.

Vision II: Major National Commitment to Distributed Education Research

A second, quite different vision of how we might address urban education needs is based on a different premise about the nature of attainable knowledge in education. This view was articulated by Cronbach (1982) and is widely shared among practitioners and education researchers. This premise is that the important knowledge that will lead to the improvement of education systems will be found locally, not nationally. This position does not necessarily deny that major regularities exist, but it asserts that rather than trying to understand contextual influences across a range of contexts, a more feasible way to proceed is to investigate local regularities within specific local contexts. This position has the virtue of adapting research to focus attention on the specific perceived problems in specific localities.

This vision suggests that research effort should be decentralized and situated in the urban settings in which education actually occurs. Perhaps the best exemplar of this research strategy is the Consortium on Chicago School Research, previously the Chicago Consortium on Urban School Research (http://ccsr.uchicago.edu/content/index.php). This is a relatively small research center (with 21+ professional staff and 12–15 support staff for a total of about 35 staff). However, it is very important that the Consortium is located at the University of Chicago and a crucial part of its operational model is that it is a partnership of a major research university to study urban schools. The model embodied in the Consortium has been widely discussed and is beginning to be emulated in other large cities. For example, there is now a major commitment to urban school research in New York, The Research Alliance for New York City Schools in partnership with New York University (http://steinhardt.nyu.edu/research_alliance/), that is modeled after the consortium.

The Consortium has been largely responsible for improved data systems and research infrastructure for studying Chicago schools. There is ample evidence (in the form of consortium research reports) that there is better information about the functioning of Chicago schools and a greater capacity to study the system. We should note that there is currently no compelling evidence to show that this approach has been effective in improving the *functioning* of Chicago schools.

Nevertheless, there is reason to believe that this model will be even more widely emulated. As we noted, New York City, in collaboration with New York University, has already adopted the model. Recently there was a meeting of representatives from 19 large urban school districts at the Chicago Consortium to discuss the consortium model and how it might be implemented in their cities. Perhaps more important is that the new secretary of education, Arne Duncan, was previously in charge of the Chicago Public Schools, where he evidently had a favorable opinion of the Consortium, since he appointed its director John Easton to be the director of the Institute of Education Sciences, the research arm of the United States department of education.

Infrastructure Requirements

It might seem that this vision of commitment to education research would have smaller infrastructure requirements and be easier to implement than the vision of a large-scale, centralized education research enterprise. This is arguable. While the Consortium in Chicago has a relatively small staff, this vision requires each city to study itself to arrive at strategies for improvement of urban education. For example, to establish a consortium-like operation in any cities in the nation would likely require a research operation at least the size of that in Chicago (20+ professional staff and at least half that many support staff). This may in fact be optimistic because the Chicago Consortium exploits its partnership with the University of Chicago for recruitment of staff, staff training, and unpaid consultations. The University of Chicago has one of the finest social science research faculties in the world, a resource every city does not have.

Putting aside advantages that the Chicago Consortium has but that are difficult to quantify, it would appear that a staff at least as large as that in Chicago would be required to carry out a parallel mission. Establishing a Chicago Consortium–like operation in the 100 largest cities in the nation would therefore require over 2,100 researchers and over 1,000 additional support personnel. Of course this is a minimum that assumes no additional research capacity would be added at any level above that of individual cities. It is hard to imagine that additional state, regional, or national capacity would not be needed, for two reasons.

First, even if actual research findings were not believed to be generalizable beyond the sites in which they were discovered, it is likely that there would be impetus to share methodological or procedural lessons learned among research centers. Second, not all of the 100 largest cities have a university with substantial research capacity nearby to support the effort. Analysis of the 100 largest cities in the United States suggests that 9 of them do not have a university nearby (within 50 miles) that is classified by the Carnegie Foundation for the Advancement of Teaching as being a research university. Only 71 of the 100 largest cities in the United States have a university nearby that is classified by Carnegie as having very high research capacity. The cities that do not have a nearby university with substantial social research capacity will have to find some way to obtain the support that the University of Chicago provides to the Chicago Consortium. This will necessarily come in the form of more extensive internal research staff or some other means of obtaining technical support. One can envision this as a new function for regional education research laboratories, or new institutions created by states, regions, or the federal government in partnership with some of these other agencies.

Therefore we conclude that this vision would also require at least an additional 2,000 researchers and probably somewhat more. While this is a lower figure than that generated in conjunction with the vision of a centralized research enterprise, it is at the same order of magnitude. We turn next to the question of where these education researchers might be found.

HUMAN CAPITAL FORMATION IN EDUCATION RESEARCH

The main argument of this chapter is that the human capital infrastructure for improving urban education needs substantial enlargement. In this section we address the supply of human capital to meet those needs. We argue that the human capital needed is a sufficient set of education researchers trained to at least the PhD level in education or the allied social sciences (e.g., sociology, economics, and possibly psychology). We examine PhD production in education critically, comparing it to production in other social sciences. The results are not encouraging, suggesting that while the production of education PhDs is substantial, the number of well-trained PhDs intending a research career is much smaller, barely enough to replace the current and (much larger) projected losses of faculty in the next decade as the cohort of faculty hired during the 1960s reaches retirement.

Training at the Level of a PhD Is Essential

The human capital infrastructure for urban education research is the set of researchers who have the skills, interest, and availability to carry out studies of urban education. This includes most prominently those trained in schools of education, but it also includes, to a lesser extent, those trained in the allied social sciences who have an interest in education. I take the position that research on education is at least as difficult as research in chemistry, biology, or economics and therefore the qualification equivalent to an academic research degree (a PhD) is a reasonable expectation for education researchers if we are to make real progress.

The proposition that education is at least as difficult as research in other sciences is arguable. However, if educational problems were substantially less challenging, then it follows that scientists that had been successful in other fields should be able to make rapid progress on education, if only they directed their attention to education. I invite those who dispute the proposition that educational problems are at least as complex as those in the sciences to provide evidence of education problems that have yielded to the efforts of distinguished scientists who have, at times, dedicated themselves to solving education problems. We know of math and science reform efforts that were driven by the premise that scientists could quickly solve education problems, but the supporting evidentiary base does not exist. For example, in international comparative studies like TIMSS, there is some evidence of national progress over time in math, but also evidence that other nations may be progressing faster than the United States.

Therefore we argue that one way to measure the production of human capital infrastructure in education research is to measure the production of PhDs. Fortunately, the Survey of Earned Doctorates has been collecting information about the production of doctoral degrees in the United States since the early 20th century. We turn to this source of data for our analysis of human capital formation in education.

Production of PhDs in Education

Table 24.1 shows the production of PhDs in education between 1950 and 2007. The table also shows PhD production in two allied social sciences (sociology and economics, and in psychology) and in two physical sciences (chemistry and physics) for comparison. It shows a dramatic increase in production over that time period, more dramatic in education than in any of the other fields. For example, 3,737 PhDs produced in 2007, which is four times as large as the number produced in economics and is almost as large as the number produced in the fields of chemistry and physics combined. Hence it might appear that there is ample capacity to add a few thousand PhDs to the education research workforce within a few years.

We argue that these figures are deceiving, however, for three reasons. First, not all PhD recipients have any intention of securing employment in research. Second, not all PhD recipients have received a level of research training that would enable them to successfully pursue a research career. Third, even those who intend to pursue research and are adequately trained may decide to do so outside the United States (this is obviously often the case for the large numbers of foreign graduate students who train in the United States).

Not All PhD Recipients Pursue Employment in Research

The PhD in many fields, but in education in particular, is the credential required to enter or advance in several nonresearch career tracks, such as administration or management. Consequently, many of the PhD recipients will not be involved in research and never intended to be. This is especially true in education, where many administrative career tracks (such as superintendent positions) require a PhD, even though there is little or no research involved in those careers. It seems likely that the reason that the median age of PhD recipients is nearly 10 years older (about 40 as opposed to about 30 in other fields) is that many of the PhD recipients have returned to graduate school after some career experience to burnish their professional credentials. Since 1962, SED has asked PhD recipients what their

Table 24.1. Research Doctorate Production in General Fields: 1950–2007

Field of study by selected characteristics	1950–1954	1955–1959	1960–1964	1965–1969	1970–1974	1975–1979	1980	1981	1982	1983	1984	1985	1986	1987	1988	1989	1990	1991	1992
Education	6,394	7,089	9,609	17,945	26,739	18,592	3,738	3,739	3,635	3,617	3,337	3,413	3,313	3,337	3,187	3,067	3,230	3,391	3,402
% Minority[a]	n/a	n/a	n/a	n/a	10.0	13.2	13.1	12.6	14.6	12.4	13.1	14.1	13.8	12.0	11.3	11.7	10.8	11.4	12.1
Median age at doctorate[b]	34.5	38.8	38.2	37.8	36.4	35.3	35.9	36.3	36.2	36.8	37.3	37.7	38.4	38.9	39.4	40.1	40.4	41.1	41.2
Economics	1,516	1,564	2,160	3,333	4,359	4,219	767	824	761	813	793	811	859	821	852	898	862	885	910
% Minority[a]	n/a	n/a	n/a	n/a	3.7	5.8	9.7	9.7	9.2	6.5	10.5	9.2	8.6	8.9	7.8	9.1	10.7	8.9	9.3
Median age at doctorate[b]	31.5	33.2	32.5	31.3	30.2	30.6	31.1	31.0	31.2	31.3	31.4	31.7	31.5	31.8	31.9	32.1	32.3	32.2	32.3
Psychology	2,753	3,394	4,351	6,618	11,370	14,770	3,098	3,358	3,158	3,346	3,255	3,117	3,126	3,170	3,074	3,208	3,281	3,250	3,259
% Minority[a]	n/a	n/a	n/a	n/a	3.2	5.9	6.9	6.3	7.2	7.2	7.5	6.6	7.8	7.6	7.8	7.6	8.5	9.1	8.9
Median age at doctorate[b]	27.5	31.6	31.2	29.9	29.2	30.0	30.7	31.4	31.5	32.0	32.3	32.6	33.0	33.2	33.8	33.7	34.0	34.1	34.2
Sociology	791	766	925	1,613	2,975	3,381	600	605	568	525	515	461	491	423	449	436	428	465	495
% Minority[a]	n/a	n/a	n/a	n/a	5.7	9.0	9.8	10.0	10.8	10.1	11.7	12.4	12.6	9.2	12.5	17.7	17.4	14.0	11.8
Median age at doctorate[b]	33.5	33.8	33.9	32.8	31.6	32.2	33.1	33.5	33.7	34.4	34.6	34.8	35.3	35.8	36.3	36.5	36.3	36.3	36.3
Chemistry	5,175	4,789	6,005	8,580	10,120	8,078	1,538	1,612	1,680	1,758	1,765	1,836	1,903	1,975	2,013	1,970	2,100	2,194	2,213
% Minority[a]	n/a	n/a	n/a	n/a	3.0	4.3	3.7	4.7	3.2	4.1	5.9	5.0	5.1	5.3	5.8	5.6	5.3	5.6	5.2
Median age at doctorate[b]	28.0	28.0	28.3	27.8	28.1	28.5	28.3	28.3	28.3	28.7	28.7	28.9	29.2	29.1	29.4	29.2	29.5	29.6	29.8
Physics	2,418	2,300	3,387	5,912	7,338	5,208	862	906	912	928	982	980	1,078	1,137	1,173	1,161	1,265	1,286	1,403
% Minority[a]	n/a	n/a	n/a	n/a	2.2	3.8	4.0	3.0	5.1	4.5	5.0	4.2	4.9	3.9	4.6	3.5	2.8	4.0	4.4
Median age at doctorate[b]	27.7	29.1	29.1	28.7	29.0	29.4	29.5	29.1	29.7	29.6	29.7	29.8	30.0	30.1	30.1	30.1	30.2	30.2	30.1

n/a = not applicable; data on race/ethnicity was not collected until 1973.

[a] Minority excludes Asian, white, non-Hispanic doctorate recipients who did not indicate their race, and those with unknown race/ethnicity. Percent is calculated based off the total number of doctorate recipients with known race/ethnicity.

[b] Only includes cases with a valid year of birth.

Note: Since 1973, excludes recipients of the Doctor of Education (EdD) with the exception of EdDs from Harvard University.

Source: NSF/NIH/USED/USDA/NEH/NASA, 2007 Survey of Earned Doctorates.

Field of study by selected characteristics	1993	1994	1995	1996	1997	1998	1999	2000	2001	2002	2003	2004	2005	2006	2007
Education	3,305	3,445	3,438	3,504	4,000	4,084	3,367	3,396	3,399	3,339	3,639	3,513	3,429	3,549	3,737
% Minority[a]	12.3	12.3	13.7	14.5	14.8	17.0	15.5	16.8	16.9	18.4	20.3	20.0	19.2	18.1	19.7
Median age at doctorate[b]	41.6	42.1	42.2	42.7	42.8	42.9	41.5	41.5	40.9	41.0	40.8	40.3	39.7	39.3	39.0
Economics	930	939	979	1,008	1,030	1,001	926	948	927	908	932	959	1,061	1,030	993
% Minority[a]	9.8	7.2	8.4	9.7	9.2	11.4	11.8	11.2	12.4	13.0	11.8	13.8	12.5	15.2	14.4
Median age at doctorate[b]	32.0	32.7	32.2	32.1	32.0	31.8	31.7	31.7	31.8	31.7	31.7	31.7	31.6	31.6	31.1
Psychology	3,420	3,380	3,428	3,495	3,556	3,665	3,668	3,615	3,399	3,199	3,275	3,244	3,286	3,238	3,278
% Minority[a]	8.6	8.8	9.9	11.0	11.3	12.6	13.0	13.3	13.7	14.2	14.2	15.3	14.8	16.3	16.6
Median age at doctorate[b]	33.9	33.3	33.7	33.4	32.7	32.5	32.3	32.2	32.1	32.1	32.2	32.2	32.0	31.8	31.7
Sociology	513	525	540	517	577	549	544	617	566	547	597	580	535	577	575
% Minority[a]	14.3	12.0	13.2	12.0	14.0	14.2	16.9	18.3	19.4	19.6	21.2	15.3	19.4	17.5	17.4
Median age at doctorate[b]	36.3	36.1	36.3	35.7	34.8	34.6	34.3	34.4	34.3	34.5	34.7	34.8	34.7	34.5	34.7
Chemistry	2,137	2,257	2,162	2,149	2,148	2,216	2,132	1,989	1,982	1,923	2,040	1,986	2,126	2,361	2,328
% Minority[a]	5.5	6.1	5.2	5.9	6.1	5.9	7.6	7.7	8.5	7.2	7.9	8.0	8.1	8.4	10.4
Median age at doctorate[b]	29.8	30.0	30.2	30.0	29.7	29.6	29.6	29.8	29.7	29.2	29.6	29.5	29.5	29.5	29.5
Physics	1,399	1,549	1,479	1,485	1,400	1,378	1,271	1,204	1,198	1,123	1,080	1,184	1,331	1,369	1,554
% Minority[a]	4.0	3.8	3.9	5.2	4.6	3.6	4.1	5.4	5.2	6.9	6.3	6.2	6.9	6.0	7.9
Median age at doctorate[b]	30.5	30.7	30.6	30.6	30.5	30.1	30.3	30.4	30.3	30.6	30.3	30.6	30.5	30.5	30.3

primary employment responsibilities will be. The proportion of PhD recipients in education that have responded "research and development" has been much lower than in other social or physical sciences. For example, in 2006 only 9.9 percent of the PhDs in education responded that they would be employed primarily in research and development. The comparable figures of sociology and economics are 37.2 percent and 54.9 percent and the comparable figures for chemistry and physics are 65.1 percent and 71.0 percent. Note that the phrasing of the question changed slightly between 2003 and 2004, so the apparent increase in 2004 in the number of individuals planning research employment is likely an artifact of that change in the wording of the question and not a sudden increase in the actual number of those planning research employment. We argue that a better estimate of the human capital available for education research is provided by the number of PhD recipients that plan research employment, rather than the overall number of PhD recipients.

Not All PhD Recipients Are Well Prepared for a Research Career

Interest in research and development aside, we argue that the number of education PhDs does not accurately reflect the number of individuals who are *well prepared* to pursue a research career. Education research, like other forms of research requires hands-on training that is best provided in an apprenticeship setting. American universities vary substantially in their capacity to carry out research. For this reason, in 1970, the Carnegie Foundation for the Advancement of Teaching developed a classification of colleges and universities for use in higher education research. It is based on empirical data on colleges and universities, and was first made available in 1973, and was updated several times, most recently in 2005. Over the last several decades, the Carnegie Classification has been the leading framework for describing institutional diversity in the study of United States higher education. The 2005 framework includes three categories of research-intensive universities: doctoral research universities (DRU), research universities with high research activities (RU/H), and research universities with very high research activity (RU/VH). These categories essentially subsumed the Research I and Research II categories used in older Carnegie classification schemes. These categories include 84 institutions classified as DRUs, 103 classified as RU/Hs, and 96 classified as RU/VH. Each of the institutions awards at least 20 doctoral degrees per year and, collectively, these 283 universities carry out the most and arguably the best doctoral training in the United States.

We argue that it is difficult to train research apprentices in settings where little research is being conducted (see, e.g., Feuer, Towne, & Shavelson, 2002). Therefore in considering the available human capital for education research, it is appropriate to restrict our attention to those trained in universities that have some minimum research capacity. Here we will use the three Carnegie classifications of research universities given above. Note that this is still a very broad list of institutions not often considered among the elite research universities (for example, it includes the University of Phoenix–Online Campus, Nova Southeastern University, and Oral Roberts University).

Not All PhD Recipients Plan to Work in the United States

PhD recipients do not all intend to work in the United States. Many foreign graduate students pursue graduate study in the United States but return to their home countries after receiving their graduate degrees. These PhD recipients are therefore lost to the United States human capital supply, and we argue that they should be excluded from consideration.

Production of PhDs in Research-Intensive Institutions Who Plan to Work in U.S. Research

If we compute the number of PhDs who have been trained in research-intensive universities and plan to be employed in research and development in the United States, the picture changes rather dramatically. Table 24.2 shows the number of PhDs who have been trained in research-intensive universities and plan to be employed in research and development in the United States over the period 1962 to 2007. It shows that while the number of research PhDs in education has been rising, the number is less than 10 percent of the total number of PhDs in education. For comparison, the percentage of chemistry or physics PhDs that meet these criteria is approximately half the total number of PhDs, and this is low primarily because of foreign students returning to countries abroad. Although almost four times as many education PhDs are produced as economics PhDs, the number of PhDs from research universities intending to work in research in the United States is about the same in these two fields.

The figures in Table 24.2 should give some pause to those anticipating that human capital needs of education research will be easily met. The requirement of an additional 7,000 education researchers discussed in connection with a large centralized research effort would require about 20 years to supply at current rates, even if all of the new PhDs were used to increase capacity and none were necessary for replacement of retiring personnel in universities and existing research operations. Even the lower figure of 2,100+ additional researchers discussed in connection with a distributed urban research effort would require at least 7 years to supply at current rates, again assuming that all of the new PhDs were used to increase capacity and none were necessary for replacement of personnel in existing research operations. This assumption is, of course, wrong. There is already evidence that schools of education are experiencing difficulty in filling faculty positions and there is reason to believe that this situation is likely to continue without a massive expansion of the education research enterprise (see, e.g., Wolf-Wendel, Baker, Twombly, Tollefson, & Mahlios, 2006).

How Much Can Supply Be Increased?

If demand for education research personnel increased, it is likely that there would be a concomitant increase in supply as scarcity bids up prices for research personnel. During the 1960s, during a period of massive increase in the scale of higher education in the United States, there was a doubling or tripling of the production of PhDs in research universities going into research and development. This expansion occurred in each of the disciplines listed in Table 24.2. There has been similar growth during the last decade (from 1997 to 2007); thus, doubling PhD production again (or perhaps a somewhat greater increase) is not impossible in the next decade. However, merely doubling production would still leave major gaps in the human capital infrastructure for urban education research. It is not clear that such a substantial increase in supply could be achieved without a sustained effort and investment in increasing the supply of human capital in education research.

One source of the additional researchers that might be needed would be the allied social sciences (e.g., economics, psychology, and sociology). The supply of psychology PhDs produced in research universities and destined for a research career is somewhat larger than (roughly double) that in education; the supply of economics PhDs is about the same size as that in education; and the supply of sociology PhDs is smaller (about half the number of education PhDs). However, all of these fields have needs of their own, and none is focused primarily on the problems of improving education in general or urban education in

Table 24.2. Research Doctorate Production 1962–2007 at Research Universities Intending Research Employment in the United States

Field of study by selected characteristics	1962–1964	1965–1969	1970–1974	1975–1979	1980	1981	1982	1983	1984	1985	1986	1987	1988	1989	1990	1991	1992	1993	1994
Education	189	968	1,375	965	187	186	162	159	140	147	150	145	139	153	152	173	176	155	148
% Minority[a]	n/a	n/a	6.8	8.5	5.5	6.6	11.9	7.0	12.9	6.8	8.1	8.4	8.0	5.9	10.6	8.1	7.4	9.0	12.2
Median age at doctorate[b]	36.1	35.1	33.2	32.9	33.7	33.8	35.4	35.1	35.6	36.7	36.4	37.5	37.6	37.2	37.8	38.6	38.3	40.0	39.2
Economics	296	618	731	801	181	213	165	169	173	169	202	184	201	224	181	177	171	166	186
% Minority[a]	n/a	n/a	2.7	3.3	5.1	4.0	4.3	6.1	8.8	3.0	2.6	5.0	7.5	6.8	6.7	7.6	7.1	4.8	7.0
Median age at doctorate[b]	31.3	30.6	29.5	29.7	29.7	29.7	30.0	29.6	29.4	29.8	29.6	30.5	30.3	30.3	30.8	30.3	30.8	30.1	30.5
Psychology	524	1,065	1,082	1,175	275	282	237	233	257	252	244	208	217	241	231	203	198	193	241
% Minority[a]	n/a	n/a	1.9	4.9	5.6	3.2	6.0	8.2	4.7	6.7	5.0	5.8	9.4	7.9	8.3	4.9	8.6	10.9	11.6
Median age at doctorate[b]	30.6	29.5	28.7	29.4	30.1	30.1	30.2	31.0	31.0	31.7	32.0	31.4	31.7	32.0	31.7	32.4	31.6	31.7	31.7
Sociology	104	260	338	434	90	95	90	66	78	74	67	62	62	54	62	62	54	60	53
% Minority[a]	n/a	n/a	D	7.1	D	D	7.0	7.6	14.1	8.2	9.0	D	D	9.6	19.4	8.2	D	10.2	D
Median age at doctorate[b]	33.4	31.2	31.0	30.7	31.9	32.8	32.8	33.3	33.7	33.7	33.7	33.0	36.4	33.8	33.8	34.5	34.8	35.9	34.1
Chemistry	1,489	3,147	2,210	2,029	535	610	629	536	489	528	524	454	448	479	483	445	389	374	333
% Minority[a]	n/a	n/a	3.4	3.8	1.4	2.4	2.1	1.9	4.3	4.2	2.9	4.0	4.9	4.0	2.9	5.4	3.9	5.6	4.5
Median age at doctorate[b]	28.3	27.8	28.0	28.3	27.8	28.0	27.8	28.3	28.5	28.2	28.4	28.7	28.8	28.7	28.5	28.7	29.6	29.3	29.4
Physics	864	2,018	1,353	941	195	246	217	202	195	223	195	165	178	153	136	145	121	112	117
% Minority[a]	n/a	n/a	2.2	2.4	3.3	D	2.3	4.1	3.7	D	3.7	D	2.9	D	D	4.3	4.1	8.0	6.0
Median age at doctorate[b]	29.0	28.8	29.4	29.7	29.6	29.0	29.3	29.5	29.8	30.3	29.5	30.0	30.0	30.0	31.0	29.7	30.4	30.8	31.0

D = suppressed to avoid disclosure of confidential information. n/a = not applicable; data on race/ethnicity not collected until 1973.
[a] Minority excludes Asian, white, non-Hispanic doctorate recipients who did not indicate their race, and those with unknown race/ethnicity. Percent is calculated based off the total number of doctorate recipients with known race/ethnicity.
[b] Only includes cases with a valid year of birth.
Note: Since 1973, excludes recipients of the Doctor of Education (EdD) with the exception of EdDs from Harvard University. This table only includes doctorate recipients who earned their doctorate from a research university according to the 2005 Carnegie classification system (Carnegie codes 15–17), and who have definite postgraduation plans in the United States in which their primary work activity will be research and development.

Field of study by selected characteristics	1995	1996	1997	1998	1999	2000	2001	2002	2003	2004	2005	2006	2007
Education	155	179	160	160	190	205	187	191	199	272	317	328	358
% Minority[a]	11.6	13.4	14.5	15.4	12.6	13.2	15.7	13.1	16.8	18.8	18.4	18.1	18.8
Median age at doctorate[b]	38.3	37.6	36.7	38.5	37.1	36.7	35.9	37.7	35.6	35.5	35.3	35.6	34.7
Economics	186	182	185	216	220	240	248	211	231	248	325	267	321
% Minority[a]	6.5	8.8	7.6	7.0	8.7	8.0	6.9	13.0	9.7	10.2	14.2	13.1	14.1
Median age at doctorate[b]	30.9	30.5	30.2	30.6	30.4	30.7	31.0	30.8	31.0	30.9	30.6	30.7	30.4
Psychology	199	205	220	252	230	263	267	254	244	559	700	714	679
% Minority[a]	11.1	11.3	9.5	9.1	11.3	11.4	12.1	14.3	13.9	15.1	14.9	11.4	13.9
Median age at doctorate[b]	31.3	31.8	32.0	31.0	30.8	31.7	30.9	31.3	31.6	31.1	30.5	30.3	30.5
Sociology	68	72	82	75	95	110	107	95	86	146	145	156	155
% Minority[a]	10.3	13.9	18.5	D	8.6	15.5	12.1	12.6	19.0	11.6	20.0	14.1	15.5
Median age at doctorate[b]	33.6	33.9	32.0	32.4	33.7	33.5	32.6	32.6	33.4	32.9	32.9	32.8	33.1
Chemistry	272	336	338	429	420	389	464	403	390	957	1,127	1,204	1,140
% Minority[a]	6.6	3.3	5.1	5.9	7.4	9.0	6.7	7.5	5.4	7.4	6.6	7.0	9.3
Median age at doctorate[b]	29.6	29.8	29.3	29.1	29.1	29.5	29.5	29.1	29.4	29.2	29.2	29.3	29.3
Physics	128	181	212	232	186	199	259	146	124	507	606	629	704
% Minority[a]	6.3	3.3	5.2	3.1	D	5.5	4.7	7.0	6.5	6.6	5.5	6.1	7.0
Median age at doctorate[b]	30.3	30.2	30.6	30.3	30.7	30.2	30.3	31.0	30.6	30.1	30.1	30.0	30.0

Source: NSF/NIH/USED/USDA/NEH/NASA, 2007 Survey of Earned Doctorates.

particular. Therefore it is difficult to tell how much the allied social sciences may contribute to reducing the shortage of education researchers. At most it seems plausible that their combined contribution would not be as large as that made by education programs. This still leaves a considerable gap.

We also note that while educational problems have an inescapably interdisciplinary character, each discipline brings its own emphasis to research. The focus of sociology and economics on institutions leads naturally to a characterization of researchable problems that focus on institutions, much as psychology tends to focus on individual behavior to the exclusion of institutions. While these are all parts of human behavior that have important implications for education, problems of curriculum and instruction are also central to education and these are not natural objects of research in the allied social sciences. Thus, too much reliance on the allied social sciences poses the risk that the focus of education research could be directed away from core issues of curriculum and instruction toward other topics more congenial to researchers trained in other disciplines.

The potential danger is twofold. We say potential because it is not clear that either of these is a real danger, indeed they may both be potential strengths of a different education research enterprise. The first potential danger is that if many of the problems of education are problems of what is taught and how it is taught, then the remedies most likely lie in examination of curriculum and instruction and not in institutional studies. The second danger is that for research to be used, it must be considered relevant by policymakers and practitioners. This latter group in particular is likely to view research that is too far afield from problems of instruction as irrelevant to their concerns, even if it has the potential to produce real benefits.

Production of PhDs in Critical Subfields

We have considered the production of education researchers in general, but education research has many specialties and most education researchers (like most researchers in the disciplines) specialize in one or at most a few of them. Many specialties will be needed to solve the nations pressing problems in urban education. Acute shortages in any one of them could hamper a program of education research. Unfortunately fine-grained data on many education specialties is not available from the SED (or any other source of which we are aware). However, data is available form the SED on several technical fields that, in our experience, are essential in education research and have historically been in short supply.

One such area is educational assessment, testing, and measurement. Specialists in this field are essential for developing, implementing, and interpreting information not only from cognitive tests, but also from affective, attitude, and behavioral measurements that are increasingly figuring in efforts to understand instruction in classroom teaching, to develop measures used in accountability systems, and to develop meaningful data collection systems for managing school systems. With the current emphasis on policies involving test-based accountability systems and the development of better education information systems, the importance of this area seems likely to expand considerably. This field is represented in the SED by one subfield code in education (educational assessment/testing/measurement) and another in psychology (psychometrics and quantitative psychology). The number of PhDs reported in these fields each year is so small that they fall below the threshold for data disclosure in many individual years. We combined the data from both and represent it as the data on the combined field even though quantitative psychology is a somewhat different field that often has little relevance to testing and assessment. Thus the numbers in this field represent an overestimate of the number of research professionals in measurement, assessment, and psychometrics. For simplicity of reference, we call this field "measurement" in this report.

A second technical field that is likely to be in short supply is the field of educational statisticians and research methods specialists. Such personnel are essential to support the parts of a research operation that is quantitative and will rely on statistical analysis as one important research method. Statistical methods are not and should never be considered the only tool that is essential in education research. Qualitative methods of various kinds, particularly when used in conjunction with statistical methods are essential to build a comprehensive understanding of education systems. For example, qualitative and mixed-methods studies have been a central part of the Chicago Consortium effort. However, we would argue that statistical studies are essential to understand the functioning of large urban school districts. They are essential, for example, to gain extensive understanding of operations that may involve dozens or hundreds of buildings and thousands of students and to provide comprehensible summaries of functioning. This technical area is represented in the SED by one subfield in education (educational statistics/research methods) and another in the general social sciences (social statistics). For simplicity of reference, we call this field "educational statistics" in this chapter.

A third technical field that is somewhat more amorphous than the other two is public policy analysis within the general social sciences. Note that public policy analysis is a social science field, but it includes the analysis of public policies (such as defense policy, environmental policy, or financial policy) that are not even narrowly social policies. Education policy analysis is a subfield (and a small one) of public policy analysis, but education policy analysis has emerged as a crucially important research enterprise that is seen by many in education as vital for carrying out research that can lead to the development of sound practices. While this crude attempt to quantify production of education policy analysts probably substantially overestimates supply, the figures that emerge are so low that they indicate an evident need for greater supply in this area. We should note that data on production of PhDs interested specifically in education should improve in subsequent years due to the addition of a category for education policy analysis in the SED starting in 2008.

Table 24.3 shows the production of PhDs in education, PhDs in the areas of assessment/testing/measurement, and psychology PhDs in the areas of psychometrics and quantitative psychology (the field we refer to as measurement) from 1958 to 2007. It also shows the production of PhDs in education statistics and social statistics (the field we refer to as educational statistics) from 1960 to 2007 and social science PhDs specializing on social policy analysis from 1983 to 2007. The choice of years reflects when the questions differentiating these subfields were added to the SED questionnaire. Note that the numbers here are, of course, much smaller than for all PhDs, with only 90 measurement PhDs, 94 educational statistics PhDs, and 210 public policy analysis PhDs produced in 2007. While the numbers of measurement and public policy PhDs produced appear to be increasing over the last decade, the number of educational statistics and research methods PhDs appears to be declining.

As in the case of the data on PhD production in all fields, not all of even this limited number of PhDs will enter research employment in the United States or will be well prepared to do so by virtue of training in research universities. Like PhDs in education generally, these groups are somewhat older than PhDs in the disciplines generally, approximately 35 years old as compared to about 30 years old in the other disciplines represented in this study. Moreover, many of them do not plan employment in the United States or if they plan employment in the United States, they do not plan employment in a research and development setting.

Table 24.3. Research Doctorate Production 1962–2007 in Technical Subfields

Field of study by selected characteristics	1958–1959	1960–1964	1965–1969	1970–1974	1975–1979	1980	1981	1982	1983	1984	1985	1986	1987	1988	1989	1990	1991	1992
Measurement and psychometrics[a]	74	151	367	653	536	97	104	89	68	70	61	72	54	72	53	54	42	53
% Minority[b]	n/a	n/a	n/a	3.5	6.8	D	D	13.1	7.4	14.3	11.9	8.6	D	D	D	D	D	13.2
Median age at doctorate[c]	31	33.2	32.1	31.5	31.9	33.1	32.3	34.1	33.8	34.7	33.8	34.5	35.3	35.8	35.4	36.4	36.0	38.0
Educational/Social statistics[d]	—	60	404	967	615	109	117	124	123	129	122	112	117	94	120	118	102	84
% Minority[b]	—	n/a	n/a	3.3	6.8	4.7	4.5	12.1	7.0	5.8	12.6	12.7	7.5	5.6	5.6	7.1	7.9	D
Median age at doctorate[c]	—	36.0	32.1	31.3	32.2	33.2	33.3	33.3	33.7	34.3	33.8	34.6	34.8	35.4	35.1	35.0	37.2	34.9
Public policy analysis (social science)[f]	—	—	—	—	—	—	—	—	69	54	70	81	83	73	79	87	111	107
% Minority[b]	—	—	—	—	—	—	—	—	D	11.3	13.0	15.2	12.8	13.4	7.7	18.4	15.3	13.6
Median age at doctorate[c]	—	—	—	—	—	—	—	—	34.5	33.3	35.9	35.8	36.0	37.3	36.4	37.0	36.0	36.8

Field of study by selected characteristics	1993	1994	1995	1996	1997	1998	1999	2000	2001	2002	2003	2004	2005	2006	2007
Measurement and psychometrics[a]	42	48	37	52	54	53	66	57	48	49	57	70	66	61	90
% Minority[b]	D	16.7	D	D	D	D	12.7	9.8	D	11.1	D	13.2	11.5	D	13.3
Median age at doctorate[c]	35.7	35.6	32.7	33.8	35.7	37.3	33.9	35.9	35.0	32.4	34.4	36.5	35.8	35.7	35.1
Educational/Social statistics[a,d]	100	106	100	115	111	116	125	113	110	119	108	88	74	90	94
% Minority[b]	6.0	7.8	D	13.3	7.4	9.2	7.8	11.2	9.3	15.0	10.2	12.2	15.9	13.1	20.0
Median age at doctorate[c]	35.1	34.1	34.5	36.2	34.4	32.9	34.0	33.4	35.9	33.5	35.0	33.6	34.3	34.7	33.1
Public policy analysis (social science)[e]	98	94	94	104	127	96	125	137	140	145	145	145	161	171	210
% Minority[b]	15.3	9.7	14.1	13.5	7.5	13.8	12.9	14.4	16.3	16.8	16.5	14.5	18.4	22.1	17.1
Median age at doctorate[c]	38.7	39.2	38.8	37.6	36.0	37.9	36.7	38.2	37.0	38.6	37.9	37.8	38.7	36.8	35.6

— = subfield was not on the questionnaire field of study list during this time, see notes below.

D = suppressed to avoid disclosure of confidential information. n/a = not applicable; data on race/ethnicity not collected until 1973.

[a] Measurement and psychometrics is comprised of "Educational assessment/testing/measurement" and "psychometrics and quantitative psychology." The subfield "edu-cational measurement and statistics" was introduced in 1962. In 1983 it was separated into two subfields: "educational statistics/research methods" and "educational assessment/testing/measurement." Both of these subfields use data from "Educational measurement and statistics" from 1962 to 1982. The subfield "psychometrics" was introduced in 1958; "quantitative psychology" was introduced in 1983. In 2004, these subfields merged to form "psychometrics and quantitative psychology." In the Infrastructure Project Data Request tables, 1958–1982 only includes counts for "psychometrics"; 1983–2003 includes counts for both subfields combined.

[b] Minority excludes Asian, white, non-Hispanic doctorate recipients who did not indicate their race, and those with unknown race/ethnicity. Percent is calculated based off the total number of doctorate recipients with known race/ethnicity.

[c] Only includes cases with a valid year of birth.

[d] Educational/social statistics is comprised of "educational statistics/research methods" and "statistics" (social science), which was introduced as a separate subfield in 1967.

[e] The subfield "public policy studies" was introduced in 1983, it was rename to "public policy analysis" in 1993.

Note: Since 1973, excludes recipients of the Doctor of Education (EdD) with the exception of EdDs from Harvard University.

Source: NSF/NIH/USED/USDA/NEH/NASA, 2007 Survey of Earned Doctorates.

Production of Critical Subfield PhDs in Research-Intensive Institutions Who Plan to Work in U.S. Research

If we compute the number of PhDs who have been trained in research intensive universities and plan to be employed in research and development in the United States, the numbers of PhDs produced in the three critical subfields becomes considerably smaller. Table 24.4 shows the production of PhDs from research universities who plan research employment in the United States in the areas of assessment/testing/measurement and psychology PhDs in the areas of psychometrics and quantitative psychology (the area we refer to as measurement) from 1958 to 2007. It also shows the production of PhDs in education statistics/research methods and social statistics (the area we call educational statistics) from 1960 to 2007 and social science PhDs specializing on social policy analysis from 1983 to 2007. Note that the numbers here are, of course, much smaller than for all PhDs, with only 35 measurement PhDs, 31 educational statistics PhDs, and 44 public policy analysis PhDs produced in 2007.

The figures in Table 24.4 suggest that it will be difficult to supply the human capital needs of education research in these critical subfields. Some indication of the potential demand in this field is that 2 of the 21 professional staff at the Chicago Consortium are psychometricians or measurement specialists. This suggests that the vision of a decentralized urban education research infrastructure could require more than 200 additional PhD-level psychometricians or measurement or assessment specialists. The rate of PhD production from research universities in measurement appears to have increased somewhat in the last decade. However, even at this increased rate of production, the requirement of 200+ new measurement specialists is 7 years of production even if all of the new PhDs were used to increase capacity and none were necessary for replacement of retiring personnel in universities and existing research operations. It is hard to imagine that demand for measurement professionals will not grow substantially as a consequence of test-based accountability policies at the state and national level, regardless of whether the education research enterprise expands at all.

How Much Can Supply Be Increased?

Historical data is equivocal about the degree to which supply of measurement professionals could be increased. During the massive increase in the scale of higher education in the United States in the 1960s, there was an increase in the production of PhDs in research universities in the specialties of measurement and education statistics. However, even at the high point of this expansion, the production of measurement and educational statistics PhDs has never exceeded its level in recent years, although it declined substantially in the 1980s and 1990s. This raises serious questions about the capacity of research universities to produce substantial additional PhDs in these areas.

Unlike more general research training, training in measurement, particularly, and educational statistics to a lesser extent are quite specialized. Such training is essentially not done in other of the allied social sciences. Thus the allied social sciences (e.g., economics, psychology, and sociology) are unlikely to be a source of trained researchers in these fields. Some individuals in measurement and educational statistics are trained in departments of (mathematical) statistics. The scale of such training is hard to estimate, but it does not seem to be large. Moreover, the production of statistics PhDs is not large and appears to be declining among those born in the United States.

Public policy analysis is the one technical subfield in which PhD production at research universities seems to be increasing. Thus it may have the most potential of any of these fields to increase production internally. Moreover, educational policy analysis usually draws heavily on economics and sociology. Thus these fields might be a source of trained researchers to supply needs in education policy analysis, again with the caveat that research training in these fields is at a scale similar to that in education, so the amount of an excess research training capacity in these fields is not obviously large.

Production of PhDs in Other Critical Subfields

We chose these three technical subfields of measurement, educational statistics, and educational policy analysis in part because of their importance to education research, but also because data was available about production of PhDs in these fields. They are clearly not the only subfields of education research that are crucial for developing a knowledge base to address improvement of urban education. There are clearly others that are needed but for which there is little data.

One example is qualitative ethnographic research. It is clear that high-quality qualitative studies are as essential as high-quality statistical studies to understand the functioning of education systems (see, e.g., Eisenhart & DeHaan, 2005). The training required to produce skilled qualitative researchers is at least as intensive as that required to produce skilled quantitative researchers. It requires at least as much investment by mentors in the training process (in fact, because of the nature of the work, it may require more investment of mentors' time to train a qualitative researcher). It is likely that some individuals in sociology and anthropology as well as education might be carrying out research of this kind. Unfortunately, we were unable to find subfield codes in the SED that we felt sufficiently identified qualitative/ethnographic education researchers. Thus we have little purchase on production of PhD researchers in this area.

Another example is research on instruction. We argued previously that the study of instruction in the classroom context is likely to be an area in which intensive research is necessary. Note that this area would include both those involved in quantitative/statistical studies of classroom instruction as well as those involved in intensive ethnographic studies. Some individuals in psychology as well as those in education might be pursuing research on instruction. Yet we found no clear way to identify in the SED researchers specializing in the area of classroom instruction.

Yet another area in which research is crucial is the area of curriculum, as distinct from instruction. The study of what should be taught, of coherent sequencing, the planning of relating curriculum objectives in one area to those in other areas are all crucial topics about which there are many unanswered questions, but here again it was unclear from the SED how to identify individuals primarily concerned with research in these crucial areas of education research.

There are undoubtedly other areas of research that will be identified as crucial that we have not mentioned. It seems unlikely, however, that the current form of the SED can shed much light on production of researchers in more specialized areas than the ones we have identified here.

CONCLUSIONS

The research infrastructure needed to improve urban education in the United States is woefully inadequate. Current proposals for addressing this inadequacy range from large centralized efforts to smaller decentralized research efforts situated in urban locations. Either approach on the scale proposed would imply increasing the number of PhD education

Table 24.4. Research Doctorate Production 1962–2007 in Technical Subfields at Research Universities of Students Intending Research Employment in the United States

Field of study by selected characteristics	1962–1964	1965–1969	1970–1974	1975–1979	1980	1981	1982	1983	1984	1985	1986	1987	1988	1989	1990	1991	1992	1993
Measurement and psychometrics[a]	37	114	178	174	31	34	25	20	19	16	25	13	19	18	14	12	12	11
% Minority[b]	n/a	n/a	D	5.4	D	D	D	D	D	D	D	D	D	D	D	D	D	D
Median age at doctorate[c]	31.7	30.9	30.4	30.8	34.2	30.9	35.7	31.8	32.6	34.3	31.8	37.9	34.9	34.9	38.8	37.6	36.5	36.6
Educational/Social statistics[d]	14	106	205	173	33	31	30	24	22	24	22	23	20	29	21	30	13	17
% Minority[b]	n/a	n/a	D	4.8	D	D	D	D	D	D	D	D	D	D	D	D	D	D
Median age at doctorate[c]	32.7	31.2	30.8	31.4	33.3	33.5	35.7	34.2	34.7	32.7	33.6	36.3	34.2	35.2	34.5	37.6	32.9	39.0
Public policy analysis (social science)[f]	—	—	—	—	—	—	—	6	10	9	19	14	13	17	16	20	18	13
% Minority[b]	—	—	—	—	—	—	—	D	D	D	D	D	D	D	D	D	D	D
Median age at doctorate[c]	—	—	—	—	—	—	—	32.2	31.6	34.4	33.8	33.9	36.8	32.0	37.4	35.4	34.5	36.8

Field of study by selected characteristics	1994	1995	1996	1997	1998	1999	2000	2001	2002	2003	2004	2005	2006	2007
Measurement and psychometrics[a]	21	10.0	15.0	13	15	15	11	14	18	15	18	28	31	35
% Minority[b]	D	D	D	D	D	D	D	D	D	D	D	D	D	D
Median age at doctorate[c]	35.9	31.4	33.7	36.2	35.4	33.9	34.2	33.9	31.6	31.7	37.8	34.1	33.9	31.7
Educational/Social statistics[d]	20	19	29	27	26	26	34.0	27	28	26.0	24	23	35	31
% Minority[b]	D	D	D	D	D	D	D	D	D	D	D	21.7	14.3	D
Median age at doctorate[c]	32.8	37.4	36.6	31.3	32.9	32.3	33.1	34.7	30.9	33.8	31.6	33.7	34.0	31.5
Public policy analysis (social science)[e]	13	24	14	21	21	17	26	23	29	22	35	41	45	44
% Minority[b]	D	D	D	D	D	D	D	D	D	D	D	12.2	11.4	11.4
Median age at doctorate[c]	41.2	35.1	38.0	32.8	37.7	33.7	38.0	34.8	33.3	33.4	32.9	36.5	34.8	34.2

— = subfield was not on the questionnaire field of study list during this time—see notes below.

D = suppressed to avoid disclosure of confidential information. n/a = not applicable; data on race/ethnicity not collected until 1973.

[a] Measurement and psychometrics is comprised of "educational assessment/testing/measurement" and "psychometrics and quantitative psychology." The subfield "educational measurement and statistics" was introduced in 1962. In 1983 it was separated into two subfields: "educational statistics/research methods" and "educational assessment/testing/measurement." Both of these subfields use data from "Educational measurement and statistics" from 1962 to 1982. The subfield "psychometrics" was introduced in 1958; "quantitative psychology" was introduced in 1983. In 2004, these subfields merged to form "psychometrics and quantitative psychology." In the Infrastructure Project Data Request tables, 1958–1982 only includes counts for "psychometrics"; 1983–2003 includes counts for both subfields combined.

[b] Minority excludes Asian, white, non-Hispanic doctorate recipients who did not indicate their race, and those with unknown race/ethnicity. Percent is calculated based off the total number of doctorate recipients with known race/ethnicity.

[c] Only includes cases with a valid year of birth.

[d] Educational/social statistics is comprised of "educational statistics/research methods" and "statistics" (social science), which was introduced as a separate subfield in 1967.

[e] The subfield "public policy studies" was introduced in 1983, it was renamed "public policy analysis" in 1993.

Note: Since 1973, excludes recipients of the Doctor of Education (EdD) with the exception of EdDs from Harvard University.

Source: NSF/NIH/USED/USDA/NEH/NASA, 2007 Survey of Earned Doctorates.

researchers by as few as 2,000 to as much 7,000 to 8,000. Such a research infrastructure is not unprecedented in the biomedical sciences, to name one example. We argue that education research is at least as complex as other areas of scientific research and therefore requires research training at a comparable level: that of a doctorate in education or a related field. However, meeting the human capital needs for a serious research program of this magnitude will not be easy.

While the current level of production of education PhDs (3,700 per year) suggests that only modest expansion would be needed to produce a large enough number of PhDs with training in education, this number is deceiving. A better indicator of the human capital available for education research is the number of education PhDs produced each year in research universities who plan careers in research and development in the United States. This number is only about a tenth of the total number of education PhDs each year (about 360 in 2007). While this number has increased in the most recent decade, it has never been much higher than the current level, even in the early 1970s, when the production of education PhDs reached its all-time high in the United States. The number of PhDs in education from research universities who intend a career in research exceeds the corresponding number of sociology PhDs, is about the same as the corresponding number of economics PhDs, and is less than the corresponding number of psychology PhDs. Even if we assume that no new PhDs would be needed to replace retiring faculty, existing education researchers, or any other growth in local, state, or national research organizations, at current rates of production of PhDs in education, it would require 7 to 20 years to produce the number of education researchers needed to staff a serious reform.

Some substitution of PhDs trained in allied social sciences (economics, psychology, or sociology) may help meet some of the human capital infrastructure needs of education research. However, it is wise to recognize that these fields do not produce dramatically larger numbers of PhDs than does education, and they have their own human capital needs. Thus it may be unwise to expect that the allied social sciences can easily fill the human capital gap that may emerge in the next decade.

Education research relies on many specialties in addition to research generalists. We examined production of PhDs in three of these subspecialties: measurement and psychometrics, educational statistics and research methodology, and policy analysis. Our analysis of each of these subspecialties included individuals who earned their PhDs in areas other than education. Researchers in these subspecialties are in short supply. This was particularly true for PhDs who were trained in research universities and planned employment in research and development in the United States. Historical comparisons suggest that it will be very difficult to meet demand for measurement specialists and education statisticians, because the rate of PhD production in these areas has never been substantially higher than it is today, and because there is little prospect of substitution of individuals trained in other disciplines for those specifically trained in measurement and psychometrics and education statistics.

The purpose of this analysis is not to declare that the human capital needs of urban education research cannot be met. It is to declare that they have to be systematically addressed. This will require a commitment to gather better data on training programs, their productivity, and the ways that they can be made more productive. The Institute of Education Sciences (IES) has allocated considerable resources to predoctoral and postdoctoral training programs in education research that are intended to support committed education researchers and draw young scholars from allied social sciences into the field. These programs may be partially responsible for the recent increase in the number of individuals earning education doctorates in research universities and intending a research career. However, it appears that more investment will be needed to provide the human capital infrastructure required for a research enterprise on the scale that has been proposed here and that is probably necessary, and that should be a national priority.

We suggest several courses of action that could be undertaken immediately:

- There should be a comprehensive survey of education research doctoral training programs in the United States, to determine what kinds of research training are actually available, and to the extent possible what the quality of that training might be.
- There should be a group convened to propose steps to strengthen research training in education. This group might build on the Carnegie Endowment's work on strengthening the doctorate.

A strategic plan should be created for enhancing human capital development in education research to support the enlarging research effort in education. The plan should include specific policy recommendations which might include training grants or coordination among agencies such as the Institute of Education Sciences, the National Science Foundation, and the National Institute of Child Health and Human Development, which fund the bulk of federally supported education research. Such a planning process would need to involve the key agencies that would implement elements of the plan.

REFERENCES

Cronbach, L. J. (1982). *The evaluation of educational and social programs.* San Francisco, CA: Jossey Bass.

Eisenhart, M., & DeHaan, R. (2005). Doctoral preparation of scientifically based education researchers. *Educational Researcher, 34,* 3–13.

Feuer, M., Towne, L., & Shavelson, R. (2002). Scientific culture and educational research. *Educational Researcher, 31*(8), 4–14.

Janowitz, M. (1969). Sociological models and social policy. *Archives for Philosophy of Law and Social Philosophy, 55,* 307–319.

Wolf-Wendel, L. E., Baker, B. D., Twombly, S., Tollefson, N., & Mahlios, M. (2006). Who's teaching the teachers? Evidence from the National Survey of Postsecondary Faculty and the Survey of Earned Doctorates. *American Journal of Education, 112,* 273–300.

25

The White House Office of Urban Affairs

Regionalism, Sustainability, and the Neglect of Social Infrastructure

Ronald Walters

In the past 30 years, urban policy has been on the backburner of the American agenda, an outgrowth of the rise of the neoconservative movement. Since its capture of the national political system in 1980 only limited approaches to urban issues that are critical for the future of the country have been possible. Indeed, the Institute on Race and Poverty at the University of Minnesota Law School (1997) gives us the following data on the reduction of governmental interest in urban policy: "Between 1980 and 1992, subsidized housing funds declined by 82%, economic development assistance by 78% and job training by 63%." The pressure created by this loss of financial resources forced cities and inner-ring suburban political jurisdictions to enact higher taxes, as federal resources shifted to support middle-class, largely white, populations moving to outer-suburban and exurban locations.

The result was a white suburb–black city paradigm of regional residence that was characteristic of a new neocolonialism where essential regional decisions were made to favor the movement of the white population with its personal wealth and privilege along with corporate wealth out of urban areas. In an important article on this subject, Howell Baum, a University of Maryland Professor of Urban Studies, cites Massey and Denton as characterizing these settlements created by sprawl as at least the "new American Apartheid," leaving Baum (2004) to conclude that "sprawl was mainly a movement of White households," even though some blacks moved into the inner-suburban ring during this period as well (p. 18). A great attraction, however, was that sprawl was highly lucrative, as developers created modern living units on smaller spaces of land, and thus, the pursuit of the American dream became a powerful political force. In this process, older residential areas were left behind and residents suffered from resource withdrawal and its implications. This was the urban environment to which candidate Barack Obama addressed his proposed White House Office of Urban Affairs in the campaign of 2008, kept it through his transition to the presidency and launched it in February 2009.

The act of creating an office in the White House to coordinate urban policy was first attempted by President Richard Nixon, who established the Urban Affairs Council, which he wanted to be equivalent to the National Security Council in function and importance, largely because of the mounting problems in the inner cities that had expressed themselves through substantial violence (Shull, 1999, pp. 140–141). He wanted the Council to be used to develop strategies enumerated in the Kerner Commission Report on the cause of that violence and to address housing blight and abandonment in these places as an advisory structure through which he would implement policy in the cabinet agencies. In 1969 it was initiated, and he gave concurrent leadership of this effort to Arthur Burns and Patrick Moynihan, but the two failed to collaborate effectively, especially after the release of Moynihan's proposals for welfare reform. This led to the demise of the Council and it was succeeded by the Domestic Council in March of 1970, headed by John Ehrlichman. Thereafter, most presidents kept the Domestic Policy Council and vested in one special assistant the task of monitoring urban policy.

This chapter will assess the emerging direction of the White House Office of Urban Affairs in terms of two main variables that have been enunciated as fundamental to its work, regionalism and sustainability, in an attempt to determine to what extent they will impact the vexing problems of race and poverty in the urban areas as relevant factors in the health of metropolitan areas and the policies geared to their enhancement.

THE WHITE HOUSE OFFICE OF URBAN AFFAIRS

The Launch

During the 2008 presidential campaign, candidate Barack Obama's proposal for a White House Office of Urban Affairs included a lengthy list of issues that it would tackle in traditional areas such as housing, education, poverty, crime, and employment. He confirmed his intention to establish such an office in a June 21, 2008, speech at the annual meeting of the U.S. Conference of Mayors in Miami, Florida.

True to his promise, as president, on February 19, 2009, he issued Executive Order 13,503 (2009), establishing the office, the functions of which are

> to provide leadership for and coordinate the development of a policy agenda for urban America across executive departments and agencies; to coordinate all aspects of urban policy; to work with executive departments and agencies to ensure that appropriate consideration is given to such departments and agencies to the potential impact of their actions on urban areas; to work with executive departments and agencies including the Office of Management and Budget to ensure that Federal Government dollars targeted to urban areas are effectively spent on the highest-impact programs; and to engage in outreach and work closely with state and local officials, with non-profit organizations, and with the private sector, both in seeking input regarding the development of a comprehensive urban policy and in ensuring that the implementation of Federal programs advances the objectives of that policy.

The coordinating function of the new office was highlighted by the addition of cabinet agencies that would come under the new order, such as: the departments of Treasury, Justice, Commerce, Labor, Health and Human Services, Housing and Urban Development, Transportation, Energy, Education, and the Environmental Protection Agency.

That same day, the president appointed Adolfo Carrion of New York City, the former Bronx Borough president, as director of the new office and Derek Douglas, director of New York governor David Paterson's Washington office, as special assistant. Carrion, a person of Puerto Rican descent and an urban planner by training, received high marks from New York City–based observers for his role in fostering low- and moderate-income housing construction in the city's poorest borough and some criticism for having supported a new Yankee Stadium in the area (Shulman, 2009). Upon his selection, Carrion explained that his office would become a catalyst for cities becoming economic centers to help pull the country out of the recession and improve American competitiveness in the global markets. His office in the White House reports to the president through both Valerie Jarrett and Melody Barnes concurrently; however, the Office of Management and Budget adds to the quartet of offices that are the immediate screen for urban policy along with Barnes's White House Domestic Policy Council and the National Economic Council. Ultimately, Derek Douglas was appointed to the Domestic Policy Council and the Office of Urban Affairs itself came to be comprised of a small staff of five persons.

On July 13, 2009, the Obama administration's Office of Urban Affairs hosted a "roundtable" that was the kick-off of a "listening tour" planned to assess "best practices in communities" and determine how "the federal government can serve as an effective partner in developing competitive, *sustainable* (my emphasis) and inclusive communities" (The White House, 2009a). He indicated that the tour would visit cities such as Denver, which has planned for a significant expansion of its population by installing an innovative public transit system; Philadelphia, which has pioneered the development of "urban agriculture" that brings fresh foods into underserved areas of the city; Kansas City, Missouri, which focused on transforming low-income communities through a green growth strategy, and others.

At the initiation of the tour, President Obama directed the quartet of offices associated with urban policy to conduct a comprehensive policy review, the first in the past 30 years, underscoring the era when there began the neglect of urban policy (The White House, 2009b). He also reported the formation of a new interagency partnership on sustainable communities, led by Shaun Donovan, secretary of Housing and Urban Development, Ray LaHood, secretary of Transportation, and Lisa Jackson, administrator of the Environmental Protection Agency. In addition, he highlighted the fact that his administration had taken action in the national budget passed in the spring, to invest in two urban projects. One of these was designed to further the "Promise Neighborhood" concept developed by Geoffrey Canada, who developed the Harlem Children's Zone, and the other was Choice Neighborhoods, which modeled new housing strategies for diverse situations. However, this budget also broadly supported nearly $30 billion of projects that fell into urban or metropolitan areas such as the following:

- *Housing*: $1 billion to strengthen access to affordable housing through Community Development Block Grant funding increase; $4 billion for public housing capital fund; $2 billion to strengthen rental assistance properties; $2 billion to stabilize neighborhoods by purchasing foreclosed homes; and $1.5 billion to prevent homelessness.
- *Workforce development*: $3.95 billion to strengthen workforce development skills and summer jobs.
- *Green jobs*: $5 billion for weatherization assistance for low-income families and job training in this field.
- *Transportation*: $1 billion to improve transit infrastructure and $8 billion to initiate high-speed rail service between regions.

The "Guiding Principles" of the office included the element that cities and their regions could become engines of economic growth for the regions and the nation, and that in order to effect this growth, urban policy must change to eliminate the silos and operate in an interagency, interactive fashion. President Obama became somewhat more specific in his remarks, saying:

We also need to fundamentally change the way we look at metropolitan development. For too long, Federal policy encouraged sprawl and congestion and pollution, rather than quality public transportation and smart, sustainable development. And we've been keeping communities isolated when we should have been bringing them together. (The White House, 2009b)

Ostensibly, this would be the mandate of the new interagency partnership on sustainable communities where Housing, Transportation, and Energy would work together.

The Listening Tour

Initiating the tour, Adolpho Carrion sounded the theme that it was designed to begin a national discussion on urban policy and that it would begin by meeting with the stakeholders, experts, and public officials at the local level. To this extent, he invoked the president's view that "Washington can't solve all the problems . . . that change begins not from the top down, but from the bottom up" (Carrion, 2009a).

Kansas City, Missouri, September 14

Rep. Immanuel Cleaver has initiated a project, known as the Green Zone in Kansas City that has been approved by the city council, which appropriated $1 million for planning. It will focus on 150 blocks of the city where the quality of life is substandard, the population heavily minority, and seek to address the attendant social problems. The plan envisages the substantial financial assistance of $200 million from the stimulus package funding to be focused into this area with the hope that it will be an incentive for private funding to invest as well. It is designed to attract local residents to participate in the weatherization of homes, bus and rapid transit construction where transit managers indicated a need for training operators in the urban core because of the shortage, the use of alternative energy, and revamping neighborhood infrastructure (Abouhalkah, 2009; Carrion, 2009b; Nusbaum, 2009).

Chicago/Dubuque, September 17

The traveling group of cabinet officials visited a site in the Garfield neighborhood of Chicago where training and day care were contained in one building, where the building was also located on a bus line. It continued with a luncheon with the Chicago Metropolitan Planning Council, which covers a six-county region with more than 1,000 corporate and community leaders. The same day, the tour went to Dubuque, Iowa, where a historic millwork district was transforming into a residential area of mixed-use housing, with several transit options and a strong environmental footprint.

Denver, September 18

Here, the tour focused on a public housing project, the South Lincoln Park Homes Development, sponsored by the Denver Housing Authority, a mixed-use facility that includes business, education, and entertainment units in areas that offer walking proximity and light rail access. Director Carrion presented this project, which included the Union Station with $10 million from the stimulus funds (Associated Press, 2009; Environmental Protection Agency Press Office, 2009).

Philadelphia, September 23

Philadelphia was the site where the Fresh Food Financing Initiative (FFFI) was spotlighted. In 2001, the Food Trust, a nonprofit organization that advocates increased access to healthy food in the city, developed a chart showing underserved areas without supermarkets. An entrepreneur, Jeff Brown, built a series of ShopRite stores through the cooperation of the FFFI, a state and local community partnership that focuses on locally produced food and workers who live in the neighborhood. The tour visited the ShopRite Store at 52nd Street near Parkside Avenue (Clark, 2009).[1]

Flagstaff, October 1

The group visited a business incubator at the Northern Arizona Center for Emerging Technologies and the Southwest Windpower manufacturing warehouse. These facilities were known to have spurred technological growth in the state with the incubator having been built with $3.2 million of city funding and $2.3 million from the State Economic Development Administration. It had served 11 clients and 30 affiliate members and raised more than $30 million in private investment and $18 million in government grants (Ferguson, 2009).

Near the beginning of the tour, Carrion reiterated in the White House Blog the concept that

> we need to ensure that there is a more direct relationship to municipalities, to counties, to regions. And those federal investments require that there be partnerships between all levels of government, and that there be public-private partnerships as well. . . . The three lenses that we're looking at this through are: Are we making places more economically competitive? Are we making places more environmentally sustainable? And are we creating places that are providing opportunity for more people? (Burt, 2009)

The goal of the office, and by inference the Listening Tour, was to discern in what ways the operations could enhance the function of cities and metro areas in becoming more economically competitive and environmentally sustainable and in providing enhanced opportunity for residents. This initiative appeared to attempt to highlight successful models to advocate their replication in metros across the country utilizing aspects of the philosophy examined below.

Administration's Urban Philosophy

While a candidate for the presidency, Barack Obama's proposal provided only brief references to the philosophical direction his urban policy would take. However, in a speech before the U. S. Conference of Mayors, he indicated that urban policy should be focused on metropolitan growth rather than on inner-city crime and poverty:

> Yes we need to fight poverty; yes, we need to fight crime and yes, we need to strengthen our cities. But we also need to stop seeing our cities as the problem and start seeing them as the solution. Because strong cities are the building blocks of strong regions, and strong regions are essential for a strong America. (Obama, 2008)

This view became the underlying rationale of the Office of Urban Policy presented in the president's remarks, which launched the listening tour in several cities in the summer of 2009 and in which he expressed the desire to "develop a new urban policy vision that views cities and metropolitan communities from the perspective of opportunity and possibility rather than a collection of problems to be managed" (The White House, 2009b). This effort by the Obama administration would be addressed to a new era in which the old social problems persisted, but in which economic instability and globalization were key features of the American landscape.

In the work of Bruce Katz, director of the Metropolitan Policy Program at the Brookings Institution, one finds many of the concepts presented in the president's June 21, 2008, speech before the U. S. Conference of Mayors, carried into the transition committee on which he served, and emerging in the initial presentations of the president and the director of the Office of Urban Affairs. Katz confirmed the importance of metro regions with data that substantiates their status in such measures as the size of the economies, the majority of patents, the amount of seaport tonnage, their connection to the global economy, and other indices. This supported his advice that the perspective of the Office of Urban Affairs should be based not on sociological problematics, but on its promise to become the engine of American economic growth and innovation.

One week before the president issued his executive order establishing the Office of Urban Affairs, Katz (2009) made a speech at the New York University School of Law in which he confirmed these concepts and set forth five tasks for the office that was to come:

- *Paradigm and Bully Pulpit*: set an urban and metropolitan vision for the United States and communicate it with the full power and prestige of the White House.
- *Policy Review and Assessment*: subject the federal government to a full scale policy review to assess the extent to which the current mix of policies and programs, forged in earlier decades and ossified over time, adequately meet the 21st [century] power and potential of metro America.
- *Policy Design and Implementation*: develop, advocate for and ultimately implement next-generation federal policies that empower major cities and suburbs to collaborate on problem-solving, and "join-up" related issues of domestic policy, such as economic and workforce development, transportation, energy, and housing.
- *Transparency and Accountability*: re-establish the federal partner as a platform for information rich and evidence driven government, to unveil urban assets, drive metropolitan markets and inform public and private decisions.
- *Partner and Performance*: build a different kind of relationship with the vast network of urban and metropolitan partners in the United States with new tools, new ways of identifying, rewarding and diffusing innovation and a new ethic of performance.

Katz's view was that because many of the federal and state policies were misaligned, the new resources being made available for economic recovery could be better spent by a coordinated strategy among not only state, federal, and local government, but among federal government agencies as well. To this end, Katz focused on the need for innovation in urban policy as administered by the Department of Housing and Urban Development. Here, he referred to the "Promise Neighborhoods" proposal adopted from the Harlem Children's Zone model, where resources are focused on an area to affect transformation of a neighborhood. He also cited the successes of HOPE VI, an older HUD program, and suggested that the administration would build on this through its own "Choice Neighborhood Initiative" that would address the rehabilitation of distressed housing stock in low-income neighborhoods.

The rationale for his focus on "policy implementation and design" in the previous listing is this:

To grow sustainable metros, the federal government should join up transportation, housing, and energy and environmental policies. These policies often work at cross purposes today. Transportation programs generally invest outside core areas of metros, while housing policy continues to favor concentration of affordable housing. Environmental policies often make redevelopment costly and sprawl easy. (Katz, 2009)

The connection of this style of coordination, associated with lower levels of government, is regarded by Katz as a "radically different approach to federalism" that leverages planning and resource implementation from the bottom up. Katz's view that because population, business development, and employment are moving from central cities and inner suburbs, causing slow growth patterns while suburbs are rapidly developing, policy should unite both in consideration of more regional metro planning and development.

However, in the five tasks previously listed, one notices the absence of advocacy for the sociological dimension that has troubled urban growth and promoted the movement of growth to the suburbs, even though, Katz (2009) says, in words almost identical to those of candidate Obama one year earlier, that "yes, we need to fight poverty. Yes, we need to fight crime. Yes, we need to strengthen our cities. But we also need to stop seeing our cities as the problem and start seeing them as the solution" because they are "the building blocks of strong regions." Nevertheless, understanding that many of the social problems associated with cities have now become suburbanized, without a conceptual framework that does not include a more robust role for the Office of Urban Affairs in this issue area, it would appear to complicate how those "building blocks are strengthened" so that they enhance the role of the regions.

What we see, then, is that the actions of the president in alluding to the regional focus of his urban policy and creating the interagency partnership on sustainable communities on July 13, 2009, were consistent with the philosophy recommended by Bruce Katz to the Office of Urban Affairs. It has accepted these two dominant concepts, one that asserts regionalism as the new framework of special considerations, and "sustainability" and the substance of that frame. Below, I will briefly assess the Baltimore experience with regionalism in the guise of its policy of Smart Growth and then discuss sustainability, both in an effort to understand how the new office might approach its task in a manner that simultaneously deals with race as one of the most potent reasons why urban policy declined, and how it fits into the aims of the administration for its resurrection.

SMART GROWTH POLICY IN MARYLAND

Evolution of Smart Growth

President Barack Obama made reference at the outset to the concept of "smart growth" as a regional program used to fight sprawl, congestion, pollution, and the use of transportation to bring communities together. Such an experiment was attempted in the state of Maryland beginning in 1997. Using the vehicle of an editorial in the main newspaper, the *Baltimore Sun*, Governor Parris Glendening (1995–2003) justified his new Smart Growth Initiative that he proposed to the State Legislature in 1997 by referring to the factual record, which showed that in 25 years, at the rate of current growth, the state would lose half of its farm land and one-quarter million acres of its forest ("State Agenda," 1996). He viewed the attempt to build infrastructure into areas where sprawl was occurring as unsustainably expensive in the long run and that upgrading existing schools was 54 percent less expensive than building new ones. So, his initial proposal included $72 million for transportation funds focused on existing communities and job creation tax credit for businesses to provide jobs in the target revitalization areas, and $46 million to rehabilitate decaying commercial districts and to support mortgage assistance for those wanting to purchase homes in older areas of the state's cities and counties. In this respect, 33 communities were targeted, but they were not necessarily in low-income areas (Mirabella, 1996). Land use dominated the principle features of the program:

1. Mix land uses;
2. Take advantage of compact building design;

  3. Create housing opportunities and choices;
  4. Create walkable communities;
  5. Foster distinctive, attractive communities with a strong sense of place;
  6. Preserve open space, farmland, natural beauty, and critical environmental areas;
  7. Strengthen and direct development toward existing communities;
  8. Provide a variety of transportation choices;
  9. Make development decisions predictable, fair, and cost-effective; and
 10. Encourage community and stakeholder collaboration in development decisions. (National Center for Smart Growth Research and Education, 2011, p. 14)

His proposal, eventually titled "The Smart Growth and Neighborhood Conservation Initiative," became law in 1997, a key feature that allowed its passage, however, was that the governor allowed zoning authority to remain in the hands of local officials. Over the ten-year period from 1997 to 2007, however, its success was decidedly mixed.

In the context of the gubernatorial election of 2002, the outgoing, term-limited Governor Parris Glendening's Smart Growth policy became a key aspect of the political debate for his successor ("Build on Success," 2002). While acknowledging that Maryland had not been spared from the suburban growth that had taken place nationally in recent years, he defended his Smart Growth policy as having been effective in stemming the tide of sprawl by directing growth into certain areas, such as Baltimore City's west side, where a new housing project rehabilitated formerly abandoned buildings. He also pointed to the attraction of corporate investment to the city by the Preservation Tax Credit and dramatic increases in funding to protect the state's best farmlands and natural waterways.

In any case, a conclusion by one observer was that much of the original vision of the Initiative had not been realized since the major failure of Smart Growth was that it did not retard suburban growth, such that despite the national reputation Maryland had earned for this policy innovation, its population continued to move to the outer suburbs while the inner suburbs stagnated. This conclusion also applied to the city itself, since one of the consequences he cited was that "Baltimore is struggling to hold together school system and tax base while Baltimore County is racing to develop new strategies to revitalize older neighborhoods" (Green, 2004, p. 1A).

The source of the information for the above assertion was a study by the National Center for Smart Growth at the University of Maryland in 2007, which indicated that it was not clear why the program was not more successful in inhibiting suburban growth (Knapp & Frece, 2007). In any case, a November 2008 study released by the same organization found that Smart Growth was a failure and purported to find some answers for this conclusion (Rein, 2009). The study said that while the idea for Smart Growth was conceptually sound, it was lacking in implementation such that it had failed to restrain growth in the 10 years of its existence and that just as many Priority Funding Areas (PFA) existed before the law's enactment as afterward (Lewis, Knaap, & Sohn, 2009). Lewis et al. believed that the causative element was the failure to pass statutory requirements for PFAs to become a mandated part of planning by local jurisdictions and that the program required a larger budget to provide more substantial incentivized leverage for local jurisdictions to comply.

The Racial Effect of Smart Growth

The 2000 Census provided information used by Thomas Hylton (2003) to assess the effectiveness of Smart Growth, and he noted that it was not having a positive impact on segregation in the city of Baltimore, as five whites left for every black. Hylton then argued that Smart Growth could be utilized to stop racial segregation, pointing to the model of home construction in the city of Columbia, Maryland. There, builders of one of the few modern planned cities designed a mixed-use pattern of housing, where 10 percent of home construction had to include low-income affordable units. This effectively precluded ghettoization by race.

Race, therefore, was a serious variable to consider in the construction and success of Smart Growth plans, especially in residential housing. For example, the Public Justice Center released a study also in 2000, on data covering the period 1995–1997 that indicated a severe racial discrepancy in the denial rate for mortgages in Baltimore by race, with 40 percent for blacks and 24 percent for whites. The author of the study, Calvin Bradford, concluded that HUD had "actually contributed to the destruction of these minority neighborhoods and they are supposed to be charged with the enforcement of fair housing and the elimination of programs with discriminatory effect" (Nusgart, 2000, p. 2C).

Many of the African American residents of the city therefore, could not naturally take advantage of the incentives of the Smart Growth program to rehabilitate their own communities, and those who could move were therefore moved into the county's inner-ring, many facilitated by the subprime mortgage market that eventually collapsed.

The conclusion of the ACLU study of 2000 was confirmed by a decision of a federal district court in January 2005, the result of a 10-year suit also by the ACLU, and the decision was rendered by Judge Marvin J. Garbis. He said that HUD officials had been "wearing blinders" that kept them from looking beyond the city of Baltimore to disperse public housing residents (Siegel, 2005a, p. 1A). This was an especially audacious view in light of the 1999 decision of the Fifth Circuit Court of Appeals, which ruled in favor of homeowners, finding that the development of new scatter-site public housing in predominantly white areas violated the equal protection rights of white homeowners (*Highlands of McKamy IV and V Community Improvement Association, et al. v. Dallas Housing Authority*, 1999). From the bench, Judge Garbis admonished HUD by stating that it was "high time that HUD lived up to its statutory mandate" but also implied that there was a community-level aspect by opening the door for stakeholders to come together and seek a solution, saying, "Maybe there's a way that people can recognize that we're all together in this region" (Siegel, 2005a, p. A1). Obviously, Judge Garbis understood that just as white racial resistance to the distribution of public housing residents had influenced the policies of a sitting U.S. senator, it had likewise influenced the policies of HUD.

The Glendening Smart Growth plan appeared not to factor in the reality that without aggressive funding of race-oriented issues such as upgrading neighborhood housing and the Baltimore schools the migration of especially white parents from the city would continue. Howell Baum wrote in 2004, "Failing schools and racial segregation contribute to urban sprawl which contributes to crowded suburban schools, congested highways, air pollution and the loss of open space" (Rodricks, 2004, p. 1B). He pointedly says that neither the Smart Growth movement nor its thinkers have connected to the fact that as middle-class white families move to the suburbs, they also contribute to "residential segregation, school segregation, impoverishment of the city, deterioration of public services, and reduced participation in and competence for government and civic affairs"—in short, "urban problems that are not on the Smart Growth agenda" (Rodricks, 2004, p. 1B). Baum's view was that

> Smart Growth says little about race, even though part of the motivation and much of the effect of sprawl has been to segregate metropolitan areas racially. . . . By ignoring urban education and race, Smart Growth cannot control suburban growth. (Baum, 2004, p. 14)

Thus, although Glendening did increase support for education, the concept of "full funding" for schools was not debated until the 2002 elections when the Thornton Commission issued its plan. Before then, a report by the Maryland Budget and Tax Policy Institute (2004) found that although education funds increased, their effectiveness was severely undercut by decreased funding in areas related to the educational performance of children and youth, such as: after-school care, child care, health care, and higher education.

By not factoring racial interests into Smart Growth, perhaps it collaborated with white racial resistance to black in-migration in suburban areas. A *Baltimore Sun* journalist painted an interesting story of the racial resistance of whites in Baltimore County, by reporting on a meeting at an American Legion Post where the aim of the discussion colored by several derogatory racial references, was to object to urban renewal plans that had the potential of bringing in blacks. In fact, he pointed out that in 1994, the "Moving to Opportunity" Program caused racial hysteria among suburban whites with the specter of federal subsidies fueling the movement of thousands of poor black public housing residents into their neighborhoods, so strong that U.S. Senator Barbara Mikulski killed the funding for the program (Carson, 2000).

The lack of racial sensitivity or deliberate collusion to limit black mobility may have led Governor Glendening to allow counties to retain zoning authority, which meant that based on their own local prejudices, they could obfuscate the intension of Smart Growth to be racially inclusive—and so they did. Indeed, Gerrit Knaap, director of the University of Maryland's Smart Growth Center indicated that one of the central reasons why many states have not been willing to try Smart Growth is that towns and counties would have to give up some authority and "nobody wants to give up power" (Kobell, 2006, p. 15A). That power, in this case, prevented the out-migration of blacks and supported their growth and segregation in the city, at least until the dam began to break in the 1990s and beyond.

Nevertheless, there were also positive and negative political factors that kept African Americans in the city of Baltimore. One was the lack of economic resources as indicated by the city data for 2003 that of 10,852 active vouchers, 90 percent were utilized by black families and over 90 percent were for rental units in the city (Siegel, 2005b). However, there was also a level of commitment to the city suggested by the fact of their recent political power. Having gained the ability to elect an African American mayor, members of the school board and city council, they saw an opportunity to use this power for their own growth and development.

A negative factor was that the politics of redistricting in Baltimore County was hostile to black in-migration. After the 2000 census, the Baltimore County Council noted the growth of the black population by creating a Council district 59 percent black (Green & Nitkin, 2001). However, the American Civil Liberties Union sued on the grounds that the percentage should have been at the constitutional level of 65 percent and that the distribution of blacks into other districts was done to disallow them to threaten white incumbents. Moreover, the growth of blacks in the suburban city of Towson, a college community, prompted the Baltimore County Council, which had maintained a long history of resistance to the growth of the black population, to devise a redistricting plan to split the city into three other districts.

Conclusion

A number of factors placed great pressure on the leadership with the civic responsibility of public policy to assist in the rehabilitation of the city and especially its low-income residential areas. Unfortunately, even though Governor Glendening suggested that one of the successes of Smart Growth was a funneling of funds into the development of Baltimore's urban core, even there, such funding routinely neglected the neediest neighborhoods.

One implication of this was that the funding did not contribute to poverty reduction, for although at the time of a study by the Maryland Budget and Tax Policy Institute, based on 2005 census data, Maryland was considered the second most affluent state in the nation, poverty had continued to grow unabated from 7.3 percent in 2001 to 9.8 percent in 2005 (Maryland Budget and Tax Policy Institute, 2006). This growth in poverty occurred despite a period of economic recovery beginning in the late 1990s. Moreover, the Institute report indicates that Baltimore City had the highest rate of poverty at 22.6 percent compared to an overall 8.2 percent average for the state as a whole. The inevitable conclusion is that the version of Smart Growth that does not pay substantial attention to vulnerable populations in the city's core may not only sacrifice its immediate objectives but may also contribute to the failure of important long-term goals of regional policy. This does not auger well for its use as a comprehensive urban planning device.

That racial issues should have been a robust aspect of the planning process in a regional framework is indicated by the severe outcome in Maryland when several homes in Charles County's Hunter's Brooke development being built for affluent black and Hispanic families migrating into the southern part of the state were set afire by lower-income white youths in the December of 2004 (Garland & Schaffer, 2004).

THE SUSTAINABILITY DEFICITS

Given the discussion above, it is possible to reach the conclusion that if the city of Baltimore struggled, in significant part, because of the dynamics of sprawl, then the metro was not healthy and therefore, not "sustainable" as a unit in terms of the new conception propounded above by Katz. In another perspective on this subject, Professor Julian Agyeman's examination of the concept of "sustainability" indicates that it is possible to determine its origins from international development theory as one of the paths that settled on the quality of ecosystems as relevant to the quality of life. Although he suggested that this led to prioritizing economic sustainability and environmental livability standards above all, in this debate there emerged a social justice perspective that reinserted the condition of humanity into the environment, which came to be the anchor of the environmental justice movement.

These concepts moved precipitously into nations and their public policies; many kept the original formulation of "sustainability" as witnessed in the Smart Growth movement. However, Agyeman and his colleagues Bullard and Evans (2002) concluded that states and localities in the U.S. adopted something of a synthesis in the perspective of "the need to insure a better quality of life for all, now and into the future, in a just and equitable manner, whilst living within the limits of supporting ecosystems" (p. 78). But they also believe that "most fall short of addressing social justice and equity concerns as pivotal" (Agyeman, Bullard, & Evans, 2003, p. 38). They proceed then, to assert that communities need to sustain growth and development by protecting and enhancing the use of natural resources in order to promote economic success necessary to meet social needs by reasserting social justice concerns into the five areas of: land use planning, solid waste, toxic chemical use, residential energy use, and transportation.

This is consistent with Portney's (2001) view that social justice concerns are not ancillary, but are a necessary precondition for cities to become sustainable. In fact, he found in a multivariate analysis that the percentage of African Americans residing in the city was one of the important variables that related to the issue of sustainability. The fact that the status of a racial group is salient in his study suggests that a degree of racial polarization exists within the city, and in Scott Bollens's (1998) terms, the governing ideology in a polarized city constitutes a barrier to an "ethnic group's claim to penetrate public policy" (p. 191). He says, further, that "when there is a single dominating ethnic group in control of the government apparatus, the morality-based doctrines of that ethnonational group regarding sovereignty and cultural identity will merge with the state's urban policy" (p. 191). This is a way of suggesting that where whites constitute the majority, policies of "new urbanism," Smart Growth, and so on represent the sovereign ideologies that serve the interest of that group and, as such, marginalize the interests of those of groups that are sociologically subordinate within the political system.

The fact that Bollens eventually neglects formulating race or ethnicity into the policy/programmatic formulae of sustainable growth is reminiscent of Katz's understanding of these issues, in particular his refusal to elevate them to the level of saliency that other variables enjoy in his regional framework. Below, I will discuss this issue in more specificity as it relates to rationales of the criticality of the racial variable in regionalism and sustainability.

REGIONALISM, RACE, AND POVERTY

One of the major theorists who has influenced the reconceptualization of regionalism not only to include but also to enhance attention to issues of race, racism, and poverty has been John Powell, the former founder and director of the Institute on Race and Poverty (IRP) at the University of Minnesota Law School, now director of the Kirwan Institute at the Ohio State University. Under his leadership, the IRP (1997) produced a significant paper that contains much of his thinking on this subject. Addressing the Maryland case, the IRP paper suggested that sprawl was, in part, a consequence of race and racism in that although the Maryland experiment on Smart Growth established growth limits within municipal boundaries or the existing geographical infrastructure, it "only made it more expensive to abandon the core city" for the state and neither did it "stop the abandonment of racial minorities living in concentrated poverty."

The definition of sprawl is the unplanned movement of populations beyond urban and suburban jurisdictions in ways that challenge the social, environmental capacity of infrastructure to service them. The processes that create it are interactive. On one hand, white flight is motivated by two factors, one of which appears to involve racial dynamics such as conflict, negative racial perceptions, and desire not to integrate within neighborhoods and institutions such as schools. However, it also involves the positive attraction of whiteness. Rich Benjamin (2009) says that whites are not drawn to places he calls "Whitopia" in the exurbs just because they are populated with other whites. He says,

> Rather, the place's very Whiteness implies other perceived qualities. Americans associate a homogeneous White neighborhood with higher property values, friendliness, orderliness, cleanliness, safety, and comfort. These seemingly race-neutral qualities are subconsciously inseparable from race and class in many Whites' minds. Race is often used as a proxy for those neighborhood traits. (p. 19)

In any case, the process of migration is one in which the services that depend upon affluence such as retail establishments, employment, and social organizations follow them into the new living spaces, creating new communities that are largely white. Indeed, Bill Frey (2007) of the Brookings Institution finds data that indicates the movement of white populations beyond the suburbs at a rate even faster than their out-migration from cities.

On the other hand, the result of white migration is to leave black communities poorer. The resource shift intensifies the negative socioeconomic status of many left behind, contributing to a general drag on the quality of life in the neighborhoods and the city, and the general ability of people living in those neighborhoods to acquire a style of life that allows them to fulfill their own sense of the American dream.

Zoning

Politics and public policy are very often the legal and institutional instruments utilized to maintain this problem, such that when whites, as in Baltimore County, resist the movement of blacks into their suburban areas, local exclusive zoning is used to check their ability to acquire affordable housing either public or private, because of the restrictions on housing acreage or population per unit codes. Powell believes that, specifically, "exclusionary zoning requirements are portrayed as necessary to maintain a legitimate neighborhood aesthetic, when in reality that aesthetic is White and non-poor" (IRP, 1997). As seen in the discussion on Maryland above, a form of exclusionary zoning was supported in the 1975 Supreme Court ruling on *Milliken v. Bradley* that overturned the Detroit metropolitan desegregation plan, finding that the white suburbs had not contributed to the segregation of Detroit City schools. This decision made regional school integration more difficult and preserved the white racial sanctity of suburban schools (IRP, 1997).

This issue promotes the problem of fragmentation, an overlay of sprawl, in various places, where policies of selective investment by government units have emphasized the enhancement of environmental space as the definition of a "sustainable community." In Powell's terms, sprawl and fragmentation, supported by zoning policy amount to a "conspiracy to deny people of color equal access to the good things of America" (Finley, 2002, p. 25).[2] If he is correct, this "conspiracy," either intended or unintended, has become an enormous impediment to the fair distribution of resources, since the movement of whites and the resource trail that follows them may defeat concepts of diverse community, balance of resources, and other elements of regional harmonious growth and development.

One of the antidotes to the problem of sprawl could be that of "balanced growth." As the health of the inner-core of cities is important to the general city's health, the condition of the general city is important to the viability of the region. Paul Peterson (as cited in Harding, 1999, p. 676) argues that cities "die" if people leave in numbers large enough that they are deserted or otherwise become dysfunctional. Cities, however, may also "die" from within, even as people maintain residence there. He argues that resolving the economic problems of each city in a metro sets up a competitive set of relations among them that tends to make the regional balance unstable because each unit must compete for external economic resources and the success of some cities would appear to produce a situation of status inequality in others.

The Issue of Community

There is in the title of the IRP paper on this subject the inference that what must be created is "Metropolitan Communities." Although, as Powell suggests, early theorists of urban policy recognized the implicit responsibility to resolve the relationship between racial segregation and urban vitality, few modern analysts appear to give urgency to the much larger problem of the relationship of a captive urban black population of significant size to the ability of the region to resolve many racial issues and subsequently to use the captive resource of this population in the process of contributing to the viability of the region, the state, and the international community. The creation of community in this context will be exceedingly difficult for several reasons, and thus, I will discuss several impediments to its realization.

First, there is the problem recognized in the IRP paper that the "good life ideology" exists in minds of both whites and blacks in a way that privileges the suburbs as the model of "the American dream." However, the paper also evokes the price of this style of living as one that exists at the expense of others and says that "if this ideology were to be supplanted by a reconceptualization of the common good, then cities could begin to recover" (IRP, 1997).

Second, the IRP paper suggests that the degraded condition of urban areas has produced a negative image that has an equally negative effect on the ability of the region to attract and acquire resources with which to achieve its economic objectives. Therefore, it is recommended that one of the actions required to counter the strong resistance of whites to sharing resources is "efforts to reeducate citizens about the interdependence of regional neighborhoods and communities," a project that could "counteract the incomplete picture of the economy provided by the media" (IRP, 1997).

Edward Jepson Jr. (2005) finds cities "as systems or interdependent parts of systems that require a balance of resources and assimilation capacities with regard to their environments for continued systemic survival" (p. 168). Therefore, not only has the condition of the inner city harmed the image reputation of the region, but what is often more expensive than positive investment is the economic cost that poverty and racism has meant to the region in terms of the expenditures for social services, policing, shoring up failing schools, and caring for the infrastructure of abandoned commercial and housing units. This defeats the idea of sustainability because inherent in this concept is the idea of balance of resources expended among the various government units enhancing the civic capacity of each unit to interact for the benefit of the whole.

Third, one of the primary characteristics important in community building is significant trust, which Powell believes is one of the main difficulties in "fixing" this problem. In this regard, the research of Harvard political scientist Robert Putnam (2007) is relevant. He has found that in diverse communities neighbors trust one another about half as much as in racially homogenous communities and that all measures of civic engagement are lower in diverse communities than in homogenous communities. So, the techniques utilized in the models of communities such as Seattle, Portland, and others with low-diversity populations that have achieved a level of community cohesion must be reassessed.

Finally, as implied above in the case of Baltimore City, the sense of "community" in the regional metros must be founded on a sophisticated model that takes into consideration community independence, autonomy, and, in the case of African Americans, the quest for self-determination that has been a hallmark of the expectations of black political empowerment. Community building requires sophistication because of the complexity that the fair and just distribution of resources within the metro will not occur without politics, a demand from a city or county, negotiations among leaders, the influence of alliance groups, and conflict and consensus over goals that may be resolved at either the regional or state level.

It is necessary, in a regional context, for the city as a critical unit in the metro to have what Elaine Walker and Dan Gutmore recognize as "civic capacity," defined as "the ability of local leaders to build and maintain effective alliances among representatives from governmental, business, non-profit, and community-based sectors to work toward a collective problem solving goal" (Orr, 1996, pp. 317–318). Building civic capacity as a social project requires resources as a vital ingredient to regional sustainability and helps to define the objective of the elimination of poverty that threatens civic capacity.

This raises a question that concerns political scientists, which is the difficulty that race presents in the project of political incorporation or enhanced "civic capacity." Prince George's County, Maryland, near Baltimore City, contains the largest and most affluent African American population in the country that exercises a majority role in county political

institutions. In her study of this issue, Professor Valerie Johnson found that black representation in the county political system did not automatically result in political incorporation,
because of impediments which consisted of: divergent class interests within the African
American community, ineffective black political mobilization to increase representation
in proportion to their number in the population, inability of blacks to form a consensus
around an education agenda, and "tremendous resistance" to becoming equal partners in
the state governing coalition (Johnson, 2002). While most of these limitations on black
incorporation were anticipated by Professor Robert Smith (1996), still the last factor of
resistance to equity concerns is very often primary because control of resources takes place
outside the black-dominated political units.

While her brief discussion of the external factors of resistance is narrowly based on the
political relationships between county African American leaders and two camps of leaders
such as Governor Parris Glendening and Mike Miller, leader of the State Assembly, she summarizes the issue of incorporation thusly:

> African American political incorporation in suburban jurisdictions is complex at best. Internal
> and external factors merge to create a variety of possibilities. Full African-American incorpora-
> tion is predicated on creating intra and inter-group alliances that seek to advance the needs of
> the whole community, while taking into account diverse needs. (Johnson, 2002, pp. 142–143)

This suggests that the "civic capacity" to obtain resources and their management within
political units within metros dominated by African Americans is central to sustainability.
However, the demand for resources must also be recognized and responded to by external
actors at the effective political levels in order to develop the equity that leads to a positive
balance of resources.

CONCLUSION: IMPLICATIONS FOR
THE OFFICE OF URBAN AFFAIRS

At this point, no strategy document has been released by the White House Office of Urban
Affairs. However, one hopes that the "Listening Tour" participated in by the director of the
office and cabinet officials informs the Obama administration on the real possibilities and
difficulties of sustainable regional growth that are most certainly vested in the linkages between the urban core and its social infrastructure of neglected neighborhoods and the wider
metro region, as argued by experts in this analysis.

In this sense, the fundamental question the IRP (1997) paper asks should be entertained
by the Office of Urban Affairs, which is that in considering models of regional growth
and sustainability, "will such initiatives pave the way for the eradication of concentrated
poverty and racial segregation?" Given that this review has found that in many instances,
regional models of development were deficient in their consideration of racial dynamics,
it is clear there needs to be a robust insertion of programming especially in the context of
targeted urban policies that have the capacity to impact positively the regional framework of
metros. The adoption of this goal should immediately govern the way in which economic
resources committed to regional development are allocated to the various communities in
the construction of model projects in distinct racial communities to sensitize them to the
interactive template that is responsible for all communities benefitting from the regional
development policy. Yet a study by the U.S. Conference of Mayors (2009) discovered that
metro areas were "shortchanged" in the distribution of stimulus funds. Indeed, the emphasis

on "shovel-ready" projects, led by highway development, could result in worsening the problem discussed in this analysis.

There is at the base of this issue one of economic justice that relates regional space to the health of the social infrastructure as a vital component to a comprehensive definition of sustainability. In Powell's (1998) view:

> We need a regional approach that gives cities or communities a way to maintain appropriate control of their political and cultural institutions, while sharing in regional resources and balancing regional policymaking. We need an approach that avoids both the myopia of local, fragmented governance and the blunt regionalism exercised by an overarching unit of government, such as a county or state that can suffocate local governments (p. 20).

Sharing resources requires the civic capacity of units within the region, as we have noted, to negotiate for them often in a manner that uses the formal metro political institutions of policymaking where bargaining can take place in a framework of civic cooperation for mutual benefit. It is suggested by Harding (1999) that informal alliances may also produce significant arrangements that fuse whenever there is a need to supplement fragmented service delivery (p. 678).

However, the principle of equity should be instituted as one that recognizes the inequality in status, defined by economic resources and the success in managing them. Here, Bollens (1998) comes close to Powell in his suggestion that there should be an "equity strategy" in the planning of goals for the space involved that takes into consideration "criteria such as the ethnic group's relative size or need in allocating urban services and spending" because of their need to seek remediation and compensation for citizens who have experienced past actions that have led to their subordinate status in society (p. 192).

In any case, this chapter has discovered severe impediments to the neoliberal approach of eliminating African American residential areas from metro and regional planning policy, ignoring the substantial resources withdrawal that impact upon their quality of life and assuming that their communities may be competitive without a sufficient infusion of economic and other resources to bolster neighborhood institutions and families.

I would argue that it is, therefore, necessary for the White House Office of Urban Affairs to adopt a philosophy that privileges the social infrastructure of urban units of the metros, to the extent that the substantive content of sustainability will exhibit a justice quality that has the capacity to alleviate racism and poverty, because of the demonstrated quality of these factors not only as morally negative in themselves but also as detrimental to the achievement of the wider aims of regional public policy.

NOTES

1. In his White House Blog, Adolpho Carrion said that President Obama had made smart investment and "smart growth" a top priority for his administration as he profiled the tour visit in Philadelphia.

2. We referred to this above as the manner in which Smart Growth in Maryland collaborated with those who resisted migration to maintain limits on the opportunity structure of poor urban residents.

REFERENCES

Abouhalkah, Y. T. (2009, August 26). Green Zone requires solid follow-through. *Kansas City Star*. Retrieved from http://www.kansascity.com

Agyeman, J., Bullard, J. D., & Evans, R. B. (2002). Exploring the nexus: Bringing together sustainability, environmental justice, and equity. *Space and Polity, 6*, 77–90.

Agyeman, J., Bullard, J. D., & Evans, R. B. (2003). Toward just sustainability in urban communities: Building equity rights with sustainable solutions. *Annals of the American Academy of Political and Social Science, 590*, 35–53.

Associated Press. (2009, September 19). Officials tour Denver sustainable growth areas. Retrieved from http://www.thedenverchannel.com/news/21005895/detail.html

Baum, H. S. (2004). Smart growth and school reform: What if we talked about race and took community seriously? *Journal of the American Planning Association, 70*, 14–26.

Benjamin, R. (2009, October). Refugees of diversity. *American Prospect, 20*(8). Retrieved from http://www.prospect.org/cs/articles?article=refugees_of_diversity

Bollens, S. A. (1998). Urban policy in ethnically polarized societies. *International Political Science Review, 19*, 187–215.

Build on success of smart growth. (2002, November 20). *Baltimore Sun*, p. 15A.

Burt, S. (2009, September 17). What will make Chicago more sustainable? Retrieved from http://gapersblock.com/mechanics/2009/09/17/what-will-make-chicago-more-sustainable/

Carrion, A. (2009a, August 4). A fresh conversation on the future of American cities and metro areas. Retrieved from http://www.whitehouse.gov/blog/A-Fresh-Conversation-on-the-Future-of-Americas-Cities-and-Metro-Areas

Carrion, A. (2009b, September 14). A green vision . . . a bright future. Retrieved from http://www.whitehouse.gov/blog/2009/09/14/a-green-visionhellip-a-bright-future

Carson, L. (2000, November 26). Fear and outrage frustrate renewal cynicism. *Baltimore Sun*, p. 1C.

Clark, V. (2009, July 24). Obama officials come to applaud more Philadelphia supermarkets. *Philadelphia Inquirer*. Retrieved from http://www.groceryworkersunited.org/NEWS_072409_Obama_officials_applaud_more_Phila_supermarkets.shtml

Environmental Protection Agency. (2009, September 18). Obama administration officials wrap up sustainable communities tour with Denver visit [Press release]. Retrieved from http://yosemite.epa.gov/opa/admpress.nsf/a21708abb48b5a9785257359003f0231/4f11b331ae18270885257635006c3225!OpenDocument

Exec. Order No. 13,503, 3 C.F.R 227 (2009).

Ferguson, J. (2009, October 2). Visiting Urban Affairs officials give Flagstaff leaders high marks for their commitment to the environment. *Arizona Sun*, p.1.

Finley, M. (2002, March–April). On race and space. *Minnesota Magazine*, 22–26.

Frey, W. H. (2007, February 12). America's new demographics: Regions, metros, cities, suburbs and exurbs. Speech presented at University of Maryland, College Park. Retrieved from http://www.brookings.edu/speeches/2007/0212demographics_frey.aspx

Garland, G., & Schaffer, S. (December 8, 2004). Arson in a changing land. *Baltimore Sun*, p. 1A.

Green, A., & Nitkin, D. (2001, May 23). Council plan to redistrict is criticized. *Baltimore Sun*, p. 1B.

Green, A. A. (2004, April 9). Maryland's fastest growing suburbs get farther from cities. *Baltimore Sun*, p. 1A.

Harding, A. (1999). North American urban political economy: Urban theory and British research. *British Journal of Political Science, 29*, 673–698.

Highlands of McKamy IV and V Community Improvement Association, et al. v. The Housing Authority of the City of Dallas, 169 F.3d 973 (5th Cir. 1999).

Hylton, T. (January 15, 2003). Use smart growth to fight segregation. *Baltimore Sun*, p. 13A.

Institute on Race and Poverty. (1997). Regionalism: The creation of urban dysfunction and strategies for recreating metropolitan communities. Minneapolis, MN: Author. Retrieved from http://www1.umn.edu/irp/publications/regionalism.htm

Jepson, E. J., Jr. (2005). Sustainability: Much more than business as usual. *State and Local Government Review, 37*, 166–171.

Johnson, V. C. (2002). *Black power in the suburbs: The myth or reality of African American suburban political incorporation*. Albany: State University of New York Press.

Katz, B. (2009, February 12). The White House Office of Urban Policy: Form and function. Speech presented at New York University Law School, New York, NY. Retrieved from http://www.brookings.edu/speeches/2009/0212_housing_katz.aspx

Knapp, G., & Frece, J. W. (2007). Smart growth in Maryland: Looking forward and looking back. *Idaho Law Review, 43*, 445–473.

Kobell, R. (2006, July 2). Regional approach to growth. *Baltimore Sun*, p. 15A.

Lewis, R., Knaap, G., & Sohn, J. (2009). Managing growth with priority funding areas: A good idea whose time has yet to come. *Journal of the American Planning Association, 75*, 457–478.

Maryland Budget and Tax Policy Institute. (2004, September). *New report highlights the need to sustain Maryland's education finance initiative* [Press release]. Retrieved from http://www.marylandpolicy.org/html/research/thorntonrelease.asp

Maryland Budget and Tax Policy Institute. (2006, August). *Despite four years of economic growth, poverty in Maryland increases* [Press release]. Retrieved from http://www.marylandpolicy.org/documents/PovertyPressRelease_000 .pdf

Mirabella, L. (1996, July 10). State spends to slow sprawl. *Baltimore Sun*, p. 1B.

National Center for Smart Growth Research and Education. (2011). *Indicators of smart growth in Maryland.* College Park, MD: The National Center for Smart Growth Research and Education. Retrieved from http://www.smart growth.umd.edu/research/pdf/SartoriMooreKnaap_MDIndicators_010611.pdf

Nusbaum, E. (2009, September 7). Kansas City's Green Impact Zone: A model for community investment. Retrieved from http://northwesthub.org/kansas-city-green-impact-zone-143

Nusgart, R. (2000, May 17). Study finds huge disparity in loans to blacks, whites, mortgages in Baltimore. *Baltimore Sun*, p. 2C.

Obama, B. (2008, June 21). A metropolitan strategy for America's future. Speech presented at the U.S. Conference of Mayors, Miami, FL. Retrieved from http://www.realclearpolitics.com/articles/2008/06/a_metropolitan_strategy_for_am.html

Orr, M. (1996). Urban politics and school reform. *Urban Affairs Review, 31*, 314–345.

Portney, K. E. (2001, August). *Taking sustainable cities seriously: A comparative analysis of 23 U. S. cities.* Paper presented at the annual meeting of the American Political Science Association, San Francisco, CA.

Powell, J. A. (1998). Race and space: What really drives metropolitan growth. *Brookings Review, 16*(4), 20.

Putnam, R. D. (2007). *E pluribus unum*: Diversity and community in the twenty-first century. *Scandinavian Political Studies, 30*, 137–174.

Rein, L. (2009, November 2). Study calls Md. smart growth a flop. *Washington Post*, p. B1, B4.

Rodricks, D. (2004, February 26). Erlich realizes we all have a stake in city's schools. *Baltimore Sun*, p. 1B.

Shull, S. A. (1999). *Presidential policy-making: An end-of-century assessment.* Armonk, NY: M. E. Sharpe, Inc.

Shulman, R. (2009, February 20). White House Urban Affairs chief picked. *Washington Post*, p. A2.

Siegel, E. (2005a, January 7). Judge criticizes pooling poor in the city. *Baltimore Sun*, p. 1A.

Siegel, E. (2005b, January 31). In Dallas, vouchers and hope: Decision in rights case is a model in Baltimore. *Baltimore Sun*, p. 1A.

Smith, R. (1996). *We have no leaders: African Americans in the post–civil rights era.* Albany: State University of New York Press.

State agenda to stop sprawl. (1996, June 26). *Baltimore Sun*, p. 13A.

U.S. Conference of Mayors. (2009, June 12). *Economic study shows: U. S. metropolitan areas shortchanged in stimulus infrastructure spending* [Press release]. Retrieved from http://www.prnewswire.com/news-releases/economic-study-shows-us-metropolitan-areas-shortchanged-in-stimulus-infrastructure-spending-62109882.html

The White House, Office of the Press Secretary. (2009a). *President Obama announces next steps in development of urban and metropolitan agenda: Announces national conversation on urban and metropolitan policy; calls for review of federal policies that impact urban and metropolitan America* [Press release]. Retrieved from http://www.whitehouse.gov/the -press-office/president-obama-announces-next-steps-development-urban-and-metropolitan-agenda

The White House, Office of the Press Secretary. (2009b). Remarks by the president at urban and metropolitan policy roundtable. Retrieved from http://www.whitehouse.gov/the-press-office/remarks-president-urban-and -metropolitan-roundtable

26

Toward Civic Responsibility and Civic Engagement

Beyond the Business of Parallel Play

William F. Tate IV

As I reflect on the content presented in this volume, many thoughts emerge that might be offered in this final commentary. However, I focus my discussion on two thoughts. The first thought is related to the critical need to develop research and practice pathways as part of civic regimes aimed to improve schools, communities, and neighborhoods. By research and practice pathway, I envision a mutually informing set of interactions among scholars, civic leadership, and education professionals with the goal of supporting children and by extension their families. My second thought is related. It is essential for current and future generations of leaders in social science, including education researchers, civic reformers, and educators, to move beyond the business of parallel play in their professional lives. Instead, the challenge will be to create, lead, support, and sustain collective, interdependent hubs of intellectual capital organized to ameliorate social maladies. Aristotle (trans. 1924) noted, "Some people do not listen to a speaker unless he speaks mathematically, others unless he gives instances, while others expect him to cite a poet as witness." All three methods will be advanced as part of this final commentary, focusing on moving beyond parallel play in education research.

The term *parallel play* is often associated with the research of Mildred Parten. Her 1932 article in the *Journal of Abnormal and Social Psychology* is both a critique and advance of knowledge focused on genetic sociology and psychology. Her attention to parallel play in this particular research article is fascinating. In light of my goal here, I am using the term *parallel play* to describe human behavior where one individual is absorbed in his or her own activity while demonstrating a tendency to play beside rather than with another individual. I recognize that the term is generally linked to young children and their development. However, in today's technology-rich world, it is very common to observe a young adult completely engaged in a video game while other individuals watch the video game, talk on a cell phone, read a Facebook message, and/or tweet. My point is that parallel play extends beyond young children. I submit that education and related social science and social services are in many cases, by way of custom, folkway, organizational design, and reward systems, cultures of individuals engaged in parallel play. This should not be viewed as a strictly negative phenomenon. There are times when independent scholarship is vital to individual intellectual development. However, at the risk of pushing this comparison too far, I submit that groups can engage in parallel play. For example, psychologists will only play with psychologists.

Economists will only play with economists. Curriculum specialists will only play with curriculum specialists of their ilk. Higher education professionals will only play with higher education professionals. Teacher educators will only play with teacher educators. I hope you get the point. Very impactful interventions, supports, and leadership are usually present when parallel play is not the norm of a learning organization. If the goal is to produce a civic regime engaged in a collaborative problem-solving journey where success is measured by the amendment of challenging social problems, then interdisciplinary and interagency action should be a point of emphasis in the mode of operation.

What do I mean by interdisciplinary? The word *inter* has one definition that includes "to bury the remains of a corpse in a grave or tomb" (American Heritage Dictionary, 1985, p. 669). The same source provides another definition of *inter* as a prefix: "between or among." Both of these definitions will inform my discussion. Note that the latter definition of the term *inter* provides a mathematical framing—two or more. The American Heritage Dictionary defines *disciplinary* as "of or pertaining to a specific field of academic study" (p. 402). These definitions all come together in the NIH Roadmap for Medical Research description of interdisciplinary research, which states, "Interdisciplinary research integrates the analytical strengths of two or more often disparate scientific disciplines to create a new hybrid discipline. . . . With roadblocks to potential collaboration removed, a true meeting of minds can take place: one that broadens the scope of investigation . . . yields fresh and possibly unexpected insights, and gives rise to new interdisciplines that are more analytically sophisticated" (National Institutes of Health, 2005, p. 9).

In essence, interdisciplinary research and related development buries traditional disciplinary practices, which are often akin to a disorganized set of cottage industries. Scholars and education professionals are typically categorized into distinct, departmentally based areas of expertise. The NIH description is a call to build on and move beyond "parallel play" in research and development.

A sage colleague once stated, "Ignorance of history is the mother of invention in education." The NIH call for interdisciplinary collaboration is not new in terms of shaping my viewpoint. My thinking on collaboration among education professionals has been influenced by the insight, and a particular remark, of Edmond Gordon. His comment is especially relevant, as his scholarship informed the introduction of the content in this book. Professor Gordon (1970) stated:

> The decade of the 1960s has been marked by tremendously increased concern for the education of underdeveloped segments of the population. . . . The problem has not subsided in response to a declared intent to attack it. The complexity of this problem became clearer when it became evident that simple changes in the quality of facilities, increase in the personnel assigned and services provided, or modest shifts in curriculum emphases, did not effect significant improvements in the quality of learning. Educators are just beginning to realize that they confront tremendously complex problems when they seek to reverse the negative impacts of educational deprivation, social insulation, ethnic discrimination and economic deprivation. Increasingly, it is sensed that the problem is not simply pedagogical but involves all aspects of the community. (p. 1)

According to Gordon (1970), a noted psychologist, the challenge of educating so-called "socially disadvantaged children" is not simply a matter of pedagogy, but rather it involves all aspects of the community. His remark is clearly a call for research and development that includes pedagogically related inquiry as well as a broader range of community factors—economic, political, and social. In point of fact, his 1970 remark mirrors the NIH description of interdisciplinary research. It screams the admonition to move beyond parallel play.

As a past president of the American Educational Research Association, my sincere hope is that education researchers and developmental scientists will team with other social scientists, lawyers, and social services and health professionals as well as others motivated to make a difference for children and their families. American history provides an important insight. While helping to advance the establishment of this remarkable republic, the poet and statesman Benjamin Franklin remarked on July 4, 1776, at the signing of the Declaration of Independence, "We must all hang together, or assuredly we shall all hang separately." In keeping with this wisdom, I urge you, the community of scholars and professionals interested in schools, communities, and neighborhoods, to "Engage Together." It is our civic responsibility.

REFERENCES

American Heritage Dictionary (2nd Collegiate Edition). (1985). Boston: Houghton Mifflin.

Aristotle. (trans. 1924). *Metaphysics*. W. D. Ross (Trans.). Retrieved September 19, 2010, from http://classics.mit
.edu/Aristotle/metaphysics.html

Gordon, E. W. (1970). (Ed.). Education for social disadvantaged children. *Review of Research in Education, 40*(1), 1–179.

National Institutes of Health. (2005). *NIH roadmap for medical research: Research teams for the future—NIH backgrounder*. Bethesda, MD: National Institutes of Health. Retrieved from http://nihroadmap.nih.gov/interdisciplinary/

Parten, M. B. (1932). Social participation among preschool children. *Journal of Abnormal and Social Psychology, 27*, 243–269.

Index

About the Contributors

Walter Allen is Allan Murray Cartter Chair in Higher Education and Distinguished Professor of Sociology in the UCLA Graduate School of Education and Information Studies. His research and teaching focus on comparative race, ethnicity, and inequality; diversity in higher education; and family studies. He has produced more than 150 publications and is a regular consultant for government, corporations, and the courts on diversity, equity, and excellence in society.

Angela E. Arzubiaga is associate professor in the School of Social Transformation at Arizona State University. Her research focuses on sociocultural perspectives on family life and home-institution connections, comparative understandings of difference, the education of children of immigrants, and immigrant families' adaptations. She was a University of California President's Postdoctoral Fellowship recipient and an awardee of the International Society for the Study of Behavioral Development (ISSBD). Additionally, she was Spencer and Bernard Van Leer investigator on the Children of Immigrants in US Preschool: Parent and Teacher Perspectives and the Children Crossing Borders (CCB) studies.

Miguel Ceja is associate professor in the Department of Educational Leadership and Policy Studies at California State University, Northridge. His research focuses on issues of access and equity in higher education for students of color, college choice, diversity and campus racial climate, and community college student success. He holds a bachelor's degree in political science and a master's and PhD in higher education and organizational change, all from UCLA.

Anna K. Chmielewski is a PhD candidate in the Stanford University School of Education. Her research interests are between- and within-school segregation in the United States and in cross-national comparison, tracking and ability grouping, socioeconomic achievement gaps, and international education policy.

Linwood H. Cousins is a social worker and cultural anthropologist. He studies the cultural characteristics of race, ethnicity, and social class among African American families and communities, with an emphasis on how culture shapes schooling and racial identity. He currently serves as director of the School of Social Work at Western Michigan University.

Davido Dupree is a research psychologist, trained in cognition and development. His research explores the themes of resiliency in cognitive development among youth of color and the relationship between identity and cognitive development. He is currently a lecturer in the University of Pennsylvania's Graduate School of Education and a research and evaluation consultant for projects designed to promote the healthy psychological, social, and cognitive development of youth of color.

Jacquelyn Duran taught elementary school in California for six years before becoming a doctoral student in the Sociology and Education Program at Teachers College, Columbia University. During that time, she completed a master's degree in educational foundations at California State University, Los Angeles. Her research interests are Latino children and their adaptation processes in public schools. She also works at Teachers College and is co-director of the Hollingworth Science Camp for elementary school–aged children.

Evellyn Elizondo (PhD, University of California Santa Cruz) was a postdoctoral fellow in education at the UCLA Graduate School of Education and Information Studies at the time of writing her chapter. She has since accepted a position as the director of research and evaluation at the Bakersfield City School District in California. Her work focuses on minority academic achievement throughout the educational pipeline, identity, efficacy, and institutional racism.

Ingrid Gould Ellen is professor of public policy and urban planning at New York University's Wagner Graduate School of Public Service and co-director of the Furman Center for Real Estate and Urban Policy. Her work focuses on housing policy, neighborhood change, and the causes and consequences of segregation.

Suzanne Fegley received her PhD in developmental psychology from Temple University in 1997. She has been teaching and mentoring students in the Graduate School of Education at the University of Pennsylvania for the past 13 years. During that time she has been actively involved in numerous research projects looking at ways to promote resilience among racially and ethnically diverse groups of children and youth. She also works with schools and other youth-serving organizations in an effort to promote culturally and developmentally sensitive supports for children and families. Her research interests include, among other things, the development of self-understanding, identity, resilience, and skin color perceptions and attitudes.

George Galster is the Clarence Hilberry Professor of Urban Affairs at the Department of Geography and Urban Planning, Wayne State University. He earned his PhD in economics from MIT. He has published over 150 scholarly articles, primarily on the topics of metropolitan housing markets, racial discrimination and segregation, neighborhood dynamics, residential reinvestment, community lending and insurance patterns, and urban poverty. His authored and edited books include *Homeowners and Neighborhood Reinvestment; The Maze of Urban Housing Markets; The Metropolis in Black and White; Reality and Research; Why NOT in My Back Yard? The Neighborhood Impacts of Assisted Housing; Life in Poverty Neighborhoods;* and *Quantifying Neighborhood Effects.* He is the fifth consecutive generation of George Galsters to live in the city of Detroit.

Olivia Golden, an institute fellow at the Urban Institute, has previously been assistant secretary for children and families in the U.S. Department of Health and Human Services

(1993–2001), director of the Child and Family Services Agency of the District of Columbia (2001–2004), and director of state operations for New York State (2007). Her most recent book, *Reforming Child Welfare* (2009), offers original prescriptions to improve the lives of the most vulnerable families and children.

Courtney Grzesikowski received her master's of education in sociology and education from Teachers College, Columbia University, in 2011 with a concentration in education policy. In 2008, she received her bachelor's of education from the University of Miami, majoring in special education and sociology. Her research interests include educational equity, teacher quality, policy reform, mixed methods, school desegregation, and intercollegiate athletics. She currently works for a nonprofit organization in New York City.

Kris D. Gutiérrez is professor of learning sciences and literacy and holds the Inaugural Provost's Chair at the University of Colorado, Boulder. Her research examines learning in designed learning environments, with particular attention to students from nondominant communities and English learners. Gutiérrez is a member of the National Academy of Education and is the immediate past president of the American Educational Research Association and the National Conference on Research on Language and Literacy. Gutierrez was a member of President Obama's Education Policy Transition Team and was recently appointed by President Obama and confirmed by the U.S. Senate to be a member of the National Board for the Institute of Education Sciences.

Shirley Brice Heath, Margery Bailey Professor of English and Dramatic Literature and professor emerita of linguistics at Stanford University, studies learning environments within families and under-resourced communities. She also examines ways of learning in studios, rehearsal zones, and laboratories and illustrates the importance of sustained visual attentiveness and role assignation within project work. She is the author of the classic *Ways with Words: Language, Life, and Work in Communities and Classrooms*.

Larry V. Hedges is the Board of Trustees Professor of Statistics, Education and Social Policy, and Psychology. He has published over 150 research papers and nine books. A major area of methodological work has been the development of statistical methods for combining evidence from multiple empirical research studies (meta-analysis) in the social, medical, and biological sciences. His work in psychology has focused on the role of uncertainty in cognitive processes involved in estimation, categorization, and discrimination. His sociological work has largely concerned the social distribution of cognitive test scores, their changes over time and their relation to schooling and other social processes. His work on educational policy concerns the relation of school resources to educational outcomes such as academic achievement and the development of evidence-based social policy.

Kathryn Hill is currently a PhD student in the sociology and education program at Teachers College, Columbia University, and a graduate research assistant for CURE (the Center for Understanding Race and Education). She holds a bachelor's degree in history and literature from Harvard University and a master's in sociology and education from Teachers College. Her research interests include curricular tracking, education policy, and school restructuring.

Mark Hogrebe is an institutional researcher in the Department of Education, Washington University in St. Louis. He directs the St. Louis Regional Database Project, which compiles data and research about K–12 attainment and other educational indicators. His interests include research and evaluation methodologies in applied settings, education in science and technology fields, and using GIS to give geospatial perspective to educational data.

Odis Johnson Jr. is currently assistant professor in African American studies and faculty associate at the Maryland Population Research Center at the University of Maryland. Dr. Johnson's research in educational policy, urban studies, and the sociology of education has been supported by fellowships and grants from the National Academies Ford Foundation Fellowship Program, the Spencer Foundation, the American Educational Research Association, and the National Science Foundation. He offers courses in program evaluation, policy analysis, and urban/community studies. His work appears in the *Review of Educational Research* and the *Journal of Public Management & Social Policy*, among other peer-reviewed journals.

Nathan Jones is a research scientist in the Understanding Teaching Quality Center at ETS. His research focuses on teacher-quality/teacher-labor markets, specifically the role of policy in shaping beginning special education and general education teachers' work environments. He earned his BA from Northwestern University and his PhD from Michigan State University. Recent publications have appeared in *Teachers College Record* and the *AERA Handbook of Education Policy Research*.

Carol D. Lee is the Edwina S. Tarry Professor of Education and Social Policy at Northwestern University. She is the former president (2009–2010) of the American Educational Research Association, a member of the National Academy of Education, a former president of the National Conference of Research in Language and Literacy, and a former fellow at the Center for Advanced Studies in the Behavioral Sciences. She is also a founder of four schools (preschool through high school) spanning a 39-year period. Her research focuses on cultural and ecological supports for learning and development.

Henry M. Levin is the William Heard Professor of Economics and Education at Teachers College, Columbia University, and David Jacks Professor of Education and Economics, Emeritus, Stanford University. He is a specialist in the economics of education.

John Logan is professor of sociology at Brown University and director of the multidisciplinary initiative on spatial structures in the social sciences. He is also the outgoing vice president of the American Sociological Association. He currently leads a national team of investigators in US2010, a study of changes in many aspects of American society as revealed by new census data, supported by the Russell Sage Foundation.

Jill McNew-Birren is assistant professor in the School of Education at Marquette University. She completed her PhD at Washington University in 2011. Jill's research explores intersections between science education, socio-scientific contexts of education, and environmental policy.

Roslyn Arlin Mickelson is professor of sociology and public policy at the University of North Carolina at Charlotte. Mickelson's research focuses upon the political economy of schooling and school reform, particularly the relationships among race, ethnicity, gender, class, and educational processes and outcomes. With funding from the National Science Foundation and the Ford Foundation, Mickelson has investigated school reform in the Charlotte-Mecklenburg Schools since 1988, including how the resegregation in the Charlotte-Mecklenburg Schools is affecting educational equity and academic achievement for all students. Currently, Mickelson is writing a book synthesizing social and behavioral science research on the effects of school and classroom composition on educational outcomes. Her previous book is *Children on the Streets of the Americas: Globalization, Homelessness, and Education in the United States, Brazil, and Cuba.*

Jerome E. Morris is professor in the College of Education and a research fellow with the Institute for Behavioral Research at the University of Georgia (UGA). He also serves as the director of the Race, Class, Place and Outcomes Research Group and the Urban Education Research Group at UGA. The nexus of race, social class, and the geography of educational opportunity captures the single coherent theme of his research and scholarship. He is completing a Spencer Foundation major research grant that focuses on the educational experiences of black adolescents in black suburbia in the U.S. South. Morris is the author of *Troubling the Waters: Fulfilling the Promise of Quality Public Schooling for Black Children,* and he has published extensively in leading research journals such as the *American Educational Research Journal, Teachers College Record, Anthropology and Education Quarterly,* and *Educational Researcher.*

Sheri R. Notaro graduated from Washington and Lee University in 1994 with a bachelor's degree in psychology, summa cum laude, and then attended the University of Michigan in Ann Arbor, where she completed a doctorate in developmental psychology and an MPH in health behavior and health education. At Washington University in St. Louis, she served as associate dean of the Graduate School of Arts and Sciences and as adjunct assistant professor for the Center on Urban Research and Public Policy (CURPP). For several years, Dr. Notaro taught an urban studies course concerning health disparities among urban populations in the United States. Now at the Graduate School at Cornell University, Dr. Notaro is associate dean for inclusion and professional development, working to promote the success of graduate students. She continues her affiliation with CURPP at Washington University in St. Louis.

Deirdre Oakley is associate professor of sociology at Georgia State University. Her research focuses primarily on how social disadvantages, often created or reinforced by urban policy choices, are compounded by geographic space. Her areas of interest include housing, education, and economic development policies. She is currently working on a collaborative project funded by the National Institutes for Health (NIH) and the National Science Foundation (NSF) examining the impact of public housing elimination in Atlanta.

Michael A. Olivas is the William B. Bates Distinguished Chair in Law, University of Houston Law Center. He is the author of 13 books, including *No Undocumented Child Left Behind.* He is a member of the National Academy of Education and the American Law Institute, the only scholar to have been elected to the two honor academies.

Katherine O'Regan is associate professor of public policy at the NYU Wagner Graduate School of Public Service, where she teaches and does research on issues at the intersection of poverty and space—the conditions and fortunes of poor neighborhoods and those who live in them. Her current research includes work on a variety of affordable housing topics, from whether the low-income tax credit contributes to increased economic and racial segregation to whether the presence of housing voucher households contributes to neighborhood crime rates. Among other things, she serves on the board of the American Real Estate and Urban Economics Association, the editorial board for the *Journal of Policy Analysis and Management,* and the research advisory board for the Reinvestment Fund.

Stephen W. Raudenbush, EdD, is the Lewis-Sebring Distinguished Service Professor in the Department of Sociology at the University of Chicago and chairman of the Committee on Education. He received an EdD in policy analysis and evaluation research in 1984 from Harvard University and was a professor in the School of Education at the University of Michigan from 1998 until 2005. He is a leading scholar on quantitative methods for studying child and youth development within social settings such as classrooms, schools, and neighborhoods. Raudenbush is best known for his work on developing hierarchical linear models, with broad applications in the design and analysis of longitudinal and multilevel research. His interests also include assessing the quality of social environments, designing studies to improve those environments, and analyzing data for these studies.

Douglas Ready is assistant professor in the Department of Education Policy and Social Analysis at Teachers College, Columbia University, and a faculty affiliate with Columbia's Quantitative Methods in the Social Sciences program. A sociologist of education, his research examines how policies and practices influence educational equity and access.

Sean F. Reardon is associate professor of education and (by courtesy) sociology at Stanford University. His research focuses on the patterns, causes, and consequences of social and educational inequality.

Allison Roda is a PhD student in sociology and education at Teachers College, Columbia University, and has been a research associate for the Center for Understanding Race and Education (CURE) for the past four years. She is interested in school choice policy, social stratification, and school segregation. Her dissertation focuses on New York City parents' perceptions of schools with self-contained gifted-and-talented and general education programs.

Robert J. Sampson is the Henry Ford II Professor of the Social Sciences at Harvard University and director of the Social Program at the Radcliffe Institute for Advanced Study. His most recent book—*Great American City: Chicago and the Enduring Neighborhood Effect*—will be published in late 2011.

Amy Ellen Schwartz is director of the Institute for Education and Social Policy and professor of public policy, education, and economics at the Wagner School and Steinhardt School, New York University. An applied economist, her research focuses on issues in urban policy, education policy, and housing, and current projects focus on issues of student mobility, immigration, and the relationship between the current housing crisis and student outcomes. She has served as a consultant to a variety of public and not-for-profit organizations, including the Federal Reserve Bank of New York and the Campaign for Fiscal Equity. She is past president of the American Education Finance Association, and is a member of the editorial board for Education Finance and Policy and the board of the Committee on the Status of Women in the Economics Profession of the American Economics Association. Her research is currently funded by the National Institutes of Health, the MacArthur Foundation, and the William T. Grant Foundation, among other foundations and government sources, and has been published in academic journals in economics, education, and public policy.

Margaret Beale Spencer, PhD, is a developmental psychologist, applied researcher, and the Marshall Field IV Professor of Urban Education in the Department of Comparative Human Development at the University of Chicago. She is the recipient of numerous awards, author of more than 100 articles and chapters, and PI on numerous federal- and foundation-sponsored scholarships supporting her culture- and context-focused program of research. Her theory-informed research focuses on and explores identity processes and resiliency outcome prediction for youth living under various conditions of risk and privilege.

Leanna Stiefel is professor of economics and education policy at New York University's Wagner and Steinhardt Schools, where she is also associate director of the Institute for Education and Social Policy (IESP) and director of the Master's in Education and Social Policy Program (ESP). Her current research interests include the effectiveness of small high schools and STEM high schools, the relationships between student mobility and academic outcomes, and the effects of food policy and foreclosures on student performance. Her work has been published as books and journal articles and been supported by the U.S. Department of Education, the Spencer Foundation, and the MacArthur Foundation, among others.

William F. Tate IV is the Edward Mallinckrodt Distinguished University Professor in Arts & Sciences at Washington University in St. Louis. He served as president of the American Educational Research Association in 2007–2008. His research interests include the application of geospatial and epidemiological models to problems related to education, human development, and health.

Brian Tinsley is a doctoral student in applied psychology and human development at the University of Pennsylvania. He earned his bachelor's degree in psychology at Howard University. His research examines how adolescent perceptions of societal biases influence the relationship between self-efficacy and academic achievement/vocational aspirations.

Anne Velasco served as a qualitative researcher and MSEP's project manager. She received her MA in sociology and her MSW from the University of North Carolina at Charlotte. Currently, she is a social worker practicing in North Carolina.

Ronald Walters (July 20, 1938–September 10, 2010) was an internationally distinguished expert on African American leadership and politics. He held faculty appointments at several universities including as professor and chair of the African and Afro-American Studies Department at Brandeis University and the Political Science Department at Howard University. He also was professor of government and politics at the University of Maryland. Dr. Walters served as director of the African American Leadership Institute and Scholar Practitioner Program, and was a distinguished leadership scholar at the James MacGregor Burns Academy of Leadership. A productive and accomplished scholar, his seminal work, "Black Presidential Politics in America," won the Ralph Bunche award from the American Political Science Association. This book served as a blueprint for the historic Democratic primary campaign of the Reverend Jesse Jackson. Professor Walters served as a campaign manager and consultant for the Reverend Jesse Jackson during his two presidential bids and was a policy adviser for Congressmen Charles Diggs and William Gray. His books, articles, and public service reflect a lifetime commitment to the advancement of underserved groups throughout the world.

Miya Warner is a doctoral student in sociology and education at Teachers College, Columbia University. Her research focuses broadly on the influence of policy on educational equity and access. Her dissertation examines the implications of urban small-school reform for disadvantaged students' access to a rigorous, college-preparatory curriculum. She is also a research associate for the Center for Understanding Race and Education (CURE) at Teachers

College, working on a mixed-methods study of changing demographics in suburbia and its impact on public education. She is coauthor of several forthcoming publications, including "The Story of Meaningful School Choice: Lessons from Interdistrict Transfer Plans" (forthcoming) in Gary Orfield and Erica Frankenberg's *School Choice and Segregation*. She has presented at numerous research conferences, including the annual meetings of the American Educational Research Association (AERA) and the Eastern Sociological Society (ESS) and is the recipient of an educational policy doctoral fellowship from Teachers College (2011) and a doctoral fellowship from MDRC (2011).

Amy Stuart Wells is a professor of sociology and education and the director of the Center for Understanding Race and Education (CURE) at Teachers College, Columbia University. She is also the director of the Building Knowledge for Social Justice Project (2009–2011) at the Ford Foundation. Her research and writing has focused broadly on issues of race and education and more specifically on educational policies such as school desegregation, school choice, charter schools, and tracking, and how they shape and constrain opportunities for students of color. Wells's current research project, "Metro Migrations, Racial Segregation and School Boundaries," examines urban-suburban demographic change and the role that public schools and their boundaries play in who moves where.

Terrenda White is an educator and current doctoral student in sociology and education at Teachers College, Columbia University. She also serves as a part-time research associate at the Center for Understanding Race and Education (CURE), led by Dr. Amy S. Wells. Her research interests include education policy, social inequality, and critical pedagogy.

Brian Williams is assistant professor in the Department of Early Childhood Education at Georgia State University in Atlanta, Georgia. His scholarly pursuits focus on the intersection of science education, urban education, and multicultural education. Specifically, he is interested in the ways in which issues related to race, ethnicity, culture, and class influence teaching and learning in science classrooms.

Gail Wolfe is a doctoral candidate in education at Washington University in St. Louis. Her dissertation examines the history of public school programs for pregnant girls in Washington, D.C., and Chicago. Gail's research interests include history of education, urban education, and gender studies.

John T. Yun is associate professor in the Gevirtz Graduate School of Education at the University of California, Santa Barbara (UCSB) and director of the University of California Educational Evaluation Center (UCEC). His research focuses on issues of equity and evaluation in education, specifically patterns of school segregation, the effects of school context on educational outcomes, the importance of evaluation to everyday school practice, and the educative/counter-educative impacts of high-stakes testing.